ELVIS PRESLEY
Caught in a Trap

Spencer Leigh

Published by McNidder & Grace
Aswarby House
Aswarby
Sleaford NG34 8SE
United Kingdom
www.mcnidderandgrace.co.uk

First published in 2017
©Spencer Leigh
www.spencerleigh.co.uk

All rights reserved. No part of this work may be reproduced or transmitted in any form or by any means, electronic or mechanical, including photocopy, recording, or any information storage or retrieval system, without permission in writing from the publisher.

Spencer Leigh has asserted his right to be identified as the author of this work in accordance with the Copyright, Designs and Patents Act 1988.

Every effort has been made to obtain necessary permission with reference to copyright material. The publisher apologises if, inadvertently, any sources remain unacknowledged and will be glad to make the necessary arrangements at the earliest opportunity.

A catalogue record for this work is available from the British Library.
ISBN: 9780857161659

Designed by Obsidian Design

Printed and bound in the United Kingdom by
Short Run Press Ltd, Exeter, UK

About the author

Spencer Leigh was born in Liverpool in 1945 and still lives there. He is an acknowledged expert on popular music, both as a broadcaster and journalist. His *On The Beat* programme has been on BBC Radio Merseyside over 30 years and he is regularly featured in *Record Collector*, *Now Dig This* and *Country Music People*. His many books include *Best of the Beatles: The Sacking of Pete Best*, *The Cavern Club*, *Love Me Do to Love Me Don't: The Beatles on Record*, *Frank Sinatra: An Extraordinary Story* and *Simon and Garfunkel: Together Alone*, all for McNidder & Grace. He is an Honoured Friend at Sir Paul McCartney's Liverpool Institute of Performing Arts (LIPA) and he has a Gold Badge of Merit from the British Academy of Composers and Songwriters Spencer continues to live with his wife Anne on Merseyside.

Chapter 12. Get Those Stakes up Higher	**204**
I. Viva Rock Vegas	204
II. Got a Lot o' Livin' to Do, 1969	207
Chapter 13. Desert Life	**222**
I. Crazy Words, Crazy Tune	222
II. Got a Lot o' Livin' to Do, 1970–1972	226
Chapter 14. My Baby Left Me	**249**
I. Burger King	249
II. Got a Lot o' Livin' to Do, 1973–1975	251
Chapter 15. I Can't Seem to Stand on my Own Two Feet	**267**
I. What If…	267
II. Got a Lot o' Livin' to Do, 1976–1977	273
Chapter 16. I Was Coming Back Anyway	**287**
I. Goin' Up, Goin' Down	287
(A) The Imitation Game	287
(B) Elvis Lives	288
(C) Family Matters	290
(D) Stage and Screen	294
II. Got a Lot of Livin' to Do, 1977 to the Present	297
Acknowledgements	302
Bibliography	304
Appendix 1: To Think I Did All That – An Elvis Presley Discography	307
Appendix 2: Elvis For Everyone	334
Answer Versions	334
Sampling Elvis	334
Songs About Elvis While Elvis Was Alive	335
Songs About Elvis Once Elvis Was Gone	335
Tribute Albums	338
Acknowledging Elvis – Songs	340
Acknowledging Elvis – Cultural References	341
I Can't Believe It's Not Elvis	341
Notable Cover Versions	343
Index	346

Contents

Foreword by Russell Watson vii

Introduction: Stranger than Fiction ix

Chapter 1. Tupelo Honey 1
   I. Old Times They Are Not Forgotten 1
   II. Got a Lot o' Livin' to Do, 1935–1948 12

Chapter 2. Long Distance Information 18
   I. Tennessee Saturday Night 18
   II. Got a Lot o' Livin' to Do, 1948–1954 25

Chapter 3. Here Comes the Sun King 30
   I. First Time Out 30
   II. Got a Lot o' Livin' to Do, 1954–1955 35

Chapter 4. The Year that Rocked the World 52
   I. The Abominable Showman 52
   II. Got a Lot o' Livin' to Do, 1956 57

Chapter 5. The Million Dollar Quartet 79
   I. The Myth 79
   II. Got a Lot o' Livin' to Do, 4 December 1956 81

Chapter 6. Winter, Summer, Springtime Too 86
   I. Meanwhile Over in Britain 86
   II. Got a Lot o' Livin' to Do, 1957 96

Chapter 7. Army Bunk, Army Chow, Army Clothes, Army Car 111
   I. The Willing Conscript 111
   II. Got a Lot o' Livin' to Do, 1958–1960 117

Chapter 8. I Slipped… 130
   I. I Ain't Never Did No Wrong 130
   II. Got a Lot o' Livin' to Do, March 1960–December 1960 137

Chapter 9. I Stumbled… 152
   I. El's Angels 152
   II. Got a Lot o' Livin' to Do, 1961–1963 156

Chapter 10. I Fell… 173
   I. Home Taping 173
   II. Got a Lot o' Livin' to Do, 1964–1967 175

Chapter 11. Comeback Very Special 193
   I. All I Gotta Do Is Act Naturally 193
   II. Got a Lot o' Livin' to Do, 1968 197

Foreword

by Russell Watson

I'm delighted to have been invited to write the Foreword to Spencer Leigh's brand new biography of Elvis Presley. He hoped I could add something about Presley's vocal range and technical ability. I feel privileged to be a part of this book, as I know Spencer writes with honesty and integrity and a genuine love for his subjects.

Presley had one of the great pop voices of all time, along with the likes of Roy Orbison and Nat King Cole, whose voices were completely distinctive. Whereas Orbison had an incredible range, which spanned over three octaves (including his falsetto) Elvis wasn't that far behind him. However, he hardly ever used the falsetto area of his voice. Presley's was a more raspy, throaty, rock sound and he was one of the pioneers of this style.

In the early stages of his career when the vocal folds were obviously younger and had much more elasticity, his vocal range was considerably more expansive; it sounded effortless, with hardly any vibrato. In later recordings, where his range had lessened, the sound was more mature and the vibrato more obvious. It was still just as distinctive though (probably more so). You can clearly hear this if you take the early recording of 'Hound Dog' and compare it to say, 'The Wonder of You'. The difference in the vocal tone, its quality and the vibrato generated are poles apart. It was less rock'n'roll, more chest than head voice, nowhere near as raspy. Dare I say it, more classical in approach.

I was interested to read recently that Elvis loved Dean Martin. Dean also had an incredibly distinctive voice and we all know and remember how he sang the phrase, 'That's Amore'. You can hear Elvis applying a similar style in some of his songs. Might I add, emulation being the highest form of flattery...

The author mentioned that some critics had said Elvis was out of tune on some of his songs, namely 'Love Me Tender' and 'The Girl of My Best Friend'. He asked for my opinion on this. Okay, if you listen to 'Love Me Tender' properly, you will find that it is the guitar that is out of tune, not Elvis! Listen to the first few chords and it sounds like the bottom three strings are out of tune. Elvis is in tune! Yes, there are a couple of flat notes in 'The Girl of My Best Friend' but it doesn't matter, as the imperfections in a human voice are what makes it so beautiful. To analyse notation to this level demonstrates a lack of connection with the music in any instance.

These days everything is perfect and you can use highly sophisticated computer technology to manually tune the voice, but to me the voice loses its natural beauty and soul if too much of this trickery is applied. It's the imperfections that make a voice unique and special. Take Nat 'King' Cole as a perfect example. In many of his photos, Nat can be seen with a cigarette in his hand. I'm not an advocate of singing and smoking but I'm sure that beautiful, raspy, warm-sounding voice had come about through his smoking and the imperfections that created. It made him unique and instantly recognisable, still to this day and just like Mr Elvis Presley.

If you had just landed on this planet and had no idea who Elvis Presley was, you might listen to a song and say, 'That's good', but if you walked into an arena and watched him perform, it would be a different beast altogether. Part of his appeal was his incredible stage presence. If you want to know what the 'X Factor' really is, watch Elvis Presley in the 1968 TV special. Nobody else has what he had in that moment in time. Truly a voice for all generations!

Russell Watson
May 2017

seen many of them and I would estimate that 80% go for the Vegas look, although the younger Presley was the one who changed the world. That tells you more about the *faux* Presleys than Presley himself: if you are overweight and over 30, you can only be the Vegas Presley. I like the ones who present their tribute with humour: there is a Scotsman who works as Elvis McPresley and enters to the music of 'Scotland the Brave'.

The huge presence of the fat Elvis impersonators distorts history. We can't take them seriously and as a result, it diminishes Elvis' stature as a primary influence on rock'n'roll and what then happened in the 1960s. Elvis, it must be said, didn't help himself either, through the dismissive way he performed some of his early successes.

There are those who sincerely believed, certainly in the years after his death, that Elvis was still alive. Could he possibly have faked his death? Was he still around? There was no evidence for this and most of us took it as a running joke – but for some it was taken seriously. Such rumours hadn't happened since the death of Adolf Hitler.

A more worrying movement was the concept of Elvis as the godlike figure at the head of a new religion, the alternative Jesus, if you like. What had made followers think he might be super-human? *Caught in a Trap* will reveal that he was all too human.

How did Elvis achieve this godlike status? What set him apart from other key performers of the mid-50s: Little Richard, Chuck Berry, Ricky Nelson, Roy Orbison, Pat Boone, Johnny Cash, Carl Perkins, and Jerry Lee Lewis? Don't answer that; it's blindingly obvious with all those guys, but it's also clear that the rock'n'roll explosion would still have happened without him. It would have been very different as there was no other obvious leader in the pack, no-one else who had charisma in bucketfuls – Eddie Cochran could match Presley's looks, but he died when he was 21. I suspect that Colonel Parker knew that from the outset and that is why Elvis very rarely worked with any of the other leading figures in rock'n'roll. He neither appeared in multi-artist exploitation films nor toured with any rock'n'roll package show. When Jayne Mansfield was filming *The Girl Can't Help It,* she was asked to go see Presley in a nearby studio and offer her services in exchange for a cameo appearance. Sadly, no one knows what happened next, but the cameo never happened.

Although all the artists that I mentioned are renowned, they had difficulty in maintaining their popularity. The same could have applied to Elvis. He made one pathetic film after another on auto-pilot, fully aware that they were not worthy of his talent. To compound the liability, for several years Elvis just released singles and albums of dreadful soundtrack songs. How could the artist who cut 'Heartbreak Hotel' and 'It's Now or Never' have been happy with 'Do the Clam' and 'Song of the Shrimp'? Although he made these dreadful movies and songs, it did not appear to harm his status as The King.

I am writing this introduction in August 2016, before I've started the book, so I've no idea where this will go, but I suspect that Elvis should be given credit for some things that are not acknowledged at present. Top of my list is his helping to bring about changes in attitude towards race in America, and top marks to him if this is correct.

However, there are a couple of things which make me cautious. In the late 1970s, the Sun rockabilly artist Charlie Feathers came to the UK. It was his first visit away from the South and I was the first journalist to interview him here. I was horrified by his views on race, which I didn't include in my feature. I have a feeling that after that interview, he was told by the promoter that people don't say things like that in Britain,

INTRODUCTION
Stranger than Fiction

'There are three requirements for a happy life. The first is having someone to love, the second is having something to look forward to, and the third is having something to do.'
Elvis Presley to hairdresser Patti Parry

On Tuesday 16 August 1977, and shortly before his next round of concert dates, Elvis Presley collapsed and died in the bathroom of his home in Memphis. He was 42 years old. The media went into overdrive. On the news, there were pictures of fans weeping and late-night vigils. There were special supplements in the newspapers and experts analysed his career – the good and the bad, but never the ugly. Once again, Elvis Presley was the biggest-selling record artist on the planet.

Twenty years later, on Sunday 31 August 1997, 36-year-old Princess Diana died in a late-night car chase in Paris, while trying to shake off the ever-present paparazzi. Again, there was blanket coverage on the news, even greater than Presley's, because the news infrastructures had advanced significantly; there were so many implications for the Royal Family – and there was so much mystery about it. Like Presley, Diana could be a divisive figure but overwhelmingly, she was greatly loved.

I would never cry for someone I didn't know personally but I can understand the grief, even hysteria, although I wondered why was there so much of it. I am convinced that it all stems from Elvis. The Brits are famously reserved and at the time, the coverage of his death from America was thought flashy and over the top, but such displays have now become the norm – so the dedicated admirers ensured that Diana had a greater display of public affection than Elvis.

The death of Elvis has become the standard for subsequent deaths of much-loved international figures, be it John Lennon, Michael Jackson, Prince, David Bowie or George Michael. There had been nothing like it at the time but this has become the default position for major celebrities who pass away. It serves as a strong example of how our media-led society is changing. There might even be an exhibitionistic or competitive edge about it – you know, 'My grief is greater than your grief.'

Contrast this with the very dignified funeral procession for President John F. Kennedy in 1963 and the stiff upper lip approach for Sir Winston Churchill in 1965. If we are to look to the past for anything to match the reaction to Elvis Presley's funeral, it would be the sobbing fans after the death of the silent screen glamour boy Rudolph Valentino in 1926.

There are other special factors relating only to Elvis. The ETAs, the Elvis Tribute Acts, for starters. There are so many of them – in pubs and clubs and even stadiums. I've as his subsequent interviews were more measured. I wonder if Elvis would have been like that if he hadn't made it.

Secondly, why was Elvis' band and all his so-called Memphis Mafia white? I may find exceptions like the Sweet Inspirations who provided backing vocals but, on the face of it, Elvis wasn't an equal opportunities employer. Off the top of my head, his only black employee was his housekeeper Nancy Rooks, and that in itself brings to mind racial stereotyping.

Then there is his repetitive approach to work. Unlike Frank Sinatra, who divided his time between being a businessman and making records, films, TV specials and concert appearances, Elvis tended to do one thing at a time. In the 60s it was one weak film after another and in the 70s it was endless concert tours. Elvis might moan, but he did as he was told or at least, what Colonel Parker told him to do.

Despite Elvis giving TCB pins to his associates, it was Colonel Parker who took care of business. When Elvis wasn't working, he wanted to party and have fun. This sense of excess surfaces with his numerous girlfriends, his childish pranks and his huge appetite. He would regularly eat twenty slices of bacon for his breakfast – yes, you read that right – and this is before we get to fried peanut butter sandwiches, banana splits, or buttermilk biscuits with chocolate gravy.

I suspect that Priscilla Presley, an intelligent woman grounded in reality, realised that he was caught in a trap and had to leave him. His lifestyle was too much for her. Elvis' sexual behaviour will have to be examined, because she was so young when she met Elvis, and I am unsure what the conclusion will be.

Caught in a Trap is the extraordinary story of Elvis Presley. How did it go so right and why did it go so wrong? Shortly before his death, three of the bodyguards who tended to his needs and kept him company wrote a book, *Elvis – What Happened?*, and we will be discussing how he viewed this and whether it had an impact on his life – and even his death. The book was scandalous and revelatory but was it true? We'll find out, but we'll start at the beginning and see how this extraordinary phenomenon came to be.

I've just looked at the time. I have a watch which has Elvis Presley on its face and I will be looking at it thousands of times as I write this book. Some people have watches which can show movies, send tweets, and take pictures. All I want is a watch that tells me the time and gives me a picture of Elvis. On stage. In his prime. 1956.

As fans sign their letters, Elvisly yours,

Spencer Leigh

Notes on text

By and large, English spelling is used throughout the book, such as theatre for theater.

Some of Elvis' songs are known by different titles. For consistency, 'That's All Right, Mama', 'Party', 'A Fool Such as I', 'Devil in Disguise' and 'His Latest Flame' are used throughout. Elvis certainly loved songs with brackets in their titles whereas I've always thought them a sign of indecisiveness: the songwriters should make up their minds!

Elvis had a grandfather Jessie D or Jesse D and a twin brother Jessie or Jesse. Clearly the twin was named after the grandfather and the memorial at Graceland is for Jessie Garon Presley. Some books have Jessie for the grandpa and Jesse for the twin, but I think Jessie is best for both. It does look odd though, as Jessie is generally used as the spelling for a female name in the UK.

CHAPTER 1
Tupelo Honey

'I was probably stupid enough to believe that having the same birthday as Elvis Presley actually meant something.'
David Bowie

I. Old Times They Are Not Forgotten

On 28 November 1970, the 30-year-old singer/songwriter Mickey Newbury was booked to play during the opening week of the Bitter End West. He had played the famous Bitter End club in New York and now the business had expanded to California.

Just one man and a guitar, he came from Texas and this was his west coast debut. He had written two big hits ('Just Dropped In' for Kenny Rogers and the First Edition and 'She Even Woke Me Up to Say Goodbye' for Jerry Lee Lewis) and he had released his own album, *Looks Like Rain*.

It was Thanksgiving weekend and he wanted to make a good impression. He'd had an idea and thought that a liberal audience in Hollywood would accept it, but now he wasn't sure, especially as he had noticed the black folk singer, Odetta, in the audience. He certainly had good intentions, but they could be misconstrued.

Mickey Newbury was going to perform his own songs, but as it was Thanksgiving weekend, he thought he would take a chance. Right away. First song in. If he lost them, he would struggle to win them over, but if they responded positively, he'd be home and dry. He walked into the spotlight, acknowledged the applause and started singing very quietly and confidentially, 'Oh, I wish I was in the land of cotton.'

What was he doing? This was a favourite song in the South and sung before the fighting at Gettysburg during the Civil War in 1863. After the South had been defeated, President Lincoln had asked to hear it. However, the song had later been outlawed: it was, after all, a song favoured by white supremacists, although its lyrics were not racist.

Odetta was stunned, but she appreciated that Mickey Newbury was doing it differently. It was no longer a march, but a sad, sombre reflection of a soldier who might be killed in battle.

Without pausing for applause, Newbury balanced it with a song from the North, 'The Battle Hymn of the Republic', which was 'John Brown's Body' with new words written by Julia Ward Hope in 1861. His voice cried out, 'Glory glory hallelujah'.

He finished his American trilogy with a tender ballad, 'All My Trials', which had been recorded as 'All My Sorrows' by the Kingston Trio in 1959. It had been a small hit for Dick and Deedee in 1964 and it was on albums by Pete Seeger, Joan Baez, Peter, Paul and Mary and the Seekers.

Then he was done. There was silence, as no one was sure if there was going to be more. Mama Cass was the first to yell her approval. Then the whole audience stood up, applauding furiously. Afterwards, Kris Kristofferson said, 'Mickey could destroy a room full of people.'

Mickey Newbury put 'An American Trilogy' on his next album *Frisco Mabel Joy* – it was released as a single, and although it made the US Top 30, many radio stations would not play it. Elvis' wife, Priscilla, heard the track and told Elvis about it. He loved it and knew he was born to sing it. He may have recalled 'Dixie' being played by an army band when he sailed to Germany in 1958. He would have heard Andy Williams sing 'The Battle Hymn of the Republic' at Senator Robert Kennedy's funeral in 1968.

Elvis would sometimes perform songs live before he recorded them. The audiences loved 'American Trilogy' but Colonel Parker wasn't sure. To him, it was just some Civil War songs that had been strung together by Mickey Newbury. Parker, who never discussed his own background, couldn't see its attraction: he rarely commented on Elvis' song selection, but this time he told him, 'You're making a mistake, Elvis. Who wants to be reminded of the Civil War?'

In truth, Parker was incensed that Newbury had taken three songs in the public domain and put his own name and the Acuff-Rose publishing imprint on them. Parker didn't see why Newbury should make one cent from Presley's performances.

For once, Elvis stuck up for himself and he decided that an atmospheric live recording of 'An American Trilogy' would be the best way to release it. 'An American Trilogy', recorded at the Hilton International in Las Vegas, was released as a single in April 1972. Again, radio stations were unsure and it only reached No.66 on the Hot 100, a poor showing for The King. Not to worry; it became a key song in his stage performance – it was a song that said, 'This is who I am, this is what I believe'.

His shrewd manager Colonel Parker had missed an opportunity. If Elvis had held back the single for four years, it would have coincided with the bicentennial celebrations. With the right marketing, Elvis could have had the biggest hit of his career.

In 1776, the Declaration of Independence had been followed by the world's first written constitution. The second amendment, which was adopted in 1791, was the right to keep and bear arms, something Elvis Presley wholeheartedly supported.

Britain lost the war and America became a country in its own right. There was, however, further conflict with the British during the Napoleonic wars, which included the Battle of New Orleans. Napoleon was defeated at the Battle of Waterloo in 1815 and sent into exile and since then, Britain, America and France have been on the same side.

The USA covered a vast area, with some states bigger than many countries and in many instances the states were only united by name. A policy of westward expansion was taking place in America and the indigenous population, mostly American Indian, was shamefully treated, being forced westwards themselves to the designated Indian Territory, effectively to Oklahoma.

Their original land had been sequestered by the pioneers, who were taming the wilderness as they went, many settling in the Appalachians, including the forefathers of Elvis Presley.

The southern climate was ideal for cotton but that cotton had to be harvested, which entailed slavery, usually on giant plantations. The plantation owners became immensely wealthy and the southern states prospered.

Although two consecutive Presidents came from the South: Abraham Lincoln (Kentucky) and Andrew Johnson (North Carolina), they were both opposed to slavery. Indeed, in 1861, Lincoln succeeded James Buchanan on an anti-slavery ticket. Along with the legislature of the day, they thought that the southern states should not be allowed to make their own decisions on such a contentious issue. The South, naturally enough, thought that they were meddling in their affairs.

The first state to secede was South Carolina in December 1860 and then Mississippi three weeks later. By the end of January, Florida, Alabama, Georgia and Louisiana had followed. Then Texas, Virginia, Arkansas, North Carolina and Tennessee. Missouri and Kentucky were declared to have seceded by their supporters but their governments still supported the Union. The states that seceded are grouped together as Dixieland.

The mighty Mississippi ran through several states from South to North and was a key means of transport. The state of Mississippi itself was low-lying, but a garrison on a hill at Vicksburg overlooking the river was seen by Lincoln as 'the key to the Confederacy'. After a seven-week siege, it fell to General Ulysses S. Grant on 4 July 1863, which meant that the North could dominate the river and eventually win the war, although there were some huge battles along the way. Lincoln was to declare the Fourth of July a national holiday, but it was not celebrated in Vicksburg for a hundred years.

The North had won the war although in a way, the war has never ended. The South nursed resentment and indeed much of it was in ruins. The total death toll was around 750,000 and many more were injured. The southern economy was wrecked. The slaves had emancipation but what would they do?

Large plantations were divided into small shareholdings and the tenant farmers, mostly black, would work the land for a proportion of the proceeds. It was not profitable work. The disparity in wealth between the white and black citizens has not been solved to this day.

We turn specifically to the state of Mississippi itself where Elvis Presley was born and I want to show how significant its culture was to him. The state covers 50,000 square miles, which is half the size of the UK, and today's population is around 3 million. It is low lying and everything is well below 1,000 feet. This being America, they still want to claim some mountains, say everything over 800 feet, and Woodall Mountain is very lucky at 807 feet to have that designation.

About 20% of the state's residents lived in Jackson, which was torched three times in the Civil War, although the Governor's mansion and the city hall were both spared. In more recent times, Jackson has been the subject of a biting duet recorded by both Lee Hazlewood and Nancy Sinatra and by Johnny Cash and his wife, June Carter. It remains a large city but it has now expanded over a wider area.

Mississippi, with good reason, is associated with the blues. The slaves had brought with them songs about their experiences in Africa and they were soon singing about what was happening around them, their only instruments being harmonicas and acoustic guitars. There would be spiritual songs praising the Lord, although they had little to thank him for, and there would be blues, which told it like it was.

The bluesman Charley Patton was probably born just outside Jackson in 1887 and his status as a blues singer and guitarist has increased with the years. One of his grandmothers was a Cherokee. He was raised on the Dockery Plantation near Ruleville, north of Jackson, which had been created out of swamp wilderness in 1895. Each of

Dockery's tenants was given a mule and 10 acres – today the norm is one man and a tractor for 1,000 acres – and they would spent their earnings at the company store. Many of Patton's songs were about what he saw around him, such as the devastation caused by the boll weevil.

He pioneered the two-part single with 'Prayer of Death', 'Dry Spell Blues' and, most famously, 'High Water Everywhere' (1927) which was about the levees breaking their banks. He spent most of his life in Sunflower County and died there, being buried in Holly Ridge in 1934.

Also in 1927, and in total contrast to 'High Water Everywhere', the advantages of the Mississippi were celebrated by Oscar Hammerstein in his song, 'Ol' Man River' which was magnificently sung by Paul Robeson in *Show Boat*. This song made valid points about atrocious working conditions, which was courageous for a Broadway musical. It was the first fully-integrated production on Broadway.

The general routine for the black workers and sharecroppers was working hard during the week, going to a juke joint on Saturday and seeking forgiveness for Saturday's sins on Sunday. The word 'juke' (originally 'jook') came from an African word for disorderly, and the bars were a mixture of dancing, drinking and prostitution.

Black or white, people liked singing about what was happening around them. There are a lot of folk songs about the railroad and many of them are about crashes, as this was not the safest means of transport. Casey Jones was a railroad man for the Illinois Central Railroad and he was killed in 1900 when his passenger train collided with another at the station in Vaughan, Mississippi, just north of Jackson. His train was travelling at 75mph when he saw that another train was on the same line at the station. He applied the brakes and warned the passengers with his whistle. The other fireman jumped out and the trains collided at 35mph with Jones as the only casualty. The damage could have been much worse and Casey was depicted as a folk hero and there are many songs about him. There is a Casey Jones Museum at Vaughan, Mississippi.

Arthur 'Big Boy' Crudup was born in Forest, Mississippi, just east of Jackson in 1905. He had various agricultural jobs but he was a good, expressive singer and he was encouraged to learn the guitar when he was 32 years old, his first guitar having a broken neck. He was never especially proficient – all his recordings are in E – but he was an excellent songwriter. He recorded many tracks for Victor Records in the 1940s including 'Mean Ole Frisco' (1942) which was taken up by B.B. King in 1959 and has become a blues standard.

On 6 September 1946 Crudup recorded 'That's All Right' (1946), also known as 'I Don't Know It', with Judge Riley on drums and Ransom Knowling on bass, although it was the 1949 version, titled 'That's All Right (Mama)', that Elvis knew best. That was the first-ever 45rpm release by a black performer and it was issued on orange vinyl. Because Crudup accepted $100 for each session, he never saw any royalties, a moral for any aspiring musician.

Victor let him go in 1954, the very year that Presley joined Sun and recorded Crudup's 'That's All Right, Mama', for his first single. In view of Elvis's alleged mother fixation, it's apt that a song with 'mama' in its lyric should be his first single, although the lyric refers to a girlfriend and not a mother.

Presley subsequently recorded 'My Baby Left Me' and 'So Glad You're Mine' but Crudup was cheated out of royalties and, it must be said, Presley did nothing about it.

This as we will see was by no means an isolated incident. Crudup returned to farming and did occasional gigs but not at harvest time. He had the nickname 'Big Boy' for many years and then he was billed as 'The Father of Rock'n'Roll.' Crudup died in 1974, and his family did receive some royalties after his death.

If there had been a court case over the song, I could imagine some clever lawyer saying that Arthur 'Big Boy' Crudup wasn't entitled to anything as he had based 'That's All Right, Mama' on 'Black Snake Moan' by Blind Lemon Jefferson.

Another bluesman, Elmore James, was born close to Jackson in Richland, Mississippi. He made his recording debut with his best-known recording, 'Dust My Broom' in 1952 but the song had come from Robert Johnson. His slide guitar riff has been copied by numerous rock bands.

Jackson is pretty well in the middle of Mississippi and to the north is Clarksdale, founded by John Clark in 1848. This city could with some conviction claim to be the home of the blues. In 1903, the bandleader W C Handy was waiting for a train at the nearby Tutwiler station. As he waited, he heard a black man playing his guitar by running a penknife across the strings. He was singing, 'I'm goin' where the Southern cross the Dog', which sounds baffling until you learn it refers to two railroad companies, the second being Yellow Dog. Handy stole the line and wrote his own 'Yellow Dog Blues'. Handy spent a couple of years in Clarksdale soaking up its culture or nicking ideas for songs, depending on how you look at it. In his teens, Elvis Presley would see R&B performers at the Handy Theatre, which had been named after him, in Memphis.

Gertrude Pridgett, who was born in Columbus, Georgia, in 1882, was the first blues singer to find national success. She worked as Ma Rainey which is appropriate as she is regarded as the Mother of the Blues. Her stately version of 'See See Rider', later known as 'C.C. Rider', and referring to a country circuit preacher was recorded in October 1924 with Louis Armstrong on cornet. It was revived by Ray Charles in 1949 and became an R&B hit for Chuck Willis and LaVern Baker. The song has developed into a rock'n'roll standard and Elvis used it to open his concerts. Why should Elvis have fallen in love with a preacher?

Bessie Smith, who was born in Chattanooga, Tennessee in 1894, had been discovered by John Hammond and recorded for the Columbia label. In January 1925, she recorded W.C. Handy's 'St Louis Blues', again with Louis Armstrong on cornet, in New York City, a contender for the greatest record ever made. The song became a blues standard and Bessie Smith was known as the Empress of the Blues. In 1937, she and her driver and lover, Richard Morgan, collided with a truck just outside Clarksdale. Her record producer, John Hammond, wrote in the jazz magazine, *Downbeat*, that she had been refused treatment at a white hospital and the delay probably caused her death. This was untrue. She was taken to an Afro-American hospital in Clarksdale where her right arm was amputated. She died without regaining consciousness."

Over 7,000 people lined the streets of Clarksdale for her funeral cortege but, despite her success, she was buried in an unmarked grave, unmarked that is until 1970 when Janis Joplin bought a headstone. This event is recounted in Dory Previn's song, 'Stone for Bessie Smith'. Janis Joplin said, 'Bessie showed me the air and taught me how to fill it.'

The famed blues man Son House, born in Clarksdale in 1902, was already alive when Handy was there: John Lee Hooker followed in 1917 and Ike Turner in 1931.

Muddy Waters, born in Rolling Fork, Mississippi, met Son House in a blues club in Clarksdale and was able to further his career. ZZ Top made a guitar from wood in Muddy's old cabin. Elvis could have recorded any number of Muddy's songs but the only one we know about is 'Got My Mojo Workin".

Nobody knows exactly what happened to Robert Johnson. He was born just below Jackson in Hazlehurst in 1911, but it was in Clarksdale that he made a deal with the Devil. At midnight. At the intersection of Highways 49 and 61. Satan appeared in the form of a large black man, tuned his guitar, sang a few songs and disappeared. It's a variation of the Faustian pact and I don't believe it. Someone was having him on, but the important point is that Johnson himself believed this and it came out in his music: 'Cross Road Blues', 'Me and the Devil Blues' and 'Hellhound on My Trail.' Elvis Presley recorded a variation of his final recording, 'Milkcow's Calf Blues', from 1937.

It wasn't the Devil that did for Robert Johnson, but what was in his trousers. He had been carrying on with the wife of a juke joint proprietor in Greenwood. He was playing there on 13 August 1938 and he drank some whisky poisoned with strychnine. He left the stage when he became delusional and he died three days later, the first member of the 27 club. He was buried close by in a church graveyard in Morgan City. (Don't be confused by these names: Morgan City only has a population of 250. It's like the so-called mountains in Mississippi.)

As I was writing this, I broke off to read the latest *NME* and there is a picture of Justin Bieber on stage with a jacket that has 'Bigger than Satan' on the back – so this reverses the story and the Devil in 2016 would want a deal with him.

I was hoping to get to the bottom of the Robert Johnson story as David 'Honeyboy' Edwards was coming to play in Birkenhead in the north-west of England in 2008 at the age of 93. The promoter said that I could talk to him before the show but 'he does get very tired these days'. I arrived early and went backstage. His dressing-room door was open and there was David 'Honeyboy' Edwards fast asleep on a chair. I tiptoed away and waited for the concert. I wasn't surprised – he was doing nine gigs in ten days.

Honeyboy didn't look a day over 80 and he did very little talking. Probably unknowingly, he repeated songs and his singing and his playing were somewhat erratic. Quite often I couldn't make out what he was mumbling but he did include a line about 'Bo Diddley died tonight'. He sang 'Sweet Home Chicago' which he is reputed to have written – when you're the last man standing, you can claim anything – but that song is usually associated with Robert Johnson.

Robert Johnson was on the verge of a breakthrough. He had been discovered by John Hammond and he would have been part of the *Spirituals to Swing* concert at Carnegie Hall in December 1938, which introduced sophisticated New Yorkers to the blues. His place was taken by Big Bill Broonzy, who sang as he ploughed the fields with his mule. Indeed, he was introduced as a Mississippi plough-hand.

Broonzy became an influential bluesman, introducing the blues to Britain and playing at the new Cavern club in March 1957. He fell off the train at Lime Street Station and he was introduced as 'Big Bill Bruised Knees'. How he must have loved that Liverpool humour. He could match them though. Broonzy went into a transport café and asked if everything was with chips. On being told it was, he said, 'In that case I'll have a double Scotch with chips.' He died the following year.

Robert Johnson's recordings have aged well and 'Sweet Home Chicago' had a new

Elvis Presley: Caught in a Trap

lease of life in the film, *The Blues Brothers* (1980). Both Peter Green and Eric Clapton have recorded albums of his songs and the Rolling Stones recorded 'Love in Vain'.

A story to equal Robert Johnson's has to be Sam Cooke's. Sam Cooke was born in Clarksdale in 1931 and he had a voice to rival Elvis Presley's. Between 1951 and 1956 he sang with the Soul Stirrers, a major gospel group. They recorded for the Specialty label and their producer, Bumps Blackwell, wanted Sam to record secular material. On paper, 'You Send Me' has a trite lyric but Sam Cooke did so much with it and this led to a succession of major pop hits including 'Chain Gang' and 'Cupid'. Inspired by 'Blowin' in the Wind', he wrote about Civil Rights in 'A Change is Gonna Come', a courageous record for a mainstream pop performer.

It seems as though there were several Sam Cookes as his output is so varied. His voice is so different on his two live albums; one sweet and sophisticated to match the Copacabana night club and one from the depths of Harlem on which he sounds like Wilson Pickett – a fantastic recording.

In December 1964, Sam Cooke took a girl to a motel in Los Angeles and she stole his clothes and his money. He chased after her and believed that the owner was shielding her. Terrified at being confronted by the angry and trouserless Cooke, the owner shot him. There have been conspiracy theories but the most obvious explanation is probably the truth: she was scared and shot him.

In 1933 Harold Lloyd Jenkins was born close to Clarksdale at Friar's Point with his father naming him after a silent film comedian. After hearing Elvis Presley on Sun Records in Memphis, he asked the proprietor Sam Phillips for an audition and he was to record for him. He chose the name Conway Twitty from looking at road maps: there is a Conway, Arkansas and a Twitty, Texas. Moving to MGM in 1958, he had a transatlantic No.1 with 'It's Only Make Believe' and Peter Sellers was to parody him as Twit Conway. The record is so like Elvis that many believed it was Elvis under a pseudonym. Indeed, my guess would be that Conway wrote the song after hearing Elvis sing 'Lonesome Cowboy' in *Loving You* (1957) and combined it with Paul Anka's '(All of a Sudden) My Heart Sings'. Elvis even croaked like Conway in his song and Conway turned this into a trademark, overdoing it for his country hits. Elvis never sang 'It's Only Make Believe' but Glen Campbell gave it the Vegas treatment.

Clarksdale is seen as a musical city, holding an annual blues festival. You can stay at the Shack Up Inn and get the full sharecropper's experience in a rustic cabin, which might be taking the heritage tradition a little too far. The actor Morgan Freeman opened a plush restaurant, the Madidi, but it closed in 2013 after 12 years.

Dropping down south from Clarksdale about 40 miles, there is another musical hotspot around Greenwood. The soul singer Betty Everett was born there and her sometime singing partner Jerry Butler was born nearby in Sunflower, both in 1939. Elvis was to record Butler's song 'Only the Strong Survive'. Butler had a wonderful voice but he left the music business for politics.

Riley B. King was born close to Greenwood, in Indianola in 1925. He quit sharecropping and went to Memphis where he became known as the Beale Street Blues Boy, later Blues Boy King and then B.B. King. He became a radio disc-jockey and he was recording from 1949. He topped the *Billboard* R&B chart for five weeks with '3 O'Clock Blues' in 1952. Ike Turner played piano on another 1952 success, 'Story from My Heart and Soul'. He was recording at Sun before Elvis and he called his guitar

Lucille – well, every one of his guitars was called Lucille. He played 15,000 gigs.

About 50 miles from Greenwood is Greenville where the creator of the Muppets, Jim Henson was born in 1936. There is a museum with his pre-Kermit figures on display. The Muppets were to run *Great Moments in Elvis History* with such lines in Elvis Caesar as 'Friends, Romans, countrymen, lend me your steers' and the response to 'Et tu, Brute?' is 'No, I ate three.'

Close to Greenwood is the small community of Winona, where Roebuck Staples was born in 1914. He learnt guitar through listening to Charley Patton. He became known as Pops Staples as he formed a family group with his daughters; Pervis, Cleotha, Yvonne and Mavis. They became known for such spirituals as 'Uncloudy Day', 'Will the Circle Be Unbroken' and an original song from Roebuck, though based on a spiritual, 'This May Be the Last Time' (1960), which was reworked by the Rolling Stones. Mavis Staples nearly married Bob Dylan. In the 1970s they became more commercial and politically conscious with 'Respect Yourself' and 'I'll Take You There'.

The film *Ode To Billie Joe* (1976) was shot north of Jackson in Greenwood, but nobody paid much attention to it, still preferring to wonder what Billie Joe McAllister threw off the Tallahatchie Bridge. What does it matter? It's fiction, but the bridge is real enough. The song was written and recorded by Bobbie Gentry, a dead ringer for the late 60s version of Priscilla Presley. Bobbie's real name was Roberta Lee Streeter, and she was born just south of Tupelo in Chickasaw County, Mississippi in 1944. In 1967, she was signed by Capitol Records and the intention was to put her funky 'Mississippi Delta' out as a single. It was based on a local children's rhyme 'Niki Hoeky', which has been recorded in various forms by Redbone, P.J. Proby and Aretha Franklin. She came up with a story song for the B-side, 'Ode to Billie Joe', and the 45 was quickly flipped and became an international hit. Bobbie was married to the singer Jim Stafford but only for a year – presumably she didn't care for spiders and snakes. That's nothing – there had been panthers and bears on the Mississippi Delta as late as 1900.

The population of Mississippi is around 60% white and the overall impression is of hillbillies and rednecks. This is the problem with Albert Goldman's biography of Elvis Presley where the New York professor goes out of his way to mock the southern way of life and Elvis never stood a chance.

A simple example is the way in which the language of the South is mocked. Pat Boone told me of the problems in maintaining his university education whilst singing rock'n'roll. 'I had transferred from North Texas State to Columbia University in New York. This is one of our great universities and Randy Wood was asking me to do Fats Domino's 'Ain't That a Shame'. I said, 'I know it's a hit song, but can't we change the title to 'Isn't It a Shame'? We tried it but it didn't sound like rock'n'roll. I wound up recording it as 'Ain't That a Shame'. I was majoring in English with a No.1 record and I thought, 'They are going to expel me for this.' They didn't and 'ain't' became a good word. It's now in the dictionary.' This enlightening quote sums up Pat Boone's attitude to rock'n'roll and, if I'd thought quicker, I would have said, 'But what about Fats Waller's 'Ain't Misbehavin'', which was written in 1929?'

But 'ain't' ain't exclusively southern. It can be found in Dickens but it was used in the South, along with more specific terms like 'y'all' for 'you all'. People were 'fixin' to do' things, even 'fixin' to die'. If there was an abundance of something, it could be 'a mess of...' which led to New Yorker Doc Pomus writing 'A Mess of Blues' for Elvis. He

Elvis Presley: Caught in a Trap

knew Elvis would be hooked by the title.

There are many ways in which southern speech is different. I have interviewed many male southern singers and they invariably call their father 'Daddy'. Elvis referred to Vernon Presley as 'Daddy'. I don't know any adults in the UK who do that and indeed, it would sound very strange if they did.

Surprisingly for the civilised world, education was only made mandatory in Mississippi in 1982, but there were certainly cultural hotspots in the state. Up in the North and just 50 miles from Tupelo is Oxford. It deliberately chose its name in the hope of having the state university located there and indeed, the University of Mississippi opened in 1848. The timing was bad as the city was torched in the Civil War.

The university came to be known as Ole Miss and in 1962, James Meredith became the first black student to enrol at Ole Miss. This caused riots and two people died during the fighting. The Governor of Mississippi, Ross Barnett, supported segregation and his supporters had a badge which said, 'NEVER'. At his graduation, Meredith wore the badge upside down. The schools in Mississippi were not integrated until the late 60s and there is still tension today.

The Nobel prize-winning novelist, William Faulkner, lived in the area and wrote about it. He concluded, 'I discovered that my little postage stamp of native soil was worth writing about and I would never live long enough to exhaust it.' His books were frequently set in the fictional Yoknapatawpha County and his most famous novel is *The Sound and the Fury* (1929). Faulkner lived at Rowan Oak in Oxford from 1930 until his death in 1962 and his former home is open for tourists.

The playwright Tennessee Williams grew up around Columbus, Mississippi and then moved to Clarksdale. His plays including *A Streetcar Named Desire* (1947) and *Cat on a Hot Tin Roof* (1955) are as hot and steamy as the climate. He could have remained Tom Williams but he chose Tennessee, the state in which his father was born. Marlon Brando established his reputation through Williams' work and the thought of appearing in something by Williams, who lived until 1983, must have crossed Elvis' mind. It would have been a movie, as Elvis lacked the discipline to star in a Broadway play.

Joel Williamson in his book *Elvis Presley – A Southern Life* concludes, 'It was precisely because the culture wracked its people with such emotional violence over generations that its artists in the twentieth century achieved such power in interpreting humanity in America.' The chief artists in his opinion were William Faulkner, Tennessee Williams and Elvis Presley, who had lived within 40 miles of each other.

Alongside these greats, I would place the music of the Band. No other music group has captured the feel of the South so dramatically and that most of their songs were written by Robbie Robertson, who was raised in Canada, makes this all the more remarkable, although admittedly their drummer and often lead singer Levon Helm claimed that Robbie had been listening to his stories. There is no better way of immersing yourself in the South than by listening to their second album, *The Band*, recorded in 1969.

Despite all the positive aspects of the expansion into the South, it has to be said that the treatment of the indigenous population by the white settlers was shameful. There were conflicts with many of the tribes and in Mississippi the French wanted to build a village with a tobacco plantation. Some African slaves supported the Natchez in their opposition but they were beaten by the French with their allies from the Choctaw tribe, which gives you an idea of how shaky the alliances were.

There is an historic route, 440 miles long, called the Old Natchez Trace which stretches from the city of Natchez to Nashville, Tennessee. As it goes through Jackson up to Kosciusko, you are reaching the birthplace of Oprah Winfrey in 1954. As it happens, the visitor centre of Old Natchez Trace is in Tupelo, which is the halfway mark. The road is used by cyclists as commercial vehicles are banned.

There was a huge dance hall for the black community in Natchez, and Walter Barnes and his Royal Creolians were appearing in April 1940. The owner had decorated the hall with Spanish moss and fairy lights and sprayed them with mosquito repellent. He nailed the windows shut and locked the back exit so that nobody could get in without paying. The place was full and a wayward cigarette started a blaze. Over 200 died in the conflagration, including most of the band, and Howlin' Wolf sang about it in 'Natchez Burnin' (1956).

Big Joe Williams was born in Crawford in 1903 and his father was a Cherokee, Red Bone Williams. After an argument, his father threw him out and this might have influenced his bad-tempered blues songs. He rambled a lot, argued a lot, played a nine-string guitar of his own creation and recorded two blues classics, 'Baby Please Don't Go' and 'Crawlin' King Snake'. Bob Dylan played and sang back-up on his 1962 album, *Three Kings and a Queen*, and he was a mentor to Mike Bloomfield. He made little money and died in a caravan back in Crawford in 1982.

Arguably the prime mover at Chess Records was Willie Dixon, who had been born in Vicksburg in 1915. He played bass and could produce records but his main skill was as a songwriter and he wrote 'Little Red Rooster' and 'Hoochie Coochie Man'.

Bo Diddley was also with Chess. He was born Ellas Bates (later McDaniel) in McComb, Mississippi, north of New Orleans in 1928. He started as a boxer where he received the sobriquet Bo Diddley, and he worked the clubs in Chicago. He recorded a demo of 'Bo Diddley' in 1954 and recorded it at Chess in 1955. Bo Diddley is known for his beat and his custom-made guitars. Bo was once asked if Elvis had copied him and he replied, 'If he copied me, I don't care and more power to him. I'm not starving.'

Bo was less generous in his praise for other artists, whom he regarded as stealing his 'shave and a haircut, two bits' sound, though he himself had purloined it. Buddy Holly used his rhythm for 'Not Fade Away' and as if to admit the point, also recorded 'Bo Diddley'. The Everly Brothers sang his praises. Bo Diddley was a major influence on the British R&B groups around 1963/4 and The Animals sang about him visiting their local club in 'The Story of Bo Diddley'. The song, 'Mockingbird' has a lot in common with 'Bo Diddley' and Bo also wrote 'Love is Strange', but using his wife's name.

When all is going well, the cities around the mouth of the Mississippi are tourist resorts. Jimmy Buffett was born on Christmas Day, 1946 in Pascagoula, very close to Biloxi and as his song says, he is the 'son of the son of a sailor'. He tells of the grandpa's life in 'The Captain and the Kid'. His father was a naval architect, often taking Jimmy on sailing trips. He came to prominence with the splendidly-named album *A White Sport Coast and a Pink Crustacean* in 1973. He moved to Key West and he has released numerous albums about 'wasting away in Margaritaville'. Don't be misled by his good-for-nothing image; He is a highly astute business man and a top-ranking performer. He has some Margaritaville resorts and before the flooding you could stay in one in Biloxi. Elvis Presley never exploited his fame like this and think how much more famous he was than Jimmy Buffett and how much more successful his records were than 'Margaritaville'.

Elvis Presley: Caught in a Trap

In 2015 Buffett received an honorary degree from the University of Miami and, wearing flip-flops, aviator sunglasses and an academic gown, he told the students that 'sitting on your ass in front of a screen' is not surfing and to 'get out and see the world.' The full speech is worth checking out on *YouTube*.

Chris LeDoux was born in Biloxi in 1948 and he became a rodeo champion, especially in bareback riding. He has released many albums about his rodeo life and being promoted by Garth Brooks has brought him to a wider public. A more contemporary group, 3 Doors Down, was formed in Escatawpa, just up from Pascagoula.

Despite natural resources, the people of Mississippi still experience considerable poverty and the situation has not been helped by extremes in climate. Flooding is common and although giant levees have been built to protect the farmland, they sometimes fail.

In 2005, there was massive flooding around New Orleans and you will recall those extraordinary shots of boats in trees. The town of Waveland, Mississippi was wiped out, but it is gradually being restored.

The Mississippi legislature appreciated that casinos could help their economy but the legislation was such they were not allowed on land. Hence, they were built offshore, mostly around Biloxi. Ironically, with Hurricane Katrina, many of the floating casinos were tossed inland. New, land-based casinos have since been permitted.

As far as I can tell, no major musicians were born in Tupelo before Elvis Presley, but a couple came close.

Tammy Wynette was born Virginia Pugh in Tremont, 25 miles east of Tupelo on 5 May 1942. She picked cotton as a child, married at 17 and trained as a hairdresser. She was pilloried for saying she would support her husband right or wrong in 'Stand by Your Man', but her own life was more complicated than that as she was married several times and her second biggest single was 'D.I.V.O.R.C.E', which was wickedly parodied by Billy Connolly. No matter what she did, her strident voice was always defiantly country. As Billie Jo Spears remarked, 'You can't go pop with a mouthful of firecrackers.'

Close to Tupelo, Chester Burnett, who became Howlin' Wolf, was born in West Point, Mississippi, in 1910. He was singing in the forces and then on a Memphis radio station after the war, also working as a disc jockey. Sam Phillips recognised his potential but Wolf made deals with the Bihari brothers in California and the Chess brothers in Chicago. He settled in Chicago but his earlier releases were made by Phillips and set the template for his later work. He said his main influence was Charley Patton but nobody, absolutely nobody, sang like Howlin' Wolf, whose voice was as abrasive as it was dramatic. At six foot six and well over 20 stone, he also looked fearsome, the sort of musician who always got paid: indeed, he was financially astute.

I have been selective in the names that I have cited in this introduction but it is true to say that Elvis was born into a very rich musical community, immersed in gospel music and the blues and with the most innovative sounds coming from black singers. Unlike the Beatles, whose main inspiration came from outside their homeland and included Elvis himself, Elvis found it on his doorstep. He was totally influenced by local culture and he was able to bring it to the world with his own unique twist.

Although blues is often seen as a downbeat music, many performers were daring and exciting. In his song, 'Graceland', Paul Simon says that the Mississippi Delta was shining like a National guitar. That image shone through the best of Elvis Presley's work.

II. Got a Lot o' Livin' to Do, 1935–1948

Much has been written about the relationship between Elvis and his mother, Gladys, and surprisingly little about Elvis and his father, Vernon. No matter how derogatory the articles and books about Elvis may be, none of them question Elvis' love for his parents, nor theirs for Elvis. Several writers have attempted to make something of it – did he have an unnatural love for his mother and did their intense devotion contaminate all his relationships with women? Or is this just wishful thinking on behalf of the authors? Every writer wants to uncover something sensational in his subject's past but he shouldn't distort the facts to do so.

Whilst the truth behind the relationship of Elvis and Gladys may be more conventional, Elvis' family tree is remarkable. When he became famous, a reporter asked Vernon and Gladys about their background but they could only go back a couple of generations. That's nothing unusual, as most people know little about their great-grandparents.

Reviewers praised Jerry Hopkins' biography, *Elvis*, for being 'thoroughly researched and meticulously detailed', but this 1971 biography contained little about Elvis Presley's antecedents. For all his faults, Albert Goldman was the first to document Elvis' Cherokee ancestry, and, had Elvis been alive, I am sure he would have thanked him for it, though not for the rest of the book. Elaine Dundy spent many months in Tupelo researching her unique *Elvis and Gladys*. Elvis, who had a tremendous sense of humour, would have been enthralled to read about his background, yet he died knowing little of his heritage. How sad that he didn't spend some of his wealth in acquiring the knowledge for himself.

We can trace Presley's family tree back to Morning Dove White, a full-blooded Cherokee on his mother's side. In the early nineteenth century, there were not enough white southern girls to go around, so many hot-blooded males took Indian brides, and the Cherokees intermarried extensively. This ancestry can be seen in Gladys Presley's dark eyes and hair: consider how convincing Elvis was as a half-caste in *Flaming Star*, but in purely statistical terms, he was only 3% Cherokee.

No Cherokees infiltrate the Presley, originally Pressley, line, which can be traced back to Scotland. Andrew Presley from Greenock moved to Ireland because of the highland clearances, that is, the change from arable to sheep farming. Once in Ireland, the family encountered hardship during the famine and they moved to America in 1745.

I must thank my friend, the blues expert Bob Groom, for linking some things which had never occurred to me. He thinks that the family name, Presley or Pressley, may originate from Wales, the famous Land of Song. In Pembrokeshire, there is a range of hills called the Preseli Mountains – and only a few miles to the west is an area known as St Elvis with a St Elvis Farm.

And yes, there really was a St. Elvis (possibly Eilfyw or Eilfw in Welsh), who was the Bishop of Munster and had baptised St. David, who is now the patron saint of Wales. Bear in mind too that Gladys is a Welsh name and that Elvis was friendly with Tom Jones: why did he love his accent?

There was a 17th-century politician Sir Gervase Helwys, who was a lieutenant at the Tower of London but got embroiled in a murder plot and was hanged in 1615. Could the name Helwys have become Elvis with the years?

Elvis Presley: Caught in a Trap

What a rum lot they are in that family tree: they seem randy as hell and nobody knew about birth control. On Vernon's side, there's Dunnan Presley Jr, a Civil War deserter who was married four times simultaneously, and Dunnan Jr's daughter Rosella Presley with her brood of illegitimate children. One of her sons was Jessie D. McDowell Presley (1896–1973), Elvis' grandfather. A slim, handsome man with raven black hair, he was raised in poverty and his only ambition was to buy an expensive suit. If J.D. knew who his father was, he never said, but why's the McDowell in there? Could it be that his grandson should really be Elvis McDowell? Another of Rosella's sons, Noah, was Mayor of Tupelo, when Elvis was born in 1935.

On Gladys' side, there's John Mansell, who abandoned his wife, Elizabeth, and his 'other wife' (her sister) and all their assorted children. Gladys' own parents were first cousins. Some Jewish blood was introduced into the tree by Nancy Burdine and this may have led to Gladys being buried with a Star of David on her grave – Elvis joked that she was 'covering her options', but he thought the same way himself. By similar statistics, Elvis had 6% Jewish blood.

Going back to Andrew Presley in 1745, it is possible to follow another line of the family and reach Thomas Presley in 1860 who was a registered slave owner around Kosciusko, some 50 miles from Tupelo. Among his slaves were two boys, who were mulattos (mixed race) and living with their mother. It is possible that Thomas Presley was their father. One of those boys is Oprah Winfrey's great-grandfather, and so Oprah and Elvis could be distantly related. On the other hand, slaves were often given the surnames of their owners, so the fact that there is a Presley in her family line is not proof of a sexual liaison.

Despite Andrew Presley Jr (1754–1855) making it to 101, there are numerous early deaths in the family tree. Two of Gladys' brothers, Travis and Johnny, died young – both heavy drinkers and prone to brandishing knives and guns. Sexual promiscuity is rife throughout the family tree, so Elvis inherited this from his forefathers. Among the many children, there are three sets of twins (two on Gladys' side, one on Vernon's), so it is not surprising that Vernon and Gladys had twins.

Both their families had settled around Tupelo (pronounced Too-pello), which had a population of around 30,000. The city had been named after a tree that was known in the area. Its bark was very good for woodcarving and its gum was used in furniture. The natural food included polk salad.

Gladys Love Smith – the Love being a family name – was born on a farm in Pontotoc, ten miles from Tupelo, on 25 April 1912. She worked in the fields, she loved singing in church and she liked dancing. She was enraptured by Jimmie Rodgers' music, her favourite track being 'Mean Mama Blues'. Tiring of farm life, she moved to East Tupelo – the poor side of Tupelo – in 1932, stayed with relations and worked at the Tupelo Garment Factory for $2 a day.

Vernon Elvis Presley – the Elvis because his mother Minnie Mae liked the sound of the name – was born in Fulton, Mississippi on 10 April 1916. Elvis was not a unique name, but it was not commonplace: a bit like Spencer really. It is an anagram of lives, veils and evils, but, try as I may, I can't make anything significant from that.

Another Elvis, Elvis Costello, comments, 'All his family had names that look like anagrams! Some of them may have suffered from being spelt wrong on electoral registers. He had lots of relations with very unusual names but maybe a lot of people in the South did. People came to America with Irish and Hungarian names and they either wrote them down incorrectly or deliberately changed them so they would be easier to assimilate.'

Vernon dropped out of school and had no regular job when he met Gladys. They both liked singing in church and roller-skating and after a two-month courtship, they were married on 7 June 1933. Because official record-keeping was poor, they could lie about their ages – even on the marriage certificate, Vernon is 22 and Gladys 19. In reality, Vernon was 17 and Gladys 21, which, for that time and place, was old for a first-time bride.

Elvis himself didn't know Gladys' true age until her death. In keeping with this bizarre family tree, Vernon's brother, Vester, married Gladys' sister, Clettes, in 1935. Vernon, with Vester and his father's help, built their first home on the Old Saltillo Road. The plot and the materials cost $150. Vernon himself was in and out of jobs – he wasn't stupid but he was work shy.

Gladys stopped making shirts when she fell ill, which we can now see was the consequence of carrying twins with a bad liver. The factory had a collection for her and gathered $10. They bought sheets and blankets for the baby – they didn't know it would be twins. They didn't give cash as they knew Vernon would drink it away.

At 4am on 8 January 1935, Gladys Presley gave birth to Jessie Garon, the Jessie being after Vernon's father. Jessie had been out drinking and he was drunk when he arrived at their shack. He congratulated them on the birth. Vernon said, 'Goddammit, Daddy, can't you see the baby is dead?'

The doctor stayed around and then at 4.35am, the second child was born. Elvis said that there was a strange blue light around the moon, but we don't know who told him that or if he made it up. Elvis also said, 'If my twin brother had lived, do you think the world could have handled two?'

Jessie Garon was already dead by the time his brother came into the world. It was typical of the time and the place to give twins matching names – hence, Jessie Garon and Elvis Aaron, and Elvis' second name was after Aaron Kennedy from the First Assembly of God church.

Vernon placed Jessie's body in a shoe box and buried him in an unmarked grave. How much emphasis do we place on the twin and his effect on Elvis Presley's life? In the first Elvis biopic starring Kurt Russell in 1979, Elvis talks to his twin but this seems fanciful. None of his associates mention this. Lamar Fike says he was working with Elvis for some years before he even knew there had been a twin.

It does, however, seem that Gladys said, 'When one twin dies, the one who lives gets the strength of both.' This was supposed to give encouragement although it may have been taken the wrong way. Biographer Ray Connolly: 'Elvis wasn't the only person to have been a surviving twin but I don't think other mothers brought it up the way that Gladys Presley did. She kept talking about it and telling him that he had inherited all the good properties of the one who died. His mother doted on him. She always told him he was special – she didn't really know that but in actual fact, he was. He was a weird bloke from the start: when he was 16 at school he was in outlandish clothes. He was wearing clothes that black guys were wearing on stage. In his own mind he was a star.'

The big stars of Las Vegas were Liberace, Frank Sinatra and Elvis Presley. Liberace and Presley were surviving twins and Sinatra was an only child, as his mother couldn't have further children. They all adored their mothers and loved displaying their wealth. Both Liberace and Presley would display their jewellery and ask audiences if they loved it; 'You should do,' they'd remark, 'You paid for it.'

The shack where Elvis was born was sturdy as it survived a tornado when he was one year old and is still standing as a tourist attraction in Tupelo, admittedly in a new location. The outhouse has not survived and there's not much to see: a two-room shack with each room measuring 15 feet by 15 feet. Still, the Tupelo Mississippi Flash was born there.

The address is now 306 Elvis Presley Drive and is part of a 15-acre complex with a museum and a memorial chapel. It is reputed to have 100,000 visitors a year; that's 300 people a day going into that little shack which seems excessive to me, but maybe some are just visiting the grounds.

There is a marker there for the Mississippi Blues Trail, which is highly unusual for a white performer, another one being for Mose Allison. You can visit the long-standing Johnnie's Drive-in for a hamburger and a Coke, just as Elvis would have done.

Holly Springs, Mississippi was ideally placed for Elvis fans by being midway between Tupelo and Memphis. A local eccentric and Elvis collector, Paul MacLeod renamed his home, Graceland Too, filled it with Elvis memorabilia and opened it to the public. He named his son, Elvis Aaron Presley MacLeod. As well as being the tour guide, MacLeod would impersonate The King, and in his off-duty hours, he would log all the Elvis references he could find in the media.

Graceland Too was the No.1 tourist attraction in Holly Springs (population 8,000) but in July 2014, Dwight Taylor knocked on his door at 11pm, demanding money. He broke the glass on the front door and forced his way inside. When he refused to leave, MacLeod shot him. MacLeod cooperated with police and no charges were filed. Two days later, MacLeod was found dead on the porch. He was already unhealthy and the stress had killed him. The contents of his home have been auctioned. Graceland Too is no more.

Excuse the diversion, but there are so many ways this story can go, and we will come across a large number of gun-related incidents. Back to Elvis One. I don't know whether you want to know this or not but it is clear from remarks made on stage that Elvis was uncircumcised.

In 1937, Vernon sold a hog to his landlord for $4. Unhappy with the price and egged on by Gladys' feckless brother Travis, he altered the cheque to $14. He was caught and he, Travis and another friend were each sentenced to three years in prison. This was excessively hard but typical for poor southerners who had to be kept in line.

You must have seen the picture of the three-year-old Elvis with his parents. Elvis wears a hat and overalls and even then has that trademark curl to his upper lip. The picture is posed and no one is smiling and it has the same stark reality as Grant Wood's *American Gothic*, which was painted in 1930. Why do they look so sad? Why is Gladys gripping Vernon's shoulder? Why is the background a cement wall? Possibly the picture was taken at the police station as a keepsake for Gladys.

Vernon was taken to the Mississippi State Prison which was 50 miles away in Parchman. The prison had been built (by prisoners!) in 1901 and effectively the convicts were worked like slaves. They had to work on the farm, hence the name Parchman Farm.

In 1927, Son House had been in a juke joint when a customer started shooting, wounding him in the leg. Son House shot back and killed him. For this he was sentenced to 15 years in Parchman Farm, but the evidence was reassessed and he was out in two.

The blues singer and guitarist Booker T. Washington White was born about 20 miles from Tupelo in 1909, and his name was shortened to Bukka White. He was recording from the early 1930s but his career was side-tracked in 1937 when he was ambushed one night by a group of thugs. He stood his ground and shot one of them dead. He was sent to Parchman Farm for two years but the Governor took him off normal work duties and had him form a prison band. He was there at the same time as Vernon but we don't know if they met. When he was released he recorded 'Parchman Farm Blues'. This is not the same song as the jazzy 'Parchman Farm', first written and recorded by the white blues artist, Mose Allison, on an album wittily entitled *Local Colour* in 1957. That song has been recorded by Georgie Fame, John Mayall's Bluesbreakers and John Hammond, the blues-singing son of the afore-mentioned John Hammond.

Parchman had an infamously strict regime and you would have thought that the inmates had neither the strength nor the inclination for sex. However, the Governor in the late 1930s wanted to eliminate homosexuality and he introduced conjugal rights. Vernon qualified for this and so most weekends, Gladys and the young Elvis would make the 100-mile round trip to Parchman so that Vernon could enjoy jailhouse cock.

It is known that on at least one visit , Elvis didn't wave goodbye to Vernon, but, heck, he was only three years old and how would you feel if you'd been left with a warden whilst your parents went to the married quarters?

Things were bad for Vernon and equally bad for Gladys. She could not maintain the payments on their shack and it was repossessed in 1938. She moved in with a cousin who looked after Elvis while Gladys worked in a laundry.

Elvis said in 1956, 'I've always liked music. My mother and dad both liked to sing. They tell me that when I was about three or four years old, I got away from them in church and walked up in front of the choir and started beating time.' Interesting that Elvis should pick that age as that is when Vernon was in prison.

Vernon found it hard to get work once he was released, after 18 months' incarceration, in 1939. He did work in a shipyard in Pascagoula on the Gulf Coast for some months in 1940 and the family lived next door to Vernon's uncle, Sales, and his wife, Annie, but both families were to return to Tupelo. Then in 1942, he found regular employment, building a prisoner-of-war camp 200 miles away. A tax bill has come to light for 1943 showing that Vernon and Gladys had earned $1,232 and had to pay $12 tax.

Gladys had a miscarriage and was not able to have further children. As their only living child, Elvis looks out of place in that heavily populated family tree.

A misrepresentation: Gladys walked Elvis to Lawhon Elementary School every day and then to Milam Junior High. This continued until Elvis was in his teens, so was she overly protective towards him? She might have been but that is not the evidence for that. Vernon saw no value in book learning: in his view, you learned a trade by working with others. Gladys, on the other hand, appreciated the advantages of being educated and wanted to ensure that Elvis didn't abscond. She was determined that Elvis should graduate, which he did. Although Gladys walked him to school, Elvis came home alone.

No one needed to force Elvis to go to church. The Presleys attended the First

Assembly of God church and Elvis, young or old, never doubted his faith. It was a country church that only seated 50. Nowadays the building has a new home as part of the tourism site. Donna Presley Early, Elvis' cousin said, 'We are part of the Assembly of God and it is great. We enjoy the music and we clap our hands. Music can touch your heart like nothing else can and going to church is like going to a concert.'

Elvis never mentioned his dad's prison record. Gospel singing became the foundation of his work. He recorded many gospel songs and frequently he began recording sessions by singing old-time hymns. On a more superficial level, he got his wiggle from the emotional outpourings of the Pentecostal preachers. He was instructed in fundamentalism and he wrote his comments and thoughts in several Bibles.

Elvis befriended the local celebrity, country singer Mississippi Slim (Walter Horn). When only eight, he was performing with him on local radio in Tupelo. He was less confident when it came to speech. He didn't have a bad stammer and I thought it was simply Elvis speaking before he had collected his thoughts. Ray Connolly thinks otherwise, 'Elvis was the one who said he had a stammer, although in America they call it a stutter. He would get stuck over certain letters, t-t-t-t. I had a much more severe stammer and I would get locked on the words and it was terrible. I don't know how I got over it. It is something to do with electrical circuits in the brain. School was a nightmare for me and it was still bad at university. Elvis had a repetitive thing and it would come out on stage. As soon as I met Elvis, he noticed straight away that I had a stammer, and he was very kind to me.'

The Tupelo Hardware Store has been at 114 W. Main Street since 1926. It was an all-purpose store and Elvis bought his first guitar there, admittedly a cheap and nasty one for $8 for his tenth birthday but it got him started. To commemorate this purchase, the Tupelo Hardware Store sells inscribed guitar picks as souvenirs.

Significantly, the young Elvis had wanted a rifle rather than a guitar. When some jealous school children cut the strings, others clubbed together to buy new ones…and Elvis wished that he'd had that rifle. His musical talent was recognised, as he received an A in music from Milam Junior High.

The country singer Red Foley had written and recorded a doleful song about the life and death of his dog, Old Shep. Elvis loved 'Old Shep' and performed it at every opportunity. In 1945, a teacher entered him in the Mississippi-Alabama Fair and Dairy Show, which took place West of the town. It was Elvis' first large audience – up to 2,000 people – and Elvis tugged at the heartstrings and came fifth. The winner, Shirley Jones, was from the same school and Elvis sang duets with her on school shows. Elvis remembered the day more for the beating he got from his mother for going on 'dangerous' fairground rides.

Memphis, Tennessee is 50 miles north-west of Tupelo, Mississippi. Vernon had found regular work in Memphis and the family decided to move. Elvis would soon be in his second hometown.

CHAPTER 2
Long Distance Information

*'Before Elvis hit it big, a bunch of us used to meet on Beale Street.
We told him that he wouldn't go anywhere with a name like Elvis Presley:
he'd have to change it. In 1954, Elvis Presley couldn't even
spell Memphis: in 1957, he owned it.'*
Ronnie Hawkins

I. Tennessee Saturday Night

In terms of size, Tennessee is a little bigger than Mississippi but it has twice the population with six million inhabitants and two particularly large cities – the capital Nashville (650,000 citizens) and Memphis (655,000). After them, it's a significant drop to Knoxville and Chattanooga with around 180,000 apiece.

Tennessee is landlocked, surrounded by eight other states, and going clockwise from the top left corner: Missouri, Kentucky, Virginia, North Carolina, Georgia, Alabama, Mississippi, and Arkansas. The state's name comes from a Cherokee word for 'river of the great bend', a reference to the Little Tennessee River on the eastern side of the state.

The Mississippi River forms the western boundaries of the state and because the fertile Mississippi Delta reminded the office-bearers of the Nile, the name 'Memphis' was taken from Egypt. This link has never been forgotten as a 32-storey pyramid was built and opened in Memphis in 1991. Its principal client was the National Basketball Association but the standards for the arena were not met, and, in a bizarre turn of events, the NBA built another arena elsewhere in Memphis. The Pyramid was closed for several years but now it is having some success with shops and a hotel: there's still a long way to go.

Unlike the state of Mississippi, there are great variations in the height above sea level and as a result, parts of Tennessee are shrouded in a thin haze, famously in the Blue Ridge Mountains of Virginia, another part of the Appalachians. The Smoky Mountains lie to the east with five mountains over 6,000 feet. Gatlinburg is the gateway to the mountain ranges and is the place for the showdown in Johnny Cash's 'A Boy Named Sue'.

During the Napoleonic wars, the Tennesseans were particularly willing to volunteer and General Andrew Jackson used the recruits with great skill to win the Battle of New Orleans in 1815. The victory was commemorated by the country singer Jimmy Driftwood in 1959, and a cover version from Johnny Horton topped the US charts. A British outing from Lonnie Donegan was a UK hit but Lonnie changed the lyric and put the British commander, Colonel Pakenham (actually Sir Edward Pakenham) on the wrong side. He died in the battle and his body was returned home, preserved in a keg of rum.

Elvis Presley: Caught in a Trap

In the 1840s when the USA was in conflict with Mexico, it again called for volunteers, hoping to recruit 3,000 men from Tennessee. Thirty thousand applied and so Tennessee was christened 'The Volunteer State'. Mexico was vanquished with a considerable loss of land and prestige. However, the state's greatest frontiersman, Davy Crockett was killed defending the Alamo.

Following the route marked by frontiersman Daniel Boone, European immigrants migrated from the Appalachian Mountains and further westward, displacing the native American tribes, which in less politically correct days were known as Red Indians. In 1830, Andrew Jackson signed the Indian Removal Act and five tribes (Cherokee, Choctaw, Chickasaw, Creek and Seminole) were forced to relocate to a newly-created Indian Territory west of the Mississippi. This journey was later named the Trail of Tears. Many of them didn't make it, dying along the way. This inhuman behaviour defies rational explanation today but at the time it cleared the southern states for settlement.

One of those cities, Chattanooga, on the Tennessee side of the border with Atlanta was well poised for development. The city had the magical combination of river and rail – the Tennessee River and the 'choo choo', naturally – but its growth was stymied when the neighbouring Atlanta in Georgia built an airport.

Although Tennessee was to secede during the Civil War, the population was conflicted, leading some family members to support opposite sides. With the exception of Virginia, there were more Confederate soldiers from Tennessee than any other state, and yet at the same time, the state provided more soldiers for the Union than the other rebel states combined. There were over 1,400 battles or skirmishes within the state of Tennessee so clearly, the good people of Tennessee enjoyed a fight.

The Band brilliantly captured the times in 'The Night They Drove Old Dixie Down', written by Canadian Robbie Robertson but partly based on what Levon Helm heard as he was growing up. During the Civil War, Virgil Cain's 18-year-old brother becomes a Confederate soldier and is shot by a Yankee. The charismatic general Robert E. Lee comes by looking for more Confederate recruits and Virgil leaves his wife and his farm to enlist. They go to Richmond, Virginia and the city is soon in flames. The Civil War is over and the South has lost.

The individual southern states were readmitted to the union only after they had abolished slavery and given the black population the right to vote. Tennessee was quickly back in the Union, but giving democratic rights to all its citizens was a deliberately slow process as the politicians found ways of blocking their privileges through literacy tests. Indeed, it took 100 years for the legislation to be rescinded.

In the 1920s prohibition was in effect in many states including Tennessee – today, there are still some counties which forbid alcohol. One of them, unpredictably, is Lynchburg, the home of Jack Daniel's. As this is a dry county, hard liquor can only be sold in souvenir gift packs at the distillery.

There were many tobacco plantations in Tennessee, so unwittingly they gave a deadly export to the world. Something more deliberate happened during the Second World War – the first atomic bomb was developed in Tennessee under the so-called Manhattan Project, and later used with devastating effect on Japan. Maybe the horrifying results of this were not grasped by the American public as in 1957, Wanda Jackson released a single, 'Fujiyama Mama', in the worst possible taste:

'I've been to Nagasaki, Hiroshima too,

*The same I did to them, baby, I can do to you.
I'm a Fujiyama mama and I'm just about to blow my top.'*

Somewhat ironically, politicians and businessmen subsequently courted the Japanese and persuaded Nissan to build the world's largest automobile assembly plant in Tennessee.

The introduction of nuclear warfare came to be known as the Big Bang but in a very different way, Tennessee was responsible for several Big Bangs in popular music, three major ones being 'the Bristol sessions', the first noteworthy country music recordings in Bristol in 1927, the development of the blues along Beale Street in Memphis, and the first recordings by Elvis Presley in 1954 at Sun Studio.

The first country recordings had been made in the early 1920s and most of them seem to be by Vernon Dalhart, a Texan recording in New York with an extraordinary number of aliases. In 1927, Ralph Peer of Victor Records went on a field trip to Bristol in East Tennessee and recorded Jimmie Rodgers (born Meridian, Mississippi), the Carter Family (from Virginia) and the Stoneman Family (also from Virginia) in what would later become known as 'the Bristol sessions.'

Jimmie Rodgers was known as 'The Singing Brakeman', as he had originally worked the railroads until a chest condition forced him to resign. His songs include 'The Soldier's Sweetheart' (recorded by Peer in 1927), 'Muleskinner Blues' and 'T for Texas' but he died from TB in 1933 when he was only 35. In May 1955, Elvis Presley performed at the Jimmie Rodgers Memorial Day celebration in Meridian.

At the time of the 1927 recording sessions, Ernie Ford was an eight-year-old in Bristol; he went on to become a bombardier in World War II, flying missions in Japan. When the war ended, he became a popular TV entertainer as Tennessee Ernie Ford, the stage name proudly revealing his origin, although his hillbilly humour would be embarrassing to hear today. His many hit records include 'Shotgun Boogie' (1951), which can be seen as a forerunner of rock'n'roll, the class ballad 'Give Me Your Word' (1955) and 'Sixteen Tons' (1956), written by Merle Travis about his family experience of being paid in tokens for the company store and being fleeced twice. Ford was a religious man and Presley was impressed how well his spiritual albums sold: *Hymns* (1956) reached No.2 on the US albums charts and was on the listings for 277 consecutive weeks.

Nashville became the state capital in 1843, which did wonders for its growth. The Tennessee State Capitol building was built by a mixture of artisans, convicts and slaves. It was unusual for the state itself to employ slaves and this is the largest project on which they were used.

Being in the centre of the state, the central plateau around Nashville was seen as a strategic vantage point during the Civil War. It was location, location, location and after the war, the city prospered.

Bristol, although having a twin city in Virginia across the state line, didn't have the infrastructure and Nashville became the self-proclaimed country music capital of the world; more latterly Music City USA, which is appropriate as so many genres of music are now recorded there, although country is still the main one.

Nashville has been at the centre of country music since the start of the weekly radio show, *Grand Ole Opry*, which began on WSM in 1925. It was originally called *Barn Dance* but following an opera programme, a witty announcer said that it was time for the *Grand Ole Opry*, and it stuck. Top performers were expected to forgo their

Saturdays and play for reduced fees in order to put *Grand Ole Opry* on their billings, a brilliant move by the programme makers. The evening shows were split into segments hosted by a star performer and sponsored by an advertiser.

In Elvis' time, the show was broadcast from the Ryman Auditorium. The Ryman had been built by local businessman Thomas Ryman, in 1890 and had originally been dedicated to spiritual music. The *Opry* was there until 1974 when it was moved to the new Opryland complex. The Ryman was shut for some years but it was revamped and reopened in 1994. They have a very impressive list of forthcoming attractions, mostly rock, pop and country, but for sure there wouldn't have been World Music nights in the 1950s.

We will come to Elvis' appearance on the *Grand Ole Opry* in the next chapter but he heard the show as he was growing up. He told Hank Williams Jr. that when he walked on stage, he knew he was standing where Hank Williams stood.

As Elvis listened to the show as an adolescent, he had no idea that its biggest star, the smooth balladeer Eddy Arnold, known as 'the Tennessee Plowboy', was managed by Colonel Tom Parker. While Eddy was singing his No.1 country hits like 'Anytime' (1948), 'Don't Rob Another Man's Castle' (1949) and 'I Wanna Play House With You' (1951), the penny-pinching Parker was doing business backstage, talking to other managers and running up WSM's phone bill on calls he should have been making from his own office.

There was a fondness for mentioning southern states in country songs as it sold records. Eddy Arnold had a country No.1 with 'Kentucky Waltz' in 1951 and he had a hit with 'Tennessee Stud' in 1959, a song about a horse, not a well-hung gent, I might add. Indeed, the hit songs about Tennessee included 'Tennessee Waltz' (Cowboy Copas and Pee Wee King, 1948, a pop hit for Patti Page – and the State Song), 'Tennessee Border' (Red Foley, 1949), 'Tennessee Polka' (Pee Wee King, 1949), 'Tennessee Saturday Night' (Red Foley, 1949) and 'Tennessee Flat-Top Box' (Johnny Cash, 1962).

The word 'Mississippi' didn't sing as well – too many sibilant s's – but Red Foley with the Dixie Dons took 'M-I-S-S-I-S-S-I-P-P-I' to No.1 in 1950 and later there were pop successes called 'Mississippi' for John Phillips of the Mamas and the Papas (1970) and Pussycat (1976).

Just as there are more caves in Tennessee than any other state, there is a higher proportion of professional musicians in Nashville than anywhere else. The so-called Nashville Cats were celebrated by the Lovin' Spoonful in a hit single in 1967. Most could not read music but an alternative system was devised which circumvented the problem, no doubt helped by the observation that country music was described by songwriter Harlan Howard as 'three chords and the truth'. The Nashville cats who played on Bob Dylan's *Blonde on Blonde* in 1966 were back in the studio the following week playing standard country fare.

Much of that standard country fare was down to Chet Atkins who had been born outside Knoxville, Tennessee in 1924. He was country music's greatest guitarist, often playing melody and rhythm at the same time, but he was also a key producer for RCA, devising the warm, much copied 'countrypolitan' sound for middle of the road artists such as Jim Reeves and Eddy Arnold. Financially, it would be hard to question his judgement, though many saw it as the death-knell for country music.

Many outsiders saw Nashville as gaudy and tacky and certainly Webb Pierce's guitar-shaped swimming pool and Conway Twitty's Twitty City (which is in Hendersonville) seemed ripe for satire. Who on earth told Hank Snow that his hairpiece was a good fit? Snow, a grouchy performer, had an argument with his fiddle player before a show one night, leading to the musician skilfully dislodging his wig with his bow. All they gotta do was not act naturally and when Buck Owens came to Liverpool Empire in the 1960s, he said backstage, 'I want to see the Beatles and catch me some pussy', possibility an indication of what he had heard about Maggie May in Lime Street.

When the satire came, it came hard. Robert Altman's 1975 film, *Nashville*, was as funny as it was savage, blurring reality and fantasy and showing just how hypocritical some performers were. It was produced by Jerry Weintraub, who had delivered the $2m budget in three days, but there must have been concerns that they would need a lot more if they lost libel actions. Unquestionably, Henry Gibson as Haven Hamilton was playing Hank Snow for all it was worth, both personally and musically. Fortunately for them, Snow refused to see the film, saying, 'I have better things to do than see a movie where somebody is supposed to be playing me.' He must have been told about its contents as he added, 'I'm not pompous at all. I'm just a quiet, bashful country boy.'

But salvation was around the corner. Willie Nelson had written hit songs but he had been trying to make it as a performer for years with his behind-the-beat vocals and Django-like guitar. He ditched his suit, grew his hair and moved to Austin, where he teamed up with another rebellious figure, Waylon Jennings, for Outlaw Country. Their records were honest and hard-hitting, without the inevitable sweetening of the standard Nashville product. Willie discovered that you didn't have to look a million dollars to make a million dollars.

Other artists joined them and in the end, Outlaw Country became a brand like any other. Some magnificent performers and songwriters are associated with it – Townes Van Zandt, Guy Clark, Jerry Jeff Walker, Kris Kristofferson and Steve Earle.

Singers and songwriters had come to Nashville to make it, which meant relatively few country stars had been born there. But times are changing, as Miley Cyrus, daughter of Billy Ray, was born in Nashville, as was Hillary Scott, the daughter of Linda Davis and co-lead singer of Lady Antebellum. Antebellum, incidentally, is a generic name for the southern architecture seen in *Gone with the Wind*, a classic example being Graceland, although that was built in 1939.

These days, the more wayward folk and country artists are branded together as Americana, an odd name that somehow includes the very British Billy Bragg. Country music today is very slick, professional and usually soulless – a young audience has lapped up the TV series, *Nashville*, without realising it is a satire, or is it? It's hard to tell especially as I've been so bored that I have never made it through one episode.

The most brilliant example of self-satire, self-promotion and indeed self-preservation has to be Dolly Parton who was born in Sevierville outside Knoxville in 1946. Her remarkable figure continues to defy gravity and amidst all the showmanship and jokes, she is an exceptionally gifted performer and songwriter. Her songs include 'My Tennessee Mountain Home', 'Jolene' and 'I Will Always Love You', which she wrote when she abandoned her singing partner, the ultra-tacky Porter Wagoner. Her Dollywood theme park attracts 2.5m visitors a year and is far more ambitious than the usual country star attractions.

Let's go walking in Memphis, the name of which is an amalgamation of two

Egyptian words meaning 'enduring and beautiful'. The frontier town is now a very large inland port and is the barbecue capital of the world. It is famous for blues, soul, Sun Records and Elvis Presley. But Memphis had immense problems in 1878 when Yellow Fever claimed over 5,000 lives. The city was declared bankrupt and its charter was revoked until 1893.

Robert Church had been born in Memphis to a white, steamboat owner and a black mother. Following the epidemic, he bought property at greatly reduced prices and in turn, he used his profits to bring life back to the city. He opened a bank which lent to the community. In the process, Church became the first black millionaire in the South.

The heart of the black music scene was around Beale Street where workers relieved the boredom of picking cotton all day long. They played as hard as they worked, seeking out juke joints and getting drunk on cheap corn liquor. An evangelist commented, 'If whisky ran ankle deep, you could not get drunk quicker than you can on Beale Street today.'

Prostitution was rife. The blues musician Sunnyland Slim recalled, 'Memphis used to be a barrelhouse town. It was the greatest town in the world for pimps and hustlers. That's where a whole lot of people got jailed.'

Most of the Beale Street musicians were singers and guitarists who would play house parties for a few dollars. There were jug bands where a musician would blow across the mouth of a bottle to create a bass sound. The best-known group was Gus Cannon's Jug Stompers who made the original version of 'Walk Right In'.

When the politician Ed Crump was running for office in 1910, he had W.C. Handy write him a theme song. Handy wrote 'Mr. Crump', which was later given a lyric by George Norton that referred to Handy's own band and showed Beale Street's darker side. It is now called 'Memphis Blues' and the best-known recording is by Louis Armstrong.

Arguably the greatest female soul singer, Aretha Franklin, was born in Memphis in 1942, but she was raised in Detroit and mostly recorded in New York.

Although called Memphis Minnie, Lizzie Douglas came from Louisiana. Big Bill Broonzy told her 'You play guitar like a man' and indeed she married three male guitarists. Her tracks include 'When the Levee Breaks' (1930), 'Bumble Bee' (1930) and 'Me and My Chauffeur Blues' (1941).

A highly distinctive R&B singer known for the grunts in his vocals, Bobby 'Blue' Bland was born a few miles outside the city in 1930 and he often sang while B.B. King played. His records were anything but bland.

Tina Turner was born 30 miles from Memphis in Nutbush. Sleepy John Estes was born close by in Ripley in 1899 and died in Nutbush in 1977. By then Nutbush was famous for its city limits, immortalised by Tina Turner in 1973 in one of the funkiest records ever made.

Among the many blues musicians associated with Beale is Peter Chatman, better known as Memphis Slim, who was born in the city in 1915. He was a fine boogie pianist. Post-war he recorded blues for black listeners but he found acceptance with white audiences and he moved to Paris in 1962 and became popular during the British blues boom. He was six foot six and he surely had the longest fingers of any blues pianist. When he died in 1988, his body was taken back to Memphis.

In 1916 W.C. Handy wrote 'Beale Street Blues' which was supremely recorded by Louis Armstrong on *Louis Armstrong Plays W.C. Handy* (1954). Armstrong told Handy, 'You wrote it so well that the notes play themselves.' The expanded edition of the album, released in 1997, includes a vintage interview with W. C. Handy. It is an unexpected pleasure to hear him and he says of Armstrong, 'There was something in that voice that appreciated the pride of race.'

'Beale Street Blues' celebrates the street but it doesn't hold back on the details:
'If Beale Street could talk, if Beale Street could talk
Married men would have to take their beds and walk
Except one or two, who never drink booze
And the blind man on the corner
Who sings the Beale Street Blues.'

Beale Street was redeveloped in the 1970s so it is not the same today, but A. Schwab's Dry Goods Store is still there. It used to sell voodoo powder and you can still buy Mojo Hands for good luck, but who knows what the bags contain.

Piggly-Wiggly, the first supermarket chain in America was started in Jefferson Avenue by Clarence Saunders in 1916. He had developed a self-service system and he believed that if he were cheaper than his rivals, the public wouldn't mind serving themselves. There was a turnstile entry which forced customers to move in one direction and it was hard to return to an item. In a highly innovative and much copied move, he put impulse purchases like candy by the cash registers.

The name came about because, whilst travelling on a train, he had seen some piglets pushing and wriggling to get under a fence. Maybe the ridiculous name went against him, but the chain store was declared bankrupt seven years later. There is now a homage to the store at the Pink Palace Museum in Memphis, illustrating the evolution of the supermarket, and possibly also the evolution of shoplifting.

One of the quirkiest (and quackiest) traditions in America continues to this day. Twice a day at the Peabody Hotel in Union Avenue, five ducks waddle across the lobby, accompanied by their Duckmaster and watched by tourists with their mobile phones. The ducks spend their day in the fountain and at night they live on the roof. Are they wondering if one day they will be on the customers' plates?

Songs about the city include Chuck Berry's 'Memphis, Tennessee' where Chuck wants to make contact with his young daughter and the Rolling Stones' 'Honky Tonk Women' which has an exceptional opening line, 'I met a gin-soaked bar-room queen in Memphis.'

Rosanne Cash, the daughter of one of Sun's leading artists, was born in Memphis in 1955 but her place of birth was not the main reason for her considerable talent.

The instrumental act, Booker T. and the M.G.'s, is famous for 'Green Onions' and organist Booker T. Jones, bass player Donald 'Duck' Dunn and drummer Al Jackson Jr were all born in Memphis. Indeed, M.G. stood for Memphis Group. They became the studio band for another local label, Stax, and when they recorded their take on *Abbey Road*, they called the album, *McLemore Avenue*, which was the studio's location, a few miles outside the city centre. Musicians who have recorded there include Otis Redding and Isaac Hayes (born 20 miles away in Covington, 1942) and a colourful example of the funkiness of the area is King Curtis' single, 'Memphis Soul Stew' (1967). Dusty Springfield's landmark album is *Dusty in Memphis* (1968), although the vocals we hear were recorded in New York. Stax Records went through some bad business deals and possibly its final blow was securing Lena Zavaroni's contract, a sure sign that management had lost the plot.

The Box Tops, a group of white boys from Memphis made the single, 'The Letter', with a stunning lead vocal from 16-year-old Alex Chilton. The letter was a popular form of communication back in 1967 and the single topped the US charts for a month. Who knows, maybe it inspired FedEx to set up their headquarters in Memphis in 1971.

II. Got a Lot o' Livin' to Do, 1948–1954

Because of the lack of employment opportunities for Vernon Presley in Tupelo, the family moved to Memphis, taking with them Elvis' paternal grandmother Minnie Mae, in 1948 when Elvis was 13. Elvis, sounding like a Steinbeck creation, later said, 'We were broke, man, and we left Tupelo overnight. Daddy packed all our belongings and put them on top and in the trunk of a 1939 Plymouth. We just headed to Memphis. Things had to be better.' Well, it wasn't that good. Vernon found work loading cans in a paint factory, but a bad back put him out of action. Gladys revelled in her job as a hospital orderly. This was ideal for her friendly and sympathetic nature. It was suggested that she train as a nurse, although she didn't pursue this.

The Presleys lived on a housing project, sharing one room with a toilet down the hall. Again, many have said that it was unnatural that the growing Elvis should sleep in the same room as his parents, but what else could he do? Thousands of families were in the same position.

Although Elvis continued with his schooling, he was also working in a cinema in Memphis from 1950. Memphis was a city that was strong on blues music. He became infatuated with the blues, hanging out on Beale Street, soaking up the fashions. He was taken with Lansky Brothers, a gents outfitters, which opened in 1946. His first purchase was a white tuxedo for the school prom, but he loved bright colours. There is a photograph of him in a blue jacket with a brown collar and he loved the mixture of pink and black – this also applied to Cadillacs. Bernard Lansky, a master salesman, said of Elvis, 'Everything suited him.'

Elvis received strange looks at school as he was different from the other boys. He was not mocked to his face as his friend Red West protected him. Everybody knew he could sing. He was still singing 'Old Shep' and he would perform solos in the Christmas carol concerts.

Elvis' report card for 1951 has come to light and it is grim reading. He has failed in English, and American History (is there any other?) and his best subject is woodwork. A life of carpentry beckons: now who else was a carpenter? Vernon advised him to become an electrician as he didn't know a guitar player who was 'worth a damn'. This is identical to Aunt Mimi's admonishment to John Lennon, 'The guitar's all right, John, but you'll never make a living from it.'

Nevertheless, Elvis Presley did graduate from Humes High. He worked as a cinema usher and then for Precision Tools, eventually taking his father's advice and working for a small electrical company in Memphis, Crown Electric. At first he was a deliveryman, driving the same truck that the singer Johnny Burnette had driven the year before.

Curiously, there is an article supposedly written by Elvis in the *Radio Luxembourg Book of Record Stars*, dated 1962, in which Elvis says that he got a job at a dollar an hour in a defence plant: I have no idea what this is about and whether the feature is genuine – it could have been a factory that was working for the military in Korea or could have been a tag that stuck after World War Two. In the same article, Elvis says of his relationship with Gladys, 'I could wake her up in the middle of the night if I was worried about something. She'd get up, fix me a sandwich and a glass of milk and talk to me.' That quote sounds genuine enough.

Samuel Cornelius Phillips was 12 years older than Elvis Presley although to Elvis, it would have seemed more. He had been born in Florence, Alabama on 5 January 1923 and it is fitting that such a famous record producer should have been born so close to Muscle Shoals. Sam worked as an announcer and radio engineer in both Decatur, Georgia and Nashville, Tennessee and quickly became adept with recording equipment.

In January 1950 he started his own business, the Memphis Recording Service, at 706 Union Avenue, a block away from Beale. He started recording local artists singings blues and R&B and he leased the product to the Chess brothers (Chess label) or the Bihari brothers (Modern, RPM). He didn't like the bland white music of the day and he wanted to capture the 'gutbucket sounds' of black musicians. He wanted the studio recordings to have the atmosphere of a cooking band on Beale. I don't believe it myself but it is said that the uneven ceiling contributed to the unusual sound.

Ike Turner's Kings of Rhythm band featured his cousin, Jackie Brenston. On 5 March 1951 they recorded a car song, 'Rocket 88' for Sam Phillips. It was largely instrumental with three short vocals: its energy level has made Phillips call it 'the first rock'n'roll record', but then the first rock'n'roll record would have to be something he'd made. The band damaged an amplifier in transit and although it buzzed, Sam thought it added to the sound. The record was released on Chess and topped the R&B charts, but there was internal friction as Ike Turner resented his subsidiary role. 'I always liked that record,' said Little Richard, 'and I used the riff in my act. When we were looking for a lead-in for 'Good Golly Miss Molly', I did that and it fitted.'

Sam Phillips recorded B.B. King, Rosco Gordon and Howlin' Wolf. He was a white man who loved the blues and R&B. He felt that he was helping race relations and that he was doing God's work.

Whether doing God's work extended to his private life is uncertain. He had a wife and two children, but he also had mistresses and would regularly visit brothels. That apart, he could work an eighteen-hour day at the studio.

Phillips had set up his own Phillips International label in 1950 but he only released one single, 'Gotta Let You Go' by the one-man band, Joe Hill Louis. The song sounds like early rap and there is no melody to speak of. Only 300 copies were pressed for local sale and he didn't know how to take it further.

By 1952 he was ready to try again. He was certain that the Chess brothers and the Bihari brothers were getting the better of him and he wanted to record, manufacture and release his own records.

He started his Sun Records imprint with a slow-burning instrumental, 'Drivin' Slow' from the 16-year-old saxophonist, Johnny London. It's good and atmospheric and it sounds as though London is playing his sax in the corridor, which gives it an eerie feel.

It's odd that the first Sun record to be successful has an Elvis connection. Sam had recorded an answer version to Big Mama Thornton's hit single, 'Hound Dog'.

Willie Mae 'Big Mama' Thornton, born in Montgomery, Alabama in 1926, had been recording without much success and was asked to work with Johnny Otis' band in Los Angeles. Two young songwriters, Jerry Leiber and Mike Stoller, were to supply the songs. Said Leiber, 'She was the biggest, the baddest, the saltiest chick you could ever see. I had to write a song for her that basically said, 'Go fuck yourself!" Hence, 'Hound Dog', which was recorded as a mid-tempo blues with novelty sounds. At first, Big Mama refused to growl because she didn't like being told how to perform a song.

'Hound Dog' was a No.1 R&B hit. John Stewart, later with the Kingston Trio, recalled, 'When I was at high school, I had to go to downtown L.A. to get the records I wanted from a black record shop and the radio stations called them 'race records.' I liked Big Mama Thornton who did 'Hound Dog'. Rock'n'roll came from country and western, gospel and the blues. You English became great aficionados of the blues. Look at Eric Clapton, he is steeped in the blues, much more than a lot of the 1950s rock'n'rollers. They knew of it but they weren't consumed by it like he and a lot of other English players were.'

Within a few days, Sam Phillips had come up with the answer version, 'Bear Cat', which joined it in the Top 10. It was recorded by a Memphis disc-jockey, Rufus C. Thomas Jr, billed as Rufus 'Hound Dog' Thomas Jr. He said, 'It was a great song to do. It was a copy but there wasn't anything she could do about it.' Well, maybe not Mama Thornton, but Peacock Records was owned by a gangster, Don Robey. He didn't find it amusing and claimed copyright infringement (which in a way was the point of answer versions) and Phillips had to concede. Phillips was a tough, stubborn individual but no match for Robey. Big Mama Thornton was to record her own answer versions with 'I Smell a Rat' and 'Just Like a Dog (Barking up the Wrong Tree)'. She died of alcoholism in 1984.

Rufus Thomas' follow-up single, 'Tiger Man' had more originality in that it ploughed the same furrow as 'Hound Dog' without copying it. It wasn't a hit song at the time, but Elvis Presley was to see its potential.

Next, an inside story. When Johnny Bragg was 17, he caught his girlfriend making love to his best friend. She fought with him and in order to explain her bruises to her parents, she accused Bragg of raping her. The police beat him until he signed a confession. The girl retracted her story but not before Bragg had been charged with six other rapes. He was found guilty of them all. Bragg was given six 99-year sentences to run consecutively (594 years, should he live that long) and he was sent to the notorious Tennessee State Prison. He was assigned to make prison clothes and when the authorities thought he was not working quickly enough, the guards tied him to a ring suspended from the ceiling and beat him unconscious with their leather belts.

But Johnny Bragg had a lovely tenor voice and a natural ear for harmony and he had enjoyed singing in church. When he heard the prisoners singing spirituals, he did not understand why they could not be as well-ordered as the groups he had heard in church. He formed The Prisonaires vocal group with other convicts – their first performances were serenading prisoners before execution. Bragg would stay behind to loosen the straps on the condemned men and clear up the mess.

Bragg became known as 'Bucket Head' as he wrote songs with a bucket on his head to simulate echo. Nashville stars would sometimes perform at the prison and when Bragg met Hank Williams, he asked, 'Do you ever sing songs written by other people?' 'Depends,' said Hank, 'Are you one of those other people?' He sang him a song which he bought for $5. The song eventually became 'Your Cheating' Heart', a country standard but Bragg had sold his copyright.

In the winter of 1953, Bragg was walking across the courtyard to his duties in the laundry with a burglar, Robert Riley. The rain was beating down and Bragg said, 'Here we are just walking in the rain and wondering what the girls are doing.' Riley said, 'That's a song.' With a few minutes Bragg had written two verses and was convinced it was a hit. As he was illiterate, he asked Riley to write it down in exchange for a writing credit.

The Democratic politician Frank Clement became the nation's youngest governor when he was 32. He appointed James Edwards as the new warden and ordered him to make the place tolerable. As soon as Edwards heard The Prisonaires, he informed Clement that this could help their reforms. In an unprecedented move, The Prisonaires were allowed to perform under armed guard at churches and civic functions and then on local radio. The audiences came out of curiosity.

In June 1953, Sam Phillips produced The Prisonaires' first single, 'Just Walkin' in the Rain'. The song's elegant but simple arrangement ensured it sold well in Nashville and Memphis and made the nation's R&B Top 10. It looked as though the whole prison had caught the bug of performing and writing songs. Sam Phillips possibly picked up two songs from white inmates, 'Without You' and 'Casual Love Affair', which he later rehearsed with Elvis Presley. Meanwhile, Johnnie Ray had picked up on 'Just Walkin' in the Rain' and turned it into a No.2 US pop hit. It topped the UK charts in 1956, preventing Elvis Presley from having his first UK No.1 with 'Hound Dog'.

In November 1953 Sam Phillips recorded Little Junior's Blue Flames with an original song, 'Mystery Train', credited to Herman Parker, who was Little Junior, and Sam Phillips. It was probably only written by Parker, but then he had based it on 'Worried Man Blues' by the Carter Family from 1930.

Sam Phillips' releases show his adventurous spirit but he was plagued with doubt and with debt. He said, 'I drove 60,000 miles one year from Maine to California setting up distribution. I didn't have any money, I'd sleep in YMCAs. I wanted to get first-hand opinions from each distributor and disc jockey and to get their feel for what we had done.'

One way to add a little income was to make local recordings. These were the days before mass-produced tape recorders and most Memphis residents had have heard their own voices. Sam Phillips had the slogan, 'We record anything – anywhere – anytime'. A member of the public could sing two songs, given to them on a 10-inch 78rpm acetate, for $4 and he might also record church services (weddings and funerals) or other location work.

Sam Phillips felt that this cut down on the search for new singers. He knew the local talent would want to hear themselves. In essence, he would hear what they had to offer and charge them $4 for the privilege. He enjoyed helping them, encouraging them to believe in themselves.

This kind of facility was often seen at fairgrounds – see Graham Greene's novel, *Brighton Rock* – but it was rare for professional labels to offer this service. As it happens, another Mr. Phillips, Percy Phillips, offered this service, just outside the centre of Liverpool. The Quarrymen – who became the Beatles – recorded two tracks there in mid-1958 for under £1, actually 17s.6d.

Elvis Presley: Caught in a Trap

Elvis had seen the sign and he wondered what his voice sounded like. He loved the music on Sun Records but he saw himself as Dean Martin. He loved Dean's lazy, slurred delivery, especially on his 1950 hit, 'I Don't Care If the Sun Don't Shine'. Sinatra was tremendous, but he worked on his technique while Dean sounded like he couldn't care less.

It's said that the record was made for Gladys' birthday. She would have enjoyed the songs chosen, but her birthday was in April. However, why shouldn't Elvis just give it to her as a present? The most likely explanation is that his friend, Ed Leek, whose father was a doctor, gave him $4 and thought he might be able to get the song played on local radio.

Regardless, this 18-year-old truck-driver carrying his guitar went through the doors at Sun Records on 18 July 1953 to hear his voice for the first time.

One way and another, Sam wasn't always at 706 Union Avenue, but it didn't matter as his secretary Marion Keisker knew how to work the equipment.

'Who do you sound like?' she asked.

'I don't sound like nobody,' said Elvis.

What does that mean? Was Elvis being modest or bragging? Almost certainly he was being modest, but you never know. When he repeated this story to the Hollywood reporter, Dane Marlowe in 1956, he added, 'I was a teacher's pet at school and didn't know how to be modest.'

There was a machine that cut the record as you sang so there were no facilities for correcting mistakes. No pressure then. Marion checked the level between voice and guitar. Elvis paid his $4 and the lathe swung into operation.

The hound dog man's big start.

'My Happiness' had been a big song in 1948 for Ella Fitzgerald, the Pied Pipers with June Hutton, and John and Sandra Steele. Elvis' voice is sweet and professional with a slight falsetto on 'any place at all'. He sounds so plaintive, so assured and so unmistakably Elvis. Elvis had it all together before any record producer worked on him. If you have not heard this track before, play it on *YouTube* where it comes with the official video, made by Disney, showing pictures from the Presley archive.

He was never to record the song again, which is a shame as he sang it well. It was a hit for Connie Francis in 1959, which came at the right time for the songwriter Betty Peterson, whose finances were in a bad way due to family illness.

The other song, 'That's When Your Heartaches Begin' had been introduced in 1937 by Shep Fields and his Rippling Rhythm Orchestra, but that version sounded too jolly for a song of lost love. The version that attracted Elvis was by the Ink Spots from 1941. This song was not so successful for Elvis as he starts too high and he sounds drunk in his deep-voiced narration. He ends by saying, 'That's the end'.

There was just the one copy of the record which was bought by Jack White, formerly of the White Stripes, in 2015 for $300,000. Jack had played a cameo as Elvis in the Johnny Cash satire, *Walk Hard: The Dewey Cox Story* (2007).

Marion Keisker made a note 'Good ballad singer' and when Sam Phillips returned she told him about 'the kid with the sideburns'.

Elvis had left the building.

CHAPTER 3

Here Comes the Sun King

'I was an overnight sensation. A year after my first recording, they called me back.'
Elvis Presley on stage, 1970s

I. First Time Out

We all know that 'That's All Right, Mama' was Elvis Presley's first Sun record and that it was a very impressive start to his recording career. Although it only had local success at first, it was a turning point in the development of popular music.

But how does this debut stack up to other stars, past and present? Here we compare 'That's All Right, Mama' to other recording debuts which are listed in date order.

There is the question as to what is a first record – with Elvis it could be 'My Happiness' and similarly with others, it could be their first home recording, if it has surfaced. This listing includes both but by and large, it is the first commercial outings. Was it immediately apparent that these artists would become major stars? Admittedly, this question is being asked with hindsight as we know what happened to each and every one of them.

We all have to start somewhere – so let's see how many stars started at the top. Just for fun, there is a rating for the tracks, going from 1 to 10, with 10 being the most impressive.

Harry James and his Orchestra featuring Frank Sinatra – 'From the Bottom of My Heart' (1939)
On 13 July 1939, Harry James and his Orchestra had a recording date at the Roseland Ballroom in New York City. They had a new vocalist and they recorded 'From the Bottom of My Heart'. When it was first issued as a 78rpm, the label read, 'Harry James and his Orchestra with vocal refrain'. The singer doesn't come in for 50 seconds but then there is a sweet and romantic verse from Frank Sinatra. It's Frank on his best behaviour, but the potential is clear and it is a 7.

Hank Williams – 'I'm Not Coming Home Anymore' (1942)
Hank Williams was 18 years old and wondering whether he should sound like Roy Acuff or Ernest Tubb but on this showing, he sounds like a young Hank Williams trying to sound older. The song was recorded in the Highbridge Radio and Shoe Shop in Montgomery, Alabama in April 1942 and probably played on radio station WSFA. It is Hank's first known composition and is about a man leaving his family because his wife has been cheating, a neat twist so early in his career. There are too many crackles and hisses to enjoy it fully but it's a good song, worth a 6, so why didn't Hank revive it during his MGM years?

Hank Williams – 'Calling You' (1947)
Hank Williams' first single, released in 1947 on the small Sterling label, was a gospel song he had written and he performed it with call-and-response from the Willis Brothers. It sounds like Hank all right and *Billboard* referred to the 'real spiritual qualities in his pipes'. The B-side, 'Never Again (Will I Knock on Your Door)' is typical of his 'love lost' compositions. He got better at it but I agree with *Billboard*, so score it a 7.

Ray Charles – 'I Love You, I Love You' (1949)
Eighteen-year-old Ray Charles fronted a jazz trio, very much based on Nat 'King' Cole's. This is a confident debut of a song written by someone Ray knew in blind school. The B-side is Ray's own, 'Confession Blues' where Ray sounds much older than his years. A confident start but nothing too original about it, but 6.

Al Martino – 'Here in My Heart' (1952)
Inspired by his friend Mario Lanza, Al Martino showed enormous confidence on his first recording, made when he was 25 years old. Just listen to the final notes! It was released on the small BBS label in Philadelphia and transferred to Capitol for national distribution. When the UK published its first sales chart in November 1952, it was No.1 and yet a few weeks before, Al Martino was totally unknown. Al Martino went into hiding when the Mob wanted a slice of his career and he never regained the momentum. Still a powerful 8.

Elvis Presley – 'My Happiness' (1953)
See previous chapter, but the voice and the sincerity is there. A 7.

Elvis Presley – 'That's All Right, Mama' (1954)
One vocalist, two guitars and a stand-up bass, no drums, and yet it remains one of the most dynamic records ever made. Producer Sam Phillips realised that adding echo increased the excitement. A lot of things came together here, all channelled through an astonishingly good-looking boy. It was a brilliant debut that led the way for Elvis and the whole of popular music. Sun Records' rising sun logo was never more appropriate than here. The film director David Lynch described it as like 'being hit by a truck filled with happiness'. An unqualified 10.

Chuck Berry – 'Maybellene' (1955)
Chuck Berry had been working as a guitarist in several bands around St Louis, Missouri but he was desperate to record his own songs. He impressed the Chess brothers in Chicago and his first single was about fast cars and fast women (that is, the very essence of Chuck Berry) and called 'Maybellene'. It was a confident composition with Chuck adding to the dictionary with 'As I was motivatin' over the hill'. It's an immensely confident performance, although the song doesn't have a great guitar riff like 'Roll Over Beethoven' or 'Johnny B. Goode'. As well as being a No.1 R&B hit, it made the US Top 10, so it was an astonishing debut for a black performer in 1955. Definitely a 9 and I might have gone the full 10 if I liked the song more.

Barbra Streisand – 'You'll Never Know' (1955)
When holidaying in a resort in the Catskills, Barbra Streisand's mother wanted to make a private recording with a local pianist and she told Barbra that she could sing something as well. The 13-year-old Barbra sang 'You'll Never Know' with a confidence that belied her years, confidently playing with the phrasing of the song, but you might think it was

a boy soprano. She said, 'I had planned a simple ending but I got carried away.' Clearly a talent to watch. Barbra's first record did not come until some years later, after she had already been on Broadway and performed on major TV variety shows. Already a 7.

Everly Brothers – 'Keep-A Lovin' Me' (1956)
Chet Atkins liked the sound of the two brothers and saw how they could make teenage records which could appeal to country fans. He couldn't justify a whole three-hour session with them and he told them to turn up at the end of a session by Carl Smith. Carl's group, the Tunesmiths, heard the four songs that Don Everly had written and accompanied them straight away. No second takes, that was it, and it was all done and dusted within half an hour. It's hillbilly and like Hank Williams, but those harmonies are in place. A solid 6.

Gene Vincent – 'Be-Bop-A-Lula' (1956)
Who'd ever heard of a girl called Be-Bop-A-Lula and what are red blue jeans? The song had been based around a comic book heroine, Little Lulu and written by a patient in the next hospital bed to Gene Vincent, Donald Graves. Gene gave him $25 for the song and he sang it on the radio in Norfolk, Virginia. In May 1956 he and his musicians went to Nashville and cut it with producer Ken Nelson for Capitol. The drummer Dickie Harrell screamed because he wanted his mother to know he was there. Oodles of echo and a classic debut unlike anything that had gone before (except 'Heartbreak Hotel'). Clearly Gene had great potential but he was beset by personal problems and couldn't build on his success. As for the record, a stunning 10.

Buddy Holly – 'Blue Days – Black Nights' (1956)
Strongly influenced by Elvis Presley's success, the hot kid on the block in Lubbock was signed to US Decca and invited to Nashville to record with his musicians. The best track was a risqué 'Midnight Special', which was held back at the time. The single was 'Blue Days – Black Nights' from Lubbock songwriter, Ben Hall. The song was well recorded, with Sonny Curtis copying Chet Atkins' style on the guitar break. The *Billboard* reviewer said, 'If the public will take more than one Presley or Perkins, as it well may, Holly stands a strong chance.' It's an excellent rockabilly record but it's just as well that it didn't make it, as he adopted a more defiant, less country style for 'That'll Be the Day', his chart-topper with the Crickets the following year. Definitely something there, so 8.

Tom and Jerry (Simon and Garfunkel) – 'Hey Schoolgirl' (1957)
Sixteen-year-olds Paul Simon and Art Garfunkel trying to sound as much like the Everly Brothers, as possible, and it worked. The single climbed into the US Top 50 and sold 100,000 copies. Tom and Jerry were has-beens at 17. Whatever happened to them? 6.

The Quarrymen (Beatles) – 'That'll Be the Day / In Spite of All the Danger' (1958)
There is a tourist plaque to mark Percy Phillips recording this in his home studio in Kensington, Liverpool, in 1958. Considering how naff a lot of British rock'n'roll was at the time, this is a decent cover of the Crickets' hit. The B-side, written by McCartney / Harrison is of more interest and the song is structured around 'Tryin' to Get to You'. Worth a 7 and they hadn't even gone to Hamburg.

Johnny Kidd and the Pirates – 'Please Don't Touch' (1959)
Johnny Kidd had written both songs for their first single, recorded on 18 April 1959,

Elvis Presley: Caught in a Trap

and released on 8 May. They were 'Please Don't Touch' and 'Growl', but the group's manager, Guy Robinson, added himself as a songwriter to create the amusing but misleading credit of Heath Robinson. As with Gene Vincent's 'Be-bop-a-Lula' and Elvis Presley's 'That's All Right, Mama', 'Please Don't Touch' was a very impressive recording debut. It defined his signature sound, very rhythmic but tough and menacing. The song referred to 'shaking', a common theme in Kidd's lyrics. The growl at the end has been copied from Conway Twitty's 'It's Only Make Believe'. The B-side was even called 'Growl' and was a continuation of 'Please Don't Touch', but dynamic in its own right. The single only reached No.26 on the UK charts, but it's worth a 7.

The Beach Boys – 'Surfin'' (1961)
The Pendeltones recorded their first single at Hite Morgan's home studio in Hollywood in September 1961 for the small Candix label. They had a song written by his son Bruce, 'Luau', lined up for the A-side, but when Dennis Wilson remarked, 'No one has written a song about surfing', lights lit up all around. Brother Brian wrote 'Surfin'' and it sounds like a doo-wop record with surfing lyrics and Four Freshmen harmonies. When the single was released, the Pendeltones were surprised to find that they had become the Beach Boys. Making No.75 on the US chart, the Beach Boys were up and running and the components of their glorious surfing hits were in place. An 8.

Bob Dylan – *Bob Dylan* (1962 LP)
There are numerous tapes of Bob Dylan performing in friends' apartments but nothing was released at the time. When he was signed to Columbia Records in November 1961, he cut a whole album for producer John Hammond in two days. It's just Bob with his guitar and harmonica and the tracks included 'House of the Risin' Sun', which inspired The Animals. His own songs were talking blues and a tribute to Woody Guthrie. It could only be Dylan, no doubt about that; he's 20 and sounding 70, and nobody else was sounding like that in 1961 (except some old blues men). Most of us wanted to follow him down. 9.

The Beatles – 'Love Me Do' (1962)
You could write a whole book on the Beatles' recordings before October 1962, the official releases being with Tony Sheridan, but this is where they stood on their own eight feet. The talent is unquestionably there and although 'Love Me Do' is a fairly routine R&B song, the vocals and the playing are so attractive. The single made the UK Top 20, giving the impression that with the right song, they would go far. An 8 but I could be persuaded to go higher.

The Kinks – 'Long Tall Sally' (1964)
The Kinks' new manager Larry Page was told by the promoter Arthur Howes that the Beatles were storming audiences with 'Long Tall Sally', and yet they hadn't put it on record. Rather than use a Ray Davies song for their debut single, Page told the band to work up 'Long Tall Sally', which they perform to the rhythm of 'Lucille'. It's okay and sold reasonably (No.42 in *Melody Maker*) but it needed a harder, more uninhibited sound. Not to worry: it would soon be all Ray and all of the knight. A 5.

The Beefeaters (Byrds) – 'Please Let Me Love You' (1964)
Roger McGuinn, David Crosby and Gene Clark were working as the Jet Set and when asked to make a single, they didn't want it to prejudice a more permanent deal. The Beatles had stormed America and so they wanted an English name, which they found on the label of a gin bottle. Folk-rock with Beatle harmonies and 'Oh yeah, oh yeah, oh

yeah'. Give them 5, but the magic, swirling ship is only a year away.

Tom Jones and the Squires – 'Chills and Fever' (1964)
Tom had been singing around the clubs in South Wales for some years and he had built up a powerful singing voice. He took Ronnie Love's moderate US success, 'Chills and Fever' (1961, US 72) and added his own spin, singing it far, far better than the original. Not a hit, but unmistakably Tom Jones and success was only another single away. As we shall see, Elvis greatly admired Tom but despite his tremendous talent, popular music would have been just the same without him. A 7.

Davie Jones and The King-Bees (David Bowie) – 'Liza Jane' (1964)
The washing-machine millionaire, John Bloom, backed this band and helped them secure a Decca contract. A *Juke Box Jury* panel of Diana Dors, Jessie Matthews, Charlie Drake and Bunny Lewis (how knowledgeable can you get?) voted this fairly routine British R&B track a Hit. As a result, David gave up his day job in an advertising agency, as pop stars didn't catch the 8.10 from Bromley every morning. Dick James could have had his publishing but he told the publicist Les Conn to get 'this long-haired git out of my office'. Not a bad single but nothing that says David Bowie about it, and he went through an Anthony Newley phase before he got there, so only a 4.

Bluesology (Elton John) – 'Come Back, Baby' (1965)
Elton John takes the lead vocal on his own song, 'Come Back, Baby' although 'the only love I've ever had' is taken from Arthur Alexander's 'You Better Move On'. It's okay but had Elton realised that somebody else should be writing his words? No real indication that this is Elton John; the vocal mannerisms came later, so 4.

Bobbie Gentry – 'Ode to Billie Joe' (1967)
Bobbie Gentry's original song was seven minutes long and Capitol producer Kelly Gordon reduced to it to five verses and four minutes, thereby adding mystery – will we ever know what was thrown off the Tallahatchie Bridge? It topped the US charts, sold three million copies and Bobbie won three Grammys (Best solo female performance, best contemporary vocal, and best new artist). An eerie arrangement from Jimmie Haskell stokes up the tension. A brilliant debut, couldn't have been better so 10 out of 10 for that. Trouble is, Gentry was never as inventive again.

Elton John – 'Young, Gifted and Black' (1970)
At the same time that Elton was developing a solo career, he was making ends meet by recording covers of potential hits for the cheapo-cheapo *Chartbusters* album series. The idea was to sound as much like the original artist as possible but Elton sounds like Elton John even when singing 'Young, Gifted and Black', which is worth a 7.

Bruce Springsteen – *Greetings From Asbury Park, N.J.* (1973)
After making scores of demos in New York and London, Bruce Springsteen finally made his debut in 1973 with an album of his own songs including 'Blinded by the Light' and 'Growin' Up'. Full of energy and crammed with lyrics, this was Bob Dylan revved up. A remarkable debut to be sure, but his songs had become more measured and he knew where he was going lyrically, melodically and stylistically by the time of *Born to Run* (1975). You could also say that he was overdressed on the album cover. Still, this debut album certainly said: 'I'm open for business' and many wanted to come inside. An 8.

Kate Bush – 'Wuthering Heights' (1978)

Dave Gilmour of Pink Floyd had spotted Kate's potential when she was only 14 and encouraged her to continue songwriting and take dance lessons and singing classes. After her O-levels (10 passes), she impressed EMI with her catalogue of 60 songs. She wrote 'Wuthering Heights' after seeing the film on TV. The song was a testament to the range and force of her voice as she became Cathy with a high-pitched wail. She was the spirit who had returned for Heathcliff. It was so far off the beaten track that anything could have happened but she had a UK No.1 and a highly unusual career beckoned, almost as strange as David Bowie's. Her recording debut had been so well-planned that she seemed like a seasoned performer but it was her first record so an 8 for that, my drawback being the amount of artifice that surrounds her and her songs.

Amy Winehouse – 'Stronger Than Me' (2003)
It's hard to ignore hindsight when we look at Amy Winehouse today and her drug use and tortured relationships prompted many of her songs. She looks amazing in the video for her first single, 'Stronger Than Me', a jazz-edged soul ballad about a wayward boyfriend. Maybe she saw herself as a rebooted Billie Holiday as it does have a 1940s night club feel about it. The single only made No.71 but the potential is unquestionably there. Shame she didn't take her own advice with 'Rehab'. A 9.

Adele – 'Chasing Pavements' (2008)
Adele posted some demos online in 2007 and such interest was shown in them that she won a Brit before she had even released a record. Her debut album, *19* (her age at the time), was released in January 2008 and she had a UK No.2 with 'Chasing Pavements'. She is a so-called blue-eyed soul singer like Dusty, but despite millions of album sales, there is nothing truly distinctive about her and maybe that vocal is too calculated – the result, perhaps, of stage school. Still, it's an astonishingly confident start, so 8.

II. Got a Lot o' Livin' to Do, 1954–1955

Sam Phillips didn't grasp Elvis Presley's potential immediately. Elvis had gone into the Memphis Recording Service in July 1953 and he may have returned twice before Sam took any notice. This suggests that Elvis was liking what he was hearing. In January 1954, perhaps as a birthday present to himself, he returned and recorded two country songs, 'I'll Never Stand in Your Way' and '(It Wouldn't Be the Same) Without You', on a two-sided 78 rpm.

'I'll Never Stand in Your Way' was a bitter-sweet song, rather like 'Half as Much', that had been recorded by Billy Walker and given a lavish pop treatment by Joni James. '(It Wouldn't Be the Same) Without You' had been recorded by western actor Jimmy Wakely and gone pop with a former vocalist from the Louis Prima band, Lily Ann Carol. The best recording of 'I'll Never Stand in Your Way' is by Ray Charles on *Modern Sounds in Country and Western Music, Volume 2* (1962).

In interviews, Marion Keisker had mentioned another acetate, 'Casual Love Affair', but the recording has never emerged. What's more, I can't find any song of this title on the songwriting websites, ASCAP and BMI, so, more than likely, it is a mistake. It is unlikely that Presley would have walked into Sun with an original song.

In any dictionary of quotations, you will find Sam Phillips' oft-repeated wish to Marion Keisker and indeed to anyone who would listen, 'If I could find a white boy who could sing like a black man, I'd make a million dollars.' There were many black artists who had crossed to the pop charts (Louis Armstrong, Ella Fitzgerald, the Ink Spots), but Sam was probably referring to the watered-down versions of R&B songs by white artists that had become pop hits. If he could have found a white boy who could give the songs the same feel as the originals and ooze sex appeal, his troubles would be over. Marion had the answer but Sam didn't like being told what to do. Eventually he relented and decided to find out for himself.

The majority of the performers on Sun Records had been black but Sam did record some white acts. He had cut some sides for the 4 Star and Gilt Edge labels and released a few singles on Sun. The Ripley Cotton Chompers recorded 'Blues Waltz' (Sun 190, but oddly, Sam had started his label with Sun 174) in September 1953. Sam put 'hillbilly' on the label to indicate that it was a country record. A few months later he released Earl Peterson, Michigan's Singing (and yodelling) Cowboy with 'Boogie Blues' (Sun 197).

In 1992, Jim Dawson and Steve Propes wrote a fine book, *What Was the First Rock'n'Roll Record*, published by Faber and Faber, and since then, there have been several CD collections posing the same question. There are many contenders, including Fats Domino's 'The Fat Man' from 1950, which is little different from his later style; 'Rocket 88' by Jackie Brenston with his Delta Cats recorded at Sun in 1951; and several possibilities from Muddy Waters, Hank Williams and Johnnie Ray. There is no definitive answer and I like to cite Frank Sinatra's 'The Huckle Buck' (1949) if only because Frank hated rock'n'roll so much.

Under various names, Bill Haley and his musicians had been recording since 1947. Originally a country band specialising in western swing, they had had some success with their white cover of 'Rocket 88' and they were finding a young audience as Bill Haley and his Comets. They recorded some dance tunes like 'Rock the Joint' and 'Crazy, Man, Crazy' for the Essex label and they moved to the more prestigious US Decca label in 1954. On 12 April 1954 they recorded 'Rock Around the Clock' at the Pythian Temple studio in New York City. The song had been recorded previously by Sonny Dae and his Knights and its rhythm owed much to Hank Williams' 'Move It on Over', but it received little publicity and didn't sell. Haley's producer Milk Gabler knew it was a hit song. They cut the song with a great guitar solo from Danny Cedrone, inspired by Les Paul's work on 'How High the Moon'. The single was released in May 1954 and it, too, didn't sell initially. The record label said it was a 'novelty foxtrot', but we record fans knew better and this dance record became the clarion call for the new music, rock'n'roll.

The following month, 34-year-old Danny Cedrone fell down a flight of stairs and broke his neck. He never knew the impact that his record would make as an international chart-topper and the first great rock'n'roll hit. Bill Haley, a pudgy 30-year-old, seemed a most unlikely person to be spearheading teenage music but that's the way it was. His looks and personality undoubtedly made it easier for Elvis Presley as the figurehead for rock'n'roll.

It is surprising that two key records of rock'n'roll – 'Rock Around the Clock' and 'That's All Right, Mama' – were made, quite independently, within a few weeks of each other.

In May 1954, Sam released a single by a six-piece country band, Doug Poindexter and the Starlite Wranglers. Poindexter was a good country singer and he and his lead guitarist, 22-year-old Scotty Moore, had written 'My Kind of Carryin' On' (Sun 202). It sounds risqué for its time as Poindexter sings 'You cute little bugger', only he doesn't sing that at all – it is 'You cute little booger', a light-hearted southern term for somebody irritating. (Another Sun artist, Onie Wheeler, cut 'A Booger's Gonna Getcha' in 1956.) It sold 300 copies, all locally, as Sam didn't have inroads into the country market. They would have been fun to watch as their bass player Bill Black dressed in hayseed clothing and was the comedian of the group.

Winfield Scott Moore III, known as Scotty, was born in Gadsden, Tennessee, a small community close to Jackson, on 27 December 1931. He had been playing guitar since he was eight and he formed his first band in the navy. He played a hollow-body Echoplex and with the Starlite Wranglers, he was developing his own style, incorporating what he had heard on R&B records.

Sam Phillips was impressed by Scotty's talent and enthusiasm and he thought that Scotty should check out Elvis Presley and see what he had to offer. Scotty invited Elvis to his home and asked Bill Black to join them. Sam had a demo of a ballad, 'Without You', that might suit Elvis. Elvis may have worked on it, but we don't have any recordings – but then Sam did, on occasion, erase what he didn't want and reuse the tape.

Scotty Moore: 'Elvis came over to my house and he sang Eddy Arnold, Al Hibbler, pop, country, blues – all stuff he had learned off the radio. Bill Black, who lived down the street from me, came over and we told Sam that he had a nice voice and could sing anything. Sam set up recording sessions at night 'cause Bill and I had day jobs. We were there to provide background music, just to see what his voice would sound like on tape. This was an audition and that's why the whole band didn't go in – it was just the three of us.'

On 5 July 1954 at the Sun Studios in Memphis, Elvis, Scotty and Bill started with 'I Love You Because', a romantic ballad written and recorded by the blind singer, Leon Payne and a hit record for Ernest Tubb. They were serious about recording this song, as several takes have been preserved, but Elvis was unsure about whether to include a narration. Scotty played some jazzy chords, very much in the Willie Nelson style of later years.

They tried a second ballad, 'Harbour Lights', written in 1937 by the Irish lyricist Jimmy Kennedy and the Austrian composer Wilhelm Grosz. The song had been recorded by Rudy Vallee, Bing Crosby and Guy Lombardo and had been a US hit No.1 for Sammy Kaye in 1950. This time Elvis was whistling.

Neither whistling nor narrations did it for Sam Phillips and he wanted something up-tempo. Scotty Moore: 'We tried anything anybody could think of and that he knew the words to, and we came up with 'That's All Right, Mama', by chance, by luck if you will. It's refreshing to hear it now. It's so simple, there's no production to speak of and it's just three guys doing the best that they could.'

Elvis knew several songs by Arthur 'Big Boy' Crudup and he had suggested 'That's All Right, Mama' from 1946. Sam had taken a break and by the time he returned, Elvis, Scotty and Bill had a solid rhythm going. Eureka!

'What are you doing,' asked Sam Phillips.

'We don't know,' they replied.

'Well, whatever it is, go back to the beginning.'

Sam turned on the recording machine and the rest is hysteria.

Commentators have had a field day with this recording: after all, the 'mama' in the song switches from a mother to a girlfriend. Is it so significant? I don't think so. This blues song lent itself to a new arrangement: there is no social significance in its title and the fact that it became Elvis' first record, although there's no doubting the perfect symbolism.

It's surprising that one of the greatest rock'n'roll records was made without drums. There are only three instruments: an electric guitar, an acoustic guitar (Elvis) and a double-bass. Sam Phillips made it more exciting by adding slapback, an electronically delayed echo: that is, playing the music back on itself a split second later.

Elvis is surprisingly high-pitched and he has so much rhythm in his voice. The lyrics have been changed so that the 'mama' in question switches from mother to girlfriend. He has reworked Crudup's verse about 'the life you're living' and changes it to 'the gal you're foolin' with'. It's possible that the lyrical changes were unintentional: Elvis may not have heard the record for some time. Crudup didn't mind the new version, later saying that 'He made it into a hillbilly record but I liked it.'

Sam Phillips knew he had captured something magical. He told them to return the next evening and they would work on something else. Just one song was chosen that second night or, to put it this way, only one song was retained.

Bill Monroe, as much as anyone, was the father of bluegrass music and he had been a regular on the *Grand Ole Opry* since 1939. He was a dour, stubborn man who had written and recorded a waltz to his home state, 'Blue Moon of Kentucky', in 1946 while Flatt and Scruggs were in his band. At first Elvis recorded it slowly like Monroe, but he sounded uneasy. They sped it up and at the end of a fast take, Sam said, 'That's different, that's a pop song.' Purists mightn't like it but any controversy was publicity, and Sam had two fine sides: 'That's All Right, Mama' and 'Blue Moon of Kentucky'.

In 1970, when Elvis was asked, 'Do you ever pull out any of those old records from the Sun label and listen to them?' he replied, 'They sure sound funny, boy, they gotta lotta echo on them.' Sun's slapback echo, which was based on a tape delay, was an important feature, and echo would play its part in rock music for evermore. John Lennon was never happy unless he had it on his voice. Fellow Sun performer Charlie Feathers said, 'Knowing how to use and record that slapback is important. You had dead mikes when Bing Crosby used to sing and everything was smooth and level. You had much more of an edge with a slapback.'

Even though it would take Sam a couple of weeks to arrange pressing and marketing, he took an acetate to 28-year-old Dewey Phillips (no relation) who fronted the radio show, *Red Hot And Blue*, for WHBQ in Memphis on 7 July. He was so impressed that he told Sam that he would play it that evening. Elvis, bashful about hearing himself on the radio where his friends would hear him, went to the cinema and watched a 1946 Oscar-winning film about veterans coming home from war, *The Best Years of Our Lives*, starring Fredric March and Myrna Loy.

Not only was Dewey impressed with the forthcoming single but so were the listeners. They called the station wanting to know when this record would be available. Dewey played it again – and again. He put out a call for Elvis to come on the show, and Vernon went to find him. When he finally arrived, Dewey told him how much he loved the record and played it again. Elvis signed Dewey Phillips' acetate, his first autograph.

There was no hurry to get Elvis on the road. His first known appearance was at the Bon Air, a little honky-tonk in Memphis, on 17 July 1954. Doug Poindexter played with his Starlite Wranglers and Elvis was a guest vocalist.

The single was released on Sun 209 on 19 July 1954. It sold well locally and was No.4 on the city's sales chart. Sam Phillips did not have the contacts for wider distribution as he had been concentrating on black singles and he should have leased it to a major label. Although it sold 20,000 copies, it failed to make the US country charts, possibly because the chart compilers didn't consider it country. It didn't sell enough to make the pop charts either.

What should be on the R&B chart, what on the country and what on the pop? Although they may have been compiled with the best of intentions, they can now be seen as a form of segregation: effectively, let's isolate the black records. Nat 'King' Cole put it very succinctly: 'Madison Avenue is afraid of the dark.'

But what genre was Elvis? Pop, R&B, country or a mixture of all three? B.B. King said, 'I saw Elvis at Sam Phillips' studio and he sounded very country to me. He didn't sound black to me at all.'

Broadcaster and singer, Rufus Thomas: 'I couldn't see Elvis' potential at first – he was a white boy trying to sing black and it didn't reach me, but after he got himself together, I was the only black disc-jockey who was playing his records. Then the station stopped me from playing Elvis because they thought that black people did not like him. There was an all-black show that WDIA gave every year for black handicapped children because there were no schools for them. We took Elvis to one of the shows and the black people stormed the theatre and wanted to get to him. I went back to playing Elvis as obviously the Programme Director didn't know what people wanted to hear. If you are choosing your music because of the colour of someone's skin, it is just plain stupid.' The show to which Rufus was referring was be the WDIA Goodwill Revue at the Ellis Auditorium in Memphis on 7 December 1956.

The single sold enough for Elvis to go shopping. He told Dane Marlowe in 1956: 'I got my driving licence at 17 and bought my first Cadillac after 'That's All Right, Mama' started to sell. It was a used model and the first night I took it out, it caught fire. Sure, it was ruined. That's life.'

At the end of July 1954, Elvis was added to a Slim Whitman show, promoted by Bob Neal, at the Overton Park Shell, an open-air amphitheatre in Memphis. Slim Whitman was a huge country star who had made the pop charts with 'I'll Take You Home Again, Kathleen' and 'Indian Love Call', although his 'Cattle Call' curdled the milk. Slim was 30 but seemed older. So far, 1954 had been a great year for him as he was riding high with 'Secret Love' and 'Rose-Marie', but then he came to Memphis. He recalled, 'I'd heard 'Blue Moon of Kentucky' but all I really knew was that a fella called Elvis Presley was going to be on the show. I could hear he was doing well so I went into the wings and I could see he had his own way of doing things. Back then he was singing to the same people as us, but the news got around and the teenyboppers started coming.'

An up-and-coming country performer, Billy Walker, was on the bill. He was enjoying his first country hit with 'Thank You for Calling'. 'Elvis said to me, 'I'm nervous. I can't keep myself from shaking,' and I guess doing those movements was how he let his nervous energy out. He made his nervousness part of the act. I thought he was dynamite from the word go and he knocked the audience out. I remember going back to the *Louisiana Hayride* and telling Horace Logan about him. He tried him out and soon had him under contract.'

Bob Neal was an avuncular DJ in his mid-thirties who worked on WMPS in

Memphis and had a record store and a talent agency, Memphis Promotion at 160 Union Avenue. Back then disc jockeys often had conflicting or dovetailing interests (depending on how you view it) and Alan Freed and Dick Clark were extreme examples.

Bob Neal's wife, Helen, was at the Overton Park show and told him, 'This isn't just another singer. This boy's different.' Bob checked him out and found that Scotty Moore was his manager but in a very loose way. For example, it was only on the day of the show that Elvis, Scotty and Bill realised that they were not in the American Federation of Musicians – they joined just before they appeared.

Elvis was entitled to a 3% royalty on retail sales of the single but Scotty and Bill only got session fees, hence the more stage shows the better – they had agreed 50% for Elvis and 25% each for Scotty and Bill after expenses. Scotty wasn't keen on a manager claiming 15% but after a few months, he realised that Bob Neal would get them considerably more work. Indeed, Scotty has revealed that his total earnings for 1954 were only $2,250 and most of that came from working at a dry cleaner's.

In the middle of August 1954, Elvis returned to the Sun studios and the only track to be retained was his version of a 20-year-old Hollywood song, 'Blue Moon'. It was a strange choice and an even stranger recording. Lorenz Hart had tried different lyrics for one of Richard Rodgers' melodies and his fourth attempt, 'Blue Moon', hit home. It was a huge success for Helen Ward with Benny Goodman and his Orchestra. Elvis' version was as weird as anything Captain Beefheart was to record. Possibly, it is Elvis trying to be Slim Whitman and getting it wrong, which is often how creativity occurs. His 'Blue Moon' was eerie, drenched in echo and intensely atmospheric. If it had been released at the time, no one would have known what to make of it. Even now, it is defiantly one of a kind.

The next session on 10 September 1954, led to six songs being recorded. At first they tried a slow ballad associated with the blues singer Lonnie Johnson, 'Tomorrow Night'. It's a good, romantic performance from Elvis. It was not issued at the time and in 1965, it appeared in a dreadful, overdubbed version. Seek out the original which was finally released in its unadorned state in 1985. Around the same time, LaVern Baker was recording the same song for Atlantic in New York City, being released on the B-side of her hit, 'Tweedle Dee'.

Jimmy Wakely wrote and recorded 'I'll Never Let You Go (Little Darlin')' in 1943 and this is Elvis having fun, as he loved going from a slow tempo to a fast one. Then there is the up-tempo 'Just Because', first recorded by Dick Stabile in 1937. Most likely, Elvis knew the polka treatment by Frankie Yankovic and his Yanks. Elvis takes this at a very brisk tempo. A line I didn't get for some years was 'You laughed and called me ole Santa Claus'. Elvis attempted 'Satisfied', a gospel song, written and first recorded by Martha Carson and then a 1953 single for Johnnie Ray. Elvis' recording has been lost and although there is supposedly a version on *YouTube*, it's not Elvis, but an imitator.

The New Orleans singer/songwriter, Roy Brown, performed his spirited 'Good Rockin' Tonight' on a show with Wynonie Harris's band. Wynonie, a fine R&B showman, was so impressed that he recorded it himself in December 1947, and both versions were successful. With the omission of the verse about 'Sweet Lorraine' and 'Sioux City Sue', the song became a rock'n'roll anthem. Wynonie's original rocks almost as hard as Elvis and much more convincingly than Pat Boone. Roy Brown himself sounds like Elvis on his 1952 cut, 'Hurry Hurry Baby', but his career came to a sharp stop after

Elvis Presley: Caught in a Trap

being ostracised for suing his manager.

Elvis loved many popular singers of the day including Dean Martin, Johnnie Ray and Dinah Shore and so did the other rock'n'rollers. They were respectful and there were no interviews in which they said they wanted to knock them off the charts. Contrast this with the punk rockers of 20 years later who publicly loathed contemporary heroes like Rod Stewart and Yes.

Elvis called Dean Martin his favourite singer, and there is an element of Dino in many of Elvis' ballads. He was the straight man to comedian Jerry Lewis, but he carved his own career as a smooth Latin balladeer. His early hits include 'Powder Your Face with Sunshine', 'If', 'That's Amore' (with lyrics written by Jack Brooks from Liverpool), 'You Belong To Me" and 'I Don't Care If the Sun Don't Shine' from the film, *Scared Stiff,* which was given a cheerful Dixieland arrangement. It had originally been written for Walt Disney's *Cinderella* but had not been used. Elvis gave it a radically different arrangement for Sun, but later he did revert to the Dixieland sound in *King Creole*.

The last songs from the session comprised the next single (Sun 210) – 'Good Rockin' Tonight' and 'I Don't Care If the Sun Don't Shine'. As you can tell from the catalogue numbers, there had been no Sun releases since 'That's All Right, Mama' two months previous. Admittedly, the summer is a slow period for sales but why wasn't Sam Phillips releasing product by his regular performers like Little Milton, Rufus Thomas and The Prisoners? Some say that he had found the Holy Grail and lost interest in everybody else. Whilst that's possible, the answer is simpler than that: cash flow. Selling records was a cut-throat business. Sam relied on distributors to put his records into the stores but they were slow to pay and he had cash-flow problems. He knew he stood a good chance of breaking into the white market with Elvis Presley and then his problems would be over.

Between August and November, Elvis played about a dozen shows at the Eagle's Nest in Memphis for $10 a night. They worked out well and he built up a following, but a booking in Gladewater, Texas was a disaster. Elvis, Scotty and Bill travelled 250 miles there and 250 miles back to play for 20 people.

On 2 October 1954 it was the big one: Elvis had landed an appearance on WSM's weekly *Grand Ole Opry*. It was broadcast live from the Ryman Auditorium and the programme was split into segments with Elvis being allocated to Hank Snow's portion of the show. Backstage, it wasn't so hot. Bill Monroe had heard Elvis' 'Blue Moon on Kentucky' and wanted to break his jaw. Once Elvis had hit it big, Monroe recast his arrangement of 'Blue Moon of Kentucky' to match Elvis'.

No one knows for certain how Elvis came to be booked for the *Opry*, but it could be that Colonel Parker was involved at this early stage. Hank Snow told me, 'Tom Parker suggested that we opened a booking agency together. We called it both *Jamboree Attractions* and *Hank Snow Enterprises*, and he said to me, 'I know a young feller Elvis Presley who is tearing the hearts out of teenagers in those clubs. We ought to bring him to the *Opry*. He did 'Blue Moon of Kentucky' on my late show on the *Opry*, but he didn't disturb the audience very much. They didn't understand what he was doing and he went away very discouraged. That was the only time he was ever on the *Opry*.'

Hank Snow introduced him as the Hillbilly Cat, but it seems that this cat was not up to scratch. Jim Denny, who booked the performers for the *Opry* and had fired Hank Williams in 1952, told Elvis that he should go back to driving a truck.

Not to worry. *Grand Ole Opry* was followed that very night by another country show, *Ernest Tubb's Midnight Jamboree*, broadcast from his record store. It's not good programming to have the same person on consecutive shows but never mind. Ernest asked Elvis on air what his ambitions were, and he said, 'I'd like to make some money so I can buy my mother and Daddy a nice house to live in.' That's playing to the gallery for you, although he was to do just that.

Ernest Tubb was not as conservative as the other performers and had been the first to use electric instruments on the *Opry*. He told Elvis: 'Don't worry, you did a fine job. The audience doesn't get it yet but they will.' When Elvis returned to Memphis, he wrote Ernest a letter thanking him for being the only person who had been nice to him in Nashville.

The rival show to the *Opry*, though not as popular, was the *Louisiana Hayride*, broadcast for KWLH from the Municipal Memorial Auditorium in Shreveport. The show had made its impact by taking on Hank Williams after the *Opry* had fired him for bad behaviour. It was less conservative than the *Opry* and featured more rising stars, so it was the right place for Elvis Presley, even though his music was so radical.

Dominic Joseph Fontana, known as D.J., had been working as a drummer around Shreveport wherever he could, sometimes laying down the beat for striptease artists, which helped when playing for Elvis' bumps and grinds. He reflects: 'I was the first drummer on the *Louisiana Hayride* and, like the *Opry*, they were trying to modernise it a bit. We started with a snare drum with a stick and a brush and we introduced the rest of the kit bit by bit. Eventually, we had the whole kit on the stage. A lot of artists didn't want a drummer because they were from the old school, which was fine by me. Sometimes I sat there for four hours playing nothing at all.'

On 16 October 1954, Elvis Presley was introduced by Frank Page during the *Lucky Strike Guest Time*. Page referred to his first record sky-rocketing up the charts (which it wasn't) and Elvis then performed 'That's All Right, Mama' and 'Blue Moon of Kentucky'. A recording of his performance exists and you can tell that this time, Elvis had it nailed.

D.J. Fontana recalls, 'When Elvis came on the *Hayride*, he looked stranger than most with his purple shirt and sideburns, ducktail and greasy stuff. He was a good-looking kid and he had a charisma about him, but he didn't do too well because it was a country-orientated older crowd. They saw him running across the stage and decided he was a nut, but after a couple of weeks, they were telling their kids, 'You gotta see this boy'. The crowd changed completely – we got the young kids coming in and that helped him a lot.'

Presley did well enough to be invited back the following week. They returned for a third time on November 6. Elvis' only ever commercial was on the *Hayride* that night. He plugged Southern Maid Donuts and sang the jingle,

'You can get them piping hot after 4pm,
You can get them piping hot,
Southern Maid Donuts hit the spot,
You can get them piping hot after 4pm.'

But not if Elvis was there first! Sadly, like most of his *Hayride* performances, a recording doesn't exist.

Another up and coming artist Sleepy LaBeef performed alongside Elvis on the

Hayride: 'Elvis was performing one night with Scotty and Bill – it was before D.J. Fontana came along with the drums – and it was dependent upon Elvis playing rhythm guitar while Scotty played lead and Bill the upright bass. He broke some strings on his guitar and he called to the wings for another. His reputation as to how he would work a guitar over had preceded him, so George Jones told him where to go, he wasn't borrowing his guitar. My wife was very tender-hearted and she lent him my guitar. He scratched it and defaced it. If I'd known how big he was going to be, I would have kept the guitar, but I sold it for $90, and, even then, I only collected $50 of it.'

Elvis, Scotty and Bill signed a contract with the station manager, Horace Logan, to appear for 47 of the next 52 Saturday nights on the *Hayride*. Elvis would receive $18 for each appearance and Bill and Scotty, getting a reasonable $12 each. The contract was witnessed by Vernon and Gladys Presley.

In 2004, there was a CD release on Red Line called *Concert Anthology 1954–1956*, which featured seven of Elvis' appearances on *Louisiana Hayride*. You can tell that both the band and the audience are enjoying themselves and you can hear Bill Black yelling on 'I Don't Care If the Sun Don't Shine' as he mounts his double-bass or performs some other crazy antic.

Even on the first songs in October 1954, the girls are screaming for Elvis. He performs 'Hearts of Stone' and 'Tweedle Dee', neither of which he cut for Sun. He gives jokey song titles and says he is 'sick, sober and sorry'. The bonus CD takes the vocals from six songs and gives them a new backing from Danny B. Harvey and two of the Stray Cats – Lee Rocker and Slim Jim Phantom. They give Elvis a hotter accompaniment and they work surprisingly well.

Elvis undertook a short West Texas tour with Tillman Franks and Billy Walker, who recalled, 'I took him on a tour with me to West Texas. 'That's All Right, Mama' had been a big record in Memphis but it hadn't sold anywhere else. Now he was on the *Hayride* which had two 50,000 watt stations carrying it and we played West Texas which was 600 miles from Memphis. They agreed to play for $150 a day plus $10 car expenses.'

At last Sam Phillips was issuing new Sun singles although the releases by Malcolm Yelvington ('Drinkin' Wine Spo-dee-o-dee') and the one-man band, Dr. Ross ('The Boogie Disease') were not big sellers.

Sam Phillips owned a recording studio, but he did not record Elvis Presley as often as you might expect. Although the long-playing album was coming into fashion, Sun Records had not released any of them and so Sun only needed eight tracks a year – four singles. The next session was on 10 December 1954 and Elvis recorded three (or was it four?) songs.

The first was a gem: 'Milkcow Blues Boogie', which had been recorded by Sleepy John Estes (1930) and Kokomo Arnold (1934). It's a blues song that would be politically incorrect today: a poor farmer has lost his cow, but that cow turns out to be his woman. Elvis has fun with the song, starting slow and then speeding up, and making that wonderful observation, 'Hold it, fellas, that don't move me. Let's get real, real gone for a change.' Elvis sounds very hip and maybe Elvis' greatest acting performance was as himself.

This curious song became a rock'n'roll favourite, being recorded by Eddie Cochran, Ricky Nelson and Jody Reynolds. Going on a few years, there is a terrific version from

Steve Marriott's All Stars.

Paul McCartney: 'When I first heard Elvis' records, I had no idea what the roots of songs like 'Milkcow Blues Boogie' were. For some time, I assumed that he'd written them himself. Then I found out it was the black guys like Arthur 'Big Boy' Crudup.' That's an odd comment from Paul as I'd have thought he would have been reading the labels.

Next up was some Texas honky tonk; 'You're a Heartbreaker', which had been written and recorded by Perk Williams with Jimmy Heap's band in 1952. A slow, ballad version from Jo Ann Greer with trumpeter Ray Anthony hadn't been a hit. Elvis found a third way to do the song – it's very playful, with Elvis dropping some lines and changing others.

We can see exactly how Elvis worked, with the numerous takes of a slow burner, 'My Baby's Gone'. Two local musicians, Stan Kesler and Bill Taylor had written this song around a jingle for Campbell's Soup. It wasn't quite working and so Elvis, Scotty and Bill upped the tempo and changed it into 'I'm Left, You're Right, She's Gone'. Sam Phillips may have had faith in the original interpretation as he made a copy of 'My Baby's Gone' for Dewey Phillips to play on WHBQ.

On 18 December 1954, Elvis Presley was back in Gladewater, Texas for a live broadcast of *Louisiana Hayride*, which has been preserved, but presenting Elvis at the *Hayride* was a logistical nightmare. D.J. Fontana: 'Hank Snow and Webb Pierce would be the headliners because they'd had No.1 records. They put Elvis on right before the intermission and when he got through, everybody was outside looking for him, so then they asked him to close the show.'

It was hard for even established country stars to follow Elvis Presley. Scotty Moore: 'The hard part for Elvis was that he was a fan of all these guys. He loved country music and he had a respect for his elders. He didn't like them having a bad time because of him.'

Hank Snow: 'Elvis was a good Christian boy, he didn't smoke, he didn't drink and he was very, very polite – an example of the good, true, honest American boy. He and my son Jimmie were about the same age, so they would chum around together. He would sit in my home and play the piano and sing songs, just another great kid. We did several tours together and I could see he was headed for stardom.' His son, Jimmie Rodgers Snow, who had been named after the pioneering country singer, became a minister and then denounced rock'n'roll.

Singer and songwriter Mitchell Torok: 'Elvis had such appeal and such charisma. The black hair was falling on his face and he wore pink shirts with black ties, and black and white shoes. Before Elvis, it had been string ties, rhinestones and cowboy boots. You put a picture of Ray Price next to Elvis Presley and you'll see what I mean. Elvis was booked to close the first half on a lot of the touring shows, but the fans would still be screaming for him when the main act came out and they had to change it round.' This comment suggests that Elvis was experimenting with hair dye rather earlier than we might think.

Elvis celebrated his twentieth birthday with his third single which combined 'Milkcow Blues Boogie' with 'You're a Heartbreaker' (Sun 215). On the same day, Sun released some very good black gospel from the Jones Brothers ('Look to Jesus') and a rewrite of 'Shake, Rattle and Roll' from Billy 'The Kid' Emerson, 'Move, Baby, Move'.

Elvis Presley: Caught in a Trap

Emerson was an excellent blues writer and his 'Crazy 'bout an Automobile' became a mainstay of Ry Cooder's stage act. The B-side of his single was 'When It Rains, It Pours'.

In January, coming back from a gig in Arkansas, Elvis, Scotty and Bill had no money on hand to pay for petrol and they asked a cinema if they could play between movies for $5.

On 31 January 1955, Elvis played at Bethel Springs, Tennessee. The drummer W.S. Holland, who later played for Carl Perkins and Johnny Cash, was there. 'The first time I saw Elvis was in Bethel Springs. We were playing a little club down that way, and we knew that Elvis, Scotty and Bill were coming to the high school gym. We asked if we could start a little late and we went and saw him. At that time, he didn't seem much greater or much different from anybody else, but I soon realised that he had the right look, the right movements and a lot of things that the rest of the guys didn't have.'

Carl Perkins was playing with his brothers, Jay and Clayton, on that show. Clayton thought Elvis was gay and Jay thought he was a sissy, but Carl thought, 'He's got a contract with Sun Records,' and was determined to get one for himself.

Eddy Arnold had had a country hit with 'I Wanna Play House with You' and this phrase inspired a new blues song, 'Baby Let's Play House', which was written and recorded by Arthur Gunter in 1954. Elvis loved its coy smuttiness and he recorded it on 5 February 1955. Bradford musician Brendan Croker: 'Who in England would have said, 'Baby, let's play house'? It's American language at its best and a beautiful description of a future sexual relationship.'

Elvis' stuttering performance is a classic and once again, you can tell that he is having fun in the studio. Johnny Burnette liked it so much that he totally ripped off the record in 'Oh Baby Babe' for Coral in 1956. The Beatles stole a verse from the song for 'Run for Your Life'. At the same session, Elvis recorded Ray Charles' 'I Got a Woman' and 'Tryin' To Get to You', which had been recorded by the Eagles in 1954, but he was to return to these songs later.

Colonel Parker had a satellite office for Jamboree Attractions in Chicago and Scotty, not realising it was Parker, wrote to the company asking about gigs in Chicago. Parker's right-hand man, Tom Diskin, sent him a condescending reply, 'There are few outlets for hillbilly entertainers in this area around Chicago.'

That might have been that, but Parker himself realised Presley's potential after seeing him in Memphis at the Ellis Auditorium on 6 February 1955 when he was fourth on the bill. Parker told Presley that he wouldn't get anywhere with Sun.

Later in February 1955, Elvis was playing in San Angelo, Texas, watched by Jerry Naylor from the Crickets: 'I saw Elvis Presley, Scotty Moore and Bill Black come to the centre of the stage and start with 'That's All Right, Mama' at the San Angelo Auditorium and the audience was on its feet. They were shouting for him and his legs were shaking and the girls liked that. He knew he had something to give and I knew I was seeing the world change.'

There is a live recording of Elvis Presley at the Eagle's Hall in Houston on March 19 of that year, and both 'I Got a Woman' and 'Baby Let's Play House' are in his repertoire. From around this time, there is a live performance of 'Shake, Rattle and Roll' and a studio outtake of the Clovers' 'Fool, Fool, Fool' which rivals Charlie Feathers for its hiccupping.

Charlie Feathers: 'Buddy Holly tried to get on Sun and he would listen to my records. He would listen to me with my hiccup and he put it into 'Peggy Sue', so who copied who?' But what about Elvis Presley's 'Baby Lets Play House' (1955) and Gene Vincent's 'Woman Love' (1956) and 'Lotta Lovin'' (1957)? As well as having a great hiccup, Elvis is close to breaking down with laughter on his recording of 'Baby Let's Play House'

'Baby Let's Play House' and 'I'm Left, You're Right, She's Gone' was released as the fourth Sun single in April 1955. All singles today have absurd barcodes as catalogue numbers but diehard fans know the numbers of Elvis' Sun singles by heart, this one being Sun 217. Also, the Sun singles credit Scotty and Bill.

As yet, Elvis Presley had not appeared on the US country charts. Marty Robbins, nearly 30 years old, had had a few country hits for Columbia. Talk about opportunism but he copied 'That's All Right, Mama', using Presley's lyrics, adding some fiddles and reducing the echo, so Marty didn't come across this song for himself. Marty took it to No.7 on the US country chart, even though Elvis was not represented at all. He followed it with Chuck Berry's 'Maybellene', a straight rock'n'roll performance which made No.9.

In May 1955, some big shows were lined up for Elvis, supporting Hank Snow on the *All Star Jamboree,* promoted and arranged by Colonel Parker. Country singer Wanda Jackson: 'I wrote to my cousins who lived in the south-western part of Texas that I would be working with Webb Pierce and someone called Elvis Presley. They wrote right back, they couldn't believe it, and could they get backstage and meet him. Because I'm female, I was like the rest of his fans. He was so great, he was so dynamic and he had such charisma. We dated for a little while and we became very good friends.' Sorry, I couldn't get Wanda to say what 'good friends' meant.

Country performer Tommy Collins: 'In Jacksonville, Florida, someone had built a stage at the home place of the baseball team, the Diamonds, and the show was headlined by Andy Griffith with Ferlin Husky, Marty Robbins and myself. When Elvis performed, people started coming in from the bleachers and they were going crazy, they were trying to tear his clothes off. Andy Griffith said, in his North Carolina drawl, 'It's an orgy', and even Colonel Parker was not prepared for this reaction. There was very little security, very few policemen, and I remember one woman who was in her forties trying to tear off one of Elvis's shoes. Colonel Parker picked Elvis up, put him on his shoulder and started knocking his way through the crowd to get him to safety.'

The local publicist for the tour was Mae Boren Axton, who was highly impressed with the effect that Elvis had on audiences. She interviewed him and told him that she would like to write his first gold record.

In June 1955 Elvis, Scotty and Bill were booked into the Radio Ranch Club in Mobile, Alabama. Ray Sawyer, who found fame in Dr. Hook, was there: 'Elvis was the first country rocker. They booked him into a big honky tonk in Mobile, Alabama, and he was supposed to start at eight o'clock, but it was ten o'clock and he still wasn't there. Everybody was getting mad and cussing, and then a pink Cadillac pulled up at the front and everyone ran to the door. Scotty and Bill were in the front, and Elvis got out with a pink coat and that look that he had. Bill and Scotty went straight to the stage; all they had was one amp 'cause Elvis didn't play through an amp – he played acoustic guitar and Bill played upright bass. As they got ready, Elvis went back and forth through the audience, didn't say nothing, just walking, looking at people, 'cause this was before the people went nuts. He had only had a few records out and everything he did came from black music – Fats Domino and Joe Turner, 'Shake, Rattle and Roll' and 'Flip, Flop and Fly'. We all knew he was something special. I was 19 years old and a drummer at the time and he came to the end of the bar and ordered a beer and put a cigar in his mouth. He was only two people away from me, and I wanted to say, 'Hey, man, do you need a drummer?' I often wonder what would have happened if I'd asked him. He might have said, 'Yeah, boy, let's go'.'

At long last, the compilers at *Billboard* had determined that Elvis Presley's releases qualified as country and from July, 'Baby Let's Play House' could be listed, reaching No.5 in a four month period with 'I'm Left, You're Right, She's Gone' on the listing for three weeks.

Stan Kesler, who often worked at Sun, had a new song, 'I Forgot to Remember to Forget', which he had written with a new Sun performer, the rockabilly singer, Charlie Feathers: 'Stan Kesler had a tune that he wanted to show Elvis, 'You Believe Everyone but Me', but I didn't think it was suitable. He mentioned another title, 'I Forgot to Remember to Forget', but he didn't have anything else on it. I said, 'Man, that's an unusual title. Let's get on with this song.' We put it on a home recorder and we took it to Sam Phillips, and he didn't like it at all. I took it to Elvis and he said, 'You'll never write a song as good as this again."' Charlie, meanwhile, had kept 'You Believe Everyone but Me' for himself: it would have been fine for Elvis but I guess Charlie wanted his own piece of the action.

Charlie would never be more than a footnote in the history of popular music but in June 1955, Sun Records released the first single by Johnny Cash, 'Cry! Cry! Cry!' and 'Hey, Porter'. It took its time but in November, it was in the US country charts.

Although Elvis liked 'I Forgot to Remember to Forget', he wasn't sure about it – maybe it was too conventional for him. Anyway, Elvis cut it on 11 July 1955. As well as Elvis, Scotty and Bill, there was drummer Johnny Bernero, who played in a western swing band and worked for Sam at $15 a session. Bernero could have toured with the trio but he didn't want to leave his wife and family and his job across the road at The Memphis, Light, Gas and Water Corporation – he kept Memphis going.

Next Elvis moved onto 'Mystery Train', which had been recorded by Little Junior's Blue Flames for Sun in November 1953. Little Junior was Herman Parker and both he and Sam were credited, although the track was derived from the prison song, 'Worried Man Blues', recorded by the Carter Family in 1930.

Little Junior's Blue Flames' treatment is bleaker but less intense than Presley's, which raised the tempo. The inspiration for Scotty Moore's guitar riff can be found on the B-side of Little Junior's record, 'Love My Baby'. Sam Phillips was to say, "Mystery Train' was the greatest thing I did with Elvis.' They completed the session by returning to 'Tryin' to Get to You' with Elvis on top form.

The fifth and final Sun single, 'I Forgot to Remember to Forget' and 'Mystery Train', was released in August 1955 on Sun 223. Released on the same day was the first single from a new Sun artist, Carl Perkins – 'Let the Jukebox Keep on Playin'' and 'Gone Gone Gone'. Had Sam Phillips found another Elvis and indeed, an Elvis who could write his own songs?

Perhaps because it was more conventional, 'I Forgot to Remember to Forget' topped the US country charts for five weeks and was on the listing for nine months. In addition,

'Mystery Train' made No.11. Paradoxically, Junior Parker had been frustrated by having no new releases on Sun in 1954 and had moved to Duke.

Over in New York, the songwriter Mort Shuman heard 'Mystery Train' for the first time: 'I was in a bar with Doc Pomus and he asked me to play 'Mystery Train' by Elvis Presley on the jukebox. I was very interested because it was something new, something different and the beat was really driving, really great. Doc was flipping out. He thought Elvis was the greatest.'

Rockabilly performer, Sleepy LaBeef: 'I loved the real, get-down-and-get-it, freight-train sound of Elvis on Sun Records. He got the beat from the old southern gospel songs and the only thing that was different was the lyrics. I'd had the same experience of singing in the southern churches, where they really put their body and soul into what they were doing.'

British musician Joe Brown: 'The Sun records are amazing 'cause it comes straight from the heart. You can hear it, it's straight from the heart onto the tape and that's the end of it. No highfalutin producer has got his greasy hands on it and mucked it around.'

On 3 August 1955, Elvis Presley returned for a homecoming concert in Tupelo. An astonishing 22,000 turned up and the National Guard had to control them. He was given the key to the city by the mayor, which was shaped like a life-size wrought iron guitar. He wore a velvet shirt made by his mother.

The excitement was mounting and the UK rock'n'roll Marty Wilde says, 'There's a wonderful album with Elvis doing 'Tweedle Dee' and 'Maybellene' on the *Louisiana Hayride*. The magic aura comes across and you can tell that he desperately wants success. It's absolutely impossible to keep that fire in your belly all the time, and it's no surprise that he lost the buzz by the time he had left the army.'

D. J. Fontana: 'Elvis had some shows in East Texas, which was only 100 miles away from Shreveport and the *Hayride,* and he asked me to play drums. He kept giving me work when they could afford someone else. They weren't making much money. I was the highest paid guy in the band at the time. I was getting $100 a week: they had to pay for the transportation and the rooms and they were splitting the rest three ways. Elvis, Scotty and Bill often didn't have anything left and I'd be loaning them ten bucks. It was that tight.'

Rock'n'roll singer Tommy Sands: 'We worked on shows together around Houston and Shreveport. He was thrilling the crowds even when he was unknown. He would be on stage for no more than 30 seconds and the girls would be out of their chairs and rushing the stage, just like they did later when he became famous. The Beatles had success like that too but it wasn't the same kind of female adoration that Elvis enjoyed. Colonel Parker wasn't really interested in the music but he loved the idea of somebody who would excite the public whatever they might be doing.'

On 15 August 1955, Elvis Presley agreed his first contract with Colonel Parker, but the arrangement with Bob Neal continued until 15 March 1956. After that, Bob Neal ran his talent agency and he managed Johnny Cash from 1958.

At first Elvis was playing country shows but he needed a different audience. Colonel Parker signed him to a demanding contract: demanding because all the onus was placed on Presley: 'As a special concession to Colonel Parker, Elvis Presley is to play 100 personal appearances within one year for the special sum of $200 including his musicians.' As Elvis was still under 21, the contract had to be signed by his parents. Vernon approved

Elvis Presley: Caught in a Trap

but Gladys was suspicious and there are few photographs of her with the Colonel, and none where she seems to be at ease.

In September 1955, Elvis Presley had his final Sun session with the Billy Emerson blues song, 'When It Rains, It Pours'. You can hear Elvis' laughter when a take goes wrong and he makes a joke about Carl Perkins. They didn't finish the recording because Sam wanted to discuss business with Elvis, perhaps because the Colonel wasn't around. Elvis was to return to the song in 1957.

On 8 September 1955 Elvis signed a new contract with the *Louisiana Hayride*; this time he was getting $200 for each appearance. This illustrated the bargaining power of Colonel Parker, but it was also restrictive. Parker wanted to make him a major star so why tie him to Shreveport each week?

Tommy Sands: 'I remember one very bright thing that Elvis said to me while we were waiting to go on stage at the *Louisiana Hayride*. I was worried about something and he said, 'I've got a rule, Tom, I never worry about things I can't control.' That has stuck with me through the years as it is very good advice.'

On 15 October 1955, Elvis played the Cotton Club in Lubbock, Texas. Sonny Curtis went with Buddy Holly: 'Elvis was wild, man, he was something else. I couldn't believe my eyes. There was so much magnetism there. We all freaked and fell immediately in love with him. Buddy Holly, in particular, fell in love with Elvis's style and the day after Elvis left, we started playing his music. Buddy played the part of Elvis, and I was Scotty. I already had a Chet Atkins style, which is roughly what Scotty Moore was doing. That's where you employ the thumb to play the rhythm, and you play the melody with the fingers. You have the rhythm and the melody going at the same time, and so one guitar player can sound like two.'

These days nobody calls the clean-cut and clean-living Pat Boone a rock'n'roll singer but he was one of the first rock'n'roll stars and he had his first US hits with 'Two Hearts' (No.16) and a cover of Fats Domino's 'Ain't that A Shame' (No.1) in 1955. To say he wasn't a rock'n'roll singer is changing history – he was, but he wasn't a good one, being better suited to romantic ballads with a beat such as 'I'll Be Home' and 'I Almost Lost My Mind', both 1956 hits.

Bill Haley and his Comets' record of 'Rock Around the Clock', but not the group itself, was included in a film about juvenile delinquency in the Bronx, *The Blackboard Jungle*, which starred Glenn Ford and a young Sidney Poitier. Well, when I say 'young', I should explain that this school has the oldest looking pupils I've ever seen. The J.D. (juvenile delinquents) movie (as the genre came to be known) was proclaimed degenerate and it was withdrawn from the Venice Film Festival. The controversy didn't hurt it as soon youngsters were going to the film and jiving in the aisles whenever 'Rock Around the Clock' was playing.

In October 1955, Elvis was up north playing in Cleveland with Pat Boone and Bill Haley and the Comets. How appropriate that they should be in Cleveland, now the home of The Rock And Roll Hall of Fame. Haley had the biggest record of the year with 'Rock Around the Clock', while Boone, six months older than Elvis, had broken through and gone to No.1 with his cover of Fats Domino's 'Ain't That a Shame'.

Pat Boone says of Elvis, 'We were two Tennessee boys and the first time we met, he was my supporting act in Cleveland, Ohio. The industry people thought he was going to be a star, and I'd heard one of his records, (Sings) 'Blue moon of Kentucky, keep on shinin'' on a country jukebox in Texas. He didn't sound like a rock'n'roller to me, so I thought the promoter, Bill Randle, had really missed this time. Elvis went on ahead of me. He was shy until he got on stage, and then he just exploded. At first, the Cleveland high-school kids didn't know what to make of him with his turned-up collar and his long, greasy hair swooped down on his forehead. Elvis originally put his collar up to hide some acne on his neck. He looked like a guy that would be on a motorcycle or from the poor part of town. He'd sing his song and say, in a hillbilly twang, 'Thank you very much and now I'd like to do another number for you…', and these kids would be covering their mouths and snickering. But when he began to sing again there was an electricity about it. They liked him very much and I had to follow him. I might have had a hard time with my narrow tie, little button-down shirt and white buck shoes, but I'd had a couple of hit records.'

Unlike Pat Boone and Bill Haley, Elvis defined the attitude and the swagger of rock'n'roll. Pat Boone was uncomfortable with being at the head of a teenage rebellion, while Bill Haley looked way too old. Haley had no idea what to do next and despite some good records, all he could do was rock around the clock again.

On 17 November 1955, Elvis, Scotty and Bill were interviewed before a show in Texarkana, Arkansas which also featured Johnny Cash. Bill Black, under Colonel Parker's orders, was handling the photo concession and said, 'I will have four or five million of them.'

Now that Parker had control of Presley, he could put his record contract on the market. Decca offered $5,000, Dot $7,500, Mercury $10,000, Columbia $15,000, Atlantic $25,000;, and then RCA-Victor clinched it on 20 November 1955 with $35,000 and a $5,000 advance against royalties for Elvis himself. Elvis bought his mother a pink Cadillac, although she couldn't drive. 'You may have a pink Cadillac, but don't you be nobody's fool,' warns Elvis in 'Baby Let's Play House'.

It doesn't sound much for Elvis' contract, but it was an unprecedented figure for the time. The contract passed over his Sun recordings, whether released or not. Losing no time, RCA reissued the 'Mystery Train' single on December 2 and reissued the other four on December 20.

It is now known that the deal was more complicated than RCA's press office made out. Steve Sholes at RCA detested Colonel Parker but was persuaded by the music publishers, the brothers Julian and Jean Aberbach, that this was the way forward.

The Aberbachs had launched the Hill and Range publishing company in 1943 with an emphasis on country music. 'Blue Moon of Kentucky' was one of their songs. They put up $15,000 of the purchase price in exchange for Presley recording many more of their songs, which we come to in the next chapter. They set up Elvis Presley Music and Gladys Music, with Presley owning 50% and brothers Julian and Jean owning 25% each. When Elvis got his cheque, which turned out to be an advance against royalties, he bought himself a pink Cadillac. Elvis was becoming a Cadillac salesman's dream.

The selling of Elvis Presley's contract is regarded as one of rock's great mistakes, but it was a considerable sum and Sam Phillips wanted the money to expand his business – he built a second studio – and he also felt that he had potential stars in Carl Perkins and Johnny Cash. The balance he invested in a new hotel chain, Holiday Inn, which made him rich, so maybe it was not so dumb after all.

Sam had great visions for Sun – in December 1955, he released Charlie Feathers'

'Defrost Your Heart'; Johnny Cash's 'Folsom Prison Blues'; and Carl Perkins' 'Blue Suede Shoes'. Within a few months, he would have Roy Orbison and Jerry Lee Lewis on his books.

The Sun roster can therefore be seeing as nurturing different strands of rock'n'roll; Sam Phillips did not want everyone to sound the same and his greatest contribution was in encouraging self-expression. Presley covered all bases and Cash was always more country than rock. Feathers and Perkins are associated with rockabilly, a label which combined rock with hillbilly, the old name for country music. Carl Perkins said, 'Rockabilly is a country man's sound with a black man's rhythm.'

By and large, rockabilly is white country music played by southern boys, usually with an up-tempo beat. The teenage lyrics tend to be playful and inconsequential. Much of the early Elvis on Sun is rockabilly. It is the intermediate stage to commercial rock'n'roll.

Charlie Feathers didn't want much else. He said, 'The Elvis that I knew died in '55. RCA didn't know how to record Elvis. 'Heartbreak Hotel' sounds bad when compared to anything he did at Sun. You listen to 'Heartbreak Hotel' next to 'Mystery Train', oh lordy, no. I wish you could have seen Elvis with Scotty and Bill: the band he had when he died was just a dime-a-dozen band.'

CHAPTER 4

The Year that Rocked the World

'Hearing Elvis for the first time was like busting out of jail.'
Bob Dylan

I. The Abominable Showman

Just how important was the relationship between Elvis Presley and his manager, Colonel Tom Parker? How would Elvis have fared without him? On the face of it, they didn't have much in common, except for wanting to establish 'Elvis Presley' as the world's No.1 star. Well, they both liked over-eating too, as Colonel Parker embodies the archetypal bloated, cigar-chomping manager with no interest in his client's music or indeed his welfare.

The first extraordinary fact was that Elvis never knew Parker's true background. He thought that his manager was Colonel Thomas Andrew Parker, born in West Virginia on 26 June 1909. He was an orphan, raised by his uncle who ran a touring show, the Great Parker Pony Circus. When Parker was only seven, he had his own pony and monkey act.

All lies, except for the date of birth.

Parker's true story only came to light after Elvis' death. Is it feasible that Presley didn't know? Yes, it is. Elvis Presley was bad at keeping secrets and if he had known, he would have told his friends – the so-called Memphis Mafia – and his relations. For this reason as well as many others, Colonel Parker was determined that Elvis should not learn the truth.

Elvis may have suspected something. Why was Colonel Parker so against him touring abroad or even going on holiday? What was that accent? Elvis hadn't met many people from West Virginia but he knew that they didn't speak like Parker. He had trouble with his r's and his s's, but maybe he had a speech impediment. It must have crossed Elvis' mind to have a private investigator check out his background, but he never did.

So, just who was Colonel Parker?

He was Andreas Cornelius van Kuijk (van Kick), known as Andre, who was born on 26 June 1909 but in Breda, south of Rotterdam in the Netherlands. He was the fifth of nine children and the family looked after some stables. Andre was looking after horses from a young age (so that's partially correct).

His father died when he was 16 and Andre went to Rotterdam and probably sailed to America as a stowaway, although he could have worked his passage. He could speak some English and he befriended a family in New Jersey, living with them for a while. He returned home in 1927 but didn't settle: he wanted to live in America and so he went back two years later, this time for good. His family never saw him again, although at first he did send money to his widowed mother. His mother died in 1958 – the same year as

Gladys Presley – and she had no idea where her son was or what he was doing. None of the family knew until one of them saw his photograph in a magazine in 1961, but even then they didn't make contact.

Some researchers have tried to explain his behaviour and the most intriguing explanation is that he left Holland the day after a 23-year-old girl, Anna van den Enden, was murdered in Breda. Her husband, like Andre, had a carnival background, so he probably knew them. However, I have seen nothing that specifically links him to the crime, so this is speculation.

This was around the time of the Wall Street Crash and the Great Depression and perversely, Andre probably viewed a move to the USA as an opportunity. When things are bleak, people want to be entertained and cheap carnival fun was the answer. However, he did not want to be deported and, in an unlikely move, he joined the US army. He was posted to the Schofield Barracks in Hawaii, which must have taken him by surprise, and he served in the coastal artillery for two years. Is there not a mixture of both Sgt Bilko and Bilko's commanding officer in Parker's behaviour? Parker liked bellowing, 'That's an order!' The bombast and the truculence could have been a cover for the insecurity of living with a secret.

Andre wanted an American name, and when he left the forces and settled in Tampa, Florida in 1932, he took on the identity of an officer, Colonel Tom Parker. With a nod to his real identity, he became Colonel Thomas Andrew Parker. As Elvis sang, 'Dreams come true in Blue Hawaii.' Andre van Kuijk had joined the US army in 1929 and emerged at the end of two years as Colonel Tom Parker.

Parker met Marie Mott, the daughter of a blacksmith, a dark-haired beauty eight years older than he was. She had been married twice and had two children, Robert and Billy, one given up for adoption. No marriage certificate has been unearthed and it is possible that, in 1935, the couple simply placed their hands on the Bible and had a carny wedding. She did help with his business at first and although they had no children, Parker did accept Bobby as his own.

Tom and Marie weren't often seen together in public and they tolerated each other. He would twist her first name Marie into Miss Rie (Misery), a joke which wore thin with the years. She showed more affection for her cats than for him and in one incident, she asked him to get her cat off the roof. Parker aimed the garden hose at the cat and turned it on. The startled cat jumped from the roof and fortunately wasn't hurt.

At first, Parker made his living at carnivals, befriending snake dancers, contortionists and bearded ladies. He developed all kinds of scams: when he had a hot dog stall, he would have a frankfurter peeping out of each end but only coleslaw in the middle. If anyone complained, he would point to a frankfurter on the ground and say, 'You dropped it.' He delighted in duping the public, looking more and more like W.C. Fields, whose 1941 film, *Never Give a Sucker an Even Break*, could have been Parker's credo.

Parker never gave a sucker an even break. He would read the obituary pages and turn up at a widow's house with a Bible embossed with the deceased's name, claiming that they had ordered it and would she pay for it? This only resulted in a few dollars profit but it was the sheer enjoyment of tricking people that Parker enjoyed. That enjoyment never left him.

During a slow period in the carnival trade, he became Tampa's dog catcher, and again his mind was working overtime. So many people loved their pets, so why not start

Spencer Leigh

a dog cemetery?

He and some associates started the Royal American Carnival Show. It was an unusual carnival in that they would travel by rail, with Parker training recruits in the towns they would visit. He could teach someone how to read palms within half an hour. He put the word 'Royal' in the title as this would play well in Canada. Although he never left the mainland, he went to Canada and Mexico because passport controls were lax.

Parker trained a young elephant on a leash. At first, it couldn't break away but then later when it could, when Parker had dropped the lead, it didn't have the inclination to do that: it had been conditioned to do as it was told. There you have it: Parker and Presley in a nutshell. Look at how the hussars carried out Lord Cardigan's orders in the charge of light brigade even though their instincts would have told them they would die. It was the same with Presley: he obeyed Parker. Whatever the result, it was better than driving a truck in Memphis. He lacked the confidence to break away from him, ignoring the fact that he was doing well before the two had even met.

The carnival employed reasonably familiar singers and Parker befriended Gene Austin, who had recorded 'My Blue Heaven', becoming his manager for a while. He did promotional work for Roy Acuff, the country singer who established the mighty Acuff-Rose music publishing organisation. He enjoyed seeing how the wily Acuff operated and Parker found he couldn't better him.

Parker got to know Jimmie Davis, the Governor of Louisiana, who had been a country singer and had written the standard, 'You Are My Sunshine'. He told Davis that he wasn't a real colonel and Davis said, 'That doesn't matter, I'll make you one' and so he became an honorary colonel. Whether Davis was legally able to do this is open to question (almost certainly not), but from then on he was officially Colonel Tom Parker. One advantage of being a colonel was that you could get a hotel room easier than a civilian.

He managed a touring show headed by Pee Wee King and the Golden West Cowboys and featuring country crooner Eddy Arnold and comedienne Minnie Pearl. Following this, he managed Arnold himself. Arnold was very popular at rodeos and livestock shows, but there was a 20% entertainment tax for singers at these events. Parker realised that this could be avoided if Arnold toured with animals; in other words, if Arnold became an animals act. So, if you booked Eddy Arnold for a rodeo, you had to have Colonel Parker's Incredible Dancing Chickens. Parker ignored the fact that this would be demeaning work for a real colonel.

It sounds terrible and it would have been worse if you saw it – today he would no doubt have been arrested. He would put a hot plate under some straw and place the chickens on it. The band would play 'Turkey in the Straw' and the birds would leap up and down. The audience would laugh and then Parker would announce Eddy Arnold. It's demeaning for Eddy Arnold too, come to think of it, and how come this wasn't a fire hazard?

In what can be seen as a dry run for Elvis, Parker got Arnold parts in two feeble films, *Feudin' Rhythm* (1949) and *Hoedown* (1950) and had him play the Sahara in Las Vegas, an unlikely venue for a country star. Arnold was paying Parker 25% commission and for this, he expected exclusivity. In 1953, when he found that Parker was signing other performers, he wanted out. Parker conveniently had, or feigned, a heart attack. Parker told him that he would have to pay $50,000 for breaking the contract,

Elvis Presley: Caught in a Trap

but Arnold saw through him. Although he found a new manager, he kept him on as a booking agent as he knew how to get work. Parker then struck a deal with Hank Snow. He managed him and together they formed Hank Snow Entertainments so that they could handle other performers. They would assemble profitable touring packages, sometimes starring Snow, sometimes not.

Parker had the idea of making the teenage singer, Tommy Sands, a cowboy star. He covered him in dirt and made him walk several miles to a diner. Parker would be waiting there, eating a meal, and Sands would pass the acting test if he could scrounge a free meal from the manager. Tommy Sands recalls, 'He did get my parents to sign a contract but my mother was never a favourite of Colonel Tom Parker's and vice versa. There was a lot of conflict and it's like Gladys Presley. They both disliked the controlling factor in his personality.'

Although Parker arranged some early bookings as a country artist and secured a record deal with RCA, he soon gave up managing Sands, although he was responsible for his breakthrough. In 1957, *The Singin' Idol*, a TV play with songs, had been written for NBC with Elvis in the title role. By then, Parker had priced Presley out of the market, but he recommended Sands, who won a gold disc for one of the songs, 'Teen-Age Crush'. Ironically, the manager in the TV play is as dominant as Parker.

On the various country shows, Parker had often seen the sisters Mary and Patti Diskin and got to know their brother, Tom, who looked after them, He was a quiet, gentle man, reliable and not a decision maker. He was soon working for Parker, even living next door to him. Parker relied on him – he could smooth things over and get things done – but he drank more than he should. Diskin came out of the Presley story better than anyone. He didn't gamble and held onto his money and died a rich man.

A fellow promoter, Oscar Davies, had recommended Elvis Presley to Parker. Parker had little interest in the music itself but when he saw Elvis Presley in February 1955, he realised that he ticked all the right boxes to become a major teenage star – looks, sex appeal, voice and stage charisma. The new teenage market was looking for a hero: Marlon Brando and James Dean had made their mark in the cinema but Bill Haley didn't have the looks or the youth to be anything other than the leader of a dance band. Parker thought that Sam Phillips had no real vision – he had what he wanted but he didn't know what to do with it. Elvis Presley should be with a major label and on *The Ed Sullivan Show*. Hence, Parker got himself into a position where he could control what Elvis did next.

As Elvis was under 21, his parents would have to sign on his behalf. The Colonel got Hank Snow to soft talk Gladys Presley. Parker visited the house with two contracts – one with Snow and Parker's company and one with Parker alone. Parker could appear honest if necessary and he persuaded them to sign. Cunningly, Parker switched them, so that she and Vernon signed the second contract.

Elvis Presley's biographers are often critical of Parker's management and with good reason, but everybody gives him credit for spotting how talented he was. Come on: how can he be a visionary genius for something that was so blinking obvious? Thousands of teenagers at the concerts had spotted his potential before the Colonel and he had already made some records. Elvis' career was more advanced than the Beatles at the time they met Brian Epstein. I doubt that Parker would have been able to handle the Beatles, as John Lennon would have tried to intimidate him as he did with everyone else.

Many older people didn't care for Presley so he was reviled and revered in equal measure, but nobody doubted his originality. Indeed, when the country star Webb Pierce saw Elvis Presley on the same bill as himself in 1954, he muttered, 'Son of a bitch. That boy could put us all out of business.' Colonel Parker would see to that. Indeed, the country performers suffered in the musical explosion while the black artists enjoyed an expanded audience.

Colonel Parker was a cold fish and it is hard to feel any warmth towards him. He would dress as Santa Claus for Christmas cards from Elvis and the Colonel, but apart from his bulk, there was nothing Santa-like about him. Many people thought of him as a 'miserable old bastard'. The most telling photograph of Elvis and the Colonel has Elvis pointing a gun at him.

The Colonel would frequently tell Elvis, 'You are like a son to me and I love you' and he would call him 'My boy'. Elvis was to call Colonel and Mrs. Parker 'the finest people in the world' and he sometimes upgraded the Colonel to an admiral. He was impressed by the Colonel's dedication: when he asked the Colonel to help Ann-Margret by managing her career, the Colonel said no, he had enough to do managing Elvis.

Johnny Rogan, the author of a study of rock management, *Starmakers and Svengalis* says, 'There are so many functions that a manager has to perform and it comes down to personality in the end. Many of the desired qualities for a manager are mutually exclusive. There is no blueprint. Some managers are indulgent and treat their artists like children. Others have them running around, and both are good managers. A good manager will be getting success for the artist and doing it in whatever style suits their personalities the best. You can be a sugar daddy but if you are naturally aggressive like Don Arden, you are an autocrat and can still make lots of money. Expansionism was the name of the game for both Larry Parnes and Brian Epstein. Brian has been criticised for one thing, and one thing only – people say he should have made more money for the Beatles. Integrity was his watchword. He didn't bother with tax avoidance schemes, which was a good thing.' Nobody would ever use the word 'integrity' when describing Colonel Parker.

As we will see as the book develops, Colonel Parker would set up the deals and Elvis would carry them out, sometimes grumbling but never criticising those in authority. If the money was there, Elvis would do it and there are many times when he should have exercised artistic control. Then again, he liked earning money as much as Parker did, even if there was a cold war between them.

Colonel Parker had the perfect client in Elvis Presley because Presley was malleable and Parker, most of the time, knew what buttons to press. Presley was extremely loyal, which is an admirable quality but not when it came to Colonel Parker. Elvis had millions of fans but Parker saw them as millions of suckers. He was a carny 'til the day he died.

If, for example, someone was expecting a tip, Parker would say, 'Would you like cash or a good meal?' If the answer was a good meal, Parker would hand over a pre-packaged meal from his last flight. When someone was caught stealing leaves from Graceland and selling them as souvenirs, Parker let him off as he admired his ingenuity.

When Colonel Parker and Brian Epstein met in 1965, it would have been fascinating if they had agreed to a job swap for a couple of years. Colonel Parker would have kept the Beatles on the road; he wouldn't have wanted anything as radical as *Revolver*, especially 'Tomorrow Never Knows' and he would have exercised his military rank over *Sgt Pepper*. Brian Epstein, on the other hand, would have sent scripts back to the studios and insisted that Elvis had roles worthy of his talent. He would have restored relationships with Jerry Leiber and Mike Stoller and he would have had Elvis back on the road, playing stadium gigs.

Both Epstein and Parker took more than the standard fees from their clients. The average at the time would be 15%, but Epstein took 25%, saying that he was also acting as the Beatles' agent. Parker was taking 25% at first, which was soon raised to 50%, but he was also doctoring the figures and had several side deals – the extent of his scams is not known. Presley never asked for an independent audit, or, if he did, Parker would have talked his way out of it – once a carny, always a carny. This is why Parker liked Vernon Presley as Elvis' business manager as he would have been befuddled with Parker's accounting.

There may be worse examples too. Would Buddy Holly have done that final tour of the mid-west had he not been fleeced by his manager, Norman Petty? Roy Wood thought he owned his own house but it turned out to be in Don Arden's name.

In the end, Parker or Epstein is a simple but personal choice. I know if I were a performer, I would much prefer to be managed by someone I could trust who would respect artistic decisions, namely Brian Epstein, even if the financial deals weren't always the best. Although good things can be said for Parker, he was too motivated by money and considering how faithful Elvis was, he deserved better. Colonel Parker was marketing Elvis like a fairground attraction and he was no classier than Colonel Sanders who was marketing his product in a bucket.

II. Got a Lot o' Livin' to Do, 1956

Almost without question, 1956 was the key year for musical development in the twentieth century. The music scene at the end of 1956 was quite different from the start of the year, and we witnessed the upsurge of rock'n'roll as well as doo-wop in the States and skiffle in the UK. Elvis Presley, Little Richard, Gene Vincent and Chuck Berry were the trendsetters, combined with the growth of independent record labels and the rise of specialist concert promoters and disc-jockeys, notably Alan Freed.

Bill Haley and his Comets had fired the starting gun as 'Rock Around The Clock' was a huge, global success in 1955. For the first months of 1956, Haley still had hit singles and the film, *Rock Around The Clock* did big business, but already the clock was striking twelve. Haley heralded in the new music but by mid-1957 he was yesterday's news, never to regain his former glory.

The groundswell for what happened in 1956 had been set earlier, but the one thing that made the big difference was the change in demographics – records were being bought and appreciated by teenagers and that in itself led to a transformation in the music.

Nobody had thought about teenagers much before 1956. Look in the Bible – there isn't a clue as to what Jesus was doing during his teenage years, and that's pretty much how it was for 2,000 years. Nobody took any notice of teenagers, even if the name was Jesus. Okay, Joan of Arc was 19, but look what happened to her. She wanted to separate the French from the English so she was campaigning for Frexit 600 years too early.

The first use of the word 'teen-ager', then hyphenated, was in *Popular Science*

Monthly in 1941 where a journalist wrote, 'I never knew teen-agers could be so serious.'

In the post-war years, teen-agers were serious young men and women. They had no culture of their own and they would aspire to be like their parents: steady, stable and conformist. There were no concessions to teenage tastes until the rise of Frank Sinatra in the early 1940s with his fans, the bobby-soxers, but even he didn't sing about teen-agers. The first record to acknowledge the phenomenon was T-Bone Walker's 'Bobby Sox Blues' in 1947.

There were insipid hit records in the mid-50s such as 'Teen-Age Crush', 'A Teen-Age Prayer' and 'The Teen-ager's Waltz', as if teen-agers wanted waltzes. Although there was plenty to rebel against, James Dean's detachment came as a shock in *Rebel Without a Cause* (1955). By the end of 1956, teenagers knew exactly what they wanted, and fathers everywhere would be echoing the phrase, 'Bloody teenagers'.

James Dean himself was killed in a foolhardy crash in 1955 and the other stars of *Rebel Without a Cause* fared little better. Sal Mineo was stabbed to death in 1976 and Natalie Wood drowned in 1981, all three deaths having an air of mystery surrounding them.

The floodgates opened in 1956 with the first generation of teenage stars, most of whom were in their early twenties, and the charge was led by Elvis Presley, who turned 21 on 8 January 1956.

Once with RCA, Elvis' anti-authoritarian image was exploited to the full: he wasn't the first young rebel but, unlike Marlon Brando and James Dean, he could sing. Rock'n'roll was promoted as rebellion – rebellion against existing forms of music, rebellion against authority, rebellion against the older generation, and most importantly, rebellion against one's parents.

This must have sat uneasily with Presley. He loved country music, R&B and even crooners like Dean Martin. He was law abiding and a regular churchgoer. He was polite to his elders, addressing them as 'sir' or 'ma'am', which was possibly a legacy from the downtrodden south, and he was devoted to his parents. Ironically, most of the major rock'n'rollers – Elvis, Buddy Holly, Jerry Lee Lewis, the Everly Brothers, Ricky Nelson – not only loved their parents, but also received their wholehearted support. No star was antagonistic towards his background until Bob Dylan came along and even that was something of a pose.

Elvis' relationship with his fellow performers isn't clear as, following Parker's orders, he kept his distance. He never went on rock'n'roll package tours, even as the main act; he had his own friends and associates, and he never appeared alongside chart rivals in a rock'n'roll musical. His image wasn't of Elvis as the boy next door but of Elvis as a godlike figure whom fans would adore. Parker's plan worked, as Elvis was at No.1 for 25 weeks of the year in 1956 and during that time, he sold 12 million singles and 3 million albums in the US alone. That was 60% of RCA's total sales.

As for Elvis, he already had four Lincolns and Cadillacs, yet only a year earlier, RCA would not authorise $35,000 for his contract and Steve Sholes had to go into partnership with the Aberbachs.

Steve Sholes, an RCA executive who came from Washington, was determined to build up the label's country division. Sholes had built the first major studio in Nashville and he wanted to make it pay. His plan was to have Elvis as his main performer in the country division as Elvis could make country appealing to a younger audience. Eddy

Arnold had crossed over to pop and Elvis could do something similar.

He talked with his friends, the music publishers Jean and Julian Aberbach, who had formed the company Hill and Range. If they fronted some of the money, he would ensure that Presley would record new songs which would be placed with them – Hill and Range put up $15,000.

Elvis was sorry to leave Sun but pleased to be with RCA. He had only released five singles in 18 months while RCA were already talking about one of these new-fangled LPs. Some of his favourite performers – Hank Snow, the Blackwood Brothers and Arthur 'Big Boy' Crudup – recorded for RCA.

Steve Sholes had learnt from his mistakes. Six months earlier he had taken Jim Reeves' contract from Abbott, but Abbott had stockpiled tracks before he left so that Reeves was competing against himself. This time the price included all the back catalogue, whether released or not.

As well as being an exceptional guitarist, Chet Atkins worked on sessions at RCA and was learning record production. He said, 'Steve Sholes conducted the buyout from Sun, and he was very smart as he bought all the masters. He didn't get the demo of 'My Happiness', but he didn't know about it at the time. He called me after he had got the contract and said that he was going to record Elvis and he wanted me to get a band together, which I did.'

It wasn't quite a fresh start for Elvis Presley. He spent the first days of January playing small town gigs with Johnny Cash and Carl Perkins. Carl was most impressed: 'Elvis did not look like Mister Ed, like a lot of the rest of us.'

On January 6, he played the gym at Randolph High in Mississippi. The days of playing small gigs would soon be over. Elvis turned 21 just two days later but there is no record of him celebrating the event. This is unlike Presley. Maybe the wheels were turning too fast and he was too busy to celebrate.

Like Colonel Parker, Steve Sholes had realised that Elvis Presley was much more than a country act and had mass appeal. He could spearhead the new music, offering an alternative to Bill Haley. The RCA executives were unsure: Sholes' job was on the line if their investment was not recouped within a year. It's surprising that Sholes was worried about this. Even if Presley did not have crossover appeal, he would still sell to the country market. RCA took out a full page in the trade paper, *Billboard,* calling him, 'The most talked-about new personality in the last 10 years of recorded music.'

Whilst retaining the feel of the Sun records, Sholes wanted a fuller sound and he asked Chet Atkins to arrange it. Elvis Presley wanted to use the vocal group, the Jordanaires. Atkins demurred: RCA had signed the white gospel quartet, the Speer Family, and Atkins preferred them. However, not all of them wanted to sing on secular records, and so Atkins had the makeshift trio of Gordon Stoker from the Jordanaires with the brothers, Brock and Ben Speer. Gordon Stoker recalls, 'I knew Brock and Ben and liked them, but I said to Chet, 'Brock is a bass, Ben is a lead and I'm a first tenor, so who's gonna sing baritone?' Chet said, 'Don't worry it won't make any difference'.'

RCA had one of the most successful country labels; its Nashville studio was in constant use. In 1955 they had taken a lease on a second studio, a decommissioned church at 1525 McGavock Street, which was still owned by the Methodists. Atkins felt that in this building it would be easier to duplicate the echo, and hence the excitement, of the Sun recordings.

Phillips had used two tape recorders with a slight delay, but Atkins with his engineer, Bob Ferris, was moving into Heath Robinson territory. Scotty Moore recalled, 'The studio had a real long, huge hallway right down the front of the building with a tile floor and some glass. They had this great big speaker at one end and a microphone at the other and a sign telling people to be quiet when they came through the door.'

The Coca-Cola dispenser was declared off limits as the rattle could ruin a take.

Presley was heading for the top of the country charts with 'I Forgot to Remember to Forget' and everyone should have been full of confidence. It wasn't so: nearly everyone was paranoid or apprehensive. Sholes knew that some executives were out to get him. Sun Records had just released Carl Perkins' original version of 'Blue Suede Shoes' and Sholes wondered if he had bought the right act. Chet Atkins wasn't sure whether he could better the Sun sound.

Elvis, Scotty and Bill were cutting a record outside of Sun Studios for the first time: Moore learnt to play by copying Atkins' style and didn't relish playing in front of him. When he asked Atkins for guidance, Atkins said, 'I'm just playing rhythm. You go on doing what you've been doing'. D.J. Fontana felt adrift, knowing he was in a city of musicians. If he wasn't up to scratch, Atkins only had to whistle for a replacement. Floyd Cramer, who had come from the *Louisiana Hayride* and knew Presley slightly, had settled in Nashville with his young wife and was wondering if he had made the right move. Only Bill Black seemed confident, chewing gum and cracking jokes.

Scotty Moore remembered, 'It was a larger studio than Sun's and more regimented – they called everything by a take number and we weren't used to that at all. We would sit around at Sun, eat hamburgers and then somebody would say, 'Let's try something'. Sam used tape echo to make it sound like there was more of us than there was. He kept Elvis's voice close to the music, treating it like another instrument, and the vocal on country and pop records was normally far out in front. Elvis liked it Sam's way: he kept saying, 'Don't make me too loud, keep me back'.'

No photographer had been invited, but Presley was wearing pink trousers with a blue stripe, and he was deferential, addressing authority figures as 'Sir'. He had confidence in his voice but was uncertain about his guitar-playing, especially in front of Chet Atkins. Here was someone who had played with Hank Williams.

Gordon Stoker knew Elvis as they had met when the Jordanaires played Memphis with Eddy Arnold. They warmed up with a couple of gospel favourites, which were not recorded. The red light went on for Ray Charles' R&B hit, 'I Got a Woman'. It was a shrewd, easy choice as Presley sang it in performance and had devised a slow, bluesy ending. It was sung infectiously, but Presley was moving around so the levels on his voice varied, especially when he dropped to his knees. Sholes said, 'Hold it son, you're gonna have to stand still while you sing.' Presley retaliated with 'I'm sorry, Mr. Sholes, I don't feel right standing still.' Sholes added another microphone so that Elvis could move. Another problem was Elvis's guitar. He was playing his new Martin D-28 percussively, and it was bleeding into his vocal microphone. Atkins gave him a felt pick, which brought a softer sound. After eight takes, they had the master. Even Cool Hand Atkins was impressed. He told his wife to come down, 'You'll never see anything like this again. It's just so damn exciting.'

The generally accepted story about 'Heartbreak Hotel' is that Tommy Durden showed Mae Boren Axton a cutting from the *Miami Herald* about someone who had committed suicide, leaving a note saying, 'I walk a lonely street.' This led to them writing 'Heartbreak Hotel' within half an hour. Thanks to diligent research by Randy Boswell, we now know that Durden's cutting was not from the *Miami Herald* and was about Alvin Krolik, an aspiring author and painter who supported himself through petty crime. On August 20, he had decided to rob the Busy Bee Liquor and Tackle store in El Paso. He picked the wrong place as the owner had killed eight would-be robbers. This made it nine. The story appeared in several newspapers including the *El Paso Herald-Post*. Crucially, Krolik had a failed marriage and had described his unpublished autobiography with the words, 'This is the story of a person who walked a lonely street'.

Axton and Duren wrote the song in half an hour, cranking up his misery by having the bellhop constantly crying and the desk clerk dressed in black. Isn't this a great idea for a themed hotel? Well, maybe not. Axton recorded a cheap demo with the singer Glen Reeves. Elvis had gone to the Disc Jockey Convention in Nashville and Mae played him the song. He asked to hear it again and again and said that he wanted to record it.

The choice of 'Heartbreak Hotel' was problematic for Steve Sholes. He knew it was right for Elvis but Mae Axton, who knew the business, refused to give the song to Hill and Range. However, when Glen Reeves had cut the demo, she did offer him a co-writing credit by way of payment. He said, 'Naw, that's the dumbest song I've ever heard' and took the cash. Mae told Colonel Parker that she would keep the song but Elvis could have a third of the songwriting. 'Fine by me,' said the Colonel, knowing that this would help his own bank balance.

If I was permitted to put my name on a song I didn't write, then 'Heartbreak Hotel' would do nicely. Admittedly, Presley had put his personality into the song but that didn't justify co-authorship. Joe Cocker transformed 'With a Little Help from My Friends' but the songwriting credit remained with Lennon / McCartney. Presley wasn't the first artist to receive such a credit – both Al Jolson and George Formby are tarnished for having their names on songs they didn't write, but they laughed all the way to the bank.

'Heartbreak Hotel' started with Elvis, accompanied by a walking bass from Bill Black, going 'Waalll, since ma baby left me', which was reminiscent of Willie Dixon's work with Muddy Waters. Scotty Moore played some assertive chords and Cramer's piano was pattering like rain. Elvis broke down at the end of each verse, effectively method acting like James Dean. The song was nailed on Take seven, but as most of the original tapes were wiped, we haven't a definitive account as to how it came into being. The influence of Johnnie Ray's 'Cry' is self-evident and indeed, the song could be regarded as a parody of 'Cry'.

Donald Clark, Frank Sinatra's biographer, has described 'Heartbreak Hotel' as 'a disgraceful recording for 1956. It sounds like it was made underwater in a breadbox.' Frank couldn't have said it better himself. On the other hand, Paul McCartney has called it 'perfect': 'It's as if he is singing from the depths of hell. His phrasing, the use of echo, it's all so beautiful.'

Presley's dirt-seeking biographer, Albert Goldman, told me: "Heartbreak Hotel', which is an extravagant and highly exaggerated account of the blues, was more a psychodrama than a musical performance. As such, however, it was an extraordinary novelty and it moved rock music into another imaginative space. Had Elvis been able to continue in that genre, he could have been counted as one of the great creative forces of rock'n'roll, rather than just its master image.'

The final song for the day was 'Money Honey', a cover of an R&B hit by the Drifters. It is a humorous, hard luck story, and Presley carried it well, helped by Cramer's hammering notes. After three hours, they had three recordings and broke up, contentedly, for the day. Gordon Stoker and the Speers had been paid for doing nothing, but they came into their own the next day.

Hill and Range had nothing so far. They had given Elvis ten new songs for Christmas listening and he had rejected them all. As nobody else made anything of 'Automatic Baby', 'Shiver and Shake' and the rest, Elvis was probably right. Maybe Hill and Range's writers hadn't got the measure of him yet, so Sholes had told the Aberbachs to forget rock'n'roll and to supply two new ballads. This worked and the songs were recorded the following day: Don Robertson's 'I'm Counting on You' and Claude DeMetrius' 'I Was the One'. Nothing earth-shattering about them but they were good solid songs which Elvis sang well, and he was to return to these songwriters.

Floyd Cramer added distinctive variations on 'I'm Counting on You' (at 17 takes, the most troublesome song) and there is a big sound on the throbbing 'I Was the One' (nailed in seven) with Presley going into falsetto. Again there are parallels with Johnnie Ray, and Presley was so pleased with 'I Was the One' that he even preferred it to 'Heartbreak Hotel'. Presley left Memphis for a week's touring with Hank Snow: it would be the last time that he would support anyone and the last time he would work with Snow.

Sholes took the five tracks to New York – two R&B covers, two ballads and a weird original – and played them for his bosses. They did not care for them and suggested that he should have a further session. He talked them into releasing 'Heartbreak Hotel', and if it did not sell, then he would push the less provocative 'I Was the One', the Hill and Range song on the B-side.

The single was released in the States on 27 January 1956, and Sam Phillips was unimpressed, calling it 'a morbid mess'. It was so atmospheric and although it became the second defining hit of the rock'n'roll era, it was totally different from 'Rock Around the Clock'. Presley could have sung 'Rock Around the Clock' with ease but Haley would have been lost on 'Heartbreak Hotel'.

Although 'Rock Around the Clock' is regarded as a fairly inane lyric, not sexual in any way, just listen to it again. It is as raunchy as any of the black songs from the period – quite possibly even Haley himself had not realised this.

The New York songwriter, Paul Evans, who was to write for Elvis, has fond memories of 'Heartbreak Hotel': 'I used to listen to the older singers like Perry Como, Doris Day and Nat 'King' Cole with my family, but once I had discovered Elvis Presley, I was banished to the basement with my own radio. I can still hear my father shouting, 'Turn that damn radio down'. This was the first music to belong to just one generation. Rock'n'roll was a parting of the ways and a weapon in our hands. Our generation celebrated our music and nobody else's.'

'Heartbreak Hotel' was parodied by Stan Freberg for Capitol in June 1956; in Freberg's version, the singer rips his pants ('third pair today'), the echo chamber goes wrong, and the band wanders into a different tune. You could argue that another Capitol record, Gene Vincent's 'Be-Bop-A-Lula', was another parody of 'Heartbreak Hotel'. Both Goodman Ace and Bob Hope found humour in reading out the lyrics on US TV, while the song itself was parodied by the Addams Family.

Elvis Presley: Caught in a Trap

The following week Elvis was back down south with Hank Snow, which was the last time that Elvis would work as a supporting artist. Snow liked Elvis but he bitterly resented Parker who had cut him out of the Presley deal.

Parker had wanted to present Elvis Presley on the hugely popular *Ed Sullivan Show*, but the 54-year-old Sullivan was unimpressed with rock'n'roll. He had tolerated Bill Haley with 'Rock Around the Clock' but he had been appalled by Bo Diddley. At rehearsal, Bo Diddley had sung about himself and Sullivan told him to change it, that he should sing a standard instead. Come the night, Ed Sullivan introduced Bo who started to play some Rodgers and Hammerstein – just a few notes before he hammered into 'Bo Diddley'. Ed banned him for life and told Colonel Parker, 'I'd rather run a one-hour test card than have Elvis Presley on my show.'

Maybe the brothers and old-time bandleaders Jimmy and Tommy Dorsey felt the same way but they thought he could raise the ratings for their *Stage Show* on CBS. The ratings had to improve and sometimes they didn't even have enough applications for studio audiences. The staff would go into Times Square and hand out tickets.

On 28 January 1956, Elvis made his first appearance on national TV performing a Joe Turner medley of 'Shake, Rattle and Roll' and 'Flip, Flop and Fly' as well as 'I Got a Woman', all for $1,250. It was odd that he was not singing his new single – 'Heartbreak Hotel' coupled with 'I Was the One' – but he felt happier making his debut on national television with familiar material.

Elvis stayed in New York City for recordings with his regular group plus Shorty Long on piano. The three sessions produced eight songs, mostly for his first album – 'Shake, Rattle and Roll', Carl Perkins' 'Blue Suede Shoes', Lloyd Price's 'Lawdy Miss Clawdy', Little Richard's 'Tutti Frutti', 'I'm Gonna Sit Right Down and Cry (over you)', 'One-Sided Love Affair' and two records very much in the Sun vein, Arthur Crudup's 'My Baby Left Me' and 'So Glad You're Mine', both now published by Presley.

Elvis made five more appearances on *Stage Show* in February and March, doing two songs every time and performing 'Heartbreak Hotel' three times. Most of February, he was performing stage shows with country acts in Florida. Charlie Louvin of the Louvin Brothers was also on the bill: 'He was becoming a phenomenon, getting bigger every day. They created one big glittering sign from one side of the stage to the other that simply said, 'E-L-V-I-S'. They had even dropped the name 'Presley' and nobody could follow him – you did good even to get through your show. His management got lots of kids to scream 'WE WANT ELVIS' from the start of the show until he came on. If you put a great performer with an extremely smart manager, you've got a winning combination. I knew Colonel Parker well. He would sell his mother if it would advance his artist: there was nothing he wouldn't do. He wanted to make $50,000 a week from an artist and if you couldn't make that, he didn't want to mess with you.'

Folk singer Tom Paxton caught Elvis when he was playing Oklahoma: 'I was a student at the University of Oklahoma in 1956 when Elvis was exploding. He came to Oklahoma City. The hall seated 5,000 and he did two shows, totally sold out. Elvis was so new that the promoters didn't know what he was and so the entire supporting bill was of country and western acts, and I mean hardcore country and western. Well, nobody suffered the fate that these poor people suffered. They were playing to 5,000 kids who wanted Elvis and nothing but Elvis, and it was simply awful for them. When Elvis came out, the place went spare and what fascinates me in these days of sonic overkill, where the mistaken belief is that loud equals exciting, is that Elvis Presley's entire gear consisted of one microphone for his voice and none for his guitar. The Jordanaires had one microphone between the four of them, the standing bass had a microphone, the guitar player had a little suitcase amp, and the drums had no microphone at all. Elvis' mike was through the PA and that was it, 25 watts or something like that, but it was adequate. It was an amazing performance, just fantastic.'

At first, 'Heartbreak Hotel' entered the US country chart and stayed No.1 for 17 weeks although it was hardly a country record. 'I Was the One' independently reached No.8 which seems odd as you couldn't buy one without the other but airplay was accorded some weight. Maybe some stores actually recorded 'I Was the One' as the selling side.

Oddly, 'Heartbreak Hotel' didn't break onto the pop listings, namely the *Billboard* Hot 100, until 10 March 1956. In April it went to No.1 and stayed there for eight weeks. 'I Was the One' made No.19. Then the song got onto the R&B chart where it reached No.3, a remarkable achievement. The message was clear: Elvis was appealing to teenagers across the board.

His first album, *Elvis Presley*, was released in the US on 13 March 1956. The cover featured a black and white photograph of Elvis in full flow taken by William S. Randolph. ELVIS ran down the left hand side in pink lettering with a green PRESLEY across the bottom. It was so perfect, so simple. The lead track was 'Blue Suede Shoes'. Seven of the tracks had been recorded for RCA and five were previously unissued Sun tracks. The opening track was Elvis' reworking of Carl Perkins' 'Blue Suede Shoes', as good an opening to a debut album as the Beatles' 'I Saw Her Standing There'. Unlike Carl Perkins, who sings the song in stop / start fashion, Elvis rushes the words, not pausing for breath and pushing up the excitement.

Elvis Presley sold 100,000 copies in the first week and became the first rock'n'roll album to top the US album charts. As albums were more expensive, Elvis was also appealing to working teenagers and twenty-somethings.

Now that Elvis was 21, he could sign his own contracts and Colonel Parker drew up another management agreement, still bamboozling him of course. Parker had his own contractual problems, as he had committed Presley to weekly appearances on the *Louisiana Hayride* and by April 7, he was only making his seventh appearance of the year. Parker broke the contract and with reluctance, he gave them $10,000 for the privilege.

Meanwhile, Sam Phillips was doing well at Sun. Johnny Cash had the makings of a major country star and 'Folsom Prison Blues' was so good that many thought him the next Hank Williams. He had his rebellious streak too – rather than dress in rhinestones, he wore black and he became 'The Man in Black'.

W.S. Holland played drums for Carl Perkins: 'Certain groups paired off and got to be close friends, like the Johnny Cash group and the Carl Perkins group. Carl and John were in the back seat of John's car one day, an old 1953 Plymouth, and Marshall Grant and I were in the front. One of them had his feet on the back of the front seat, and John was talking about how he had to keep his boots shined in the air force. He said to Carl, 'You ought to write a song about suede shoes'. Later on, we were playing in Tommy's Drive-In, out here in Jackson. They danced real close to the bandstand, and Carl heard this boy tell this girl, 'Don't step on my new shoes'.' That gave him the idea for 'Blue Suede Shoes'.'

Elvis Presley: Caught in a Trap

'Blue Suede Shoes' was released as a single by Perkins in December 1955 and it topped the US country charts in April 1956. It climbed the pop charts and the only record keeping him off the top was 'Heartbreak Hotel'. It's very much white rock'n'roll but still it made No.2 on the R&B charts. Despite what commentators write, black record-buyers were buying white records.

Disaster struck on 22 March 1956 as Carl Perkins was nearly killed. 'Blue Suede Shoes' was climbing the charts and the band was travelling from West Virginia to perform on *The Perry Como Show* from New York City. W. S. Holland recalls, 'We had a new car ordered but it hadn't arrived and we had borrowed an old Packard limousine from a dealership in Memphis. I did most of the driving and there was myself and Carl, his brothers Clayton and J.B, and our manager back then, Dick Stuart. We had the guitars and upright bass in the car with the drums in the trunk, but there was no room for the cases. We went to Norfolk, Virginia and did a show that night and that was the first time I met Gene Vincent. He didn't yet have a recording contract but he was at our show. We left Norfolk and there weren't regular places to stop and get a Coke or refreshments. I drove until daylight and I stopped at a service station to get a Coke out of the machine, and I really wanted that cold bottle on my face to wake me up. Dick Stuart woke up and said, 'Do you want me to drive?' He took the wheel, and Clayton was in the middle in the front seat and I was on the outside against the door, with Carl and J.B. in the back. Dick may have gone to sleep as he ran into a pick-up truck. The guy in the truck was going to collect some people to help him work on his farm. Our car went off the highway, tore out a long section of guard rail and turned over and over, coming back round on its wheels. When I woke up, I was sitting on the white line in the highway with not a scratch or a bruise on me. The door I was leaning against had been completely torn off, and the top was smashed with the bass in splinters. Carl was lying in a ditch of water and so I jerked out the back seat of the car, laid it beside him and rolled him up onto that seat to get him out of the water. J.B's neck was broken, Clayton's arm and leg were cut real bad and Dick and Carl were hurt real bad. The guy driving the truck died shortly after we got to hospital. I was the only one who didn't get a scratch and my set of drums was the only thing that wasn't broken. I can't explain that.'

Elvis Presley sent Carl a telegram on behalf of his musicians to his hospital in Delaware: 'We were all shocked and very sorry to hear of the accident. I know what it's like for I've had a few bad ones myself. If I can help you in any way, please call me. I will be at the Warwick Hotel in New York City.'

Elvis' motives over 'Blue Suede Shoes' have been questioned but he recorded the song on January 30 and sang it live on the Dorsey show on March 17, but not on March 24, which also happened to be the day of the Como show. It wasn't issued as a single until Carl's version was high in the charts and so I don't think there was any intention on Elvis' part to steal his thunder. Colonel Parker didn't insist on any publishing deals and so if anything he was helping Carl by bringing him additional royalties – and what's more, Elvis loved the song and wanted to sing it.

On April 3, Elvis performed for a TV variety show hosted by the laconic comedian, Milton Berle, and broadcast for the crew of the carrier USS Hancock, which was docked in San Diego, California. Elvis segued 'Shake, Rattle and Roll' into 'Heartbreak Hotel' and then performed 'Blue Suede Shoes', which he called his latest single. It would have been better to have sung it as a 'get well' to Carl Perkins and it looked as though Steve

Sholes had said, 'Let's get this out.' Elvis performed a fine version, here closer to Perkins' arrangement as opposed to the tougher sound he had on record, and Bill Black fooled around on the double-bass. The song was already in the charts and although Presley made the US Top 20, it was largely ignored.

Elvis was the subject of a comedy skit by Milton Berle in which Milton played Melvin, the twin brother who taught Elvis all he knew. This seems rather tasteless but probably the writers didn't know of Jessie Garon.

Although he continued to perform, it took years for Carl Perkins to recover from his accident. He became disillusioned: he started drinking hard and the death of J.B. from cancer in October 1958 robbed him of any ambition. Five years later, by promoting his songs, the Beatles did him more good than any therapy.

On April 14, Elvis was back in the RCA studios in Nashville for a potential hit that just happened to be published by Gladys Music. This strong romantic ballad, 'I Want You, I Need You, I Love You', introduced us to the husky Elvis.

At the session, Elvis was given a gold disc for over a million sales of 'Heartbreak Hotel'. The new single displaced Pat Boone's 'I Almost Lost My Mind' at the top of the US charts and the B-side, 'My Baby Left Me', was listed at No.31. Both sides were shown on the R&B and country charts and 'I Want You, I Need You, I Love You' was another country No.1.

Starting April 23, Elvis Presley had a month's residency at the New Frontier Hotel, Las Vegas, a stupid mistake by Colonel Parker but he was personally seduced by the idea of playing the tables. If he could establish Presley in Vegas, Parker could enjoy months of paid holiday a year – well, maybe not, because he was bound to lose.

Las Vegas was an expanding city built on largely male pursuits (gambling and hookers) – at the time it appealed to the middle-aged and elderly, not so much the young. There was only a small resident population and anyone under 21 was not allowed in a casino; so, how could the young fans see him?

Two years earlier Ronald Reagan had played the New Frontier. He told jokes, sang with a quartet, danced with showgirls and read poems. It's embarrassing to think of a future President acting the fool but then he wasn't much better in office. You could get by in Vegas so long as you were a celebrity, in his case a film star, and the audience could get to know you.

This was an important factor that Elvis didn't know in 1956 but appreciated in the late 60s. His first appearances were seen as a disaster as audiences didn't want 'Heartbreak Hotel', 'Blue Suede Shoes' and 'Long Tall Sally'. When he returned in triumph in 1969, it was a very different Elvis and the show was all about being Elvis. His indiscreet raps became legendary – the audience was seeing the man, admittedly with some loss in integrity as the performances of his early hits were often a travesty, but we'll come to this.

There was nowhere for Elvis to hide: the show was just Elvis, the comedian Shecky Greene, some showgirls and Freddy Martin and his Orchestra. Shecky's jokes were more attuned to Dean Martin's audience than Elvis': 'Johnny was a good boy, never smoked, never drank, never dated. On his graduation day, his parents asked him what he wanted. Johnny replied, 'A drunken broad who smokes.'' Yes I know, but Shecky was a resident comic in Vegas for years and Elvis was paid off after two weeks.

A novelty showband, Freddie Bell and the Bellboys, who were to have a rock'n'roll hit with 'Giddy-up-A Ding Dong', were playing Vegas, and they caught each other's acts. Freddie Bell: 'Elvis didn't do well at all. They had to play with Freddy Martin's big band and Elvis didn't have a Vegas act. He was a good performer with a good style but the audiences were into Sinatra. We did some rock'n'roll but there was choreography and a show around us. If I had done pure 50s rock'n'roll without the choreography and without the salesmanship, it wouldn't have worked – and Elvis was just singing. I saw him three times and we became good friends.' Seizing a photo op, the outlandish and outrageously gay Vegas star Liberace wanted to meet Elvis, no doubt hoping Elvis would be yearning in the same way.

Elvis only did half of the month's engagement as he was paid off. His final performance at the Venus Room in the New Frontier on May 6 was recorded but not issued at the time. Hearing it today, the 13-minute set with four songs is by no means the catastrophe you might expect and Elvis is enjoying 'Money Honey' with Freddy Martin and his Orchestra. 'Heartbreak Hotel' ends with an additional yell, 'Long Tall Sally' has that favourite Presley trick of starting slowly and going wild, and D.J. Fontana goes bananas in 'Blue Suede Shoes'. Elvis' characteristics are in place – the deliberate wrong word that is quickly corrected, the occasional stuttering and the fake song titles – here 'Take Back Your Golden Garter, My Leg Is Turning Green' and 'Get Out of the Stables, Granny, You're Too Old to be Horsing Around'. Elvis acknowledges the celebrities in the audience – Ray Bolger (the scarecrow in *The Wizard of Oz*), Phil Silvers (who barks out a Bilko command – Prez must have thought Parker was in the room instead of at the tables) and Roy Acuff (pushing Acuff-Rose songs, maybe?). The audience may be too old to scream (though senior citizens scream for Tom Jones today) but he takes a bow. He did all right.

Elvis may have been paid off but at the end of May he was No.1 on six different charts in the same week in *Billboard* magazine. His album, *Elvis Presley*, was the biggest-selling album in RCA's history.

The one good thing that came out of Vegas was when Elvis saw Freddie Bell's act. They were performing a comic 'Hound Dog'. Freddie Bell: 'I had the single by Willie Mae Thornton. It was a man-hating song and the lyrics were thought to be objectionable – they wouldn't play it on the pop stations. Bernie Lowe, who later had Cameo Records, asked me to record it and I said, 'The pop stations won't play it.' He said, 'Well, change the words.' So I went home and rewrote the lyrics and made it about a dog and a rabbit. It came out on Tree Records and it was successful on the East Coast. They brought me to the Sands in 1953. Elvis heard my version and wanted to do something similar. I said, 'That's okay, go ahead and record it.' I knew it would be a smash. I asked Mercury to issue our version as a single so that we could pick up some tail sales. They prevaricated for ten weeks and by then Elvis' version was a smash. Elvis copied my choreography too, the grinding that I did on stage. There was a lot of humour in what he did but of course it was sexy too.'

The FBI is a detective agency, part of the US Department of Justice, and it investigates matters which concern the United States as a whole as opposed to specific states. I don't know if Elvis Presley's appearances at the Mary E.E. Sawyer Auditorium in La Crosse, Wisconsin on 14 May 1956 were any different from usual, but they incensed the arts editor of the *La Crosse Register*. He felt that his newspaper had not revealed the full extent of Elvis' barbarity and said, 'I feel an obligation to pass on to you my conviction that Presley is a definite danger to the security of the United States.' His two reporters and four other media people 'all agree that it was the filthiest and most harmful production that ever came to La Crosse for exhibition to teenagers.' Elvis Presley's actions were 'sexual self-gratification on the stage' and the authorities should have stopped the first show and cancelled the second: 'Perhaps the hardened police did not get the import of his motions and gestures, like those of masturbation or riding a microphone.'

The writer concluded that Presley 'may possibly be both a drug-addict and a sexual pervert.' After the show, the fans were at the Stoddard Hotel, causing havoc until 3 am. Two girls went to Elvis' room and the FBI is told that he autographed their thighs. He added, 'I am convinced that juvenile crimes of lust and perversion will follow his show here in La Crosse.' Elvis Presley Fan Club meetings should be watched as they may 'degenerate into sex orgies'. No way – but the horrifying thought is that this writer was probably completely serious.

The opinions of the arts editor of *La Crosse Register* were way beyond reasonable comment and could well have been actionable, but the Colonel probably saw them as good for business.

On June 5, Elvis Presley gave the most controversial performance of his career. He appeared on *The Milton Berle Show* from Hollywood and he sang his current hit, 'I Want You, I Need You, I Love You' and unrecorded 'Hound Dog'. He used the stand-up microphone as a prop as he frenziedly gyrated around the stage. Bill Black placed his double-bass between his knees and banged it with his hands. The audience reaction is fascinating as you can hear them sigh, scream and laugh: it got people in different ways, but it certainly got them.

The controversy was immense. There had been much in the media about rock'n'roll causing riots and encouraging juvenile delinquency. 'Hound Dog' was a moral outrage and churchmen, politicians and parents said that Elvis was depraved and should be banned from performing.

Jack O'Brien wrote in *Journal American*: 'Elvis Presley wiggled and wriggled with such abdominal gyrations that burlesque bombshell Georgia Southern really deserves equal time to reply in gyrating kind. He can't sing a lick and makes up for vocal shortcomings with the weirdest suggestive animation short of an aborigine's mating dance.'

When you look at the bookings schedule for the 1950s, you realise that Parker kept Elvis in the smaller cities and he hardly ever played New York. I've no idea why this should be. The money must have been there and it makes no sense but you have to think like Colonel Parker. Certainly Elvis was going off-script when he told one reporter: 'I'd like to help with the Hungarian uprising, I'll go over there and sing to the people if it'll bring peace.'

But Elvis did play Los Angeles. John Stewart from the Kingston Trio: 'I saw Elvis Presley at the Pan Pacific Auditorium in L.A. right after he had done 'Hound Dog'. He still had the stand-up bass and the Jordanaires, and it was unbelievable. I was shaken by the concert. I had never seen anything like that in my life. There was so much energy coming from the stage, his voice was so strong and he was having so much fun.'

Canadian radio DJ, Red Robinson: 'Bill Haley was a most unlikely star and he was in his 30s when he had the hit records and I remember saying to him off tape in June 1956 'You must be overjoyed at having all these hits. You are big everywhere.' He said,

'Red, it's all over. This young good-looking guy from the south, the Hillbilly Cat, is going to bury us."

Jazz guitarist Barney Kessel, who later worked on rock records including Elvis Presley's: 'Elvis Presley was an entertainer and he was selling sex. He gained attention through being a white man who was able to emulate the body movements and the singing of black artists. Also, he was extremely handsome and many women were attracted to his masculinity. He did it very well, but very little of it was original. This has led to a lot of other people doing the same thing, such as Bruce Springsteen. He puts a bandana on his head and screams 'Born in the USA', but I wouldn't walk across the street to see him. He's not my idea of a Boss. He's doing Elvis Presley, and so are Rod Stewart and a lot of others. Elvis Presley is doing the black artists, so people are responding to the third or fourth carbon copy of a letter rather than the original.'

As far as we know, Gladys didn't object to her son's pelvic thrusts. She was more concerned that fans would get out of hand at his concerts and injure him. Elvis told her, 'Mama, if you feel that way, you'd better not come along to my shows because that stuff is gonna keep right on happening – I hope.'

Elvis was a target for satirists. Two disc-jockeys, Bill Buchanan and Richard Goodman, compiled a two-part single, 'The Flying Saucer' using drop-ins from hit singles for the jokes. Asked what he would do if he saw a flying saucer, Elvis said he would walk to the end of Lonely Street to Heartbreak Hotel. It's not funny in print, but it was a Top 10 U.S. single and they had follow-ups too. Some record companies accepted the joke but Colonel Parker did not like the unlicensed use of his client's records in this way.

Now jokingly called Elvis the Pelvis (with a twin brother Enis), Elvis was no more uninhibited than the southern preachers. However, a wiggling torso on a sexy 21-year-old had a completely different effect. Gladys smarted at her son being denounced as obscene and was bitterly hurt when ministers attacked him: one described him as 'a new low in spiritual degeneration'.

Presley would be performing in Memphis at Russwood Park on Independence Day and he promoted this on Wink Martindale's *Top Ten Dance Party* where he was upstaged by an OTT Dewey Phillips with his guitar. Martindale, later to make 'Deck of Cards', asked Presley if he had expected to be a singer and got the reply, 'I didn't expect to get out of Humes High School.' He praised the Platters', 'Magic Touch' and 'Great Pretender', saying, 'They don't make prettier records than that.'

On July 1, Elvis had another TV booking, this time a step up, as it was *The Steve Allen Show* from the Hudson Theatre in New York and he knew that much of the country would be watching. Again, he was to sing 'I Want You, I Need You, I Love You' and 'Hound Dog' but NBC, fearing controversy, wanted to cancel the appearance. In the end, Steve Allen's team discussed with Colonel Parker what should happen. There was to be no 'bumping and grinding'. The best way to build on the publicity was to be deliberately uncontroversial and Elvis, as if in a scene from the worst movie, sang 'Hound Dog' to a Bassett hound. Presley wore a tuxedo and the hound was on a stool wearing a top hat and bow-tie. Oh, such japes: how they must have laughed and even though it is now a famous clip in television history, it was a betrayal and denial of who Elvis was.

The Steve Allen Show marked the first time that Elvis and his band had worked with the Jordanaires – Gordon Stoker had been on Elvis' sessions and was now joined by Hugh Jarrett, Hoyt Hawkins and Neal Matthews. The ratings were exceptionally high, trumping Ed Sullivan who had based his show around John Huston's new film, *Moby Dick,* starring Gregory Peck as the peg-legged Captain Ahab, so viewers of both shows were looking below the waist.

After *The Steve Allen Show*, Elvis returned to the Warwick Hotel for a split-screen telephone interview with Hy Gardner for WRCA-TV. Elvis admitted that he only got five hours' sleep a night; hardly surprising when he was on TV at 11.30pm.

The next day Elvis went to RCA for the session of his life – Elvis and his band, the Jordanaires and the pianist Shorty Long – would record three very different tracks: 'Don't Be Cruel', 'Anyway You Want Me' and 'Hound Dog'. The session was photographed by Alfred Wertheimer so we have classic shots of Elvis at work. Even though the session was produced by Steve Sholes, Elvis knew what he wanted. No doubt he had been watching Sam Phillips at Sun and seen how he worked. He did, however, want to get away from the rockabilly echo as he felt his voice would sound better without excessive reverb.

By now Elvis had performed 'Hound Dog' around twenty times on stage. It had started out as a skit but he loved the screaming and thought he should treat the song seriously. What we have is a strong, powerful recording where Elvis sounds like he means business. The slower, more sensual version had been kicked out in touch in favour of an all-out assault on your ears, although he was to play around with the slower version in his 1970s concerts.

As well as their harmonies, the Jordanaires added handclapping, but Gordon Stoker told me, 'Shorty Long played piano on 'Don't Be Cruel' and 'Anyway You Want Me' and we went 30 minutes over. He had to go to another session and so I played piano on 'Hound Dog'. If you play 'Hound Dog' and listen to the turnarounds, the 'aahs' we sang were horrible. It was the worse sound we ever got because they didn't have a pick-up on the piano. They could only record on two tracks and they couldn't pick my voice and they couldn't fix it later.' On the other hand, D.J. Fontana was pleased. 'I like 'Hound Dog'. I thought I played some pretty good triplets on it.' Bruce Springsteen said in 2016, 'We still base our snare drum sound on 'Hound Dog'.'

I find this confusing because RCA's studio and session numbers show that 'Hound Dog' was recorded first with 31 takes, then 'Don't Be Cruel' with 28 and finally 'Anyway You Want Me' with 12. This seems remarkable: Elvis Presley sang 71 songs that day, only he didn't, as RCA counted false starts and performances that stopped halfway through because of wrong notes.

The RCA approach was radically different from Sun's. At Sun, the musicians and Sam Phillips would continue until it sounded right. With major studios like RCA, the sessions were booked in three-hour slots, so Shortly Long may well have had a session after his time with Elvis. These songs were taking longer than usual to record (and we'll come to that in a minute) but as the RCA studio was probably not booked after Elvis, Steve Sholes decided to continue: Shorty left and Gordon Stoker took over on piano. Elvis thought he could improve on 'Hound Dog'. They had a few more attempts and the final one, Take 31, was the single with Gordon Stoker on it.

Otis Blackwell had written 'Don't Be Cruel' in 1955 and offered it to the Four Tunes who, fortunately for us, turned it down. When Elvis heard the demo, he wanted to record it and the arrangement was developed with the Jordanaires in the studio. This is why they did not feel happy until Take 28. The power of the percussion is reduced as D.J. was simply hitting Elvis' leather-clad guitar with his sticks. Bill Black's bass, especially at the start, is exceptionally effective, and listen to how much mileage Elvis gets out of a simple 'Mmmmm'.

Colonel Parker told Otis Blackwell that the song had to be published by Hill and Range and that Elvis should be the co-writer. For every $100 the song earned, Blackwell would receive $25, but he accepted the deal, as no deal meant the song would only go to a lesser artist.

The Jordanaires have more claim as co-writers than Presley as they created wordless vocals which weaved around what Elvis was singing. Gordon Stoker: 'He liked what we did, and we liked what he did, so it was very much a family deal. We loved him and he trusted our judgement. We had done the same for Hank Snow and Red Foley and it actually takes a lot of brains to go 'doo-wah, doo-wah, doo-wah'! It was unusual at the time but it must have been okay as it has been copied so much. With 'Don't Be Cruel' the arrangement was a combination of what Otis Blackwell imagined and what we came up with. We had something that Elvis liked and it all came together.'

Next up was a new ballad, 'Anyway You Want Me' from the music publisher and songwriter Aaron Schroeder with Cliff Owens, actually Clyde Otis under a pseudonym. 'I remember doing that song,' says Gordon Stoker, 'and saying to the other guys, 'This guy can really sing." There are some tasty guitar licks from Scotty Moore.

It was a great day for rock'n'roll, and for Memphis. Over in Nashville, Elvis' neighbours, the Johnny Burnette Rock'n'Roll Trio cut their classic, 'The Train Kept A-Rollin''. Johnny and Dorsey Burnette looked like the boxers they were and like so many brother acts, there were frictions within the band. Dorsey was to walk away because Johnny was credited as the front man.

'Hound Dog' and 'Don't Be Cruel' were rush-released for the next single and both sides were listed together on the *Billboard* Hot 100. The single was No.1 for 11 weeks as well as being a double-sided country and R&B No.1.

Colonel Parker had seen how Frank Sinatra had become both a record and film star and he thought Presley could do the same. What's more, the two big actors with teenage followings, Marlon Brando and James Dean, couldn't sing – Marlon had tried in *Guys and Dolls* (1955) and fallen flat on his face. Pat Boone had sung the theme song for *Friendly Persuasion* (1956), a fine ballad 'Thee I Love', and would be making films once he had finished his studies. Parker wanted to get in there fast and he arranged a meeting with Hal Wallis.

The film producer Hal Wallis liked to jest that he was born at the start of the century and so his destiny was clear, but he was born in Chicago in 1898. He worked as a salesman for a heating company but in 1922 he managed a cinema in Los Angeles. This led to a job arranging publicity for Warner Brothers and he made a great success of *The Jazz Singer* with Al Jolson in 1927. The following year he was a studio manager and soon after that, a production executive. He worked on *Little Caesar* (1930), *The Maltese Falcon* (1941), *Yankee Doddle Dandy* (1942) and *Casablanca* (1942). He encouraged Humphrey Bogart and the dance director Busby Berkeley. Leaving Warners after an argument over who should accept the Oscars for *Casablanca,* he set up his own company, Hal Wallis Productions.

Wallis was a stocky, well-dressed man with little humour. It took him some time to appreciate Jerry Lewis' style and he sacked him for ineptitude without realising that the silliness and the little-boy voice were part of the act. It could however be argued that not laughing at Jerry Lewis showed that he did have a sense of humour. He struck gold with the Dean Martin and Jerry Lewis films and he encouraged Dino to sing. Elvis came along just as Dean and Jerry were breaking up.

Wallis later produced *Becket* (1964), *Anne of A Thousand Days* (1969) and *True Grit* (1969) and his final film was *Rooster Cogburn* (1975). He was married to Martha Hyer and died in 1986 at the age of 88. Unfortunately, none of the big historical roles came Presley's way.

Presley had seen *Rebel Without a Cause* several times and could act whole scenes from the script, but that wasn't his audition piece. When he met Hal Wallis at Paramount, actually on April Fool's Day, he was asked to read from a new script, *The Rainmaker*. He was reading the part of Jimmy Curry and acting with Frank Faylen, who wasn't wanted that day for another Wallis production, *Gunfight at the O.K. Corral*. Because Burt Lancaster and Katharine Hepburn had already been allocated the starring roles in *The Rainmaker*, Wallis realised that the supporting role would be a waste of Presley's box-office potential and it would be better to schedule a film around him.

Elvis was given a contract for three films with Paramount. Elvis' fee for the first film would only be $15,000, but there was much negotiation and re-negotiation as Elvis became a world-famous star, and Colonel Parker was always looking for backhanders for his cooperation. Wallis himself was up for a piece of the action. Before he had settled on his first film for him, *Loving You*, made in 1957, he leased him out and recouped his initial outlay. Wallis arranged for Elvis to take a supporting role in a western, *The Reno Brothers*, made by Twentieth Century-Fox, where he would be given a love interest and could sing a few songs. One of them led to the film being retitled *Love Me Tender* and in terms of marketing, that supporting role became the leading role. The film was being made in black-and-white but was shown in widescreen CinemaScope, although it was little more than a B-feature. The filming started on August 22.

Elvis' debut played up his southern roots. Convinced that his brother Vance (Richard Egan) has died in the war, Clint Reno (Elvis) has married his brother's girl, Cathy (Debra Paget). Vance had organised the robbery of an army payroll and now the war was over, Vance wanted to return the money to avoid prison – but he had a job persuading his associates. In the shootout, Mike Gavin (Neville Brand) shot and killed Clint: as it happens, Neville Brand was one of the most-decorated soldiers in World War II. There was an alternative ending in which Elvis lived, but Fox didn't go with this.

As the critic Ramsey Campbell commented, 'Most of the second half consists of the cast riding around the same bit of landscape and somehow missing one another.' The most dramatic moment was not filmed – Elvis' horse bolted and Elvis was knocked to the ground by a large branch. When Elvis wounded his brother, he looked shocked. This was for real. He had a gun which fired blanks and Richard Egan set off a trip wire which was so realistic that Elvis wondered if he had picked up a real gun.

In the ensuing gunfight, Elvis is killed – and when it came to common sense, Twentieth Century-Fox were on the rocks. Why have Elvis being so ungallant to a girl? Why have the girl prefer Richard Egan to Elvis? Why kill off Elvis in his first film? These are examples of what fans don't want. You could argue that there was a resurrection, as

Elvis is seen superimposed on the final credits singing 'Love Me Tender'. The *Monthly Film Bulletin* of the British film Institute said that this ending would only appeal to 'connoisseurs of the grotesque'.

The Times on *Love Me Tender*: 'Elvis Presley has a small mouth which can fall easily into a pout of sulkiness. He sings with a kind of outside mandolin, with jerks that suggest a species of St. Vitus's dance and breathlessness natural to the end of a cross-country race. There is some attempt to keep his style down to the 1860s but it has a way of escaping and certainly the ecstatic moans set up by the muslin-dressed maidens at the county fair whenever he waggles his knees indicate that time has somehow slipped forward a matter of 90 years or so.'

Directed by Robert Webb, *Love Me Tender* was set in 1865, so Presley could hardly sing rock'n'roll. In theory at least, the musical director, Ken Darby, wrote four songs. The most significant is 'Love Me Tender' but its authorship is complicated.

George Poulton had been born in Cricklade, near Cirencester, England in 1828. His parents immigrated to New York and he was a good musician who became a teacher. He had an affair with one of his students and was tarred and feathered. He wrote a beautiful romantic melody 'Aura Lee', which was given a lyric by his lawyer friend, William Fosdick. This became a song of yearning for the Union army in the American Civil War. John Ford had it as a recurrent theme in *The Long Gray Line* (1955) with Tyrone Power and Maureen O'Hara.

It was perfect for *The Reno Brothers* and Ken Darby gave it new words, 'Love Me Tender'. The song was now in public domain, so Ken Darby could claim the full credit. Only he didn't. Colonel Parker wanted Elvis' name on there, but there was a further problem. Ken Darby was a member of ASCAP and Presley had been registered with its rival, BMI. Under their rules, ASCAP and BMI composers were not allowed joint credits. Ken Darby resolved this by registering his wife Vera Matson with BMI, so the credit for 'Love Me Tender' reads Matson – Presley. Sometimes in concert, Elvis would attribute this song to Stephen Foster, so he didn't even know whose work he was stealing.

The same composing credit was given to three new songs for the production, 'We're Gonna Move' (proto-rockabilly and based on 'This Ole House'), 'Poor Boy' (pelvic thrusts and screams), and 'Let Me', the last two songs at a fundraiser for a new schoolhouse. None of the cast notices that Clint has invented rock'n'roll, but then, in a night scene where Cathy is crying, there's a car in the background: surely the characters would have commented on that.

The soundtrack was conducted by Lionel Newman, Randy's uncle, and the instruments included accordion and banjo. As well as the single of 'Love Me Tender', there was to be an EP (extended play) of four songs. In the same year, Ken Darby arranged Rodgers and Hammerstein's score for the film, *The King and I* and won an Oscar.

Pat Boone, way out of his depth, had had US hits with Little Richard's 'Tutti Frutti' and 'Long Tall Sally'. Don't take my word for it: just listen to the way he sings 'ducked back in the alley' and compare it to Richard. Pat Boone however saw nothing wrong in covering black music. 'Those records couldn't get played on the white radio stations. I couldn't change that but by doing their songs, I brought attention to these artists and the original versions, and they acquired a bigger audience. In most cases, they wrote their own songs, so they were delighted that I was doing them, no matter what they may say today, as they were getting songwriting royalties. Little Richard never criticised me in 1956 as I was a catalyst bringing artists like him to mainstream America.'

Bobby Vee: 'Pat Boone is not responsible for the way our country was, he was just a guy looking for some material. It could be said that he introduced the white population to black R&B and black rock'n'roll. They might not have heard it otherwise until much later. The upper mid-west where I grew up was agricultural and I came to rock'n'roll through country music. I was listening to the country station and they started playing Elvis Presley and Carl Perkins. I didn't hear the Moonglows and the Spaniels and all those other great doo-wop groups until a couple of years later when I got into the business and started going to New York City and working at the Brooklyn Paramount. Some of these wonderful groups had been harmonising for ten years or so, but I hadn't heard them.'

What is ignored in the debate is that Elvis Presley also recorded Little Richard songs – 'Tutti Frutti', 'Long Tall Sally', 'Rip It Up' and 'Ready Teddy' – and so surely he is as much at fault as Pat Boone. However, Richard regarded this as the ultimate accolade, telling *Rolling Stone*, 'I thank God for Elvis Presley. I thank the Lord for sending Elvis to open the doors so I could walk down the road.' When Richard left rock'n'roll in 1958 to become a minister, Elvis sent him a gold-embossed Bible, which he had autographed. Says it all really, though Little Richard was also prone to autographing Bibles.

When Elvis went to Radio Recorders at Hollywood to cut his second album, which would be called *Elvis* and released in October, he sang three Little Richard songs: 'Rip It Up', 'Ready Teddy' and 'Long Tall Sally'.

There was another rocker from Otis Blackwell, 'Paralysed', who had to share his credit with Elvis. Otis Blackwell was just unlucky or gullible, as Elvis' Sun colleague, Stan Kesler, didn't have this problem. Elvis had dated Barbara Pittman, one of Sun's few female singers, and she recorded the demo of Stan's song, a ballad 'Playing for Keeps'.

We know what the country star Webb Pierce thought of Elvis and now Elvis recorded his song, 'How Do You Think I Feel', a sad composition with a light-hearted, rhumba arrangement. There was the country standard, 'When My Blue Moon Turns to Gold Again', recorded by Cindy Walker (1944) and Tex Ritter (1952).

Chet Atkins had written a tearjerker 'How's the World Treating You'. 'I wrote that with Boudleaux Bryant,' said Chet, 'a great writer who wrote for the Everly Brothers. I came up with the melody when I was in New York City around 1952– it was one weekend when I had nothing to do. I had the title too and I played it to Boudleaux and he wrote the words. Eddy Arnold did it first and it was such a thrill when Elvis did it.' There is a version by the Beaver Valley Sweethearts from the same period, not a name that most female duos would choose.

Jerry Leiber and Mike Stoller didn't rate 'Love Me'. They had written it as a parody of country music and it had been recorded by Willie and Ruth for their Spark label in 1954. They couldn't believe that Elvis would treat it seriously. A warm romantic ballad, 'Anyplace Is Paradise', came from Joe Thomas, a former sideman for Jelly Roll Morton and Cab Calloway.

Aaron Schroeder had submitted 'First in Line', co-written with Ben Weisman. You may not have heard of Ben Weisman, but you will, as he wrote more songs (56) for Elvis Presley than anybody. Most of them are known for the wrong reason, but he could be good and 'First in Line' is an okay ballad. So far as I know, Elvis never praised his work.

Elvis cut his childhood favourite 'Old Shep' in one take, bearing in mind his

Elvis Presley: Caught in a Trap

schoolmistress' advice at Humes High: 'Sing the words slowly so that people can pick up on the story.' One track, 'Too Much', was held back for a single and the other 11 were combined with an earlier cut, 'So Glad You're Mine' for his next US album, *Elvis*.

Oddly enough, I have *The Elvis Presley Album of Juke Box Favourites*, published by Aberbach for 2/6d (12p) in 1956. It features five songs which they published: 'Blue Suede Shoes' and 'I'm Left, You're Right, She's Gone' (both published by Hi Lo Music with rights assigned to Aberbach), 'I Was the One' (published by Ross Jungnickel but rights to Aberbach); 'My Baby Left Me' (published by Elvis Presley Music, an Aberbach subsidiary) and 'Tennessee Saturday Night' (published by Home Folks and assigned to Aberbach). What a tangled web they wove. The Aberbachs intended Presley to record 'Tennessee Saturday Night', a 1949 hit for Red Foley, but either it never happened or the tapes went missing.

There is an interview with Elvis in 1956 in which he talked about other Arthur Crudup numbers including 'Cool Disposition' (1944), which would have suited him fine, and 'Hey Mama, Everything's All Right' (1947), which is similar to 'That's All Right, Mama'.

By now, Ed Sullivan realised he had been hasty in dismissing Elvis in such a superior manner. He wanted Elvis, and Colonel Parker would make him pay. Ed Sullivan negotiated three appearances and the cost was $50,000. At the time, Frank Sinatra would have charged $20,000 per show and the Beatles did three appearances for $18,500 in 1964. In truth, the publicity was so substantial that Elvis would have been well-advised to do it for free.

In August 1956, Ed Sullivan was hospitalised after a head-on collision while driving to his holiday home in Connecticut. So for five weeks, *The Ed Sullivan Show* had guest hosts – Phil Silvers, Red Skelton, Patti Page, Kirk Douglas and, on September 9, the Yorkshire-born actor, Charles Laughton – a strange choice, but he was on Broadway in *Major Barbara* and had Sunday night off. Laughton had famously been a guest on the show in 1949 when he read, with great effect, from the Bible. So it was that a man who was born in Scarborough in 1899 and was famous for playing the hunchback of Notre Dame introduced Elvis Presley on the biggest variety show in America, to a verified audience of 54 million.

Had anybody realised just how wildly inappropriate Charles Laughton was? Couldn't anyone have written him a decent script and said, 'Go out and play a TV host.' Indeed, it was Elvis Presley, not Charles Laughton, who sent Ed Sullivan a get well soon message. Maybe Laughton was hoping he would get well slowly so he could host another show. It's hard to express how hopeless he was – and bear in mind that Ed himself wasn't great. Looking like Alfred Hitchcock, Laughton recites a few limericks and reads James Thurber's comic take on *Little Red Riding Hood*, saying, 'In presenting something for everyone, I feel we have neglected the children.'

It is a curious show, mixing the classical with the popular, with considerable disdain. Charles Laughton introduces the acrobatic Brothers Amin ('two agile young men', he says lasciviously), operatic soprano Dorothy Sarnoff, a cabaret singer currently on Broadway, Amru Sani, comedy vocal act the Vagabonds, tap-dancers Conn and Mack, conjuror Carl Ballantine (who waggles a string of cards and says, 'Elvis Presley') and Toby the Dog, the sort of act that wins *Britain's Got Talent*.

Those who stayed awake saw Elvis Presley. Charles Laughton has a stone-cold audience in New York which neither laughs nor screams when he is mentioned, although they applaud an ad for the new Lincoln. Elvis couldn't be released from his Hollywood commitment and so he is performing in Los Angeles in front of screaming fans. Charles Laughton has Presley's four gold records and says that Mr. Sullivan will present them at the first opportunity.

Ed Sullivan liked his star turn on early, as well as having the final spot. Here Elvis starts with a confident 'Don't Be Cruel', realising how even a simple curl of the lip can get fans screaming and slows down for a restless 'Love Me Tender' – why does he suddenly go into marching movements? For his second stint, he does 'Ready Teddy' with musicians around him rather like the *Comeback Special* of 1968, and Gordon Stoker on piano. He closes with a truncated 'Hound Dog' – had he been told the show was over-running and to keep it short? At least, he wasn't singing to Toby the Dog.

Suzi Quatro: 'I first saw Elvis Presley on TV when I was five years old and I knew that I wanted to be him. I was so inspired by him and I wanted to sing rock'n'roll. Then in 1964 I watched the Beatles' first performance on *The Ed Sullivan Show* and I wanted to start an all-girl band – and we did!'

The show was not screened in the UK but *The Times* said on 15 September 1956, 'Elvis Presley's first appearances on television were disliked by so many viewers that his subsequent career in the medium seems doubtful.' A Californian police officer commented; 'If he did that in the street, we'd arrest him' – but then again, if Charles Laughton had recited speeches from *King Lear* in the street, he might have also been arrested.

Chet Atkins: 'Elvis used to come to the studio with clippings from the newspapers. He was laughing about them because most of the time they were incorrect. A lot of the big-time gossip columnists didn't like him and made fun of him. He laughed at that but I'm sure it hurt him too.'

Elvis now had his famed gold lamé suit but he only wore it a couple of times, as he found it uncomfortable and he took to wearing the jacket with dark trousers. On September 26, Elvis Presley returned to Tupelo for two performances at the Mississippi-Alabama Fair and Dairy Show. Considering Tupelo was only a small town, you realise that most of the audience of 22,000 had travelled some distance, not just for Elvis, but for the prize cows on display. He followed this with dates in Texas and played to 26,000 at the Cotton Bowl Stadium in Dallas.

On September 28, RCA announced that advance orders for the 'Love Me Tender' single were over half a million. In October, it became the first record to enter the *Billboard* chart at No.1 (excepting the record on the very first chart which happened to be 'I'll Never Smile Again' by the Tommy Dorsey Orchestra with Frank Sinatra in 1940). The B-side, 'Anyway You Want Me', also made the Top 20. The *Love Me Tender* EP was listed on the singles chart with 'Poor Boy' reaching No.24.

Appreciating that he had commitments, in July 1956 Elvis Presley asked the Memphis Draft Board to give notice of if and when he would be drafted. *Billboard* in October 1956 reported that Elvis was due to be inducted into the army in December. It said that 'after a shortened basic training, he is slated to join Special Services.' He could keep his sideburns. Elvis was annoyed with the Draft Board for releasing this story, but it wasn't their work. The whole shebang was invented by Col Parker, although Elvis never knew it. The thought of Elvis giving free concerts as part of Special Services appalled

Parker, so what was he playing at?

Many current and former servicemen complained about this easy option, although it was standard for entertainers. Col Parker told his gullible client that, to assuage criticism, he should do the full monty, no Special Services for him. The US army was as surprised by this suggestion as Elvis himself.

Also in October 1956, Elvis was involved in a fist fight in Memphis. Elvis had been hit first and had fought back well. The two assailants were fined.

When Elvis returned to *The Ed Sullivan Show* on October 28, Ed was hosting the programme and Elvis was in the studio. He repeats 'Don't Be Cruel' and 'Love Me Tender' and this time he's allowed a full 'Hound Dog'. Elvis has the Jordanaires around him as he sings 'Love Me' and he is having fun. There is the English cabaret singer, Joyce Grenfell, a children's choir from Northern Ireland with no indication as why they have been invited, a Spanish ventriloquist Señor Wencas whose lips keep moving, and Unus, an Austrian who could balance his body on the tip of his finger.

A 40-foot cut-out of Elvis Presley was positioned above the marquee of the Paramount in New York. Size was important as it had to be higher than Marilyn Monroe's on Loew's State Theatre for *The Seven Year Itch* in 1955. When the film opened around the country, it recouped its entire production cost of $1m in three days, another record.

The single, the EP and the album were all big sellers and as if that wasn't enough, another EP was issued with 'Love Me' (which some must have confused with 'Love Me Tender') as the lead track. 'Love Me' from that EP made No.2 on the Hot 100 and 'When My Blue Moon Turns to Gold Again' was listed at No.19.

Colonel Parker wanted the kids' pocket-money – all of it. He didn't want *ad hoc* fan clubs appearing everywhere – he required a coordinated effort and he recruited Hank Saperstein to control them. Saperstein was ahead of the game: he was skilfully manipulating the kids to buy any old junk as long it had *The Lone Ranger* or *Wyatt Earp* logos. Traditionally, fan clubs didn't make money: they were loss leaders to promote the artists but Parker didn't see why they shouldn't be money-spinners. At its peak, fans were joining at the rate of 4,000 a day.

Soon there were T-shirts, belts, watches, pens, magazines, bubble-gum cards and badges with exclusive items and discounts for fan club members. Parker realised that some people loved to hate Elvis so you could buy 'I love Elvis' and 'I hate Elvis' buttons, badges and patches. He was making money out of the people who didn't like Elvis – that's marketing for you! When Elvis did his shows, Parker himself would be selling glossy photographs at 10 cents a pop. Oh, pop, what about some Elvis Pepsi? All the knick-knacks for Hugh O'Brian as Wyatt Earp were pushed into second place.

Elvis had a marketing suggestion of his own. He wanted to look as good as possible on the screen and his favourite actor was Tony Curtis with his jet black hair. Elvis dyed his sandy hair and it was never its natural, lighter colour again. The one product that they didn't market was the Elvis Hair-Dye, available in just one shade, but it is surprising that Elvis was never derided for colouring his hair. Perhaps it was because the result looked so good.

Elvis was the world's most eligible bachelor. Different girls were linked to him almost every month. Gladys accepted her son's succession of girlfriends, although she did tell him to settle down, get married and open a furniture store. She and Vernon had been hoping that he would marry a local girl, Dixie Locke, but he was on the road so much that she found another boy. She asked Gladys to tell Elvis.

Although magazines like *Confidential* blew the gaff on film personalities, there were few attempts to discredit rock'n'roll stars. Unlike today, Chuck Berry's indiscretions, which landed him in jail, were hardly mentioned by the press of the day, so much so that Berry was able to deny it for years. *NME* journalists have told me that although they were aware of Gene Vincent's alcohol intake and wild lifestyle, they wrote blander pieces because that is what the readership wanted.

An investigative reporter could have had a field day with Elvis Presley's background. Elvis would have been humiliated if his father's prison sentence had come to light – and there might have been a series of revelations, as Jerry Lee Lewis' father had also done time. Elvis daringly flaunted the family secret by making *Jailhouse Rock*. Maybe it was one of the Colonel's little jokes: perhaps he was saying to Vernon, 'Don't you dare cross me.'

On 15 December 1956, Elvis returned to the *Louisiana Hayride* for a special performance at the Louisiana Fairgrounds. It was a benefit concert for the Shreveport YMCA, although, knowing Parker, Presley will have been paid. Tickets were $2 and money was used to buy a swimming pool. This, his fiftieth appearance on the *Hayride*, was his last. At the end of the show, the MC Horace Logan said, 'Elvis has left the building.' In 2005, that microphone was sold for £24,000.

Elvis Presley was only 21 years old but already he was halfway through his life. The Beatles and Bob Dylan were still at school and they were making notes.

CHAPTER 5
The Million Dollar Quartet

*'Sam Phillips didn't record the Million Dollar Quartet. I did.
Sam was next door in Taylor's restaurant.'*
Jack Clement

I. The Myth

Put Elvis Presley with another superstar and very little happens. The TV Special with Frank Sinatra in 1960 was a damp squib and nothing, absolutely nothing, of importance happened when Elvis met the Beatles in 1965. Bob Dylan had an inconsequential meeting with Elvis which he wrote about in 'Went to See the Gypsy'. Maybe Elvis didn't fancy jamming with Bob as he did say on stage in Vegas, 'My mouth is so dry it feels like Bob Dylan spent the night in it.'

The most frustrating meeting of all has to be when Elvis Presley showed up at the Sun Studios on 4 December 1956 and jammed with Carl Perkins and his session pianist, Jerry Lee Lewis. Johnny Cash was around but apparently Christmas shopping was more exciting than a jam, and maybe it was; after all, Johnny Cash was now earning good money. Nevertheless, the resulting session with Elvis, Carl and Jerry Lee has plenty of fire but they are not always on mic and the overall sound could have been improved.

The Million Dollar Quartet could have been so much more – and now it is. A Broadway, West End and Las Vegas success, *Million Dollar Quartet* began in Chicago in 2008. It was touring the UK in 2016 and my comments relate to the London production at the Noel Coward Theatre in June 2011.

With scant regard for history, this jukebox musical speculated what might have happened if Elvis Presley, Carl Perkins, Jerry Lee Lewis and Johnny Cash had had a mammoth jam session. Judging by the audience reaction (mostly pensioners the night I was there), *Million Dollar Quartet* is here to stay and will be staged and restaged for many years. Indeed, it was in Liverpool in February 2017 with, get this, Jason Donovan as Sam Phillips.

By and large, *Million Dollar Quartet* ignores what the musicians put down that day and substitutes a mammoth session where the four artists perform 50s hits, whether or not they had even been written at the time. There is witty repartee and some drama between the performers and the show, which features 24 songs, runs for 1 hour 45 minutes without an interval. I did wonder if I had been given the right programme, as the first seven pages were about *Betty Blue Eyes* and there was very little to set the show in context. Quite apart from rock'n'roll, 1956 was a significant year in world history, but there was not a political comment in the show.

Without doubt, the dominant musician in the show was Jerry Lee Lewis, played by

Ben Goddard in comic style, more Jerry Lewis than Jerry Lee Lewis. I was wondering how anyone could work with someone like this and which one of Elvis, Johnny and Carl was going to knock him out. I had my money on Carl, but the answer was none of them. Goddard's one-dimensional performance, though funny at first, became tiresome, and I was unsure about the cast approving of his chasing young girls.

Still, there was a good rant when the very religious Jerry Lee wondered if he was singing the Devil's music – in reality, a conversation at a later date which was taped by Sam Phillips – and there was a wonderful one-liner to Carl Perkins, '88 keys beats six strings any ole time.' Goddard performed a fine version of 'Real Wild Child' but, judging by the applause, it was 'Great Balls of Fire' and 'Whole Lotta Shakin' Goin' on' that the audience wanted.

Similarly, Oliver-Seymour-Marsh as Carl Perkins wasn't best served by the script. Did Carl Perkins really resent Elvis Presley doing 'Blue Suede Shoes' when, after all, he would be collecting songwriting royalties? Maybe he did and that could explain why Elvis didn't record any more of his songs. If so, Carl was shooting himself in the foot. (Oh, he did that for real in 1966 anyway.)

In any event, Elvis could hardly be blamed for Carl's rapid decline from stardom in 1956 which was partly attributable to his car accident and his hard drinking. In the show, Carl performed 'Matchbox', 'Who Do You Love', 'My Babe', 'Honey Don't' and 'See You Later Alligator', and Seymour-Marsh played excellent guitar solos while the rest of the quartet were singing backing vocals and playing their instruments.

I had my doubts about the portrayal of Johnny Cash in *Million Dollar Quartet*. Would the country star have wanted to take part in a rock'n'roll jam session? Would he have even known 'I Hear You Knocking'? Derek Hagen captured Cash's personality but he was portrayed as a man with a secret. Sam Phillips wouldn't let him record an album of gospel songs and so he had signed with Columbia rather than re-signing with Sam. In the play's most dramatic moment, he told Phillips he was leaving. Hagen captured Cash's voice perfectly as he sang 'Folsom Prison Blues', 'Sixteen Tons', 'I Walk the Line' and 'Riders in the Sky'.

By all accounts, Elvis Presley was amazingly charismatic. All eyes would be on him when he entered the room. Although Michael Malarkey was very good, he lacked that charisma. Put it this way: he's no Tim Whitnall, who was so good in *Elvis* in 1977. He would only look like Elvis Presley with the lights out. Malarkey came over as just another tribute singer as he performed 'Memories Are Made of This', 'That's All Right', 'Long Tall Sally' and 'Hound Dog'. He was okay but not Elvis.

On the original tapes, Elvis talked about Jackie Wilson imitating him in Las Vegas and then did his impersonation. I wish that this golden moment had been included and expanded for the stage show.

It is unusual these days to see a show with effectively just one stage set. At the end, Elvis sat at the piano with the others around him and Sam Phillips took a picture. The actors froze as the magic photograph of the four of them on 4 December 1956 was shown. The applause was for the way that they had recreated that moment.

However, if you look at the uncropped version of that photograph, you will see a girl sitting on the piano. Who was she? It was Elvis' girlfriend, Marilyn Evans, a dancer from the New Frontier in Las Vegas. Here, Elvis' girlfriend was called Dyanne and, played by Francesca Jackson, she sang 'Fever' and 'I Hear You Knocking'. There were two other musicians in supporting roles: Gez Gerrard as Carl's brother, Jay, on bass and Alex Yates as W.S. Holland on drums. The songs that the quartet performed together were 'Blue Suede Shoes', 'Brown Eyed Handsome Man', 'Down by the Riverside' and 'Peace in the Valley'.

The book by noted researcher Colin Escott and Floyd Mutrux (director of *American Hot Wax* and *Urban Cowboy*) was written tongue-in-cheek. It does mess with the truth – but they are after a deeper truth in that they are trying to nail the relationship between the four musicians and Sam Phillips at the birth of rock'n'roll.

Sam Phillips, played by Bill Ward, acted as narrator and he maintained that the four performers were never as happy as they had been on that afternoon. Certainly they had their share of misery, much of it self-inflicted, but what of Phillips himself? In the play, he sold Elvis for $40,000 because he wanted to invest in a new hotel chain, Holiday Inn, but if he was such a good businessman, why did all four performers joke about Sun's poor distribution? I wasn't sure about RCA negotiating for him to produce Elvis again. Again, I was expecting this to be resolved by Elvis telling him that he didn't want it.

The show ended with the Million Dollar Quartet performing in Las Vegas. This was a production for coach parties who wanted a rave-up rather than serious music fans.

II. Got a Lot of Livin' to Do, 4 December 1956

Life had always been tense and dramatic for Carl Perkins. His father Buck was a poverty-stricken sharecropper in Tiptonville, Tennessee, raising three sons with his wife, Louise: James Buck (Jay or J.B, born 1930), Carl Lee (born 1932) and Lloyd Clayton (born 1935). Even when they were nine or ten years old, they were picking cotton. Jay and Carl would do as they were told but Clayton was regularly beaten by his father for misbehaviour. Carl was not as strong as the other brothers, as the after-effects of pneumonia and scarlet fever had damaged his lungs.

Carl Perkins' background is revealed in his songs – in 'Movie Magg' he takes a girl to the cinema riding together on horseback and 'Dixie Fried' is the story of a tough, barroom fight. These are not skilfully-crafted Brill Building songs but songs that resonate with references to his own experiences and lifestyle.

Indeed, he could have had a field day writing about life as he knew it. For example, Clayton had lied about his age and joined the marines when he was only 14. When the truth was discovered, he returned home but his instructor told him, 'We've money invested in you and we'll be calling you back.' When Clayton realised that he didn't want to return, he shot himself in the foot, knowing they would not want an injured serviceman. He threw away the plaster cast and his foot became swollen and infected. He treated it by drinking whiskey and gradually it did, miraculously, get back to normal.

The Perkins brothers formed a country band with Carl and Jay encouraging each other on lead and rhythm guitars respectively, while Clayton played the stand-up bass loudly and aggressively, without much musical skill. He got by as it gave the band some attitude.

Sam Phillips recognised Carl Perkins' talent but the brothers were ill-suited to the teenage market. Jay was a steadying influence but Clayton was wild and uninhibited, someone who would fight at the merest provocation. Carl wanted to be like Jay but feared that he was turning into Clayton.

In 1953 Carl had married Valda Crider and in March 1956, they were expecting their third child. 'Blue Suede Shoes' was shaping up to be a hit: Elvis Presley had covered it and this would lead to much-needed royalties.

So life was tense in the band even before the car accident in March 1956. Carl had a fractured skull and a broken shoulder, Jay a broken neck and Clayton minor injuries. When Jay saw Carl in hospital, he was surprised as he had been told that Carl had been killed. These were strong, tough, resolute people but it was still remarkable that the band was back on the road, with a replacement for Jay, a month later. When Carl opened on the Big D Jamboree tour on April 23, he told the audience, 'It's a boy!' and launched into 'Honey Don't'.

When Jay returned to the line-up, he was plagued by recurring headaches and became addicted to painkillers. He was no longer the peacemaker between Carl and Clayton and when they worked with Johnny Cash, they found that Cash encouraged Clayton's idiocy.

The new recording sessions at Sun had been inconsistent. Carl was back in action in May with the magnificent 'Boppin' the Blues' and the tough 'Dixie Fried', both of which made the US Country Top 10; 'Boppin' the Blues' crossed over to the pop charts, stalling at No.70. His 'Pink Pedal Pushers' was all too obviously an attempt to rewrite 'Blue Suede Shoes' but 'That Don't Move Me' is lame and half-heartedly performed. His version of 'Lonely Street' is so bad that it is hard to tell whether he is copying Carl Belew's song or writing his own and his voice is so rough on Louis Jordan's 'Caledonia' that he must have been drinking. On the session tapes for another dodgy recording, 'Her Love Rubbed Off', Carl mutters, 'Let's get this son of a bitch finished.' Carl wants to go home – or to the nearest bar. For all its faults, it's a wonderfully angry and defiant track, the forerunner of what in the late 70s would be called psychobilly.

Sam Phillips had had a busy year at Sun and he brought in a young producer, Jack Clement, to help him. By now, Sam was mostly recording white artists, but there were sessions with Rufus Thomas and Rosco Gordon. Johnny Cash was becoming a major country music star; his own song, 'I Walk the Line', had topped the country charts for six weeks and had been a pop hit, making No.17 on the *Billboard* Hot 100.

Sam Phillips recognised that Carl Perkins was losing his drive and he thought he had the answer. Jerry Lee Lewis was the same age as Elvis, being born in Ferriday, Louisiana. He was an exceptionally talented but arrogant entertainer, his fiery piano playing full of flourishes and glissandos. He and his father had come to Memphis in November, hoping that Sam Phillips would be impressed. He was and his first single, 'Crazy Arms', was released in November 1956. Sam asked Jack Clement to work with him. Jerry Lee stayed in Memphis doing honky tonk dates and, as he wanted some money for Christmas presents, he told Sam and Jack that he would undertake session work.

And so it was on Tuesday afternoon 4 December 1956 that Carl Perkins was cutting new tracks at Sun. Sam Phillips thought that the addition of Jerry Lee might make them sound more commercial and that it would move Carl away from his standard rockabilly sound.

Carl had never met Jerry Lee before and he could sense that the very self-assured Jerry Lee would soon be having a ruckus with Clayton. Carl had a new song, 'Your True Love' and Jerry Lee immediately saw how he could enhance it. It was a good lively performance although Carl isn't always on key. Sam Phillips declared, 'That's a hit, Carl'

Elvis Presley: Caught in a Trap

to which Jerry Lee added, 'That song ain't worth a damn.' Jerry Lee would have to be careful, as not only where the three Perkins brothers there but also Buck Perkins who wanted to see how a record was made.

Carl asked his dad about a song he used to sing, 'Matchbox', originally recorded by Blind Lemon Jefferson in 1927. Buck sang what he knew and Carl repeated the verses while Jerry Lee added a boogie riff. They took a little break so that Carl, aided by Early Times Kentucky whisky, could complete the lyric. They went for a take and Carl took two instrumental breaks on his guitar: he would have given one to Jerry if the bastard hadn't been so smug. It was a little rough and they would do it again before release but Sam declared, 'That's a smash – it sounds like the South is gonna fight the North again!'

They would have done another take that day but there was an unexpected visitor: Elvis Presley. Carl hadn't seen Elvis for a year and he was now a major star, indeed the biggest star in the US. He looked different, his hair, once sandy, was jet black. He starred in the biggest film at the US box office, *Love Me Tender*, and he had taken a few days' holiday in Las Vegas with Colonel Parker. He had come from Vegas with one of the showgirls, the stunning Marilyn Evans, whom he described as his 'house guest'.

Elvis was in no hurry and he said he would like to hear a playback of what they had been doing. He heard 'Matchbox' and called it a killer track and he praised Jay and Clayton for their backing vocals on 'Your True Love'. The downside of the Million Dollar Quartet is that they had interrupted a very good session.

Sam Phillips saw a photo-op. He called Johnny Cash and asked him to come to the studio double-quick. Then he rang the local newspaper, *Memphis Press-Schmitar*, and asked them to send a photographer, who happened to be George Pierce. A reporter, Bob Johnson came along as well as his friend, Leo Soroca from United Press International.

Elvis sat at the piano and doodled a few notes. Jerry Lee said, 'I didn't know you could play' but wisely refrained from passing comment on his ability. When Johnny Cash arrived, a press photograph was taken of Elvis at the piano, with Carl on guitar and Jerry Lee and Johnny Cash behind him. Marilyn was sitting on the piano but the photo is usually cropped. When it appeared the following day, Bob Johnson wrote, 'If Sam Phillips had been on his toes, he'd have turned the recorder on when that very unrehearsed but talented bunch got to cutting up 'Blueberry Hill' and a lot of other songs. That quartet could sell a million.' Hence, the phrase, the Million Dollar Quartet.

What Johnson didn't know is that the tapes were turned on, and the musicians must have known that as, by and large, they are singing into the microphones. Of course what they were doing was only for fun as Elvis was on a different label now and RCA would never have permitted this, had they known. Indeed, they could have confiscated the tapes.

After the photo session, Elvis asked if there was an acoustic guitar around. Charles Underwood, who wrote 'Ubangi Stomp' for Warren Storm, said he had one in his car.

Johnny Cash had to pick up his wife Vivian when she finished work and they were going shopping. There are no known tapes of him singing with the Million Dollar Quartet, but he recalled singing 'Blueberry Hill' and 'Isle of Golden Dreams' with them. They must have been singing this when the photograph was taken. We know that he wasn't around later as Elvis says, 'Takes Johnny Cash to do this', as he gets to grips with 'On the Jericho Road'.

In a WHSmith music magazine interview in 1993, Johnny Cash told Max Bell, 'The story goes that I wasn't there except for the photo call. It isn't true. The truth is that I was present throughout the session which started with me and Elvis singing a lot of gospel tunes. Since Jerry played the hottest piano, obviously we had to let him sit down. The liner notes say that my voice isn't heard because I'd left the studio. In fact, they had lost the tapes. I wish they would set the record straight.'

So the famed Million Dollar Quartet is really the Million Dollar Trio. They are backed by the Perkins band on occasion and another Sun artist, Smokey Joe Baugh, adds his bass voice to 'I Shall Not Be Moved'. Baugh had recorded a novelty song for Sun in 1955, 'The Signifying Monkey', a cleaned-up version of something bawdy.

By now, you must be thinking that the world and his wife were at Sun Records that day – with no security either, just Marion Keisker by the door. We don't know for sure but the complete rundown is likely to have been Sam Phillips, Jack Clement, Carl Perkins, Jay Perkins, Clayton Perkins, Buck Perkins, W.S. Holland, Jerry Lee Lewis, Johnny Cash, Charles Underwood, Elvis Presley, Marilyn Evans, Bob Johnson, George Pierce, Leo Soroca and Smokey Joe Baugh. There are 10 known photographs from the afternoon.

W.S. Holland says, 'Many times I have thought, 'Boy, I would have given anything if whoever took those pictures had just angled the camera round three or four feet and myself and Clayton and J.B. would have been in the picture. Jack Clement just turned on the recording machine and that's the reason that you don't have a good sound, we were just playing whatever we thought and didn't have any idea that someday it would be billed as the Million Dollar Quartet. We didn't even know that the recording machine was even on. If we had, we might have tried a little bit better. If you listen to the CD, it starts and stops just like a jam session.'

Sam Phillips and Jack Clement watched what would happen. For the next 50 minutes, the musicians performed over 35 songs, rarely doing complete takes and often only singing snatches. Nevertheless, it is a remarkable smorgasbord of southern music – country, gospel, blues and rock'n'roll.

The star of the tape is unquestionably Elvis. He talks about being in Vegas and how he had seen Billy Ward and his Dominoes. Their lead vocalist was Jackie Wilson who did a hilarious impression of Elvis singing 'Don't Be Cruel', which amused Elvis so much that he saw it four times. He talks about him doing a big ending: 'All he needs is a building to jump off'.

Elvis impersonates Jackie Wilson impersonating Elvis Presley and he also has a stab at impersonating Bill Monroe ('Little Cabin Home on the Hill') and Ernest Tubb ('I'm With a Crowd but so Alone'). Marilyn Evans has her moment as she requests 'Farther Along'.

Carl takes the lead on Wynn Stewart's 'Keeper of the Key' with Carl and Jerry adding harmonies and he comments, 'I'm gonna cut that record', which he did. Among the gospel songs is 'Peace in the Valley' which Elvis was soon to record, but he wasn't sure about Faron Young's 'Is It So Strange'. He says, 'Ol' Faron Young sent me this song to record. He wouldn't give me none of it, he wanted it all.' (Laughs) It's a revealing comment as it shows Elvis knew exactly what Colonel Parker was doing with music publishing.

Elvis starts the blues track 'Reconsider Baby' but no one knows it well enough for it to take shape. Come 1960, this would be one of his best-ever records.

They show their love of Chuck Berry by singing 'Brown Eyed Handsome Man' three times and 'Too Much Monkey Business'. Elvis reveals that Pat Boone's latest hit, 'Don't Forbid Me', had been offered to him first. He performs a full version of his own 'Paralysed'. Jerry Lee performs his single, 'Crazy Arms' and he finishes the session on his own with short versions of four songs as Elvis and Carl are saying goodbye.

Copyright restrictions prevented these tapes from being heard for 30 years and inevitably, bootlegs surfaced. Indeed, the first bootleg I heard must have been from a sixth generation copy as they sounded so bad. In the official 1990 CD issued, marketed as an Elvis Presley album by BMG, it sounded much better.

I do think that the *Million Dollar Quartet* show would have worked if they had stuck to the original tapes and shown what had happened, but I accept that it would have been less of a jukebox musical. It would however give a truer picture of rock'n'roll history. Elvis Presley called the day 'a barrelhouse of fun'. He was right.

One of the interesting aspects of the tapes is that Jerry Lee, who was unknown at the time, saw himself on a par with Elvis, while Carl was happy to take a back seat, preferring to play guitar licks than sing.

A couple of years ago in a TV documentary, Rich Hall showed the photograph of the Million Dollar Quartet and said that it showed 'Jesus, Buddha, Muhammad and Carl Perkins.' That was a cruel, cruel joke, but it was much funnier and much sharper than anything in the play.

CHAPTER 6
Winter, Summer, Springtime Too

'We were all kids and it's strange that people analyse the historical aspects of what we did. If anything, we helped to popularise the sound of a guitar so that people no longer confused it with a banjo.'

Phil Everly

I. Meanwhile Over in Britain...

I love rock'n'roll, always have, but I am sure I loved rock'n'roll all the more when I was young for knowing that my elders hated it, really hated it. My father thought it was an abomination and for some unknown reason, particularly loathed the Everly Brothers. Maybe it was because there were two of them. When he said that Duane Eddy was too lazy even to write some words, I retorted that Stravinsky only wrote instrumentals: he said, 'You cheeky little sod' and cuffed me.

Dad never changed his mind about rock'n'roll and indeed, I can't recall anyone over 30 who thought that the new music was any good. One school chum told the careers officer that he wanted to be a rock'n'roll singer. 'You've already got too many qualifications,' said the teacher, 'You don't need to be able to read or write.'

Okay, it sounds like I've been watching the touring version of *Hairspray* (which I have), but kids who go to that will find it hard to believe that life was really like that. Today, for example, parents go out of their way to enjoy the musical tastes of their children. As it turned out, some of the brightest minds of the generation worked in rock music.

So far we have looked at the rise of rock'n'roll, and Elvis Presley in particular, in the US in the mid-1950s. I want to explain Elvis Presley's success in the UK – it is somewhat different to the US as he didn't come over on tour and we didn't see his TV appearances.

Whenever I see the bright yellow Sun label today, it excites me. It is nearly always a sign of quality, but prior to Johnny Cash and Carl Perkins singles in 1956, there was no outlet for its output in the UK. After that time, various tracks were released on the London-American label. None of Elvis Presley's Sun releases in 1954/5 were released in the UK at the time, so they were never heard on the BBC. Later, they came out as album tracks and occasionally as singles, but they were not advertised as older material, which meant that we in Britain did not hear Elvis in chronological order and it never occurred to us (or to me, at any rate) that they were out of sync. There was a sound but unexpected reason for this, which was due to internal politics within the record companies.

In 1899 Francis Barraud painted a portrait of a terrier listening to a cylinder player, although he soon substituted a wind-up gramophone. The picture was purchased by the

Gramophone Company in the UK and used for their label, His Master's Voice (HMV). By 1901, it was similarly featured by Victor (later RCA-Victor) in the US, and HMV and RCA had an arrangement whereby the two companies gave each other the first option on their releases. HMV became part of the vast EMI organisation. In the early 1950s, HMV was doing well with two American balladeers, Perry Como and Tony Martin, both RCA recording artists.

EMI's biggest rival was Decca, a British company which had begun by manufacturing wind-up gramophones. It had a US counterpart, which discovered Bing Crosby, but the companies became separate in the build-up to the Second World War. They maintained links to license each other's products and UK Decca released Bill Haley on its Brunswick label.

Elvis Presley's first RCA single, 'Heartbreak Hotel', was a game-changer and it was sent to HMV's label manager, 43-year-old Wally Ridley for immediate release in the UK. He revealed, 'RCA Victor sent me everything they released in America in the pop or country and western fields, and my job was to decide what should be released here on HMV. Steve Sholes, who was a real sweetheart of a feller, wrote to me one day and said, 'I'm sending you six sides. You won't understand a word but do yourself a favour and release two of them because this man is gonna be very big indeed'. He underlined the last words. I poked my ear into the set, I turned it up, I turned it down, nothing – the only words I could make out were 'heartbreak hotel'. I released it and HMV got the worst reviews it had ever had for a record. The chiefs wanted to sack me for releasing it. Radio Luxembourg wouldn't play it and nor would the BBC. Jack Payne wrote half a page for the *Daily Express* saying, 'How dare they release such rubbish'.'

The UK bandleader Cyril Stapleton informed the *Daily Express* readers in May 1956 that 'Elvis Presley's record of 'Heartbreak Hotel' should be appearing in the best sellers soon – despite the fact that you can't understand a word he's singing about.'

The *New Musical Express* took the advertising money but reviewer Geoffrey Everitt dissed the product. 'If this is singing then I give up and furthermore if this is the stuff that the American record fans are demanding, I'm glad I'm on this side of the Atlantic. For a breath of fresh air, we turn to Billy Cotton and his Band...'

This was echoed by Steve Race in *Melody Maker*: 'Rock and roll is the antithesis of all that jazz has been striving for...good taste and musical integrity.' He was to say of 'Hound Dog': 'I fear for this country. It ought to have the good taste to reject music so decadent. It is not pleasant to watch a whole generation of British teenagers associate themselves with the cheapest music even America has yet produced.'

The show business writer, Dick Tatham, was to write a biography of Elvis Presley but he had this to say in *Record Mirror* in 1956: 'The incomparably incomprehensible Mr. Presley realises, for example, that 'Heartbreak Hotel' called by any other name would sound just as ear-catching. He is probably aware that the lyrics are so inane, it doesn't matter whether you hear them or not.'

This is *Melody Maker's* review of Elvis Presley's first UK album, *Rock'n'Roll*, with the reviewer wondering if Presley was a gospel singer: 'I have listened to these pieces with an increasing horror. They certainly didn't remind me of the excellent Rosetta Tharpe, but I had in mind one cold night on a friend's farm when one of the cows became entangled in some barbed wire and we had to wade through the mud to try and extricate the suffering animal.'

These are reviews from music papers bought by teenagers. A more serious publication, *The Gramophone*, regularly gave the likes of Elvis Presley, Bill Haley and Little Richard bad reviews if they bothered to review their new releases at all, while both Pat Boone and the Big Ben Banjo Band attracted positive comments. It's been fascinating to read reviews I never saw at the time and, as long as they are well expressed, I don't mind reviewers holding totally different opinions to me. To quote John Oakland, the reviewer for *The Gramophone*, 'I've never gone into much detail over the average rock'n'roll disc because I honestly believe that one sounds much like another, and that people who go for that sort of thing aren't likely to read what I write, or even read this journal at all.'

If you only went by the reviews, you might assume that the whole of the UK hated Elvis. The music was treated as if it came from outer space. The record industry had ignored the fact that teenagers might like to have some music for themselves. Author Ray Connolly was raised in Ormskirk: 'I was obsessed with rock'n'roll from the age of 15 when I first heard Elvis. Before that I had been obsessed with popular music anyway. I had gone to see Guy Mitchell at the Liverpool Empire and I went with my mother and my aunt when I was 12. When I heard Elvis, it was like the scales had fallen from my eyes and I thought, 'This is my life.' At the time it was assumed that anyone who liked rock'n'roll was semi-moronic. John Lennon thought differently and I thought differently. When I went to university, students didn't like pop music. It wasn't intellectual enough and low culture and they liked trad jazz, which I always hated. Eventually I found a job where I was writing about popular music, which was great, and through that job I met Elvis and the Beatles and so I was very lucky.'

Folk singer Martin Carthy also sees that it was a social revolution. 'I was 14 or 15 when rock'n'roll came along, the sort of age where something is either going to leave you stone cold or knock you over – and it knocked me over. When I look back on Bill Haley, Lonnie Donegan, Elvis Presley and Gene Vincent, I can see that rock'n'roll and skiffle represented something very important – the idea that ordinary people could make music. For the first time, you didn't have to be a trained musician to make music.' In a sense, Martin Carthy is wrong as there are generations of troubadours, minstrels and music hall performers who had no formal training at all, but I know what he means.

Soon to be one of the UK's rock'n'roll singers, Terry Dene was based at HMV's impressive record store in Oxford Street, London: 'I was working as a record packer at the HMV shop, and every morning we used to listen to the new records. I saw a label with Elvis Presley's name on it and I thought, 'What a strange name. I wonder if I'm pronouncing it right.' We played 'Heartbreak Hotel' over and over every morning until the management told us that we had to stop. I'd never seen a photograph of him. I didn't know whether he was black or white, but I knew he sounded great. When I eventually saw him in *Love Me Tender*, I knew I could do that and I wanted to sing those sorts of songs.'

Wee Willie Harris was similarly impressed. 'I used to go to a record stall down the market in Bermondsey. I was standing there one day when, all of a sudden, I heard this record – (sings) 'Well, since my baby left me, I found a new place to dwell' – all very high-pitched. I thought it was Johnnie Ray with a new song but the guy said it was Elvis Presley. I said, 'I like that. I'll buy it.''

It seems that nearly everybody heard 'Heartbreak Hotel' by chance. George

Harrison told BBC Radio 2, 'I was riding along on my bicycle and heard 'Heartbreak Hotel' coming out of somebody's house. What a sound, what a record; it changed the course of my life.'

The BBC included minuscule portions of rock'n'roll in its schedules but EMI ensured that the record was among the selections in jukeboxes in coffee bars and slot machine arcades. It could be heard on evening shows from Radio Luxembourg, but unlike today where you can listen to any song on demand, in 1956 most people depended on luck. However, you could go into a record shop and ask to hear a record in a listening booth, with a view to purchasing it.

Paul McCartney told *Q* magazine: 'I'd seen an ad for 'Heartbreak Hotel' in the *NME* and I had to go into a record shop and listen to it through headphones in one of the booths. It was a magical moment, the beginning of an era.'

But you couldn't go into a listening booth if you were only 11 years old.

I saw the title 'Heartbreak Hotel' by Elvis Presley in the charts and the exciting cover picture of him in full flow on the cover of the *NME*.

The title, the name and the look promised so much and I could sense that this could open the door to a magic kingdom, but I went for weeks without hearing it. Then one day I had a cold and was in bed. I switched on the radio for *Housewives' Choice*, a dreary programme as the good housewives of the UK shunned rock'n'roll and preferred David Whitfield (Decca) and Ronnie Hilton (HMV) – and it was followed by a religious pep talk, *Five to Ten*. This particular morning, an irate vicar denounced the vilest, most repulsive, most appalling record he had ever heard. The singer would rot in hell and his name was Elvis Presley. I'm exaggerating but that's what he wanted to say. He played 30 seconds of 'Heartbreak Hotel' and that was enough to change my whole life. And that is the important point – I am sure that we all knew that this was not a silly craze or teenage fad. Elvis would remain with us for the rest of our lives.

The record also healed the sick, as I left my bed and went to a store and bought it (5/7d or 28p, should you be interested).

'Heartbreak Hotel' went to No.2 in the UK but Elvis was deprived of the top slot by his biggest rival at the time, Pat Boone. Although Pat Boone is derided today (and even back then), he did have good taste in picking his songs and the Flamingos' doo-wop classic, 'I'll Be Home' suited his warm, romantic voice. A lot of sons and young husbands had been conscripted, so this song resonated with meaning.

A friend's mother had Pat Boone's record and she was mystified by the nonsense on the B-side, 'Tutti Frutti'. Little Richard's original had not been released in the UK, but there was something appealing about someone singing 'Awopbopaloolop Alopbamboom' even though Pat Boone was chanting it like a children's rhyme. Who were La Bostrie and Penniman, the names under the title of the record? How could two people have written a song with such nonsensical lyrics?

Pandora's box had been opened. The summer of 1956 was brilliant. EMI had first option on product from the US Capitol label and along came a record that was even more outrageous than 'Heartbreak Hotel', Gene Vincent and the Blue-Caps with 'Be-Bop-A-Lula'. The lyric combined the nonsense of 'Tutti Frutti' with the echo of 'Heartbreak Hotel' and Vincent sounded as though he was singing from the bottom of a well. Could a girl really be called Be-Bop-A-Lula and how could she wear 'red blue jeans? I'd never met a girl with 'flying feet'.

What a record! The *NME* reported that the BBC had banned its B-side, 'Woman Love'. If Gene Vincent wasn't actually singing 'fucking', then he was getting close to it. The single was banned, the first *bona fide* American rock'n'roll classic to be so treated. 'Let's face it,' said a BBC spokesman, 'it's a bit suggestive and anyway, you can't understand what he's saying.' It's akin to the controversy in 1969 over Desmond Dekker's 'The Israelites' where Dekker might have said, 'My wife and my kids, they fuck off and leave me.' As far as I know, nobody ever asked Vincent or Dekker what they were singing.

Vincent even made the Top 30 with the follow-up, 'Race with the Devil', the scariest, edgiest record ever released up to that point: the chilling story of a terrified member of a hot-rod gang having a road race with Satan. 'I've had a wild life, so they say,' sang Vincent, 'But I'll outrun the Devil on Judgement Day.' We had no idea what was going on, but it sure was spooky. Vincent was the same age as Presley but he looked haggard and older: no wonder if this was how he lived his life. More please and oh, by the way, just what were hot-rods?

It wasn't until November 1956 that anything by Little Richard was released in the UK. His Specialty singles were leased to Decca and released on their London-American label. The first was the frenzied 'Rip It Up', but his thunder was stolen by Bill Haley and his Comets who took it into the Top 10. Then London-American combined Richard's first US hits on one single, 'Long Tall Sally' and 'Tutti Frutti', which made No.3 early in 1957. As my father used to say, the lunatics had taken over the asylum. I wouldn't say he was right but he did have a point.

Little Richard's biographer, Chas White: 'Little Richard looked outrageous in *Don't Knock The Rock*. This bizarre figure came out with a lascivious face, plenty of make-up, greasy hair, a high pompadour and really wild eyes. He was playing a baby grand and he put his foot on top of it and started hammering the keys. Our piano at home was a sacred instrument that you walked around and my aunt played hymns on it. Little Richard was belting the heck out of it and screaming his head off and when he finished he bowed as if he had played a Chopin nocturne. It was unbelievable.'

The accepted protocol was for a performer to release four singles in a year, so it was surprising that we were bombarded with new product from Elvis Presley – indeed, HMV released six Elvis singles in 1956. This was not down to marketing but company politics.

Decca UK had originally released Capitol's product but the American independent had switched to EMI and had enormous success with Frank Sinatra, Nat 'King' Cole and Dean Martin. Decca had payback by wooing RCA, telling the company it could have its own UK label if it went with Decca. This was agreed in March 1956 but it wouldn't take effect until June 1957. As a result, EMI released as much as the market could take before the lease expired and for some mysterious reason, they went a few months beyond that too. Hence, the market was saturated with Elvis singles, EPs and LPs; all good stuff too.

These are the singles that HMV released in the UK with their chart placings:

March 1956 Heartbreak Hotel / I Was the One (HMV, No.2) The build-up was slow as it took two months to make the charts.

May 1956 Blue Suede Shoes / Tutti Frutti (HMV, No.9) A straight rival to the Carl Perkins single, which entered the charts a week earlier and made No.10.

July 1956 – I Want You, I Need You, I Love You / My Baby Left Me (HMV, No.14)

Elvis Presley: Caught in a Trap

Elvis had three records at once in the UK Top 20. This was a US No.1, so its UK sales had been hampered by too much Elvis on the shelves.

September 1956 – Hound Dog / Don't Be Cruel (HMV, No.2) The *NME* only listed Hound Dog but *Melody Maker* had it as a double-sided hit.

November 1956 – Blue Moon / I Don't Care If the Sun Don't Shine (HMV, No.9; B-side, No.23) The first of Elvis' Sun tracks to be issued in the UK. It was an inspired choice, making the Top 10.

December 1956 – Love Me Tender / Anyway You Want Me (HMV, No.11) This had been held back until the UK opening of the *Love Me Tender* film.

February 1957 – Mystery Train / Love Me (HMV, No.25) A wonderful track, but there is so much Elvis around that it only sold moderately.

March 1957 – Rip It Up / Baby Let's Play House (HMV, No.27)

April 1957 – Too Much / Playin' for Keeps (HMV, No.6)

June 1957 – All Shook Up / That's When Your Heartaches Begin (HMV, No.1) Elvis' first UK No.1 and not before time.

First RCA single, Teddy Bear / Loving You (No.3, B-side No.24)

August 1957 – Paralyzed / When My Blue Moon Turns to Gold Again (HMV, No.8) Neither side had been a single in the US. RCA may have taken umbrage but the fans loved these singles as it was another Top 10 hit.

Second RCA single, Party (No.2, B-side No.17)

October 1957 – Lawdy Miss Clawdy / Tryin' to Get to You (HMV, No.15, B-side No.16)

On the *NME* chart for 2 November 1957, Elvis had seven titles in the Top 30: Party (4), Teddy Bear (12), All Shook Up (16), Tryin' to Get to You (20), Got a Lot o' Livin' to Do! (21), Loving You (24) and Paralysed (26).

Third RCA single, Santa Bring My Baby Back to Me / Santa Claus Is Back In Town (No.7)

January 1958 – I'm Left, You're Right, She's Gone / How Do You Think I Feel (HMV, No.21) Again, a Sun track as an A-side and it does okay.

Fourth RCA single, Jailhouse Rock / Treat Me Nice (No.1) – Advance orders of 250,000 and the first record to go straight into the UK charts at No.1, so long as you don't count the No.1 on the very first chart, Al Martino's 'Here in My Heart' in November 1952.

From this moment, RCA had control of the release schedule.

The situation was similar to that of the Beatles with their first US releases. Once they eventually had a hit in the US in January 1964, other labels which had been granted licenses for their earlier product reissued them, leading to the Beatles having the entire Top 5 in the *Billboard* Hot 100 one week in April 1964. In both cases, the overkill didn't hurt the artist and that was because the product was so strong.

Wally Ridley at HMV was losing an American Elvis but was he now looking for a British one? 'No. When I heard Presley, I listened to what was behind the voice. I decided that the UK would take three years to find musicians who could even begin to play like that, let alone find a singer up front to do it. Everybody would be copying him anyway and we'd only be second-best. I left it alone and stuck with what I knew. Right in the middle of all this nonsense, I had 'St. Therese of the Roses', which had nothing to do with rock'n'roll but sold a quarter of a million for Malcolm Vaughan. If a song is well-written, has a clear, clean message and is delivered with sincerity with a good quality performance, good orchestration and a good sound, then you can sell and sell.'

Bill Haley and his Comets had introduced rock'n'roll to the UK and the first British acts were Tony Crombie and his Rockets and Art Baxter and his Rock & Roll Sinners, examples of jazzmen who were dumbing down for a quick killing. They did okay in the ballrooms but nobody wanted their records.

Still, Britain had to have its own rock'n'rollers and the first success went to a young merchant seaman, Tommy Steele: 'I was never the sex symbol. I was always 'the boy next door'. It wasn't intentional: it was just me being me, just like Presley was being Presley, and that's the way he came out. The easiest way to be is yourself. I never went looking for screams by gyrating and quivering my lower lip. In Sweden they had a poll to find out who was the best rock'n'roller – and, believe it or not, I beat Elvis. That was purely on my personality, I think – my records weren't as good as his.'

Guitarist Brian Gregg: 'Tommy Steele was supposed to be our answer to Elvis, but he quickly became a George Formby character and no-one took him seriously as a rock'n'roll singer. Terry Dene had more aggression and a better voice for rock'n'roll but there were personal problems and until Cliff Richard came along, there wasn't anybody really.'

That included Larry Page, who was billed as the teenage rage and recorded an embarrassing cover of 'That'll Be the Day': 'I was born in Hayes, Middlesex and packing records for EMI was the only job that was going there. I started taking singing lessons and, initially, I thought I was going to be another Ronnie Hilton or Perry Como. The minute rock'n'roll hit, I thought, 'Forget the lessons and get out there and do something'. The pianist who played for me at my recording test was Terry Stanford who became Russ Conway, and I was signed for EMI, started recording for EMI and continued packing records, including my own.'

Here's the Methodist minister, Lord Soper, watching the first BBC first pop show to feature rock'n'roll: 'I'm perplexed by *6.5 Special*. I can't understand how intelligent people can derive any sort of satisfaction from something which is emotionally embarrassing and intellectually ridiculous. I heard one songwriter say that his song said as much as a Shakespeare sonnet. That is what I call invincible ignorance.'

Twenty-five year old Jack Good was the director of the BBC's teenage show, *6.5 Special*. 'Tommy Steele was so good that I didn't mind that he didn't have this threatening aspect, which I always like in a rock'n'roll artist. Tommy wasn't on *6.5 Special* very much because the BBC wouldn't pick up his option. They said that rock'n'roll was going to be finished in nine months and so he would be a liability. Two months later we couldn't afford him because his price was more than double the whole budget for the show. I was on £18 a week myself and we had 12 million viewers. They tolerated me for a year and then kicked me off. They said rock'n'roll was dying and skiffle was dead and the programme had to reflect that. I disagreed, so we parted company.'

Did Jack Good, an Oxford graduate who had studied Shakespeare, think rock'n'roll had as much value as the Bard? 'Well, no, I didn't think that. I was a dedicated Shakespeare fan. It's like whisky: you don't think of it as having much value, but boy, is it fun sometimes.'

The playwright Alan Bleasdale had been a rock'n'roll fan. 'British rock'n'roll to me was summed up by Tommy Steele, Terry Dene and Cliff Richard. I never collected

British rock'n'roll records, ever. I didn't think they were fit to tie the guitar straps of the Americans. I did buy a Lonnie Donegan record once, and, much to my shame, Frankie Vaughan's 'Green Door', but I didn't buy British rock'n'roll because it wasn't rock'n'roll to me. Marty Wilde, come on.'

'It's lovely to hear my old records,' says Tommy Steele, 'It's almost like an art form now, isn't it? We were nowhere near as musically accomplished as the lads today. We knew nothing about chord sequences and how to find different ideas within the confines of a chord sequence. With us, it was straightforward chords and emphasising the second and fourth beat to the bar. 'Come On Let's Go' was more ridiculous than anything Presley ever did. That was when the engineer really did find out how to go to extremes.'

More than anything Jack Good wanted Elvis on *6.5 Special*. Scriptwriter Trevor Peacock: 'I always remember Jack Good ringing up Colonel Parker, trying to get Elvis to appear on *6.5 Special*. They agreed some huge figure like £10,000, which was, of course, totally unpayable. Jack said, 'All right, ten thousand' and Parker replied, 'Well, that's my cut. Now, regarding the fee for the boy himself...' It was £250,000 for one appearance, which was totally crazy. So, Elvis never did anything over here.' Similarly, talk of Elvis coming for the promoter Harry Foster was nothing more than that – talk.

By and large, the British artists were wise in keeping away from Elvis' songs. There was no point in becoming an Aunt Sally unless you recorded for the Embassy label. This label was distributed through Woolworth's stores and the singles offered two contemporary hits for four shillings (20p) performed by competent singers with cheapo-cheapo backings. You could buy Shorty Mitchell singing 'All Shook Up' or the Canadians with 'Blue Suede Shoes'. Most artists were using pseudonyms and Shorty Mitchell was the composer and arranger, Geoff Love and the Canadians were the stalwarts of the BBC Light Programme, the Maple Leaf Four. This in its way was the start of tribute acts and a touring show, *Disc Doubles*, featured singers as Elvis and Sinatra. The Belfast singer, Ronnie Carroll, who had a single with 'The Wonder of You' long before Elvis, had his first job darkening his face and becoming Nat 'King' Cole for a show, *Hollywood Doubles*.

In the 1950s, it was a brave man who covered one of Presley's own records; almost artistic suicide. Clinton Ford had leanings in folk, jazz and country and he covered one of Elvis Presley's country sides. 'I loved 'Old Shep' and I was singing it at Butlin's because I was a Redcoat in '57, '58 and '59. It used to go down well and I thought I must record it. Oriole didn't like the song – they said it was too slow, too dreary and too long, but eventually they let me record a shortened version. I wanted a steel guitar and a choir on it but they preferred a rock'n'roll group with two saxophones. It was a terrible version but it went in the charts. RCA saw what was happening and immediately released an Elvis EP with 'Old Shep' as the main track.'

Being a good-natured bloke, Clinton said he would give his royalties from 'Old Shep' to the Battersea Dogs Home. It made the charts and poor Clint missed out. This was one song which didn't have royal patronage – Clint heard that the Queen told a member of her household to turn off *Housewives' Choice* because the presenter was playing 'Old Shep' and she had lost a corgi.

BBC presenter Brian Matthew: 'Clinton Ford is an old friend of mine and he was regularly appearing on *Easy Beat* on Sunday mornings, a show I produced and introduced myself. I was compering a live show from the Royal Albert Hall and Clint didn't want to sing 'Old Shep'. I made him change his mind and he was met with hooligans shouting, 'We want Elvis! Get off!' This was live on air from the Royal Albert Hall. He stopped singing and he said in an American accent, 'I'm gonna finish this song if it kills me.' That did the trick and they applauded and yelled. It was a lovely moment.'

Despite these curious cover versions, the British fans were never attracted to cheap tat. Colonel Parker asked Hank Saperstein to visit Britain with a view to licensing Elvis products here. He set himself up in a London hotel but nobody wanted to buy into this. Brian Epstein was later criticised for giving away the rights to market the Beatles and his mistake had been looking at it from the British perspective: he hadn't grasped the potential of the market.

Sheila Prytherch from the Vernons Girls sang 'All Shook Up' on *6.5 Special:* 'I came from classical singing lessons and I had Elvis on a T-shirt. I had to shake my boobs and sing 'I'm all shook up' and I nearly died of embarrassment. I thought my singing teacher would drop dead.'

Ann O'Brien continues, 'I had 'Elvis' written on a pair of jeans on my backside and Mary had 'Presley' written on her bum. We had to jump in front of the camera with our bums showing 'Elvis Presley'.'

When Private Elvis Presley was stationed in Germany, he met the girls' agent, Stanley Barnet and asked him about 'those swingin' girls', possibly attracted to the name, as his father was called Vernon.

Despite its huge success in America, neither the BBC nor ITV took *The Ed Sullivan Show*: the BBC was limited by charter to the number of American imports it could broadcast and chose *The Perry Como Show*, which was certainly more professional and had a more engaging host. ITV simply thought that their own *Sunday Night at the London Palladium* was better, which it unquestionably was. The continuity in Sullivan's show was hampered by its stilted and inexpressive host: I know that this was part of the fun for Americans, but it looked incompetent to outsiders.

So if the UK fans wanted to see Elvis, they would have to go to the cinema, first to *Love Me Tender*, which despite the contortions, was Elvis in 1865. The queues had lined up in Times Square for the film but not in the UK. You had to find the film first as it was withdrawn after four days in Windsor due to fans booing Presley on screen. Tim Thomas wrote to the *NME:* 'I have never seen anything so funny as Elvis trying to act. I squirmed when I saw his half-closed eyes, greasy hair and curled lip.'

Elvis was defended by Jennifer Ross in *Hit Parade:* 'Since when has it been essential to hear a singer's words? Can you hear what Caruso sings? Of course not.' Especially if he's singing in Italian.

The film *Rock Around the Clock* seems quaint today but rock'n'roll was once a revolutionary force and it set the wheels in motion for Little Richard (who was in the follow-up *Don't Knock the Rock* and also, *The Girl Can't Help It*) and Elvis Presley. Taking their cue from Edward VII's reign, some youths with sideburns dressed in long, velvet-collared jackets, combined with drainpipe trousers, white socks and crepe soles. They became known as Teddy boys and they were often fighting or ripping up cinema seats. My mother said that I couldn't go to *Loving You* on my own as I might get caught in a riot, but she didn't mind taking me to it. She spent every moment wondering if some Ted was about to knife her in the back.

After talking to a cinema manager, Lord Auckland told the House of Lords about a cinema manager he knew. 'The other week he showed, because he was forced to show it by his circuit, one of these rock'n'roll films, with Elvis Presley or some such star; and after the showing some of his regular patrons said, 'Why the blazes do you show this kind of stuff here? I have been patronising this cinema for many years and I shall think twice about coming again.' He had to reply that his circuit ordered him to show this film. Here, I think, is a case where circuits should arrange for a public local poll to be taken, so that the right kind of film is shown in the area.' Ah, an early plea for independent local cinema.

Zealous cinema managers stopped dancing in the aisle and, in Liverpool, hundreds of exuberant fans were chased from the ABC in Lime Street to the Pier Head. Lord Boothby said on the BBC's *Any Questions*, 'What worries me is that a fourth-rate film with fifth-rate music can pierce the shell of civilisation. The sooner this ridiculous film is banned the better.'

Lord Boothby also said that 'one of the purposes of us old fogies is to stop young people being silly'. You can rely on a Lord to say something silly, especially one whose knowledge of adult delinquency came from his friends, the Krays.

Jack Good created ITV's fast-moving *Oh Boy!* which was far slicker than its American counterparts, but had to make do with British artists. Jack Good discovered Cliff Richard: 'Franklyn Boyd, who published 'Schoolboy Crush', brought it round to me. It was a real drippy song, and I hate drippy songs. I asked him to put on the other side and then I went, 'What's that? What's that? You idiots, that's the side I want for *Oh Boy!* I've got to have this boy.' I auditioned Cliff and he wanted to be like Elvis. I told him to shave off his sideburns, which he didn't want to do, and to drop his guitar, which he didn't play very well at the time. I got him to be mean, moody and magnificent.'

Cliff Richard: 'I was a carbon copy of Elvis. All I had was a leg, a guitar and a lip. Jack didn't like that and he didn't want me to be too much like Elvis. He made me cut off my sideburns. He liked me to be moody but that wasn't because he wanted me to copy Elvis. He didn't think I looked as good when I smiled. However, I don't think that I ever did look moody. Awkward perhaps, but not moody.'

Wally Whyton from the skiffle group, the Vipers: 'Cliff was imitating Elvis like mad but he could do it with conviction. That's the real art of doing it; if you can't do it with conviction, you don't get away with it. The kids wanted Elvis but they would settle for an imitation and that was Cliff. He soon became his own man.'

Oh Boy! was a huge success and remains a benchmark for TV music shows. Jack Good discovered Billy Fury, who was as close to a British Elvis as we ever had. He was often writing his own material, a forerunner to the coming messiahs.

Guitarist Big Jim Sullivan: 'I thought Billy Fury was great, a nice unassuming guy who put on a good show. He'd be at the side of the stage, twitching and waiting to get on there. Billy had seen the Presley films and he was taking it a bit further. He got down on the floor with the mike stand and was rubbing it against his body. The more he did it, the more the girls liked it but the guys in the audience didn't like him at all. One night at Glasgow, when he was gyrating, they ripped the big brass ashtrays off the stage and threw them at him. One of them made a nasty dent in Colin Green's guitar and it could have killed him.'

Joe Brown: 'Jack Good wanted to make an album of Billy's own material and he played me the early Presley stuff with Scotty Moore playing guitar and he said, 'Pick up on those licks', which I had done anyway. It was a strange musical line-up for *The Sound of Fury* but it worked very well. Reg Guest was on piano, Bill Stark on acoustic bass, Alan Weighell on electric bass and myself on guitar. Using two basses was a very shrewd move because the Americans had that rockabilly sound with the slap bass and we didn't have any players that could slap the bass and keep the thing in tune as well. Jack just used the acoustic bass for the 'dum-dum-dum'. *The Sound of Fury* was a very good album and we did the whole thing in a couple of hours.'

While he was in Hollywood in 1960, the middle-of-the-road romancer (and template for Tom Jones) Frankie Vaughan met Elvis Presley, and his recollection shows that Presley knew what was happening in the UK: 'We'd go to the Commerce Room for lunch and after lunch we'd play handball. I saw a game going on and there was a ball very high in the air and I went for it and another guy was running for it. It was Elvis and we both wound up on the floor. He said, 'You're Britain's Frankie Vaughan' and I said, 'You're Elvis Presley' and he said, 'That's right.' We became pretty friendly then. To be honest, I hadn't rated many of the rock'n'roll singers although I loved Fats Domino and Little Richard, but I always thought that Elvis had that little bit extra and I loved 'Heartbreak Hotel'. I can see now that there was a good southern feel in all he did.'

II. Got a Lot o' Livin' to Do, 1957

On 4 January 1957, Elvis Presley had to report to the Kennedy Veterans' Hospital in Memphis for a physical examination to assess his suitability for the forces. No problems there as Elvis was classified 1-A. He would not be called immediately and there would be negotiations with Colonel Parker before the details were finalised.

For his own part, Elvis had no desire to be bawled at from dawn to dusk and to lose his superstar status. Colonel Parker listened to Elvis' complaints and then did what he had already decided. Gladys Presley was horrified. She didn't even like her precious son playing competitive sports in case he was injured.

It mightn't go down too well with fellow recruits but Elvis had said that he liked stuffed teddy bears. Presumably this was a joke that had misfired but his young female fans took it seriously and sent them to him. On his third appearance on *The Ed Sullivan Show* on 6 January 1957, he thanked fans for giving him 282 teddy bears, no great number when you consider he is Elvis Presley and the size of America, but by drawing attention to it, he was encouraging donations. Eventually the teddy bears were given to children's hospitals.

The New York songwriters, Kal Mann and Bernie Lowe, jumped on the bandwagon by writing '(Let Me Be Your) Teddy Bear' for Elvis and it was included in his second film, *Loving You*. By then Mann and Lowe had established their own Elvis, Charlie Gracie, and his hit, 'Fabulous' is an acceptable rewrite of 'Don't Be Cruel'.

As Ed Sullivan had previously shown Elvis Presley in full flight, why did he have a change of heart? Apparently, Ed had been told that Elvis was putting something down his trousers to emphasise his manhood. There is no evidence that Elvis did this but some rockers did: Billy Fury, for one. Even if he did, it was highly unlikely that he would have done so on national TV. Still, Ed Sullivan was concerned enough to instruct the producer to only show Elvis from the waist up.

The production notes which come as a DVD extra in the box set for the Sullivan shows, indicate a floor covering of a large record was requested. As the floor was never seen, this was an unnecessary expense and an indication that the 'waist up' was a last-minute decision. If Elvis had realised he would be filmed this way, surely he would have changed his presentation. As it stands, it looks daft.

Whatever, it is a strange performance. In the opening medley of 'Hound Dog', 'Love Me Tender' and 'Heartbreak Hotel', Elvis looks more manic than sexy and the puffed sleeves don't work. The setting was odd as Elvis is performing in in front of a musical motif with the Jordanaires dressed as tour operators.

Elvis returns to sing 'Too Much' and 'When My Blue Moon Turns to Gold Again' in the middle of the show. He closes with the spiritual, 'Peace in the Valley', written by Rev. Thomas A. Dorsey in 1939 on a train travelling from Indiana to Cincinnati. It had been a million seller for Red Foley, Pat Boone's father-in-law, in 1951, Apart from Elvis, there is a stunning performance from the British ventriloquist Arthur Worsley with his dummy Charlie Brown, although they make out it was the other way round.

Mister Ed reveals that Elvis is about to film *Running Wild* in Hollywood with Hal Wallis. Before that there is to be a charity show for Hungarian relief and Ed endorses him to the mums and dads of America by saying he is 'a fine, decent, young man.' Elvis encouraged the public to give generously to Hungary, who had turned on their Soviet rulers, and he was made an honorary citizen of Budapest.

Within a week of *The Ed Sullivan Show*, RCA released 'Too Much' as a single. The original 'Too Much' had been recorded in 1955 by Bernard Hardison for Republic, an R&B label based in Nashville. It was written by the owner of the label, Bill Beasley, but his secretary Lee Rosenberg was listed instead, because they had intended to pitch it to Decca, a label that was in litigation with Beasley. The co-writer was Len Weinman, who played the song to Steve Sholes. It hadn't been a hit but Elvis saw its potential, although he dropped the bridge in favour of a guitar solo from Scotty Moore.

Scotty Moore revealed, 'We had gone through 'Too Much' a couple of times: I had the solo down and it was in a strange key for a guitar. Elvis thought he could do it better and when we did it again, I got lost, but we didn't stop playing. We didn't have multi-tracking and as we couldn't re-do a solo, I kept going and somehow managed to come out at the letter A as I was supposed to. When Elvis heard the playback, he turned to me with a little smirk and said, 'You're gonna have to live with that for the rest of your life.' He really liked that take and he didn't just choose it to annoy me.'

Scotty's contribution is the best part of the record, which is held back by a sluggish beat. Nevertheless, 'Too Much' topped the *Billboard* chart, although it is often ignored today. It is rarely performed and Elvis never sang it in his Vegas years: he had so many hits that he could afford to ignore a No.1.

The other side was a country ballad, 'Playing for Keeps', written by Stan Kesler and featuring neat interplay between Elvis and the Jordanaires. It was a very attractive performance and made No.21 in *Billboard*.

Colonel Parker was not keen on crediting anybody but Elvis Presley on his records and he had dropped "Scotty and Bill' from the singles. 'Too Much' – 'Playin' for Keeps' was the first single to credit the Jordanaires, but he had a reason for this. As the name suggests, the Jordanaires were a well-known gospel group and Presley was keen to make a gospel album. It was an improbable move from someone who was shocking the nation but it matched Ed Sullivan calling him 'a fine, decent, young man.' Many commentators say that Elvis was a changed man after he had been in the forces, but the indicators were already in place. Colonel Parker had established the brand and saw how Elvis could develop into an all-round entertainer. Not just yet though as there was money to be made from rock'n'roll.

Vernon and Gladys loved singing gospel songs with Elvis: somewhere there must be tapes of them singing together, and sooner or later, his estate is going to release them.

The Jordanaires' contribution to Elvis' records has been debated and sometimes they sound old-fashioned. At their best, they bring a doo-wop sensibility to Elvis' records. They ooh and aah in the right places on the ballads 'I Want You, I Need You, I Love' and 'Anyway You Want Me' and add classic harmonies to 'Don't Be Cruel', 'All Shook Up', 'Teddy Bear', 'Treat Me Nice' and 'I Beg Of You', although the finest example is 'Stuck On You', made when Elvis returned from army service in 1960. It is hard to think of these songs being performed in other ways as their contributions are as memorable as the King's and despite Presley's overwhelming presence, these records are team efforts. Many other performers used the Jordanaires including Ricky Nelson ('Poor Little Fool', 'Lonesome Town, 'Travellin' Man'), Jimmy Dean ('Big Bad John') and Conway Twitty ('It's Only Make Believe'). They made many albums and singles of their own, but usually of a gospel nature and not intended for the mainstream.

Presley's musical schizophrenia was evident in the next sessions which merged gospel with rock'n'roll. For 10 days in January, Elvis Presley spent many hours in Radio Recorders in Hollywood working on the soundtrack for *Loving You*, then called *Stranger in Town* (and later *Something for the Girls* and *Lonesome Cowboy*), as well as potential singles, album tracks and gospel songs. There were further sessions in February, really to rework a couple of songs but also to add new performances. The sessions featured Scotty, Bill and D.J. with the Jordanaires plus pianist Dudley Brooks, who had written for Benny Goodman and Count Basie. Gordon Stoker played organ on the spirituals.

The first religious song was recent: Frankie Laine's million seller from 1953, 'I Believe', written by Ervin Drake, who was to write 'It Was a Very Good Year'. It's a very emotional song, but just who is singing this song? 'Every time I hear a newborn baby cry': is this man a doctor? Most people have never heard a newborn baby cry apart from their own.

Another recent song, 'It is No Secret', was written by Stuart Hamblen and first recorded by Red Foley with the Andrews Sisters. There are two ballads from Rev. Thomas A. Dorsey: 'Peace in the Valley' and 'Take My Hand, Precious Lord'. Dorsey wrote the latter after his wife had died in childbirth and Presley's voice is exceptional. RCA knew that the performances could have a wider appeal than the southern gospel market if the marketing was right. With the exception of 'I Believe', these beautiful songs were largely unknown outside the south and not known at all in the UK.

By far the biggest song from the session, 'All Shook Up' was written by Otis Blackwell after someone had shaken and spilt a bottle of Pepsi (the clean version) or after someone had told him how it felt to have V.D. (the dirty version). Both David Hill and Vicki Young had recorded it in 1956, without commercial success. When it was released as a single, it was combined with a dramatic reading of 'That's When Your Heartaches Begin' including a narration. There is much to be said for the modesty of Elvis' original performance on Sun, but the success of this one led him to 'Are You Lonesome Tonight' after he had left the army.

'That's When Your Heartaches Begin' owed something to Johnnie Ray as well as the Ink Spots and revealed that Elvis had a great voice for narration. Notice the effect of him saying, 'into your – aah – love affair and yeah, that's when your heartaches begin.' Brenda Lee, Jack Scott and the Flamingos also mixed singing and speech. And couldn't Elvis have done a great job on Commander Cody's 'Mama Hated Diesels'?

Elvis recorded a jaunty rocker from Rose Marie McCoy, 'I Beg of You', and an R&B ballad recorded by Marie Knight, 'Tell Me Why'. Faron Young's 'Is It So Strange' has a poignant, high-pitched vocal and you can sense Elvis' shoulder shrugging on 'Have I Told You Lately That I Love You', a song written on a hospital bed and recorded by Gene Autry, Bing Crosby and Tex Ritter.

Most surprisingly, Elvis sang a raunchy, R&B song recorded by Smiley Lewis a year earlier, 'One Night of Sin'. This was about visiting a prostitute for the first time: 'One night of sin is what I'm paying for' and 'Don't call my name, It makes me feel so ashamed'. Presley must have sung this for fun – it would have been unthinkable as an official release. It says something for record company security that it didn't escape into the media.

A month later they had worked out a new version of the song. The title was shortened to 'One Night' and now it was about somebody pleading for his girlfriend to spend the night with him. Still pretty risqué, but it could be released.

Dudley Brooks played piano triplets on 'Blueberry Hill', which is solid enough but lacking Fats Domino's personality and clipped delivery. Elvis was partial to Ivory Joe Hunter's recordings as, like Elvis, he appealed to both R&B and country markets. This time Elvis sang 'I Need You So', which Hunter had written and recorded in 1950. He returned to Billy 'The Kid' Emerson's 'When It Rains, It Pours', which he had tried at Sun and was now called 'When It Rains, It Really Pours'. One other track, 'Don't Leave Me Now', was held back for the next film, *Jailhouse Rock*.

Byron Raphael and Trude Forsher had worked on a ballad, 'Castles in the Sand', with a professional writer. Elvis liked it, sang a few bars, decided that it wasn't for him and started singing Bing Crosby's 'True Love', which Cole Porter had written for *High Society* in 1956. He had been singing 'Loving You', noted the similarity and sang it impulsively.

The primary purpose of the sessions was to put down the score for *Loving You*, and Elvis would mime to the recordings on screen. An extraordinary amount of time was spent in getting the songs for *Loving You* right. Admittedly, three different arrangements of the title song were needed for the film but the number of takes, often not complete, is high. We don't know how many takes there were for 'Lonesome Cowboy', but the totals for the others were 'Teddy Bear' (13), 'Hot Dog' (17), 'Mean Woman Blues' (21), 'Party' (sometimes with additional lyrics) (28), 'Got a Lot o' Livin' to Do!' (41) and 'Loving You' (90), which does seem excessive but some of the takes were only a few seconds long. An officially released double CD of the film score, released in 2006, contains 56 versions of 'Loving You'. It is listenable but you tire of the voice indicating 'HZ – Take 3' and so on. There's laughter, so the multiple takes don't bother Elvis too much. He even sings, 'I will spend my whole life through hating you.'

Although the Presley camp knew many country songwriters, 'Lonesome Cowboy' was written by the Brill Building team, Sid Tepper and Roy Bennett. There is a French double-CD, *Elvis Chante Sid Tepper & Roy C Bennett*, but there is not one hit single amongst them and they often gave Elvis songs unworthy of him. The double-CD includes a demo of 'Wife No.99', a novelty song which Elvis was wise to reject.

This was the first Tepper and Bennett song that Elvis recorded but they also wrote 'One More Day' for the film, which was sung by the actor, Mickey Shaughnessy. Jesse Mae Robinson wrote the rave-up 'Party', sometimes known as '(Let's Have a) Party'. 'Party' is chastised for being such a short hit single – just 86 seconds – and yet there is an additional verse in the film which could have been included.

RCA's financial figures for 1956 had been good, largely because Elvis had sold 12m singles and 3m albums in his first year for them. There was a lot of criticism of Elvis but some of the old guard accepted his music. In March 1957 the country's leading jazz musician, Louis Armstrong, said that he planned to record with Presley: 'You'd be surprised what we could do together.' It would have been a dream ticket but Parker wouldn't have endorsed it. Indeed, a cameo from Armstrong would have fitted nicely into *King Creole*.

In 1957 it was reported that Elvis had said, 'The only thing Negroes can do for me is shine my shoes and buy my records.' Elvis had said no such thing – it was fake news – and, probably prompted by Colonel Parker – he then gave an interview about his love of black music and culture to *Jet* magazine. The magazine concluded, 'To Elvis, people are people regardless of race, colour or creed.' This criticism of Elvis never completely disappeared and some rap records have been very critical of him.

Rock'n'roll was helping to bring about cultural changes. The social commentator Professor Terry Hamblin says, 'Elvis helped to build support for desegregation. White teens were saying, 'We don't agree with our parents.' They liked Chuck Berry and Little Richard and so they saw African-Americans in a different context and it built support for the desegregation that we saw in the 1960s.'

This was also good news for the black record labels. Professor Hamblin continues, 'The black record labels wanted the tracks to cross over to the white audiences. They wanted them to listen to the Coasters' singing 'Yakety Yak' or Chuck Berry singing 'School Day'. We were all being hassled by our parents and white teenagers could say, 'I can relate to what this artist is singing about'. The music is colour blind for the audience listening to it.'

On March 22, RCA released a new single, 'All Shook Up' coupled with 'That's When Your Heartaches Begin'. 'All Shook Up' topped the US charts for eight weeks, replacing a cheerful and effortless Perry Como single, 'Round and Round', also on RCA and a throwback to the early 50s. Eventually 'All Shook Up' was supplanted by Pat Boone's revival of 'Love Letters in the Sand', complete with highly engaging whistling, but 'All Shook Up' had sold 2.3m copies in the US.

Elvis continued touring and fellow performer Ben Hewitt saw him in April 1957. 'I saw Elvis at the Buffalo Auditorium and I had a seat about ten rows from the stage. I never heard him. From the time that Scotty Moore, Bill Black and D.J. Fontana walked out on that stage, I never heard a thing. Maybe they were just up there going through the motions because I don't think anybody heard them. It was one continuous scream for the whole 30 minutes. I saw his mouth move and I saw the band's fingers working but I never heard the music.'

Elvis wanted Bill Black to play the new electric bass as it had a different tone and offered greater volume. Bill was unhappy and was to throw a Fender across the studio

Elvis Presley: Caught in a Trap

while they were recording the soundtrack for *Jailhouse Rock*.

'All Shook Up' was Elvis' first UK No.1 but at first glance, the *NME* charts look mystifying. The single entered at No.24 on 15 June, disappeared the next week, and returned at No.7 the following week. A special issue of 'All Shook Up' had been pressed for sale to US forces in Europe and in error, this appeared on a list for UK record stores, who naturally placed orders. Some of these orders were serviced, hence the single coming in at No.24. EMI realised their mistake and withdrew the single, officially releasing it a week later.

RCA had decided how to treat Elvis' spiritual recordings. They would issue an EP of four songs, *Peace in the Valley*, and he would make a Christmas album which would combine religious and secular songs. The EP was released at a controversial moment: the first Elvis / Nixon meeting. An 18-year-old marine, Hershel Nixon, accused Elvis of pulling a gun on him in a restaurant in Memphis and shouting, 'I'll blow your brains out, you punk.' Clearly, Elvis should have been in the frame for *Dirty Harry*.

Apparently, Nixon had accused Presley of ignoring his wife, and Presley pulled the gun on him. Presley told the police that it was only a replica and he sent Nixon an apologetic telegram in which he detailed his fear of strangers. It was so paranoid and off-line that it can only have been written by Presley himself. He invited Nixon to his show in St Louis and the marine was similarly contrite. Such incidents drew Presley even more into his cocoon and already the so-called Memphis Mafia was forming around him who, for some years at least, would be bound by a code of loyalty.

In April 1956, the Presleys had moved to 1034 Audubon Drive in Memphis, a fine house costing $40,000. There was not enough privacy and now, a year later, they had to move. He sold the property for $55,000 and bought Graceland at a knockdown $102,000, although it needed attention. Graceland – doesn't it sound like a funeral home?

Graceland was a mansion three miles south of the city centre in the suburb of Whitehaven. The property resembled a colonial home from the *Gone with the Wind* era, but it had been farmland during the Civil War. The land was originally owned by S.E. Toot who owned the newspaper *Memphis Daily Appeal* and he named the farm, Graceland, after his daughter, Grace. The house was built in the 1930s by the then owners, Dr. and Mrs. Thomas Moore. It had two storeys and 23 rooms. Their daughter, Ruth, sold Graceland with 13 acres of land to Presley. Another 600 acres were sold to developers and this eventually became Elvis Presley Boulevard; so much for seclusion. Nowadays Graceland is on a four lane highway, located at 3764 Elvis Presley Boulevard, and the grounds include a car museum and hangars for aircraft.

Elvis completed the purchase on 10 April 1957 and moved in with Vernon and Gladys. He took three weeks' holiday in April 1957 to choose the décor and determine what was to be done. He wanted a wall around the property. He painted the building blue and gold so it glowed in the dark. In other words, you can see me but you can't come in.

Elvis never intended to be a recluse, as recluses don't have six-car garages, and Graceland remained his great constant for the rest of his life. He never wanted to move, although he had second homes for expediency.

He chose the interior decor with his parents and it displays the tastes of people who have suddenly come into money. Why did he want the initials 'E.P.' everywhere, even embossed in gold on his piano? Was this the Liberace influence?

A lot of it was tacky and I wonder how someone who had such great taste making records – at least, up to that time – could have wanted, say, red telephones with rhinestones. Maybe he had seen them in the homes of country stars and thought that was how it was done. He was impressed by Webb Pierce's guitar-shaped swimming pool. In 1957, *Woman* magazine in the UK reported that Elvis 'designs furniture and is kind to his parents.'

The photographs of Gladys reveal a different story and show how unhappy she was. She worried for her son – he might be torn apart by fans or die in a plane crash – and she felt like a prisoner. She distrusted Colonel Parker and she might go for weeks without seeing her son, although he would ring her every day.

A return to Tupelo for one of Elvis' concerts made her realise how she preferred the old days. She was drinking heavily, mostly beer and vodka. Nothing annoyed Elvis more than accusations that his mother drank: in 1971 one fan outside Graceland asked him to sign Jerry Hopkins' biography, *Elvis*. Elvis threw it into the road and said, 'These people who write about me don't know nothing. The only thing that guy got right was my name.' On the whole, Hopkins' book was sympathetic and much worse was to come.

In March 1957, Colonel Parker went to Washington and told William Arnold, the commander of the Fifth Army, to regard Elvis' induction as a wonderful opportunity for army recruitment. He said, 'If the hero of today's youth is prepared to do his bit, then so will everyone else.'

No-one was a match for the rock'n'roll spin-doctor who saw this as free, positive, international publicity for Elvis Presley. Parker was concerned over criticism, especially from the church, of Elvis' outlandish performances: this would show that Elvis was a good, all-American boy. It would be two years out of Elvis' life but his career would last longer as a result.

As if on cue, Frank Sinatra wrote for *Western World*. No doubt it was ghosted, but it accurately conveyed his views: 'My only deep sorrow is the unrelenting insistence of recording and motion picture companies upon purveying the most brutal, ugly, degenerate, vicious form of expression it has been my displeasure to hear and naturally, I'm referring to the bulk of rock'n'roll.'

And just why don't you like it, Frank? 'It fosters almost totally negative and destructive reactions in young people. It smells phony and false. It is sung, played and written for the most part by cretinous goons and by means of its almost imbecilic reiterations and sly, lewd – in plain fact – dirty lyrics, it manages to be the martial music of every side-burned delinquent on the face of the earth.'

From the end of March and going into April, Elvis undertook concert dates, mostly in the mid-west and Canada. He had given up on his gold lamé suit but not before a photograph was taken which became the cover for *50,000,000 Elvis Fans Can't Be Wrong*, his second collection of million sellers, released in February 1960. Much later this cover was copied by Jon Bon Jovi for the collection, *100,000,000 Bon Jovi Fans Can't Be Wrong*: he's joking, isn't he?

Rivalling Elvis for popularity, but in a very different way, was the evangelist Billy Graham. In 1957 he embarked on a marathon 16-week crusade at Madison Square Garden, known as the 100 Day Crusade. The comedian Lenny Bruce remarked, 'If he really wanted a challenge, he'd go to Vegas'. In New York, the highlight was hearing George Beverly Shea singing a Swedish song that had been translated by two missionaries, 'How Great Thou Art'.

Billy Graham often featured popular singers in the crusades, notably Pat Boone in the US and Cliff Richard in the UK. In 1957, Tennessee Ernie Ford had US Top 10 albums with *Hymns* (No.2) and *Spirituals* (No.5) and another in 1960 *Nearer the Cross* (No.5). Pat Boone made No.21 on the US album charts with *Hymns We Love,* released at the same time as *Elvis' Christmas Album,* and he had a No 4 single with the spiritual 'A Wonderful Time Up There' in 1958. To mark his retirement in 2005, Boone wrote and recorded 'Thank You Billy Graham' with guest appearances from Kenny Rogers and LeAnn Rimes. Bono, with a comment for every situation, said that Billy Graham was the 'voice of sanity'.

The only shows that Elvis played outside the US were in Canada, where the fan-mania was as strong as in America. There was fierce opposition to Elvis performing in Ottawa and the Catholic ministers urged parents to stop their children attending. As a result only 3,500 turned up for the early show at the stadium but it was a capacity audience of 8,500 for the second.

While in Ottawa, he told a radio DJ that he had eight cars – four Cadillacs, a Lincoln and three sports cars – so his six-car garage was already too small. He added something so off-piste that it could have been his Lennon – Jesus moment. He said, 'I'm not perfect. There was only one perfect man and that was Jesus Christ. The people didn't like him, you know, they killed him, and he couldn't understand why. I mean, if everybody liked the same thing, we'd all be driving the same car and be married to the same woman, and it wouldn't work out.' Welcome to the wonderful, wacky world of Elvis Presley.

Thirty-one year old Bob Richards, the pole-vaulting parson who had won three Olympic medals, defended Elvis, saying that when he was young, he was in a gang and he had 'fought, sworn and stolen fruit.' Well, the new delinquents weren't known for stealing apples.

And so to *Jailhouse Rock*, directed by Richard Thorpe, who made *The Student Prince* with the semi-operatic star Mario Lanza, another of Elvis' favourites, It was written by Guy Trosper who had been Oscar-nominated for *The Pride of St Louis* (1952). This had a strong script which gave Elvis a chance to emulate Marlon Brando, James Dean and Montgomery Clift as a vulnerable, damaged character full of pent-up aggression. It was a serious role and he knew he shouldn't parody himself as often as he did.

The recording sessions for the songs did not get off to a good start. As usual, Elvis warmed up by singing gospel songs with the Jordanaires. An MGM representative felt he was wasting time and told him to get on with it. Elvis walked out of the studio and wasn't seen for the rest of the day.

Once MGM had apologised, Elvis got to work, meticulously getting the songs right. There are two officially-released, double-CDs of outtakes from the *Jailhouse Rock* sessions – and yet there are only six songs. Including false starts, there are 164 different takes. It is good to hear how 'Treat Me Nice' developed – it was too fast at first and Elvis slowed it down. He dropped the Jordanaires singing 'Hi baby' and 'Hey baby' during the same song. When he stumbles on 'Young and Beautiful, he says, 'You better get Pat Boone in here quick.'

Jerry Leiber and Mike Stoller had been commissioned to write songs for *Jailhouse*

Rock. They came up with the title songs, 'I Want to be Free', 'Treat Me Nice' and 'Baby I Don't Care'. To this was added a high school song, 'Young and Beautiful' and the aforementioned 'Don't Leave Me Now', both from Aaron Schroeder. Schroeder was a key New York publisher and very good at editing songs and coming up with ideas. He was to write, 'Scooby-Doo, Where Are You?'

Five songs were to make up the *Jailhouse Rock* EP, while 'Treat Me Nice' was on the B-side of the 'Jailhouse Rock' single. The songs were recorded with Dudley Brooks on piano, called Cuddly Dudley by Elvis.

There were three songs which were submitted and apparently not recorded – 'Young Hearts' (Sid Tepper, Roy Bennett), 'Wha'cha Gotta Lose' (Edward Thomas, Fred Wise) and 'Oh My, You Lied' (David Hill). This was the same David Hill who recorded the original 'All Shook Up' and he was to write for Elvis as David Hess. The plinkety-plink 'Young Hearts' was a country hit for Jim Reeves, and 'Wha'cha Gotta Lose' became nondescript doo-wop for the Del-Vikings.

This was followed by the shooting of the film itself. Elvis was briefly hospitalised when he swallowed one of the caps from his teeth. Incidentally, much was made of Elvis having a haircut when he joined the forces but he had had his hair cut in *Jailhouse Rock*, though he is wearing a wig in this scene.

Jim Denny from the *Grand Ole Opry* visited him on the set and said, 'I always believed in you.' When he had gone, Elvis said, 'Does that son of a bitch think I've forgotten that he broke my heart?'

On July 8, Elvis met aspiring actress Anita Wood, but they steered clear of the opening of *Loving You* at the Strand Theatre in Memphis the following night. Instead, they went to a special midnight screening with Vernon and Gladys. The romance made the press and already there was talk of her becoming Anita Presley. At the same time, Elvis was dating other girls and one had to climb out of a bedroom window at Graceland when Anita returned early. Elvis gave Anita a sapphire and diamond ring, another example of his ostentatious spending; really these gifts meant little to him. Anita was to win the *Hollywood Star Hunt*, a media event, although she rarely appeared in films.

In both colour and VistaVision, *Loving You* was a huge success from the start. Hal Wallis had paid for Elvis and for Colonel Parker as a 'technical adviser'. Presumably Parker told the screenwriters Hal Kanter (later to find success with *All in the Family*) how to be a manipulative and money-grabbing manager with little feeling for the artist.

A more appropriate starring vehicle for Elvis than *Love Me Tender*, *Loving You* is the Elvis story, somewhat off-kilter – from truck-driver to star with Lizabeth Scott, a woman, in the Colonel Parker role. The script came from a short story, *A Call from Mitch Miller*, by Mary Agnes Thompson, which appeared in *Good Housekeeping*.

A former country star, Tex Warner (Wendell Corey), has a roadshow with his Rough Ridin' Gamblers in support of the crooked Governor, Jim Tallman. He longs to return to the bigtime and he and his ex-wife and manager, Glenda Markle (Lizabeth Scott) see Deke Rivers (Elvis Presley) as their meal ticket. Deke joins his hayseed show and has girls screaming. Glenda manipulates an anti-Deke feeling amongst parents to create controversy. A jealous boyfriend taunts Deke in the diner with 'Go ahead, Sideburns, sing.'

In one sequence, Deke Rivers tells Glenda that his real name is Jimmy Tompkins and he takes her to a graveyard to show her the tombstone marked 'Deke Rivers'. The inscription reads, 'He was alone but for his friends who miss him', and the new Deke wants to live up to that.

Deke sees how he is being manipulated ('I ain't no monkey in a zoo') and walks out of a national TV show but is wooed back. He returns to sing 'Loving You' to his girlfriend Susan Jessup (Dolores Hart) and then does a wild 'Got a Lot o' Livin' to Do!'. Scotty, Bill and D.J. had cameo roles and the Jordanaires join them for the final number. In 2016, the red trousers with white piping that Deke wore in the film fetched $42,000.

Gladys Presley can be seen in the audience for 'Got a Lot o' Livin' to Do!' She wears a blue dress and sits behind the woman with her feet in the aisle. Some prints have a shot from the stage in which both Vernon and Gladys can be seen.

Elvis' first screen kiss was with the fan Daisy Bricker (Jana Lund) backstage in Amarillo. Her next film was *High School Hellcats*. In 1959 Dolores Hart wrote an article for *Photoplay*, 'What It's Like to Kiss Elvis?' Possibly not so great, as four years later she retired from her Hollywood life to become a nun.

By the time of the premiere, Elvis had a hit single from the film, the double-sider 'Teddy Bear' and 'Loving You'. 'Teddy Bear' knocked off 'Love Letters in the Sand' from No.1 and stayed for seven weeks. 'Loving You' made the Top 20.

The biggest threat to Elvis Presley was making his mark. Ricky Nelson appeared in a weekly sitcom based around his family, *The Adventures of Ozzie and Harriet*. His father was the bandleader Ozzie Nelson and he managed his sons, Ricky and David. The sitcom was hugely popular and, incidentally, Ozzie and Harriet Nelson were the first couple in a TV series to be shown sleeping together in a double bed.

Once his voice had broken, Ricky Nelson had just turned 17 when he made the Top 10 with both sides of his first single, 'A Teenager's Romance' / 'I'm Walkin'', and he had five other hit titles before 1957 was out. He was exceptionally good looking but his nasal voice lacked Presley's range. However, he stuck with what was comfortable – and in a sense, he was the boy who wanted to be Carl Perkins. His first album, *Ricky* (1957), included 'Boppin' the Blues' and 'Your True Love' and his 1957 hit, 'Be-Bop Baby' wasn't written by Carl Perkins but sounds like it should have been.

Keith Richards said that he didn't buy Ricky Nelson records, he bought James Burton records, and he was certainly a huge influence on young guitarists. James Burton: 'Ricky Nelson was at Imperial Records and he heard the bass player James Kirkland and me working with Bob Luman. The next day he sent a telegram to our house in the valley inviting us to meet his parents. He wanted us to play with him on his family TV show and we liked that, as he had a real smooth voice and he let us play as we felt. That solo in 'Hello Mary Lou' is just what came into my mind at the time. He didn't like me playing with other artists. Even though Johnny and Dorsey Burnette wrote songs for him, he didn't like me playing on their records.'

On many records, Ricky is accompanied by the Jordanaires. Neal Matthews from the Jordanaires: 'We were moonlighting with Ricky Nelson and at first we didn't tell Elvis. We were on the sound sets of Elvis' films during the day and then we worked with Ricky at night. We didn't tell Elvis but he knew it was us as soon as he heard the records.'

In many ways, Charlie Gracie's 'Fabulous' on Cameo is the hit record that Elvis Presley never made. Charlie says, 'Bernie Lowe gave me 'Fabulous' and asked me to sing it like 'Don't Be Cruel'. I don't like to copy people but Bernie was the boss and if

Spencer Leigh

I didn't do what he said, he'd go to the street corner and find another kid. He'd been looking for an Elvis Presley or Rock Hudson type so how he found me, short and ugly, I don't know.' Come on, Charlie, don't be modest. 'I'm not being modest. There were hundreds of singers who were better looking than me. I took no notice of the fan letters. I'd got my mirror.'

At the end of August 1957, Elvis toured the north-west. At the Memorial Stadium in Spokane Coliseum in Washington, he gave his longest show to date – 18 songs. The following day he was at the Empire Stadium in Vancouver, playing to 26,000, his biggest audience to date, with only the public address system used for football matches. Elvis had invented arena rock. Elvis Presley liked screaming crowds because 'they cover up my mistakes.' This contrasts strongly with the Beatles, especially George Harrison, who never liked the screaming: maybe they didn't make mistakes.

Red Robinson is a Canadian disc jockey who met Bill Haley, Elvis Presley, Buddy Holly, Eddie Cochran, Gene Vincent and the Beatles and his interviews have been preserved. It is said that you can get to anyone in the world with six degrees of separation but by meeting Red, you are a handshake from almost everyone in popular music. At this time, he was obsessed by asking everybody how long rock'n'roll would last.

In 1956 he was a frequent host of the TV programme, *Cross Canada Hit Parade*. He was the compère for Elvis in Vancouver and there for the Beatles in 1964. He is the only person alive who has hosted shows for both Elvis and the Beatles. Red hosted the press conference: 'Both of us were sitting on a table top looking out at the press and behind all the press was Colonel Parker. When somebody asked him a question, Elvis might look to the Colonel to see how to answer it. When the show got started, he had to wait an hour because of the warm-up acts and I found him more down to earth than anybody I'd met. He was interested in me – where did you go to school, are you dating, do you like football, what kind of car do you drive. It was just two young guys talking and there were no airs about it. Of course he had vanity, a lot of it, but he had no conceit and that's the truth. He opened his dressing room door and invited a policeman inside. He wanted to borrow his handcuffs and he jokingly handcuffed me to the shower rail. He hid the key and laughed and laughed.'

Before he performed, Elvis drove around the stadium in a black Cadillac with the top down. He was wearing his gold lamé jacket, black shirt, black trousers. He smiled and waved. Behind him on the stage, Colonel Parker had placed a banner, 'Greater than ever, Elvis Presley in *Jailhouse Rock*'. Elvis performed for 30 minutes but the audience was out of control and they had to stop. The same thing happened with the Beatles in 1964.

Elvis' appearance at the Multomah Stadium in Portland, Oregon was equally out of control and Elvis was asked to leave the stage. The police restored order and Elvis was allowed to continue.

Elvis and his musicians needed cheering up after all this mayhem and what better than recording a Christmas album in September? Steve Sholes even supplied a Christmas tree and gifts.

The record industry was thinking that there could be a new genre of rock'n'roll songs for Christmas. The big hit in 1956 had been Harry Belafonte with the very traditional 'Mary's Boy Child', but there had been contemporary offerings – Eddie Cochran was impersonating Elvis and playing guitar for the Holly Twins on 'I Want

Elvis for Christmas' – 'You ain't nothing but a reindeer' – and Little Lambsie Penn stated 'I Want To Spend Xmas with Elvis', written by Bobby Darin – so two major artists were starting their careers in tribute trivia.

Elvis had been very impressed with the high-voiced female on Ferlin Husky's 'Gone'. It was Millie Kirkham and he asked Steve Sholes to bring her to Hollywood. She was six months pregnant and not keen to fly, but the money would be useful. She worked well with the Jordanaires and her voice can be heard in particular on the non-seasonal ballad, 'My Wish Came True', written by Ivory Joe Hunter. Millie thought the result comic but it sounded great.

The other out of season song was Jerry Leiber and Mike Stoller's 'Don't', a more well-mannered version of 'One Night'. Leiber and Stoller had given this song directly to Presley, much to Parker's annoyance and another black mark against them. They also gave him 'I'm a Hog for You, Baby' but he didn't record this one, enabling the songwriters to give it to the Coasters in 1959.

Millie Kirkham is also featured on 'Blue Christmas', a song associated with Ernest Tubb and one which Elvis was to call 'my favourite Christmas song out of all the ones I've recorded'. Elvis sang 'White Christmas', 'I'll Be Home for Christmas' (both associated with Bing), 'Here Comes Santa Claus' (a faster version of the Gene Autry favourite) and two carols, 'Silent Night' and 'O Little Town of Bethlehem'.

Elvis thought that the pop hit would be a new song, 'Santa Bring My Baby Back to Me', written by Aaron Schroeder and Claude DeMetrius and he fancied recording some Christmas blues. As Leiber and Stoller were around, he asked them to write one – just like that. Within half an hour, they had 'Santa Claus Is Back in Town' in which Santa is not coming in a sleigh but 'a big black Cadillac'. Colonel Parker said, 'What took you so long?' Elvis loved it and gave it a sensational workout. It was funny and exciting and should have been an A-side.

This was not the season of goodwill. Scotty and Bill had been disenchanted for weeks; they enjoyed the work but they were not receiving the rewards. Colonel Parker took the view that he could replace them at any time. On September 21, they left but D.J. stayed. With concert dates coming up, the famed country guitarist Hank Garland stepped in for Scotty. D.J. suggested Chuck Wiginton for bass, who played on the *Louisiana Hayride*. He was a bank clerk during the day but he took leave to go to Graceland for two days' rehearsal.

At the end of September, Elvis was back at the Mississippi-Alabama Dairy Show and Fair in Tupelo, this time a benefit for the Elvis Presley Youth Recreation Centre. When he appeared in Los Angeles, the LAPD told him that he could not wiggle.

The single of 'Jailhouse Rock' was released in September to be followed by the *Jailhouse Rock* EP. The single topped the US charts for seven weeks, giving him 26 weeks at the top of the charts in 1957. The *Jailhouse Rock* EP was not listed on the chart in the way that *Love Me Tender* was, but it sold over a million.

Like *Loving You*, *Jailhouse Rock* is another film about a young, talented singer being exploited. In *Jailhouse Rock*, Elvis played an ex-con, Vince Everett, whose guitar took him 'from shame to fame': a show-business story of rage to riches. Vince Everett is jailed for killing a man accidentally in a bar brawl. He befriends Hunk Houghton (Mickey Shaughnessy) who teaches him how to play the guitar. He gets into further trouble and, stripped to his waist, he is flogged (fans wept at this). Leaving jail, he sets about pursuing a career in music.

In a scene reminiscent of Sun Records in 1954, he sings 'Don't Leave Me Now' blandly and then is encouraged to rough it up. Unfortunately, 'Don't Leave Me Now' is taken from him by an underhand record company and passed to their star, Mickey Alba.

Bobby Vinton: 'I used to sing Elvis' songs in my band, but it was the film of *Jailhouse Rock* which really impressed me. In that film, he starts his own record label and presses the copies up. That was a really neat idea and I wanted to do the same.'

Vince is embittered and when a crowd reacts against him, he smashes his guitar – whereas the real Elvis would have won them over. He makes his way forward with the help of record plugger, Peggy Van Alder (Judy Tyler). When Hunk is released from prison, he gets a job as his gofer; Hunk sees how twisted he has become and hits him to bring him to his senses. He nearly loses his voice (the same plotline as Sinatra's current film, *The Joker Is Wild*), but in true Hollywood fashion everything works out fine and he croons 'Young and Beautiful' (this film's 'Love Me Tender') to Judy Tyler. In reality, there was no Hollywood ending as Judy Tyler was killed in a car crash in July 1957.

Being an MGM film, you might expect lavish sequences with stunning choreography, but *Jailhouse Rock* is in black and white and only the title song is given a Hollywood workout. That shows what Elvis could have done, given half the chance. For an alternative approach to 'Jailhouse Rock', see the hilarious sequence in *The Blues Brothers*.

The *Monthly Film Bulletin* said, 'The title number, very much over-staged, has a certain primitive verve.' Lenny Henry has called 'Jailhouse Rock' 'a euphemism for sex' and he is probably right. Prisoners are segregated by sex and hence, all the dancers are male, so when No.47 says to No.3 'You're the cutest jailbird I ever did see', you can imagine what the jailhouse rock is going to be. The song is wonderful anyway – how can anyone top Jerry Leiber's line, 'The whole rhythm section was the Purple Gang'?

The real Purple Gang was formed in Detroit during prohibition. Shifty Henry is a Leiber/Stoller reference to a jazzman, John Henry, that they knew in LA. Sad Sack was the name of a comic book character.

The crisp, witty dialogue has stood up well. Elvis is asked at a cocktail party, 'How long have you been in the music business?' and he replies, 'About a week.' He leaves when asked to comment on atonality in the work of Dave Brubeck. (Don't blame him – I'd leave too.) He argues with his agent outside the house and then kisses her. She says, 'How dare you think such cheap tactics would work with me?' and he responds, 'Them ain't tactics, honey, that's just the beast in me.'

Reviews tended to be unkind: John Tynan in *Down Beat* thought it was 'A deadly dull effort based on the premise that the god of rock'n'roll can do no wrong.' *The Times* said, 'Physically Mr. Presley has the right presence for the part but at no time does he ever suggest inner turbulence, and the peevish, petulant face suggests no emotion.'

All Elvis fans have come to love this film, but not Elvis himself. He commented on *Jailhouse Rock* in 1976, 'I'm embarrassed to see it now. All those rockers in England will be very hurt about that 'cause this one's their classic.' The rockers are right – Elvis was at his best and displayed a considerable acting talent which should have been developed.

In October, Elvis played the East coast and John Stewart of the Kingston Trio saw him. 'I saw Elvis Presley at the Pan-Pacific Auditorium in LA and that was right when 'Hound Dog' was out. He still had the stand-up bass and it was unbelievable. I was shaken by the concert. I had never seen anything like that in my life. There was so much energy coming from the stage, his voice was so strong and he was having so much fun.'

Also there was Maurice Kinn, the founder of *NME*. He had been a former boxing reporter and that never left him: 'Presley sets out with a sadistic intent to arouse the fans to fever pitch'. He called it 'sheer mass hypnotism of an amazing kind.'

Kinn had a few words with Presley himself and he was better at landing punches then his US counterparts. Kinn asked why his name was often on the sheet music and record labels. Elvis replied, presumably when Colonel Parker wasn't around, 'I have never written any part of a single song, but often people bring me material and offer me one-third of the royalties if I record their song. If the composition is considered suitable – and only if it's suitable – I make a disc and collect one-third share of the composer's royalties.' Did it not occur to Elvis that this was grossly unfair? Maybe it did but it didn't bother him. Presley knew some writers like Jerry Leiber, Mike Stoller and Stan Kesler but Parker didn't want Presley to meet songwriters. Shortly after this interview, Presley's name stopped appearing on song credits so possibly he had a word with Colonel Parker about it, but the deals continued, More of this anon.

When Kinn asked Elvis to name his favourite singers, there was Dean Martin naturally, but he also praised Pat Boone, Tommy Sands and the new kid on the block, Ricky Nelson. Pat Boone: 'Elvis and I were supposedly rivals but that was not our doing – it was the record companies and the media. We came from the same state and had similar backgrounds, but he was the rebel and I was the conformist. We often appeal to the same fans but for different reasons.'

In November, Elvis Presley sailed to Hawaii for three shows – two at the Honolulu Stadium, which was a boxing arena, and one for servicemen at Schofield Barracks, Pearl Harbour. Tom Moffatt and Ron Jacobs of KHVH had set up stunts with a fake Elvis which gathered huge crowds. The fake Elvis went to Honolulu Stadium and took applause at half-time. Colonel Parker was furious: 'There are no Elvis imitators, there is only one Elvis.'

On 19 November, *Elvis' Christmas Album* was released. It was the Christmas sessions plus the *Peace in the Valley* EP as it was thought that the spirituals sounded like carols. In the US it was a gatefold album with a portfolio of Elvis pictures. There wasn't any cynicism about this as Elvis loved Christmas and always would. He loved giving presents although it was difficult to know what to give the man who had everything. (A burglar album, perhaps?) Colonel Parker had hoped that the album would establish Elvis as an all-round entertainer, but there was an unexpected backlash.

As far as Irving Berlin was concerned, Bing Crosby had recorded the definitive version of 'White Christmas' – warm and inviting and full of good intentions. Presumably he hadn't heard the Drifters' take from 1954 as that was Elvis' template. He was having fun and even included an impersonation of Johnnie Ray. Irving had constructed his own Berlin wall against Elvis and he personally rang the directors of the top American radio stations and asked them not to play such rubbish: this only helped publicity and sales.

There was some envy about this – Elvis and his gang were putting the old-time songwriters out of work. In 1961 Richard Rodgers was horrified at the up-tempo, fun-packed treatment of his romantic ballad, 'Blue Moon', by the Marcels and even when the record was topping the US charts and thereby making him a tidy sum, he was condemning it. A notable exception among the old-time songwriters was Johnny Mercer, who entered into the spirit of new music and wrote Pat Boone's 'Bernadine'.

What's more, some clergymen thought that Elvis was not treating 'Silent Night' (written 1818) and 'O Little Town of Bethlehem' (written 1868) with proper respect and complained on behalf of the long-dead composers. The ministers criticised his breath control: Elvis would never be in their church choirs.

Elvis' Christmas Album was the ideal Christmas gift, although some complained it was wrong that such a depraved artist should be appealing to children in this way. The album sold a million, topping the charts and displacing the soundtrack for *Around the World in 80 Days*. It was a major seasonal seller for the next decade. The biggest-selling Christmas single for 1957 was not Elvis but Bobby Helms with 'Jingle Bell Rock'.

That year Elvis received the one Christmas present he didn't want: his formal notice to join the US army. He was ordered to report to the induction centre in Memphis on January 20 but was slated to start filming *King Creole* at the same time in New Orleans. Colonel Parker said he would sort it out.

Elvis spent his first Christmas at Graceland – and it snowed. He invited several of his relatives, placing $15,000 in large denominations on his bed. Was this a test? After Christmas, he found that $1,000 was missing and he thought he knew the culprit was: no Cadillacs or jewellery for the thief.

On December 27, he was given a deferment until March, so that he could make the film. The official letter from President Eisenhower said, 'Greetings, you have been chosen to have the honour to serve your country'; a polite way of saying you had been drafted.

In an attempt to widen his image and approval rating, Presley had allowed himself to be drafted into the US army. It would have been easy to escape the draft, but Colonel Parker thought it was a good career move. The simple fact that I know his military dog-tag (53310761) shows how effective this was. Those who say that Colonel Parker was always short-sighted are wrong: he knew that being with Uncle Sam would pay off once he was demobbed.

Elvis ended the year with a concert in St Louis. The concerts were winding down and the world's greatest concert attraction would stop performing. He could so easily have completed his duty within a few months by giving concerts to the troops but Colonel Parker insisted on no special treatment. Elvis, however, was to have his own interpretation of that and the military and private life of Private Elvis Presley was unlike that of any other soldier, before or since.

CHAPTER 7

Army Bunk, Army Chow, Army Clothes, Army Car

'A good soldier has his heart and soul in it. When he receives an order, he gets a hard-on.'
The Caucasian Chalk Circle, Bertolt Brecht, 1945

I. The Willing Conscript

Why on earth did Elvis Presley join the army?

Conscription is compulsory military service, most often in the army, and its origins can be traced back to ancient Egypt. It is rare for a country to demand universal conscription, that is, recruiting all males who are physically fit and within given ages, even in wartime. It is sometimes selective, perhaps by a national lottery, a sweepstake nobody wants to win.

There are exemptions, possibly for the medical profession, farmers, fishermen, clergy and government workers, which can mean that the army depends on the lower classes. There can be deferments for students and those looking after a family.

Russia on the other hand had a policy of 'you, you and you' and those they chose might be away from home for decades. The numbers came and went but around 1920, there were 5.5m in the Russian army. The Soviets also introduced military training in schools with two years' service at 18 and refresher courses.

The treatment of conscientious objectors is controversial and it may be difficult to determine how deep-rooted their beliefs are: is it draft-dodging under another name? Few would disagree with exemptions for the Amish and the Quakers, although they might be given some non-combatant work.

Until the late 1940s, conscription only applied to males. Israel and then China widened it for both sexes. China discovered that enforcing a strict national service was financially draining.

The armed forces may not be large enough without conscripts but a volunteer force is likely to have more *esprit de corps* as the soldiers are there willingly. They will be more disciplined, as short term conscripts come and go. Invariably, the senior officer ranks, and hence the training of recruits, will be undertaken by professional soldiers.

There have been many instances of bullying, which senior officers should control. The 1950s ITV series, *The Army Game*, made light of this and certainly this series could not be remade today. Many servicemen have left the forces mentally scarred from treatment by sadistic officers.

By way of contrast, the US series, *The Phil Silvers Show*, showed how incompetent the US army was, with their officers upstaged by the scheming Sgt. Bilko. Did the Soviets view this comedy series as a documentary? A significant part of the Russian arsenal was propaganda and the Soviet authorities would never have permitted a similar series about their forces.

Besides being a fighting force, there are social benefits attached to conscription. The conscripts get fit, eat healthily, learn a trade and are submitted to discipline and regimentation, which are useful attributes for civilian life. Arguably though, it is better for a civilian to learn a trade – that way you don't risk losing your life. The forces do not encourage free thinking as you're told what to do.

Both the Union and the Confederates used conscription in the American Civil War (1861–5). The war was fought over slavery and many thought that ordering civilians to join an army was tantamount to slavery itself. For the next 50 years, the USA only had one minor war against Spain, and most action was seen in conflicts with the Native Americans.

After that, the USA did not reintroduce conscription until World War I. Both Britain and America legislated for conscription and then withdrew it when the war was over.

After World War I, Germany was forbidden to have an army greater than 100,000, but Hitler ignored that by introducing two years of compulsory military training from the age of 18. By not stopping Hitler early on, he was able to march on Poland and in 1939, the world was again at war. The USA were very concerned when Germany conquered France and did not favour a Europe controlled by Germany and Italy. Conscription was reintroduced and it was even favoured in polls amongst American students, who were amongst the most likely to serve.

Under the Selective Training and Service Act of 1940, all males between 18 and 45 had to put themselves forward and those chosen would serve for the remainder of the war plus six months. The Act was administered under Major Lewis Hershey, who remained in his post until 1969.

The singers Frank Sinatra and Dick Haymes both avoided national service: Frank through a hearing problem (!) and a phobia about crowds (!!) and Dick Haymes by being born in Argentina. Many thought Frank was displaying cowardice and had duped and/or bribed the medical examiner, and everybody thought Haymes was being absurd. Sinatra's career recovered but Haymes' never did.

By 1945, the nature of warfare was changing as America discharged two nuclear bombs in Japan to bring about the end of the conflict. Around 200,000 Japanese civilians were killed, and there has been much debate as to whether this was the right action or not.

It was hoped that peace would prevail after such a devastating war as no one envisaged anything like that happening again. Everybody expected peace, and conscription in the US was dropped, although it remained in the UK.

There had been an uneasy but vital alliance between the USA and Britain with the Soviet Union during the war, and it soon fell apart. The Soviets introduced Communist governments in the eastern European countries it had 'liberated'. Both Britain and America were wary and knew that the Soviets wanted to spread their ideology to the western world.

Even if the countries were not fighting physically or with nuclear weapons, they could be using propaganda to gain the upper hand. Look at the fear that gripped Hollywood in the early 1950s as Senator Joe McCarthy held witch hunts for Communists in the entertainment industry.

Elvis Presley: Caught in a Trap

The author George Orwell was superb at coining phrases ('Big Brother', 'Room 101') and he devised the 'Cold War' in 1945. Not to be outdone, Churchill supplied the phrase, the 'Iron Curtain'. Orwell saw the world becoming a nuclear stalemate, with just a few superpowers possessing weapons which could obliterate mankind in seconds.

The Cold War led to the formation of NATO (North Atlantic Treaty Organisation) which resisted any advancements of the Soviets in Europe. It had the concept that an attack on one country was an attack on all.

President Eisenhower proposed a nuclear test ban treaty but as America was in the lead, Russia was hardly likely to accept. At that time, only America had exploded nuclear bombs, but in 1949 Russia undertook a nuclear test, indicating that both sides had effective weapons. Under the terms of the peace treaty, Germany was not allowed to develop nuclear weapons which holds good to this day.

Japan had previously governed Korea but in 1945, the country was split, with the North under Russian rule and the South under American rule, but then becoming a republic in its own right. Both sides wanted a united Korea and tensions were high.

In 1950 the communist North attacked the South with Soviet support and captured their capital Seoul. With the backing of the United Nations, the US sent troops to help the South, often using conscripts, and they were assisted by British troops based in Hong Kong. For the first time, America allowed student deferment when recruiting forces.

The United Nations Assembly called it 'a police action' rather than war, but General MacArthur pushed forward and over a million Chinese troops were put on alert.

The death of Stalin, some say authorised by the Politburo, in 1953 eased the situation and for a short time, Russia was less dictatorial. An armistice was declared in 1955 and the two countries have been separate ever since.

Nikita Khrushchev came to power and denounced Stalin, but he was just as keen for Russia to be a major world player and he felt that his country would be humiliated if it could not match America's fire power. By way of consolation, in 1961 Yuri Gagarin became the first man in space.

There were some benefits to the west when the two main Communist blocs, the Soviet Union and China, fell out with each other around 1960.

Eisenhower tried to make friends with Khrushchev and invited him to the US. Unfortunately, the schedule was not well chosen. Khrushchev visited Frank Sinatra on the set of *Can-Can,* who told him, 'The movie is about a bunch of pretty girls and the fellows who like pretty girls.' Caught in a rare smiling moment with the dancers, Khrushchev said, 'This is what you call freedom but it's only freedom for the girls to show their backsides. It's capitalism that makes the girls that way.'

The next day Khrushchev called the film 'lascivious, disgusting and immoral', but it should be noted that he hadn't rushed away. Back home, Khrushchev told his associates that Russia didn't need to lift a finger as America would bury itself. He disliked their ostentation and their flashy cars: Why did these people always have to be on the move? Weren't they content?

Khrushchev hadn't appreciated that many Soviet citizens were envious of American culture. They liked what they heard clandestinely about the TV shows, the comic books and above all the music. If you were caught with an Elvis record, you would be punished, so it was all the more exciting to hear them.

The TV producer Leslie Woodhead, who wrote a fascinating book, *How the Beatles*

Rocked the Kremlin (Bloomsbury, 2013), was a soldier in Berlin at the same time as Elvis Presley was conscripted. One night they met two young Russian soldiers who wanted to defect. Leslie could speak a little Russian and when he asked them why, he was told, 'Our officers won't let us listen to Elvis Presley.' Leslie adds, 'The Russians could hear our music and our culture on Radio Luxembourg, the BBC World Service and the Voice of America, on short-wave radio in the middle of the night. What came out of those crackling radios obviously grabbed their attention and there was something about the sound that contained the sound of freedom. Although he didn't say so, I think Khrushchev was seduced by what he saw in America and he recognised that it was a threat.'

In later years, President Eisenhower was to criticise the development of nuclear weapons, saying that many companies were profiteering from the arms race which he described as 'mutually assured destruction'. It's unfortunate that he hadn't come to these views while he was in office.

The armed peace was expensive, paid for in taxes and creating panic. Neither the Soviets nor the Americans wanted to give way over anything and their countrymen supported these aims.

Hungary had been liberated from Nazi rule by the Soviets in 1945 but the country tired of its new rulers. In 1956 there were student demonstrations demanding the withdrawal of Soviet troops, which turned into a major uprising. Russian tanks were sent to the capital Budapest and over 2,500 protesters were killed.

Elvis Presley supported the uprising when he was on *The Ed Sullivan Show* and he performed a benefit concert for relief, a highly unusual move for Presley and even more so for Colonel Parker, who generally nixed charity concerts (unless his boy was getting his standard fee.) It's possible that Parker was thinking that Presley could escape national service by showing how useful he could be as a civilian.

Being a celebrity did not necessarily protect you, as the baseball star, Willie Mays, was called up, and many black vocal groups had constantly changing line-ups as their members came in and out of the forces including The Drifters and The Coasters.

Even though there was a nuclear threat, Major Hershey argued for conscription to remain. He encouraged recruitment as those who volunteered had some say in where they were posted and so could keep out of the firing line.

At first the idea of doing a few special shows for the troops appealed to Colonel Parker, but then he realised the enormous PR potential if Elvis did regular service. He would be in the forces for two years: the media would be fed regular stories about him. He would come out of the forces as a hero, the All-American Boy made good, and he could clean up. He could see it now; he could rub it in through Elvis appearing on a Frank Sinatra TV special – Elvis wouldn't have to say anything but the older generation would know that Frank was being humiliated.

Parker knew that there would be no trouble with Presley. He was a good, able-bodied, clean-living American boy. Although he was often called a rebel, he had none of the argumentative, anti-establishment characteristics of Marlon Brando or James Dean.

If the USA had been at war when Elvis joined in 1958, Colonel Parker (and indeed, Elvis) might have been less keen to serve, but Parker was fairly sure he would arrive back in one piece. He would never have allowed him to serve if it had been a few years later and there was the chance of him being posted to Vietnam. On the other hand, with what

Elvis Presley: Caught in a Trap

we know now about Elvis' posthumous earning capacity, Colonel Parker might not have been too grief-stricken if anything had happened to him.

Parker must have had the G.I. blues with Elvis' posting to Germany: this hadn't been in the script. For a start, he would be close to the Russian border and secondly, as he had no intention of leaving the US himself, Elvis would be out of his control.

Germany was partitioned into four allied zones after the war, with the zones being policed by the Soviets, the Americans, the British and the French. Around 1960, 80,000 troops from the UK were in Germany, which was a third of its total force. Russia by comparison had a military force of over five million.

To counter-balance NATO, Khrushchev signed a treaty with East Germany to allow Russia to use its sites for missile installation. In August 1960, after a riot in Karl-Marx-Stadt – now Chemnitz – Elvis Presley himself was declared an enemy of the people by the East German government.

Berlin, which had been devastated during World War II, became a divided city with its two parts, East and West, being divided at first by barbed wire and then a wall. This was partly to stop citizens in East Germany escaping to the West.

There the troops from the East and the troops from the West faced each other and it was potentially lethal. It would only take a rebel panzer attack to spark another war.

The crooner Eddie Fisher had made records while he was in the forces but Parker did not like this concept and he seemed neither in nor out. Similarly, Clyde McPhatter would cut records and even appear on stage in military uniform.

As it happens, Buddy Knox was called up before Elvis Presley. He had had his first hit in 1957 with 'Party Doll' and he was managed by Norman Petty. Petty encouraged him to make records during his leave and issued the singles as Lieutenant Buddy Knox, the label billing being a surprise to Knox. He still had hit records and maybe Petty should have thought this through by giving regular updates on his boy's progress.

Buddy Knox said, 'The week `Party Doll' hit No.1, the army decided that they needed me real bad, and it meant that we couldn't come to England where 'Party Doll' was a hit. We had the London Palladium and European dates lined up. The contracts went into the garbage can and I got drunk for the first time in my life. It broke the band up.'

From November 1961, Don and Phil Everly trained for the Marine Corps and graduated in March 1962. Contrary to the standard arrangements, they were allowed to serve together, an odd move considering the tensions between them. That was it: they were then on stand-by.

The Four Preps mocked the rival groups joining Uncle Sam in 'The Big Draft' (1961). The Barron Knights revamped this for the UK as 'Call Up the Groups' (1964) a plea for the draft to be reinstated to eliminate their competition.

In the 1950s, conscription continued in the UK where every fit male aged between 18 and 26 did national service, with two years of active duty and four years in the reserves. The test cricketer, Colin Cowdrey, was turned down because of flat feet, causing the MP Gerald Nabarro to say in Parliament, 'There is no excuse for evading national service.' He had to apologise to Cowdrey, who had been willing to participate.

Thinking of doing its own Elvis, the UK planned a recruitment campaign with the singer, Terry Dene, but he had mental problems and should never have been enlisted. It was the flipside of Elvis, a national disaster. Terry Dene: 'I knew before I went in the forces that there was an element of risk. I'd had a long record of being medically unfit, but because I was a big success, a lot of that was pushed under the surface. I had to go out and be this star, but underneath I was very shy and nervous. When I was confronted with the army, my call-up was delayed. I decided that I wanted to go in because I was getting letters saying I was a coward – I was sent white feathers in envelopes. When things did go wrong, they went wrong in a very short space of time. I came under medical supervision and they put me in a military hospital. In the end I was told, 'We're terribly sorry about this, there's been a mistake', meaning 'You shouldn't have been here in the first place.' What a cock-up.'

Terry Dene's time in the army became a major news story. Terry Dene: 'It was brought up in Parliament and everyone was wondering why they had taken 'Screwball' in the first place. It was very nasty publicity. I came up before the army board and they asked me if I would get my job back. I said, 'You tell me.' They knew they had handled the whole thing very badly and that I had to face the vultures, as it were, by being exposed to the press. They offered me an army pension as compensation but I turned it down.'

Dene became a laughing stock and it ruined his career. Marty Wilde escaped national service because of fallen arches and, wait for it, severe corns. Marty Wilde: 'I went for my medical and had my interviews but they didn't take me in the end. I was discharged on medical grounds, which was partially true. They said I had a malfunction in my foot and so I couldn't march, but they just needed a good excuse not to have me there. They didn't want to catch another cold. It wouldn't have been so bad for me because my father was ex-Sandhurst and he put me in the picture and I could have made a go of it. I'm glad it didn't happen though as it would have held back my career.'

The main reason for wanting to boost recruitment was because conscription was about to be abolished. That happened in 1960, so we will never know how John Lennon would have fared in the army, which would be a perfect subject for a West End play. On the other hand, national service proved to be very beneficial for the Kray twins – it turned them into gangsters.

In 1962, the Soviets were spotted making military installations in Cuba and for a few tense months, it looked like the world was on the brink of war. Khrushchev backed down, probably because of the threat of retaliation as nobody could predict what would happen when nuclear bombs were released. In 1963 there was a Test Ban treaty, which banned testing above ground, but who knew what was happening below ground. The Soviet Union was still building its arsenal and it was an open secret that America was carrying out nuclear tests only 100 miles from Las Vegas.

Vietnam was a French colony but after the battle of Dien Bien Phu in 1954, it was divided in two and by the 1960s the Communist North wanted to control the South, who asked America for assistance. At first they sent military advisers but in 1964 Congress approved war and conscripted soldiers were sent to Vietnam.

Many in America opposed this war and hence, draft-dodging and the pubic burning of draft cards was not seen as cowardice. This split the country. Young eligible males moved to Canada including the singer/songwriter Jesse Winchester. Canada, like the UK, had abolished the draft in 1960. The film, *Alice's Restaurant* (1969), offers a good picture of the counterculture. As Country Joe sang, 'What are we fighting for?'

Who knows what the US government was thinking when they served draft papers on Muhammad Ali, possibly the greatest of all boxers. Maybe an Elvis rerun, only in this case Ali would show support for an unpopular war. However, Ali opposed the war in Vietnam and refused to be inducted. This led to a protracted court case which led to Ali being vindicated in 1971. By then the war was over and he was too old and had been out of the ring too long to be the champion he once was.

The Vietnam War ended in 1973 and the US turned to an all-volunteer military force. As a contingency plan, males between 18 and 25 were required to register; that has now been extended to females.

As the years went by, Mikhail Gorbachev made strong moves to end the Cold War and his actions also led to the break-up of the Soviet Union, with democracies being introduced. Russia is no longer a Communist country but it is strongly led by Vladimir Putin, and at the time of writing (May 2017), it appears that Russia's cyber-crimes could have influenced the US elections.

Putin himself enjoys western culture and is a fan of Abba. Without a doubt, western culture has drawn the East and the West together and they are not two completely different entities anymore. Russia even takes part in the Eurovision Song Contest, although not in 2017 because of the host nation.

I can see the links between the East and the West every day in Liverpool where fans from Russia and other former Communist countries long to know everything about the Beatles. They must visit Memphis and feel the same way about Elvis. So well done, Elvis. He may have done more than any other serviceman to make the world a safer place. Maybe that was his greatest role.

But there is still the nuclear threat, which at present seems insurmountable. To think that this stand-off can go on forever without some accident or deliberate action is nonsensical.

II. Got a Lot o' Livin' to Do, 1958–1960

Having secured his deferment from the army, Elvis started shooting his fourth film, *King Creole*, on 20 January 1958. The film was based on a best-selling novel by the pulp fiction writer, Harold Robbins, *A Stone for Danny Fisher*, written in 1952. It was currently an off-Broadway success. In 1961, Robbins would publish his most famous book, *The Carpetbaggers*.

King Creole was directed by Michael Curtiz, who made the Oscar-winning *Casablanca* and he gave *A Stone for Danny Fisher* plenty of style. Shot in black and white, the end result is close to *film noir*.

Many changes were made to the book – Danny Fisher is not a boxer but a singer and the location has been switched from New York to New Orleans. Most of the film was shot amongst the clubs on Bourbon Street and in keeping with the surroundings, Elvis has a Dixieland jazz accompaniment crossed with rock'n'roll. The bluesy 'New Orleans' was written by Sid Tepper and Roy Bennett, who had converted Elvis' slightly stuttering speech into a vocal performance.

The film is packed with dramatic weight and Elvis called this 'the best part I've ever had'. He was right. A few years earlier, the book had been considered for James Dean and, like Dean in *Rebel without a Cause*, Elvis played a moody delinquent. He didn't always win and fans cried when he was beaten up and shot, although he pulled through in the end. It was the last film in which Elvis played a rebel and he deserved an Oscar nomination. Elvis would grow up for his future roles but he was so vain that he never played a character older than himself.

It is a strong cast too with Walter Matthau (real name Walter Matuschanskayasky) as a nightclub owner, Vic Morrow (who was in *The Blackboard Jungle*, 1955) and Carolyn Jones, later Morticia Addams from *The Addams Family,* as a gangster's spooky moll, looking like the singer Keely Smith. Elvis' girlfriend, a waitress Nellie, is played by Dolores Hart, who became a Benedictine nun in 1970. The girls in Elvis' films are not unattractive but they are often unlikely choices. Put it this way: the girls went to the movies to swoon at Elvis and, in theory, the fellas should have fancied his girlfriends. I don't think this happened.

Maybe Sophia Loren should have made a guest appearance. She met him on the set in February 1958 and though they had never met before, they were soon snogging happily in front of a photographer.

Nobody liked the title *A Stone for Danny Fisher* and at different times, the film was going to be *Sing, You Sinners* and *Danny*. Indeed, a title song, *Danny*, was written and recorded for the film, but it was not released at the time. There's a moment where Elvis is about to yodel but then thinks better of it. This is when he would have sung 'Danny'.

Instead, in 1959 the song appeared on Cliff Richard's live album, *Cliff!*, and was the B-side of Marty Wilde's UK hit, 'A Teenager in Love'. In 1960, it was given a new title, 'Lonely Blue Boy', and when it became a US Top 10 hit for Conway Twitty, it was filled with his characteristic groans. Considering that the soundtrack album of *King Creole* only contains 11 tracks, none of them longer than 2 minutes 17 seconds, surely Elvis' version, which is excellent, could have been a bonus track. Not to worry, the album was No .2 in the US and No.1 in the UK.

There is the menacing 'Trouble' (Leiber / Stoller) but Presley is usually miming rather than performing the songs live, and it shows. He's all over the place on 'Dixieland Rock' and his poor miming ruins an excellent performance. There are the rock-a-ballads (a 1958 term) 'As Long As I Have You' and 'Don't Ask Me Why' (US No.23 as a B-side). While Elvis serenades the girls in a department store and distracts them 'Lover Doll', his cronies (including Vic Morrow) are shoplifting, certainly a novel way of stealing. There is the romance of 'Young Dreams' and the school hymn, 'Steadfast, Loyal and True', later revived by Aaron Neville.

Elvis wasn't confident about the title song, another Leiber / Stoller, which was, I think, the first song to liken a guitar to a gun. It had a rapid-fire guitar solo from Scotty Moore. Elvis sang the tongue-twisting lyric quickly and exited with a Dixieland flourish. A great track in my opinion but Elvis preferred the frantic 'Hard Headed Woman' as a single,which was another US No.1 and yet hardly heard in the film. Both songs were A-sides in the UK with both singles making No.2.

But Elvis was lucky. The Head of Religious Broadcasting at the BBC considered placing 'Hard Headed Woman' on the banned list as it made fun of biblical tales. The BBC did not want an outright ban on an Elvis Presley single and so the single could be played with special permission from the Assistant Head (Light Entertainment).

In 2011 Suzi Quatro released a cover version of 'Hard Headed Woman': 'I had been working with some young musicians, say, between 18 and 25. The tracks had come out really well and then I said, 'Let's do 'Hard Headed Woman' because we'll really see how your chops are. Nobody can teach you how to feel this one properly.' – and boy, did they! I was very impressed.'

Paul McCartney criticised Elvis' version of 'Hard Headed Woman' for 'that dreadful great big trombone in the middle of it.' Derek Johnson of the *NME* was unimpressed with the whole song. 'I am frankly amazed at how he gets away with it. Except for a big-band accompaniment instead of a small group, this record sounds exactly the same as a dozen others he has made.'

This is unfair and the score suggests that Elvis could have made some imaginative and experimental records if he'd wished. Take the bayou song, 'Crawfish', an evocative duet with street vendor Kitty White. The song was later revived by Marianne Faithfull and it would be great to hear it by Tony Joe White. Joe Strummer called it his favourite Elvis song.

When Jack Good was producing Billy Fury for Decca, he recorded the eerie, almost ghostly 'Wondrous Place', written by Bill Giant. It was as sexy as hell, particularly when Billy had a sharp intake of breath just before the title line. It is now regarded as a classic track but back in 1960, it was too weird for a high chart placing. Jack Good recalled, 'I had a demo of Bill Giant's 'Wondrous Place' and it struck me immediately that it had to be done by Billy, though a lot of his good records were his own compositions. We both agreed that we wanted a steamy bayou thing: shades of Elvis Presley's 'Crawfish'. It was a wonderful stage number and Billy was terrific on stage. He was so quiet but when he put on the gold lamé suit, it was as though there was somebody else inside.'

Billy Fury was the closest the Brits had to an Elvis. Alvin Stardust: 'Billy wrote all the songs on *The Sound of Fury* but, more to the point, all those songs were classics. Then he did 'Wondrous Place' which to me had everything that 'Heartbreak Hotel' had.'

When *King Creole* was shown at the Odeon in Marble Arch, London, plaster fell from the ceiling and eight people were slightly injured, so Elvis did genuinely bring the house down.

While Elvis had been making *King Creole*, 'Don't' / 'I Beg Of You' had been issued as a single with both sides making the Top 10, and 'Don't', although a rather candid song, being on top for five weeks, and also a UK No.2.

A Brill Building lyricist, Russell Moody, wrote 'Wear My Ring around Your Neck' and took it to his friend, the Broadway composer, Bert Carroll. Bert was working on a ballet and said he hadn't got time. 'It'll only take you ten minutes,' said Russell. 'This will be an ideal song to pitch to Elvis. The girls will be wearing Elvis rings around the neck while he's away.' Okay, said Bert, and wrote his ten-minute melody. Russell then learnt that Elvis wasn't recording any more new songs before he went in the army, so Russell took it to Pat Boone. If Pat Boone didn't like it, then perhaps it could be a novelty song for Perry Como. Before any of this happened, there had been a change of heart and Elvis would do it after all.

'Wear My Ring around Your Neck' was a US No.2 and a UK No.3, but UK audiences didn't get the song – teenage boys didn't give their girlfriends friendship rings. It had connotations for Elvis himself – would Anita wear my ring while I'm in the forces?

The B-side, 'Dontcha Think It's Time', was popular, making the US Top 20 in its own right. Ben Hewitt: 'Clyde Otis asked me to do a demo for Elvis. We kept playing 'Dontcha Think It's Time' in different keys until we found one where I sounded like

Elvis, the band sounded like Elvis' recording band, and the vocal group sounded like the Jordanaires. That way, when Elvis heard it, he would more or less hear himself doing it, and it worked: Elvis recorded the song.' The song had a similar raunchiness to 'One Night' and the author Michael Gray has written, 'Elvis was saying, 'Let's fuck' years before John and Paul were wanting to hold your hand.'

Elvis Presley returned to Memphis in March and gave two shows at Russwood Park, home of the Memphis Chicks baseball team. As he left the stage on the second show, he threw a diamond ring into the audience. They were his only concert performances of the year. The stadium burned down two years later and Elvis didn't appear on stage again until 1961.

The last thing the fans wanted was Elvis to join the army. Millyon Bowers, who headed the Memphis draft board, said, 'A crackpot called me out of bed last night and complained that we didn't put Beethoven in the army.' Well, Beethoven wasn't American, Beethoven wasn't alive and Beethoven with his hearing loss wouldn't have passed the medical.

As Elvis had a few days until he had to enlist, he rented out the Rainbow Rollerdome for late-night partying with his buddies. Elvis knew that the rollercoaster car stopped at the top of the ride. He got off and climbed down the perilous structure. When the car reached the bottom, the operator wondered where Elvis had gone and feared for his safety, but Elvis was right behind him. Elvis had the recklessness of James Dean.

'Elvis died the day he went into the army,' said John Lennon. Perhaps 24 March 1958 rather than 3 February 1959 was the day the music died.

At 6am on 24 March 1958, Elvis reported for duty at the Memphis Draft Board, along with 12 other recruits. Elvis had brought along his mum and dad, his girlfriend (Anita Wood), his manager (Colonel Parker) and a couple of his chums, as you do. Not to mention all the fans and reporters.

The recruits were taken on an army bus to the Kennedy Veterans Hospital to be prodded, poked and evaluated by their medical team. They were returned in the afternoon for the induction ceremony. Sgt Walter Alden was one of the officers: his daughter, Ginger, was three and will play a part in the story, but not yet.

Private Elvis Presley was to be paid $78 a month, the only money he would earn between now and his death that wasn't reduced by Colonel Parker's commission. It wasn't so big a drop in earnings as he still received record royalties.

Presley was put in charge of the other recruits and at 5pm, they set off to Fort Chaffee, Arkansas, some 260 miles away. They arrived six hours later. No time to sleep in though. 'Where's your teddy bear?' asked one soldier.

5.30am – Your morning call, Private Presley. Five hours of aptitude tests and then a regulation haircut. Well, not quite a regulation one – Elvis always looked great. Presumably the aptitude tests went well as Presley was scheduled to drive tanks, which delighted him. In a highly symbolic act, a star is shorn by the camp's barber, James Peterson – he still looked a star.

At a press conference, Colonel Parker, not missing a trick, held red balloons advertising *King Creole*. Elvis put on a brave face but he felt the way his mother looked – very much under the weather. 'I don't think rock'n'roll will die out before I get back and if it does, I'll sing ballads,' he surmised.

On 28 March 1958, Elvis went by army bus to Fort Hood, Texas to receive eight weeks basic training. Elvis was now off limits to the media. He was assigned to A Company, Second Medium Tank Battalion, Second Armoured Division, once under the control of General Patton: now that would have been an intriguing confrontation.

Fort Hood housed 23,000 soldiers and it must have been difficult for Elvis – think how many men, filled with envy, would like to provoke the King. Maybe Sgt. Bilko gave them ideas, as that night's episode of *The Phil Silvers Show* was called *Rock And Roll Rookie*.

The so-called 'basic training' went well with Elvis being concerned that the gunfire might affect his hearing. He was commended for his marksmanship but his written tests were not good enough for officer material. He said, 'I never was any good at arithmetic. That's Colonel Parker's department', little realising that he was commenting on the costliest mistake of his life.

Elvis finished his basic training with twenty-mile long marches in the Texas sun. The first was an ordinary route march, the second combined walking with running, and the third was with an 85-pound combat-pack on his back, so congratulations were in order. It rained continuously during the bivouac week – the platoon was kept on the move, deprived of regular sleep, to simulate the feeling of warfare. Many recruits collapsed but Elvis kept on going. There could have been a drama when Elvis encountered a poisonous snake in his tent, but then he was used to Colonel Parker.

Rex Mansfield had joined the army in Memphis on the same day as Elvis. They became close friends in Fort Hood and on a day off, he, Elvis and Lamar Fike went to an air hostess training centre and selected the girls they wanted.

Elvis had two week's holiday at the end of his basic training and he would then receive a posting. Colonel Parker had wanted to book some concerts, but Elvis told him to forget it. He planned to relax, but agreed to two days of recording sessions with his friends.

Elvis Presley's only studio recordings during his army service were made at RCA in Nashville. He turned up in service dress but then Elvis always liked uniforms. The dream team was Hank Garland and Chet Atkins (guitars), Bob Moore (bass), Floyd Cramer (piano), Buddy Harman and D.J. Fontana (drums) and the Jordanaires. Hank Garland was up there with Chet Atkins, a wonderful guitarist who had played the solo on Red Foley's 'Sugarfoot Rag' (1950).

Five songs were recorded and three were new, 'I Need Your Love Tonight', 'I Got Stung' and 'A Big Hunk o' Love', which sounded as though it had been written for *King Creole*. Then there was 'Ain't That Loving You Baby' (written by Clyde Otis and Ivory Joe Hunter in 20 minutes) and Hank Snow's '(Now and Then There's) A Fool Such As I' (an excellent revival). Ray Walker of the Jordanaires: 'Elvis could adapt to whatever he had to do. I know he didn't like 'I Got Stung' as he joked about it, but he sang it in the right way.'

All five tracks would become hit singles, but for the moment the *King Creole* soundtrack was receiving media attention. The film itself opened in America to great commercial success. Other top films of the year were *No Time for Sergeants* and *A Farewell to Arms*.

Not many of the ticket sales were in Mexico – there was an anti-Elvis backlash because he was supposed to have said, 'I'd rather kiss three black girls than a Mexican.' This seems offensive to almost everyone and although Elvis was unlikely to have said it, it was reported that he had. There were protests outside cinemas and public burnings of his records. By way of contrast, *The Times* in December 1958 reported that 500 schoolchildren had been asked about hero worship and whom they most admired. Sir Winston Churchill was top, Elvis was third but as 'your own mother' was second, it was a curiously flawed survey.

Elvis Presley bought Graceland in 1957, but Vernon and Gladys, not to mention his paternal grandmother Minnie Mae, wanted to be with Elvis, and so they left Graceland and flew 600 miles to Killeen, some three miles from Fort Hood, and into rented accommodation, thereby enabling Elvis to sleep outside the base.

There is a home recording of Elvis playing 'I Understand (Just How You Feel)', a doo-wop song from the Four Tunes based around 'Auld Lang Syne'. He accompanied himself on piano and ended with that big voice which he was to use so powerfully in Vegas. Quite a bit of background noise – I don't think anyone was paying much attention.

Gladys, who was drinking heavily and swallowing diet pills, became ill and returned to Memphis for hospital treatment. She had chronic hepatitis. The army was reluctant to let Elvis visit her and he threatened to go AWOL, but when they realised she was gravely ill, they let him go.

Elvis was at his mother's bedside for 36 continuous hours. On 14 August, his father told him to take some rest so he went to the movies with three girls (this is Elvis-world). While he was there, his mother died, just 46 years old, and Elvis became inconsolable. It is possible that Elvis blamed Vernon as he had not been at her bedside when she died.

It was a personal tragedy and possibly a commercial and artistic one, as Gladys was the only one who saw through Colonel Parker. Now Colonel Parker took control and, in what can be seen as a dry run for 1977, he allowed hundreds of mourners to file past the coffin and all but turned the funeral into a circus.

Only a day later, Elvis was overcome with grief at Gladys' funeral. He threw himself on the coffin, his cries alternating between 'Everything I have is gone' and 'She's not dead'. Vernon Presley expressed his grief rather differently. Within a week, he bedded the first of several women.

Elvis loved his parents and was devastated by Gladys' early death, but I don't think it was an unnatural relationship. If he had been so devoted to his mother, would he have gone on tour: wouldn't he have stayed home and sacrificed everything for her? Mind you, I can't think of a single performer who has sacrificed everything for his mother. It's a contradiction in terms. You can't become famous unless you leave the house.

According to Jerry Hopkins' biography, 'Elvis' world collapsed like a sandcastle in the burning sea'. Maybe it did for a short time, but, come on, he was in the army and had to return to the job in hand.

Elvis was posted to West Germany as part of a NATO exercise. The Cold War was on but I don't think that anyone at the time thought it could escalate into a real war. If the Americans considered this a threat, why did they allow servicemen to bring their families? Even stranger, Elvis took his dad and his granny as well as his Memphis buddies, Red West and Lamar Fike. The entourage did not include his current girlfriend, Anita Wood, nor Colonel Parker, who had his own reasons for not leaving America. Elvis was the only private in the US army to employ a Colonel.

Elvis took the train from Fort Hood to Brooklyn and before setting sail to Germany

Elvis Presley: Caught in a Trap

on 22 September 1958, talked to the media. The best-selling spoken word EP, *Elvis Sails*, consisted of three interviews on board USS General Randall: one for the press, one for a newsreel and one with Pat Hernon. The EP reached No.2 on the US EP charts. Examples of Elvis' wit: 'What is your ideal girl?' 'Female, sir.' (Laughter and applause: note too that the Beatles would never call reporters 'sir'.). Some of the newsreel footage was shown in a curious British feature film, *Climb Up the Wall* (1960), starring the British disc-jockey Jack Jackson and directed by Michael Winner.

For the rest of September, Elvis and 800 recruits crossed the Atlantic. Elvis shared a cabin with another recruit, Charlie Hodge. Together they sang 'I Will Be Home Again', and they sang country songs at a ship's concert. Charlie became a lifelong friend, the only Memphis Mafioso who was one of his musicians.

Elvis saw the White Cliffs of Dover, but the USS Randall set anchor at Bremerhaven, West Germany. The troops were taken to barracks built by Hitler for his SS troops at Friedberg, 20 miles north of Frankfurt. Elvis would be based there for the rest of his army service, some 17 months. His first job was driving a jeep for Captain Russell of D Company of the 1st Medical Tank Battalion of the 3rd Armoured Division. Their motto: 'Victory or Death', playfully shortened to VD.

Almost straight away, Elvis was given a 'sleeping-out pass' which meant that, unless he was on night duty, he could return to his family some 15 miles away at a hotel in Bad Neuheim at 5pm. Some days he snuck out for lunch. If anything was going to alienate him from his fellow soldiers, it would be that. Just as well that he was sleeping off the base as he had brought his mother's nightgown with him, though what he did with it is a mystery.

Captain Russell found that the attention that Elvis was getting was unbearable and so Elvis was switched to the scouting platoon. He was to be a reconnaissance Jeep driver, which meant that he led the way for the convoys.

But did Elvis want the attention? Elvis couldn't tolerate the fact that the King of Saudi Arabia and his 32 wives were getting more consideration than him at the Hilberts Parkhotel in Bad Neuheim. Elvis' entourage moved to another hotel in the same area but after complaints about noise from other residents, they looked for a luxury home or apartment to rent.

Largely because of Elvis, Bill Haley and his Comets had become passé in Britain and America but not in Germany. There were riots in Berlin, Hamburg and Essen, and Haley considered cancelling the dates because of poor protection from the police. Elvis in army uniform went backstage to see them in Wiesbaden (October 23) and Mannheim (October 29). He told Haley that he was bored with army life and he considered joining them on stage for 'Shake, Rattle and Roll'. The police forbade it, fearing a full-scale riot. That would have been as nothing compared to Colonel Parker's reaction.

Meanwhile Colonel Parker, spinning from a distance, wanted a positive story about Elvis helping the disabled. The magazine wanted a pretty girl in the photoshoot, somebody the fans could identify with, and 16-year-old typist Margit Bürgin, is chosen. As Elvis' gutsiest single, 'One Night' was being issued, Elvis followed its lyric by having a fling with Margit. Unbeknown to Elvis and according to later reports, she had an abortion.

There were no more home comforts of any variety, as Elvis left his friends and family for an army tent close to the border with Czechoslovakia, so he was surprisingly close to the Soviets. One of the officers gave Elvis Dexedrine to stay awake on guard duty – it may have been his first exposure to drugs, although some say he tried his mother's slimming pills. Always favouring excess, he soon has a quart pot of Dexy's midnight runners.

On 27 November 1958, Elvis was promoted to Private First Class. He was up to his knees in mud at the Grafenwöhr training camp and he remarked to a fellow soldier, 'Boy, do I hate this shit.' Nevertheless, Elvis looked immaculate in all his army photographs: thank Lamar and Red, who cleaned his boots and pressed his uniforms throughout his stay in Germany.

In December the Elvis entourage moved into a three-storey house surrounded by a picket fence at Goethestrasse 14, Wiesbaden. Another of Elvis' girlfriends, Elisabeth Stefaniak, who spoke both English and German, was invited to live there – but as a secretary being paid $35 a week. She handled the 10,000 fan letters arriving every week and Elvis called her 'Miss Postage Stamp'. Plagued by fans, Elvis agreed to sign autographs between 7.30 and 8.00pm, and a notice to this effect was put outside the house.

Following his colonel's orders, Elvis Presley had turned down an invitation to entertain the troops over Christmas with Bob Hope. Instead, he had a blue Christmas – all he wanted to do was talk about Gladys.

Elvis wrote to Anita Wood and sent her a poodle for Christmas. He said he would marry her on his return. He told her to play Tommy Edwards' 'Soldier Boy', which was written in Korea in 1951, and make it their record. Elvis didn't mean a word of it.

Country singer Bobby Bare, about to be drafted, wrote and recorded a parody of Elvis' induction, 'All American Boy'. Because Bobby was unavailable for promotion, it was released under a friend's name, Bill Parsons. 'I got drafted six months after Elvis and I wrote 'All American Boy' the same week that I went into the army. It was a combination of myself and Elvis, any rock'n'roller who gets drafted, you know. They take away his guitar, cut his hair off and make him a GI. I cut a demo but it was given to the radio stations with my buddy's name, Bill Parsons, on the record. He was at the same session cutting a different song. He called me up and said, 'What am I going to do? They've put my name on your record and I've been asked to do *American Bandstand*.' I said, 'I can't do anything, I'm in the army. You take the money and run. It'll be forgotten in six weeks'. He did the show, lip-syncing to my record which was impossible to do, being a talking blues. I hoped he'd buy me a new car when I got out, but neither of us made any money on it.' The single entered the US chart, climbing to No.2, but was only a minor UK hit, being covered on LP by Marty Wilde.

On 8 January 1959, Elvis' 24th birthday, Dick Clark had a live telephone link with Elvis on *American Bandstand*. He told Elvis, 'The folks at home certainly haven't forgotten you.'

In January 1959, Vernon and Elisabeth were injured in an accident on an autobahn. With no evidence but fuelled by paranoia, Elvis believed the accident had been caused by sexual favours being granted in the car. Elvis had an unusual relationship with Elisabeth because she was both his secretary and his girlfriend. Priscilla's book refers to a girl who was paid to have sex with Elvis and if this is Elisabeth it is plainly wrong. She had a full-time job dealing with his fan mail.

Elisabeth had been born in Germany and her stepfather was stationed at the same base as Elvis. According to her account, she was both Elvis' secretary and lover. Scores of girls would be coming and going to Elvis' bedroom and when they had left, he would knock three times on the wall and she would spend the night in his arms. She said that Elvis didn't want full sex as he feared paternity suits, but she did want to marry him. (The inspiration for 'Crawfish' has to be *Porgy and Bess* and Elvis was living a life of Orgy and Bess.)

Elvis' friend Rex Mansfield, who was with him in Germany, wanted to date Elisabeth but felt he could not ask her while she was in this strange relationship. Eventually it petered out and Rex dated Elisabeth and married her in June 1960. Elvis never spoke to them again.

The British army's ill-fated decision to recruit a rock'n'roll singer, Terry Dene, had been a disaster. He broke down after two days in January 1959, his former fans derided him as a wimp and questions were asked in Parliament. Perhaps seeing the UK fiasco, Colonel Parker issued a ridiculous press release, allegedly written by Elvis and entitled *My Army Life Is Fine*. The press release praised Colonel Parker.

Elvis was singing 'I Need Your Love Tonight' and Vernon was feeling the same way. In March 1959, Devada (Dee) Stanley, ten years older than Elvis, was divorcing her husband, a hard-drinking army sergeant. She fancied a relationship with Elvis but settled for Vernon. Elvis was not amused: Gladys was being betrayed.

By April, Dee and Vernon were making love in Vernon's bedroom every night. As Dee shrieked with pleasure, Elvis pounded the piano as hard as he could. Unable to take anymore, he ordered Vernon to return to Memphis on the pretext of taking care of business (TCB, his favourite phrase), though Vernon soon returned.

In May 1959, Anthony Newley starred in a mickey-take of a pop star in the British army, *Idle on Parade*. Ironically, the film and the ballad, 'I've Waited So Long', turned him into one. Newley became a master songwriter and entertainer, based in Vegas, although Presley never recorded any of his songs.

Also in May, Anita Wood wrote to Elvis while on tour with Robert Goulet. Goulet added a P.S. – 'Hey, Elvis, don't worry! I'm taking good care of Anita!' Elvis was furious and years later, when he saw Goulet on TV, he put a bullet through the screen.

This could be fake news but an actress, Kim Tracy, long after his death, revealed that Elvis' idea of foreplay was to say, 'The snake is coming to get you.' It did as, according to her testimony, she became pregnant but later had a miscarriage. Lamar Fike said that he never saw her all the time he was in Germany.

On 1 June 1959, Elvis achieved Specialist Fourth Class. Pretty obvious what his speciality was. Elvis was picking up girls and discarding them – maybe he wasn't the great lover that some assume. People in love with themselves are rarely good at loving others.

During night manoeuvres, Elvis tried to heat his tank (for once, I'm not writing in sexual metaphors.) He failed miserably and nearly killed himself with carbon monoxide fumes. He was taken to Frankfurt Military Hospital and the *NME* had a front page headline, *Presley Statement from Sick Bed*. But not really, 'He was too ill to speak to us.'

Elvis had tonsillitis. Milking this for all it was worth, the *NME* then had the front page headline, *Presley Vanishes*. 'Where is Elvis?' was the question fans were asking. 'We don't know,' said the *NME*. He was officially on sick leave but he had gone to Paris in a chartered plane with Charlie Hodge and some friends.

Elvis went to the Lido night club where he befriended George and Bert Bernard, a comedy mime act who had made the film, *Gobs and Gals* in 1952. Their set piece was a parody of Yul Brynner and Deborah Kerr in *The King and I*. One night at the Lido after closing time and to everyone's surprise, Elvis sat at the piano and performed 'Willow Weep for Me' and some favourites for the staff.

During their ten-day visit, the gang went to the Folies-Bergère, the Café de Paris, the Carousel, the Moulin Rouge and the Four O'Clock Club. At the Four O'Clock Club, the good ol' boys took an entire chorus line back to the Hotel Prince de Galles for a jolly roger. It was not all sex though – Elvis started his karate lessons in Paris but declined an invitation to visit the Louvre with his Memphis boys. Maybe he stayed home and played 'Mona Lisa' instead. Neither Elvis nor the French Elvis, Johnny Hallyday, made any attempt to contact each other. Elvis was enjoying himself so much that he almost missed his deadline to return to base. He hired a Cadillac to get back on time which costs him $800.

Elvis had a Frankfurt special with a contortionist. He spent several hours in a bedroom with her and according to Lamar, he came out wringing wet. Elvis had arranged a girl for Lamar but she turned out to be a transvestite.

The impresario Bill Kenwright maintains that Elvis made a day trip to the UK and was shown the sights by Tommy Steele, but how this could be done without anybody else knowing defies belief. I suspect that Tommy had been winding Bill up but to what purpose? It also would be out of character for Elvis to go sight-seeing: if Tommy had lined up some girls, it might have been another matter.

Elvis had another hit single with 'A Big Hunk o' Love' but it was not his finest moment. During his time in Germany, Elvis only had one Top 20 entry on the German charts. This was when 'I Need Your Love Tonight' climbed to No.15. Elvis didn't have a No.1 in Germany until 1969, which was 'In the Ghetto', a record that missed the top in both England and America.

In July 1959, some old recordings were marketed for an album, *A Date with Elvis*. Although not making new recordings, Elvis agreed to photo-shoots, as the front cover showed him in army uniform in a sports car. However, this wasn't the real 'date with Elvis'. On the back sleeve was a calendar for 1960 with his proposed release date from the army – March 24 – circled.

There was only one previously unissued recording on the album: 'Is It So Strange', cut in 1957 and delayed because Parker wanted Faron Young to relinquish some of his songwriting royalties, which he did. Elvis had plenty of time on his hands and could easily have made records if asked. However, Colonel Parker was adamant that Elvis shouldn't sing as he wanted to negotiate a good deal with RCA for his return.

Elvis had a Grundig tape recorder and from time to time recorded himself on piano; he was working on gospel songs with a view to a religious album. Some of his home recordings have now been issued: 'Danny Boy', 'Soldier Boy', 'The Fool', 'Earth Angel' and 'He's Only a Prayer Away'. Elvis comes across as a competent pianist but often the balance isn't right as there is too much piano. Still, Elvis never anticipated that these tracks would be offered for purchase. There is a particularly good version of 'I'm Beginning to Forget You', a Jim Reeves B-side, with Elvis playing guitar.

In August 1959, Captain Joseph Paul Beaulieu arrived in West Germany and was stationed at Wiesbaden, living off the base with his wife, Ann, and his step-daughter, Priscilla (born 25 May 1945). A 28-year-old airman under his control, Currie Grant, moonlighted as a compère at the Eagle Club. His wife, Carole, was Tony Bennett's sister. Currie often visited Elvis and, as part of his friendship, he procured teenage lovers for Elvis. He soon discovered that he could only have his way with them *before* they met Elvis. Once they had sampled the King, they lost all interest in him.

Although she was only 14, Currie was delighted when the beautiful Priscilla asked if she could meet Elvis and he wanted to try his luck first. The Beaulieus exercised little parental control in allowing her out at night with a married man. Priscilla maintains in her book, *Elvis And Me*, that Currie tried to rape her but, if so, why did she continue to see him?

Elvis' current girlfriend was a 15-year-old beauty, Heli Priemel. Once again, it looks like under-age sex and hence, statutory rape. Then he had a brief fling with a 22-year-old film actress Vera Tschechowa, who invited him to spend time in Munich with her and her mother, Olga. Olga was a noted film actress and friend of the Führer, still speaking fondly of him. Fascinated, Elvis intended to visit them during his next vacation.

Why did the Beaulieus allow their 14-year-old daughter to visit a 24-year-old sex symbol? Elvis had been topping the charts with the lascivious 'One Night' and his name had been linked to beautiful models and actresses. Maybe Ann Beaulieu was living her own dreams by letting her daughter have a blind date with Elvis. Whatever the reasons, their only constraint was a midnight curfew. Well, there was school the next day.

On their first meeting in September 1959, Elvis was playing Brenda Lee's 'Sweet Nuthin's'. He sang 'Rags to Riches' and 'Are You Lonesome Tonight' to her and asked what she thought about the new boys on the block, Fabian and Ricky Nelson. He was struck by her facial resemblance to Gladys and himself and the fact that her hairstyle (deliberately) replicated Debra Paget's in *Love Me Tender*.

Not wasting a moment, Elvis took her to his bedroom, but even Elvis appreciated that she was only 14. I'll wait until next time, he thought, just fondling her instead. Priscilla wrote, 'His kisses set me on fire but he would never take advantage.' Priscilla returned home at 2am, and her mother was thrilled that she has kept Elvis's interest up (if that's what you call it) for so long. He had also eaten five bacon and mustard sandwiches. He called her Cilla or Little One and he liked her answering back.

By October, Elvis and Priscilla were seeing each other three or four times a week – and the bedroom door was firmly closed behind them. He told Priscilla that he hated his father dating someone new but he used Vernon to tell Captain Beaulieu of his good intentions – they bought the good Captain a car, so make what you will of that. When Priscilla's school work started to suffer, Elvis had the solution: take some Benzedrine.

The film producer, Hal Wallis, visited Elvis to talk through his first post-army film, *G.I. Blues*. It would be loosely based on his army life, including location shots in Germany but they would be filmed with an Elvis stand-in: it wouldn't look good for Elvis to be filming while still in service. Elvis, a docile creature in front of authority, agreed. Wallis had no idea that Elvis' real life was far more dramatic and comedic than anything he could propose.

Hal Wallis had plans to make a western, *Rodeo*, with him and to loan him to 20th Century-Fox for a film about a Mississippi gambler who won a showboat in a card game.

Meanwhile, 1,000 Yorkshire fans petitioned Elvis for a UK concert. Rumours abounded that Elvis might star in the Royal Variety Performance, but again, Colonel Parker would never agree to a charity show.

In November 1959, Dr. Laurenz Landau, an unqualified doctor, told Elvis that he could rejuvenate his skin with aromatherapy – Elvis, remember, was only 24-years-old. Presley thought that the German weather might be damaging his skin and was impressed with Landau's proposed treatment. The con-man wrote, 'It is my cherished ambition to give you a complete new skin and I swear to achieve this within the quickest possible time. Please don't worry about the small wrinkles on your forehead – you will not age.'

A complete sucker, Elvis began treatment. The so-called doctor washed Elvis' face with his mixture of leaves and herbs. He snooped around, taking photographs and recordings whenever he could.

Elvis and his guardians went to the Moulin Rouge nightclub in Munich, with Elvis staying with Vera Tschechowa and her mother. Elvis sang an impromptu 'O Sole Mio' with the bandleader, but added that he was not supposed to sing while in the army. Surely, the army would have preferred him singing to his other indiscretions. Elvis was photographed with cooks, lavatory attendants, strippers, prostitutes and possibly transvestites. Elvis even French kissed a stripper – now and then, there's a fool such as I. Rudolf Paulini, showing amazing integrity for a photographer, didn't sell his pictures at the time, but the seedy collection can be found in *Private Elvis* (Fey Books, Germany, 1978). Elvis looked like a guy who'd been having non-stop sex, which of course he had.

On 22 December, Elvis sacked Dr. Landau for trying to feel his manhood and threw him out. He returned two days later and told Elvis that he had compromising photographs and tape recordings and he would tell the world about Elvis and Priscilla, although Landau thought she was 16. In short, blackmail.

Presley agreed to pay Landau $200 for the treatment received and a further $300 for him to fly to London. He did not leave and he demanded a further $250 and after that, $2,000. At this point, Presley contacted the FBI and told them of the blackmail. According to their file, 'Presley assures us that this is impossible as he was never involved in any compromising positions.' No one at the FBI thought to check up on Priscilla's age.

The FBI decided to do nothing that would 'involve Elvis Presley in an unfavourable light since Presley had been a first-rate soldier and had caused the Army no trouble during his term of service.' Come to think of it, does anybody ever see Dr. Landau again?

Elvis gave Priscilla a gold and diamond watch and a ring inlaid with pearls and diamonds. Priscilla gave Elvis some bongo drums. He was delighted – or said he was. Years later, Priscilla found several sets of bongos in Graceland.

It was freezing cold in January. Elvis faked a high temperature to get out of manoeuvres, so he was a decent actor after all.

Elvis never became a five star general, but he was made a buck sergeant, commanding a three-man reconnaissance team. As the prospects weren't that good, he decided against enlisting for a further term.

In February 1960, Elvis and Priscilla were getting serious. According to *Elvis and Me*, 'I begged him to consummate our love. He quietly said, 'No, someday we will, but not now. You're just too young'.'

In March 1960, Elvis left many of his papers and possessions in Germany and planned to send for them at a later date. They include a gospel LP on which Elvis had scrawled, 'Lamar, keep your fucking hands off this LP!' and a letter to the music publisher, Freddy Bienstock: 'At the moment, I am at the top of my profession. If I record shit like this, I'll be at the bottom.'

There was a press conference before he left Germany. Quite out of the blue, Elvis told the press about his '16-year-old girlfriend', Priscilla, and said he had only ever seen her at her parents' house, an indication that he knew he was doing wrong. Every newspaper wanted a photograph, but no-one checked the details or her age. There is something to be said for today's intrusive press, as nowadays this story would not have been under wraps. When questioned by the press, Paul Beaulieu backed up Elvis's story and told Elvis that he didn't want to say anything to embarrass him.

According to her autobiography, *Elvis and Me*, Priscilla again begged Elvis to have penetrative sex but he wanted to wait, giving her one of his army uniforms as a keepsake. Priscilla maintained that she was a virgin bride on their wedding day seven years later. It does appear that Elvis divided his female friends into nice girls and playthings as this seems the only way to describe his behaviour. The concept of the virgin bride ran very deep with Elvis, though only if the virgin bride was his.

Sgt. Elvis Aron Presley left Germany and Priscilla waved him off. The plane stopped for refuelling at Prestwick Airport, outside of Glasgow. For a few minutes, Elvis walked on British soil – or at least on Scottish tarmac. He shook cold hands with sturdy fans and there were photographs in the NCO's office. There is a Harp Rock Plaque on the site today.

At 7.40am on 3 March 1960, Elvis arrived at McGuire Air Force Base, near Fort Dix, New Jersey in a snowstorm. The army held a press conference and he was surprised to meet Marion Keisker again. She had left Sun Records and was a captain in the air force. The welcoming party included Colonel Parker, Nancy Sinatra (whom he was about to work with), Jean Aberbach and representatives from RCA.

On returning home, he showed the press his final pay packet of $109.54. He weighed 13 stone and was much more muscular than when he enlisted. Elvis wore an extra stripe on his discharge, thus promoting himself to staff sergeant, no doubt a trick learned from Colonel Parker.

On 5 March 1960, nearly three weeks early, Elvis Presley was discharged from the US army at 9.15am. He spent the day talking to Colonel Parker and then he was joined by Lamar Fike and Rex Mansfield for a train to Washington, travelling in a private carriage. The next morning they took the Tennessean which left Memphis at 8am. Elvis waved to the crowds at every station. Because of the snow, the journey took all day and he was to return to Graceland on the morning of 7 March. He held a press conference and then went to see for the first time the stone angels on his mother's grave.

Then he went to see the *Holiday on Ice* show at the Ellis Auditorium in Memphis. He liked it so much that he went the following night to a 'negroes only' performance. Being Elvis, he was allowed to conduct the orchestra with a special lighted baton. He invited the whole cast to Graceland.

All in all, I am surprised at the lax discipline of the US armed forces in West Germany. At times, it seems more like Dad's Army than the world's supreme fighting force. I am sure that Elvis would have been better behaved had Colonel Parker or his mother been around. Elvis is lucky to have escaped Germany without several court martials, paternity suits, criminal charges and a hefty prison sentence. Had the journalists then been as inquisitive and as investigative as today, his career would have been ruined.

CHAPTER 8
I Slipped...

'It's now or never, my love won't wait'
Elvis Presley hit, 1960

I. I Ain't Never Did No Wrong

A highly controversial study by the American taxonomist Alfred Kinsey, *Sexual Behaviour in the Human Male*, was published in 1948. He and his researchers had spoken to thousands of males about their sex lives. The participants, all volunteers, had been frank and intimate. Faced with this evidence, nearly every rational reader would have reached the same conclusion: namely, men were sexually driven, lustful creatures who seized opportunities as they arose, though possibly constrained by moral or religious principles, or even the possible consequences.

Kinsey's technique was questioned: he had only used volunteers, so how representative was this of the whole? The real picture could be different. This was true but it was doubtful if it would be substantially different. The criticisms were made by critics who wanted to invalidate his research.

The prudish American public, as a whole, did not like the conclusions and the picture it painted of society. *Life* magazine said it was an 'assault on the family as a basic unit of society, a negation of moral law, and a celebration of licentiousness'. This was arguably true. Kinsey was placing no moral criticisms of his subjects and he was treating both homosexuality (then illegal) and extra-marital affairs as normal behaviour.

Maybe Kinsey didn't need all that research. The evidence was in the popular songs of the day. People bought songs about sexual relationships which were often franker you might expect. Here are a few examples: there are many more.

Cole Porter's 'Let's Do It' (1928) compared human lovemaking to animals mating and 'Love for Sale' (1931) can only be about prostitution. The prospect of sex after a long time away excited Ella Fitzgerald in 'Bewitched, Bothered and Bewildered' (a 1956 record but written in 1940): the words were written by Lorenz Hart, a repressed, depressed homosexual. Noël Coward as good as told the world he was gay in 'Mad about the Boy' (1932), although he passed it to a girl singer. In the 1930s George Formby was making a living out of double entendres with 'With My Little Stick of Blackpool Rock' and 'With My Little Ukulele in My Hand'.

All kind of shenanigans were described in the black blues and R&B market. Leadbelly accused his friend of 'Diggin' My Potatoes' (1946); Wynonie Harris had a 'Lovin' Machine' (1952); and Billy Ward and his Dominoes paraded their sexual prowess in 'Sixty Minute Man' (1951). Clyde McPhatter fronted the Drifters on 'Such a Night', which became a major pop hit for Johnnie Ray in 1954. The BBC banned the record but that didn't prevent Johnnie Ray from reaching the top.

Undeterred, Kinsey continued his research and published *Sexual Behaviour in the Human Female* in 1953. This was even more problematical as he pointed out the double standards in society and that women were as sexually motivated as men. The TV evangelist Billy Graham accused Kinsey of promoting immorality and one minister said that he was leading us 'out in the fields to mingle with the cattle and become one with the beasts of the jungle.' Wasn't this what Cole Porter was saying with his song, 'Let's Do It'?

The criticism hit Kinsey where it hurt, as much of his funding was withdrawn. He died in 1956 and he has to be congratulated for bringing certain things to the fore: namely, that everybody has a sex life (no matter how repressed), that adolescents were becoming sexually aware at younger ages, that women should be more comfortable with their sexuality, and that there needed to be a greater understanding of homosexuality.

In a way, Kinsey was starting the sexual revolution, which was advanced by Gregory Pincus who pioneered the contraceptive pill which, in the early 60s, made it possible for couples to have sex without fear of pregnancy. As one deeply religious wit put it, this was The Pill's Grim Progress. There was also Hugh Hefner with his magazine, *Playboy*, with its first centrefold in 1952 going to Marilyn Monroe. Its success encouraged further magazines like *Penthouse* and several manuals on sexuality.

In the UK, the zoologist Desmond Morris published *The Naked Ape* (1967) and *Intimate Behaviour* (1971), which confirmed much of what Kinsey was saying.

Although Elvis Presley never admitted it, his gestures, particularly his pelvic thrusts, were designed to excite teenage girls. Right from the start, it amused him and on his TV appearances in 1956, he was often close to laughter. Other performers didn't get it quite right because they didn't have his looks (Gene Vincent, Carl Perkins), they overdid it (Little Richard's screams) or they looked silly (Chuck Berry's duck walk). The best practitioners, outside of Presley, were Eddie Cochran (US) and Billy Fury (UK).

Presley was all about sexuality but the press rarely wrote about his girlfriends, so much so that the *NME*'s Alley Cat column made several stinging comments, all implying that he wouldn't get married because he was gay. He was friendly with the actor Nick Adams who had worked with James Dean and it was thought that they might have been more than friends. His life was so well – shielded that the Alley Cat (usually Maurice Kinn) was even making such comments in 1965. Nobody knew about Priscilla.

When somebody has the keys to the sweet shop, they will gorge on its contents, and that is the story of Elvis Presley. Here are some of the girlfriends I know about.

In February 1954 he met 15-year-old Dixie Locke at the Rainbow Rollerdrome in Memphis. She became his steady and discussed marriage with him. She broke it off because she didn't see him enough but she became the President of the first Elvis Presley fan club.

In what seems like a genuine interview, Elvis told David Williamson of the *NME* that he had only been in love once and it was with Dixie. He gave her his school ring: 'In Tennessee a girl has to be pretty special for that.' While Elvis was on tour, she was dating other boys and she returned his ring. This interview, dating from April 1959, does not mention Anita Wood.

1955 was a musical year. As well as the receptionist June Juanico, he dated three country singers: Anita Carter (from the second generation Carter family), Wanda

Jackson and Barbara Pittman (who was on Sun).

In 1956 he dated at least three Vegas showgirls, Marilyn Evans, Kathy Gabriel and Sandy Preston, and the singer Kitty Dolan, whom he met in Vegas. Other dates included Kate Wheeler and Sharon Whiley.

When he got to Hollywood, he had no success in dating Debra Paget and in a rare public moment of self-doubt, he said, 'I sent her flowers, I was nuts about her, but she wouldn't even give me the time of day.' Possibly he couldn't believe that someone would turn him down.

Then he dated Natalie Wood, who had been in *Rebel without a Cause*. They became serious and Elvis took her home to meet his parents. They planned to elope to Las Vegas but Colonel Parker and Gladys Presley talked him out of it.

In 1957 it was Arlene Bradley, who claimed to have dated him for the next six years, and a Hollywood actress, Joan Bradshaw. Once again he had the hots for a Las Vegas dancer, this time Dorothy Harmony, and he tried to get her a role in the film, *Hot Rod Rumble*. He dated Barbara Hearn who can be seen in an audience scene in *Loving You*.

He dated the dancer Rita Moreno and Dolores Hart, who was in *Loving You* and *King Creole*. He called Dolores 'whistle britches'. It is speculated that she became a nun because of her unrequited love for Elvis.

Elvis had the mother of a weekend with the famed stripper, Tempest Storm. She then beguiled Herb Jeffries (the 'bronze buckaroo' who recorded 'The Devil is a Woman'), becoming his second wife in May 1959. Jeffries came with her to London in 1961 where she stripped at Paul Raymond's Revuebar, albeit billed as 'Elvis Presley's girlfriend'. I wonder if Colonel Parker knew about that. I was only 16 and living in Liverpool, but if I'd been a little older, I'd have been tempted to see her out of curiosity. She was the first person to cash in on her closeness to Elvis Presley: well, maybe not if you are taking your kit off in a Soho dive. But not for long.

Paul Raymond expected his girls to go from fully clothed to completely naked in 60 seconds, but Tempest Storm had a slow act, only removing her gloves in the first minute. Raymond told her to speed up as this was not the London way. In 1967 Herb Jeffries wrote and produced the film, *Mundo Depravados*, for Storm, which has become a cult film.

Elvis enjoyed this world but he also felt comfortable with young girls and he liked the company of three Memphis teenagers, Gloria Mowel, Heidi Heissen and Frances Forbes, who were all 14. There was nothing sexual about this, and possibly he liked to meet young fans to see how he could appeal to that age-group.

In 1957 Elvis met the first girl he wanted to marry, 19-year-old Anita Wood, a glamorous blonde who could act and sing. Her first record was 'Crying in the Chapel' and there is a bootleg tape of Elvis and Anita fooling with 'Who's Sorry Now'. Apparently, Colonel Parker vetoed their marriage as it could harm his fan base. She married the football player, Johnny Brewer, of the Cleveland Browns.

Other girlfriends before the army included June Wilbank, Yvonne Lime, Jana Lund and Venetia Stevenson, who was to marry Don Everly.

Once he was in Germany with the army, he found time for night manoeuvres with the Russian actress Vera Tschechowa, the dancer Anjelika Zehetbauer and 16-year-old Margit Buergin, whom he called 'Little puppy'.

There's more to come, but we'll stop it there for the moment as I'm sure you've got the picture. Elvis was a highly charged, highly experienced sexual animal, and his whole stage act was based around sex – warm, romantic ballads ('Love Me Tender', 'Loving You'), lewd songs about carnality ('One Night') and wild, gyrating performances.

There is no doubt that Elvis enjoyed intimate relationships with glamorous females and he appears to have enjoyed foreplay more than the act itself. It was all good fun with consenting adults and there is no evidence that Elvis forced himself upon anyone.

And then Elvis met Priscilla, and here we hit the problem. She was only 14 at the time they met.

The Russian-American novelist, Vladimir Nobokov, published his most famous novel, *Lolita*, in 1955. It told of a professor's passion for a 12-year-old girl and it led to the term 'Lolita Syndrome'. Nabokov wrote the screenplay for the 1962 film directed by Stanley Kubrick, which was a *tour de force* for James Mason with his remarkably creepy voice. His quarry, Sue Lyon, is a 16-year-old girl, which radically and deliberately changes the nature of the story.

It is probable that the producers feared the original book was such a sensitive subject that nobody would want to see it. A cinemagoer might feel uncomfortable as he watched or if he saw someone he recognised in the audience. Even with a 16-year-old in the title role, it would be difficult for the film to find an audience.

Although there have been several high profile, historical child abuse cases in recent times, some situations were tolerated then, although it would seem unacceptable today.

The attitudes of pop stars to their fans was different. It would be a remarkable star who asked a groupie for her birth certificate. So maybe what I am recounting is symptomatic of the times and things are different today.

And not just in Britain and America. Jacques Brel wrote 'Jackie', a fantasy about his younger self wanting to be famous and become 'the procurer of young girls'. Serge Gainsbourg had many suspect projects including 'Lemon Incest' with his daughter, Charlotte, and an album about under-age sex, *Histoire de Melody Nelson* (1971), with Jane Birkin.

Records often indicate the climate of the times, notably 'Jail Bait' by Andre Williams (1957). The lyric includes such choice lines as '15, 16, 17, that's jail bait' and 'You'll get one to three.' There is a definite feeling in the song that the girl is encouraging the boy. In 1974 the lead singer of the Drifters, Johnny Moore was singing 'Every night, I pick you up from school, 'Cause you're my steady date' but you can argue that Johnny Moore in his forties was playing the part of a 15-year-old boy. In 1976 the Sutherland Brothers and Quiver were extolling 'The Arms of Mary': 'She took the things of boyhood, and turned them into feel good.' And how about 'My Sharona from the Knack in 1979? 'Never gonna stop, give it up, such a dirty mind, I always get it up, for the touch of the younger kind.'

The most infamous example of the Lolita syndrome in the rock'n'roll era is with Jerry Lee Lewis. Jerry Lee's career was doing fine with Sun Records as he had international hits with 'Whole Lotta Shakin' Goin' On' and 'Great Balls of Fire', again two songs that were sexually charged.

Jerry Lee had married a preacher's daughter, Dorothy Barton, in 1952 when he was only 16 but he left her for the club life. That same year he got Jane Mitcham pregnant and her brothers forced him to get married. It was a shotgun wedding but he was still married to Dorothy. Somehow he was able to get a divorce and before the year is out,

Jane had given birth to Jerry Lee Lewis Jr.

Jerry Lee and Jane fell out over his womanising, which became excessive once he had chart hits. In 1957 he became infatuated with his second cousin, Myra Brown, the daughter of his bass player, Jay Brown. On 12 December 1957, with 'Great Balls of Fire' shooting up the charts, Jerry Lee married Myra in Hernando, Mississippi. It was not reported as a news story in the States.

Jay wanted to kill Jerry when he first heard about his activities but then he realised he could see the world through his talented son-in-law. He gave Myra a beating instead.

Around this time, the southern states had been amending their marriage laws to fall in with the rest of the civilised world. The age of consent was rapidly being accepted as 16 years. Mississippi was the last of the southern states to amend its law and so many couples were making their way across the state line to get married. In 1957, the legislature in Mississippi raised the minimum age for women from 12 to 15 and for men from 14 to 17 and it looks as though Jerry Lee Lewis and Myra Brown were married just before the age limit was raised.

But once again, Jerry Lee was already married – or was he? Did that second marriage count because it was bigamous? Did this new marriage count? As sure as hell, the supremely arrogant Jerry Lee Lewis couldn't care less.

Jerry Lee came to the UK for a 37-date tour, with two shows a night for Lew and Leslie Grade with the Treniers in May 1958. This had the makings of being a great rock'n'roll tour. It was quite the family outing as Jerry Lee and Myra came with her father Jay as bass player, Jay's wife Lois and Myra's sister, Rusty. There was an ominous warning when the plane carrying them had to make an emergency landing in Ireland because the engine had caught fire.

A replacement plane took them to London and Jerry Lee held a press conference. Someone asked him how old Myra was. Sensing a problem, he said 15 but even that was a cause for concern. The *Daily Mail* then revealed the truth.

'Age doesn't matter back home,' said Myra, 'You can marry at 10 if you can find a husband.' The story became front page news, although no one had researched the full story of that rather dodgy second marriage. Early marriage ran in the family: Jerry Lee's sister, Frankie Jean, had been married at 12 and was now pregnant at 15.

The police came to the Westbury Hotel and examined Myra's passport in the presence of her parents. Myra admitted she was waiting to hear from Mississippi about the legality of their marriage. Somewhat undeterred, Lois said, 'The first my husband and I knew about this marriage was when we found the certificate in a drawer at home. If I find it is not valid, they will get married again quickly. I will insist on that.' Probably not, as the law had changed.

Clearly not taking any advice from publicists, Jerry Lee told the media, 'I was a bigamist at 16. My marriage to Jane was invalid. I married Dorothy when I was 14. I was just a brat and didn't know what I was doing. She was a good girl but I left her because I was too young to get married. Then I met Jane who was as wild as the wind. I met her before my divorce from Dorothy so I married her bigamously.'

The reactions to all this could have gone either way. British mums and dads were horrified by the story and the teenage fans could have defiantly supported Jerry Lee but not a bit of it: the entire country was outraged. The Teddy Boys who had loved his records barracked his shows, shouting 'Baby-snatcher' when he appeared on stage,

Elvis Presley: Caught in a Trap

and somebody rolled a pram on stage. After three days, Jerry Lee returned home and the tour limped on for a short while with British replacements. Jerry Lee had lost an estimated £35,000.

This was an opportunity for the adults' hatred of rock'n'roll to come to the fore. What were these Americans doing over here anyway? Questions were asked in the House of Commons, leading to this splendid exchange:

Sir Frank Medlicotte: 'Is my Right Hon. Friend aware that great offence was caused to many people by the arrival of this man with his 13-year old bride, especially bearing in mind the difficulty that others have in obtaining permission to work here? Will he remember also that we have more than enough rock'n'roll entertainers of our own without importing them from overseas?'

Minister of Labour (Iain Macleod): 'This was, of course, a thoroughly unpleasant case, which was ended by the cancellation of the contract and the disappearance of the man. But, at the time the matter was before my officers, it was purely a question of a permit for employment, and his case was treated under the ordinary arrangements which apply to anybody.'

Commenting on the Jerry Lee Lewis controversy in the *Daily Mail* and widening her criticism, Eve Perrick complained about 'semi-literate latter day wandering minstrels, roaming the country to entertain hordes of other semi-literate minors'.

What is the solution? Perrick says that the Chancellor should impose 'such a heavy tax on gramophone records made by unknown, under-age and untalented rock'n'rollers that their price will be too high even for the teenage market.'

What a lunatic idea. Looking at the records released around that time, you might have to pay an extra two shillings for Marty Wilde's 'Endless Sleep' or the Kalin Twins' 'When', but how about a discount if you bought Kathie Kay's 'Hillside In Scotland'? Elvis Presley was very definitely not unknown, but I would think that Eva Perrick would want to impose a super supertax on 'Hard Headed Woman'.

She had a close ally in Leslie MacDonnell, a director for the Moss Empires circuit. He said, 'We will ban those singers who have to make about 30 attempts of one song before the technicians have enough good material to make a single record.' How exactly will he find how many takes Tommy Steele made of 'Singing the Blues' or Cliff Richard of 'Move It'? In any event, the country's most insecure singer was Michael Holliday, whose style was based around Bing Crosby.

The Jerry Lee scandal travelled back to the States and his career, for the moment, was over. Jack Clement, Barbara Pittman and George Klein, with a wry sense of humour, issued a cut-in single in the style of Buchanan and Goodman called 'The Return of Jerry Lee'. There was no intention to issue it but Sam Phillips loved it and put it out. At one point, Klein asks Jerry Lee how he proposed to Myra, and Jerry Lee answers, 'Open up a-honey, it's your lover boy me that's knocking.'

With irony piling upon irony, Jerry Lee had cut the title song from a teen film, *High School Confidential*. It was a terrific rock'n'roll record with some madcap piano playing and it was still issued as a single. It made No.21 in the US and No.12 in the UK, so some fans were still buying his records.

For a couple of years, Jerry Lee could only play small clubs dates in the southern states for reduced fees, but then he returned to the charts with a revival of Ray Charles' 'What'd I Say'. By then Myra was 16 and as they were portrayed as a loving couple, all was forgiven.

In 1962 Jerry Lee returned to the UK for a tour for Don Arden but a few days before the tour, Jerry and Myra's son, Steve Allen (named after the TV host), drowned in their pool. His arrival in the UK was delayed because of the inquest and the funeral. Astonishingly, Jerry Lee did not want to cancel the tour: he had something to prove. He came to the UK and Myra followed a week later. Don Arden's publicist, Ken Pitt, had an idea: 'Jerry told me that she was a very religious little girl. She read the Bible every day and it was her bedtime reading. I suggested that she should be carrying that when she stepped off the plane as she would get a better reception, and of course she did.'

But Ken Pitt found that working with Jerry Lee was difficult. 'He was just uninterested. He didn't want to talk to anybody and he wasn't interested in anybody else. When he sat at the piano, he would play in his own inimitable style and that was marvellous but whenever he came off the stage, he might say, 'Hiya, how y'doing?' to me but I don't think he really know who I was or what my function was.' Still, his wild, rocking performances drew huge acclaim and Jerry Lee Lewis was back.

In the mid-60s the obstinate and arrogant Jerry Lee Lewis moved over to country music and has been a successful touring attraction ever since, but the length and the quality of his performances depend very much on his mood. He has now been married seven times and has had to cope with the death of close family members. He once went to Graceland to shoot Elvis Presley and there were many violent incidents in his career, but then he does call himself 'The Killer'.

Then there is Chuck Berry whose misdemeanours caught up with him in December 1959. He was arrested for taking a 14-year-old Native American, Janice Escalante, across the state line for immoral purposes. The girl was going to be a hooker at his club.

Chuck Berry was fined $5,000 and given a five-year sentence. It was determined subsequently that the judge had been racially biased and the sentence was reduced to three years. Chuck was able to record some songs while his appeal was being heard and one of them, wisely not released at the time, was a song about a young girl growing up, 'Adulteen'.

From February 1962 to October 1963, he was incarcerated. Significantly, and unlike today, it never occurred to him that the public might take against him because he spent his time learning accountancy (so he could manage his own business) and writing new songs. When he asked the prison guard for an atlas, the staff thought he was planning his escape. Not so – he was writing 'The Promised Land', a song that Elvis would record.

The key point is that Chuck Berry was 100% correct, even more than 100% in fact. When he came out of prison, he found that he had an increased following. The Beatles, the Rolling Stones and other British groups were singing his songs and soon he was back recording new ones, making the charts and successfully touring the UK. If any journalist asked him about prison, he would simply say that he had never been inside.

Chuck became so skilful at his accountancy that he was able to work the system. In 1979 he went to a party at the White House just before he served four months for tax evasion.

It could be perilous to be in the spotlight. Rockabilly singer Ben Hewitt: 'A guy in North Florida did some record hops as me and because most people didn't know what I looked like, he got away with it. One night he drove a 14-year-old girl home. They hugged and kissed, she said no, he said yes, and he raped her. She told her parents who told the cops, and they picked up the guy and threw him in jail. This guy rang up Irving Green of Mercury Records in Chicago, saying he was me and demanding money. Irving stormed into Clyde Otis' office and asked what kind of fool Clyde had hired. He shouted, 'Who is this clown, Ben Hewitt?' Clyde said, 'You'd better ask him, he's sitting right across the table from me.' Had I not been in the office at that moment, I could have been named in the papers as a rapist.'

In the previous chapter, I described how Elvis and Priscilla met when she was only 14. She desperately wanted to meet him and encouraged an airman to introduce her. We don't know what happened between them, but she continued to see him because she wanted to meet Elvis.

There seems to be an attraction to younger girls amongst the rock stars. Roy Orbison opened 'Goodnight' with the phrase, 'My lovely woman child' and recorded a song called 'Child-woman, Woman-child'. Gary Puckett and the Union Gap performed 'Young girl, get out of my life' and both Steve Lawrence and Mark Wynter sang 'Go Away Little Girl'. Neil Diamond and Cliff Richard sang 'Girl, You'll Be a Woman Soon'. There is nothing to connect them to any untoward practices but they were appealing to young audiences who loved to fantasise and hear messages like this.

Consider too the songs with 16 in them – 'Sixteen Candles' (Crests, 1958) and 'Happy Birthday Sweet Sixteen' (Neil Sedaka, 1961). A British vicar wanted the Sedaka record banned, as he realised why Sedaka wanted her to be 16.

P.J. Proby, a Southern rocker based in the UK since the mid-60s, knew Presley and recorded songwriter demos for his approval. He thought there was nothing unusual about Elvis and Priscilla's relationship and indeed, the tabloids had a field day with P.J's young girlfriend.

Priscilla's mother and stepfather appear to have encouraged the liaison. Even if they didn't know of his many affairs, surely a vulnerable young girl should not be seeing a 24-year-old man who was seen as a sex god without a chaperone, and allowed to stay out until midnight.

We know that he gave her drugs and certainly had serious sex with her even if he did not go the whole way. We know from his behaviour that he knew that, at the very least, his actions could be misconstrued.

We don't have the lowdown on most of his relationships but a couple of the girls have said that they did not have full sex with Presley. Maybe he was worried about future paternity suits, but these were the days before DNA tests, so it was easy for somebody, whether or not she had had sex with him, to make a claim if it would ensure a better life for her child.

Nobody else but Priscilla knows what happened in the bedroom but she should never have been there. We can be fairly sure that Priscilla in her autobiography, *Elvis and Me* (Century Hutchinson, 1985), is showing Elvis in the best possible light, but even in doing that, she is giving enough grounds for Elvis to have been arrested. She did after all write: 'Our relationship remained chaste, though we came awfully close to consummation.'

II. Got a Lot o' Livin' to Do, March 1960–December 1960

Elvis was back and there was much speculation as to what would happen next. He was seen as a model patriot and being 25 it was never on the cards that he would continue as a rebellious, headline-grabbing rock'n'roller.

By 1960, for one reason or another, all the leading rock'n'rollers, with the exception of Fats Domino, were out of action. Although there were excellent, second-generation rock'n'rollers (Freddy Cannon, Brenda Lee, Jack Scott, Larry Williams), the fashion was for good-looking, clean-cut boys singing drippy beat-ballads. They got their breaks on Dick Clark's *American Bandstand,* a daily TV show broadcast live from Philadelphia. It was a mimed show with live dancers, who became celebrities in their own right. Brian Hyland recalls, '*American Bandstand* was a very important show for breaking records. The kids would get home from school at four o'clock and turn it on.'

British TV producer Jack Good: 'We all thought that the show must be great – you know, Chuck Berry refers to it in 'Sweet Little Sixteen'. I went to the States in 1959 and I have to tell you that *American Bandstand* was the most boring show I have ever seen. Terrible, terrible, terrible, and I hated Dick Clark 'cause he looked so slick and so smooth and he was selling commercials for spotty girls. I don't think he contributed anything to rock'n'roll, but he understood a cash register.'

Many new idols came from the Tri-State area and several were of Italian extraction, owing as much to Al Martino as to Elvis Presley. Compared to 1956, it was dullsville but then New Elvis was like New Labour: the radical originality had been sanitised. After being demobbed, Elvis never shook his pelvis again, except in jest, and even recorded twist songs – the brain-dead but enjoyable dance which, for a time, upstaged rock'n'roll.

The crossover artist is Ricky Nelson: was he the last of the old rockers or the first of the new breed? Lead guitarist James Burton: 'Ricky Nelson was at Imperial Records and he heard the bass player James Kirkland and me working with Bob Luman. The next day he sent a telegram to our house in the valley inviting us to meet his parents. He wanted us to play with him on his family TV show and we liked that as he had a real smooth voice and he let us play as we felt. That solo in 'Hello Mary Lou' is just what came into my mind at the time.'

In 1958 Ricky Nelson topped the US charts with 'Poor Little Fool', supposedly written by Sharon Sheeley but is the writing credit correct? P J Proby: 'There was a boy of 16 who claimed that he had written 'Poor Little Fool' and was going to take Sharon to court, so we invited him over with his mother to dinner and there was Ricky Nelson, with Johnny and Dorsey Burnette. The boy came in and he was gob-smacked as there was his idol, Ricky Nelson, and they had a great meal. Sharon played the perfect hostess and the boy went away and dropped the lawsuit. It could have turned nasty as the Burnette brothers were heavy dudes so maybe he sensed that something might happen to him.'

Jerry Lee Lewis scathingly called 1958 to 1963 'the era of the Bobbys', regarding Bobby Darin, Bobby Vinton, Bobby Vee and Bobby Rydell as interchangeable. Bobby Vee: 'Yeah, and don't forget Bobby Goldsboro. There was a ton of us. It's the American name. There are more Robs or Bobs in America than anything else.'

The Bobby-sox heroes, who made their US chart debuts or consolidated their careers while the Cat was away, were white male solo singers – in other words, the opposition, what Elvis was returning to in March 1960. It was as though Pat Boone had won.

Bobby Darin, whose talents were as awesome as Elvis' own, was the most talented of the Bobby-soxers, whether or not called Bobby. Neil Sedaka: 'You can't really touch

Bobby Darin, he was in a class by himself. He was my idol and he had a very polished supper club act. I wanted to do that kind of cabaret act myself, and when I did the Copacabana, it went very well.'

Paul Evans: 'I knew Bobby Darin and even before 'Splish Splash', I knew that he had something. Conversations would stop when he walked in a room and heads would turn in his direction. I would have bet on him becoming a big star. He thought had it all but so what, he did have it all. He was never rude and he was never so cocky that you didn't like him.'

Mort Shuman had started writing with Doc Pomus: 'The first song that got things rolling for us was 'Plain Jane', which we wrote for Bobby Darin on the newly-formed Atco label. Bobby was very much into rock'n'roll at the time but he had a lovely ballad voice and did some of our demos.'

Roger McGuinn, who later founded the Byrds: 'Bobby Darin hired me as a back-up singer to play 12-string guitar and sing harmony when he was doing some folk music. He also opened up a publishing company in the Brill Building and hired me as a songwriter. He was very driven and he was an amazing artist. He could play the drums, vibraphone, piano and guitar, and he could tap dance and do impressions too. He was always very professional, always on time with a pressed suit and shoes shined and just ready to go. In that respect, he was old school like the vaudeville artists from the 20s. I never heard him say that if he was good now, what would he be like when he was Sinatra's age, but he was cocky, no doubt about that.'

Frankie Avalon, in reality Francis Avallone from Philadelphia, had his first hit in 1958 with 'Dede Dinah' and topped the US charts with 'Venus' in 1959. Bobby Vinton: 'I heard 'Venus' on the radio and I loved it as it was such a new sound. It had a good echo and I loved the way that they used an acoustic guitar. It was a great song with a nice gimmick and I used to sing it with my band.'

Mort Shuman: 'Pete De Angelis and Bob Marcucci from Philadelphia were going great guns with Frankie Avalon, and they came rolling into New York. They told us, 'We've got this new kid called Fabian, and we would like to make him a peppermint-flavoured Elvis Presley.' They wanted to create an anti-septic scene with a pussycat Elvis. Fabian was, and still is, a lovely guy but he was not the greatest rock'n'roll singer that ever came out. We wrote 'I'm a Man' and he did the best he could and it went into the Top 40. I can't criticise it as I recorded it myself in London and I can't believe how bad I was. Joe Brown saved it with his guitar solo.'

Doc Pomus: 'Fabian was getting a lot of attention at record hops, but his first records hadn't sold anything. The problem was to make records for a feller who didn't have, in the legitimate sense, a voice. In other words, he had to practically talk the lyrics. We took a couple of songs that we had written for Presley – 'I'm A Man' and 'Turn Me Loose' – and watered them down. Presley hadn't rejected the songs – we never even gave them to him – and Fabian got lucky with them.' (The Presley lyrics have been recorded by Adam Faith, who, until I told him, hadn't realised he was singing anything different from Fabian.)

Mort Shuman: 'Turn Me Loose' was originally written for Presley with a much stronger, harder lyric. Pete De Angelis had asked me for a song for the kid and our publisher said, 'You've got this great song. I don't think Elvis is going to do it. Why don't you tone down the lyrics a bit, make it more teen-oriented and we'll get Fabian to do it?'

It became a different thing for Fabian, but that's showbiz. We went into the studio and I played piano on the session. Fabian did his best and it was enough to get by.'

Fabian was the classic pretty face and a pompadour. Lou Christie: 'Fabe is a nice person, a very nice person, and he did appeal to a lot of people. He did have a magical quality about him. Bob Marcucci was impressed by the way he looked and it was the beginning of merchandising people.'

Bobby Vee: 'We would all agree that Fabian was not a great singer. He typifies the American teenage idol and to a great degree, he was manufactured. Forty years on and he is a very good host of rock'n'roll shows: he knows how to talk to people and he's a nice warm performer.'

Duane Eddy: 'I had put my guitar down to sign autographs and I had my back turned. Some guy picked it up and carried it out of the door. Fabian saw that he had my guitar and called for the tour manager. Fabian tried to catch him but he couldn't. The guy knew the back of the hall too well. Fabian lost him but he saved my guitar.' So Fabian did something positive for rock'n'roll? 'Oh, that's unkind! 'I'm a Man' and 'Tiger' are good fun rock'n'roll records.'

Tommy Sands starred opposite Fabian (and Bing Crosby) in the 1960 film, *High Time*: 'They wanted the Fabian character to be the dark lover-boy type and since I also had dark hair, they thought I would be too much competition and they dyed my hair blond. I didn't like that at all. I had to get to make-up every morning at 4am for them to touch up my roots. They would grow out overnight and you could see the black around the edges.'

Mort Shuman: "Turn Me Loose' was in the Top 10 around the same time as 'A Teenager In Love' by Dion and the Belmonts, and so Doc and I became the flavour of the month. We had been writing together for about a year and Laurie Records told us that they had this group of little Bronx hoods – old-time punks if you like. They were kids who'd steal hub-caps, just normal healthy pursuits for teenagers in the Bronx, and they were called Dion and the Belmonts. We said we would write for them and I started going 'doowah, doowah' and 'A Teenager in Love' was born. Dion and the Belmonts recorded it, which was great for us.'

Dion: 'The teachers in my school thought I didn't know what I wanted to do but music opened my whole world. Rock'n'roll at its best was an expression of individual freedom. There was no such thing as teenagers back then, let alone teenage music. From 13 to 19, you weren't supposed to talk and then you became an adult and could listen to adult music. Rock music gave us our own culture.'

Doc Pomus: 'Dion was a great, great singer and he is the most underrated singer of all-time. So many people emulate him without realising that they are copying him. The street bends in his voice are part of the hierarchy of rock'n'roll to me.'

A difference between the first rock'n'roll songs and the teen ballads is that the singer was often prepared to play the gallant loser. Ruth Batchelor who wrote for Elvis said that his management would not even consider songs where Elvis had lost to another guy. Elvis would never have sung 'Run to Him', a 1961 hit for Bobby Vee. Bobby appreciates the social changes: 'That was the great American value system at the time. It wasn't a deliberate image but it was a pulse that was going on in pop music at the time. When you look at 1950s rock'n'roll, you have the rough edges of Eddie Cochran and Ronnie Hawkins, the songs that made people say it was going to corrupt our youth and was never going to last. By the early 60s, the major studios had gotten hold of rock'n'roll and tamed it, and that was when I got involved. The songs were more socially acceptable and spoke of values that are still alive today. I don't mind that. I liked the songs that I sang.'

So this was the brave new world for Elvis Presley. Bobby Darin was a new explosive talent and Dion had a wonderful voice, but the music of the day was blander, with teen idols with limited talent and no real commitment to what they were doing.

On Sunday 20 March 1960, Elvis went to Nashville for his first post-army session, with Steve Sholes and Chet Atkins co-producing, although the session tapes show that Elvis knew what he wanted.

Elvis was switching off from army time and tuning into Elvis time. His first session started at 8pm and went through to 5.30am. By then they had completed six songs, all of which would be released. Scotty Moore was back with him as well as Hank Garland. Bob Moore was bass, D J Fontana and Buddy Harman on drums and Floyd Cramer on piano, a Nashville A team if there ever was one.

The first song was a new Otis Blackwell song. 'Make Me Know It', very much in the same vein as Don't Be Cruel', and with an identical theme. At the time I thought Elvis was singing 'with your head and shoulders' in the chorus but I now know it is 'go ahead and show it' so the song never made sense to me.

Then he did a song that had often been on his mind – 'Soldier Boy', which had been recorded by the Four Fellows in 1955 and related to Korea. This was an excellent doo-wop song with a beautifully plaintive lyric from Elvis. The outtakes include Elvis whistling the tune: what a pity he didn't complete this for a bonus track.

Then there was John Leslie McFarland's 'Stuck on You', which to a degree is 'All Shook Up, Part 2'. Uh huh. Some critics have thought it half-hearted but that is the nature of the song and it has grown on me with the years. I would say that this is the best doo-wop performance ever by an act who is not a bona fide doo-wop performer.

In 1964 Mort Shuman wrote 'Little Children' with John Leslie McFarland, a hit for Billy J Kramer with the Dakotas: 'John Leslie McFarland is one of the great unknown talents. He was more than eccentric, he was mad, totally round the bend. He was a light-skinned black guy from Chicago who had no idea of right and wrong. He stole a mummy from a museum and took it on a bus. He stole a horse from a mounted policeman and took it into a cinema. He stole a plane and flew it even though he'd never flown before. How can you expect a man like that to write normal songs? We wrote 'Little Children' together and he wrote 'Stuck on You' with Aaron Schroeder, which was based on the shuffle Otis Blackwell did for 'All shook Up'. Aaron Schroeder looked like the head of an insurance company, a really dapper businessman and is hard to imagine him writing with this totally spaced-out lunatic. He wrote one song about weeds growing in the garden of love, but how can you interest Elvis Presley in a song called 'Weeds'?'

Fred Wise and Ben Weisman had written the bluesy 'It Feels So Right' and a ballad, 'Fame and Fortune', very much in the vein of 'Playing for Keeps' or 'I'm Counting on You'.

The greatest performance and one of the best of his career was 'A Mess of Blues', the first song he had recorded by Doc Pomus and Mort Shuman. Mort Shuman: "'A Mess of Blues' was a Doc Pomus expression. Doc sometimes doesn't give me as much credit as he should, but that's okay and I still give him credit. 'A Mess of Blues' was totally Doc's idea, you know, a mess of blues. Doc loved the word 'mess' and he loved the blues, so 'Since you've gone, I got a mess of blues' is a great line. It could be a mess of trouble, anything, and it's just a great Doc Pomus expression. It was a very driving, bluesy thing and it was a return to roots for Elvis.'

Like everyone else, Doc and Mort had to surrender some of their royalties to Elvis and Doc, with great humour, used to refer to it as 'the Elvis tax', but Elvis was actually taking money from a disabled man as Doc was in a wheelchair.

It was a great start to his first comeback and he topped it with his first degree black belt in karate. He and his entourage took an overnight train to the Fontainebleau Hotel in Memphis for rehearsals for his appearance on Frank Sinatra's next special for Timex, subtitled *Welcome Home, Elvis*.

The most obvious way for Elvis to push his new single would have been on *The Ed Sullivan Show*. However, Frank Sinatra's TV ratings needed a boost and his sponsor Timex suggested that he should swallow his pride and make an offer to Colonel Parker. Presley knew that Sinatra hadn't changed his views but both could see that such a combination made great commercial sense.

The stars had their own spots and they swapped songs with Frank singing 'Love Me Tender' and Elvis 'Witchcraft', both looking uncomfortable. Elvis contributed a line, just one line, to an ensemble piece, 'It's Nice to Go Travelling'.

Frank told Elvis what he has missed while he had been away, which turned out to be his *Only the Lonely* LP and Sammy Davis in *Porgy and Bess*. Peter Lawford, Joey Bishop and Nancy Sinatra contributed to the show with Nelson Riddle conducting, but the show didn't sparkle. Someone should have filmed the backstage moment when Joey Bishop asked Elvis for his autograph and Colonel Parker demanded a dollar. Still, when the show was eventually shown on 12 May (a pointless delay), the show grabbed 40% of the audience, Frank's highest ever rating.

During the show, Frank said, 'Glad to see the Army hasn't changed you, Elvis', when it must have been obvious to everybody else that it had. When Elvis eyed 19-year-old Nancy, Frank said, 'She's spoken for.' Well, I wouldn't be too sure about that.

On 23 March, the new single was released, 'Stuck on You' on the A-side and 'Fame and Fortune' on the back. It was the first Elvis single in stereo. It sold its first million copies in a couple of days, knocked 'Theme from *A Summer Place*' from the top and stayed for four weeks, when it was replaced by an even greater record, the Everly Brothers' 'Cathy's Clown', both featuring Buddy Harman on drums.' Fame and Fortune' made No.17 in its own right.

RCA was so pleased with the sales of 'Stuck on You' that they wanted a new album. They had booked him on a late night session on 3 April and the intention was to master the tracks immediately and have a new album released as quickly as possible. It would be called *Elvis is Back!* They already had 'Make Me Know It', 'Soldier Boy' and 'It Feels So Right' and they were saving 'A Mess of Blues' for a single.

The same musicians were booked along with the saxophonist, Boots Randolph, best known for his 'Yakety Sax' instrumental, which was used on *The Benny Hill Show*. His contribution was especially notable on 'Such a Night', 'Like a Baby' and 'Reconsider Baby'. The drummers, D.J. Fontana and Buddy Harman were together for 'Such a Night' and at the end, you can hear Elvis give a quiet but appreciative 'Wooo!'.

Elvis Presley: Caught in a Trap

Elvis added Charlie Hodge for 'I Will Be Home Again', written by Bennie Benjamin, the composer of 'Don't Let Me Be Misunderstood'.

There was only guitar, bass and drums for a sensual 'Fever', which followed the Peggy Lee arrangement rather than Little Willie John's original. Elvis started by saying, 'I can't get my bearings right but we've got plenty of tape.'

Elvis did two blues songs, 'Like a Baby' (written by Jesse Stone) and Lowell Fulson's 'Reconsider Baby'. There was a fierce rocker by Leiber and Stoller, 'Dirty Dirty Feeling' but it was emotionless, just going through the motions. Going back to the Sun writers, there was Stan Kesler's gospel-slanted 'Thrill of Your Love' (with Ray Walker on bass), somewhat similar to 'Peace in the Valley'. The one song that sounded like a novelty was 'The Girl Next Door Went A' Walkin'', co-written by Thomas Wayne, a Nashville performer who had his own hit with 'Tragedy' in 1959: he was the brother of Luther Perkins from Johnny Cash's band. The song had been pitched by Scotty Moore, who was working for Fernwood Studios.

'The Girl of My Best Friend' came from two Brill Building writers Beverly Ross and Sam Bobrick, although the UK writer Bunny Lewis claimed, I think without substance, that he had written it. It was put onto *Elvis is Back!* but an 18-year-old Presley soundalike, Ral Donner, covered it and took it into the US Top 20. Ral then had a million-seller with 'You Don't Know What You Got' and he made numerous records in which he sounded like Elvis. He was the best of the soundalikes and he did a narration as Elvis Presley for the film, *This is Elvis* (1981).

That in itself showed it was a remarkable session but that wasn't all. It also embraced 'It's Now or Never', 'Are You Lonesome Tonight' and a light rocker, 'I Gotta Know'. What is intriguing is the versatility of it – Elvis showed that he was at his best when given a variety of styles and moods. The outtakes show that doing so many songs didn't faze him and he was in good humour throughout.

Elvis Is Back! was a big-selling album, but it couldn't dislodge the Kingston Trio from the top with *Sold Out*.

The title *Elvis Is Back!* was about right. He was making up for lost time with his Memphis girlfriends. Anita Wood realised that marrying Elvis was out of the question, although he gave her a diamond necklace. She recorded the plaintive singles, 'I'll Wait Forever' (on Sun, released after he had left the army) and 'Memories of You'. She spent a lot of time at Graceland and although she knew Elvis had other girlfriends, she was baffled at the love letters from 15-year-old Priscilla. 'She's just a girl,' said Elvis, dismissing the whole thing.

In 1931 the director Norman Taurog won an Oscar for *Skippy*, based on a comic strip and starring his nephew Jackie Cooper, aged eight. To ensure that Jackie would cry on camera, he told him that he was about to kill his dog. The young boy finished the picture and although he continued to work for him, he harboured a grudge and never wanted to see him socially.

Taurog didn't repeat his Oscar success but he made commercial films with Mickey Rooney and Judy Garland, Mario Lanza, and Dean Martin and Jerry Lewis. He was a safe pair of hands and, now in his sixties, he was hired to make a service comedy, *G.I.Blues*, with Elvis Presley. During the 1960s he made eight more films with Elvis and when he wasn't working with Elvis, there was always Pat Boone and Frankie Avalon. You get the picture? This man was the leader of the bland.

G.I. Blues was a light-hearted, fictitious account of Elvis's army life. It made out that Elvis, or Tulsa McLean as he was called, did little army work and spent most of his time partying. The truth was somewhat different. Elvis spent nearly all his time partying. I love the credits – 'Technical Advisor, Col. Tom Parker: Military Technical Advisor, Capt. David S. Parkhurst'. Why was Capt. Parkhurst needed? Couldn't Elvis (or Parker) have told them what was wrong? The answer is the endorsement that this film was made 'with the full cooperation of the US Army'.

Around the same time, Ricky Nelson was starring in another demoralising picture, *The Wackiest Ship in the Army*, but at least that had Jack Lemmon in the main role.

Rock'n'roll came to Broadway with *Bye Bye Birdie*, a musical about how an egotistical rock'n'roll sensation, Conrad Birdie (Dick Gautier) is drafted, much to the annoyance of his agent (Dick Van Dyke) who cannot afford to marry his girlfriend (Chita Rivera). Dick plans to write a major hit for Birdie ('One Last Kiss') so that he can live off the royalties, but the big songs from the show are 'A Lot of Livin' to Do' and 'Put on a Happy Face'.

This 1960 musical was the first Broadway production to acknowledge that rock'n'roll even existed, although naturally the parents win the day. The West End production starring Marty Wilde did reasonable business, but was too American for many theatregoers.

When it was filmed in 1963, there were negotiations with Colonel Parker as the producers wanted Elvis to perform a couple of songs. Parker said the cost would be $100,000. The producers tried to talk him down. 'Tell you what,' said Parker, 'We'll flip a coin. If I lose, Elvis will do it for free and if I win, you will pay $200,000.' The producers walked away.

The film was made with Dick Van Dyke and Janet Leigh, with Jesse Pearson playing Elvis for laughs via the narcissistic Conrad Birdie. He had one reasonable ballad, 'One Last Kiss' and Ann-Margret and Bobby Rydell didn't fare much better. Ed Sullivan's role was ominous as by the time the film was released, the Beatles' appearance on *The Ed Sullivan Show* was only weeks away which truly said bye-bye to Birdie. Not to worry as Charles Strauss went on to write *Annie*.

G.I. Blues starts with Elvis showing us what he did in the tank regiment. He plays a happy-go-lucky soldier, who is transferred to Frankfurt. He is bet $300 that he can't stay the night with the iceberg dancer at Club Europa, played by Juliet Prowse. His army buddies spy on him as they go from club to club and it's embarrassing to watch today. Personally, I would have told the dancer that there would be $150 for both of us if she let me through the door.

Juliet Prowse was a leggy singer and dancer who had been in *Can-Can*. She denied an affair with Elvis, but you would, wouldn't you, if Frank Sinatra was your fiancé? Almost certainly, this only encouraged Elvis. He enjoyed Prowse's company as she had a supple body and favoured athletic sex, so we're back to that contortionist.

What was happening off-screen was more exciting than what was filmed. This was the first Elvis film where the script, the score, the location and the direction were cynical and done to order. Elvis didn't film a single frame in Germany: there were location shots and Elvis was on the Paramount lot.

Ray Walker of the Jordanaires, who all perform 'Frankfurt Special' in a train carriage with Elvis: 'We saw the whole of Germany without leaving the studio. We were

Elvis Presley: Caught in a Trap

in a three-sided Pullman car. They had a rear projection screen behind the windows and two guys had a 20-foot pole on a rack and were shaking it to make it look as though the train was moving. Things are more sophisticated today.'

The fall in standards in Presley's films started here and not with *Blue Hawaii*, which was also directed by Taurog. The title song, built around an army march, is so mundane and demoralising as it implies everything the soldiers do is pointless: 'We'd like to be heroes but all that we do here is march.'

The score is poor, although the songs come from experienced writers – Sid Tepper and Roy Bennett, Aaron Schroeder, Fred Wise and Ben Weisman, and even Sherman Edwards, who wrote 'Broken-Hearted Melody' for Sarah Vaughan in 1959. Couldn't he have given Elvis something as good as that? Certainly he could have done better than the lullaby, 'Big Boots', but I suppose it works – it sends you to sleep. His 'Didja Ever', another kids' song, is tedious, revived once by Michael Barrymore and a children's chorus for a Royal Variety Performance.

You get the impression that Freddie Bienstock assembled the writers one morning and said, 'Okay, here's the plot. Write the songs and we'll meet for lunch. This thing's set in Germany so take some operatic thing and add new words, making sure it's out of copyright.'

Sid Wayne and Abnie Silver took 'Barcarolle' from Offenbach's *The Tales of Hoffman*, but they slipped up. It was still in copyright in Europe. Not to worry – they took their lyric, 'Tonight Is So Right for Love' and changed it to 'Tonight's All Right for Love' with a new melody, this time taken from Strauss' *Tales from the Vienna Woods*. Elvis sort of filmed a new version but it looks like a paste-and-scissors job to me.

Songwriter Mort Shuman: 'There were about 25 writers under contract to Elvis' publishing companies which went through Hill and Range. He had Elvis Presley Music for BMI and Gladys Music, which was his mother's name, for ASCAP. The minute Elvis had a film, all these writers were put on call and started working like crazy. About a block and a half away from the Brill Building, there was Associated Recording where they made Tin Pan Alley demos. It was operating 24 hours a day and people were sending demos to artists all over America. There were usually three or four studio musicians around and if a writer could sing passably, as was my case, then he could do the vocals. Otherwise, you might use a session singer, perhaps a has-been R&B performer or someone up-and-coming. Loads of demos would be made for Elvis and then Freddy Bienstock would sort through them and take them to Elvis.'

The film had a 'Wooden Heart' as well as a wooden head, but that song was a No.1. Elvis' version, partly sung in German, topped the UK charts for six weeks. It was not issued as a single in the US and Joe Dowell took his cover version to the top.

'Wooden Heart' was based on 'Muss I Denn Zum Staedtele Hinaus? (Do I Really Have To Miss This Little Town?)' and after the German bandleader Bert Kaempfert considered it right for *G.I.Blues*, it was given an English lyric by three American writers. Admittedly, Elvis performs the song delightfully at a puppet show with tuba and accordion accompaniment. It demonstrates that he would have been the perfect guest for *The Muppet Show*.

Bert Kaempfert is the only person who worked with the three greats of popular music – he produced the first records by the Beatles ('My Bonnie'), he adapted a German folk song for Elvis Presley and wrote 'Strangers in the Night' for Frank Sinatra.

For a jukebox scene, Elvis recorded a new version of 'Blue Suede Shoes', this time more akin to Carl Perkins' arrangement, but it only leads to a fight, effectively over the old Elvis versus the new one. The actor who fights Elvis is Ken Becker who also fought him in *Loving You*.

His new rock song, 'Shoppin' Around', written by Tepper and Bennett, never caught fire. Before recording a take, Presley said, 'I'm gonna play rhythm on this son of a bitch.' Perhaps the best moment in the film is when Elvis sings 'What's She Really Like' without accompaniment, in the shower. He also sings 'Pocketful of Rainbows' to Juliet Prowse in a chair lift. He had trouble recording this track as, at the time, it was a rare excursion into falsetto.

The best song from *G.I. Blues* is the much neglected 'Doin' the Best I Can', a poignant Pomus and Shuman ballad that could have been a single for Presley and revived by any number of singers. It is the most overlooked song in the Presley catalogue. Mort Shuman: 'Doc and I were much into Don Robertson who was a great country writer. His output was not very large but most of his songs were spot-on, great classics like 'I Really Don't Want to Know'. We were in that mood when we wrote 'Doin' the Best I Can' and I love Elvis' recording. I feel that he was very much influenced by the Ink Spots when he did it. He is sounding like their lead singer.'

The reviews for *G.I. Blues* were reasonable and the film was a full-out international success. *The New York Times* commented, 'Gone is the wiggle, the lecherous leer, the swagger, the unruly hair, the droopy eyelids and the hillbilly manner of speech.' And that was praise, not criticism.

The Guardian said, 'He is still apt to dredge his low notes from the bottom of the barrel. But so did the artist he is faintly beginning to represent – the young Bing.' Really?

Monthly Film Bulletin said that 'Juliet Prowse deserves a better role and a more mature leading man; certainly one with more genuine fire than Elvis Presley.'

If Elvis had been cruising while he made *G.I. Blues*, he was still serious about his musical career.

The Italian aria, 'O Sole Mio', which means 'My Sunshine' was written in 1898 and was famously recorded by Enrico Caruso in 1916. In 1949, Tony Martin recorded an English version with the title, 'There's No Tomorrow'. Elvis Presley was very fond of 'O Sole Mio', but when his publishers, Hill and Range, couldn't reach a deal over 'There's No Tomorrow', they asked four Brill Building writing teams for new lyrics. The best was by Aaron Schroeder and Wally Gold and Elvis brought Mario Lanza's version of 'O Sole Mio' to the session so he knew what he had to match. For the record, Presley hits a G sharp at the end as opposed to Lanza's high B.

Ray Walker of the Jordanaires: "It's Now Or Never' was Elvis' favourite secular song and he wanted to hit those notes like Caruso or Lanza. He was proud of that.' Neal Matthews adds, "Surrender' was real good too as they showed off the range and the power of his voice. They were different arrangements for us too.'

'It's Now or Never' was a US No.1 for five weeks, but a difference in the copyright laws between the US and UK meant that its release was delayed while a resolution was reached. The US B-side, the glorious 'A Mess of Blues' became a UK A-side, reaching No.2 and was coupled with 'The Girl of My Best Friend'.

Copyright resolved, this was followed by 'It's Now or Never', which was No.1 for eight weeks and became Elvis' biggest-selling UK single. It, more than anything, marked

Elvis' change from rock'n'roll singer to adult entertainer. The UK B-side was 'Make Me Know It'.

It was now or never for Vernon Presley and Dee Stanley too as they married in Huntsville, Alabama. Elvis was nowhere to be seen but they returned to Graceland. David Stanley: 'I was four years old when Elvis became my stepbrother. Gladys had only been gone for a year and a half. It would be hard for anyone to accept that. But in my mother's defence, she never tried to be Elvis' mother, she never said I am the Queen of Graceland. Actually, my mother and Elvis had a good friendship and laughed a lot. Elvis was kind to Billy, Ricky and myself because he knew that we didn't have a choice, and my mother was very fond of Elvis.' However, Elvis wasn't to approve of Dee's plans to redecorate Graceland and she and Vernon were soon to move out but live nearby.

Of his own relationship with Elvis, David Stanley said, 'Elvis picked me up, a four-year-old kid, and welcomed me into his family. We had holidays together and I spent summers on the backlots of movies. He taught me how to play drums and how to play football. I did get a lot of attention going to school in a pink Cadillac. I would get Elvis to sign 20 pieces of paper and I would sell them at school.'

Elvis' new love was water-skiing and he had a new boat called Karate. His agility on water-skis was incorporated into the script for *Clambake* (1967).

Sam Cooke had been signed to RCA from the Keen label and like Elvis, his singles are wonderfully varied. In September 1960 he climbed to No.2 with 'Chain Gang', his 'Jailhouse Rock' as it were.

The follow-up to 'It's Now or Never' in both countries was 'Are You Lonesome Tonight'. It was written in 1926 by two Tin Pan Alley songwriters, who included a narration based on Jacques' speech from *As You Like It*. Several artists recorded it, notably Henry Burr, Vaughn Deleath (a female despite the name) and Al Jolson. In 1950, the song was revived by the bandleader Blue Barron with his vocalist Bobby Beers but a disc jockey, John McCormick, performed the narration.

Outside of publishing deals, 'Are You Lonesome Tonight?' is the only song which Colonel Parker asked Elvis Presley to record, a request emanating from Parker's wife. Elvis copied Jolson note for note and almost word for word. He recorded it late at night during a marathon session and put the lights out in order to increase his emotional feelings. Chet Atkins found Elvis' working hours interfered with his day job at RCA and so he stopped producing him after this.

Despite being a transatlantic number one in 1960 (6 weeks US, 4 weeks UK), 'Are You Lonesome Tonight?' was one of Elvis's most controversial recordings as rock'n'roll fans felt he was selling out. This was nonsense as the B-side of 'All Shook Up', for example, was another lost love song with a narration, 'That's When Your Heartaches Begin'.

Dodie Stevens recorded an answer version, 'Yes, I'm Lonesome Tonight', but the best adjustments to the lyric came from Elvis himself who sang such variations as 'Do you gaze at your bald head and wish you had hair?' in concert.

Elvis's laughing version, caught in concert in 1969, is taken by some as evidence that he was perpetually high and by others that he had a wonderful sense of humour. Elvis had simply forgotten the words, but the song title summarised Elvis's later life and became the title of a West End play by Alan Bleasdale featuring Martin Shaw as the broken King.

The B-side was written by Paul Evans, 'I Gotta Know', featuring close harmony vocals with Elvis in the middle. Paul Evans: 'To get a song to Elvis, you either had to be in New York City or Nashville. Here in New York, you would have to go to Hill and Range, a big company which controlled the music that Elvis would record. I knew the people and I played 'I Gotta Know' for them. I was very excited when I heard that Elvis had cut the song and I was dying for it to come out, then I got a call to go over and see them. Even though Elvis had cut the song, they didn't know if he would release it, and so they wanted to cut it with this new kid, Fabian. I got angry and said, 'Absolutely not' as I didn't want anything in the way of Elvis. I was surprised that they had asked my permission as normally, publishers would just do it. It worked out okay as the Presley record did very well for me.'

Paul had done his demo specifically for Elvis. 'When you do demos for specific artists, you want to sound like the artist. I did try and get that kind of mumbling, closed mouth sound that Elvis had. I learnt a lot that way. Someone gave me a song for Perry Como so I had to croon the song. You didn't know what you were going to be asked to do when you were called to do a demo.'

In the summer of 1960, Elvis Presley starred in a new western, *Flaming Star*. It was to be *Black Star* and Elvis recorded the same song but with amended lyrics as 'Flaming Star'. As the lead song on an EP, 'Flaming Star' made the US Top 20. The title was an American Indian concept that once you saw the black star or the flaming star, your number was up: a bit like getting the black spot in *Treasure Island*. The concept also appealed to David Bowie, hence the title of his final record, 'Black Star' (2016).

Two songs were dropped from the film, a cheerful song about a girl in trousers, 'Britches' and a sweet-voiced ballad, 'Summer Kisses, Winter Tears', but included on the *Flaming Star* EP. If 'Summer Kisses, Winter Tears' sounds familiar, just start singing Tommy Roe's 1963 hit, 'The Folk Singer'.

'Flaming Star' would be the title song and the only other song in the final version would be the hoe-down 'A Cane and a High-Starched Collar', which is placed in the first five minutes to get it out of the way, as it were. After that, Elvis doesn't sing a note – he's too busy killing people: indeed, he kills as many people as a Clint Eastwood character. Nevertheless, my DVD copy says 'contains mild violence'.

The film was directed by Don Siegel, who made several films with Eastwood, so possibly he was warming up. The scene where Elvis and his brother ride into town and encounter the hostile townsfolk is similar to later encounters in Italian westerns. Siegel's previous film had been *Hound-Dog Man*, a coming of age film for Fabian.

Flaming Star is a western about a half-breed torn between family loyalties. It was based on a book *Flaming Lance* (1958) by Clair Huffaker, a male writer who dressed all day everyday as a cowboy, which was unusual even by Hollywood standards. At first the script was written by Nunnally Johnson (*The Grapes of Wrath*) for Marlon Brando. Brando turned it down and the producer, David Weisbart, thought it would suit Presley. He asked Siegel to rework the script with Huffaker.

Elvis refused to wear brown contact lenses so he remained a blue-eyed half-breed. He played the son of John McIntire and Dolores Del Rio, who was Mexican. The chief Indian was played by Rodolfo Acosta, another Mexican, so ethnically this film is confusing. Elvis was called Pacer which sounds like a name from *Watership Down*.

A British actress, Barbara Steele, was going to play Elvis' girlfriend but she was

Elvis Presley: Caught in a Trap

miscast and, more to the point, towered over him. She was replaced after a couple of weeks by Barbara Eden. Eden dressed far too smartly for the film, but at least she was smaller than Elvis.

Siegel practised karate with Elvis and knew he would have no problems in fight scenes. He was however unsure about a dramatic scene where Elvis had to threaten the town's doctor. He told Don Siegel that he could have the use of his Rolls-Royce until he felt prepared. A week or later, Elvis said, 'I'm ready for that scene.'

Elvis convinced no one that he was half-Indian and the film was tiresome, mostly consisting of horsemen passing on messages to each other. Elvis played an unlikeable character: he fought dirty and it was inevitable that he was going to meet his own flaming star. The film impressed Andy Warhol and became the image for one of his most-famous Pop Art silkscreens, *Double Elvis* (1963).

The film was banned in South Africa because Elvis had an American-Indian mother in the film. The film raised valid issues about race relations but not well. The Indians were said to be savages but clearly they had a more developed sense of belonging.

Don Siegel said in 1968, 'Presley is a very fine actor, but he's given very little chance of being a fine actor. It's not a question of talent. He's in absolutely banal, stupid pictures.' This wasn't one of them but it's not too far above them.

Johnny Bragg was allowed out of prison to perform with his new group, the Marigolds at a civic event in Memphis honouring Elvis Presley. The warden, no doubt thinking it funny, had them perform an a cappella 'Jailhouse Rock'. Elvis loved it and wanted to record with them but Colonel Parker did not consider it a good career move.

While Bragg was released, he was soon back doing time again for allegedly attacking a white female over $3. He was given 10 years and his record company, Decca, dropped him for not delivering further singles. Elvis visited him and offered help, but Bragg shrugged his shoulders and said he would form another prison band. When one of The Prisonaires returned for a burglary sentence, he was delighted as he could work with him again.

Johnny Cash had left Sun Records: he felt that Sam Phillips had not given him enough attention and would not let him record a gospel album. He moved to Columbia, who let him record *Hymns by Johnny Cash*. It wasn't a big seller but he had done what he wanted. Elvis felt the same way. He had made the *Peace in the Valley* EP and now he wanted to make a gospel LP.

In a way, his most unexpected accomplishment in 1960 went unnoticed. He released a gospel album, *His Hand in Mine*, and it made the US Top 20 albums, eventually selling over a million copies.

Elvis said in an interview, 'I know practically every religious song that's ever been written.' As if to bear that out, the whole album was made over two days with his usual musicians, the majority of the songs being recorded in five takes or less. The most problematic was 'He Knows Just What I Need' with 10, so this was fast work for Elvis, presumably because he knew the songs well. At many times, he sounds like a fifth member of the Jordanaires who had released their own gospel album, *Heavenly Spirit*, in 1958. Some songs were familiar to British ears ('Joshua Fit the Battle of Jericho' and 'Swing Down Sweet Chariot') but most had not travelled to the UK.

Elvis sang both black and white gospel songs. 'Milky White Way' was a hit record by the black gospel group the Trumpeters from Baltimore in 1947. The Blackwood

Brothers were known for 'Mansion Over the Hilltop' and 'In My Father's House', here recorded with a tremendously deep vocal from Ray Walker – how Elvis loved such voices.

Stuart Hamblen's ballad, 'Known Only to Him', was associated with George Beverly Shea, who sang at Billy Graham's crusades. Elvis' vocal is magnificent and the arrangement follows the recording by the Statesmen Quartet. This is one of Elvis Presley's best records and if RCA had wanted a religious follow-up for the surprise hit, 'Crying in the Chapel' in 1965, they could have gone with this.

Elvis took 'I Believe in the Man in the Sky' from the Statesmen's repertoire, and their arranger and bass singer, Mosie Lister, wrote 'His Hand in Mine'. Elvis once played Johnny Rivers their original version of 'I Believe in the Man in the Sky' and said, 'Now you know where I got my style.'

'Crying in the Chapel' was not used on the album – perhaps it was out of keeping with the rest of the songs It had been written in 1953 by Artie Glenn from Knoxville and it was recorded by his son, Darrell. That record did well and it was covered by Rex Allen (country), June Valli (pop) and the Orioles (R&B).

In the midst of the gospel songs, Elvis recorded a new single, 'Surrender', which would be released in 1961. Doc Pomus: "Surrender' was an assignment from Elvis Presley. It was the only time that he gave us an exact assignment. Following 'It's Now Or Never', which was based on 'O Sole Mio', he wanted something based on 'Come Back To Sorrento'. I thought 'Sorrento' sounded like 'Surrender' so it worked out very well.'

Mort Shuman: 'My greatest kick was in writing the songs and making the demos and I didn't care what happened to them after that. There is a point in my demo for 'Surrender' where it breaks and we change key with me singing, 'Won't you please surrender to me?' Elvis did that exactly the way that I did it, which made me feel good. It was nice to feel that he was really listening to what we were doing.'

Ray Walker of the Jordanaires: 'Elvis didn't think he could make that final note on 'tonight'. I told him to pretend to vomit and to put an 'h' in front of 'tonight' – and it worked!'

The success of the album, *His Hand in Mine* took Colonel Parker by surprise. Elvis was more bound for Hollywood than bound for glory, but he was back in the big-time, making successful films and having hit singles.

Had the army hurt his career? Emphatically not.

Had the army changed his career? Emphatically yes.

But this was the nature of the man himself – Elvis had a wide breadth of interests. He didn't just want to record rock'n'roll. He wanted to work in country, pop, R&B and gospel – he had a fondness for Italian arias. By the end of 1960, he must have felt that he could do anything and go anywhere – New York, Nashville, Nazareth and Naples: he had so much to offer.

Elvis was thinking more and more about Priscilla. He wanted her in Graceland and he rang Captain Beaulieu to see if it were possible. He asked Vernon and Dee to contact the captain to say that they would let her stay at their nearby Hermitage apartment.

Priscilla came to Memphis for the Christmas holidays and Elvis collected her from the airport and showed her around Graceland. Her two-week stay was extended to a month and then in January she returned to school in Germany.

Elvis Presley: Caught in a Trap

Elvis could not afford to be complacent, but he was. Unknown to Elvis, as he left Germany, the Beatles came. On 17 August 1960 they played their first show in Hamburg. The new setting transformed their music and popular music would never be the same again. They were to sing a number of Elvis' songs – Paul sang 'Wooden Heart' in Germany and in German, Stuart Sutcliffe 'Love Me Tender', and Pete Best 'Wild in the Country'. Their roadie, Mal Evans, always had a copy of *Elvis Monthly* in his pocket.

Elvis had worked hard to get back on top. As we shall see, by 1964, with mediocre films and records, he was no match for the Beatles. Shagged out would be the best way to describe it, I suppose.

CHAPTER 9

I Stumbled…

'Elvis was his own, he couldn't share it with anybody and nobody knew what it was like to be Elvis. Extreme fame is extreme loneliness and he didn't have friends like you and I have friends. He had people who worked for him but that isn't the same thing.'
Ray Connolly, author *Being Elvis – A Lonely Life*

I. El's Angels

Humphrey Bogart and Frank Sinatra associated with close friends who wouldn't betray confidences. They were mostly show business personalities themselves and they were not on the payroll. Elvis Presley had a different approach with his Memphis Mafia, a jokey term given to them by the press. There was nothing Italian or indeed duplicitous about them: they were simply good ol' boys like Elvis, who enjoyed a good time and were at his beck and call. If Elvis wanted to play touch football, if Elvis wanted to go the roller rink, if Elvis wanted to spend all night at the movies, if Elvis wanted girls, they would take care of business. No doubt about it, there was an element of pimping about this job. Indeed, the Memphis Mafia did everything but wipe his bottom, and some, as we will discover, did that.

To heighten the camaraderie, Elvis gave them TCB bracelets, but he also gave them to his band and fellow performers such as Tom Jones. I don't want to overdo the JC analogy but Jesus was also a Capricorn and had 12 disciples.

By and large, Elvis felt out of place in Hollywood and so he liked a group of friends from back home around him. They thought and ate as he did. Los Angeles guitarist Barney Kessel told me, 'I found Elvis to be a very nice young man, who knew his manners. He had a problem in relating to people outside of his circle, which is why he kept an entourage from Memphis. I think they all felt strange at being in Hollywood, a very sophisticated town and far removed from their natural settings. Elvis himself had very simple tastes. He would never have gone in a French restaurant and he liked fast, takeaway food. He used to drop peanuts into his Coca-Cola and he ate candy bars.'

When Elvis was in Hollywood, he created his Elvis World in Perugia Way, Bel Air. He lived in a house, hired from the Shah of Iran and designed by Frank Lloyd Wright. It had modern furnishings as he hated antiques and would joke, 'I grew up with antiques.' His home was like a bachelor pad for the Memphis Mafia and casual sex, often with Hollywood hopefuls, was the norm.

Elvis was the first rock star with an entourage. They were yes men and they had to be as they depended on him for a living. The Memphis Mafia was a modern version of King Arthur's court, and neither Colonel Parker nor Vernon Presley had much time for them. They felt that they cost too much and that their hot-headed behaviour could land Elvis in trouble. Although the Colonel didn't care for them, he could see that they helped Elvis to get things out of his system.

They were paid about $250 a week in the 1960s which had increased to $425 by the time of his death: it was reasonable money with free accommodation and *ad hoc* presents of clothes and jewellery. The biggest perk was being with Elvis, which was a drug in itself. These were tough guys, not scared of a fight, carrying weapons and studying martial arts like Elvis. Some had hard, beat-up faces, not the sort of people you would want to meet down a dark Tin Pan Alley. They did carry guns but that was not unusual in Graceland – even Elvis' granny, sweet old Minnie Mae, packed some heat.

The musicians were not part of the Memphis Mafia as they usually had a life outside Elvis.

Who were they and why did Elvis need them? Many of them are listed below – there are more – partly because they came and went or rather were fired and rehired. Until the final months, they were intensely loyal to Elvis but then the secrets of Camelot were revealed in *Elvis: What Happened?* (1977), put together by Steve Dunleavy from conversations with Red West, Sonny West and Dave Hebler. They insisted that the book was not published to destroy Elvis but to help him. What else could they say?

Billy Smith (b. 1943) and **Gene Smith** (b. 1934) were two cousins, but not brothers, who were always close to Elvis. They sometimes slept in the same room as Elvis to prevent his sleepwalking. Gene had worked at the Precision Tool Company with Elvis and became his chauffeur. Gene's accent was mocked by the others as he would say 'cruck' for 'truck' and 'light bub' for 'light bulb', which worked against his wish to be a film actor. He left in 1969 after a pay dispute with Vernon. Billy and his wife Jo lived in a trailer on the grounds at Graceland. Billy had responsibilities for Elvis' wardrobe, ensuring that his lavish costumes were always ready, and he and Jo played racquetball with Elvis on the day he died. Gene Smith said it was not Elvis in that coffin.

George Klein (b. 1935) met Elvis at Humes High School in Memphis and was probably the first person to realise his singing potential. He encouraged him to take part in a local talent show and then, when he became a disc jockey at WHBQ, he was a strong advocate for his Sun singles. He had bit parts in *Frankie and Johnny* and *Double Trouble*. Elvis paid for Klein to have plastic surgery on his nose, one of his more unusual gifts. Elvis was best man at his wedding to Dr. Nichopoulos' secretary, Barbara Little, and he introduced Elvis to the doctor. In 1977, Elvis lobbied President Carter when Klein was arrested for fraud, but Klein was found guilty and served time. Another disc jockey that Elvis befriended, although he never made the Mafia, was Cliff Gleaves (b. 1930). He had lost a testicle in the Korean war and Elvis called him Charlie Copper Cod.

Red West, actually Robert, was born in Memphis in 1936 and met Elvis at Humes High School. Tall and muscular, he had the makings of a gifted golfer and football player and he defended Elvis in a couple of fights. True to his hair colouring, he had a fiery temper but he had also studied the trumpet and could read music. He drove Elvis, Scotty and Bill to some early gigs as well as the Burnette boys and he joined the Marines in 1956. When he met up with Elvis again in 1960, Elvis employed him as a bodyguard. He married Elvis' secretary, Pat West, in 1961. Like his cousin Sonny, he was tough and aggressive and he shielded Elvis from anything unpleasant. He had bit parts in 15 Elvis films – he and Joe Esposito are in Elvis' pit crew in *Spinout* (1966) – and he continued acting after Elvis died, co-starring with Robert Conrad in *Hard Knox* (1984). He was a good songwriter, well up with the Brill Building boys, and his songs for Elvis include 'Separate Ways', 'If You Talk in Your Sleep' and 'If Every Day Was Like Christmas'. He wrote 'A Thousand Years', the B-side of Pat Boone's US No.1, 'Moody River' (1961), which sounds like a rewrite of Elvis' 'I Want to Be Free'. He, Sonny and Dave Hebler were fired by Vernon Presley in 1976, which led to the book.

Sonny West, actually Delbert, was born in Memphis in 1938 and introduced to Elvis by his cousin, Red, at the Rainbow Rollerdrome. He ran the toughest gang in town and Elvis needed someone to drive and to keep the jealous boyfriends away. Elvis was best man and Priscilla maid of honour at his wedding to Judy Morgan in Memphis in 1971. Sonny and Judy lived in the grounds of Graceland and he maintained Elvis' cars, motorcycles and golf carts. Elvis gave him numerous Cadillacs. When Sonny was given a double-layer sponge cake for his birthday, Elvis bolted the lot at one sitting. Sonny was fired after a fight with Vernon in 1976. West has made more disparaging remarks about Elvis than the other employees.

Born and raised in Memphis, **Lamar Fike** (b. 1935) was impressed when he saw Elvis in his flashy clothes at the Sun Studios in 1955. They became friends and by 1957, he was working for Elvis, a founder member of the Memphis Mafia if you like. He was a fine organiser, ensuring that everything happened correctly, and he usually operated Elvis' stage lighting. He tried to enlist with Presley but was turned down because of his weight (20 stone, which was to increase to 25). When Elvis called him Buddha or Lard-ass, the others would join in, ignoring the hurt they were inflicting. Lamar lived with the Presleys in Germany and became a good friend of songwriter, Mort Shuman, although Shuman never met Elvis. He left in 1962 to manage Brenda Lee for a year and then moved to Hill and Range until 1972. Among the songs he found for Elvis were 'Kentucky Rain' and 'It's Midnight'. After Elvis' death, he and his wife moved to Nashviile and worked for other performers. The copyright line in Albert Goldman's *Elvis* is Albert Goldman, Kevin Eggers (who managed Townes Van Zandt) and Lamar Fike.

As a soldier in Germany, **Joe Esposito** (b. 1938) met Elvis and stayed with him until August 1977. He was Italian-American, coming from the mid-west but he fitted in fine. Elvis called him Diamond Joe and at different times he was a tour manager, bodyguard and bookkeeper. His wife, Joan, a former showgirl, was the matron of honour at Elvis and Priscilla's wedding. He had minor roles in *Clambake* and *Stay Away, Joe* and occasionally played guitar with him on stage. He and Dr. Nichopoulos started a racquetball business, Presley Centre Courts, which went bankrupt after being abandoned by Elvis in 1976. Despite suing Elvis, they all remained friends. Joe protected Elvis' reputation, firmly stating that Elvis didn't take drugs. After Elvis' death, he became road manager for the Bee Gees.

Elvis had known **Marty Lacker** (b. 1937) since Humes High School. He joined Elvis in 1960 and became his secretary and bookkeeper. He and Joe Esposito were best men at Elvis' wedding. Elvis gave him cars and jewellery and his wife Patsy blamed Elvis for turning him onto drugs. He was fired in 1967.

Charlie Hodge (b. 1935) first met Elvis on a TV show in 1956. They met up again in the army: they did basic training at Fort Hood and were assigned to Germany. Charlie lived at Graceland and took care of Elvis' personal business. They often played and sang together and they can be heard on 'I Will Be Home Again'. In 1962 Elvis had the crazy idea of recording 'Begin the Beguine' with a new lyric: Red West submitted 'You'll Be Gone' and when Cole Porter said no, Charlie wrote a new melody. It was Charlie Hodge who suggested James Burton for his stage band. Charlie played rhythm guitar with the TCB band and he would hand Elvis the scarves which he gave to the audience. Being five foot three, he was the butt of many jokes and in his autobiography, he revealed that Elvis wore lifts in his shoes. Charlie is in both *Clambake* and *Charro!*

Larry Geller (b. 1940) had a hair salon in Beverly Hills and was hired by Elvis after giving him a good hair cut in 1964. Elvis was bored with making *Roustabout* and Geller gave him several spiritual books. Elvis called him Guru because of his fascination with religion and the occult. They talked about the mystical world and Elvis was keen to contact his twin, Jessie. Colonel Parker disliked his influence on Elvis and tried to ensure there was somebody else around when they met. He was a quiet, confident man and he even suggested that Elvis should enter a monastery.

Alan Fortas (b. 1937) was a fine football player who was a bodyguard and assistant from 1958 to 1969. He managed Elvis' Circle G Ranch. Occasionally he played tambourine on stage and can be seen in the 1968 TV special.

A trained fighter pilot, **Dick Grob** (b. 1939) was in the Palm Springs police department when he met Elvis, who called him Grob the Fox. In 1969 he became the head of security, both at Graceland and on the road. Grob believed that Elvis was dying of bone cancer at the time of his heart attack.

In the 1970s, Dee Presley's sons worked for Elvis, mostly as personal assistants. Elvis called **Billy Stanley** (b. 1953) 'Charlie Manson' because of his sinister look. Billy claimed that Elvis had an affair with his wife. **Rick Stanley** (b. 1953) was arrested in 1975 for forging a prescription and he was fired after insulting Linda Thompson. He became a church minister. David Stanley (b. 1956) started working for Elvis in 1972 when only 17 and he was on duty as a bodyguard at Graceland the day that Elvis died. He maintained that Elvis was taking cocaine at the time of his death and he too became a minister.

Sam Thompson, the brother of Linda Thompson, was a former police officer, hired as a bodyguard. He got on well with Colonel Parker, which was unusual, and he became a judge.

Dave Hebler (b. 1937) was a karate champion from Pittsfield, Massachusetts. He ran a martial arts studio in Glendora, California and met Elvis in 1972. Elvis gave him a Mercedes-Benz but Vernon fired him in 1976.

A cousin of the singer Don Ho, **Ed Parker** was born in Hawaii in 1931 and became a karate instructor. After a recommendation, Elvis went to his studio in Santa Monica and studied in earnest. Ed suggested many of his stage moves. In 1973 Ed used Presley's name for a karate championship and when Elvis saw the sign, he returned home.

The King's schilling, **Jerry Schilling** (b. 1943) studied martial arts with Elvis and Elvis called him Cougar. He was his personal aide until 1976. He became a film editor at Paramount and then went into personal management, handling the Sweet Inspirations and marrying one of them. In the 2016 film, *Elvis / Nixon*, the actor playing Schilling was better looking than the one playing Elvis: he was good-looking but not that much.

Plus an honorary membership to Elvis' chimpanzee, Scatter, and maybe also Little Elvis. Elvis' favourite chat-up line was to ask a girl if she would like to see Little Elvis, which must have been like dating a ventriloquist and his doll.

Returning to sanity, a mention for two people who were not part of the Memphis Mafia but are an integral part of the story:

In 1967 one of the ladies who worked for Dr. George Nichopoulos, Dr. Nick (b. 1927) asked him to visit Elvis. He had saddle sores from too much riding and he was about to make a film. Dr. Nick gave him a doctor's note for a couple of days. Nothing wrong with that but soon Dr. Nick was giving Elvis his prescription drugs and he wrote out a prescription for eight different drugs on the day that Elvis died. He was involved with other performers, notably Jerry Lee Lewis. He was arrested in 1980 but he was acquitted of malpractice. An incensed fan tried to shoot him at a football game.

Mary Jenkins was the cook at Graceland from 1963 and is one of the few black people in this story. She would fix Elvis his meals, the normal being homemade vegetable soup, two pounds of burnt bacon, mashed potatoes and sauerkraut, plus snacks of peanut butter and mashed banana sandwiches. Elvis gave her a home and seven different cars. After his death, she wrote a book, *Elvis, The Way I Knew Him*. A delightful lady, her appearance on a TV documentary about Elvis was most touching: she described how she smuggled his favourite foods into a Memphis hospital, oblivious to the possibility that she may have hastened his death.

II. Got a Lot o' Livin' to Do, 1961–1963

Buoyed by the success of 'It's Now or Never', Elvis Presley wanted more of the same. This time it would be the Italian ballad, 'Torna a Sorrento', which was written in 1911, and had been sung by Caruso. In 1947, it was given an English lyric, 'Come Back to Sorrento', which has been recorded by many artists including Gracie Fields, Josef Locke and Dean Martin.

Mort Shuman told his songwriting partner, Doc Pomus, 'Why should I want to write for some redneck idiot who has so forgotten his roots that he thinks it's a good career move to sound like Mario Lanza? You write it, Doc, you've already got the music.'

And the title too, as Doc immediately saw that 'Sorrento' could become 'Surrender'. Mort Shuman: "Surrender' was never anything I felt great about and I was too young at the time to realise that it was a crass commercial operation. I just knew it wasn't what Doc and I could do best; which was to write original songs.'

Mort's right: Elvis Presley was the man who wanted to be Mario Lanza. They were both on RCA, they both ate to excess, they both recorded operatic arias, they both took drugs excessively and they both died at an early age. They were the Super Mario Brothers.

Elvis's record is less than two minutes long, but he does hit a high B flat, far higher than anything he'd done before. Mort Shuman: 'You're putting me on. Is it less than two minutes? That doesn't matter though. One of my all-time favourite records, 'The Letter' by the Box Tops, is unbelievably short. That was the beauty of singles. It was pure concentration, pure quintessence and you had to get everything into as short a period as possible. Everything had to be done bang, quick. When pop songs started stretching out, they lost their immediacy.'

The result wasn't as enduring as 'It's Now or Never', but it was still a transatlantic No.1. In 2001 Yorkshire's TV diva, Lesley Garrett, put Doc's words into an operatic setting and they sounded fine. The B-side, an appealing, plaintive ballad, 'Lonely Man',

Elvis Presley: Caught in a Trap

came from Elvis' next film, *Wild in the Country*.

Much has been made in the press and even by Frank Ifield himself of him being the first artist to have three No.1s in the UK. When I heard Frank say this a few years ago at the Epstein Theatre in Liverpool, I wanted to shout out 'What about Elvis?' Elvis had three consecutive No.1 records with 'It's Now or Never', 'Are You Lonesome Tonight' and 'Wooden Heart' and even followed it with a fourth, 'Surrender'. Then again, when Frank claimed to be the first artist to sell a million copies in the UK, I could have shouted 'Elvis Presley'.

Elvis Presley's films may be criticised for lacking intellectual clout, but the screenplay for *Wild in the Country* was written by Clifford Odets. He had been a leading dramatist during the Depression and his plays included *Waiting for Lefty* about a New York cab strike and *Awake and Sing*, a study of a Jewish family. *Golden Boy* (1937) became a stage musical for Sammy Davis Jr, the world's most unlikely boxer. Odets was brought into *Wild in the Country* to advance Elvis' career as a serious actor. It is in the same heavy dramatic mould as the Tennessee Williams plays of the period – lots of arguing, lots of drinking, no one happy and endless discussions.

At the time the film was unusual as there had been few scenes between a psychiatrist and her patient before this but now, compared to such a brilliant radio series as *In the Psychiatrist's Chair*, it seems flimsy. Furthermore, the highbrow claims are to no avail as Elvis acts so badly, just saying the words and putting little feeling into them. He was acting much better in *King Creole*. While making the film, the heartthrob was suffering from haemorrhoids and, arguably, they led to his poor performance. Will we ever get to the bottom of it?

Well, maybe. Hope Lange went to visit him while he was off ill and with a swift tug, she pulled away his bedsheets. 'Whoa there!' said an embarrassed Elvis. Don't know what Little Elvis thought.

The poster implied the worst, 'Lonely man...loving man...singing man', and the film was, at least, better than this. A disturbed youth gets entangled with three women: a decent girl (Millie Perkins), a psychiatrist (Hope Lange) and a wild one (Tuesday Weld). Hope Lange almost kills herself over him and an alternative ending was shot in which she died. The dialogue includes Tuesday Weld saying, 'I need a man to go to hell with.' Elvis responds, 'Paint your toenails red and run away.' Clifford Odets? I don't believe it.

Still, the film does have its fans. Doc Pomus: 'I thought some of Elvis' films were marvellous. I loved *Viva Las Vegas*, and *Wild In The Country* was very interesting. Okay, a lot of them weren't up to par but that's how it is with people who are singer / actors rather than actor / singers as the motion picture becomes a vehicle for the singing.'

This time there's not much music but it's good to have 'I Slipped, I Stumbled, I Fell' and 'In My Way', revived by Davy Kaye in 1965 and produced by Joe Meek, as well as the folky title song, only given B-side status in the US, although it was as strong as 'Love Me Tender'. Another song, 'Forget Me Never', was recorded but not used.

'Wild in the Country' was the A-side in the UK and made No.4 (a flop after four consecutive No.1s) but the B-side, 'I Feel So Bad', was a sensational bluesy performance that made No.5 in the US. Praise too for Boots Randolph's forceful sax and Floyd Cramer's edgy piano. The song had been written and recorded by Chuck Willis in 1954. Maybe 'I Feel So Bad' wasn't right for the UK market as nobody knew what a raincheck or a grip was. It may have seemed alien to UK record-buyers but it sounded great.

'I Feel So Bad' had originally been recorded for the next album, ominously titled *Something for Everybody*. Twelve songs were recorded quickly in March and 'I Feel So Bad' was put onto a single in place of 'I Slipped, I Stumbled, I Fell' which was more a novelty than a potential single.

The Governor of Tennessee declared 25 February 1961 would be Elvis Presley Day. The citation declared him to be a true man of the south and a cultural resource. On 8 March the Tennessee Volunteers made Elvis an honorary Colonel, so we now had Colonel Presley and Colonel Parker. About as bogus as Colonel Bogey, I should think.

Over at RCA, Elvis wrote his own rules. Chet Atkins: 'Mr. Sholes was aware of many of the old ballads with recitations, but Elvis had the idea of doing 'Are You Lonesome Tonight'. We recorded it at two in the morning with the lights down low to get a good mood. It was very exciting when we cut it as we all knew it was a smash, but I checked out around that time. Elvis would want to go from midnight to seven. I had to work during the day and I couldn't afford to stay up all night.' It is also reported that Atkins fell asleep at the session and Elvis was not amused.

Paul Evans: 'I was in the office of Fred Fisher Music when Elvis' people called to demand a cut-in on the copyright for 'Are You Lonesome Tonight' The publisher laughed it off but he did wind up giving him a piece of the mechanical royalties.' (That is some royalties on the physical product sold, but not on broadcasting.)

Chet Atkins was no longer there but his fingerprints are all over the album. He was fond of crossover LPs, a mixture of pop and country, known as 'countrypolitan'. Atkins did it with Jim Reeves and Eddy Arnold. Although the new Elvis album was called *Something for Everybody*, this was mostly country MOR and aimed at females who liked romantic songs. 'I Feel So Bad' wouldn't have worked on this LP. On the other hand, Don Robertson's songs were ideal. 'There's Always Me' could have been a hit single, but an outtake shows that Elvis didn't take it seriously. Instead of 'When the evening shadows fall, And you're wondering who to call', Elvis sings, 'When the evening shadows fall, And you're wondering who to ball…'

But calling an Elvis album *Something for Everybody* showed the way things were going. He was no longer a threat. Elvis had been emasculated and was becoming a family entertainer. How much Elvis was cognizant of this is open to debate.

At Sun Records, Carl Mann had rocked up Nat 'King' Cole's 'Mona Lisa' and his arrangement had been copied by Conway Twitty, whose single had gone gold. Carl Mann had recorded a new Charlie Rich song. 'I'm Comin' Home' and given it a similar arrangement, which was now copied by Elvis. It worked fine but why was Elvis, the great originator, working for Xerox?

Charlie Rich: 'I first met Elvis Presley one night-time when he was taking some underprivileged children out. I got to know him after that but we weren't buddies and I didn't run around with him. I didn't have the contacts to get a song to him but he heard a record of mine, 'I'm Comin' Home', that he liked. He wanted to record it and as Colonel Parker wanted some sort of publishing deal, something had to be arranged with Sam Phillips. It must have been some meeting because Sam didn't like to give in.'

Bobby Vinton topped the US charts with 'Roses Are Red'. 'I had an office in New York and I was listening to songwriters coming in with material. Back then, if you sang a song, you owned it. Elvis would publish every song he recorded or else he wouldn't record it. When you get to be No.1, you can ask for the publishing! I said, 'I never knew

Elvis Presley: Caught in a Trap

that, but the next song I record, I am going to say that I want the publishing'. In came Burt Bacharach and he played me a new song and my legs started shaking. As soon I heard (sings) 'Blue on blue' and the chord changes, I knew that it was unique and different and yet commercial. I said, 'Burt, it's a nice song, maybe I'll do it on an album. If I can have the publishing, it would make it more interesting.' He said, 'Gee, I just gave the publishing away. I figured that you wouldn't like it and I would get someone to run around with it.' He said, 'I'm sorry you don't like it that much', and he went out towards the elevator. I went after him and I said, 'Burt, please, that is a great song, I don't need the publishing, I just thought I'd ask', and after that, I never asked for the publishing on any song.'

Elvis revived a couple of songs from his youth: 'It's a Sin' was a country hit for Eddy Arnold in 1947 and 'Sentimental Me' from 1950 was the B-side of the Ames Brothers' 'Rag Mop'. Some songs were ordinary – 'I Want You With Me', written by Woody Harris who wrote some early successes for Bobby Darin, had no life in it while 'Judy' was a dull, rockabilly ballad, written and originally recorded by Teddy Redell.

You wonder how Priscilla's parents – and indeed Priscilla herself – must have felt when they heard 'Put the Blame on Me'. Even if Kay Twomey, Fred Wise and Norman Blagman didn't know of Presley's private life, Freddy Bienstock certainly did. If Elvis had ever been arrested over his relationship with Priscilla, he would have been asked about this song: 'You just did what I made you do, You love me and I love you.'

The USS Arizona had been sunk by the Japanese during their surprise attack on Pearl Harbour in 1941 and parts of the superstructure were still in the harbour. It had been agreed to build a memorial for more than 1,000 seamen who had lost their lives, but the Government had originally postponed the proposal because of budget constraints during the Korean war. Now President Eisenhower had agreed to a memorial but the Government would only fund $200,000 of the necessary $500,000.

Elvis Presley was asked to help and his benefit concert at the Bloch Arena in Pearl Harbour in March 1961 was his first public appearance in three years. His 15-song set included 'Reconsider Baby' and 'Swing Low Sweet Chariot' as well as his hits. The concert raised $64,000 and the memorial was built. The highly unusual walkway over the remains attracts tourists to this day.

Such an engagement was out of character for Colonel Parker but he regarded it as publicity for the next Elvis next film, *Blue Hawaii*. Two days later Elvis was working on *Blue Hawaii*.

In June Elvis had another all-night session to record five songs, none of them related to a film. There was a Don Robertson song with Hawaiian overtones, 'I'm Yours', which included a narration, and a ballad from Red West, 'That's Someone You Never Forget'. Although he didn't claim a credit, the title came from Elvis as he wanted a song to remember Gladys.

The rest were by Doc Pomus and Mort Shuman. They had written their own Neapolitan ballad with 'Kiss Me Quick'. The other two made one of the greatest singles of all-time – 'Little Sister' and '(Marie's the Name) His Latest Flame'. It showed that the flame, latest or otherwise, still burned. It was the grittiest single Elvis had made since leaving the army. Both sides made the US Top 10 in their own right and the single topped the UK charts for four weeks.

But the songs hadn't been intended for Elvis.

The record producer Snuff Garrett had invited Doc and Mort to Los Angeles to write for an album that Bobby Vee was making with The Crickets and also for some other Liberty acts. By the time they arrived, Bobby Vee had finished the album. They had written 'Little Sister' and '(Marie's the Name) Her Latest Flame' and at first they passed 'Marie' to Del Shannon, but he jettisoned this potential single in favour of his own song, 'Hats Off to Larry'. So they went to Elvis.

Mort's voice and guitar demo for 'Little Sister' shows the song to be a furious rocker, but Presley wisely slowed down the tempo. Elvis may not have appreciated its worth as he only performed the song in concert as part of a medley with the Beatles' 'Get Back'. Produced by Phil Spector, LaVern Baker's 'Hey, Memphis' is a sassy female version of the song.

The *Rolling Stone* writer, Dave Marsh, has commented that 'Little Sister' with its Scotty Moore lead guitar sounded like a forerunner to The Who. Robert Plant from Led Zeppelin performed 'Little Sister' on *The Concert for Kampuchea* at Hammersmith Odeon, while Ry Cooder's 1979 reworking with an insidious rhythm and upfront backing vocals is on par with the original.

Lots of songs have been written around the 'shave and a haircut, two bits' rhythm: 'Not Fade Away', 'Willie And The Hand Jive', '(Marie's the Name) His Latest Flame' and half of Bo Diddley's repertoire. Mort Shuman accepts that he purloined the beat. 'I did steal the Bo Diddley riff, but everybody loves Bo Diddley. There is not one blues or rock musician or fan who does not love Bo Diddley. Bo Diddley is Bo Diddley. He is something special. I once saw Bo Diddley on some dinky fair in the afternoon and yet that rhythm is one of the pillars of rock'n'roll. There's no reason why anyone else should not take it and do something with it. After the Bo Diddley rhythm, we got to the middle eight, which is totally different and something I really like. There's no reason why it is Marie, other than it flowed. (sings) 'Carol's the name, her latest flame'. You see, that doesn't flow.'

Mort continued, 'That 45 with 'Little Sister' is my favourite Elvis 45, not because we wrote them but because they were really strong songs, done well, played well and produced well. Both sides went into the Top 10 in America, and that didn't happen very often. I love Elvis' version of 'Little Sister', but if anyone did a cover version that was completely different it was Ry Cooder. I loved it, it grooved and funked along and worked really well.'

Mort Shuman's demo for 'His Latest Flame' had an unusual organ effect in the middle and Elvis rang Doc to ask him about it. Doc gave him the answer but it wasn't until later that he realised he had been talking to Elvis himself and not just somebody from the studio. It was the only time he spoke to him. As Mort remarked, 'It's said that Elvis was very generous and gave Cadillacs to his friends, but I wrote several of his hits and he never sent me a Christmas card.'

On the LP *Elvis Sings Mort Shuman and Doc Pomus*, you can hear Elvis in the studio. Mort Shuman: 'Elvis had a great time in the studio. He had lots of fun and he had a great rapport with the musicians. He didn't take himself too seriously, which is great. He had a self-deprecating attitude, but, like a lot of Americans, he could all of a sudden get very serious about something. You can see from those documentary films that Elvis was very musical. There's a lovely scene where he ad-libs a spiritual around a piano. Elvis was really good at singing spirituals and they were always there to give him succour.'

That single notwithstanding, the plan was to recast Elvis Presley as a family entertainer, hence the new film would be *Blue Hawaii*. Although *Flaming Star* and *Wild in the Country* had made money, they hadn't been huge successes, so both Hal Wallis and Colonel wanted a big, happy musical with plenty of songs and lots of laughs and where better to set it than Hawaii.

Blue Hawaii is both the end of Elvis's golden period and the start of his decline. It contained both the magical 'Can't Help Falling in Love' and the dire 'Rock-A-Hula Baby (Twist Special)'; its huge success led to a succession of cheapo-cheapo beach party movies, not just by Elvis, with identical plots. But *Blue Hawaii* itself wasn't cheap as it was made with a $2m budget.

As Patrick Humphries has written, 'You only ever got one crack at growing up, but you knew that the soundtrack to your adolescence deserved to be better than *Blue Hawaii*.'

Elvis was doing a Bing Crosby and indeed Bing had been recording and filming in Hawaii ever since 1936. His 'Sweet Leilani' had topped the US charts for 10 weeks and had been featured in his film, *Waikiki Wedding*. If younger, Bing could easily have starred in *Blue Hawaii* and sung the whole score. Bing had already recorded the title song and 'Hawaiian Wedding Song'. The surest sign that something was wrong is the one rock song, 'Rock-A-Hula Baby' which showed Elvis twisting during a party scene. Forget it – Elvis did, as he never sang it again.

After giving an old lady a music box for her birthday, Elvis sang 'Can't Help Falling In Love'. Its melody was taken from the French tune, 'Plaisir D'Amour', written around 1800. It has been recorded in its original form by Mary Hopkin and Joan Baez, but is now better known as 'Can't Help Falling in Love'.

Five new songs were written by Tepper and Bennett for *Blue Hawaii*, the best being 'Hawaiian Sunset', which could have been a standard. Their blues, 'Beach Boy Blues', doesn't work – 'I'm a kissing cousin to a ripe pineapple, I'm in the can.' The songs were decently recorded with the regular crew as well as local group, the Surfers, and the steel guitarist, Alvino Rey.

Elvis loved the routine for the dance number, 'Slicin' Sand'. The choreography was by Charles O'Curran, and his wife Patti Page was in the wedding scene set at the Coco Palms resort on the island of Kauai. Elvis sang with Patti at night in the dining-room.

'Almost Always True' is the French song, 'Alouette' with new words. Bill Haley did it better as 'Pretty Alouette' in 1958. I don't know why Colonel Parker had these songwriting deals: surely he could have tossed off the lyric himself in a tea break? In both this and 'I Slipped, I Stumbled, I Fell' from *Wild in the Country*, Elvis gives examples of how not to drive as he sings complete lines looking at the girls and not the road.

One song, 'Steppin' Out of Line', was cut from the production but used on the next album, *Pot Luck*: you can see where it was cut as Elvis says, 'You're stepping out of line' and they move onto something else. The song is about telling a 17-year-old that she doesn't have true feelings and Elvis refers to under-age sex. Elvis cures her feelings by spanking her – I am not making this up. What was the scriptwriter playing at? The girl in question, Ellie, was played by Jenny Maxwell, who had lost out on playing the title role in *Lolita* to Sue Lyon.

The audience might have been waiting for Elvis' mother to have words with him.

She was played by Angela Lansbury who was dreadfully over the top as Elvis' mother. Ironically she was 35 years old and yet her son was in reality 26. It's odd watching her in this film in 2016; I kept expecting everyone to drop dead around her.

The actor Tony Perkins had recorded 'Moonlight Swim' for RCA in 1957 but as he is known for creepy roles especially *Psycho*, it doesn't sound right. Elvis revived the song for *Blue Hawaii* and the scene where Elvis sings it with the young tourists is one of the best moments in this sugary film.

Once again, I didn't find Elvis' girlfriend, Joan Blackman, too attractive: the producers are putting Elvis with a Barbie Doll without realising that this turned Elvis into a Barbie Boy. This sounds churlish but consider the talent that was around. Elvis and Bardot: that would have been a match. Briefly, Elvis did up the ante when he made films with Ursula Andress and Ann-Margret.

The original choice for the film was Juliet Prowse as their chemistry had worked well in *G.I. Blues* and even more so off screen. She was on loan from 20th Century Fox but she sent a list of demands including the cost of a secretary, and the size of her billing meant that the producers could not agree. They replaced her with Joan Blackman while Prowse was suspended by Fox.

The *Blue Hawaii* album topped both the US and UK album charts for months and *Blue Hawaii* became the biggest film of Elvis' career. Maybe the Elvis fans preferred Elvis in lighter roles. Elvis took note; he loved rock'n'roll but he also loved money.

The main attractions were Elvis' screen wedding (cue for 'Hawaiian Wedding Song'), the scenic beauty, the pretty girls and Elvis in his swimming trunks, though not necessarily in that order. Body hair was considered unsightly and Elvis had to shave his chest – it was worth it as Colonel Parker negotiated an additional $25,000 for a bare-chested Elvis.

Blue Hawaii was either the last of the good Elvis movies or the first of the bad. Did this start the rot and did its success prompt those turgid beach party movies with Frankie Avalon and Annette? A word of caution from film critic, Ramsey Campbell: 'The decline in Elvis' films was not so apparent at the time as it now seems looking back. We are all more enlightened, much wiser and full of retrospective advice as to what should have been done back then.' It should be remembered that they played an important part in 1960s adolescence. Teenagers in the 60s could take their first dates to an Elvis film, safe in the knowledge that there would be nothing to embarrass them.

When RCA issued the album, it quickly topped the charts and they wanted to issue a single. 'Can't Help Falling in Love' was the obvious choice but Colonel Parker felt that they had missed the boat as fans would already have it on the album. He told RCA that they could only issue it if they paid royalties for a guaranteed one million sales. It sold well over a million so it didn't matter, but it was another example of his business acumen.

Elvis' version made No.2 in the US and topped the UK charts for four weeks which was great promotion for the film. 'Rock-a-Hula Baby' also made the US Top 30, but RCA should have gone with the far superior 'Moonlight Swim' for the B-side.

Andy Williams upped the tempo on 'Can't Help Falling in Love' in 1970 and took the song to No.3, followed by a soul treatment from The Stylistics, produced by its writers Hugo and Luigi, at No.4 in 1976. Elvis loved the song but followed Andy Williams' more up-tempo arrangement. He closed nearly every concert with 'Can't

Help Falling in Love' and didn't do encores. Instead, somebody intoned that Elvis had left the building, which meant he could move fast when he wanted to.

Elvis was still making singles that were not connected to films and we can view 'Don't Be Cruel', 'Stuck on You' and 'Good Luck Charm' as a trilogy or possibly as decreasing Russian dolls. Aaron Schroeder and Wally Gold wrote 'Good Luck Charm' and although it's good, Elvis was treading water. It's not exciting, and Merseybeat was around the corner. It was catchy enough to top the charts in both Britain and America, but far better was a beautiful B-side, a Don Robertson song, 'Anything... That's Part of You', performed immaculately by Elvis. Don Robertson had written the song as he was missing his girlfriend, an airline hostess: she was gone and he buried his head in her sweater. When he came up for air, he had the title for the song.

Having had such a success with *Blue Hawaii*, a sensible plan would have been a full-blown musical with big production numbers, and indeed Jerry Leiber and Mike Stoller had suggested a film version of *Walk on the Wild Side* directly to Elvis. Colonel Parker was livid – how dare they pitch a project direct to Elvis. With a couple of exceptions, Elvis would no longer record their new songs.

So no *Walk on the Wild Side*; it was back to el cheapo with the light-hearted *Follow That Dream*, the score being so lukewarm that there was no single from it. Indeed, it was based on the novel, *Pioneer, Go Home* by Richard Powell. The film's title was changed to *Follow That Dream* as none of Elvis' regular songwriters could come up with a half-decent song called 'Pioneer, Go Home', but then that would tax most songwriters.

Every character Elvis played was born in the South and this time he's a hillbilly with 'the IQ of a grasshopper', although one girl retorts that 'his shoulders make him look like a genius'. When Joanna Moore gives him a word association test and says 'Sex', he recites the one-times table. Well, it seemed amusing at the time, and Elvis does possess comic timing.

The title song started with the same beat as 'His Latest Flame' but was nowhere near as exciting. Still it was the best song by far, as 'Angel' was crass teen pop, 'What a Wonderful Life' was pure hokum (Elvis sings, 'I don't care where I'm going' – you said it, chum) and there is another song about following your dreams, 'Sound Advice'. It sounds like the songwriters had been given a self-help manual and told to make it into a musical. One song had a life beyond the musical, as fans wondered if Elvis was sending them a message with 'I'm Not the Marrying Kind', and a comparison could be drawn with Cliff Richard's 'Bachelor Boy' (1962).

Although there was no single from the film, the *Follow That Dream* EP made the US Top 20 and topped the EP chart in the UK for 20 weeks, not that there was much competition.

Jerry Leiber and Mike Stoller returned for the next single, 'She's Not You' (also written with Doc Pomus) and 'Just Tell Her Jim Said Hello' (which had been written for Johnny Cash), but it was their final single for Elvis. Although it topped the UK charts for three weeks, it only made No.5 in the US.

Doc had a Fats Domino sound in mind for 'She's Not You', but Leiber and Stoller convinced him that it would work better as a beat-ballad with a shuffle rhythm. Not wanting to waste the opportunity, Leiber and Stoller submitted an older song of theirs, 'Just Tell Her Jim Said Hello', which Elvis recorded as an easy-paced ballad for the B-side.

Elvis was, as it were, keeping three balls in the air – singles, albums and films with live appearances being kicked into touch. Most of the tracks for *Pot Luck*, the follow-up to *Something for Everybody*, were recorded in March 1962, the same time as 'She's Not You'. Steve Sholes totally missed a potential gold disc with 'Suspicion', putting the track on the album and leaving Terry Stafford to take the song into the US Top 10 in 1964. He became the third artist (after Joe Dowell and Ral Donner) to pick up on hit singles through listening to an Elvis album.

Mort Shuman: 'I didn't really think that 'Suspicion' was really right for Elvis, but to his credit, he took it and made it his own. If you play Elvis and Terry Stafford, I don't think you'll find too much to say about Terry Stafford. Oh, wait, they have that little girl's whoo. When I moved to France, I wrote 'Shami-Sha' using the same two chords and that riff on the piano.'

Pot Luck was a decent album, making the US Top 10 album charts and No.1 in the UK. Leiber and Stoller had gone but Pomus and Shuman were fine replacements. As well as 'Suspicion' and 'Kiss Me Quick', they wrote 'Gonna Get Back Home Somehow' and 'Night Rider', while Doc wrote 'I Feel That I've Known You Forever', with Alan Jeffries.

Mort Shuman: "Gonna Get Back Home Somehow' is influenced by an old Hank Williams song, 'Ramblin Man". Great song, and we just wanted to write a travelling song like it. There's something about trains that captures the imagination, no doubt about it. Doc and I were very into moving songs. 'Long Lonely Highway' is another one.'

Otis Blackwell wrote the charming '(Such an) Easy Question', while Don Robertson's 'I'm Yours' was enhanced by a narration. It was placed next to the *Blue Hawaii* outtake, 'Steppin' Out of Line', and possibly Bill Giant's 'Fountain of Love' was intended for that film. It gave the album a feeling of the islands.

Red West offered another good country ballad, 'That's Someone You Never Forget', although, unintentionally, it has a spooky start: not the Jordanaires' finest moment. Sid Tepper and Roy Bennett's 'Just for Old Times Sake' is another good ballad but the best song and the best performance comes from Paul Evans and Al Bryon's 'Something Blue', a neat twist on the wedding theme.

In recent years, Abdul Bari-Awad has been boxing as Kid Galahad, an example of fact following fiction. *Kid Galahad* was the title of a 1937 film starring Bette Davis and Edward G. Robinson and it was remade with Elvis cast in the Wayne Morris role.

By 1962, Elvis' films were aimed at his female fans and as females don't generally go for boxing movies (and this is long before *Rocky*), the brutal *Kid Galahad* was intriguing. Elvis didn't undertake much training for the role as all his wins were with straight slugs and no fancy footwork. Indeed, if more care and attention had been paid to the technical aspects, this could have been a very good film indeed.

Charles Bronson is his sparring partner and Ed Asner, after several TV appearances, makes his film debut as the district Attorney. The sturdy cast includes Gig Young (Elvis' only gig of the year) and for the second time Joan Blackman is his girlfriend. Unusually for an Elvis film, there is a plot going on without Elvis and there are many scenes in which he does not appear.

Elvis played a reluctant boxer with a heart of gold and the songs needed to be tougher for a boxing movie. 'Home Is Where the Heart Is' belongs in some cornball film and in a big romantic scene, who would want to sing 'A Whistling Tune'? In any event, that song had been left over from *Follow That Dream*. Ruth Batchelor told *Punch* about writing for Elvis: 'I would be handed a movie script and told to write only what fans expected of his image. For instance, he could never sing 'darling', only 'baby'.'

Trivia question: how many films did Elvis Presley make in Hawaii? The answer is not two – *Blue Hawaii* (1961) and *Paradise, Hawaiian Style* (1966) – but three, as *Girls! Girls! Girls!* (1962) was set on the islands. Hal Wallis and Norman Taurog were so pleased with the success of *Blue Hawaii* that they set about a similar mixture almost immediately. Elvis sings to a granny at one point – one song starts like 'Can't Help Fallin' in Love' – you can see the boxes being ticked. The one thing they missed was to put Hawaii in the title. The original title was *Gumbo Ya-Ya*, a Creole expression for everybody talking at once, so *Girls! Girls! Girls!* was at least an improvement on that.

The title song was by Jerry Leiber and Mike Stoller, which they had written for the Coasters in 1961. Even at the time it would have been considered sexist, but it was written to showcase the Coasters' comedic voices and they don't sound rational when singing these outrageous words. Elvis sings it straighter than the Coasters and Jerry Leiber added a verse for Hawaii and brought in the Twist. And what made Elvis dance like Chubby Checker in several sequences?

Although there were location shoots in Hawaii, some of the filming was done on the lot at Paramount in Hollywood. Jimmy Savile had been planning to visit Hollywood to give Elvis his UK silver discs for 'It's Now Or Never' and 'Rock-A-Hula Baby', but Larry Parnes convinced Savile that it would be better for Billy Fury to go instead. Elvis was making his eleventh film, *Girls! Girls! Girls!* and they visited the set in April 1962, while he was shooting 'Return To Sender' in the Pirates Den. His dancing moves were more Jackie Wilson than Elvis Presley, but he had seen him in Vegas.

Larry Parnes: 'Billy was the first British pop star to meet Elvis Presley and when I am involved in something like this, I set my watch half an hour forward and Billy was taking his time. We had a suite in a hotel and Billy came into the lounge. He was beautifully dressed but he was all in black. He had a lovely, black silky-looking suit. I said, 'Billy, you can't go dressed like that! Surely you should put on one of your nice, tailor-made suits and one of your lovely shirts with a patterned tie.' He said, 'Okay, I will go and change.' He changed and he looked good in whatever he wore: he held his clothes beautifully. We got to the studio and we were introduced to Elvis Presley. We shook hands and Elvis was dressed in black from top to bottom and he looked virtually identical to the way Billy had been dressed.'

And what did Larry make of it all? 'They were lovely sets. Hawaii reproduced in the Paramount studios. When I was introduced to Presley, he said, 'I am glad to meet you, sir, I understand you are the Colonel Parker of England'. I said, 'No, not quite, I wish I was.' (laughs) Colonel Parker was a very nice man. He took the trouble of phoning our hotel the following day to see if we had enjoyed ourselves.'

Billy presented Elvis with his silver discs but their conversation was even shorter and more stilted than that between Elvis and the Beatles in 1965. Billy reported, 'We didn't really say much at all but I was on the set all day watching him. He was one of the nicest people I've ever met – he called everyone 'Sir'.' Elvis told Billy that he had seen *The Hellions*, a British western set in South Africa with Richard Todd, Lionel Jeffries and Marty Wilde, five times. Fury may well have heard another song from the film, 'Because Of Love', because he released it as a single.

Spencer Leigh

Did Larry Parnes want to bring Elvis to the UK? 'Of course. I made an offer for Elvis to come to Britain, and Colonel Parker promised me that I would be the first person that he would deal with if he decided to do that. I am sure he would have kept his word. I'll give you my theory and I could very well be wrong. Elvis was a brilliant recording artist, one of the most brilliant we have ever had, and he was very good in films as an actor, but he was not a great stage performer. Billy Fury was a better stage performer than Elvis Presley, and I think that Colonel Parker was shrewd enough to realise this. He felt that it was better for Elvis not to be seen live on stage. He would just let the fans buy his records and see his films.'

This is an outrageous comment and astonishing, if true. First of all, Parnes is saying that Presley wasn't much of a stage performer and that Colonel Parker knew it and so kept him making films and records. This ridiculous statement could be disproved by Presley's triumphant return to the stage in Las Vegas in 1969. When Parnes saw him on stage, he thought, 'No, he's not as good as Billy Fury.' I think Larry is on 'cloud number nine' from 'Because of Love', and while we're about it, what exactly is cloud number nine?

As well as *The Hellions*, we can piece together some of Elvis' viewing habits. He liked watching films and his current favourites were *The Great Escape* (Steve McQueen, 1963) and *The Birdman of Alcatraz* (Burt Lancaster, 1962) and his favourite oldies were *Wuthering Heights* (Laurence Olivier, 1939), *Mr. Skeffington* (Bette Davis, 1944) and *Les Misèrables* (Frederic March, 1935). He would watch anything with James Dean and Marlon Brando but he didn't care for the Keystone Kops as he thought it was a mockery of law enforcement. Elvis knew what made great entertainment and so he was losing his self-respect with some of the films he was making.

Considering the number of girls in Elvis' films – sometimes he has to choose between three – it is odd that *Girls! Girls! Girls!* only has two when the title promises more. They are the *Playboy* Playmate, Stella Stevens (real name, Estelle Eggleston) and newcomer Laurel Goodwin (later in the pilot for *Star Trek*). Stella Stevens has the best song as she revives 'The Nearness of You', which would have suited the romantic Elvis. How odd that Elvis never recorded an album of standards.

Elvis plays a tuna fisherman and the script is waterlogged, the only curio being that Elvis speaks Chinese to his sidekick, Benson Fong. Still, Hal Wallis liked the script as he entrusted its writer, Edward Anhalt, with *Becket* in 1964 where he had to write dialogue for Richard Burton and Peter O'Toole.

Elvis is in good humour and the score is stronger than usual with 'Return to Sender', an Otis Blackwell song, which is mimed badly by Elvis. He even glances at his watch – no comment! 'Because of Love' had hit potential too and the comedy number 'The Walls Have Ears' with Laurel Goodwin works okay.

'Song of the Shrimp' was lampooned mercilessly by Townes Van Zandt in live performances. 'We're Coming in Loaded', sung on a tuna boat, was equally ridiculous, and it's unusual to find Otis Blackwell writing a point number.

Elvis sang 'Earth Boy' in Hawaiian with the young Tiu sisters but there were too many cute kids in this film, not to mention a cat, Kapoo, that could predict the weather. Still children were an increasing feature of Elvis films, an indication of where his popularity was heading. 'You know something…I should win a medal,' said Elvis at the end, 'for being the world's biggest jackass.' The joke, I think, was on him.

'Return to Sender' was a great record with the Jordanaires high in the mix, and the musicians include Boots Randolph, Scotty Moore and the jazz musician Barney Kessel. It was a US No.2 for five weeks – it couldn't dislodge the Four Seasons with 'Big Girls Don't Cry' – and a UK No.1.

Postal deliveries have always been a regular topic for songwriters – 'Death Letter Blues' (Son House), 'Sealed with a Kiss' (Brian Hyland), 'Letter Full of Tears' (Billy Fury), 'Love Letters' (Ketty Lester), 'Please Mr. Postman' (Marvelettes) and not forgetting The Singing Postman or Slim Whitman, another singing postman. Elvis recorded 'Western Union' and the punning Jerry Reed song, 'U.S. Male'. In 1993, when the U.S. Mail issued its Elvis stamp, there was a tenfold increase in the number of letters it was obliged to return, duly marked 'Return to sender – Address unknown'.

In June and July 1962, Elvis spent his time at Graceland and was frequently seen around Memphis on his motorcycles or in one of his many cars. He now had a British Rolls-Royce in his fleet. He rented fairgrounds for late night partying and he was staying up all night and sleeping in the daytime. On 6 August 1962 Anita Wood announced that she was breaking up with Elvis, although they still saw each other from time to time.

In August Elvis bought a customised Greyhound bus which would be mainly used for trips between Memphis and Los Angeles. It became a house on wheels. On its first trip, Elvis went to Hollywood for some interior scenes on *It Happened at the World's Fair* and then moved to Seattle for location shoots.

It was a sound idea to make a film at the World's Fair in Seattle but the end result is more a travelogue than a story, primarily designed to show the fair's attractions. Elvis played a charter pilot and during the film, he fell for a nurse, joined the space programme, searched for a lost uncle and got his buddy, Gary Lockwood, out of trouble. Again, there were scenes of Elvis with children, especially seven-year-old Sue-Lin. Elvis was kicked by a young Kurt Russell: years later Kurt Russell would cause further affront by playing him in a movie.

The score is songwriting by rote. Let's have a ballad here, a novelty there and a lullaby later on and every song is competent and dull. The only songwriter to acquit himself is Don Robertson but even there 'They Remind Me Too Much of You' is a rerun of 'Anything That's Part of You'. Robertson played organ on 'I'm Falling in Love Tonight' but that made it sound like a gospel song.

'Relax', wouldn't have been written if it weren't for Fever' but it had none of the sharpness of that composition. Elvis is singing romantically so surely he wouldn't say 'Defrost', making his girlfriend sound like a fridge. The best bit of the novelty 'How Would You Like to Be' is taken from 'Good Luck Charm'.

Not content with having a hit with an Elvis song, 'Suspicion', Terry Stafford was given a song which had been rejected for *It Happened at the World's Fair*. 'I'll Touch a Star', written by Dolores Fuller, who had another career as the angora sweater girl in Ed Wood's B-movies, sounds like 'Suspicion, Part 2'.

Most disappointing of all is the single, Otis Blackwell's 'One Broken Heart for Sale'. This is a return to 'Return to Sender' but lacking its wit. It only made the Top 20 in Britain and America, his weakest performance to date, ignoring reissues. It is a short record and there is an additional verse in the film but that wouldn't have saved it. It was still a Top 10 album but it didn't deserve to be. Its playing time was only 21 minutes so cynicism was in the mix.

In October 1962, Elvis got his wish. He had persuaded Priscilla's parents that she should come to Memphis. She was to live with Vernon and Dee in their house on Hermitage – well, that's the official story. She enrolled at the Immaculate Conception High School and Elvis was responsible for her education and well-being.

When she arrived in her sailor suit and white socks, Lamar said to Elvis, 'Jesus, she's cute but you'll end up in prison.' Parker thought that it might calm Elvis down and after a couple of weeks, she was sharing his bed at Graceland. Elvis gave her a puppy called Honey for Christmas, but he also gave her Placidyl and she was out for two days, an indication too that her parents weren't speaking to her every day. She has said, 'I could be brought into womanhood under his tutelage. Like a sculptor, he could shape my image and design my demeanour in ways that would bring him delight. I was the doll he loved to dress.'

As if to celebrate, *Girls! Girls! Girls!* opened nationally. Elvis saw that Priscilla was uncomfortable with Anita being around, and that romance was over. Elvis and Priscilla celebrated Christmas at Graceland and he gave her a diamond ring.

In January 1963, the filming started on *Fun in Acapulco,* though Presley remained in Hollywood. How did they manage to get the finance for this film? 'Listen, here's the pitch. We have a trapeze artist with a fear of heights so he becomes a lifeguard and is pursued by a female bullfighter'. Maybe they just said, 'Elvis'. Viv Stanshall of the Bonzo Dog Band described this film to me as *Unfun in Acapulco*: Viv covered 'No Room to Rhumba in a Sports Car' thinking its silliness suited the Bonzos' canon.

Fred Wise, who wrote 'Rhumba' as well as 30 other Elvis songs, didn't have a wooden heart at all. He found out his wife was cheating on him and in January 1966 he jumped out of a high building and landed at the feet of his wife and her lover. He wrote most of his songs with Ben Weisman, who wrote 57 songs for Elvis, far more than any other writer. Had he lived, Fred might be up there with him.

The country music songwriter Don Robertson went to the Purple Onion club in San Francisco to get a feel for flamenco and wrote 'Marguerita'. It's good to hear Elvis with a mariachi band and he could easily have made a Latin album.

Elvis plays a trapeze artist who in a moment of panic kills someone. He fled the circus to escape his past and assume a new life in a foreign country. Sound familiar?

For once, Elvis had an exceptional co-star, the Bond girl, Ursula Andress, in her first American film, straight from *Dr. No*. He was intimidated by her; she was Swiss with an incomparable figure and broad shoulders and he told his friends, 'I'm embarrassed to take off my damn shirt next to her.' She was married to the Hollywood director, John Derek, and although they flirted a little, it was Dr. No to anything else.

So much could have been done with this duo – it could have been a major success. As it is, the story is bland. In a dangerous situation, she helps him to regain his nerve.

There was a lost opportunity for an intriguing score with Mexican influences, as, despite the Four Amigos, we are drowned in pap. In one song, the lady only beats Pedro the bull because the bull fancies her, and then she kills him. How could he sing such nonsense? The songs have appalling titles – 'The Bullfighter was a Lady' and 'You Can't Say No in Acapulco' – and Elvis has to sing, 'Now I know the way a pretzel feels'. How does it feel, El? It is a shame, as country artists like Marty Robbins and Joe Ely have shown how enticingly Mexican influences can be added to American music – and couldn't Elvis have done a great version of 'La Bamba'?

Elvis Presley: Caught in a Trap

The one decent song was 'Bossa Nova Baby', written by Jerry Leiber and Mike Stoller and originally recorded by Tippy and the Clovers. It is faster than most bossa nova records and one of the most successful, although not by Presley's standards (US No.8, UK No.13). It clearly influenced 'Viva Las Vegas'.

In April 1963, RCA announced that Elvis had sold 100 million records. The following month Elvis had his first Nashville session for 14 months. He was recording songs that had nothing to do with his films, songs that hopefully would be chosen for their effectiveness on record.

In two long, overnight sessions, Elvis recorded 14 songs. In January 1964, he recut two of them and added 'Ask Me'. Elvis was with his old friends – Scotty Moore, Bob Moore, D.J. Fontana, Buddy Harman, Boots Randolph, Millie Kirkham and the Jordanaires. Although Steve Sholes was producing, this was largely a titular role as Elvis knew what he wanted to sound like. They had enough tracks for an album but there were just too many film scores to promote. Instead, the tracks were used as B-side and album fillers. In 1990, RCA put them together for a 15-track collection, *For the Asking – The Lost Album*.

A partnership of three writers at Hill and Range, Bill Giant, Bernie Baum and Florence Kaye, wrote 40 songs for Elvis, but only one of them, '(You're The) Devil In Disguise' had any significant success. It wasn't an exceptional song but it was helped by a fine performance from Elvis with a neat stop-start arrangement. To give Bill Giant his due, he did write Billy Fury's 'Wondrous Place' – if only Elvis had recorded that. The B-side was a good Otis Blackwell and Winfield Scott song, 'Please Don't Drag That String Around'. 'Devil in Disguise' was No.3 hit in the US and No.1 in the UK.

The Giant, Baum and Kaye partnership wrote an English lyric for Domenico Modugno's 'Io', which they called 'Ask Me', a superb romantic ballad which could have been an A-side.

Charlie Daniels became one of the kings of Southern boogie, but back in 1964 he was a young songwriter getting work where he could. He wrote a beautiful song with Joy Byers, 'It Hurts Me', the most sensitive song he has ever written, with a tremendous performance from Elvis and his musicians. Joy Byers was married to Bob Johnston who was to work with Bob Dylan at Columbia.

'Witchcraft' was not the Frank Sinatra song that Presley sang on the TV special but an R&B song that had been recorded by the New Orleans group, the Spiders, in 1955. It was written by Fats Domino's writing partner, Dave Bartholomew and it's odd that such a good song was not given to Fats.

There's an acceptable revival of Chuck Berry's 'Memphis, Tennessee' and Elvis played his new arrangement to Johnny Rivers. Rivers immediately picked up on it, copied it and put it out as single. It was a US hit and Elvis said, 'Let the bastard have his hit record but I never want to see him again.'

Otherwise, it was new songs all the way. 'Long Lonely Highway' was excellent Pomus and Shuman, while Paul Evans got in with 'Blue River', its concept being a maritime 'Heartbreak Hotel'. Don Robertson maintained his high standard with 'Love Me Tonight' (especially) and 'What Now, What Next, Where To'. He had got the unusual title from a Carl Sandburg poem and he taken round his demo to Johnny Cash. Johnny took it but never showed any inclination to cut it so Don gave it to the Aberbachs, who passed it to Presley.

Buddy Kaye and Phil Springer, who were to write for Dusty Springfield, wrote 'Never Ending'. Dory and Ollie Jones wrote 'Finders Keepers, Losers Weepers'. Sid Wayne and Ben Weisman wrote 'Slowly But Surely' and Bob Roberts and Paddy McMains 'Echoes of Love'. The only song that should have been ditched was 'Western Union', a shameful rewrite of 'Return to Sender', this time for the telegram service.

In July, Elvis cut the score of *Viva Las Vegas*. Elvis was smitten with his co-star Ann-Margret – she was talented, very beautiful and knew how to ride a motorbike. There were two weeks' location shooting in Las Vegas. There was talk of a romance between Elvis and Ann-Margret and the press played it up as they didn't know about Elvis and Priscilla. Elvis persuaded Priscilla that nothing had happened. She had graduated from Immaculate Conception and would attend the Patricia Stevens Finishing School. Elvis bought her a Corsair.

Viva Las Vegas is one of Elvis' best films. It was shown as *Love in Las Vegas* in the UK, because a previous film, *Meet Me in Las Vegas* (1956) with Dan Dailey and Cyd Charisse had been renamed *Viva Las Vegas* in the UK. Mort Shuman on the title song: 'I like 'Viva Las Vegas' and it worked pretty good over the opening credits. It wasn't rock'n'roll but I liked it. It was more like a samba. You know what pisses me off. The song titles aren't mentioned in the Presley pictures, let alone the writers. The only credit in *Viva Las Vegas* is for the guy who wrote the Mickey Mouse music, but nowadays you get all the songs in the credits, though they whiz by so fast.'

'Viva Las Vegas' is one of the great Pomus and Shuman songs and although it is taken as an upbeat celebration of Las Vegas, especially today when the city has become so successful and enormous. But it is at heart an ironic song – there's a reference to losing money on the one-armed bandits and the 'thousand pretty women' are surely hookers.

There isn't much of a plot but it is fun and entertaining. Elvis plays a racing car driver who goes to Las Vegas and falls in love with Ann-Margret's chassis. The chemistry between the two stars is torrid: just look at the end of the dance sequence for 'C'mon Everybody'. Ann-Margret does her best to upstage him and this is as steamy and provocative as an Elvis film will allow. For once, there is a fine Tepper and Bennett song, 'The Lady Loves Me' but the ending is weak. Sid Tepper was rung from the set and told that Ann-Margret was going to push Elvis into the pool and so could they amend the song. They would hold on for the new lyric! Tepper said, 'The gentlemen's all wet', which doesn't make sense unless you have seen the film and know Elvis has fallen backwards from a diving board (well, his stunt double has).

Though it was dropped from the film, their remake of LaVern Baker and Jimmy Ricks' 'You're the Boss' is fine, although Ann-Margret can't match LaVern Baker's voice. In the film, Ann-Margret performs 'My Rival' and 'Appreciation' and the Forte Four do a dance number written by Leiber and Stoller, 'The Climb'.

Then there is Elvis with the slow and bluesy 'I Need Somebody to Lean On', a revival of Ray Charles' 'What'd I Say' (even by then a cliché), a dance number similar to 'La Bamba' 'Do the Vega' (which was dropped from the film), and the wedding song, 'Today, Tomorrow and Forever'. Best of all is the title song by Doc Pomus and Mort Shuman. It has the hurried excitement of everything happening and it is flashy and glitzy. There are snatches of 'The Yellow Rose of Texas', and 'Santa Lucia' so why didn't RCA issue a soundtrack album?

Elvis Presley: Caught in a Trap

Elvis was so smitten with Ann-Margret that he asked Colonel Parker to manage her. Parker said, 'Okay, my time will be split 50/50 with you.' Elvis then thought it wasn't such a good idea. Ann-Margret gave Elvis a fruit machine with three guitars for the jackpot. He put it in his den at Graceland.

In September 1963, Elvis started his own football team, Elvis Presley Enterprises, with its own uniform, featuring celebrities and his inner circle. P.J. Proby who, back then, was plain Jim Smith, recalls, 'I played football every Saturday. I was on Ricky Nelson's team and we played against Elvis' team. Elvis was a quarterback and I was a running back and I would tackle Elvis and make sure he didn't make a touchdown. I can remember picking the ball out of the air when he passed to one of his ends and running the field, past Red West and all of his boys, and I made a touchdown myself. I remember Elvis saying to Red, 'Watch the barefoot boy. Watch the boy with no shoes. He's fast.' After the football game, we would go straight to Elvis' house for a night of partying and pool.'

Pat Boone didn't play football with Elvis but he did record a tribute album. 'The album, *Pat Boone Sings Guess Who*, was a tribute to Elvis because I wanted to sing some of his songs, although I didn't want to do them how he did them. I told the Colonel that I was going to make an album of Elvis' hits and that it was going to be called *Pat Sings Elvis*. He said, 'Well, we'd better talk about the royalty.' I said, 'Royalty? Oh, we'll be paying the royalties to the songwriters as usual.' He said, 'No, you've gotta pay a royalty to Elvis if you want to use his name.' I said, 'Are you kidding? He publishes most of these songs. He's going to make a lot of money off this album anyway and besides, it's a tribute.' Colonel Parker didn't buy that. He said, 'You're using his name. That's going to sell records, so you'll have to pay a royalty.' I thought about it and then I decided to call it *Pat Boone Sings Guess Who*, and we never mentioned his name once.'

MGM was the home of brilliant musicals but standards had slipped. *It Happened at the World's Fair* was bad enough but in October, Elvis not only scraped the barrel – he was right underneath it. Elvis was persuaded he should play identical cousins – one with a blond wig – for *Kissin' Cousins*. The production was held up for two hours as he had to be coaxed to leave his trailer wearing a blond wig. He thought people would laugh at him; surely not.

With a budget of $800,000 this was bargain basement filming: the budget allowed for just three weeks' filming. This was because Parker had met the infamous Sam Katzman, King of the Quickies. Standards went by the board and Parker even sent back the initial script unread: 'If you want an opinion or evaluation of this script, it will cost you an additional $25,000.' Sam Katzman had shown Colonel Parker how to economise and, with a couple of exceptions, the standards truly drop from here.

Biographer Albert Goldman: 'Elvis had no say in the movies he appeared in, any more than he had a say in any of the other major decisions in his career. He would get a script, he would examine it, he would be appalled by it, he would make devastating statements about it, and then he would go out and do it. There you have the essential Elvis Presley – he was a mule pulling a plough.'

Elvis' stand-in Lance LeGault is visible in the fight sequences and Glenda Farrell, who broke her neck during the shooting, struggled gamely on playing his mother, taking off her brace for the takes. If they had had to replace her, all that economy would have been in vain.

The soundtrack was mountain country music but of a particularly unpleasant variety. There could have been Appalachian sounds but this is Hollywood's idea of bluegrass. 'Smokey Mountain Boy' is terrible but it's amusing to hear Elvis singing about food. Did Elvis invent line dancing with 'Barefoot Ballad'? The songs are disgraceful – in 'Catchin' on Fast', Elvis is pretending to be naïve so that girls will kiss him. One love song is called 'One Boy, Two Little Girls'. A pleasant ballad, 'Anyone Could Fall in Love with You', was dropped. A bit of trivia: the leader of the love-starved mountain girls is Maureen Reagan, the daughter of Ronald Reagan. Don't worry, girls, there are two Presleys to hand.

Perhaps there needed to be two Presleys with Ann-Margret and Priscilla. When she was in London, for a royal premiere of the *Bye Bye Birdie* musical, Ann-Margret talked about her relationship with Elvis. This appeared in a Memphis newspaper with the heading, 'Elvis Wins Love of Ann-Margret'. Again, didn't that newspaper know of Priscilla? At the end of the shoot, Ann-Margret revealed that Elvis had given her a double-bed, so make what you will of that. She told Elvis she had been misquoted, but how could that be?

On 22 November 1963 President Kennedy was assassinated. Ann-Margret drove to Elvis' house in Hollywood and found him glued to his TVs. She says in her autobiography, 'We clung to each other, tried futilely to make sense of what had happened, and prayed for the future.'

Elvis had a lot more to worry about. The four moptops had been booked for *The Ed Sullivan Show*.

CHAPTER 10

I Fell...

> *'Do the Clam, Do the Clam,*
> *Grab your barefoot baby by the hand.'*
> 'Do the Clam', Elvis Presley, 1965

I. Home Taping

Since Elvis' death in 1977, RCA/BMG has been trawling the archives for unissued performances to release. Many of his 1970s concert appearances were professionally recorded so there is still a long way to go and although his introductions usually offer little insights, yet more versions of 'Bridge Over Troubled Water' or 'Can't Help Falling in Love' add nothing to his canon.

What is fascinating, however, are the home recordings that have percolated out, notably on the 1999 CD, *The Home Recordings*, which offered 22 examples admittedly only spread over 50 minutes, They were not always competently recorded and Elvis never intended anyone else to hear them so they present a unique picture of Elvis at home.

Although recorded at Sun's studio, the Million Dollar Quartet session in December 1956 with Carl Perkins, Jerry Lee Lewis and, arguably, Johnny Cash resembles a lengthy home recording. The microphones were switched on without any tests for balance, so the results are both historical and frustrating. That Christmas, Elvis met up with Red West, who was on leave from the army. They recorded themselves messing around with 'When the Saints Go Marching In', swopping lines and laughing and generally having a good time.

Just before he went into the army, Elvis was having fun with Anita Wood. He played a note on the piano and said, 'That's your key' to which she replied, 'My key?' as though she has never thought about it. She started singing 'I Can't Help It' with Elvis on piano and repeating the phrase 'Still in love with you' when it occurred. They discussed what Anita should sing if she made records. Elvis said that she shouldn't sound like Julie London, it would be better to sound like Connie Francis and they performed her hit, 'Who's Sorry Now' and the Ink Spots' 'When the Swallows Come Back to Capistrano'.

Then Elvis was at Eddie Fadal's house in Texas where they were awaiting orders to go to Germany. He took the doo-wop hit, 'I Understand (Just How You Feel)', starting in high tenor and building up to a big ending. The song, based around 'Auld Lang Syne', had first been recorded by the Four Tunes in 1953. Perhaps Elvis was considering how he could record it himself. It's a pity he didn't as it became a hit for the G-Clefs and Freddie and the Dreamers. Unfortunately, Elvis had to compete with background noise, including a crying baby.

In 1959 Elvis was at home in Germany with a Grundig recorder. He wasn't doing any sessions in Europe – even though he could have gone to London for a day and the Platters recorded in Paris – and here he sang some gospel, 'I Asked the Lord' (with a few notes from 'Jingle Bells'), which was associated with Mahalia Jackson. There was a Jim Reeves B-side, 'I'm Beginning to Forget You' and a stunning vocal on Nat 'King' Cole's 'Mona Lisa': if only he had done this in the studio.

There was a lovely version of Elvis doing 'Danny Boy', a song about a soldier who had lost his life, and then he played piano on 'Soldier Boy', written by David Jones of the Four Fellows while in Korea. He played around with Lee Hazlewood's great song for Sanford Clark, 'The Fool' – before he started, he asked 'Daddy' to shut the window to keep out the screams from the fans. Why didn't he serenade them instead? He was singing in harmony with someone here, but I don't know who.

In 1960 when Elvis was staying in Bel Air, he recorded a piano boogie of a dirty song, 'Birthday Cake'. It was Elvis as Jerry Lee but it was too muffled to enjoy. From the same time was 'Make Believe' from *Show Boat* with harmonies from Red West and Nancy Sharp, who was working on the wardrobe for *Flaming Star*. Elvis could have performed this song in his Vegas years.

I don't know the date but there is a tape of Elvis messing around with a song called 'I Wonder'. It sounds as though he is making it up on piano as he goes along and his pals are singing along with him – great fun.

We have no idea what is stacked away at Graceland and I suspect that only a small portion of Elvis' home recordings has surfaced. It is a shame that both Colonel Parker and Brian Epstein agreed that there would be no permanent record of the Beatles meeting with Elvis in 1965 either on tape, film or still photography. The very time that Elvis should have pressed Record, he didn't.

In 1966 Elvis was living in Rocca Place, Hollywood while making a film. Red West had had a few songs recorded and he wanted to make demonstration records of new ones with his friends Charlie Hodge and Glen Campbell. Elvis got involved and added a harmony or two. Were songs like 'I've Been Blue', 'It's No Fun Being Lonely' and 'Mary Lou Brown' intended for the King, or would some little-known singer receive a demo with Elvis' voice on it? Who knows, but 'Mary Lou Brown' would have worked very well for Elvis.

They were certainly superior to the songs that Elvis was being given. On Elvis' instruction, Red West took a pile of demos, put them in an envelope marked 'Shit' and sent them back to Colonel Parker. Parker was not amused. In 1965, Elvis' feeble films, records and music publishing brought in an overall total of $5m. Even the year of *Rubber Soul* and *Highway 61 Revisited*, there was still a market for 'Do the Clam'.

It is a shame Presley didn't exercise more control. He had taken a liking to French pop and he loved a song that Charles Aznavour had written, 'Venice Blue'. It would have been perfect for him but he didn't pursue it and it was successful for Bobby Darin.

Red, Charlie and Elvis had fun with the country standards, Bob Wills' 'San Antonio Rose' and the Sons of the Pioneers' 'Tumblin' Tumbleweeds'. They were putting each other off, but they laughed too loudly at Elvis' jokes: they weren't that funny but they were working for him. Still, if you were in a room with Elvis singing 'Tennessee Waltz' and he went, 'Yes, I lost my little britches', wouldn't you fall over laughing? This propensity for laughing too loud at Elvis' jokes was apparent on the sit-down section of the 1968 comeback special.

By way of contrast, there was a serious attempt at a gospel song, 'Show Me Thy Way, O Lord', another indication that Elvis' default mode was gospel. When he sang the big love ballad from *Carousel*, 'If I Loved You' to his own piano accompaniment, he was developing the big endings that he loved in Vegas.

The R&B singer Joe Henderson had recorded 'After Loving You' in 1962 and here, four years later, Elvis demonstrated how Conway Twitty might have croaked it. It's amusing and entertaining and Elvis loved the song, recording it officially in 1969.

In the studio, Elvis usually recorded his vocal with the musicians but he was given a backing tape for 'Indescribably Blue' and we can hear him working on the song, deciding what he will do in the studio. In a reverse situation, he and Charlie Hodge worked up a film song, 'Suppose', written by Sylvia Dee, and they sent it to Felton Jarvis to add the backing. Felton did that but he also redid it with Elvis and that version appeared in *Speedway* (1968).

In 1966 Elvis performed a Dean Martin song, 'Write to Me from Naples' and Guy Mitchell's first hit 'My Heart Cries for You'. Elvis was dredging the 1951 hit from his memory and he didn't recall many of the words: it was like a pub singalong. He might have heard Ray Charles' 1964 remake. Elvis fared better with 'Dark Moon', a 1957 hit for Bonnie Guitar and Gale Storm and written by Ned Miller, who wrote 'From a Jack to a King'. Elvis spent six minutes playing around with this and it is worth hearing it all on YouTube.

In 1971 Elvis recorded a piano and vocal version of 'I'm Still Here', written and recorded by Ivory Joe Hunter in 1964 as well as the Irish ballad, 'I'll Take You Home Again, Kathleen'. In 1973, he sang another Ivory Joe Hunter ballad, 'I Will Be True', this time from 1952.

Elvis ended up with professional recording equipment in his Jungle Room so much more could probably be revealed. Odd snippets have emerged such as he and Linda Thompson in 1974 singing 'Your Life Has Just Begun', a song unknown to me and spoilt by the telephone ringing. From the same year, there was a neat 'Baby What You Want Me To Do' with just Elvis and his guitar and a bunch of noisy friends who applauded at the end.

It is unlikely that much of his 20 years of home taping will ever be officially released because the recording standards are not good enough, but what does emerge is always fascinating.

II. Got a Lot o' Livin' to Do, 1964–1967

On 7 December 1963, the Beatles comprised the panel for BBC TV's *Juke Box Jury*, hosted by David Jacobs. Elvis Presley's new single, 'Kiss Me Quick' was played, and voted a hit, but their comments showed that it wasn't a hit with them. George said, 'The song's just a load of rubbish' and Ringo said he'd been 'going down the nick'. Songwriter Mort Shuman: 'If I'd been on the panel, I'd have agreed with them. We didn't write it for Elvis and I don't know why he did it. We wrote it for the Flamingos, who had the good taste not to do it. I prefer the German version of 'Kiss Me Quick' because the German lyric fits the melody much better.'

Since Elvis had left the army he had been industrious, making one film after another and recording songs in mammoth all-night sessions. His all-night sessions in RCA's Studio B in Nashville had produced 81 masters. He could record a whole album in two nights and, between March 1960 and January 1964, he had made 15 million-selling singles. In January 1964, he was given a gold record for a million-selling Christmas album, released in 1957 and making the charts every December.

His films too were commercial successes, especially *Blue Hawaii;* the top five movie stars at the US box office were Doris Day, Rock Hudson, John Wayne, Cary Grant and Elvis Presley. In 1963 Elizabeth Taylor had starred in *Cleopatra*, which became more of an event than a film: everything that could go wrong did go wrong during filming. Colonel Parker saw what was happening and didn't want his boy in any projects that could spin so alarmingly out of control. Elvis' films were quick, safe and reliable and designed to make money.

But this was a miscalculation that didn't take into account that moviegoers might tire of the product, or that new generations might see Elvis as old hat. You can sense this in the Beatles' comments; it's just as David Cameron said across the dispatch box to Tony Blair in parliament in 2005, 'You were the future once.'

Elvis was no longer as innovative as his early years but he was so far ahead of his rivals that, until the Beatles came along, he was really only competing against himself. The game-changer was the Beatles' appearance on *The Ed Sullivan Show* on 9 February 1964 to a US audience of 70 million. At an engaging press conference, they were asked 'Aren't you just four Elvis Presleys?' This enabled them to go into hip-shaking impressions of Elvis – the Beatles were certainly far more skilled at handling the press than Presley.

Presley was never sure whether the Beatles were paying him an insult or a compliment. A few months later Reg Ball from a beat group from Andover called the Troggs was to take his publicist's advice and become Reg Presley.

Pat Boone: 'I have never seen anything like the audience reaction for the Beatles. The fans would shriek from the moment they came on until long after they'd gone and you couldn't hear them perform. It was somewhat like that with Elvis and somewhat like that with me, but with us the screaming was at the beginning, at the start of a song they'd recognise, then they'd go quiet because they wanted to hear it and go crazy at the end.'

Elvis and the Colonel sent a public telegram welcoming them to America, but they can't have been happy. Elvis' new single was the second-rate 'Kissin' Cousins', which promoted an equally bland movie. In later years, RCA released the vocal track of 'Kissin' Cousins' and you can sense Elvis' frustration. Even his charity work had its problems: he had bought a former presidential yacht to give to charity and the charity would not accept it as it was unsafe.

Clive James in his book, *Fame in the Twentieth Century*, wrote, 'The secret of great success in the popular arts is to bring the punters in on the event. You have to be doing something they can do, so that they can dream they are the star for a brief moment.'

If that is true, and it probably is, then *Kissin' Cousins* was a turning point. When Presley was having his first successes on record and on film, young men dreamed of being Elvis and young girls dreamed of being with Elvis. But who on earth would identify with Elvis (either one of them) in the ridiculous *Kissin' Cousins*, which had a plot so banal it defied belief?

Even on his first photograph, Elvis has that curled lip! Gladys, Elvis and Vernon around 1938, possibly taken as a memento when Vernon was in Parchman Farm.

More family life. Tupelo, 1941.

Elvis on stage, 1956.

Col. Parker, Elvis Presley and Ed Sullivan, 1956.

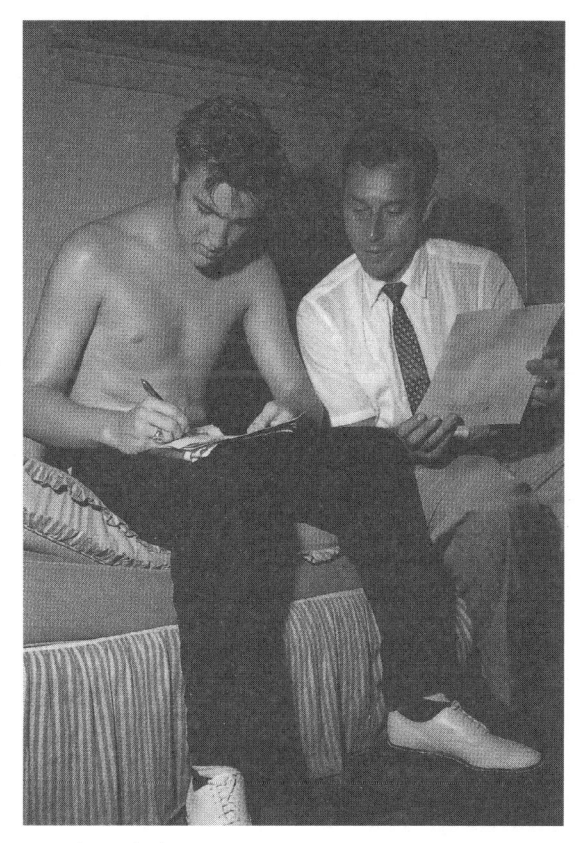

Barechested Elvis signing contract.

Elvis on stage, 1956. The sideburns had a life of their own.

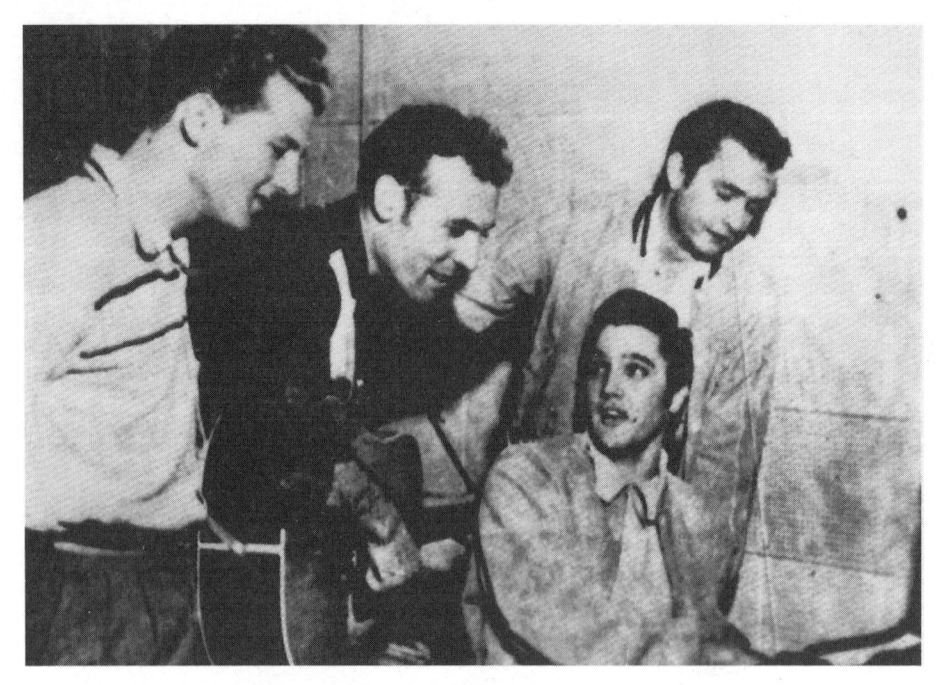

The Million Dollar Quartet, December 1956 at Sun Studios: Jerry Lee Lewis, Carl Perkins, Johnny Cash and Elvis Presley.

The Sun Studio, now a haven for tourists (Tim Whitnall).

"Presley for President", Los Angeles Airport, 1956. A joke campaign but Elvis is enjoying it. Eisenhower won.

THE KNOW-HOW ON ELVIS

REAL NAME: Elvis Aaron Presley.
BIRTHPLACE: Tupelo, Mississippi.
BIRTHDATE: January 8th, 1935.
FATHER'S & MOTHER'S NAME: Vernon & Gladys.
HEIGHT: 6 feet.
WEIGHT: 12 st. 12 lb.
HAIR: Brown.
EYES: Blue.
BROTHERS AND SISTERS: None (an identical twin died at birth).
FAVOURITE FOODS: Pork chops, brown gravy, apple pie.
FAVOURITE CLOTHES: Sports jackets and sport shirts.
NICKNAME: "Chief" as he is called by his musicians.
FAVOURITE COLOURS: Pink and black.
FAVOURITE SINGERS: Arthur "Big Boy" Crudup, Ink Spots, Frank Sinatra, Hank Snow.
FAVOURITE SUBJECT: English.
HOBBIES: Sports cars, motor-cycles, collecting teddy bears, swimming, water skiing, boxing, football.
EDUCATION: Graduate of Humes High School, Memphis, Tenn. Studied electricity at night school in Memphis.
FAVOURITE TYPE RESTAURANT: Quiet coffee bar.
DISLIKES: Formal parties, getting dressed up, crowded places.

Elvis fan magazines often carried suspect information. Surely it should be "Brothers and Sisters, 1 (twin brother died at birth)". How did anyone know the twin was identical? Elvis preferred Dean to Frank: he didn't collect teddy bears, and he loved dressing-up. He did lose 12 pounds in the army though and came out looking great.

ELVIS—UP-TO-DATE

- REAL NAME: Elvis Aron Presley
- BIRTHPLACE: Tupelo, Mississippi
- BIRTHDATE: January 8th, 1935
- FATHER & MOTHER'S NAME: Vernon and Gladys (deceased)
- HEIGHT: 6 feet
- WEIGHT: 12 st. (lost 12 lb. since entering the Army)
- HAIR: Brown
- EYES: Blue
- BROTHERS AND SISTERS: None (an identical twin died at birth)
- FAVOURITE CLOTHES: Sports jackets and sports shirts
- FAVOURITE COLOURS: Pink and black
- HOBBIES: Sports cars, motor-cycles, collecting teddy bears, swimming, water ski-ing, boxing, football
- EDUCATION: Graduate of Humes High School, Memphis, Tennessee. Studied electricity at night school in Memphis
- REGIMENT: 2nd Armoured Division, U.S. Army
- RANK: Private
- SERIAL NUMBER: 53310761

The official Elvis Presley Fan Club address is:
Miss Jeanne Saword,
24 Clarendon Flats,
Balderton Street, London, W.I

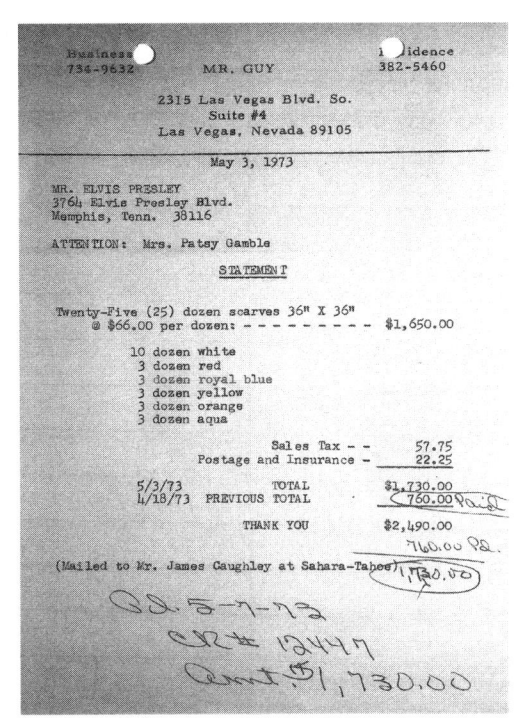

The bulk buying of scarves rather takes from the spontaneity of the event.

Elvis' final prescription, the day before he died.

Elvis McPresley, who is managed by Colonel McParker.

Elvis statue in Beale Street, Memphis (Tim Whitnall).

Elvis Presley: Caught in a Trap

The US air force is building a missile base in the Big Smokey Mountains and Lieutenant Josh Morgan (Elvis P) is sent to talk to the owner of the proposed site, the hillbilly Pappy Tatum (Arthur O'Connell). Josh discovers that Jodie Tatum (also Elvis P) is his double and they discover family links. El 1 and El 2 find girls to marry and Pappy agrees to the missile site providing there is a permanent police patrol on his land, thereby preventing the Inland Revenue from locating his moonshine still.

Despite the tired jokes and tired songs, the director Gene Nelson could have succeeded if he had put more into the scenes with El1 and El 2 in the same shot: the fight between them is lame and so obviously fake.

Nevertheless, the producer Hal Wallis was to say, 'Returns from cinemas all over the world showed one thing – *Viva Las Vegas* and *Kissin' Cousins* marked a tremendous comeback for Elvis Presley as a box-office attraction. These two films were blockbusters and we think Elvis has gained a whole new audience, an audience of all ages.' This is a curious comment to be making when he was about to renegotiate Elvis' contract. Surely he would be wanting to talk the price down, but the meaning was clear. Elvis was guaranteed money. What other star could say that?

Mort Shuman: 'Let's face it. Most of the people who were writing for Elvis were Tin Pan Alley hacks. They were born on the wrong side of the cusp as far as the Great Musical Divide was concerned. Rock'n'roll made them a good living but it wasn't something they felt deeply about. If Lawrence Welk had been popular instead of Elvis, they would have written Lawrence Welk songs. I could never have done that.'

Not to worry – in March while the Beatles were storming up the US charts and setting new sales records, Elvis was making his next film, *Roustabout*. This was one film where Colonel Parker earned his money as a technical advisor, as it was set in fairgrounds. Indeed, the scheming, rival carnival owner played by Pat Buttram could have been played by Parker himself. He might have even done it as he loved film sets and there was a huge sound stage at Paramount for this one. There are several photographs of Colonel Parker wearing Paramount's costumes, not to mention the famed shot of Elvis holding up Parker with a machine gun during the making of *Follow That Dream*.

There was invariably a 'no motorbikes' clause for the duration of a film, so, in theory, Elvis was delighted with *Roustabout*, as he wore black leather and rode a motorbike on screen. In practice, he argued with the director John Rich who wouldn't give him time off when he felt sick and who also ordered the Memphis Mafia to keep quiet. Elvis nearly walked out a couple of times.

In the script, the down-at-heel fairground staff twig that he would be ideal for the Wall of Death – we'd figured this out an hour earlier – but the rider in the sequence is so obviously not Elvis. How did Elvis feel about having a stunt man for this scene? Would he have liked to have done it himself? I suspect not, because this was a time when stars did not put themselves at risk. Elvis (Charlie Rogers) says at one point, 'I'm not biting the head off a chicken', so he could have had ten years on Ozzy Osbourne.

Johnny Meeks: 'I was in *Roustabout* with Elvis and I'll bet you never saw me. I'm a part of the band but all eyes are on Elvis. He was like that in real life. You could be standing right next to Elvis but everybody would be looking at him. He had more charisma than anyone I know.'

Mae West turned down the role of Maggie Morgan, the fairground owner, which was played by Barbara Stanwyck, and both she and Leif Erickson as her drunken husband with a huge chip on his shoulder deserved better. Still, *The High Chaparral* was only a few steps away. Early in the film, Raquel Welch makes her Hollywood debut in Mother's Tea House. She's the girl who says, 'Uh, how come they call this place a tea house?'

The original Little Egypt was Catherine Devine and she appeared at the World's Fair in Chicago in 1893. The name had been handed down and the current Little Egypt threatened to sue Paramount for allowing Wilda Taylor to appear under that name as an exotic dancer. This was an opportunity for Elvis to revive the Coasters' song, written by Leiber and Stoller. The Coasters had only made No.23 in 1961, so Elvis' fine version should have been a single. It didn't happen as perhaps the song was too far from his new image as a family entertainer.

There was nothing else of note in the score and to make it worse, Elvis sounded bored when he was performing 'It's Carnival Time' and 'It's A Wonderful World'. Who can blame him? 'There's a Brand New Day on the Horizon' was written by Joy Byers, but at least she had ripped off a decent spiritual, 'This Little Light of Mine'. A title song that was written by Otis Blackwell was not used, which may mean it was worse than the one by Giant, Baum and Kaye.

Still the soundtrack album topped the US album charts for the first week in 1965, squeezed in between the Beach Boys and the Beatles. It was less successful in the UK and Andy Gray, reviewing the film for the *NME*, wrote, 'How long can Elvis Presley stick to the same old script?' The answer was four years.

It was around this time that Presley met his hairdresser and spiritual advisor, Larry Geller, much to chagrin of Colonel Parker. Presley wanted to know why he had been blessed with such talent, even if he was misusing it, and Geller took him into the desert. Elvis saw a cloud that mutated into the face of Jesus and said, 'I'm not a believer anymore. I'm a knower. How can I make such dumb movies when I have seen the face of God?' Good question! The Colonel told him to get off 'this religious kick' and Elvis replied, 'My life is not a kick.' The Colonel wanted to oust Geller but Elvis stuck by him. A comparison can be made with the Beatles and the Maharishi and indeed, Geller was to introduce Elvis to the guru, Sri Daya Meta.

In September 1964, Elvis was made an honorary sheriff of Shelby County, Tennessee, which allowed him to make arrests and carry firearms. This was the first of many similar awards.

Elvis took a holiday in Las Vegas. He wanted to play there but he remembered 1956 and he couldn't bear the humiliation of a second failure. He saw the comedian Howie Pickles, who started joking about him. He made comparisons of Jesus and Elvis: 'Think about it, Jesus said, 'Love thy neighbour' and then Elvis says 'Don't Be Cruel'.' Then he delivered the crunch: 'Jesus was born from Immaculate Conception, and the girl Elvis lives with goes to the Immaculate Conception High School.' The audience wanted to laugh but didn't dare as Elvis was there.

'I'm a big fan of yours, Mr. Pickles,' said Elvis from the audience, 'but I don't dig that stuff about my Lord and Saviour. It don't sit right with the way I was brought up.'

That same night a woman Pickles had insulted for being too fat was killed and, with his sheriff's badge, Elvis wanted to solve the crime. His investigations took him to a new age hippie commune outside Vegas, where he agreed to perform a charity Peace Concert, much against Colonel Parker's wishes. It was a huge success and other cities wanted charity concerts, which didn't sit well with Parker. Elvis did help to solve the case but not before a friend died. As Elvis left the chapel after the funeral, Colonel Parker was waiting. He'd had enough of Elvis doing what he wanted. 'Everything's packed,' said Parker, 'We've got a movie to make, son.' Elvis walked slowly to his white Cadillac.

The last four paragraphs are all fiction but isn't it fun? I am recounting the plot of *Viva Las Vengeance*, one of Daniel Klein's Elvis murder mysteries, published in 2004. Other titles are *Kill Me Tender, Blue Suede Clues* and *Such Vicious Minds*.

Putting historical characters into a novel can be very entertaining and it is a growing trend. We like these characters, so why can't they do more than rerun their lives? No matter how many times Elvis' story is written, the ending is going to be the same, Elvis is going to die when he is 42 years old. It would be nice to change the story. A brilliant example is the Quentin Tarantino film, *Inglourious Basterds* (2009) in which Hitler is killed when a cinema catches fire and so the war ends a year earlier. The ending took viewers by surprise: although the film was fiction, they expected certain rules to be observed, namely, that Hitler died in his bunker and the war ended in 1945.

Expect a lot more historical rewrites as the years go by.

Still, back to the facts...

When you consider the wit and the ingenuity of the Beatles in *A Hard Day's Night* (1964), it is a pity that Elvis got so stuck in a rut. Although Cliff Richard was seen as the British Elvis, he did star in a lavish musical, *The Young Ones* (1961), which was more lavish than anything Elvis was in, and he followed it with the amiable *Summer Holiday* (1963). As a song, Tepper and Bennett's 'The Young Ones' was considerably better than what they had been giving to Elvis.

Elvis wasn't the only singer/actor to be caught in a rut. Billy Fury's love of animals (and girls!) came through in *I've Gotta Horse* but, despite guest appearances from some stalwart actors, the film went nowhere. Rick Nelson appeared with his wife and was directed by his dad in *Love and Kisses* (1965) but it resembled a long episode of *The Adventures of Ozzie and Harriet*. However, the idea was forming that concerts might make good movies and Steve Binder directed *The T.A.M.I. Show* from the Santa Monica Civic Auditorium in October 1964. The film featured the Rolling Stones, James Brown, Jan and Dean, and Gerry and the Pacemakers.

An indication of how Elvis felt came when he met the British actor and singer John Leyton, who was in Hollywood shooting *Von Ryan's Express* with Frank Sinatra. Elvis warmed to him. 'Elvis said to me that he would love to have been in *The Great Escape* and he was very surprised to find out that I was a singer. Somehow he got hold of one of my albums and he noticed that I had recorded 'I Don't Care If the Sun Don't Shine', which was an old song anyway. He said, 'It's better than my version, you should go back to singing'.'

Had the King abdicated? How could someone with such taste in music appear in such rubbish as *Girl Happy*? Elvis plays Rusty Wells, a nightclub singer, who travels to Fort Lauderdale for some bookings and to keep an eye on Shelley Fabares for her protective, mobster father. Hardly a believable plot – who on earth would hire Elvis as a chaperone? Elvis may have disliked his blond wig in *Kissin' Cousins* but worse was to come. In *Girl Happy*, he appears in drag – the King becomes a queen. The film is similar to *Where the Boys Are*, a 1960 film with Connie Francis and Dolores Hart, also shot in

Spencer Leigh

Fort Lauderdale.

The songs are perfunctory, even the title song, written by Doc Pomus. The hit single, 'Do the Clam', which just missed the US Top 10, was a nonsensical dance record. I know this is a beach party film but what is the point of dancing like a mollusc?

The songs are nondescript, but 'Fort Lauderdale Chamber Of Commerce' plumbs new depths for Tepper and Bennett. 'Wolf Call' with the Jubilee Four is about whistling at girls – very non-PC today – and 'Puppet on a String' is a pretty country ballad and the best of the bunch.

The film company Allied Artists, which had made the epics, *El Cid* (1961) and *55 Days at Peking* (1963), had ridiculously overspent and faced bankruptcy. They needed a quick hit for some easy money – and what better solution than Elvis Presley? They came to an arrangement with Hal Wallis and Colonel Parker, and Parker said they could cut corners even further by using existing tracks instead of commissioning a new score.

Parker cannily suggested songs that had been published by his company. Elvis mimes to these tracks but ironically, this makes *Tickle Me* one of the better Presley soundtracks. The songs, mostly cut three years earlier and published by Parker / Presley / Aberbach, include 'It Feels So Right' and 'Night Rider'.

Yes, *Tickle Me*, that's right. Elvis Presley made a film called *Tickle Me*. No wonder Allied Artists was going under if they couldn't come up with a better title than that. Everything about the film was tacky – when Elvis sings 'Long Lonely Highway' from a coach window in the opening credits, the coach is driving endlessly over the same terrain.

The producers were hoping that Elvis on a female dude ranch would attract the punters and it did reasonably well. There is some expense in a fantasy western sequence in which Elvis plays the Panhandle Kid. The other actors are unknown (another economy) and Elvis has several scenes with a clumsy sidekick, played by Jack Mullaney. This was a half-hearted attempt to duplicate the Dean Martin and Jerry Lewis relationship, and it was the highpoint of Mullaney's career.

The poster for *Tickle Me* said, 'See Elvis take on the rodeo, the robbers and the Ghost House!' Probably giving the film a connotation it doesn't deserve, we could say *Tickle Me* was Elvis Presley starring in a parody of Elvis Presley films. The truth is, *Tickle Me*, directed by Norman Taurog, was even more cheapo-cheapo than usual.

Then something unexpected happened and no, I am not going back to Daniel Klein's fiction. Elvis had recorded 'Crying in the Chapel' in 1960 but it had never been released as the copyright holders wouldn't agree to a deal. In 1965, the negotiations were reopened and a compromise reached. RCA thought they would try it as a single, knowing that at least they would have strong sales in the south. In May 1965 it climbed to No.3 in the US and topped the new *Billboard* Easy Listening chart. It sold two million copies in the States and also topped the UK charts, his first UK No.1 in two years.

How would he enjoy this new found success? Well, filming *Frankie and Johnny*, a film we will discuss shortly. When filming was over, he and the Memphis Mafia went to a motorbike showroom and rode away on ten bikes.

In August, Elvis returned to Hawaii for *Paradise, Hawaiian Style*. He played a helicopter pilot ferrying passengers around the islands, but he did none of the flying himself. While there, he and Colonel Parker visited the memorial for the USS Arizona and Elvis laid a wreath. Elvis then signed long-term deals with Hal Wallis, with RCA

Elvis Presley: Caught in a Trap

and with Colonel Parker himself. Colonel Parker would now officially receive 50% of his earnings: he was doing that anyway with his biased accounting. When this was reported in the media, Parker commented, 'I've got to make a living.'

The lead singer of Herman's Hermits, Peter Noone was at the wrap-up party at the Polynesian Cultural Centre on 18 August 1965. A short interview between them was recorded but Herman had difficulty understanding Elvis. Asked if he will come to England, Elvis says, 'Colonel Parker has a bad back. As soon as he feels better, we'll probably come over.' Asked to name his favourite group, Elvis says, 'LAPD', that is, the Los Angeles Police Department.

To celebrate Elvis' 10 years with RCA, the record company issued *Elvis for Everyone*. The cover picture was of Elvis standing next to a cash register: how blasé can you get? The contents weren't much better: a ragbag collection of leftovers from recording and film sessions, even going back to the Sun days with 'When It Rains, It Really Pours' and 'Tomorrow Night', which had a new backing track. With 24 minutes playing time and no hits, this was not so much a celebration of Elvis at RCA as a precursor for budget reissues. *Elvis for Everyone* was a Top 10 album, but only just. The album still sold 300,000 copies.

The Beatles came to America in August for a stadium tour and possibly John Lennon tried to see Elvis in Graceland on August 19. David Stanley recalls, 'I was 10 years old and there was a call from the front gate and Vester Presley, Elvis' uncle, answered the door and it was John Lennon and Brian Epstein. John mopped my head with his hand and said, 'Is Elvis home?' He wasn't, as he making a movie in Los Angeles. I was freaked out but my mother didn't let them in. She didn't want long hair in the house.'

Chris Hutchins, who worked for the *NME* and knew Parker, arranged a meeting between the Beatles and Elvis. Elvis was working on *Paradise, Hawaiian Style* and after much to-ing and fro-ing, both Parker and Epstein said yes.

As if it mattered, there was the showbiz protocol as to who would visit whom. Chris Hutchins set it up with Colonel Parker. On August 27, the Beatles would go to see Elvis in Perugia Way, Bel Air. Unlike today, press and photographers would not be invited.

The Beatles' press officer Tony Barrow recalled, 'The fact that someone from the press was involved had put the Beatles off. George said, 'If this is going to be another dirty big press party, let's forget it. We want to meet Elvis but not with a gang of photographers and radio DJs hassling us.' So the deal with Chris Hutchings was – no pictures, no taping, no leaking of details in advance. This was in his best interest as he would have the story exclusively to himself.'

The Beatles went with Brian Epstein, Mal Evans, Neil Aspinall, Tony Barrow and their driver Alf Bicknell – no one else. Roger McGuinn of the Byrds wanted to tag along but was told 'Sorry, no'. John said that he didn't want it to be a contest to see who could field the most players.

They were impressed when they saw Elvis, not just because he was Elvis but because he had a remote control for his TV. Although some had reached the UK, they hadn't seen one before. Colonel Parker's opening words were 'A chair for Mr. Epstein.' He was amazed that Epstein managed several other acts: Parker's time was devoted to Elvis. Neither of them revealed what they discussed but surely Epstein had raised the question of Elvis coming to the UK.

Alf Bicknell: 'It was exciting to arrive late at night at Elvis' home with Elvis standing at the door, shaking everybody's hands and calling everybody 'Sir'. It was a luxurious home and had an immense hall with a beautiful brick fireplace. It impressed me to see the number of people that Elvis had working for him. There were four Beatles and they had Brian, Mal, Neil, Tony and me. I used to drive the Beatles around on my own.'

The conversation was inconsequential but they discussed the problems of travelling by plane and mid-air dramas. Elvis said of his films, 'I play a country boy with a guitar who meets a few girls along the way and I sing a few songs.' Paul asked him how long it took to make a film and Elvis said, 'No more than a month if we're lucky'.

He said that when they deviated from the formula, as with *Wild in the Country*, the films didn't do as well. Elvis played a record he loved, 'Mohair Sam' by Charlie Rich, written by Dallas Frazier. He called for instruments to be brought out – Ringo had bongos – and they jammed for a little while, starting, oddly enough, with Cilla Black's 'You're My World'.

But not much happened. George shared a joint with Larry Geller. Ringo and Mal Evans played pool with Jerry Schilling and Billy Smith and had a good time. Parker and Epstein played roulette. According to Tony Barrow, Priscilla was walking around in a long dress and tiara and looking like a Barbie doll.

They were each given a pack of Elvis records as they left and a fan took a photograph of Elvis saying goodbye. As they left, John shouted, 'Long live the King!' As the limousine pulled away, John said, 'That wasn't Elvis, it was just a feller.' John told George that Presley was stoned and George replied, 'Aren't we all?' Tony Barrow was disappointed, later describing Elvis to me as 'a boring old fart'.

Elvis' cousin, Donna Presley Early: 'I wouldn't say that Elvis was jealous of the Beatles. He knew that the world was a diverse place and that people liked all kinds of music. He felt that there was plenty of room for everyone. The books that say he was jealous are wrong. Elvis certainly enjoyed the Beatles himself. He played me their records and he never played me his own! He loved listening to what other people were doing. He adored Brook Benton and he also played me the Platters and the Ink Spots. He loved gospel music and he loved the depth of J.D. Sumner's voice, as we all did.'

Elvis was invited to meet them the next day but just a few of his Memphis Mafia went. The boys were invited to their Hollywood Bowl concert but that would have been a step too far – their loyalty was to Elvis.

Alf Bicknell: 'I thought that Elvis' boys were great. They were like stars themselves and they were much more confident than us. They took us to a couple of night-clubs that were closing down for the night and they got the singers to perform especially for us. We couldn't have done that.'

John Phillips from the Mamas and the Papas was invited to Bel Air in the daytime: 'Elvis took me outside to his swimming pool. He said, 'Look at the lawn, John'. I said, 'Very nice, Elvis'. He said, 'Know what it is. It's Astroturf. You never have to cut it'. I said, 'Very nice, Elvis'.'

Perhaps it would have been better if they had met at Graceland. Elvis had bought go-karts for Graceland and he and his boys would ride around the estate or ride around Memphis on their motorbikes late at night. Perhaps to keep them in the house and somewhat safer, Priscilla gave Elvis a miniature racing set for Christmas 1965 and he would stage races with the Memphis Mafia. On New Year's Day, 1966, he invented a fireworks game for Graceland. Everyone put on football helmets and pads and then threw fireworks at each other.

Elvis was uneasy about the Beatles and I suspect it was down to education. Most of the rock'n'rollers had had a basic education and only Pat Boone of the major stars had gone to university. Rock'n'roll was seen as *infra dig* by university students who favoured jazz or folk. A few years later the Beatles came along. The Beatles had not done well at school but they had had a grammar school education and could have done better if they had applied themselves. Simon and Garfunkel were the Everly Brothers gone to college.

The Beatles' biographer, Hunter Davies remarks, 'John, Paul and George were three grammar school boys and although they didn't pay much attention in class, it had an influence on them. John and Paul were big readers – they read Lewis Carroll and this comes out in so many ways. They were intelligent and educated and hungry for knowledge. They got bored very quickly and wanted to move on, and this is why their music was always changing and developing.'

Considering how easily John and Paul mixed with people of higher formal education such as Peter Cook and Dudley Moore, it is likely the educated set automatically regarded the Beatles as intellectual and their failure at school merely demonstrated that there weren't obedient and had independent spirits.

Still, like Elvis, we must get back to the films. *Harum Scarum* in the US, *Harem Holiday* in the UK, is dreadful either way, a preposterous attempt to recast Elvis Presley as Rudolph Valentino – he even wears one of Valentino's costumes from *The Sheik* (1921) – and the result is like a bad pantomime. On the face of it, you might think it was expensive but, outside of Elvis' salary, not a bit of it. This is a Sam Katzman film and he was using sets already on the MGM lot. You will find the temple in *Harem Holiday* the same one as in Cecil B DeMille's *King of Kings* from 1927. First time it was a de Mille production, this time it was a run of de Mille production. There was just one feature which held Elvis' interest – Mary Ann Mobley, who had been Miss America.

Elvis didn't turn up at first and instead spent time with Larry Geller, as he was so dismayed by the songs. Colonel Parker feigned a heart condition to buy some time and then forced him to go.

Elvis, usually a natty dresser, looks dreadful in his green pantaloons. He plays a movie star who's kidnapped in the Middle East and it would have been preferable if they had kidnapped Sam Katzman instead. It is so tacky – one character, peeling a banana, fluffs his lines and Elvis laughs – and it's in the film. It's clichés all the way, as Elvis encounters a beautiful princess, a very small person, several belly-dancers and an orphaned slave girl. At one stage, he says, 'I'm in love with your daughter. How could I assassinate you?'

The only song that works outside the film is 'So Close, Yet So Far', written by Joy Byers and modelled on 'Halfway to Paradise' but not as strong. Oddly, this film has been shown on TV with this song omitted.

Joy Byers also wrote the best of the new songs for *Frankie and Johnny*, but that is damning them with faint praise, as the film starts with the MGM lion roaring and goes downhill from there. The only songs that cinemagoers would remember were old chestnuts, 'Frankie and Johnny', 'Down by the Riverside' and 'When The Saints Go Marching In'. Elvis' duet with Eileen Wilson of 'Petunia, the Gardener's Daughter' is appalling, but then it was meant to be a typically corny vaudeville performance. One song not recorded for the film, 'Wife Number 99' (Tepper, Bennett), exists in demo form, though not performed by Elvis, and sounds crass today.

Sam Cooke had recorded 'Frankie and Johnny' in 1963, shortly before being shot by a motel manager. There's no connection but Elvis was wary of portents so I am surprised he still cut the song. Shortly before his death, Cooke had recorded his brilliant anthem, 'A Change is Gonna Come'. Parker told Presley that Cooke had been killed by the Mafia for stepping out of line and sounding off about civil rights. There is no evidence for this but it is an example of Parker wanting to keep Elvis in line.

Still, Elvis was at the time intrigued by his new Sony video-camera and he wanted to film some high-class romps with his girlfriends, girl-on-girl if he could. Nobody knows for sure but it seems unlikely that Elvis himself was starring in his own porn movies.

The Pomus and Shuman song, 'What Every Woman Lives For', could not be more sexist if it tried. Mort Shuman: 'I was writing songs to make everyone happy and not make waves but I was already tuned out. Without knowing it, I was contributing to Elvis Presley's decline – and mine as well. Eventually I said, 'That's the end of it." Mort based himself in Europe, living in London and France, recording albums in English and French and writing such hits as 'Little Children' (Billy J. Kramer) and 'Sha-la-la-la-lee' (Small Faces).

Frankie and Johnny is set on a riverboat and several of the characters are perpetually drunk. As so often with Elvis films, jail and gambling feature prominently.

Elvis (Johnny) stars with Donna Douglas (Frankie) from *The Beverly Hillbillies* in a film based around the song, 'Frankie and Johnny'. Elvis flirts with Nellie Bly for no other reason than a fortune-teller has told him that a red-headed woman will bring him luck. Their song about their misfortunes, 'Frankie and Johnny' is the key part of their vaudeville act. Frankie always fires a blank at Johnny but one night a misguided employee swops the blank for a real bullet. The tension mounts and we think Elvis is going to die: I'm exaggerating of course – we know this can't happen in a quasi-pantomime. Frankie shoots him but the bullet bounces off his lucky charm – what is this charm made of? – and she realises that she has loved him all along. Elvis got up, dusted himself down and picked up his pay packet – $650,000 – sorry, $325,000: Colonel Parker was the big winner here.

Paradise, Hawaiian Style was intended to replicate the success of *Blue Hawaii* but this was so bad that it made *Blue Hawaii* look like *Citizen Kane*. Elvis' hair looks unnatural throughout and although this is a beach movie, we only see Elvis with a large towel around his body. It could be that Paramount weren't prepared to pay the extra for Elvis disrobing, but then Elvis had put on a few pounds and maybe he didn't want to display his physique.

Elvis' co-star should have been Shirley MacLaine but she pulled out. The last-minute replacement was a little-known British actress, Suzanna Leigh (Judy), who had just completed *Boeing Boeing* for Hal Wallis. The real action though was off-screen, as she didn't respond to Elvis' advances. He tried to win her around with a Mustang but still no-go. He was petulant when she was visited on set by the Irish hell-raiser Richard Harris. Elvis was in such a sulk that he went AWOL for a few days, much to Parker's annoyance – he blamed Suzanna. A stand-in was used for some long shots. The film, it must be said, contains some spectacular aerial photography.

On the other hand, the actress Julie Parrish (Joanna) was desperate to be in *Paradise, Hawaiian Style* as she loved Elvis. She failed the audition but noted that Hal Wallis

Elvis Presley: Caught in a Trap

had been casting for *Boeing Boeing*. She played a girl walking down the street who was pinched on the behind. Then she asked Wallis about the Elvis film and got that too, although her scene in *Boeing, Boeing* was cut, which hardly mattered as the film was boring, boring.

Elvis and Julie perform 'A Dog's Life' in which they struggle with four unruly dogs. In a helicopter. Fancy allowing dogs inside a plane without securing them in any way! Any pilot would be struck off for such behaviour. The song was equally ludicrous and Elvis laughed so much when he recorded it that it took some time to complete. There was an off-stage drama as Julie took some drugs and her right side went into a spasm. Elvis apparently healed her with a laying on of hands. Elvis' acting is especially bad. Could be drugs, but I suspect that he learnt his lines just before the scenes and rushed them out before he could forget them.

Elvis sings a nightclub song 'Scratch My Back' with Marianna Hill but this could have been sultry and sexy rather than silly. Nine-year-old Donna Butterworth sings dreadful songs with Elvis – 'Queenie Wahini's Papaya' and 'Datin'' – and she performs a full length 'Bill Bailey, Won't You Please Come Home': more padding.

One of the production numbers, 'Drum of the Islands' is sung in a war canoe by Tongans. However, the only war canoe available belonged to Samoans and they objected to Tongans being inside their boat. The producers had to break up a fight.

Elvis was impressed by a local performer, Kui Lee, who died of cancer in 1966. He recorded 'I'll Remember You', which Kui Lee had released in 1964, and he probably thought of Gladys. It is excellent and it should have been in *Paradise, Hawaiian Style*. Instead, the track was a bonus track on the *Spinout* album in 1966.

At the royal premiere for *Born Free* in 1966, the Queen asked Suzanna Leigh about working with Elvis. She said that Elvis wanted to come to Britain. Apparently, Buckingham Palace sent an invitation to a garden party to the Colonel but he ignored it. This may be apocryphal as Elvis would have wanted to go even if the date had to be rearranged.

It was back to motor racing for *Spinout*, which was released in the UK as *California Holiday*. The original title had been *Raceway*, but that was dropped. Warren Oates, who saw him on the set, praised 'his amazing ability to drive a racing car while stoned.'

Elvis races an experimental car and has trouble off track with singer Shelley Fabares and the second *Gidget*, Deborah Walley. Surprisingly, Elvis doesn't get a girl in the end, but nor do the girls go off with each other: that would have been a mind-changing ending for 1966.

The score is inconsequential but the title track was a US Top 40 single: it was full of dodgy girl / car double meanings. The B-side, 'All That I Am', was better. This musical smorgasbord includes 'Smorgasbord' in which Elvis sings, 'I'll take the dish I please and please the dish I take'. Elvis plays a double-neck guitar for 'I'll Be Back' but doesn't do much with it. Struggling to find anything remotely interesting to say about these songs, I note that he was backed on screen by a girl drummer.

The press was full of stories about Elvis being the world's most eligible bachelor and perhaps with this in mind, he was given a never-get-married song, 'Never Say Yes', written by Pomus and Shuman.

An MGM executive commented, without irony 'Elvis Presley's films don't need titles. They could just be numbered and they'd still sell.' It says an enormous amount for Elvis Presley's popularity that he could come through such a succession of films unscathed. Cliff Richard tried a similar series in the UK but soon gave up.

Elvis' new producer was Felton Jarvis, who had made hit records for Tommy Roe and he knew that Elvis' great voice deserved better material. He wanted to work to find the right songs. Felton was an affable, good-tempered man, ideal to be working with the mercurial Presley, and they talked about old cars and favourite films.

The success of 'Crying in the Chapel' had caused Elvis, the Colonel and RCA to consider another gospel set. This, in May 1966, was an opportunity for Felton to see exactly what Elvis could do with his voice. There is a photograph of Elvis socialising with Kitty Wells at RCA in Nashville and it's a shame that they didn't do something together when she was working so close to hand. It was a fantastic band including Scotty Moore, Chip Young, Harold Bradley (guitars), Floyd Cramer (piano), Bob Moore (bass), Buddy Harman, D. J. Fontana (drums), Charlie McCoy (harmonica), Boots Randolph (sax) and Pete Drake (steel guitar). As well as the Jordanaires, there was Millie Kirkham and the Imperials.

Jake Hess had left the Statesmen in 1963 and had formed the Imperials, taking their name from the Imperial Quartet which Colonel Parker used to promote. Hess insisted on a morals clause with each singer – no sexual relationships outside marriage and they must conduct themselves as personal representatives of God. No chance of Elvis joining them then, but he wanted them on the session for a very full choral sound. The result would be very different from the southern quartet feel of *His Hand in Mine* and it works perfectly on 'Somebody Bigger That You And I' and 'How Great Thou Art'. Elvis' voice is shining to the fore as on 'So High', which had been adapted by LaVern Baker in 1959 for the R&B hit single, 'So High, So Low'.

Elvis' cousin, Donna Presley Early: 'I love everything he did as I think he was the greatest entertainer who has ever lived or will ever live. 'How Great Thou Art' is my all-time favourite, but I also love 'Funny How Time Slips Away', 'Loving You' and 'Her Latest Flame'. I like hearing those outtakes where they mess up on a session and you will notice that Elvis always takes the blame himself.'

'Ol' Man River' had inspired the song, 'That Lucky Ol' Sun', written by Haven Gillespie in 1949. That in turn had inspired 'Somebody Bigger than You and I', which had been recorded by the Ink Spots in 1951 and was on the B-side of the Statesmen's 'Crying in the Chapel'.

Elvis takes his sources from both black and white gospel music, and 'Stand by Me' is a blues song written by Charles Tindley in 1905. 'Farther Along' goes back to a Missouri preacher who travelled by horse to reach his flock. Presley takes it slower than most versions of this song, perhaps to extract more from the lyric, and anyway there are plenty of up-tempo performances on this album.

How Great Thou Art was a US Top 20 album in 1967, and how great Elvis art, as it was nominated for a Grammy. This might not sound like a big deal, but Elvis had never won one. Indeed, many thought there was a deliberate policy to keep him out because he had upset the status quo with rock'n'roll in the mid-50s. This was untrue. The Grammys didn't start until 1958, so none of his early, ground-breaking records had been eligible.

In 1959, 'A Fool Such as I' was nominated for Record of the Year, but it lost to Bobby Darin's 'Mack the Knife' and Elvis could hardly complain about that. Similarly,

Elvis Presley: Caught in a Trap

in 1960 he was nominated for Best Vocal Performance with 'Are You Lonesome Tonight' and was beaten by Ray Charles' 'Georgia on My Mind', again a decision hard to dispute. His *G.I. Blues* album lost out to *The Genius of Ray Charles* in Best Vocal Performance Album, Male.

In 1959, 'A Big Hunk o' Love', which is fun but hardly a great recording, was nominated twice – once for Best Vocal Performance by a Top 40 Artist and once for Best R&B Performance – and the winners respectively were 'Midnight Flyer' by Nat 'King' Cole (his only Grammy) and 'What A Diff'rence a Day Makes' by Dinah Washington.

In 1967, Elvis was nominated for Best Sacred Performance and he received his first Grammy, beating the Browns, Red Foley, Dottie West, and George Beverly Shea with the Blackwood Brothers.

Felton Jarvis was finding great material for Elvis to record. He got funky with 'Down in the Alley', recorded by the Clovers in 1957. It is a repetitive blues with an insistent beat and Charlie McCoy and Boots Randolph wailing on harmonica and sax, respectively. Elvis must have loved the lyrics – he is going bowling with a girl until 3.30am. This wasn't released as a single and in 1970 Ronnie Hawkins recorded an equally fine version with Duane Allman that made the US charts.

Elvis' arrangement of 'Love Letters' follows Ketty Lester's but combines piano and organ perfectly. It became a US Top 20 single and make the Top 10 in the UK. Darrell Glenn, who had recorded the original 'Crying in the Chapel', had written a ballad, 'Indescribably Blue', which was given a similar arrangement to 'Love Letters' and became another US hit. By Elvis standards, these were little victories but they showed that Elvis wasn't finished yet.

The 60s folk revival had passed him by and he associated it with draft-dodging and non-patriotic behaviour but for the first time he recorded a Bob Dylan song, 'Tomorrow Is a Long Time', which he had heard on an Odetta album, and made a very good job of it.

In September 1966, Elvis made *Easy Come, Easy Go*, this time playing a US navy lieutenant Ted Jackson. As always, his mind is on girls, and in the title song, he sings, 'So many girls in every port, You gotta be a juggernaut'. This film was way too cynical when you consider that the main audience was girls. Pat Harrington Jr (playing Judd Whitman) owns a roulette wheel and in place of the numbers, there are pictures of girls with their measurements and telephone numbers. This prompts the woeful song, 'The Love Machine' and another one, 'She's a Machine', which was dropped but still recorded. Elvis is no great romancer, telling the girl in 'You Gotta Stop, 'That's right, you're wrong again'. The slow intro of this song is cribbed from 'Runaround Sue' and the best song, 'I'll Take Love', takes its cue from 'La Bamba'.

Most of the songs were written by Gerald Nelson who later made an album, *Songs I Wrote for Elvis*. I wouldn't brag about it. Well, he doesn't: the album consists of his demos for Elvis and he admits that he wrote some of the worst songs he has ever heard. He could be good though. He and his songwriter partner Fred Burch wrote 'Tragedy' for Thomas Wayne and they had originally hoped that Elvis would record that song.

The cast includes the 64-year-old actress Elsa Lanchester, who was married to Charles Laughton from 1929 until his death in 1962. She plays a lively Yogi which gives the two El's the chance to sing 'Yoga Is as Yoga Does'.

Part of the time Elvis is a deep-sea diver searching for treasure. Is it Elvis or his double in that wet suit? The treasure, like the script, is worth little, and what little there is goes to a local arts centre. Yes, Elvis supports modern performance art.

Elvis caught a cold, nothing special about that, but he was visited by Dr. George Nichopoulos, who would soon be on his payroll. This would be even better than owning that pharmacy.

Then there is the Christmas song, 'If Every Day Was like Christmas', which Red West had written with the arranger Glen Spreen. When Elvis was going to record this with the Jordanaires and the Imperials, he didn't feel at his best and he told Red to put down a guide vocal and he would add his voice later. Two days later, Elvis recorded the song and it became a UK Top 10 single in 1966. Roy Wood used the same theme for 'I Wish It Could Be Christmas Everyday'.

On Christmas Day 1966, Elvis and Priscilla announced their engagement, but isn't he really wedded to Colonel Parker? The lack of record sales, the falling audiences for his films, the punitive commission of Colonel Parker and preparing for a wedding might have caused Elvis to rein back on his spending. This is when he goes ballistic.

Elvis bought 19 horses, one for each of his staff, and at first he kept them at Graceland. Next Elvis bought a ranch, the Circle G, in Mississippi for $300,000. Donna Presley Early was Elvis' cousin: 'We lived very close to Elvis in Memphis and we used to visit Elvis at Graceland at Christmas and all that sort of thing. When he purchased the Circle G, he asked my family to move into the ranch. He sold it in 1970 and then moved us onto the grounds at Graceland, which was a fabulous place to live.'

Then Elvis bought a Lear Jet, an intriguing purchase as he wasn't touring and not travelling all that much, so what prompted this?

If Presley were married, the Colonel thought it would keep him away from Ann-Margret and her management, and stem his fixation with guns. Priscilla hoped it might make him grow up – no more water balloon fights, a reduction in his entourage, a better diet, and cutting his lavish spending. Colonel Parker probably liked Elvis spending as it kept him working.

A far better concept for a movie than *Double Trouble* would be the making of *Double Trouble*. The script called for an English heiress, but English roses, Petula Clark (a little old at 34) and Jane Asher, turned it down. The filmmakers picked the unknown Annette Day, spotted at her parents' antique stall in Portobello Road. It's hard to say what they spotted because she looks as though she is reading from an autocue – just like Elvis, I suppose – and the producers were so unhappy that a further eleven days' shooting was requested. God, it must have been bad! Check out Elvis' hands: they are bruised on occasion: don't know what happened there or whether the director, Norman Taurog, even noticed. He had lost his sight in one eye and was losing it in the other.

The English character actor, Norman Rossington, was in the cast and it might seem essential that Elvis should be in England for at least part of the story. No such luck – he remained on a sound stage in Los Angeles. Elvis plays a nightclub singer, Guy Lambert, who meets Jill (Annette Day) while he is Germany (no, he's not there either). He pursues her but leaves her alone when he finds out her age – she is only 17. How could Elvis act this convincingly?

There's some nonsense about gangsters and more nonsense as Elvis sings 'Old MacDonald' to some chickens and 'Long Legged Girl (with the Short Dress On)' to his chick. J. Leslie McFarland, who can usually be relied on for quirky songs, wrote the appalling 'Long Legged Girl', sexist to be sure, but just a dreadful song, performed with a messy, brassy accompaniment. It was considered a likely hit but it only reached No.63 in the US. There is 'I Have Only One Girl', which sounds like an outtake from *G.I. Blues* and contains a little snatch of 'It's Now or Never'.

Presley's oink, oink in 'Old MacDonald' are the least convincing pig sounds on record. Pork scratchings. Back home, he confided, . 'These damn fools have got me singing 'Old MacDonald' on the back of a truck with a bunch of animals. Man, it's a joke and the joke's on me.'

 'Old MacDonald' and 'Could I Fall in Love' were written by Randy Starr, who wrote 12 songs for Elvis. In the real world, he was a New York dentist, Dr. Warren Nadel. He didn't write any hits for Elvis but he did write 'I Know Where I'm Going' (George Hamilton IV) and the children's favourite, 'Mole in a Hole' (Southlanders). An intriguing feature of 'Could I Fall in Love' is Elvis harmonising with himself.

Neal Matthews of the Jordanaires: 'Elvis wanted songs that he got emotionally involved it and he didn't want to be recording crap. He might have been better off if he had stood up to Colonel Parker, but basically he was an easy-going guy who didn't know how to say no.'

Double Trouble was released in the spring of 1967, a time of great revolution in the music industry, building up to the Summer of Love. In 1966 Bob Dylan had released *Blonde on Blonde*, the Beach Boys *Pet Sounds* and the Beatles *Revolver.* Now they were about to release *Sgt. Pepper's Lonely Hearts Club Band*. What did Elvis make of 'A Whiter Shade of Pale'? What would be his response? As well as skipping the light fandango, he was tripping over an extension cord and he banged his head, suffering from concussion. The filming of his next film, his twenty-fifth if anyone's counting, *Clambake*, had to be delayed.

Elvis Presley plays Scott Hayward, a multi-millionaire's son who sets off to Miami to discover himself and finds powerboat racing, water-skiing and (yet again) Shelley Fabares. The first time she had told Elvis, 'I have a boyfriend'; the second, 'I'm engaged'; and the third, 'We're married now'. Elvis said, 'You're weakening, aren't you?' They got on well together, but the films held little interest.

Elvis acts in front of back-projections and with so many long shots in the power boat race, he could have been missing.

Elvis is racing a boat that had burst at 90mph the previous year and he fixed it with his miracle goop, a product that he had designed but never tested: did I tell you he is a miracle scientist too? He wins the race by topping 100 mph: the goop holds up and he gets the girl. The best moment is when his love rival challenges him to a karate fight and Elvis downs him with a punch.

His sidekick is the water-ski instructor, Will Hutchins (Tom Wilson), who supposedly sings 'Who Needs Money' with Elvis, but Will's voice was dubbed by Ray Walker. Will is incredibly annoying throughout and far more childish than the children. Elvis does well with the production number, 'Confidence', in a playground, although the song owes much to 'High Hopes'. The title song is a reworking of 'Shortnin' Bread'. After Elvis sang 'Clambake' in the studio, he burst out laughing and went into an improvised blues.

By far the best song is the country standard, 'You Don't Know Me', written and recorded by Eddy Arnold in 1946 and revived by Ray Charles in 1962. Who can say how this ended up in the film, but I suspect Colonel Parker had a financial interest. Whatever, it is a fine performance from Elvis, and the song conveys far more emotion than the cartoon characters. A fairly decent song, the bluesy 'How Can You Lose What You Never Had', was dropped from the production.

Elvis' white suit was cut into tiny pieces and given to purchasers of the boxed-set, *Elvis – The Other Sides – Worldwide Gold Award Hits, Vol. 2*. Oh, note the seam in Shelley's tights as she comes out of the pool – well, it keeps you awake, doesn't it?

A little bonus is the appearance of Jack Good, known for ITV's *Oh Boy!* and the special, *Around the Beatles*. He played a receptionist and I wondered whether he had suggested working with Elvis. 'Oh yes, but not then. I had seen Colonel Parker many times and said, 'Look, I'm the guy who should be producing Elvis. Why have you got him doing all these rubbishy pictures?' He said, 'Jack, these films make money. *Blue Hawaii* was Elvis' biggest hit'. When I was lucky enough to play in *Clambake*, I said to Elvis, 'Why are you still doing these stinking rotten awful films?' and he said, 'The Colonel has promised me that he is going to give me a good movie next'. The Colonel may have promised that, but he never delivered.'

How did Jack feel about his role behind the desk? 'Well, I should have been behind bars for the way I acted and the whole film was one of the really, really awful ones.' Look at *The Graduate* (1968), as the scene with Dustin Hoffman and Buck Henry in the hotel lobby could have been inspired by *Clambake*.

At the wrap party for *Clambake*, Elvis played bass and then sang blues and gospel with Lance LeGault. When Priscilla's stepfather, Paul Beaulieu, visited the set, he admired the two longhorns that Elvis was with. It was never a good thing to praise anything in front of Elvis as he was given them as a present.

Maybe Elvis wasn't in line with the spirit of the times by releasing *How Great Thou Art* (March 1967), 'The Love Machine' as a single, and having *Double Trouble* as his new film. Still, Elvis the Man was in line with the summer of love. At the end of April, Priscilla's family was in Palm Springs and the media sensed something was happening, but they were thrown off-track.

The next day, 1 May 1967, Elvis and Priscilla flew to Las Vegas and they were married at 9.30am by David Zenoff, a Justice of the Nevada Supreme Court, in Milton Prell's suite at the new Aladdin Hotel. The best men were Joe Esposito and Marty Lacker. It was front page news: the world's most eligible bachelor was married. Looking at the two of them together, you can see that Elvis wanted Priscilla to have dark hair like himself. David Stanley said that she used it to comic effect. With her dark hair and dark eyes, she could dress as a very convincing vampire and chase them around Graceland at Halloween.

Elvis biographer Ray Connolly: 'By the time they married she had been living with him for a couple of years. The excitement had worn off. The families had been saying, 'Make an honest woman of her' and he did. Despite all their problems, she has never said an unkind word about him and she has been very loyal to him, so I think it was hard for her to leave. Maybe if she had been older, it would have been better for them. Nowadays she goes on tours and works with the Royal Philharmonic Orchestra, and his image now is better than it ever has been. Maybe she should have managed him all along.'

The wedding created ill-feeling with the Memphis Mafia, particularly Red West, as so few of them knew about it. It could be that Priscilla didn't want them all there, that she wanted something more private. Colonel Parker told them that there hadn't been time to find a bigger room, which obviously was nonsense.

Sgt Pepper's Lonely Hearts Club Band was released on 1 June 1967 with a lavish gatefold sleeve and a front cover which showed the Beatles with some of their favourite people, but not Elvis. The artist Peter Blake was born in Dartford in 1932 and his *Self-Portrait with Badges* (1961), in which he holds a copy of *Elvis Monthly*, can be seen in Tate Britain: 'Presley was left out on purpose because if you are taking the top symbols and top idols, he would have to be there. The Beatles felt he didn't deserve to be there after all those awful films. It was probably as well as Colonel Parker would have made us pay for the use of his photograph.'

Paul McCartney told *Q* magazine: 'When the Beatles were recording, we would often ask George Martin for the Elvis echo. I think we got it down perfectly on 'A Day in the Life'.'

But in June 1967, it was business as normal for Elvis as he started work on his next film, *Speedway*, this time with a celebrity co-star, Nancy Sinatra. Neither of them looked realistic. Presley was losing weight with diet pills combined with his standard sleeping pills. Elvis plays a stock-car racer who is being hounded by a revenue official, Nancy Sinatra, for back taxes. Elvis fails to win the big race but he does get Nancy. Petula Clark again turned down an Elvis film and so did Sonny and Cher. The actors include Poncie Ponce, Harry Hickox and Harper Carter – was everybody hiding under pseudonyms?

Although Presley and Sinatra can be heard on 'There Ain't Nothing like a Song', there were no duets. There are only seven songs in all, so an opportunity was lost. Three more songs – a lullaby, 'Five Sleepy Heads' (Tepper, Bennett, Brahms), 'Suppose' and 'Western Union', which is 'Return to Sender, Part 2' – were bin-bagged. A different song called 'Western Union', was a hit for the Five Americans in 1967.

The best-known of Elvis' songs is 'Your Time Hasn't Come Yet, Baby', sung to encourage a girl growing up. 'Who Are You' which Elvis sings to Nancy, has some mellow jazz saxophone. 'He's Your Uncle, Not Your Dad' is terrible but was to advance the plot. By now, Elvis was recording his vocals to backing tracks. He didn't care. Nancy Sinatra sings 'Your Groovy Self' with a witty lyric from Lee Hazlewood. If only he had been asked to write for Elvis, especially when we know Elvis loved 'The Fool'.

Hooray! In September 1967, Elvis had a fine session for Felton Jarvis: decent songs, great musicians and strong performances, but the key to it all was singer, guitarist and songwriter, Jerry Reed, who was being heralded as the next Chet Atkins.

Jerry Reed had been born in Atlanta in 1937 and his early songs had been recorded by Brenda Lee and Gene Vincent. After army service, Reed moved to Nashville as a session guitarist and was mentored by Chet Atkins. In 1967, he had his first US country success with 'Guitar Man', a song about playing rock'n'roll in small clubs. Atkins thought it was perfect for Elvis and asked him to play the finger-picking electric guitar style he had been developing. Effectively, Jerry Reed was re-cutting 'Guitar Man' but with Elvis' lead vocal. Elvis was in such good humour that on one take, he went straight into 'What'd I Say'. Felton Jarvis knew he had a hit single. Using the same technique, they recorded Jerry Reed's 'Big Boss Man'. Jerry Reed wrote 'Tupelo Mississippi Flash', the song which established him as a country star.

Jerry Reed should have stayed, as he could have added some direction to a messy 'Hi Heel Sneakers' featuring Charlie McCoy on harmonica. Elvis began the take with a comic take on Bobbie Gentry's 'Ode to Billie Joe', a song which mentioned Tupelo.

Gentry was a dead ringer for an older Priscilla.

Elvis recorded two songs associated with Eddy Arnold – 'You Don't Know Me' and 'Just Call Me Lonesome', which is old-style lonesome with a crying steel. 'Singing Tree' is nonsense as though the writers had wanted to match 'I Talk to the Trees' from *Paint Your Wagon*. 'Mine' is a run-of-the-mill wedding song. There is a gospel song, 'We Call on Him' and a dramatic version of 'You'll Never Walk Alone' with Elvis on piano, based on Roy Hamilton's version from 1954.

In October, Elvis Presley went to Arizona to make *Stay Away, Joe*, which was good advice whatever your name. Elvis plays rodeo rider Joe Lightcloud, who visits his home reservation and helps with the Government's rehabilitation scheme. For the first time ever, Elvis is seen kissing a girl on a bed, although his mother (Katy Jurado) soon puts paid to that. At the end of the film, all the men who have lost their girls to Elvis gang up on him and the film ends with the demolition of his house. 'Man, that's what I call one hell of a fight,' says Elvis as the roof comes tumbling down.

There are only four songs – one of them is 'Stay Away, Joe' and another, 'Stay Away', is based on 'Greensleeves'. 'All I Needed Was the Rain' is a decent ballad but 'Dominick' is sung to a bull, which is gay. We laughed when Tommy Steele was compared to Elvis Presley, and now Elvis can't even better 'Little White Bull'.

Elvis and Priscilla spent Christmas at Graceland looking forward to their baby, but Elvis had itchy feet. The music world was passing him by and he was no longer relevant. He called the Colonel to wish him a happy new year: the Colonel had the answer: 'There are no good Christmas specials anymore. What did we have this year? Bing Crosby and Mitzi Gaynor. I'll get you a deal and you can make one next year. You can put some gospel songs in there. How does that sound?'

'Yeah,' said Elvis, 'and I like those Clint Eastwood westerns too. Get me one of them. No songs and lots of action.'

'Job done,' said the Colonel.

CHAPTER 11

Comeback Very Special

'Personal appearances – that's what matters.'
Rudy Vallee to Elvis Presley in *Live a Little, Love a Little*, 1968

I. All I Gotta Do Is Act Naturally

Excluding documentaries, we have covered most of Elvis Presley's film appearances by now. After 1969, he would only be playing himself, although you can argue that he never did anything else. He never played anybody older than himself, he always came from the south, he never changed his accent or manner of speech, he usually wore what Elvis Presley would be wearing, and he never wore prosthetics or altered his appearance, save for the occasional beard or blond wig. He was no Robert DeNiro or Tom Hanks, but then some great screen stars were nearly always the same – John Wayne, Robert Mitchum, James Stewart. With this in mind, just how good an actor was Elvis Presley?

The concept of entertainers in musical films goes right back to Al Jolson in the highly successful movie, *The Jazz Singer* (1927), a movie associated with the advent of sound pictures. Possibly Elvis Presley was encouraged by Bing Crosby, who starred in both light comedies and inspirational dramas, often singing a few songs along the way. He and Bob Hope were a winning combination in a series of *Road* films.

In the late 1940s / early 1950s, Frank Sinatra and Gene Kelly were a bankable duo in musical films, usually with Frank doing the singing and Gene the dancing. In 1953, Sinatra won an Oscar for his supporting role in *From Here to Eternity* and he was outstanding in a fearless role as a jazz drummer hooked on drugs in *The Man with the Golden Arm*. He clashed with Marlon Brando while they were filming *Guys and Dolls* (1955), largely because he knew Brando couldn't sing and was dragging the film down, but it was the top US film of the year with box office receipts of $9m. It easily beat Gregory Peck as Captain Ahab in *Moby Dick* ($5.2m) who gave a performance every bit as wooden as his leg. The studio played its cards well, leaking the spats between Brando and Sinatra and turning the film into a 'must see'. The ads proclaimed 'Brando sings!' and cinemagoers soon learnt he couldn't, but they'd had to pay good money to find out.

The following year, Frank Sinatra and Bing Crosby were box-office gold in *High Society* ($6.5m) and this made more money than Elvis Presley in *Love Me Tender* ($4.5m) and Pat Boone in *April Love* ($4m). The big film of the year was *The Ten Commandments* ($18.5m) – not much opportunity for songs there, but a brilliant score from Elmer Bernstein.

The big spectacles dominated the ticket sales and indeed they had to do well to recoup their budgets so there was *The Bridge on the River Kwai* ($18m), *Ben-Hur* ($17m), *Spartacus* ($13.5m), *West Side Story* ($11m) with *Mary Poppins* and *The Sound of Music* both topping $20m in the mid-60s.

For films which featured singing stars in the same period, consider *Blue Hawaii* (Elvis, $4.7m), *Viva Las Vegas* (Elvis and Ann-Margret, $4.7m), *Babes in Toyland* (Tommy Sands and Annette, $4.4m), *Bernadine* (Pat Boone, $3.7m), and *Loving You* (Elvis, $3.7m), The ensemble efforts included *Bye Bye Birdie* (Bobby Rydell and Ann-Margret, $5.6m) and *Ocean's 11* (The Rat Pack, $4.9m).

Sometimes a young star's appearance was simply an added bonus, giving the film street cred but not making much difference to the returns: *Rio Bravo* (Ricky Nelson, $5.2m), *North to Alaska* (Fabian, $4.5m), *Where the Boys Are* (Connie Francis, $3.3m) and *The Wackiest Ship in the Army* (Ricky Nelson, $3.3m),

As none of the other offerings featuring rock'n'roll stars got into the listings, Elvis Presley was easily the most commercially successful of this generation of singing actors. For seven years, from 1957 to 1966, Elvis was in the US Top 10 major box office stars, not quite matching Doris Day but easily outclassing Frank Sinatra. The only other singer to be mentioned was Pat Boone.

Boone was a cardboard cut-out of an actor, confusing his roles with his real-life persona. For example, he was married and he refused to even kiss anyone until *Journey to the Centre of the Earth* (1960), quite a handicap for a romantic lead. He did have a steamy scene with Ann-Margret in *State Fair* (1962). She's steamy and he's seen but would like to be elsewhere. Boone would never have played a delinquent in the way that Presley did, so his films were family entertainment from the start. Similarly, he never got angry and so *April Love* was too genteel. At best, Boone was an inauspicious actor but on his DVD commentary for *State Fair*, he is surprised by his own performance and says he looks like a young Tom Cruise. Should have gone to Specsavers.

Pat Boone, Ann-Margret and Bobby Darin starring in a remake of the Rodgers and Hammerstein musical, *State Fair*, was never going to work and the songs were too old-fashioned for a contemporary cast. Such an unhappy fate didn't happen to Elvis films until the late 60s – they did what they said on the can and they made money. There is, however, one wonderful line in the film when Darin's girlfriend says, 'Everybody's hair gets blown with the wind', and he replies, 'Mine doesn't.' And if you think the film is clunky, listen to Pat Boone's commentary in which he sings along with the songs.

In terms of presence and ability, Bobby Darin was a fine, dramatic actor but he was not getting into those box-office lists. He was in *Too Late Blues*, *Hell is For Heroes* (with Steve McQueen) and *Pressure Point* (playing a Nazi sympathiser!).

None of the young stars won Oscars and indeed, only one of them was nominated. In 1963, Darin was nominated as Best Supporting Actor in *Captain Newman, MD*, but he lost to Melvyn Douglas in *Hud*. Darin reflected that it was 'the most exciting event of my life. The fact that I didn't win was totally unimportant.' That wasn't true – he was furious. He thought his looks went against him and he told James Darren, 'If I looked like you, I'd be the biggest thing in Hollywood.' Still, Darin had made the Oscar nominations, something Elvis had never managed despite fine performances in *Jailhouse Rock* and *King Creole*.

Johnny Cash played a bank robber in *Five Minutes to Live* (1961) and it's obvious that he can only do things his way. *A Gunfight* (1971) with Kirk Douglas worked well, although many thought that having two endings was preposterous. Still, he made guest appearances in TV dramas and sometimes teamed up with Willie and Waylon and the boys for cheaply-made westerns, which are simply grown men playing cowboys: films as party time.

Roy Orbison could write his own songs for *The Fastest Guitar Alive* (1966) but he was a hopeless actor, totally lacking in emotion and the entire film floundered. Nothing can save a film when the lead actor is completely at sea.

Some rock'n'roll stars found themselves in rubbish. In 1960, Conway Twitty sang the abominable title song for *Platinum High School*, but the film was worse, shown in the UK as *The Rich, Young and Deadly*. Conway turns out to be the murderer and he later remarked, 'Sal Mineo said that my performance in *Platinum High School* was the best by any actor / singer that he had seen'. Maybe Sal Mineo didn't go to the movies very often.

Conway was in *Sex Kittens Go to College*, again 1960. This film boasted an intriguing cast – Mamie Van Doren, Tuesday Weld and Brigitte's sister, Mijanou Bardot. Mamie Van Doren is the head of the science department – there's type-casting for you – but she is exposed as a former stripper. Given the choice between Van Doren and Weld, I'd pick Weld anytime, but these brashy sexpots like Mansfield and Van Doren are associated with rock'n'roll films.

By and large, exploitation films were not made in the UK; usually British films were professionally made and had a supporting cast of familiar character actors. Cliff Richard was in *Serious Charge* (1959), a drama about homosexuality – a rare theme for the day – in which a new vicar (Anthony Quayle) is accused of molestation. The score by Lionel Bart included a fast-paced 'Living Doll'; Bruce Welch told Cliff to slow it down, and hey presto, it's a No.1. Cliff played a pop singer being exploited by a sleazy Soho agent (Laurence Harvey) in *Expresso Bongo* (1960). Religion is used as a marketing ploy and Cliff sings 'A Voice in the Wilderness'.

Cliff found his payday with *The Young Ones* in 1961, playing the son of a property developer, Robert Morley. Opposed to his dad's heartlessness, Cliff opens a youth club and stages a musical to raise funds. It was in the Judy Garland and Mickey Rooney tradition of let's-do-a-show and it was well-made with a decent budget, deserving of its success. In *Summer Holiday* (1963), Cliff, in his open-mesh T-shirt, and the Shadows toured Europe on a London bus. Cliff's next film, *Wonderful Life* (1964), had the misfortune to be released the same week as the Beatles' *A Hard Day's Night* and he drifted away from celluloid after that. In 1967 he made a film, *Two a Penny*, with the Billy Graham Organisation and featuring Graham himself.

In almost everything he did, Anthony Newley was a Marmite performer; extremely talented but many people couldn't stand him. He had been a child actor and he had no problem in playing Jeep Jones in *Idle on Parade* (1959), a quickie parody about pop stars being conscripted (Elvis Presley, Terry Dene). Unexpectedly, the film made Newley a teen idol and his exaggerated delivery meant that his voice was always recognisable. He was very good in the Soho drama, *The Small Sad World of Sammy Lee* (1963) and he created a sexual fantasy out of his lifestyle in the amazingly misguided *Can Hieronymus Merkin Ever Forget Mercy Humppe and Find True Happiness?* (1969). He became a Vegas favourite and it is surprising that Presley never did any of his songs, but maybe he was just too associated with the Rat Pack.

Adam Faith had more charisma as an actor than as a pop singer. He did well in both *Beat Girl* and *Never Let Go*, both 1960, and by the mid-60s that was the direction he favoured. He starred in successful stage productions of *Alfie* and *A Chorus Line* and the

TV series, *Budgie* and *Love Hurts*.

The reviews can hurt too. Pop stars in films often lead to sniffy reviews, perhaps because the reviewers knew that this was not their true vocation. One newspaper said that Elvis should be up for Worst Supporting Actor in *Love Me Tender*, which certainly was unjustified. An LA critic called Kevin Thomas called Tommy Sands 'hopelessly hammy' when he was in *None But the Brave* and accused him of nepotism. Sands went round to see him and beat him up.

Everybody jumped on board the Beatles bandwagon and their naturalistic performance in the *faux* documentary, *A Hard Day's Night* and it's self-evident that they didn't put too much creativity in *Help! (1965)*, which isn't far from being a pantomime. John Lennon fared okay in *How I Won the War* (1966), but Ringo Starr has been the only Beatle to appear regularly in films.

Bob Dylan appeared in *Pat Garrett and Billy the Kid* (1973), but despite writing the score, he didn't have much to do. It is among the greatest westerns and Kris Kristofferson is perfect as Billy the Kid. As well as being one of country music's most successful songwriters, Kristofferson was a very prolific film star, and being 80 years old hasn't slowed him down too much. Being prone to mumble, he doesn't have the greatest diction but he is astonishingly good-looking, especially with a beard, and he was unfairly tarnished with the wildly overspent *Heaven's Gate* (1981), a much-neglected film. Mick Jagger made a mess of *Ned Kelly* (1970), but he was woefully miscast as an Australian outlaw by its director, Tony Richardson: he was far better in the disturbing *Performance* (1970), where he could play a version of himself.

Tom Jones and Bryan Ferry have hardly bothered with films, but Paul Simon had a small part as a creepy record executive in Woody Allen's *Annie Hall* (1977). Carrying a film proved too much for him in *One Trick Pony* (1980), despite an excellent soundtrack. Art Garfunkel held his own with Jack Nicholson and Ann-Margret in *Carnal Knowledge* (1971), but he never looked like leading man material. A rugged Johnny Hallyday was, nevertheless, brilliant as a gunman casing a bank in a small town in *L'Homme du Train* (2001).

Barbra Streisand has had a long career in both music and films, sometimes making musicals like *Funny Girl* (1968) and *Hello Dolly!* (1969). In more recent times, she has used her fame to ensure that she is doing the projects that she wants: it is an example of the way Presley could have gone had he had Streisand's driving self-confidence.

The most stimulating example of a singer turned film star is that of David Bowie. Much of his music is other-worldly and he has enhanced his music by appearing in *The Man Who Fell to Earth* (1976) and *Merry Christmas Mr.Lawrence* (1983). In 1980 he was a Broadway sensation in the title role for *The Elephant Man*. Generally, he spaced his roles so that each one became an event in itself. It is another example of someone having confidence in himself and what he was doing.

Elvis Presley started well – he was never an angry young man but he could act defiantly. He looked good, he had a virile physique, he could fight convincingly, but he was not expressive enough to pick up on inner torment. No producer or director did anything with his strong sense of humour: you rarely see him laugh whole-heartedly and yet he had one of the most engaging laughs in the world.

From 1962, his films were largely inconsequential and although he still had his following, the public had fallen out of love with him. These poor films have affected the reputation of his early work. If he had only made the first six or seven films, he would be held in greater stead an as actor.

The later films too were casually and hastily thrown together, and part of the blame lies with Elvis himself. With the exception of Elvis himself, the budgets were low. The directors found no way to challenge him or indeed keep his interest. After the first few films, there is not a single remark where Elvis looks forward to the challenge of making some film.

II. Got a Lot o' Livin' to Do, 1968

Elvis had loved working with Jerry Reed on 'Guitar Man' and so he was asked to join a recording session in Nashville in January 1968. He brought along a new song, 'U S Male' which combined a dramatic start, a rock'n'roll beat and a witty lyric: everything Elvis liked. He arranged a rocking version of Chuck Berry's 'Too Much Monkey Business' where the lyric was updated to refer to Vietnam, though not with any political stance. Although not released, Elvis played around with 'The Prisoner's Song' and sang 'I'm a big hairy coon': these were different times.

On 1 February 1968, Priscilla gave birth to Elvis' daughter Lisa Marie, at the Baptist Memorial Hospital in Memphis. He couldn't play the doting father for too long as he had to return to Hollywood to make *Live a Little, Love a Little* for MGM, based on a book called *Kiss My Firm But Pliant Lips* – it definitely needed a new title but the one they chose wasn't impressive. The songs included 'A Little Less Conversation' by Billy Strange and Mac Davis, at the time a minor hit single, and 'Wonderful World' by British writers, Guy Fletcher and Doug Flett.

Guy Fletcher recalls, 'Freddie Bienstock at Carlin was in business with Colonel Tom Parker and this was the only way to get to Elvis. He was getting eight mailbags a week of songs by aspiring writers from all over the world. Freddie wanted to play him 'Wonderful World' which we had written for Cliff Richard. We had written it for Eurovision but 'Congratulations' became the UK entry, although Cliff had recorded it. It was reasonably successful on an E.P. but Freddie took it to Elvis and Elvis really liked it. It became the opening song in *Live a Little, Love a Little*, as he is driving a buggy over the dunes. We had to rewrite the lyric for America and I never liked the rewrite.'

Both *Speedway* and *Stay Away, Joe* were released in 1968 to poor reviews and dwindling audiences. Elvis must have wondered whether it was worth it. *Live a Little, Love a Little* did update his image as there was some sex, drugs and rock'n'roll about it. Michele Carey drugs Elvis and he is out for three days. During his dream, his dog speaks to him and he sings 'Edge of Reality'. When he comes round, he's got to make sense of the rest of the film. Elvis swears a bit and he's seen in bed with a girl (admittedly, with a board between them). The key song is 'A Little Less Conversation', although its time hadn't come yet, baby. Rudy Vallee, who used to sing through a megaphone, played the boss of his advertising agency. The boss told him, 'Personal appearances – that's what matters.' Was Elvis taking notes? *Live a Little, Love a Little* was not given a British release, evidence that his films were no longer profitable. UK Elvis fans caught up with it on video in the mid-1970s.

In April, Elvis and Priscilla spent some time in Las Vegas and saw Tom Jones in one of the showrooms. Women of all ages screamed for Tom and he mixed loud, bombastic versions of hits with sexual small talk. Elvis and Tom became good friends. Tom loved playing Vegas, especially as he was so well paid for it. He told Elvis to consider a residency in Las Vegas: compared to the inconvenience of making a movie, this was easy money. Tom didn't make movies: he could see what it was doing to Elvis.

By now there was tension between Elvis and Priscilla. I can't say because I wasn't in their bedroom, but it appears that Elvis lost interest in her because she had become a mother. P.J. Proby told me this was very common down south and he himself hadn't wanted sex with anyone who had borne children. Also, Elvis never wanted to be monogamous.

Ann-Margret married the actor Roger Smith (Jeff Spencer in *Hawaiian Eye*) on 8 May 1967. It could have been on the rebound from Elvis but if it was, it still worked as they remain married today. Elvis, that master of tact, went to her next Vegas season and told her that he still carried a flame. He had casual relationships with Quentin Dean (female!) on *Stay Away, Joe* and Michele Carey on *Live a Little, Love a Little*. Although he and Nancy Sinatra could hardly get enough of each other on *Speedway*, Nancy didn't want a relationship with a married man, even if that married man was Elvis.

It wasn't just Elvis. It takes two to tango and after only a year of marriage, Priscilla had rather more dancing lessons that she needed from Steven Peck in Los Angeles, a dancer who had prepared Tommy Sands for film roles. Joe Esposito told Elvis about them and Elvis said, 'Stay of out of her business and leave her alone'.

At the end of May 1968, Elvis, Priscilla and Lisa Marie went to Hawaii for a short holiday and they attended the Karate Tournament of Champions, hosted by his friend Ed Parker. Elvis and Priscilla met Mike Stone, an instructor who had been born in Hawaii. Elvis was immensely impressed by his skills and Priscilla liked his physique. In 1972 Stone became Phil Spector's bodyguard and then worked in security in Las Vegas, which is when we will meet him again. Elvis had gone to Hawaii to lose weight: he could diet when he had a mind to and with some exercise, he came back suntanned and a stone lighter.

Once Elvis had started making films, Colonel Parker didn't like him on TV, the fallacious argument being that fans mightn't pay to see him in the cinema. Now that his films were losing their appeal, Parker favoured a TV special but with Christmas songs. Elvis liked Christmas songs but he didn't want to be another Perry Como and Andy Williams.

Parker struck a deal with NBC: like RCA, they were owned by General Electric and the label could get, as it were, a free album from the soundtrack. The sponsor was the Singer Sewing Machine Company, so the show would effectively be aimed at housewives. The deal, oddly enough, was for NBC to finance both a TV special and a film, *Change of Habit*, which was made the following year.

Bob Finkel was a highly-experienced producer who had worked on *The Andy Williams Show*, which had won an Emmy. In April 1968, Finkel had courted controversy in a TV special, *When Harry Met Petula*, as Petula Clark had touched Harry Belafonte's arm while singing an anti-war song, 'On the Path to Glory', which in itself was contentious. It was the first time that a black man and a white woman had made physical contact on a major TV show and it shocked viewers in the southern states. It later emerged that Belafonte and Clark knew exactly what they were doing: an alternative take had been filmed where they didn't touch and this somehow 'disappeared', so that there could be no last-minute substitution.

These were turbulent times in America. Martin Luther King had been assassinated in Memphis in April 1968, and Robert Kennedy met a similar fate in Los Angeles in June. Indeed, the production of the TV special stopped when Kennedy was shot and Elvis spent the rest of day on conspiracy theories.

NBC told Finkel that as this show was a comeback for Elvis Presley, it must be truly special. He met Presley who kept calling him 'Mr. Finkel' and he felt he would have to establish a better relationship, although this was how Elvis approached authority figures. Elvis was keen to listen to suggestions.

Bob Finkel hired Steve Binder as the director for the TV special, which would be called *Singer Presents Elvis*, a ghastly title for a show now familiarly known as the *Comeback Special*. Binder had made his impact with *Hullabaloo* and he had directed the film of the all-star concert, *The T.A.M.I. Show*. Binder hadn't taken much notice of Elvis, being more impressed with the Beatles and the Stones, but Finkel told him that Elvis needed a modern edge. Furthermore, Binder liked things happening spontaneously and this could bring out the best in Presley.

But maybe it all comes down to Marie Parker's hips. She was scheduled for hip replacements and she would be in hospital in Palm Springs and then recuperating at home. For much of the preparation and shooting, Colonel Parker wouldn't be around. His acolytes, like Tom Diskin, would report what was happening, but not having the Colonel around was a huge bonus.

Binder and Finkel had worked out a theme, based around 'Guitar Man', that is, the adventures of a young singer who plays in low-rent dives, dreaming of success, meeting temptation along the way and in the end, realising he was happier in those cheap clubs, but, in keeping with the season, it would end with a plea for peace, love and brotherhood, goodwill to all men. Eventually, this story became nebulous and *Singer Presents Elvis* was a series of impressive set-pieces, the one for 'Guitar Man' being inspired by 'Jailhouse Rock'.

Billy Strange was going to be the arranger and conductor but he had other commitments and couldn't meet the timetable. He had completed two songs with Mac Davis – one for the storyline, 'Nothingville', and a reflective ballad, 'Memories', very much in the Glen Campbell mould but ideal for Elvis and the TV special.

Bones Howe took over: he had worked with Elvis before and was having success with Fifth Dimension and the Association. He told Finkel how warm and funny Elvis could be and how he loved his crooked grin. Finkel wanted an easy-going atmosphere which would provide plenty of that. The conductor would be Billy Goldenberg, who had been Barbra Streisand's accompanist. Good people one and all, and this had the makings of being a memorable TV special.

Elvis invited Scotty and D.J. to play a few oldies, but when Steve Binder heard them reminiscing in the dressing-room, he determined a better format. A square stage was set up in which the musicians would face each other but there was not enough room for D.J. to play a full kit. Instead he rapped on the back of Elvis' guitar case.

The idea was that Elvis would perform his early songs and talk and joke with his friends in front of 300 people. As well as Elvis, Scotty and D.J, there was Charlie Hodge playing guitar and Alan Fortas and Lance LeGault with additional percussion.

There were two shows scheduled for 27 June 1968, but Colonel Parker, with his mind distracted or just disinterested, had not distributed the tickets to key fans. As a result, a local radio station said Elvis was doing these shows and listeners could get in touch. Hence, some fortunate people woke up that morning not knowing they would be seeing Elvis later in the day. The muddle didn't matter as any 300 people in a room would scream and cheer for Elvis Presley, especially when he was looking so good in black leathers. Or maybe not so good – he came off stage from the first show drenched in sweat and his dresser had difficulty getting him out of the suit – Elvis had to be showered, spruced up, tidied and back in that suit, blown dry, within 30 minutes for the second show. He was using Dean Martin's dressing-room, which had never seen such activity.

Having two shows gave the producers back-up as they could choose the best performances, and many songs were not used at the time. What viewers remember is the hypnotic mantra of Jimmy Reed's 'Baby What You Want Me to Do', which ran through the performances; in fact, Elvis sang it five times in the two shows. He performed 'That's All Right', 'Heartbreak Hotel', 'Love Me', 'Blue Suede Shoes', 'Lawdy Miss Clawdy', 'When My Blue Moon Turns to Gold Again' and 'Trying to Get to You'. Elvis sounded hoarse at times which added to the excitement. There is fierce guitar playing during Rufus Thomas' 'Tiger Man', which had been written by Sam Phillips under the pseudonym of Sam Burns.

Elvis, with his usual hesitant delivery, told a wonderful story: 'Something wrong with my lip, wait a minute. Got news for you, baby, I did 29 movies like that. The police filmed the show one time in Florida, 'cause the PTA or the YMCA or something, they thought I was, uh, something. They said, 'Man, he's gotta be crazy'. The police came out and filmed the show and I couldn't move, I had to stand still, the only thing I could move was my little finger like that.' The audience loved it but the musicians were laughing too loud.

Elvis was never going to get through 'Are You Lonesome Tonight' in this set-up, and he doesn't. He changes the lyric, 'Are You Lonesome Tonight? Does your hair look a fright?' and la-dee-dahs a narration. At one stage he refers to the groups of the day like 'the Beatles and the Beards'. This is just taken as an amusing aside but it is an in-joke as Chris Beard was a writer on the show.

When they had been rehearsing, Colonel Parker had been on the set and it was his birthday on 26 June. Elvis celebrated this by reworking 'It Hurts Me' and singing, 'Is it too much to ask for one lousy, tired ol' Christmas song?', the parody being written by the show's writers, Allan Byle and Chris Beard. Parker took it in good spirit as the show was going well.

Now, as a concession to Colonel Parker, Elvis said, 'I would like to sing, uh, my favourite Christmas song.' In the televised show, this segued into 'Blue Christmas', which he performed but the remark was intended for 'Santa Claus Is Back in Town'. When he sang 'Blue Christmas', one of the musicians egged him on by shouting 'Play it dirty! Play it dirty!'

Scotty had come on stage without a guitar strap as he wasn't expecting to stand up or to swap his guitar with Elvis. As a result, when Elvis stood up, he didn't have anything to support his guitar and he improvised needing a strap to the tune of 'One Night'. It was silly but fun and it worked. Elvis himself hadn't played so much guitar since his days with Sun Records. At the end of each show, Elvis sang 'Memories' to a pre-recorded backing tape. It was a curious way to end the session, but again it worked.

Similar to 'On the Path to Glory', Bob Finkel felt there had to be a song which reflected the times and the music director Earl Brown wrote 'If I Can Dream'. Elvis thought it was too Broadway but then he realised how it could have a bluesy feel, the comparison being Sam Cooke's 'A Change Is Gonna Come'. Once he had recorded it, everyone, except the Colonel, knew it should end the show. The Colonel said no, it had to be a Christmas song but everybody including Elvis stood firm: it was a big-voiced inspirational ballad that set the scene for 'Let It Be' and 'Bridge over Troubled Water'.

Two days after the sessions with Scotty and D.J, Elvis did another two shows, this time singing early hits with L.A. musicians and an orchestra – 'Heartbreak Hotel', 'One Night', 'Hound Dog', 'All Shook Up', 'Can't Help Falling in Love', 'Jailhouse Rock', 'Don't Be Cruel', 'Blue Suede Shoes', 'Love Me Tender' and 'Baby What You Want Me to Do'. Elvis sang to a backing tape for a medley of 'Trouble' and 'Guitar Man' and mimed 'If I Can Dream'.

The intention was to decide what worked best for the broadcast. Fortunately, the leftovers would be shelved but not destroyed and in recent times everything has been released.

In addition, there were production numbers: Jerry Reed's 'Big Boss Man', 'Little Egypt', 'Let Yourself Go' (from *Speedway*), an old B-side 'It Hurts Me' and the spirituals, 'Sometimes I Feel like a Motherless Child', 'Where Could I Go But To The Lord' and 'Up Above My Head' as well as Leiber and Stoller's quasi-spiritual 'Saved'. One scene in a bordello was dropped as NBC thought it was too spicy but it was restored for video release.

The session pianist, Don Randi, a member of the Wrecking Crew, played on the TV sessions. "We were recording on a Saturday which meant time and a half for all the musicians, and some of us because of our status were getting double scale anyway. So I was making a lot of money, and if we went past midnight we were in golden time and we would clean up. We were finishing off a 10 second cue and Elvis came over to the piano and said, 'Don, I can't get this.' I put on his earphones and they had everything in there – strings horns, the lot – and it was confusing. I told them to take certain things out and only put certain instruments in there. Elvis said, 'Thanks' and it was five minutes to midnight. All he had to do was walk in the booth and we would play the cue and he would nail it in one. Elvis was walking back to the booth when the floor manager ran over and pointed at the clock. He said, 'Do you mind?' He was telling Elvis to move his ass and hurry up. Well, Elvis looked over at me and said, 'Are you hungry, Don?' I said, 'Yes, I am a bit' and he called a lunch break. So that cost the studio a lot of dollars."

Elvis was on a high: by the end of June he had his TV special in the bag. There was another film on the horizon and it held some interest for him. He had been impressed with the so-called Italian or spaghetti westerns, though most of them were made in Spain. He loved Clint Eastwood in *A Fistful of Dollars* and *For a Few Dollars More* and he wanted to make one himself. Not, of course, in Europe – this would be an Italian western made in America, but it would have that look. He'd have Clint's three-day growth; the outlaws would look unkempt: there would be long scenes in the hills; and there would be excessive violence with beatings-up, shoot-outs and a scene where Elvis is branded on the neck.

Clint Eastwood didn't give much away about his character in his films. He didn't say much: he was an observer who came to life for a showdown, but Clint conveyed his steely determination in all he did. Kyle Eastwood, his son, said he never liked his dad giving him 'that look' when he had misbehaved.

Eastwood was a fine actor who had reasoned that minimalism was the way, but Elvis Presley, presumably with little direction from Charles Marquis Warren, had decided that he only needed the look – and he just looked bland: you never had the impression that Elvis in the title role of *Charro!* had much authority.

In one scene, Presley's horse has been taken and he is walking through the outlands with his saddle. He comes across some surprisingly well-groomed, wild horses and we just know he will have the big, black stallion. He corals and trains it within five minutes, immediately riding him up a steep incline; even the Horse Whisperer took 24 hours.

The story is inexplicable with Elvis suddenly walking away from a showdown in the first five minutes and yet not being hit by a shower of bullets, but that goes with the territory for this genre. The ending is particularly ludicrous. Elvis is heading across the plains with the gang leader (Victor French) as captive and a golden cannon, worth at least $100,000, to be returned to the Mexicans. It is not even under canvas. Elvis alone is driving the horses, looking after the cannon, watching out for the bad guys and guarding the prisoner and he'll never reach his destination.

Elvis sings the title song and *Charro!* is the only film where Elvis does not sing on screen. A second song, 'Let's Forget About the Stars', was dropped. A nude scene with the leading lady, Ina Balin, stepping out of a bath and embracing Presley was similarly ditched. Instead of Ennio Morricone, Hugo Montenegro wrote the score and the film had too much music, albeit mostly repetitive, but it is well in keeping with the Italian westerns. So is the acting: the cast includes experienced western actors but the dialogue is so bad that it sounds dubbed.

Despite some publicity junkets, not involving Elvis, no one paid any attention to *Charro!* The UK release was held up until 1971 when it was mischievously released at the same time as *Elvis: That's the Way It Is*, the documentary about his Vegas comeback. As I recall, it briefly played one week at a rundown cinema where I live in Liverpool – that was it.

In October, Elvis was to make yet another film, *The Trouble with Girls (And How to Get into It)*, for MGM. This was back to the carnies, here set in 1927 and it had a tortuous journey to the screen. It was originally *Chautauqua*, the name of the fair that encouraged learning. Glenn Ford was going to star and then, in 1961, it was going to be Elvis. In 1964, his role was given to Dick Van Dyke and then in 1968, it was back to Elvis. His proposed co-star was to be Bobbie Gentry but she dropped out and the Broadway actress, Marilyn Mason came in.

The Trouble with Girls is a long way from the 'sweet love, dark lust and murderous passion' of the original project. A smartly-attired Elvis runs a travelling sideshow called the Chautauqua. He disappears for long sections of the film and he seems uninterested while he is on screen: he certainly makes no attempt to act. There are about six plots going on – one involving Vincent Price as Mr. Morality – and when a murder takes place, Presley, now Poirot, announces that the murderer will be revealed at the next show.

Billy Strange was in charge of the music and he and Mac Davis wrote 'Clean Up Your Own Backyard', which is performed with an acoustic country trio. Elvis recorded this with The Blossoms, who included Darlene Love, and a full backing and it was a moderate success (US No.35, UK No.21), but I prefer the down-home setting. Elvis sings 'Swing Down, Sweet Chariot' with the Mello Men, a ballad 'Almost' while accompanying himself on piano, and he adds a couple of lines to Marilyn Mason's 'Signs of the Zodiac'. The film is confusing in its full-length version (97 minutes) and even more so when it was cut down to 72 minutes for a UK release as a second feature.

The single of 'If I Can Dream' was released in October 1968, but the sales came once the TV special was screened on 3 December. It reached No.12, Elvis' highest chart placing in three years. The TV special itself had high ratings, as high as Elvis on *The Ed Sullivan Show*, and received critical acclaim too. One newspaper called it 'a stunning affirmation of his talent' and several used the word 'landmark'. *The Los Angeles Times* said, 'I don't think many viewers care to see singers sweat on TV.' On the contrary, I think they rather enjoyed it and anyway didn't sportsmen sweat on TV all the time?

Elvis was euphoric. He told Steve Binder, 'I'm never going to sing another song that I don't believe in. I'm never going to do another movie that I don't believe in.' Elvis knew the way to go, and this time Colonel Parker wasn't going to mess it up.

CHAPTER 12

Get Those Stakes up Higher

Elvis Presley is associated with Las Vegas as surely as Frank Sinatra, but it is a very different Vegas. Whereas Sinatra will be forever associated with his Mafia connections, this didn't happen with Elvis Presley, although there are some dubious acquaintances. Elvis appeared briefly in Vegas in 1956 and made a film, *Viva Las Vegas*, with Ann-Margret, that was released in 1964, but he didn't begin his famous concert appearances until 1969. Those five years from 1964 to 1969 made all the difference as this was when the great clean-up started, primarily due to the multi-millionaire Howard Hughes moving in and the Mob, largely but not completely, moving out.

In my book *Frank Sinatra: An Extraordinary Life* (McNidder & Grace, 2015), I told the history of Las Vegas, largely because its Mob background was intertwined with Sinatra's own career. The main members of The Rat Pack (Sinatra, Dean Martin and Sammy Davis Jr) had turned Las Vegas into an entertainment capital: it would always appeal to gamblers but now you could have a good time without losing your money, although that was always the preferred option for the hoteliers.

Hence, the ins and outs of Las Vegas are not really a part of this story and if it were I would be largely repeating Chapter 6 of the Sinatra book.

'I always want to be a millionaire.'
The reason Elvis always kept a million in cash in the bank

I. Viva Rock Vegas

Not every star masters The Look. It's not easy: Jerry Lee Lewis had cold eyes; Carl Perkins and Del Shannon lacked hair; Charlie Rich was built like a wrestler; Chuck Berry looked sleazy; Gene Vincent was disabled and his injuries made him haggard; and Roy Orbison knew he was not photogenic and took to wearing dark glasses.

But Elvis had The Look, even I think from that first photograph as a child. He was devastatingly handsome and for most of the time, svelte. Right from the start, he knew what to wear, so there are very few photographs, even casual ones taken by fans, where he doesn't look right.

It was the same with the Beatles. With the exception of those ridiculous pictures in Victorian swimsuits, they not only looked right but also looked like a group. Contrast this with almost any photograph of the Byrds, who didn't even look like friends. Admittedly, it was open warfare for much of the time but the Byrds couldn't even get it together for the camera.

Both Elvis and the Beatles were way ahead of the pack when it came to photo sessions. Maybe that was why they didn't agree to any photographs from their meeting in 1965: they weren't sure who would come out on top.

Elvis was so aware of his looks that he rarely wore anything but smart, contemporary clothes in his films – even if they were set in the 1800s. The make-up artists couldn't tamper with his face: none of his characters had scars or distinguishing features, and Elvis never played anybody older than himself. Indeed, when his characters are asked for their age, they are usually five years younger than the actual Elvis.

An odd quirk is that Elvis didn't mind sweating in public. There are five or six examples in his films where you can see Elvis' shirt with sweat under the armpits. In a similar way, he didn't mind sweating while performing as it added to the excitement – the performer, as it were, was giving his all. As a result, he didn't object to heavy stage wear which became even worse under the lights, a prime example being the black leather suit for the 1968 TV special.

There are several instances in the rehearsal sequences shown in *That's the Way It Is* where Elvis is sweating heavily under his arms. It could be early evidence of his drug-taking, especially as nobody else around him is sweating like that.

Bill Belew designed his clothes for the TV special and Elvis was so satisfied that he asked him to work on his Vegas opening in 1969 and then all his other stage appearances. Belew, who died in 2008, said, 'Bob Mackie had Cher and I had Elvis, and we had fabulous bodies to design for.'

There were two key influences; firstly, the country stars in their gaudy rhinestone suits and secondly, the outfits worn for karate. Elvis was the first performer to incorporate karate movements into stage performances so that he knew these clothes would look right. He could see where the country stars went wrong; Porter Wagoner took his stage clothes to excess – if you added electric lights, he'd have made a good Christmas tree.

Elvis' return to the stage in bejewelled white jump suits in a Nevada showroom could have made him a laughing stock but he became a trendsetter and numerous performers copied his lead. His lavish costumes were typical of the time: the Seventies was The Decade That Fashion Forgot. How had Bill Belew pulled it off?

Bill Belew was born in 1931 and studied design in New York. He designed clothes for many singers and Broadway stars, including Ella Fitzgerald and Joan Rivers. The NBC director Steve Binder was making his programmes in Los Angeles but he thought it best to use a New York designer instead of a Hollywood one as he might get something different. He asked Belew to design clothes for that Petula Clark / Harry Belafonte special and then asked him to work on Elvis Presley's.

The black leather suit was a throwback to the rock'n'roll era although it was Marlon Brando (jacket) and Gene Vincent (suit) who made the image iconic. Elvis' outfit was far more tight-fitting and stylish than Gene Vincent's which looked like it came off the peg from British Home Stores. The Beatles had worn similarly ill-fitting leather suits in Hamburg, but the influence for Presley's, although he might not have known it, was Jim Morrison of the Doors.

Presley was very pleased and he asked Belew to work on his opening in Las Vegas. Apart from the black leather suit, he had used wool for the special, and Elvis wanted something that would not be so hot. Belew spoke to friends who designed for ice skaters and told them he was looking for something similar. The ice skaters did splits and turns and lifts and Elvis would be doing his karate chops. He needed something that would not be too hot and would retain its shape. They recommended stretch gab, a form of gabardine.

The lighting in Las Vegas was not going to be as sophisticated as Broadway and so Bill kept it simple. If the clothes were white, then the lighting engineer could easily change their colour for different numbers through the use of filters. Black would not be appropriate here as it would negate any filter.

Bill decided on jumpsuits with high Napoleonic collars, pointed cuffs, wide belts and bell-bottoms. He took his cue from pictures of Napoleon with his high collars. The purpose of the clothes wasn't to distract from Presley himself and if he had high collars, it would draw attention to his face.

He added metal studs, sequins and rhinestones with some embroidery, and the first Elvis jumpsuits now look a model of restraint, although on almost any other performer it would have looked ridiculous. Like Neil Armstrong with his moon suit, Elvis needed a special suit for Planet Vegas.

Vernon Presley thought they were too expensive as the initial bill was $11,000, but polyester would look tacky and Elvis was the King. Elvis paid the bill and continued to use him. He wanted to look good whatever the cost, but he was never precious about his image. Tony Cartwright recalls, 'I saw someone once give Elvis Presley a photograph to sign. He looked at himself and said, 'That looks like Engelbert Humperdinck!' There was some similarity between them.'

The jumpsuits became more elaborate and hence more expensive as the years went by. Bill was glad that Elvis modelled his clothes for the Memphis Mafia and they enjoyed them and didn't think they distracted from his masculinity. The last thing he wanted was to dress Presley like Liberace. Sometimes the suit would be split to the waist to display Elvis' chest, and there were often cords and fringes which would shake when Elvis moved.

Sometimes Elvis wore his stage clothes in public, notably for the meeting with President Nixon in the White House in 1970. The reason that it is the most requested photograph in the official American archives is because no one had ever looked like that in the Oval Office before. Around 1971, he favoured hip, black clothing for casual wear – he had probably been watching *Shaft*.

When it came to the worldwide TV concert, *Aloha from Hawaii*, Elvis told Bill that this was a chance to make a patriotic statement and that the jumpsuit had to say 'America'. Bill suggested the outline of the country or the American flag but neither seemed inspired. He had, however, noticed an American eagle on the outside of an American embassy and Elvis loved the idea. The jumpsuit would be white and decorated with red and blue stones – red, white and blue – and the eagle would be gold.

Bill added a cape for his entrance but at rehearsal, Elvis fell backwards as the cape was too heavy. There was a frantic call to Bill for a shorter one and they only had two days to make it and get it to Hawaii. One of Bill's team took it on the plane, giving it a special seat of its own. The stewardess asked what it was. 'It's Elvis' cape,' she was told. 'Can I touch it?' she asked, and she did.

The following year Elvis wore the Peacock jumpsuit at the Forum, Los Angeles and it is on the cover of *Promised Land* (1975). In 2008, it was sold at auction for $300,000, the most expensive sale for an item of Elvis memorabilia. Among the other jumpsuits were Bicentennial, Prehistoric Bird, Sundial, Burning Love and my favourite, Enter the

Dragon, Elvis' very own Game of Thrones.

Bill Belew made over 20 different designs for Elvis – the common themes were the plunging V necks, the high waists and the bellbottom trousers. There were no pockets. Most of the designs came with a cape and Elvis generally wore them with long silk scarves.

When Elvis' weight became a problem, there was a good argument for making them all in black as black makes you look thinner. There was an even better argument for getting him out of jumpsuits altogether, but Elvis was not one for letting things go.

Elvis' weight was throwing up new problems, but Bill was still being creative. In 1977, he designed the Diamond suit. This jumpsuit contained certain stones that Elvis could press to switch on laser beams. Bill had designed it with an electrician who was into lasers and on the day of Elvis' death, they were going to test it. They didn't want Elvis to damage anybody's eyesight or, for that matter, electrocute himself. Providing it worked, it would have been the ultimate jumpsuit, but would it have been Elvis?

II. Got a Lot o' Livin' to Do, 1969

To see the new year in, Elvis and Priscilla Presley hosted a party at the Thunderbird Lounge in Memphis. Elvis and Priscilla were often on the dance floor and Elvis specifically requested the manic reworking of 'Summertime', a 1966 Top 10 for the Chess singer, Billy Stewart. Elvis never tired of hearing Aretha Franklin's 'Chain of Fools' and he loved singing 'chain, chain, chain' alongside the backing vocalists. There was live music from Billy Lee Riley, a former rockabilly artist on Sun Records, and B.J. Thomas, who was heading for the Top 10 with 'Hooked on a Feeling', produced at American Sound Studios in Memphis by Chips Moman.

A few days later, Elvis was hanging out at Graceland. After the TV special, he should have felt on top of the world and should have wanted to make a new, best-selling album. However, he was filled with despair at the prospect of dragging himself to Nashville to record with Felton Jarvis on January 13.

If you ignored the soundtracks, the gospel albums and the reissues – Elvis had only released four albums since he had left the army: *Elvis Is Back!* (1960), *Something for Everybody* (1961), *Pot Luck* (1962) and *Elvis for Everyone* (1965). Even three of those album titles suggest that barrels were being scraped. Would the new one be any better?

Freddy Bienstock and the Colonel were still pressing for the Elvis tax, that is, 50% of the publishing on the songs to be recorded, and although Elvis had plenty of songs he would like to record, he was not allowed to cut them, so ironically the Elvis tax was holding him back. Elvis wanted to make a new album, yes, and freed from a film soundtrack, he thought the new songs would be better. Bienstock certainly had some winners but not enough of them.

Sensing his frustration, both the disc-jockey George Klein and jingle maker Marty Lacker recommended American Sound Studios at 827 Thomas Street, north Memphis instead. It was a small workplace, located in the poverty-stricken, black area of the city. If you didn't mind the rats, you could make a wonderful record there.

The studio was the brainchild of a white guitarist, Lincoln Moman, known as Chips, who had been born in Georgia in 1936. Residing in Memphis since he was 14, he had worked with Warren Smith and Johnny and Dorsey Burnette. He helped found Stax

Records and worked with Rufus Thomas, Carla Thomas, the Mar-Keys and Booker T. & the M.G.'s until 1963. He left because he had not been paid correctly and when he was awarded $3,000 in settlement, he opened his own studio, American Sound, in the premises of a run-down dairy.

The studio scored with both black and white artists, including Wilson Pickett, Bobby Womack and Ben E. King. In 1967, he cut 'The Letter', a US No.1 with the Box Tops. A definitive white soul album, *Dusty in Memphis*, had been recorded there in 1968 as well as sessions with Neil Diamond which included his signature song, 'Sweet Caroline'. Moman cut hits with Sandy Posey ('Born a Woman', 'Single Girl', both 1966), who was a secretary at the studio.

Moman had written 'This Time' (a million-seller from Troy Shondell, 1961) and, with Dan Penn, the ultimate cheating song, 'Dark End of the Street' (James Carr, 1967) and, again with Penn in hand, 'Do Right Woman – Do Right Man' (Aretha Franklin, 1967). He had his own songwriting company and several writers working for him. From time to time, he took a song from Red West and asked him about Elvis.

Chips was a tough cookie, having beaten up hoodlums who attacked him in a car park. When Martin Luther King was killed in Memphis in 1968, he had stayed all night in his studio with a shotgun to hand – and he would have used it if necessary. He was no pushover.

George and Marty had suggested American Sound before, but this time the suggestion hit home. This studio had a proven hit record and it was on his doorstep. Elvis thought that Felton Jarvis might object, but quite the reverse, Felton thought that the change would do Elvis good and arrangements were quickly put into place. Within four days, it was determined Felton would produce the sessions with Chips Moman and he insisted on bringing his engineers, Al Pachucki and Roy Shockley, with him.

American Sound was a very busy studio but Chips Moman was able to accommodate Elvis, mainly because Elvis wanted to work at night and also because Neil Diamond generously postponed his next visit. Presley liked Diamond anyway and as a sweetheart deal, he cut his song, a new one, a tender love song about making love in the open, 'And the Grass Won't Pay No Mind'.

One of the factors that made Elvis special was his bringing together of white and black culture, right from the very start in 1954 with 'That's All Right, Mama'. In 1962 Ray Charles released his ground-breaking *Modern Sounds in Country & Western Music*, which had topped the US album charts for 14 weeks. As a result, the fusion of country, R&B and pop had been well established by 1969, and American Sound knew how to add a commercial gloss. This time Elvis wasn't going to do anything radically new: the aim was to just do it better than anybody else.

So Elvis' first session in Memphis since 1955 was scheduled for 13 January 1969, but Elvis had a cold on the first night, which did not improve. Fortunately, it added a rough edge to his voice and probably enhanced the tracks.

There was another problem. Elvis didn't want the songs that Felton had selected, certainly not all of them, and Marty told him that he would have a wider choice if he didn't insist on 50% of the publishing. Elvis said, 'I'll sing what I want to sing', but Marty knew how the Colonel would take this. This was rebellion.

Chips had only a few days to find good, new material for Elvis and he did a fine job, but then who wouldn't want to write for Elvis?

Elvis Presley: Caught in a Trap

The musicians too were all experienced and very much in tune with Elvis. Reggie Young (guitar), Bobby Emmons (organ) and Bobby Wood (piano) had done time in the Bill Black Combo. The others included John Hughey (steel), Tommy Cogbill and Mike Leech (bass) and Gene Chrisman (drums).

As Elvis came through the back entrance on the first night, he heard the rats scurry and he said, 'What a funky little place.' He would be there for four nights, by which time he had tonsillitis as well as a heavy cold and decided to rest. Chips worked on some overdubs and he returned for fresh sessions over six days in February, when he was in perfect voice. There were 30 completed masters, together with one-offs and bits and pieces that have also been released over the years. Elvis said to Chips, 'We've done some hits here, man' and he was right. The sessions produced two signature tracks, two more hit singles and two million-selling albums, all further evidence that Elvis was back.

Elvis was drawn to songs that reflected his own life: some authors say it was subconscious, but Elvis was intelligent and knew what he was doing. If he could relate to a song, then he could give a stronger performance.

That is certainly true of the first song up, 'Long Black Limousine', which like 'The Long Black Veil', was a cautionary tale about stepping out of line. In the song, a girl who has nothing but dreams wants to return home in a long, black limousine: we know what that long black limousine will be.

'Long Black Limousine' had been recorded by its composer, the country performer Vern Stovall in 1958. Covers came from Bobby Bare, George Hamilton IV and Jody Miller in the country field. Elvis knew the soul version from O.C. Smith on *Hickory Holler Revisited* (1968). O.C. Smith started the song like a New Orleans funeral, thereby giving the ending away, but Elvis and the musicians based their arrangement on what O.C. did next. It took nine takes to nail that coffin down and although it is melodramatic and kitsch, it is also quintessential Elvis.

Among the Hill and Range submissions were 17 songs from Mac Davis: God loves a trier. The one that really impressed Elvis was 'In the Ghetto', which had parallels with 'Long Black Limousine'. Here the dispossessed have no way out of their dilemma and indeed, Davis had unnecessarily subtitled the song, 'The Vicious Circle'. It was the perfect song to follow 'If I Can Dream', but Elvis thought it might be too political for him. Chips Moman thought it great too and while Elvis was dithering, he said, 'Look, if you don't want it, I know Joe Simon will take it tomorrow.' That had the desired effect: Elvis promptly recorded it and when he heard the playback, he exclaimed, 'Yeah!'

David Stanley: 'Elvis did 'In the Ghetto' because it was a great song and Elvis was drawn to wonderful songs. We lived in Memphis where Martin Luther King lost his life, but there is a lot of difference between that music and the music that projects anti-establishment, anti-government things. Of course Elvis was anti-war but if there was a situation that threatened the very freedoms that we had, then Elvis would be on the front line. Elvis was on the front line from 1958 to 1960. Communicating Civil Rights is one thing, but Elvis was not the person to communicate a negative. He bombed out with John Lennon and he loved Paul and George. He did 'Yesterday', 'Get Back' and 'Something' but he did a lousy job on 'Hey Jude'. I told him not to do it: I didn't think that one was him. He respected their ability but if someone said something negative about the establishment, he didn't like it.'

It is true – Elvis' version of 'Hey Jude' didn't catch fire. Wilson Pickett had just recorded it at Muscle Shoals and released it as a single and maybe Elvis thought it would be fun to do. It's like Chinese whispers: he follows Wilson Pickett who hadn't got the words right and Elvis hasn't heard them properly. It was recorded on the spot and he probably intended to rework his vocal but he never did. Pity – it could have been a *tour de force*.

There are other examples of songs being recorded on a whim throughout the sessions. At one point Elvis starts Chips' own song, 'This Time' and then goes into 'I Can't Stop Loving You'. Ray Charles' arrangement of Don Gibson's song must have been on his mind as the arrangement of 'After Loving You', recorded by both Joe Henderson and Eddy Arnold in 1962, is so similar to 'I Can't Stop Loving You'. We know from outtakes that Elvis had been toying with this song for years so he was relieved to record it at last.

You can hear how Elvis starts singing Eddy Arnold's 1947 country hit, "I'll Hold You in My Heart (Till I Can Hold You in my Arms)' with himself on piano: the drums are there and then the other musicians then join in. You can tell no one knows when Elvis is going to finish. There is another moment where Elvis starts Roy Orbison's 'Only the Lonely', but sadly, the musicians don't pick up on this. This loose feeling is similar to Bob Dylan and the Band's *Basement Tapes*.

Just because Vernon was around, Elvis went into one of his favourite songs, 'From a Jack to a King', which had been written and recorded by Ned Miller in 1957, but had been a gold disc on reissue in 1962. Elvis incorporated his stuttering into the lines, so presumably he thought this was effective. You can tell he is having fun.

It may be a weakness but Elvis was a sucker for well-written, maudlin songs, even going right back to 'Old Shep'. 'Long Black Limousine' was one and another was Mac Davis' 'Don't Cry Daddy' about a parent trying to comfort his two children after his partner had gone, but found that they were comforting him. Yet another was the ultra-sentimental, 'Mama Liked the Roses', which has become a standard for Mother's Day. It covered family life, religion, death, graveyards and horticulture in two and a half minutes: in fact, your typical country song.

Mort Shuman had stopped writing with Doc Pomus and had moved to Europe, writing hit singles for the Small Faces, Cilla Black and Billy J. Kramer. He wrote English lyrics for *Jacques Brel Is Alive and Well and Living in Paris* and appeared, a larger than life character, in the West End production. He still passed songs to Hill and Range and an excellent ballad, 'You'll Think of Me' found its way to Elvis. Mort Shuman: 'I don't know how Elvis got hold of 'You'll Think of Me'. I wrote it as a Dylany song and I almost spoke it when I sang it. It's very much in the San Francisco era. Elvis put it on the backside of 'Suspicious Minds', which was a great song – I love that chorus.'

And could Elvis have done the Brel songs he put into English? 'No, I thought Elvis should stick to rock'n'roll, country or blues because his mind was geared to that. Of course, vocally he had the mettle to do the Brel songs, but he wasn't messed up or tortured like me or Scott Walker. Elvis would have just wondered what the hell the songs were about.'

In various combinations, Bill Giant, Bernie Baum and Florence Kaye had written many songs for Elvis, but they had only come up trumps once – 'Devil in Disguise' in 1963. The commanding 'Power of My Love' is so much better than their film fodder and could have been a hit single if there hadn't been so many other contenders. Another song 'Rubberneckin'' by Dory Jones and Bunny Warren was definitely a film song, recorded for the next film *Change of Habit*, and this showed what Elvis was about to leave behind. It contains the line, 'Some people say I'm wastin' time'. You said it, Elvis.

The country singer, Eddy Rabbitt, was under contract to Hill and Range. He was a promising writer who would become a country star and Lamar Fike told Elvis that he thought 'Kentucky Rain' would be a winner. 'Kentucky Rain' found a singer wondering what had gone wrong with his relationship and Eddy's 'Inherit the Wind', the title taken from a 1960 Spencer Tracy film, was about receiving your father's wanderlust.

AMMO for Elvis: the British songwriters, Chris Arnold, David Martin and Geoff Morrow, were a UK songwriting and production team, AMMO, and they had written 'In Thoughts of You', an excellent ballad with a classical feel that was a UK hit for Billy Fury in 1965 and would have suited Elvis. Elvis recorded two of their songs on these sessions, both of love lost: the sombre 'This Is the Story' and the lilting and melodic 'A Little Bit of Green', and there would be a third before the year was out.

Chris Arnold: 'We had an office, a broom cupboard really, in Carlin Music and we were writing for Cliff Richard, the Shadows, Frank Ifield and Cilla Black. Freddy Bienstock said, 'I need some songs for Elvis, I'm going over in a week's time'. We had to get very busy very quickly and he took our songs with him. 'A Little Piece of Green' and 'This Is the Story' came out exactly as we had imagined. David had a very versatile voice and he is a very good mimic and he did sound like Elvis on those demos.'

Geoff Morrow: 'I remember Freddy Bienstock loving 'A Little Bit of Green' and off it went to Elvis. We were very excited. We should have submitted and written 150 songs for Elvis as he clearly liked the songs that we were writing. Sometimes you don't realise when you're onto a good thing.'

Chris Arnold: 'We had a diary for our appointments in the music business but on the back page any one of us could write the title for a song. 'A Little Bit of Green' was a title in the back of the office diary that Geoff had written down. We wrote the melody and the title was the only part of the lyric that we had. I said to Geoff and David, 'What does it mean anyway?' They said, 'That's your business.' I thought, 'Green? Jealousy, maybe it's about that.''

David Martin: 'Elvis loved 'This Is the Story'. I know that because he did it live in Las Vegas. He had so many songs to choose from so he must have liked it.'

Chris Arnold: ''This Is the Story' was mainly written by Geoff. He had the idea of this guy sitting by his fireside and looking at a photograph and thinking about his relationship with the girl he was losing as the theme for a book – This is the story of what happened to you and me in the last few days. Geoff wrote most of the song, and then David and I took it to the finishing line.'

Another UK song, 'The Fair's Moving On' by Doug Flett and Guy Fletcher, was tailor-made for Elvis or, at least, Colonel Parker. Guy Fletcher: "Wonderful World' was our first song for Elvis and amazingly we got a cable from Colonel Parker saying that we should write another. We had been the first British writers to be recorded by Elvis Presley. We were already basking in that accolade and then we wrote 'The Fair's Moving On'. We knew that Colonel Parker had been a fairground barker and had an act with dancing chickens. He saw Elvis at a carnival and signed him and so we thought we would write a song about that environment. It was a love affair between a fairground worker and a local girl and how upset she was that he was leaving town. The song was saying, 'Don't be sad because I'm coming back."

Chips Moman had produced an excellent single, 'Suspicious Minds', which had been written and recorded by Mark James for Scepter Records in 1968. It was an expensive horn-driven production with stylish back-up vocals and it deserved to be a hit. However, James' voice was not distinctive enough and the slow intro didn't make enough impact: after all, you have to hook listeners in during the first ten seconds. Chips knew that it was a hit song and it needed a bravura performance – it needed Elvis.

Elvis liked Mark's songs; he had written 'Hooked on a Feeling' for B.J. Thomas, and we can see how he related to it – what was Priscilla up to while he was away, that type of thing. It was about deep love, paranoia, anguish and impending loss: 'We can't go on together with suspicious minds.' Chip's arrangement was over the top but that was perfect for Elvis who was in magnificent voice. The stop / start moment is a disc jockey's nightmare but it worked perfectly.

Colonel Parker's deputy, Tom Diskin, and Freddy Bienstock knew it was a winner but wanted 50% of the song. Chips published it and refused to be browbeaten. He said, 'You will have made the most expensive demo in history if you don't release it.' The impasse was resolved by Harry Jenkins, a veep at RCA, who said that it must be released and no deal was needed. The Colonel acquiesced, 'Okay, let Elvis do what he wants to do without us. Let him do it and fall on his ass.' Chips' defiance had repercussions as he never worked with Elvis again.

Elvis and Chips knew how to bring out the best in backing vocalists and a superb example was with the shoop-shoops on 'Wearin' That Loved on Look': indeed, it could have been called 'The Shoop Shoop Song' if that title hadn't already been taken. It's an excellent performance but the song itself, written by Dallas Frazier, cribs a bit too much from 'If You Don't Come Back', a Drifters' record from 1963.

Dallas Frazier also wrote 'True Love Travels on a Gravel Road', in which Elvis reflects on life and its tribulations, and that no matter what happens, love will endure. It's a fine performance but you can sense that Elvis is shifting towards his stadium voice. The backing track for another of Dallas' songs, 'Memory Revival', was recorded but Elvis' vocal was never added: just one of those things that got lost. Similarly, there is no vocal on 'Come Out, Come Out (Wherever You Are)', which was frustrating for the little-known writers Don Thomas and Mike Millius. Beck's 'Lord Only Knows' (1997) opens with a scream sampled from a Millius album, his other shot at national recognition. Elvis had also begun to put a vocal on Mac Davis' 'Poor Man's Gold', but there was outside noise and they stopped.

There were pop singles from the early 60s that Elvis wanted to revive. 'I'll Be There' had been written and first recorded by Bobby Darin and had been thrown away on the B-side of his 1960 US hit, 'Won't You Come Home Bill Bailey'. It became the closing record at the Cavern in Liverpool and so Gerry and the Pacemakers had picked up on it and it became a US Top 20 hit in 1965.

'It Keeps Right On A-Hurtin'' was a No.3 US hit in 1962 written and recorded by Johnny Tillotson. Tillotson says, 'I was definitely influenced by Hank Williams and the way he could paint pictures with his songs. That particular song came to me because of two thoughts: one was something a girlfriend said and the other was my father's illness. I had written something intangible that people could relate to, but you don't know you are doing that. There have been 100 cover versions and Elvis' was a wonderful surprise.

Elvis Presley: Caught in a Trap

I had sent him a different song, 'Dreamy Eyes', because Priscilla had such lovely eyes and I thought he might go for it but he preferred that one so I won't quarrel with that.'

Elvis' associate from the Sun days, Stan Kesler, got a look-in with 'If I'm a Fool', a pop / country ballad, recorded by both Jimmy Clanton and Bobby Wood in 1964. It was Bobby's only chart single and in later years, when playing keyboards on Elvis tribute shows, he could legitimately sing it. However, the song is little more than a variation of 'Am I That Easy to Forget'.

In 1967, Felton Jarvis had produced the original version of 'Gentle on My Mind' for its composer, the bluegrass singer John Hartford. Glen Campbell spotted its potential and it was a moderate US hit for him in 1968. The following year, Aretha Franklin took a soul treatment of it into the charts. It was not a UK hit until Dean Martin covered it in 1969, taking it to No.2.

'Gentle on My Mind' is about a hobo walking the railway track and having a reverie about what life was like. Elvis was not normally at his best with songs that were packed with lyrics, and maybe that was why he took it slower than most singers. There was the gentle chugging of a train and its whistle, but the performance lost its impact by fading out after three minutes.

In 1950, with wonderful billing, Hank Snow, the Singing Ranger, and his Rainbow Ranch Boys, topped the US country charts for over five months with another travelling song, 'I'm Movin' On'. As in 'Gentle on My Mind', the singer has got the urge to leave his partner and move, this time back to the south. Hank Snow moves on all right as he packs seven verses into two and a half minutes: in short, (1) That big 8-wheeler, (2) That big old whistle, (3) Mr. Fireman, (4) Mr. Engineer, (5) I've told you baby, (6) You switched your engine and (7) But someday baby. In particular, verse 6 shows that his woman is in the wrong.

Before he made *Modern Sounds in Country & Western Music* in 1962, Ray Charles was testing the water with a few R&B versions of country tunes, notably 'I'm Movin' On' in 1959. He took five of Snow's verses, sung in the order (5), (1), (7), (4) and (3) and added a coda much in the style of 'What'd I Say', which he had just recorded.

Elvis started country-style but built up steam and ended like Ray Charles, but he only sang four verses (1), (7), (3) and (5). It's good but I prefer the version Chips Moman recorded with the Box Tops at American Sound. It lasts four minutes and they sing (1), (2), (3), (5) and (7).

Many of Ray Charles' songs, including 'Hit the Road Jack', were written by Percy Mayfield. Charles hadn't recorded 'Stranger in My Own Home Town' and Presley would have known Mayfield's own version from 1963. It was about coming home and being ostracised, probably for being in prison. It was too repetitive, especially as it lasted four minutes, and it needed more of a story.

The Philadelphia duo, Kenny Gamble and Leon Huff, had written 'Only the Strong Survive', which had just been recorded by Jerry Butler and was to climb to No.4 on the US pop charts. It was a fine R&B performance from Jerry Butler and if anything, it was topped by Elvis Presley. An utterly soulful performance with Presley at his dramatic best.

Another classy R&B singer, Chuck Jackson, had recorded a Burt Bacharach and Bob Hilliard song, 'Any Day Now' in 1962. It was another record that Elvis had loved and he gave it a masterly performance. He never recorded any Bacharach / David songs but surely he would have got round to them had he lived. In the 1960s, the songwriters wouldn't have given Hill and Range a piece of the action. Arlo Guthrie told me that Hill and Range had asked for a deal on 'This Land Is Your Land', the most celebrated song by his father, Woody Guthrie. Elvis wanted to record it but the family said no to a publishing agreement and Elvis didn't do it.

One of Elvis' favourite singers, Roy Hamilton, had already been booked into American Sound. As it was a daytime session, Chips saw no reason for cancellation. Quite the reverse: when Elvis heard about it, he arrived early to meet him. He generously gave him 'Angelica', written by Barry Mann and Cynthia Weil. It was a superb Screen Gems song which would have been perfect for Elvis. It had been recorded by Gene Pitney and Scott Walker, but it had yet to chart. Roy Hamilton's single was released a few months later, but he died in July 1969, having just turned 40. 'In the end, it was Oliver – God bless him – who took the song into the Hot 100.

'Without Love' had been recorded by the high-pitched Clyde McPhatter in 1957 and had been revived by Ray Charles in 1963. Both Elvis and Tom Jones recorded this song in 1969 and it was a hit for Jones. At the time Tom Jones said, 'All my hits are very big songs, very loud songs. I've got to rip them to shreds'. Well, I'd agree with that but I am not sure it is a positive attribute. Tom Jones has a fantastic voice but he can never quite escape his old world of noisy drinking clubs, and where did he get that cheesy opening? Presley treats the song with more solemnity, enhanced with a gospel choir.

Then there's the first Shirl Milete song that Elvis cut, 'My Little Friend', about remembering an old love he called his little friend – shades of Priscilla again? It's a country – rock song in the vein of 'Gentle on My Mind' though nowhere near as strong.

Bobby Russell was on a roll with 'Honey' and 'Little Green Apples' but 'Do You Know Who I Am' was a tender break-up ballad that deserved more attention, even if it was recorded by Elvis. The similar sounding 'Who Am I' was a ballad with a religious theme by Rusty Goodman from the Happy Goodman Family. On 22 February 1969, that was to be the final song that Elvis recorded at American Sound.

It is sometimes said that the country star Ronnie Milsap played piano on the American Sound sessions. Well, he did and he didn't. Some changes were made to the tracks before they were ready for release and Ronnie Milsap added a harmony to 'Kentucky Rain' and recorded a new piano part for 'Gentle on My Mind'.

While Elvis had been recording in February, Bob Dylan was making *Nashville Skyline* and he met Freddy Bienstock on a plane back to New York. Freddy told him what a magnificent job Elvis had made of 'Only the Strong Survive'. He must have been impressed, as it wasn't a Hill and Range song.

Elvis and Priscilla went skiing in Aspen, Colorado, taking Lisa Marie with them. Musically the past weeks had gone extremely well and some tremendous records had been made. The only disappointment was the 1968 Grammys where Elvis' 'You'll Never Walk Alone' had lost in the Best Sacred Performance category to Jake Hess' 'Beautiful Isle of Somewhere'.

Meanwhile, Colonel Parker was negotiating the terms for Elvis Presley coming to Las Vegas. Parker liked the idea of Elvis playing in Vegas. The right place for Parker, but was the Showroom International the right choice for Presley? Maybe because the place was so unreal. Oddly enough, on his first season, he said, "Viva Las Vegas'? That's one number I ain't gonna do.'

Parker had been involved with Vegas since the late 1940s, when he booked Eddy

Arnold in El Rancho Vegas. In 1953, Parker and Arnold had a spat at the Sahara which was owned by Milton Prell, a front-man for the Detroit Mafia. He and the Colonel were friends and Parker would discuss business with him, but Prell played upon his weaknesses. Parker liked the one-dollar slots but Prell moved him towards the heavier stuff.

Elvis liked Vegas as much as Parker, but Parker saw the public relations disasters with Frank Sinatra and the Mob, and he never wanted Elvis to be photographed with them. He was mortified when Elvis' associates came to be known, jokingly, as the Memphis Mafia, and seemed to like it. As far as I know, the only photograph of Elvis and the Mob was when Milton Prell gave him a huge cake with twin Hotel Sahara towers for his 27th birthday, clearly as a photo-opportunity.

Normally, the cabaret shows were seen as loss leaders: the husbands went gambling while the wives went to the shows. Colonel Parker could see that with Elvis, the hotel/casino could make money in its own right. He anticipated fans coming from all over the world to see Presley.

The presence of young fans for pop acts had been borderline acceptable for the management, as they might come with their parents and wallets would be lightened. When Elvis conquered Vegas in 1969, he created a different problem. Elvis' fans were adults but on the whole they were coming solely to see him and didn't want to gamble. The fans were lookie-loos, that is, people who only watched the gamblers and didn't participate. The ticket prices had to accommodate that, but Elvis was seen as a mammoth PR boost for the city.

Elvis could be the opening act for the 30-storey International Hotel, being built by Kirk Kerkorian for $60m. Kerkorian had been a pilot who had flown gamblers from California to Nevada and then established Trans-International Airlines. He bought the Flamingo but he wanted to create his own, very tasteful dream hotel (according to his tastes, that is). It was a lavish skyscraper containing a showroom the size of a large theatre, seating 2,000. Kerkorian wanted to reinvigorate New Vegas so he hadn't wanted Frank Sinatra as the opening act, though he was to book Nancy. Tom Jones, already a proven hit in Vegas, would be fine but Presley would be ideal. Parker discussed it with Presley, who wisely said that he'd rather be the second act because by then logistical problems should have been resolved. 'Good idea,' said Parker, 'We're also in a better position if the hotel isn't ready on time.' Parker told Kerkorian that he could have two bites of the cherry: the first tranche of publicity when the hotel opened and the second a month later when Elvis arrived.

It is possible that Prell was involved in the financing of this contract and it's possible that, in later years, when the Mafia was covering Colonel Parker's gambling debts, they were granted a piece of Elvis. As the years went by, Elvis might have been doing shows for free to wipe out Parker's debts.

On 13 March, *Charro!* opened to poor reviews and even poorer audiences. Not to worry, it was ignored and a few weeks later, Elvis had a hit single, his first from the Memphis sessions, 'In the Ghetto'. It climbed to No.3, his biggest single in four years. It was the same in the UK where it went to No.2. The B-side, 'Any Day Now', was revived at the same time by Percy Sledge. Percy's version became an R&B hit.

While negotiations were going on, Elvis was making what was to be his last fictional film, *Change of Habit*, a joint production for Universal and NBC. Steve Binder was directing, but Colonel Parker disliked him. He had put too many ideas into Elvis' head. Is Elvis the only actor to have come through 30 films without playing a cop? He is given some social responsibility in *Change of Habit* by being cast as a doctor. He works in the ghetto, helped by some nuns led by Mary Tyler Moore, hence the title. Elvis doesn't know they are in holy orders but if they'd told him at the outset, there would have been no story.

Mary Tyler Moore is miscast but not nearly as badly as Elvis as the young doctor bringing medical care and rock'n'roll to the ghetto. It's like a Doris Day film, but it has more bite, as one of the youths tries to rape Mary Tyler Moore. In the end, she jumps over the wall and makes the new slim-line Elvis an offertory he can't refuse. It's Elvis or Jesus, and Elvis is winning as the film ends.

The most bizarre moment in the film is when Dr. Elvis plays 'Lawdy Miss Clawdy' on the piano. He also leads a big folk-rock mass and sings 'Let Us Pray'. Again, AMMO was on call to write a song. Geoff Morrow: 'Elvis was making a film called *Change of Habit* and there was an awkward moment where he sang to a child with autism. Three or four people had had a shot at writing the song but it hadn't worked and so we were asked to come up with something.'

Chris Arnold: 'I said, 'We have to give the child the confidence to believe that they are having a conversation.' There is a line in the song that says, 'You live in silence but for once let's pretend we're talking here together, Let's be friends'. That is the message of the song. We felt 'Let's Be Friends' fitted the bill and it was duly recorded by Elvis. It was intended for the film, but somebody decided that the film was too long and the song was dropped. It had been recorded though and one day we were walking through the production department of RCA in London and we saw an album, *Let's Be Friends* by Elvis Presley on their Camden label. It was good to see the song being used and as the title track of an album.'

Geoff Morrow: "Let's Be Friends' was Chris Arnold's forte. He speaks Greek and Latin and went to Cambridge and really he is far too clever to be involved with David and I. He saw how that song could work in the most unsentimental way. There is a danger that these are finger-down-the-throat songs, but this one says, 'Let's be friends, I like you' and it is on a very normal level. Elvis did a lovely rendition of it.'

When the film wrapped at the start of May, Elvis and Priscilla went to Hawaii on holiday. They saw some karate and caught Tom Jones at Ilikai Hotel in Honolulu. Elvis came in during the second number and everyone went 'Oh look, it's Elvis', which was impish as it was Tom's audience. There are ways for entertainers to enter unobtrusively. Tom's road manager, Tony Cartwright: 'I'm sure Elvis saw Tom's massive reception and thought, 'If that's what I've got to beat, I'll beat that.' Elvis could have happily performed every song in Tom's set and done them just as well, plus he had the added advantage of those amazing looks.'

Elvis called Tom 'Sock Dick' as he thought Tom put a sock down his trousers to increase the size of his manhood when he was on stage.

By now Elvis had lost his interest in his Circle G ranch and he sold it to a local gun club. He brought the horses back to Graceland. However, they soon defaulted on the mortgage payments. In 1972, there was an auction for the property and as Vernon outbid other contenders, Circle G was back with the Presleys.

In June 1969, his first album from the Memphis sessions was released, *From Elvis in Memphis*. Although it had many influences, it worked as a cohesive whole and it is superb. It only made No.13 in the US, not quite as good as the TV special LP, but it was listed for four months. The tracks were well chosen and the album was a UK No.1. Ironically, the top US album was by his old friend from Sun, *Johnny Cash at San Quentin*, another artist who had undergone a terrific transformation. Unlike Presley, Cash wouldn't have thought twice about recording songs on social issues.

Released at the same time was *Memphis Underground* by the jazz flautist Herbie Mann. It had been made at American Sound with several of the same musicians. It was among the biggest selling jazz albums of the decade.

In June, Elvis went to Vegas to see how the hotel was progressing. The International would be the highest building in Las Vegas, with a huge, swimming pool. There were 1,000 slot machines and three theatres – the lounge, a playhouse and the showroom. The showroom was three times bigger than any other showroom in Vegas.

At the Riviera, Elvis saw Engelbert Humperdinck, who was also being handled by Tony Cartwright: 'During the show, I heard Elvis say to the Colonel, 'Let's have the two guitar players'. One was Robin MacDonald and the other was Mick Green. Mick had a shuffle beat and nobody else was playing that. Elvis wanted them and I had to nip that in the bud as Elvis was going backstage to say hello. At the end of the show, I said to Elvis, 'I overheard you talking about the two guitarists. They're with me and they're going from here to Australia. I don't want you making them an offer. Engelbert will be very upset as they have been with him a long time'. Elvis said, 'No problem at all, Tony, I won't mention it'. He was a man of his word and it was spoken like the true gentleman he was.' (Robin and Mick later discovered what they had missed.)

Tony witnessed a freakish incident where Elvis needed Red West's help to take his trousers down so that he could go to the toilet. 'When they returned, Engelbert's valet signalled to me and I said, 'What is it?' He said, 'There's a gun on the floor in the toilet'. Red said, 'Elvis must have dropped it. I'll go and get it'.'

Elvis still had to get his band together. The American Sound musicians were too busy with studio work. The previous year he had not been able to secure James Burton for his TV special because he had been working with Sinatra.

James Burton had been born in Dubberly, Louisiana in 1939 and he was playing guitar on the *Louisiana Hayride* when he was only 14. He developed a very bright, string-bending sound with Ricky Nelson – just listen to 'Believe What You Say' – and he made a smooth transition to studio musician, working on the TV show *Shindig* and playing an important part in the Bakersfield sound for country acts, notably Merle Haggard. He is known for playing the Fender Telecaster but he also played steel guitar and dobro. He says, 'Unlike a violin, a guitar can be made to do what you want to do with it, but it's not how much you play. It's what you play and how you play it.'

Elvis knew he had the right man. James Burton: 'Elvis called me in 1969 to put a band together. He called it the TCB band and I called it Taking Care of Burton. I stayed with him until the end.' Elvis had not come up with TCB – he had taken it from Aretha Franklin's 'Respect': 'Take out – TCB', and the lightning bolt for the bracelets and necklaces came from Captain Marvel.

Burton chose the musicians carefully, offering good wages so that they wouldn't lose out on session fees. The initial band was James Burton (lead guitar), John Wilkinson and Charlie Hodge (guitars), Jerry Scheff (bass), Larry Muhoberac (piano) and Ronnie Tutt (drums). The sound was enhanced by the Imperials Quartet and the Sweet Inspirations featuring Cissy Houston, mother of Whitney. James Burton: 'Elvis loved the band but he was real nervous that first night at the International. He was walking up and down so much he was wearing out the carpet. I said, 'Elvis, don't worry, it's too late to cancel'.'

There had been a no from the Jordanaires. Ray Walker; 'The International Hotel deal was set up very quickly and we were called five weeks before the opening. We were doing up to four sessions a day, plus overtime; in fact, we have done as much as 128 hours singing in a week. We couldn't do Las Vegas because we had so many sessions booked.'

'...and we had some Coca-Cola commercials,' added Gordon Stoker, 'That was more than we would have been paid by Elvis for a week's rehearsal and four weeks of shows. I think we were very fortunate as a lot of the musicians never saw Elvis before he went on stage and then of course 'Elvis has left the building'. They would rehearse with Charlie standing in for Elvis and then play the set.'

At the start of July, Elvis was rehearsing with his TCB band in July and doing daily workouts: he wanted to be in superb shape. Expectations were high and Elvis was on the cover of *Rolling Stone* for the first time: still, it was only issue No.37. The feature itself was a let-down as it mocked Presley for the hippie generation. Elvis had been interviewed on the set of *Change of Habit*. He said, 'I've got a date in Vegas and maybe another film after that. Then I'm going to try and get to Europe. I've got some good, faithful fans over there.' When asked where Colonel Parker was, he said, 'I think he's in Palm Springs. I'm not sure.'

When Barbra Streisand opened at the International, the temperature was 120 degrees, but her reception was icy. The showroom was still under construction and she told audiences that she was expecting 'some schmuck with a ladder to walk by any minute now'. There was no opening act, no showgirls and no lavish sets. Her instinct that audiences would just want to see her and not a flashy show was wrong for Vegas. She did well but it could have been better.

On 20 July 1969, Neil Armstrong became the first man to walk upon the moon, another burst of pride for America.

On 25 July, Elvis and his friends went to Barbra Streisand's final night. He told the 14-year-old David Stanley that he needed some culture. David was amazed at how good she was. Presley said to Charlie Hodge, 'That's a hell of a big stage to fill.'

On 26 July, there was an afternoon dress rehearsal and then at 10pm a special show for an invited audience. Elvis was nervous: he'd never done a one-hour show before, and soon he would be doing it twice nightly. The audience included Ann-Margret, Paul Anka, Cary Grant and Fats Domino, who as luck would have it, was playing in the lounge. Or rather, as bad luck would have it, as Domino was in Vegas almost as a custodial sentence, making good his gambling debts.

Starting 31 July 1969, Elvis played a month at the International. There were two shows a night, seven nights a week. The first show at 8pm was a dinner show and the midnight one was drinks only. Frank and Dean had reigned supreme for 10 years but Elvis was so successful that Vegas turned to rock.

It wasn't difficult to work out a repertoire. Elvis would do some early hits ('Mystery Train', 'Hound Dog', 'Blue Suede Shoes', 'All Shook Up'); new hits ('In the Ghetto', 'Suspicious Minds') and new recordings ('Inherit the Wind', 'Rubberneckin''). There would be blues from time to time – 'Reconsider Baby' and 'Baby What You Want Me to Do'.

There would be songs not associated with him – Chuck Berry's 'Johnny B Goode', Ray Charles' 'I Can't Stop Loving You', Del Shannon's 'Runaway', Willie Nelson's 'Funny How Time Slips Away', Little Walter's 'My Babe' (Elvis loved what James Burton had played on Ricky Nelson's version) and the Bee Gees' 'Words'.

Right from the start, Elvis closed his shows with 'Can't Help Falling in Love' but the arrangement was more upbeat than the days of *Blue Hawaii*. It became the perfect signature tune, especially when he had a cape, and as Elvis hadn't reissued it on a 45rpm. Andy Williams released it in January 1970: it did okay in the US but Andy found himself in the UK Top 10.

Elvis never did encores: this was when fans knew it was over – the compère didn't say, 'Elvis has left the building' at the International. How could he? He lived there. Tony Cartwright: 'It would have been easier if Elvis Presley had left the International. When they built the hotel, they built this massive suite for the starring attraction. It was five times bigger than any other suite in Vegas and it was called the 10-acre suite. It was fantastic. However, there was a flaw. No one had thought about how they would get Elvis Presley from his suite to the stage. Elvis couldn't go down in a normal elevator as he would be mobbed. He had to use the service elevator which brought his food from the kitchen. Elvis would get in that with two of his boys. The kitchen was equally massive. There would be Elvis Presley in his stage suit walking past the turkey rack, the meat rack and the sausage rack, and there was no way round this problem.'

An easier problem was what you said in-between the songs. Most singers said little of substance: it was a way of catching breath or plugging new offerings, but Vegas was different. Anthony Newley thought he knew the secret: 'The difficult lesson that you have to learn is that Las Vegas is not theatre, it is not variety and it is not even cabaret as we know it. It is something much more subtle. It is about being who you are. Sammy Davis explained it to me before I opened in 1969. He told me that I should just sing the songs that I had written and made famous and should just be myself. It became very clear to me over the years that the closer you get to being who you are, the more successful you become. The great night club performers are the ones who come out like Sammy, Frank and Dean and create an evening out of who they are: they put in asides and they stop the orchestra if they want to. That rapport with the audience is very important because then the great night club act is happening right here in front of you. It is not choreographed, it is not rehearsed, it is happening here and if something happens, you stop and you talk to the girl serving the drinks or you talk to your musical director. It is a Zen experience and the great performers know that.' (Anthony Newley could be right but I'm not sure Elvis and the Colonel knew what Zen experiences were.)

Elvis' comments weren't scripted and who knew what he would say from night to night? As we shall see in the next chapter, he was sometimes way out of order, but not in 1969. Maybe he had been working up these jokes with the boys for years, but however feeble they appear, they certainly worked on stage.

Elvis was blessed with having a great band. James Burton: 'I would make out a set list but he would never stick to it. One time he played 'Blue Christmas' in August. Elvis would change the tempos from one show to another and sometimes he did those old hits really fast. It was always hard on Ronnie Tutt who played drums but those concerts worked out great.'

Jerry Scheff: 'Elvis loved to play stump the band. He could keep in mind the key of the last song and start singing another song in another key relating to that. As we went on, I realised that he wanted to do songs that would show off his voice. He started doing 'My Way' but he didn't do new rock and roll songs. He would say, 'I can't find any I really like'.'

Elvis was very like a boxer. Once he was ready for the ring, the adrenalin was flowing and he wanted to be out there. Tony Cartwright: 'I saw Elvis on his first night at the Hilton. The band started and it was very exciting. Elvis came out and everybody stood up. It was a great reception. He sounded great, and it was unlike anything that I had seen or heard before. Elvis had a great idea with those jumpsuits. He wasn't doing many karate kicks at first but when he did those kicks, those suits were reinforced around the bum. I loved it when Elvis threw in old hits unexpectedly like 'Jailhouse Rock'. He would take requests, people could scream something out and he would do it. I saw Elvis' first 54 shows and I formed a great relationship with Colonel Tom Parker who was always out front.'

'Oh, I thought I wouldn't live through it,' says Liverpool fan Maria Davies, 'I got so excited and I was afraid of fainting. I took a deep breath in the way that guardsmen are told. My heart was pounding and my head was banging. I just thought I wouldn't live.'

Priscilla, Lisa Marie, Vernon and the Stanleys were all in LA and Presley could reach them easily. On 9 August 1969 Charles Manson and his tribe carried out their gruesome murders in Hollywood including that of the actress Sharon Tate. Presley knew one of the victims, Jay Sebring as he was a celebrity barber who had cut his hair and, indeed, had had Larry Geller on his staff.

After their arrest, Presley learnt he himself had been on Manson's hit list. He didn't know what would happen next: how many crazed, drugged-out hippies were out there? He flew his family to Las Vegas, beefed up the security and employed Hollywood's top investigator, a former narcotics cop, John O'Grady, to determine what was going on and report back.

The fact that there was so little Christmas material in the TV Special was a bonus as NBC could repeat the show at any time of the year. It was repeated on 17 August 1969 and 'Blue Christmas' was replaced by 'Tiger Man'.

By the time the month had ended, Elvis had played to 100,000 people and the gross receipts had been $1.5m. Presley himself had been paid $125,000 but his expenses included paying the band. It had been the most successful season in Vegas ever and the hotel gave Elvis a gold belt. The International was so pleased that it waived Colonel Parker's gambling losses, provided of course that Elvis returned.

Elvis and his entourage stayed an extra day so that they could support Nancy Sinatra at her opening. Frank hosted a party for his daughter and the Presleys attended. Ironically, Elvis coming to Las Vegas was not the musical event of August. That was the 'half a million strong' Woodstock festival, the music festival that defined a whole generation. There were no 50s stars on the bill but the rock'n'roll revival band, Sha Na Na, did well.

But Elvis was speaking to the Woodstock generation. His new single, 'Suspicious Minds', was a contemporary record, a new Elvis for the forthcoming 70s, and the public loved it. It was his first US No.1 since 'Good Luck Charm' in 1962. Like 'In the Ghetto', it went to No.2 in the UK. It was backed by 'You'll Think of Me', a nice gift for Mort Shuman. The dramatic 'Suspicious Minds' was perfect for live performance.

In September, Elvis and Priscilla were in Graceland but they didn't relax as they were planning interior decorations. They went to Honolulu while the decorators were in and they returned in December for the run up to Christmas. Amidst the euphoria, two films slipped out: *The Trouble with Girls* in September (bad reviews) and *Change of Habit* in November (so-so reviews).

RCA had recorded the final week of Elvis' Vegas appearances with a live album in mind. In the end, they decided on a double-album, Elvis' first, clumsily-titled *From Memphis to Vegas / From Vegas to Memphis*. This was a clever idea as the best of the Memphis songs had been chosen for the first album and so disguised the fact. Even by 1969, most live albums were disappointing but this worked well and the live shows had been recorded excellently – with a bit of studio retouching too. 'Suspicious Minds' had become an eight minute *tour de force*. The LP made No.12 in the US and No.3 in the UK.

Elvis didn't go back to American Sound Studios but in 1972, the temperamental Chips Moman left the city as he was annoyed that Memphis had renamed itself Soul City after Stax Records. One of the last albums he recorded there, *Arthur Alexander*, included the original version of 'Burning Love'. The building was demolished in 1987.

Chips Moman set up a new studio in Nashville and he co-wrote the hippie anthem, 'Luckenbach, Texas', recorded by Waylon and Willie. In 1985, he worked with Johnny Cash, Jerry Lee Lewis, Carl Perkins and Roy Orbison as the Class of '55. The track, 'We Remember the King' could be about Jesus, could be about Elvis.

CHAPTER 13

Desert Life

'Good evening, I hope my mouth will work right, you know.'
Elvis Presley on stage, 1974

I. Crazy Words, Crazy Tune

In the 1950s, Elvis said little on stage, probably because there was too much screaming, but it was evident that he had a strong sense of humour. Look at how he leads audiences into thinking they are going to hear a romantic ballad and then bursts out with 'You ain't nothin' but a hound dog'.

Elvis had seen several Vegas acts before he started his concert dates in 1969. Frank, Sammy and Dean were great entertainers who had mastered one-liners, often written by the lyricist Sammy Cahn, who had scripted Frank and Elvis' TV show. Cahn was brilliant at this, but, as far as is known, Elvis didn't want scripted remarks. Sammy Cahn would have told someone if he was working for Elvis, so I don't think he ever did. Also, his lines were not as sharp as the lines Cahn was writing for Dino: 'The girl that I marry will have to be, A nympho who owns a distillery' or 'I didn't know what time it was, I drank my watch.'

I say this because if you listen to several shows by members of the Rat Pack, you will hear the same jokes over and over: they knew what worked and kept on saying them. On the other hand, Elvis seems to be saying the first things that come into his head – he does repeat himself of course: he'd be foolish not to repeat jokes that worked – but by and large it's whatever's on his mind, and he got away with it, because Elvis was naturally funny.

Just like Frank Sinatra, Elvis spoke of his concerns, both of life around him and what was happening in the world outside. Both Frank and Elvis were much franker on stage than at a press conference.

Lyrics

'I lost my little britches to them ol' sons of bitches.' ('Tennessee Waltz', 1966: not on stage, a home recording.)

'Do you gaze at your bald head and wish you had hair?' ('Are You Lonesome Tonight', 1969 and a favourite)

'Suddenly I'm not half the stud I used to be.' ('Yesterday', 1969)

'I got three little kids and a very horny wife.' ('Stagger Lee', 1970)

'For my darling I love you because you took the pill.' ('Love Me Tender', 1970)

'I've been travelling night and day, I've been streaking all the way.' ('Tryin' to Get to You', 1970)

'Now that you're here, too bad you're queer.' ('It's Now or Never', 1970)

'Wasn't the spring, the spring became the mattress.' ('Sweet Caroline', 1970)

'This time you gave me a molehill' ('You Gave Me a Mountain', 1972)

'Look away, look away, Disneyland' ('American Trilogy', 1973: even Elvis' most serious songs weren't exempted from his humour)

'I keep streaking all the way.' ('Tryin' to Get to You', 1974)

'Captain Smith poked his Pocahontas.' ('Fever', 1974)

'Cats were born to give you fever, be it Fahrenheit or lemonade.' ('Fever', 1974)

'This is the promised land calling and the motherfucker's on the line' (Rehearsal, 19 August 1974)

'How am I doing? Guess I'm going blind.' ('Funny How Time Slips Away', 1976: Elvis was suffering with glaucoma.)

'Your lips excite me, for God's sake, don't bite me.' ('It's Now or Never', 1977: Elvis joking to the end)

'Wise men know when it's time, time, time to go.' ('Can't Help Falling In Love', 1977)

As you read the crazy lyrics, you get a feel for how Elvis' mind works. I've seen many Elvis impersonators over the years but I've yet to meet one who specialises in silly lyrics, yet it would work well.

When Elvis talks to the audience, you can't second-guess what will come next.

Elvis on his background:

'Those of you of the Caucasian race…well, we are, aren't we…it was on my draft card…Caucasian…I didn't know what it meant…Thought they were going to circumcise me.'

'Let me introduce you to my father. He's more of a ham than I am.'

'Where's granny?'

Elvis on his career:

'I was studying to be an electrician. I got wired the wrong way.'

(On doing 'It's Now or Never') 'They thought lads from the South mumbled all the time.'

'The Sun records sound funny. There's a lot of echo on them.' (1970)

On singing 'Hound Dog' on *The Steve Allen Show* in 1956: 'I didn't move a muscle the whole song. The collar was so stiff, I'd have cut my throat if I had.'

On singing 'Hound Dog' on *The Ed Sullivan Show*: 'I was 19 years old and had terminal acne.' (1972)

'Man, I was tame compared to what they do now. I just wiggled.' (1972)

'I was only singing and dancing. I led a straight, clean life and I didn't contribute to juvenile delinquency.' (1958)

'Regardless of who you are, there are people who don't like you. Look at Jesus Christ.' (1956)

'The guys in the forces got lonely as they call each other 'mother' a lot.' (1969)

'I'm leavin' – It's not the title of a song, I'm just getting the hell out of here.'

Elvis on karate

'I don't do karate in order to break bricks or boards. How many times does a brick come out and attack you?'

'When I did *G I Blues* I blocked a kick the wrong away and there I was with this big fat hand. Nothing they could do about it. They tried to put make-up on it, nothing.

It came out on the back of the album. Look at it.'

Celebrity introductions

On being told Charlton Heston was in the audience: 'I was in the dining room at Paramount studios, just came out of Memphis, and there was Moses. Charlton Heston. He was doing *The Ten Commandments*. I'd like to ask him what state of mind he had to get into for that part. He'd just talked to God and here he was in the canteen.'

'I'd like to introduce you to the Babe Ruth of baseball, Mr. Arnold Palmer.' (Elvis didn't know who Palmer was. Elvis was too impatient for golf – the 100 yards dash was more to his taste.)

When Neil Diamond is introduced, Neil stands up and sings a line from one of his songs. 'No, no, Neil's come to watch the show. He's not working tonight.' (1970)

'Brenda Lee opens at the Fremont tomorrow night. She's so little, you can miss her. Brenda, if I get a chance, I'll come over and see you.' (1971)

'My first movie contract was with Hal Wallis. Mr. Wallis made about ten of my movies. We usually close our show with a song from *Blue Hawaii* but tonight we'll do it early. I'd like to dedicate it to Mr. Wallis because he still makes very good films like *Anne of a Thousand Days* and *True Grit*.' (1971)

'These high collars, man. He originated them, 20 years ago. Billy Eckstine. It's really a pleasure, man.' (Elvis sings part of 'I Apologise', 1974)

'His hair never moves and he's a great friend of mine, Glen Campbell.' (1975)

'I'd like you to please say hello to Ann-Margret. You're beautiful. Put the light on her, man, I want to look at her. Colonel Parker is outside selling Ann-Margret pictures.' (1973)

'I had one of the biggest fights I ever had in my life with her. But I still love her, Phyllis McGuire.' (1973) (Elvis had been dating Phyllis McGuire of the McGuire Sisters in 1964 and her partner was the mobster, Sam Giancana. Elvis had been messing where he shouldna been messin'.)

Personal revelations

On Priscilla: 'Most of the stuff you read about me is junk. We're the very best of friends and we always have been. Our divorce came about not because of another man, not because of another woman, but because of the circumstances involving my career. I was travelling too much. I was gone too long.'

'John O'Grady was head of the narcotics squad in Hollywood and he has written a book. On page 166, he has three pages about me and my ex-wife Priscilla and about that paternity suit, that was a complete conspiracy and a hoax, man. No way! I had a picture taken with that chick and that's all. She got pregnant by the Polaroid. She goofed up. She named the night. That night my wife was in the audience. I ain't gonna fool around when Priscilla's out there, y'kidding me. (Laughs) If you like *The French Connection*, the Chinese Connection, the British Connection, the knee bone connection to the jawbone, the jawbone to the hambone, buy this book. When is it out, John?' (2 September 1974, Las Vegas)

'Ladies and gentlemen, I just want to say one thing. They don't give you anything if you're strung out. Last week I was made an 8th degree black belt in karate and it carries the title, Master of the Art. I couldn't face my father, Priscilla, my baby, my friends, nobody, if I was strung out and if I ever catch anybody in this hotel, bellboy, room service, maître d' telling anybody that I'm strung out, then I'll pull his goddamn

Elvis Presley: Caught in a Trap

tongue out by the roots.' This last part was yelled and as if to prove it, he coughed and spluttered on stage. 'Sorry, but if it comes up, its's gotta go, you know. It's not cool on stage, but I can't help it.' (Las Vegas Hilton, March 1975)

'You didn't know that you were coming to see a crazy man.' (The drugs aren't working)

'I don't pay any attention to rumours or to movie magazines, they are all junk. (Applause) They have a job to do. If they don't have anything, they make it up. I heard the rumours flying. You can't be sick in this town – you are strung out. I heard the rumours flying but I have never been strung out in my life, except on music. (Applause). I was sick in the hotel with a temperature of 102, and they wouldn't let me perform. Three different sources said I was strung out on heroin. I swear to God, I had the flu. Now don't get offended, ladies and gentlemen, as I am talking to somebody else. If I ever catch anybody in this hotel – bellboy, room service, maître d', telling anybody that I'm strung out, I'm gonna break your goddamned neck, you son of a bitch! (Band laughs, audience applause) That is dangerous to myself, my little daughter, my father, my friends, my doctor, even my relationship with you. I will pull your goddamned tongue out by the roots. (Applause) How many of you saw the movie, *Blue Hawaii?* This is the most requested song, 'Hawaiian Wedding Song'.'

'So those you who've never seen me before will realise tonight that I'm totally insane and I have been for a number of years.' (1970)

Elvis on being on stage:

'They're watching me, folks. They're gonna come and get me. It's just a matter of time really. They got woolly boogers all over this audience, saying 'Get him, get him.''' (Las Vegas, opening night, August 1969: start as you mean to go on)

'I'm awful sweaty. Lay it on me, kid.'

'I looked her square in the eye 'cause that was all she had – one big square eye.'

'Look at all those funky angels hanging from the ceiling. There ain't nothing like a funky angel, boy.' (Décor at the International)

'A real fine drummer Ronnie Tutt and over on the Fender bass, Jerry Scheff. Any way you look at it, that's Tutt Scheff.' (One of Elvis' favourite jokes)

'On the piano, Colonel Parker.' (Another favourite joke!)

'Couple of people want me to say hello. Hello, couple of people.'

'Well, well, well, that's all folks.'

Always wanting to make extra dollars from Elvis, Colonel Parker prepared a spoken word album for fans, *Havin' Fun with Elvis*. His RCA contract only called only for songs and so his speech was not their copyright, although it had been recorded with RCA equipment. RCA wasn't happy about this and they came to an arrangement with Parker to release it officially. It is often listed as a candidate for the worst record ever made.

In one sense it is but in another, it is immensely revealing: for this is where we see the true Elvis. Sure, he couldn't rap like Bruce Springsteen, but these comments came straight from the heart. The ones that I list above – and there are hundreds more – are often witty, descriptive and sharp. His sense of surrealism matched some singer/songwriters judged to be more intellectual. Elvis could be very funny but you note how the Sinatra menace could creep in sometimes. Elvis was tormented and he articulated that in this strange way. It was never the self-pity that you heard from other artists who had never known the same level of pressure.

Spencer Leigh

II. Got a Lot o' Livin' to Do, 1970–1972

The month in the Showroom International at Las Vegas had been so successful that Colonel Parker signed a five-year deal on a tablecloth for Elvis to return every February and August, a typical Parker move that locked Elvis into another long-term contract. Surely Parker should have realised that he was really in unchartered waters with Presley. It would have been better to see how events developed and what other offers came along, such as huge stadium gigs. Okay, sign for one year, maybe two, but surely not five. The tablecloth, incidentally, has been preserved.

The owners of the other casinos, even though they didn't have Elvis themselves, didn't want to lose him. Elvis was having an immediate effect on everybody's profitability. He was encouraging a new generation to come to Vegas and the city would be growing to over a million residents.

Gordon Stoker of the Jordanaires: 'Colonel Parker sold Elvis too cheaply and two shows a night in Las Vegas is what killed Elvis Presley. Elvis wanted the second show to be as good as the first and he took uppers to get him going and then downers, because he was so keyed up after the last show, to put him to sleep. Colonel Parker could have made the same money from one show a night.'

The sisters Maria and Gladys Davies had clerical jobs in Liverpool. They saved up their money and went to see their hero. They made three trips and saw 36 shows, which surely is no stranger than following a football team. 'I don't really think about the cost. I think of it as buying a slice of happiness,' said Maria, 'Everything's different with an Elvis show. He never did anything the same.' Vernon Presley gave them a stylish black suede waistcoat with fringes that had been worn by Elvis. They were making so much money that the Presleys could afford to give such things away.

Elvis loved communicating with fans and he would kiss them and distribute around 30 scarves in each performance. Charlie would hand them to him one by one in rapid succession and fans would crowd to the front, hoping to catch Presley's eye. Personally, I would rather have had another couple of songs but I can see how this whips up fan fever, particularly in an environment that is not used to it.

Having special clothes made for you wasn't confined to Elvis. Another Brit, Rex Martin, ran the *Worldwide Elvis News Service* which could run to 32 pages in a big week. Prior to attending the shows, he had a special jacket made with large inside pockets in which he concealed cameras and cassette recorders. Although he would keep the cassettes rolling, he would run the camera for a few seconds at a time. He was keen to photograph the girls that Elvis was kissing as selling them copies would repay his costs. One night he got carried away by Elvis' leg movements in 'Fever' and his camera was seized and confiscated. The following day Rex bought smaller equipment, but Tom Diskin had had him tailed and that night he was frisked and barred from the show.

By tipping the maitre d', Maria and Gladys were able to sit up front. Maria was impressed by the large gold belt that Elvis was wearing, given to him by The International. Maria Davies: 'Elvis loved to embarrass people. He'd been given this very large gold belt and the fan club had asked me to find out what the inscription said. He always came down to the front row and when he did, I grabbed hold of his scarf and said, 'Elvis, what's on your belt?' He didn't hear me the first time – 'Huh?' he said – and so I repeated it. This time a mischievous smile came over his face. He thrust his hips right

Elvis Presley: Caught in a Trap

into my face to allow me to read the inscription, saying at the same time, 'You gotta lotta nerve there, baby!' Well, the whole show room erupted with laughter as they'd not heard my question, only Elvis' reply. It was so funny. Even Gladys thought I'd had a brainstorm and asked him to take his clothes off.'

Elvis had been lucky as he had got through his first season in Las Vegas with few vocal problems. Working in such intense dry heat can be hard on the voice and many singers suffered 'Las Vegas throat'. Admittedly, Presley is hardly going out in the street or riding in the desert but living in air conditioning 24/7 is hardly good for you. Even such a hardened Vegas pro as Frank Sinatra had trouble with his throat, although, in his case, it would be lubricated with bourbon. Tom Jones had a machine that made steam (no, not a kettle) and he seemed to avoid the problems.

Again RCA recorded the final week of shows, and an album, *On Stage – February 1970*, was released in June. It was the first album to be released where the artist's name only appeared on the spine. All 10 songs were new to his repertoire: this was a good idea and RCA should have done the same in later years when Elvis was reluctant to go to the studio. It made economic sense too: the musicians had to be there on stage with Elvis and RCA didn't need to pay them again – it was a cheap way of making albums.

There were no original songs on the album, but the covers had been very well chosen and in most cases Elvis added something new. It began with a frenzied version of Bessie Smith's blues, 'See See Rider' (1925), and Elvis liked the way that Chuck Willis had done it in 1957: that was much slower with a female vocal group. Elvis took that arrangement but sped it up, really sped it up. The song is not about a motorcyclist but a cheating partner, with 'see see' being a play on the word 'easy'.

'Release Me' had been a crossover hit (Kitty Wells and Ray Price, country, in 1954 and Esther Phillips, R&B in 1962) but had recently been a worldwide hit for another Vegas star, Engelbert Humperdinck. They had much in common – including a love for Juliet Prowse, for starters – and Elvis' version took it back to R&B and I loved the way he sang a nonsense phrase to catch up with the band.

Although schmaltzy, his revival of 'Let It Be Me' was excellent. This song began life as 'Je t'appartiens' for Gilbert Bécaud in 1955 and was a hit in English for the Everly Brothers in 1960. You can tell it is a translation as the language is stilted, 'Don't take this heaven from one', but that adds to its attractiveness. It has a new life these days as a funeral song.

Although excellent, Del Shannon's 'Runaway' sounded odd with a guitar break instead of an organ and I would have brought Glen D. Hardin's piano to the fore. 'Sweet Caroline' was less successful with Presley going through the motions and rushing the song. Presley could relate to Joe South's 'Walk a Mile in My Shoes' but again, he never sang it seriously enough.

On Stage was a strong album with the tracks running together to make a complete show and we had many of Elvis' comments – 'Tough way to make a living, baby', 'Honey, honey, don't get physical' – and how he encouraged the musicians, 'Play it hard now', 'Play it, James' and 'Take it home'. Why was the audience applauding at the start of 'Yesterday', as it wasn't his song? Vegas audiences did like star performers singing famous songs, so was the applause really encouragement? Both 'Runaway' and 'Yesterday' had been recorded in August 1969 while the other *On Stage* sessions featured Bob Lanning on drums, not Ronnie Tutt.

There were two hit singles from the album, 'The Wonder of You' and 'Polk Salad Annie'. Glen D. Hardin: 'He was very unpredictable and you had to keep alert. He would come up with old songs from the 20s and 30s that we hadn't heard in years. One time Elvis and I were walking down a hallway and he said, 'Do you remember The Wonder of You?' I said, 'Yeah, good song'. Later that day I orchestrated it for him. Simple as that. ' (Laughs) I worked all night on the arrangements many, many times. Elvis had an extremely good range and it was fairly easy to determine what key he would want. I don't recall hitting any of those notes ever being a problem to him.'

'The Wonder of You' had been written as a gentle ballad for Perry Como, but it was given to Ray Peterson who recorded it in 1959. There were UK cover versions from the two Ronnies (Hilton and Carroll), and although both Ray Peterson and Ronnie Hilton made the Top 30, their versions were forgotten once Elvis sang it. Glen D. Hardin wrote a very powerful arrangement on which Elvis is backed by a full orchestra as well as The Imperials Quartet and The Sweet Inspirations.

Ronnie Hilton: 'During my summer season at Blackpool in 1959, 'The Wonder of You' was in the charts and it made my act that much stronger. It was like having an ace up my sleeve. When Elvis Presley brought out his version, I thought, 'That's a bit of a liberty, it's not much different to the way I did it all those years ago.' Still, good luck to him, it was a good song and it deserved to get to No.1.'

If you listen to the lyrics of 'The Wonder of You', it would be easy to take this as a gospel song, and the line 'You touch my hand and I'm a king' was perfect for live performances.

The second hit single from the album was not released as such until 1973 and then in the UK rather than the US: it was 'Polk Salad Annie', written and first recorded by Tony Joe White in 1969. What, I asked Tony Joe, was 'a razor-toed woman'? 'No, no, it's razor totin', she's carrying a razor for protection. A lot of women back in Louisiana had straight razors in their purses. Elvis came from Tupelo and he ate a lot of polk salad as he was growing up. Felton Jarvis was a good friend of mine and I was told that Elvis wanted to fly me and my wife to Las Vegas as he was recording 'Polk Salad Annie' live on stage. We hung out there for two or three days and then I saw him in Memphis. He did a lot of different cuts of that song and he always treated me real good.' When Tony Joe was introduced from the stage by Elvis, he was coming out of the rest room and zipping up his fly, not the ideal moment for having a spotlight shone on you, but Elvis would have loved that.

Elvis never did 'Polk Salad Annie' the same way twice. Tony Joe White: 'Me too, I never do anything the same way twice. Elvis said to me, 'I always feel like I wrote that song. I can go anywhere I want to with it'. I said, 'Yeah, the way you play it, it sure sounds like you wrote it'.'

Now that Elvis was performing again, the key promoter Jerry Weintraub wanted to present Elvis around the country. Parker said he could have the rights provided he came up with $1m within a week. He did. Weintraub thought he had secured the investment from the Seattle radio mogul, Lester Smith but it later transpired that Danny Kaye had put forward the money – and made a fine return on it.

No sooner was the month in Vegas over than Elvis was performing six shows at the Astrodome in Houston with over 40,000 fans at each show. The sound was poor for the first show but then it was resolved.

Elvis Presley: Caught in a Trap

Sid Bernstein: 'I worked with a company called Management Three, which exclusively did the tours for Elvis in the States. I didn't care for Colonel Parker at first; the ego drove me nuts, but then I got to appreciate his value to Elvis. He pulled Elvis through every kind of scrape, he lived Elvis, and Elvis was his only client. If he did take 50% of his earnings, he was worth it. I saw his brilliance and there hasn't been a manager like him.'

Peter Grant, the manager of Led Zeppelin, did try to book Elvis for a European tour but Parker said he was too busy. This was to lead, in 1973, to the satellite special in Hawaii, the world's first global concert.

Tony Cartwright: 'I spent a lot of time with Colonel Parker. He didn't trust anyone because everyone who came to him wanted to get to Elvis Presley. A very big promoter went behind the Colonel's back to see Elvis. He said, 'Listen, Elvis, how about doing a great big world tour? I can arrange all this.' Elvis didn't say, 'Go and see Tom Parker' but said he would think about it. When Parker found out, he blew the promoter out and had this big row with Elvis.'

The political singer/songwriter Phil Ochs, born in El Paso, Texas in 1940, had had success with 'There But for Fortune', recorded by Joan Baez, and was known for 'I Ain't Marching Anymore', 'Draft Dodger Rag' and 'Changes', but he had not attracted a wider audience like Bob Dylan. This played upon his mind and the relationship between Dylan and Ochs was always uneasy. Dylan said to him, 'You're not a folk singer, you're a journalist' and also, impressed by his savage humour, recommended him to switch to stand-up comedy.

When Ochs saw Elvis Presley in Las Vegas in 1969, it made him hyperactive and he was probably manic depressive by then. Phil sang about political change to his followers but how much more significant would it be if he had Elvis Presley's following? He ordered a gold lamé suit from Nudie's and he asked his manager, his brother Michael, to book Carnegie Hall for a concert in April 1970 billed as *Gunfight at Carnegie Hall:* in other words, he was anticipating trouble. He had played there before but the hall must have apprehensive about this concert – with good reason.

Phil Ochs was going to perform his best-known songs but also Merle Haggard's right-wing 'Okie from Muskogee', a song he knew his audience would loathe (although I would argue that Hag was being sardonic), and hits from Elvis Presley, Buddy Holly and Conway Twitty. He told the audience, 'If there's any hope for America, it lies in a revolution, and if there's any hope for a revolution in America, it lies in getting Elvis Presley to become Che Guevara.'

Michael Ochs himself wasn't sure about this. 'To me, Phil stood for original songwriting and original ideas. I didn't think he should recycle the past and it was dumb of him to put on a gold lamé suit. The idea itself was clever: he thought that the only way to get any radical change in America would be to combine the intelligence of Che Guevera with the merchandising of an Elvis Presley. He thought that if Elvis had come out against the Vietnam war, it would have ended a lot sooner.'

That wasn't the message that Elvis Presley wanted people to take from his concerts. Elvis had never come out against Vietnam and never would but there had been an element of darkness and of social concern in his hit song, 'In the Ghetto'. Phil Ochs was making his stand in 1970 despite the fact that John Lennon was heading in the very direction he wanted. Of course Ochs could have been thinking about himself. Joe

Strummer was to meet his criteria, but he too was British.

When Ochs wore his gold lamé suit, one girl shouted out 'Strip!', which led to such a brilliant ad-lib that you wonder if it was planned. 'No, I could never do that. I prefer to retain my dignity as an American citizen. I will try to wear this gold suit and sing a song of significance. I'll try to have wealth come to terms with responsibility.'

When somebody else shouted, 'Bring back Phil Ochs', he replied, 'Hi, I'm Phil Ochs!' At the end of the show, someone cried, 'Phil Ochs is dead.'

Unfortunately, this notorious show was not filmed but it was issued on LP in 1975. You can hear the audience booing, a companion of Bob Dylan's 'Judas!' tour. A documentary about it would have been telling. At one point Ochs, arguing with everyone, put his fist through the box office window and cut his thumb. He sunk deeper into depression during the 70s and he hanged himself in April 1976, leaving behind a wife and daughter. Surely someone one day is going to recreate this as a Broadway or West End play, not least because he wrote some great songs that are as neglected today as they were in his lifetime.

During the spring months, Elvis was travelling between LA, Palm Springs and Las Vegas but not performing anywhere. He bought himself a six-door Mercedes limo and listened to the demos of potential songs for his next recording session.

From 4 June to 8 June, Elvis was back in RCA's Studio B in Nashville with Felton Jarvis. Felton knew that the sessions with Chips Moman in Memphis had gone very well but he had taken a back seat and was now on his home ground. James Burton and Charlie Hodge were on the session but otherwise it was top Nashville session men – Chip Young (guitar), David Briggs (piano), Charlie McCoy (harmonica), Jerry Carrigan (drums) and the fantastically-named Norbert Putman on bass.

Elvis wasn't keen to return to Nashville but he thought he could complete his annual schedule with a few long sessions. The sessions were productive, leading to over 30 completed tracks. Many of them were used on his next album, *That's the Way It Is*, and many more on a country album, *Elvis Country* and the one after that, *Love Letters from Elvis*. In order to get enough 'country' tracks for the second one, a further four tracks were cut one day in September, but that was it – Elvis didn't need to visit a recording studio for a year.

That's the Way It Is was to be released alongside Elvis' concert film of the same name, but it was a different product. The Deluxe edition of this album, released in 2014, was spread over eight CDs.

It is a curious album: for example, Elvis' passionate version of 'Bridge over Troubled Water' sounds like a studio version (and it is) but there is applause at the end. As we near the end with Elvis, the band and the orchestra going full blast, Felton switches to a concert recording – once you have noticed this, it sounds daft. But Elvis wasn't the only one. One of the biggest albums of the decade, *Simon and Garfunkel's Greatest Hits*, does something similar.

The Barry Mann and Cynthia Weil song, 'You've Lost That Lovin' Feelin'' is in concert all the way through. It is not as strong as the Righteous Brothers' version, but then the strength of that record lay in the interplay of the two voices. On stage in August 1970, Elvis said, 'B.J. Thomas has a new record, I don't particularly like it' and then asked for the words. It was Barry and Cynthia's song, 'I Just Can't Help Believin''. It was a surprisingly spirited performance in the circumstances and was included on the album.

Elvis going 'Sing the song, baby' is as infectious as Ray Charles' saying, 'Sing the song, children' during 'I Can't Stop Loving You'.

Johnny Cymbal was best known for his novelty single, 'Mr. Bass Man' (1963) and he wrote a touching song about unmarried mothers, 'Somewhere in the Country' for Gene Pitney in 1968. He gave Elvis 'Mary in the Morning', a ballad with the feel of 'Let It Be Me' about it.

Paul Evans wrote 'The Next Step is Love', a typical Elvis ballad, and Winfield Scott, the co-writer of 'Return to Sender', brought a Latin feel to 'Stranger in the Crowd'. I was unimpressed with Eddy Rabbitt's 'Patch It Up', which was recorded in the studio although it is a live version on the album. The song is little more than a riff and the best part is Elvis' count-in, part karate grunts and part one, two, three, four.

Oddly, this album is close to being Elvis' English album, as six of the songs have UK connections. Freddy Bienstock probably found it easier to tempt British writers with the thought of an Elvis Presley cut in exchange for 50% of the publishing.

'Just Pretend' was another song from Doug Flett and Guy Fletcher. Guy Fletcher: 'The biggest one we wrote for Elvis was 'Just Pretend' and that was in his movie, *That's the Way It Is*. It's on a lot of his albums and it is used in these Elvis Presley quasi-live shows. I wrote it for his voice. I wrote it for all the intervals he liked and I sang it almost as an impersonation. We got no direct feedback but Freddy did say that everything was cool and he liked the songs. We never met him or went to see him.'

Another live track, 'I've Lost You' was written by Ken Howard and Alan Blaikley. It had been recorded by Matthews' Southern Comfort in 1970 and Elvis repeats the title line like a mantra at the end. I'd never heard a song on this subject before – namely, how a baby can spoil a passionate relationship. I don't want to make too much of this as we deal with Elvis' subsequent recordings, but he was drawn to songs that related to his own life. The reason I draw back is because the vast majority of popular songs are about falling in or out of love, so, whatever the circumstances, Elvis would inevitably be singing songs of lost love: it was his job, it's what he did for a living.

Jackie Lomax of the Undertakers was one of the first signings to the Beatles' Apple label and he recorded a Clive Westlake ballad, 'How the Web Was Woven' as a single in February 1970. Elvis recorded a fine version, but another Westlake song, 'Twenty Days and Twenty Nights', is about love going wrong and given biblical overtones.

The Italian entry of the 1965 San Remo song contest, 'Io Che Non Vivo (Senza Te)' by Pino Donaggio and Vito Pallavicini, was given English lyrics by Vicki Wickham and Simon Napier-Bell, retitled 'You Don't Have to Say You Love Me' and given to Dusty Springfield. Elvis wanted to do the song because he liked it. It is a splendidly bombastic performance but he doesn't match Dusty.

That's the Way It Is was a hit album in both Britain and America. Elvis had hit singles with 'I've Lost You' and 'You Don't Have to Say You Love Me'. The other album to emerge from the June sessions was *Elvis Country*, a Top 20 US album in January 1971, but one that failed to find a big UK market, despite a successful hit single, 'There Goes My Everything'.

This album was ruined by attempting to make it a concept album. Elvis' performance of a mountain song from the nineteenth century, 'I Was Born about 10,000 Years Ago', was chopped into segments and placed in between individual tracks for no good reason. Baby Elvis was shown on the cover so, all things considered, it must have seemed about

Spencer Leigh

10,000 years ago to him.

The packaging suggested a roots album and 'I Was Born about 10,000 Years Ago' would have been the perfect opening track. There was a down-home feel to Bill Monroe's 'Little Cabin on the Hill', but Elvis was stuck in a countrypolitan groove with Engelbert Humperdinck's 'There Goes My Everything', Eddy Arnold's 'Make the World Go Away', Tommy Edwards' 'I Really Don't Want to Know' and disastrously, Anne Murray's 'Snowbird', which he sang with all the conviction of a bus timetable. When he approached Bob Wills' 'Faded Love', he turned it into a blues – nothing wrong with that but it's no longer country. 'I Washed My Hands in Muddy Water' was a goodtime studio jam. Elvis' arrangement of 'I Really Don't Want to Know' appealed to Boots Randolph who redid it to feature his saxophone.

At long last we had Elvis' version of Lee Hazlewood's 'The Fool', and he surely loved Willie Nelson's 'Funny How Time Slips Away'. The lyric of Eddy Arnold's 'Tomorrow Never Comes' is a mystery – is this about a condemned man? The arrangement with its military drumming builds up like 'Running Scared'.

If he was tackling 'Whole Lotta Shakin' Goin' On', he should have made sure he was going to upstage the Killer.

The songwriter Shirl Milete picked up the telephone one morning and it was Elvis, who thought he was talking to Lamar Fike. He said, 'You fat son of bitch' and was complaining about something, concluding, 'It's your baby, you rock it!' When Shirl put the phone down, he realised he had a song title and as it wasn't really his title, he listed Lamar's wife, Nora Fowler, as the co-writer. It's not much of a song, the melody being a second cousin to 'Gentle on My Mind'.

RCA squeezed a third album from these sessions, *Love Letters from Elvis*. What male would buy an album with that title? He'd had a hit with 'Love Letters' so there was little sense in reworking it, and actually, the song is about love letters *to* Elvis. Still, you can't call an album, *Sinking in Schlock*.

Again, there are British writers involved such as Geoff Stephens: 'Freddy Bienstock was a very wealthy man who owned Carlin Music. I knew him well and he told me that he would get some songs to Elvis if he could publish them. I said, 'Fair enough' and we did some demos with Elvis in mind. Elvis did them okay but then he more or less did as he was told. He sometimes sounded as if he was doing the song in five minutes, but he sounded good when he did mine.'

Geoff had written 'The Crying Game' and 'Winchester Cathedral', but the songs here lack that originality. 'This Is Our Dance' sounds like a follow-up to 'The Last Waltz' and would have been better with Engelbert, while 'Heart of Rome' is typical of the bright and breezy pop purveyed by Dave Dee, Dozy, Beaky, Mick and Tich.

Another of his songs, 'Sylvia', written with Les Reed, is a decent beat-ballad, but the composers must have been asking 'Where is Sylvia?' as it didn't get released until 1977. On the outtakes for 'I'll Never Know', Elvis comments on Lamar Fike and Charlie Hodge being in the studio: 'I've got a fat guy and a midget beside me!' – funny guy!

My bugbear, Shirl Milete, wrote the inconsequential 'When I'm Over You' and arguably the worst song Elvis ever recorded, 'Life', an abysmal discourse about the creation of the world. Still, someone liked it, maybe even Elvis, as it was released as a single in the US and made No.53 in the Hot 100. The other side, Paul Rader's 'Only Believe' was little better and nudged into the chart.

Elvis Presley: Caught in a Trap

Some songs are so bad that you would think Elvis was back on film soundtracks. Indeed, Sid Wayne and Ben Weisman returned for a soppy love song, 'I'll Never Know'. I've no idea how Gerald Nelson's 'If I Were You' passed the selection process: sample lyric, 'If I were you, I'd know that I'd love me', but the song contains a reference to the Great Snowman, which could be a little aside to Colonel Parker. At least 'It Ain't No Big Thing (But It's Growing)' does have some fun about it.

There is a reworking of that skiffle favourite 'Get Along Home, Cindy' with a neat guitar solo from James Burton, but combining 'Got My Mojo Workin'' with another blues song, 'Keep Your Hands Off It' doesn't take off.

Among the outtakes, Elvis had fun with 'One Hundred Years from Now' and presumably the original songwriter didn't write 'You can kiss my ass.' Elvis adds, 'Here goes my fucking career down the drain, man.' There is a jam with an improvised song, 'I Didn't Make It on Playing Guitar'.

In addition to those three albums, there was a gospel-styled song about a love gone wrong written by Dallas Frazier, 'Where Did They Go, Lord', which made the US Top 40. In his grandest voice, Elvis revived Tony Bennett's 'Rags to Riches', while 'The Sound of Your Cry' was about leaving while the girl's asleep: it's written by Bill Giant but it sounds like Kristofferson on a bad day and the Vegas-styled arrangement is phony. That's the way it is, but did it have to be that way?

In July, Elvis was being filmed for the *That's the Way It Is* documentary in rehearsal, working with his musicians for his next month at the International. Elvis was enjoying himself and we saw them working up several songs for the stage. Elvis was singing snatches of Marty Robbins' 'Tonight Carmen' or Ernie K-Doe's 'Mother-in-law'. He performed 'Stranger in My Home Town' with swear words: this was Elvis relaxed, informal, being professional but having fun.

The golden rule in Vegas, and I have heard it so many times, is 'What happens in Vegas stays in Vegas.' This is why Elvis regarded Vegas and then his touring dates as boys' only affairs with all that that entails. But there could be more to it than that. Tom Jones' road manager Tony Cartwright says, 'A lot of entertainers don't want their wives with them on tour, not just because they want somebody else to bed, but because they can't concentrate. The wives want them to meet people or want to be taken out. Although Elvis loved Priscilla, he didn't want her around all the time and he suggested that she took her own karate lessons with Mike Stone.'

Elvis was also prone to the occasional girlfriend at Graceland when Priscilla wasn't around. If she was going away, she would put a pencil mark where her clothes were. The clothes might be removed if Elvis had somebody else in and then returned to the racks, so Priscilla would know.

In August Elvis was back at the International and eight of the shows were officially recorded. During the month, a girl called Patricia Parker claimed in an LA court that Elvis was the father of her child and demanded maintenance. Although not appearing in person, Elvis denied that he had slept with her and said it was an attempt to extract money. The court was to arrange blood tests: this took time but the child was not Elvis'. But it could have been as Elvis was sleeping with all and sundry. When the story hit the papers, Elvis said on stage, 'Priscilla knows I didn't knock that chick up last week 'cause I use birth control'. This was a startlingly honest admission, spoken as a joke, but surely evidence that Presley didn't use scriptwriters. Priscilla wasn't in the audience but it must have got back to her.

Towards the end of the month, there was a threat of Elvis being kidnapped on stage – surely a mission impossible – and there was another threat to kill Elvis on stage. The security presence was increased. The shows passed without incident and Presley, in a good mood, performed an additional 3am show on 7 September so that workers at other casinos in Vegas could see him.

Elvis would start to sing 'I Can't Stop Lovin' You' with his back to the audience. If anyone was going to take a shot, that would surely be the moment, and if they missed, Ronnie Tutt would get it.

Elvis then made his first concert tour since 1958, a week of concerts in Phoenix, St Louis, Detroit, Miami Beach, Tampa and Mobile, Alabama. He travelled with the band but they used local musicians for horns and strings. At one concert, Elvis said that he was so tired that he had to lie down on the stage – and the audience loved it. In Tampa, Elvis tangled up the words of 'In the Ghetto' and got the giggles. Anything could happen at any time. He returned to Graceland, exhausted and wanting seclusion.

Still on good terms with Priscilla, although it came and went, the couple went to Vegas in September to catch some shows. Back in Palm Springs, Elvis heard that the Veep, Spiro Agnew, was about to visit Sinatra. Toadying up to Frank, Elvis got an invitation to meet him. Elvis brought him a present – an antique gun. Agnew thanked him but said that he couldn't accept gifts whilst in office. Elvis said that he would keep it for him. In 1973 Agnew resigned over tax evasion and Elvis decided that he didn't deserve the gun.

In November Elvis had another week of concert dates – Oakland, Portland, Seattle, San Francisco, Los Angeles, San Diego, Oklahoma City and Denver. But everyone could see Elvis that Christmas, as *Elvis: That's the Way It Is* was shown worldwide, a two-hour look at the King from the inside. The most telling moment occurs in the credits. We all know Colonel Parker will be listed as technical advisor but how about the Memphis Mafia, all nine of them, listed as technical assistants?

Just like the Labour party in the 1990s, Elvis had to reinvent himself, and *Elvis – That's The Way It Is* shows the New Elvis, given a Peter Mandelson gloss by the director, Denis Sanders. Like the New Labour hierarchy, it is clear that Elvis is absorbed by self-love. No-one loves Elvis more than Elvis himself. He is not dislikeable in the film but he doesn't have the warmth of some of his film roles where he was nearly always playing the nice guy.

This is an excellent documentary about Elvis' second season in Las Vegas: he looks great and is in fine voice, and many fans regard this as the definitive Elvis film. It is brilliantly shot and Elvis sings 36 songs (including repeats). His choice of songs, whether they be early recordings like 'Mystery Train' or new standards like 'Bridge over Troubled Water', is immaculate. The pre-concert sequences capture his humour and the snatches of songs that he rehearses or jams with his rhythm section is terrific.

Elvis fans talk up going to Vegas as the biggest adventure of their lives – even a 100-year-old fan is on show, not to mention Cary Grant, Sammy Davis and Xavier Cugat. The message is clear: We still love you, Elvis. The Luxembourg fan club convention shows an Elvis impersonator at work and he is cruelly followed by the real thing. 'I'd hate Elvis to think that all the conventions were like the one in that film,' said Maria Davies. The film has since been recut and the fans have been mostly replaced by more Elvis footage.

Maria Davies told me, 'People think that we are making up for shortcomings in our own lives but I know my own life is much fuller because of Elvis. If I didn't do it, I'd probably be like 99% of the population, vegetating in front of the TV.'

In December Elvis was buying Christmas gifts – he bought 30 handguns for $20,000 and ten Mercedes for $85,000. Vernon Presley was shocked when he saw the bills and told his son that it had to stop – he would bankrupt everyone. Elvis stormed out of the room but no one could guess what would happen next.

Elvis World was certainly bizarre but it became even more so on 19 December 1970. The full circumstances are not known, as we don't know precisely what Elvis was thinking. In another life, he surely would have been a cop as he loved collecting police badges. He loathed the big rock acts of the day and how they embraced the drugs culture. He felt that they were messing with the minds of the young and he, Elvis Presley, the King, wanted to do something about it. He spoke to John O'Grady who gave him the name of John Finlator, a senior official at the Bureau of Narcotics and Dangerous Drugs. Elvis decided that this was more important than a telephone call or a letter – he would go to Washington and see him in person.

On his own.

Early on 19 December 1970, Elvis dressed in dark glasses, a purple velvet suit and cape plus his gold belt from the International, a Colt .45 in a shoulder holster and a Derringer in his boot. He was a carrying a bejewelled cane. If he was planning to go incognito, it wasn't the best of starts. If he wanted to draw attention to himself, he couldn't have done better. He even wore mascara. He drove to the airport and bought a ticket to Washington on the next flight. Being a VIP, he wasn't checked for weapons but just gave a few autographs.

This was a great adventure, he had never done anything like this before. He didn't encounter any problems – he was recognised but most people thought he must be an impersonator. Elvis Presley wouldn't be flying business class.

Arriving in Washington, he asked a cab driver to take him to a good doughnut joint and wait for him. A hoodlum wanted to relieve him of the diamonds on his hands and Elvis pulled back his jacket to reveal his gun. He felt excited: this was a great adventure.

The manager at the Washington Hotel recognised him but accepted his alias of Colonel Jon Burrows. Entrenched in his suite, Elvis paced up and down and didn't know what to do next. The good folk at Graceland were thinking the same thing – Elvis had gone missing. He was a fully grown adult: they could hardly alert the police and ask them to find Elvis.

Elvis had determined the next stage of his mission but he needed somebody to help him. Jerry Schilling had left the Memphis Mafia to work as a film editor in Hollywood. It was the weekend and he rang Jerry and told him to meet him at the airport in Los Angeles. When he arrived several hours later, Jerry rang for a doctor as one of Elvis' eyes was swollen. He was given a shot that knocked him out and enabled him to sleep. You might have thought that the boys should have kept checking out Elvis' Hollywood home on Hillcrest Road but they didn't.

At 10pm that Sunday evening, they took off for Washington with Elvis carrying a wooden box containing an antique Colt.45 as a gift for the President. By sheer good fortune, Elvis found himself next to the Republican senator George Murphy. Murphy had been a song and dance man in Hollywood musicals in the 1930s. He was therefore sympathetic to a singer showing an interest in politics.

Elvis wanted to offer his services in the war against drugs and then meet the head of the FBI, J. Edgar Hoover. Murphy said that he would help him – and Presley's ambition now had no bounds. Why not meet President Nixon himself?

Encouraged, or perhaps humoured, by Murphy, Elvis wrote a rambling letter to Nixon in which he was appalled at the drug culture, the Black Panthers, the student revolutions and the hippie community. Elvis was declaring war on the 60s, he wanted to be back in his heyday, the mid-50s. He was hell-bent on revenge.

When they got off the plane at 6.30am, Elvis, still in his outlandish clothes, went with Jerry to the White House where he handed in his letter which asked Nixon to call him at the Washington Hotel.

By now, Schilling was fearful for his own job. He wanted to ring Graceland to tell them where he was and request Sonny West in his place. Elvis said, 'Okay, you do that and wait for a call from the White House' as Elvis himself would go to the Justice building and meet John Finlator. Possibly George Murphy had arranged this. Finlator was patient and pleasant but said that the government regulations did not permit him to give Elvis a badge. Only agents of the Bureau could have a badge.

Elvis phoned Jerry to say that he had not received his badge, but Jerry gave him good news; the White House had phoned. Luckily, Nixon liked to keep an open hour in his daily schedule in case anything special occurred. President Nixon had cleared his schedule to meet Elvis. By good fortune, Nixon was about to launch a crusade against the drug culture. He called it America's No.1 problem and he could have America's No.1 star on his side, although that is not how Elvis saw it.

By the scheduled time to meet Nixon, Sonny West had arrived and Jerry had stayed on as he wanted to meet the President too. They went to the White House, but all the president's men said that only Elvis could go into the Oval Office to meet Nixon. As soon as Nixon saw him, he said, 'You dress pretty well, don't you?' to which Elvis responded, 'Mr. President, you got your show to run and I got mine.' Great answer!

The official photo of Elvis and the President is now the most requested photograph in the Government's archives. It's a great photo but it looks like Elvis is once again performing for Ed Sullivan.

Knowing Nixon's obsession with recording, their conversation must have been recorded but it has not yet been released. When it is finally cleared, it will be the comedy download of the century. Doubtless Elvis gave his views on the drug culture, the bad influence of the Beatles and the political activism of the actress Jane Fonda. Maybe Nixon agreed: young people were going to hell because of today's music stars and Elvis could communicate to the youth and get through to them.

He was opposed to today's rock stars, and the deaths of Janis Joplin and Jimi Hendrix from overdoses made his point. Presley told Nixon that he wanted to be a federal agent at large and Nixon said, 'Getting you a badge is one thing I can do.' He could overrule the Justice department.

Elvis made a small request – could Jerry and Sonny meet the President. Nixon agreed. 'You got a couple of big ones there, Elvis, I bet they take good care of you.' Nixon gave them cufflinks with the presidential seal and when Elvis added, 'They got wives too', Nixon found two pins with the same seal. Oddly, he didn't request something for Priscilla, who didn't even know of the visit.

Having been told to leave his gift with security, Nixon asked to see it and so Elvis showed him the Colt.45 in its presentation box. Nixon thanked him and said he would be in touch.

Elvis returned to Graceland for a quiet family Christmas. He spoke confidentially to David Stanley. He said, in all seriousness, that the teenager should report to him every day after school and let him know who was selling drugs and where. He didn't add that he would buy them but he might have done.

Elvis was on a lot of shopping lists that Christmas. *On Stage* was still a big album and *Elvis: That's the Way It Is* had been released. For oldies fans, there was a 4LP boxset, a relatively new innovation, *Worldwide 50 Gold Award Hits, Volume 1*, which was the deluxe gift. The UK price was £7.50 and included a portrait album. By calling it Volume 1, RCA had confidence and indeed, Volume 2 arrived for next Christmas. This time there was a bonus – an authenticated piece of one of Elvis' suits. C'mon, who's got his fly?

Somebody gave Elvis one of those laughing boxes. He loved it. He would set it off and say, 'Meet Colonel Parker', but Colonel Parker wasn't laughing. He had a very uneasy Christmas. His boy had been out on his own for the first time and met President Nixon. What would he do next?

On 28 December Sonny West married Judy Morgan with Elvis as best man and Priscilla as matron of honour.

On 30 December, Elvis returned to Washington. He didn't meet Hoover but saw his Assistant Director, Tom Bishop. Elvis said that he was prepared to give information to the FBI about Commies and junkies. McCarthyism was back and Elvis would be an informer. Bishop said he would fix up a meeting with his boss, but he wrote to Hoover: 'He is wearing his hair down to his shoulders and indulges in the wearing of all sorts of exotic dress.' Well, that's undercover agents for you.

The United States Junior Chamber, known as Jaycees, is a leadership training and civic organisation for people between the ages of 18 and 40 and every year they announce their Top Ten Young Americans. Rather late in the day, Elvis was in the honours list in January 1971 and, perhaps being flattered at still being considered a young man at 36, he decided to attend – and he would speak. Colonel Parker must have been nervous. Would Presley use this as a platform to berate other youth leaders who, in his view, were turning the country onto drugs? Elvis would never think about libel so anything could happen, especially if he was mixing his pills with drink. In the end, Elvis was ...surprisingly... humble and his short speech quoted from one of his favourite songs, 'Without Love'. Years later, when Bob Dylan received an ASCAP award, he said the same words and namechecked Presley.

In contrast to being a Top 10 Young American, he was given a Lifetime Achievement honour at the Grammys. The first winner had been Bing Crosby in 1962 and other honourees were Frank Sinatra (1965), Duke Ellington (1966), Ella Fitzgerald (1967) and Irving Berlin (1968), so he was being treated like an old master. Elvis felt exalted by the award; Glen D. Hardin: 'He was the best rock singer in the world but he also wanted to be Perry Como.' Elvis didn't attend the ceremony, but the plaque was given to him in his suite at the International where he had another month of engagements.

It wasn't a good month as he felt ill most of the time and some appearances were cancelled. When he was over, he and Priscilla went to Palm Springs, where he convalesced.

On 15 March 1971, Elvis was back in RCA's Studio B in Nashville and the intention, as last year, was four all-night sessions and to record around 30 masters. There would be a standard pop album, a follow-up to *Elvis' Christmas Album* from 1957, which was the Colonel's idea, and a religious album, his third, and largely as a concession to Elvis. As usual, Elvis wanted to record the songs in any order he fancied. He didn't want to do the Christmas album, telling Parker, 'Why can't we just repackage the old one?'

There was a problem – there's always a problem with Elvis. He had a blocked nose and some pain behind his eyes but he was in a good mood at first, fooling around with 'I Want You, I Need You, I Love You' and cutting four songs.

Ewan MacColl had written 'The First Time Ever I Saw Your Face' about his new love, Peggy Seeger, who became his wife and singing partner. Peggy recalls, 'Ewan wrote political songs and he wasn't able to write the more personally emotional songs until the last years of his life, the exception being 'The First time Ever I Saw Your Face'. He never sang it except for the one time he gave it to me. It was made for me and I sang it from then on. I first recorded it in 1963 and then, Peter, Paul and Mary, Judy Collins and the Kingston Trio did it. A lot of them changed it because 'lay with you' was too much for them. We thought Roberta Flack dragged it out and we didn't care for Elvis' version. Ewan used to say it was like Romeo at the bottom of the Post Office Tower singing to Juliet at the top. There are better pop versions – Peter, Paul and Mary came closest to it, but I still think I sing it the best. It's a shame that Sinatra never sang it as he could have done it very well.'

Elvis recorded the song alongside Temple Riser from the vocal group, the Nashville Edition. It was on the B-side of the 1972 single, 'An American Trilogy', and possibly should have been released earlier to compete with Roberta Flack's interpretation which was in the Clint Eastwood film, *Play Misty for Me*. Elvis often sang it in concert – once dedicating it to Sheila, whoever she might be (his latest flame?) – and he would start quietly and build up to an extraordinary passion, making it even more dramatic with the years. The song may not have been written for his karate kicks but it certainly got them.

Almost certainly Elvis took that song from the Peter, Paul and Mary album, *See What Tomorrow Brings* (1965), as he sang another track from that album, Gordon Lightfoot's 'Early Mornin' Rain', with Charlie McCoy's harmonica to the fore. It is about a down-and-out at an airport lamenting that 'You can't jump a jet plane like you can a freight train'. Lightfoot says, "Early Mornin' Rain' has to be a pivotal song for me. It was recorded by Elvis Presley and if a song was recorded by Elvis, it's pivotal. He did a wonderful job: his arrangement was like Ian and Sylvia's arrangement whereas there are two or three different ways of going at that song. Peter, Paul and Mary had a certain style of doing it too but they used the changes that Ian and Sylvia made and Elvis did that too. It had a great feel and it was on his album, *Elvis Now*.'

Elvis will have heard Peter, Paul and Mary's 1964 hit single, 'For Lovin' Me', again written by Gordon Lightfoot. Lightfoot doesn't perform his song these days as he regards it as too sexist, but the idea of someone who uses women as playthings no doubt appealed to Elvis. It's performed in a casual, throwaway fashion by Elvis but that is in line with its lyric.

John Newton, the captain of a slave ship, had been caught in a storm and he prayed to God that if he was spared, he would devote his life to the church. He was spared and he gave up trading slaves and became a clergyman, writing 'Amazing Grace' in 1779 about being saved. Although an English hymn, it became much more popular as part of the Southern Baptist Hymnal and it is odd that Elvis didn't record it until 1971. It is a strong version, with the Nashville Edition singing one verse with Elvis in the background. How strange that he should record a song about the shackles being lifted from his eyes at the very time he was having trouble with them.

By 1.30am, Elvis had cut four songs but the pain behind his eyes was increasing and, in an angry mood, he threw down a guitar and called it quits for the night. Someone rang Dr. George Nichopoulos, who had a practice in Madison Avenue in Memphis and was at Elvis' beck and call. He flew to Nashville and had him admitted to the Baptist Hospital in Memphis. He was to inject cortisone into his eyeball to relieve the pressure. He told Elvis that he had glaucoma and that the condition had been exacerbated by the black dye from his hair mingling with his sweat and dripping into his eyes.

Elvis relaxed for a few weeks and he and Priscilla spent some time in Hawaii. In May 1971 he was back in Nashville ready to continue recording. He was in a good mood, arriving with his police badges and showing them to the musicians.

It was May, and heck, we had better get on and make that Christmas album for December release. Corny as it sounds, Felton Jarvis had decorated the studio with a Christmas tree and presents and the Colonel had sent Elvis and the musicians a Christmas greeting. If I'd been Elvis, I'd have gone back to Graceland but he persevered.

Rather like the first Christmas album, this was to be a mixture of traditional carols, seasonal favourites, new songs and a bit of R&B, only this time it was nowhere near as good. *Elvis' Christmas Album* is a Christmas classic if that is not an oxymoron but *The Wonderful World of Christmas* is as hackneyed as its title. The title song, a new one, exploits every Christmas cliché.

With one exception.

Elvis revived 'Merry Christmas Baby', an R&B hit from 1947 by Johnny Moore's Three Blazers. The band starts playing and Elvis keeps going, creating a magical six minutes. It is a single take and at one point, Elvis says to the bass player, Norbert Putnam, 'Wake up Put'. Who can blame him? It was the middle of the night.

Three new songs were recorded, all about wanting to be reunited with loved ones for Christmas, none of them as poignant as 'I'll Be Home for Christmas', which Elvis had recorded in 1957. They were 'If I Get Home on Christmas Day' from the British writer, Tony Macaulay, 'It Won't Seem Like Christmas', released as a single, and 'I'll Be Home on Christmas Day', written by Michael Jarrett after he had smoked some weed whilst feeling sorry for himself. Elvis made it back home for the highly saccharine 'On a Snowy Christmas Night'. Red West wrote another Christmas song for Elvis but the tacky 'Holly Leaves and Christmas Trees' lacked the potential of 'If Every Day Was like Christmas'.

Tony Macaulay, an English writer who had written 'Baby, Now That I've Found You' (Foundations) and 'Let the Heartaches Begin (Long John Baldry), was given a commission by Freddy Bienstock. Freddy might have been hoping for another 'Home Lovin' Man', a song Macaulay got to Andy Williams in 1970, but it wasn't so successful. Tony Macaulay: 'When I am asked to write a song for a famous act – I walk around the house being them for a day or so. I went around going 'Huh, huh, huh' and trying to be Elvis, which given my personal talent is no easy thing. I wrote the song around the time of Vietnam and so it could be about a soldier coming home. The song talks about the fates and being 'half a world away'.'

And how do you write for Elvis? 'It's the mid and the low tones that you aim for in ballads with some fruity tones for that rich baritone and a few places where the vocal group can go 'Aaahh'. Bob Saker who did my demos was terrific. I wrote for Sonny and Cher once and he was both Sonny and Cher on the demo. He could sing it enough like Elvis to interest Elvis but not too much because that would only irritate him. Elvis could then see that he had something that would work for him.'

The British songwriting partnership, AMMO, were taking a break in America. Chris Arnold: 'Freddy Bienstock invited us to one of Elvis' recording sessions that weekend in Nashville. It was the most wonderful and unexpected invitation. Geoff and David were committed to returning home but I decided to go. I met Freddy at the Holiday Inn in Nashville and we spent a very pleasant day by the pool talking about all things musical and at 6pm we went to the RCA studio and at 6.30 Elvis came in with his entourage. They were doing songs for Christmas. Most of them were forgettable but Elvis sang them professionally and wonderfully well. Elvis loved meeting someone from England. I was in the control room and whenever Elvis came in to hear a playback, he would sit next to me and say, 'What do you think, Chris?' I had to say on every occasion, 'Sounds great to me, El.' (Laughs) He remembered our songs and he sang me the chorus line of 'This Is the Story'. We later learnt that it had been under consideration to be a single. I liked him very much. He was so friendly and so very genuine.'

Elvis was in Perry Como's territory for 'Winter Wonderland' and Bing Crosby's for 'Silver Bells' and it gave a glimpse of what that Colonel Parker TV special would have been like. 'Winter Wonderland' ended though with a great Elvis R&B vamp. Things have changed with the internet: for a time, the only place you could hear Take 1 of 'Silver Bells' was in a chapel in Tupelo.

Then there were carols, unencumbered by such things as authors or publishing rights. Elvis could stick his name on them and could take both the writing and the publishing credit. They were sung very formally with a choir and Elvis was counting the pennies. Heck, he could do a whole album of carols and shove his name on the lot.

The gospel album, completed in June, was called *He Touched Me*, although both the Christmas and the gospel albums were based in religion, Elvis was much more committed on *He Touched Me* and hence the sound is much more Elvis. He sang Andrae Crouch's 'I've Got Confidence' with precisely that and the gospel quartet stylings of 'I John' with the Imperials was a real foot stomper. 'An Evening Prayer', written by Charles Gabriel in 1900, was sung beautifully and his earlier, dynamic 'Amazing Grace' was included.

I was less happy with 'A Thing Called Love', another Jerry Reed song that had been a hit in a better arrangement for Johnny Cash. 'Lead Me, Guide Me' was associated with George Beverly Shea, while 'There is No God But God' was a revival of an Ink Spots song from 1951. The oddest track was Dallas Frazier's 'There Goes My Everything', a huge hit for Engelbert Humperdinck, which had been rewritten as 'He Is My Everything' – a tale of love lost becomes a tale of love won.

Elvis may well have decided to do 'Bosom of Abraham' after hearing Peter, Paul and Mary revive it, but then again he would know the versions from the Golden Gate Quartet (1938) and the Jordanaires (1954). It is better known in the UK as 'Rock o' My Soul', a successful B-side for Lonnic Donegan on the reverse of 'Tom Dooley'. The album was in line with contemporary Christian rock, but a little too serious. If you hear the session tapes, Elvis is having fun and surely they could have included some of his laughter.

Red West, always up for the challenge, offered 'Seeing is Believing' and a newcomer to the Elvis publishing world, Ralph Carmichael, wrote 'Reach Out to Jesus': he was an arranger who worked with the pianist Roger Williams.

The third album from these sessions was *Elvis Now*. Elvis had been thinking of recording Kris Kristofferson's 'Sunday Morning Comin' Down', but he went with a different Kristofferson song, 'Help Me Make It through the Night'. The song has been reworked in so many different spheres by so many artists, but at its heart it is Kristofferson begging for companionship, a song that could be twinned with Chip Taylor's 'Angel of the Morning'. There is some 70s schlock in Elvis' treatment, a case of more is less, but he is in fine voice and it is an excellent performance.

The rockabilly artist, Lee Denson, had given Elvis some guitar tuition and, maybe to thank him 16 years later, Elvis recorded his song, 'Miracle of the Rosary', a Catholic song to the Virgin Mary. It resembles a religious ballad from the 1950s but it's sung well with Elvis adding some harmonies. It could easily have been included on *He Touched Me*. The same applies to 'Put Your Hand in the Hand', which like 'Snowbird', was written by Gene MacLennan and was a 1971 hit for Anne Murray. Shirley Caesar won Best Soul Performance at the Grammys with this song. The melody is similar to Joe South's 1969 single, 'Walk a Mile in My Shoes'.

Again in the folk-country vein, there was Gordon Lightfoot's 'Early Mornin' Rain', and Buffy Sainte-Marie's 'Until It's Time For you To Go'. Buffy might have seemed too radical a figure for Elvis but then she was fighting for the rights of American Indians, a cause which Elvis supported.

The most enjoyable track was surely Johnny Mercer's great song, 'Fools Rush In'. This had been given a gentle rock treatment by Rick Nelson in 1963 and included a famed guitar break from James Burton. Elvis asked James to repeat it. Elvis was on cracking from. This took 24 takes to get right but it was probably because Elvis was enjoying himself.

Although called *Elvis Now* and released in 1972, the recording of 'Hey Jude' was from 1969; 'Sylvia' and the full version of 'I Was Born about 10,000 Years Ago' was from 1970. A singalong song from Jay Ramsey, 'We Can Make the Morning', made up the numbers.

As if three albums weren't enough, some tracks from these sessions found their way onto his 1973 album, *Elvis*. There was 'For Lovin' Me' and a British song from Tony Macaulay and Roger Greenaway with the same message, 'Love Me, Love the Life I Lead'. It had been recorded by the Drifters but Elvis probably didn't know that. 'Padre' was a 1958 hit from Toni Arden and a curious song for Elvis to revive. Elvis had recorded three songs at the piano – 'I'll Take You Home Again, Kathleen', which was written in 1876, and two Ivory Joe Hunter songs, 'It's Still Here' and 'I Will Be True'. Elvis jammed a 10-minute version of Bob Dylan's 'Don't Think Twice, It's All Right', although he only knew the chorus, and three minutes of it found its way onto the album.

Two hit singles also emerged from the session. First Elvis released 'I'm Leavin''. It did well on the US easy listening chart, but Elvis was disappointed, thinking it should have been one of his biggest singles. It had been written by Michael Jarrett., who wrote

'I'll Be Home on Christmas Day', and Sonny Charles from Checkmates Inc. Michael had a girl who didn't approve of him trying to find success as a songwriter: she said, 'What if your songs aren't good enough?' and Michael said, 'I'm leaving,' and realised he had a song. Elvis' vocal glided over the instrumentation, giving the record an immense amount of charm. When he finished one take, he said, 'Phew, man, it's tough, but the thing is worth working on'.

It was followed by 'It's Only Love', written by Mark James for B.J. Thomas in 1969. It only made No.51 as a US single and the UK went with 'I Just Can't Help Believin'' instead, which had recently been a US hit for B.J. Thomas – they were rewarded with a No.6 position. Also, a double-sided reissue of 'Heartbreak Hotel' and 'Hound Dog' made the Top 10 to promote RCA's new Maximillion series.

Unreleased at the time, Elvis sang 'The Lord's Prayer' with a lot of laughter at the end and he had short workouts on 'Lady Madonna' and 'I Shall Be Released'. He had his first shot at 'My Way' but knew he could do it better. Maybe he would have done it again that day but he stormed out after one of the backing singers criticised him.

In June 1971, Elvis was honoured by both Tupelo and Memphis. His birthplace on Old Saltillo Road was opened to the public and the stretch of Highway 51 from Memphis city limits to the Mississippi border was renamed Elvis Presley Boulevard.

In July, Elvis was at his best for a very successful fortnight at the Sahara Tahoe Hotel at Lake Tahoe. His orchestra leader, Joe Guerico, added the opening of Richard Strauss' *Also Sprach Zarathustra*, better known as the theme from *2001*, as a grandiose entrance. In keeping with this, his jumpsuits became even more lavish. He was using his cape to the full, thrusting his arms out and showing off his jewellery, an ostentatious display of wealth, if you like. Soon, Bruce Springsteen would determine that the way to go was with torn jeans.

After Lake Tahoe, he moved across Nevada to the renamed Las Vegas Hilton International. He was still handing out scarves but he was also distributing stuffed bears while singing 'Teddy Bear'. Excited women would grab him on stage but he was always egging them on. By the time he had finished, he had performed 85 shows in six weeks in Nevada. The hotel was reported for violating fire codes by increasing the audiences at the shows. With all the merchandise, he and the Colonel netted $1m. Elvis was so loose and the band so tight that he could happily start songs that the band mightn't know and they would find their way through it.

Glen D. Hardin enjoyed his years with Elvis. 'We had a set list but you could never know what he was going to do. Well, we knew that he wouldn't stick to the list! He used to throw water in my direction, but I never let it bother me. One time I brought an umbrella to the second show and he got a kick out of that.'

Ronnie Tutt:' It was like working with a stripper. The drummer has to watch every move to accentuate with his instrument.' Ronnie even learnt karate so that he could follow Elvis.

Their jazz-trained bass player Jerry Scheff: 'We'd race through the 50s songs. He squashed them down to the least time possible. He wanted to be taken seriously by critics. That was his vision – to ease out of the rock'n'roll business and become known for what he considered adult-type stuff.'

There was one black spot. The first serious biography had appeared, *Elvis*, by a *Rolling Stone* writer, Jerry Hopkins. Neither Elvis nor the Colonel had cooperated with

Elvis Presley: Caught in a Trap

the author, which was possibly a mistake as Hunter Davies' authorised biography of the Beatles had done them a service. He hated his family being called white trash as they were poor through lack of opportunity, not laziness. His mother was not an alcoholic. He almost certainly hated a whole lot more, but compared with what was to come, it was a sympathetic account, and Hopkins loved his music.

In November 1971, he returned to touring. He was in such a good mood when he appeared before 10,000 fans at the Municipal Auditorium, Kansas City that he performed for 90 minutes, his longest show to date.

The strain was beginning to show between Elvis and Priscilla, especially after Sonny West told Elvis that he had seen Priscilla taking a shower with Mike Stone. He told Sonny to mind his own business but he felt cuckolded. Priscilla didn't like being alone at Graceland and Elvis didn't want her on tour. He could sleep with whomever he liked, but not Priscilla.

Priscilla Presley recounts about how she admitted the affair with Mike Stone to Elvis. Elvis grabbed her and said, 'This is how a real man makes loves to a woman.' This is uncomfortable reading but although it sounds close to rape, Priscilla does not criticise Elvis for his behaviour.

The affair pushed Elvis over the edge. Nobody had taken anything away from Elvis before, least of all his wife. It was a cold Christmas at Graceland and Elvis had plans for a gun range; he wanted an arsenal of weapons, including fully automatic submachine guns. He dreamt of himself in his cape and sunglasses killing imaginary bad guys – and some not so imaginary. He was also considering buying a drugstore as a present to himself; in that way, he would have supplies of everything he wanted. Maybe he was on to something: there could have been a successful chain of Elvis Presley Drugstores in America.

Elvis had not been monogamous himself. In particular, he had met a Congressional aide, Joyce Bova, in Las Vegas in 1969 and he liked the fact that she was also a twin. They were to have a lengthy affair, mostly in 1971, which she described in her book, *Don't Ask Forever*.

On his birthday in January, Elvis told his friends that Priscilla would be moving with Lisa Marie to her own place in Los Angeles. Priscilla wrote in her memoir that she left Elvis because of his indifference and David Stanley described Mike Stone as 'a badass and lethal'.

Elvis went to the Hilton in Las Vegas for another month of bookings and then Lake Tahoe, with Jackie Kahane as the warm-up comic – as if Elvis audiences needed a warm-up. Elvis had reduced his show to 45 minutes, so there wasn't much room for improvisation.

Some of the shows were taped by RCA for an album, provisionally called *Standing Room Only*, but it never appeared. There were several songs he had not recorded previously that were associated with other performers: 'Never Been to Spain' (Hoyt Axton – a good song that Elvis would have fun with, and Elvis had never been to Spain), 'You Gave Me a Mountain' (a song of love lost, from Marty Robbins and perfect for Elvis dramatics), 'It's Impossible' (Perry Como – decent MOR revival), 'The Impossible Dream' (show tune from *Man of La Mancha* and performed much better than Peter O'Toole) and 'It's Over' (Jimmie Rodgers, not Roy Orbison – and Jimmie Rodgers, the pop singer, not the country legend: it's okay but he'd have been better with the Orbison song. In 1977 Gene Pitney cleverly combined them).

Elvis was including a brilliant version of Mickey Newbury's 'An American Trilogy' in his set. You can tell from the rapturous applause that it makes the audience proud to be American. It was possibly apt, as the Vietnam war was winding down. In later years, a flag would sometimes be unfurled as Elvis sang the song.

There was a reworking of 'Hound Dog' with wah-wah guitar, rather like Tony Joe White might do it. Elvis' 'Little Sister' was segued into the Beatles' 'Get Back' but as he did it in less than two minutes, he was not taking it seriously.

Around this time, there were rumours of a European tour. Colonel Parker denied that it was happening. James Burton: 'Elvis wanted to go, sure. There were plane-loads of people coming from the UK, Europe and Japan and he often talked about taking the show to them. He never did it but I know he wanted to.'

The Imperials were now pursuing their own career and Elvis asked his old friend, J.D. Sumner, who had sung bass with the Blackwood Brothers, to help out. J.D (actually John Daniel but folk called him Jim Dandy) gave him a record by the Stamps Quartet. Elvis loved it and invited them to join the touring party, but he had assumed that J.D. would be with them. When he learnt that he wasn't part of the group, he booked him separately, hence the billing, 'J.D. Sumner and the Stamps Quartet'. 'He wanted the slurs I always tack onto a song,' said J.D, 'I run down the scale and bottom out on the lowest note I can and still keep the harmony.'

Although no one in the inner circle was talking, the press was surmising that Elvis and Priscilla's marriage was in trouble. He had Priscilla come to Vegas for the last night on 23 February and invited her on stage. She must have gone to every show with trepidation, not knowing how he was going to react. One night for example he dedicated 'I Can't Stop Loving You' to her. Perhaps he should have invited Colonel Parker on stage to show that there were mixed feelings in that relationship too, but Parker was occupied. That large, ill-dressed man outside the showman selling glossy photos of Elvis and making extra dollars was Parker himself.

The Colonel had arranged for a follow-up documentary film, this one to be called *Elvis on Tour*, and they filmed a glorious, ten-minute recording session on 31 March where Elvis is jamming with the gospel singers, going from one song or hymn to another. Elvis loved singing bass with gospel groups and after 'Nearer My God to Thee', he says, 'I was singing bass but he covered me up. He wiped me out.' It's a pity that Elvis didn't make a gospel album as light-hearted as this as it could have been a sensation. Religious albums don't always have to be pointed at Palm Sunday.

Priscilla and Lisa Marie had now settled in the seaside community of Marina Del Ray in Los Angeles County and she was living with Mike Stone. When Priscilla asked Elvis for a divorce, he got mad.

At the end of March 1972, Elvis at RCA in Hollywood had his most consistent recording sessions since the 1950s – seven songs and all good ones, although Elvis didn't see it that way as he didn't care for 'Burning Love'.

The Texas guitarist and songwriter Dennis Linde had a home studio and he had bought drums for $90. He wanted a riff to practice on. As he had just got married, he wrote 'Burning Love' and developed its groove. He gave the song to the soul singer Arthur Alexander who cut a fine version for his *Arthur Alexander* album, recorded at American Studios early in 1972.

Linde wrote for Combine Music, which was run by his father-in-law Bob Beckham. Beckham spotted the song's potential and he passed it to Felton Jarvis, although Elvis was in no mood to rock. Graceland was surprisingly sombre as Jerry Schilling and Joe Esposito were also getting divorced.

Felton told Elvis that 'Burning Love' was a hit song. Elvis said the words were weird. Surely though 'Your kisses lift me higher than the sweet song of a choir' was perfect for Elvis. The song took its inspiration, if unconsciously, from Elvis' hit, 'A Big Hunk o' Love' which had suddenly found its way back into Elvis' repertoire, albeit performed far too fast.

Elvis, when he did record 'Burning Love', added a 'hunka hunka', a clear reference to the earlier hit. The Stamps, who normally sang gospel, must have been surprised by such an explicit song. When the session was finished, Felton asked Dennis Linde to add some guitar and his riff opens the song. It has a great Creedence feel and a strong bass line from Emory Gordy who said, 'I was embarrassed when 'Burning Love' came out. It was like a bass solo featuring Elvis Presley.'

Elvis still didn't get it. Three months later in New York City, he said, 'It's very difficult to find any good, hard rock songs. If I could find them, I would do them.' Didn't he know he had just cut a classic?

Elvis wanted songs which would reflect his sense of loss, mournful ballads about relationships breaking down. If he had recorded an album's worth, he could have released them and beaten *Blood on the Tracks* by three years. It's hard to know what were Elvis' intentions. Were these songs intended for Priscilla and he just happened to have released them? Was he hoping to win her back?

Red West knew what his boss wanted and he submitted an excellent song, 'Separate Ways', surely the best song he had written. It described life in Graceland and the second verse was about the quandary Lisa Marie would be in. It took 21 takes to get it right but the rest of the session was easier.

Kris Kristofferson's 'For the Good Times' was on its way to becoming a standard and Presley recorded a beautiful version. Kristofferson wrote it for the collapse of his own marriage – in short, we're going our separate ways, but let's have a farewell bonk.

The German bandleader James Last wrote 'Fool', which had an English lyric from Carl Sigman, the lyricist of 'You're My World'. In this song, Elvis berates himself for his behaviour: 'Fool, you only had to love her and now her love is gone'.

The best performance from the session has to be on the ballad, 'Always on My Mind', written by Mark James ('Suspicious Minds'), Wayne Carson and Johnny Christopher, who often played bass at American Sound. Wayne and Johnny worked in a little room above the studio. One day when Wayne's wife wanted him, he said, 'But honey, you are always on my mind'. They knew they had a song and when Mark came in, he added the bridge. Wayne was planning to put it on his own album, but Red said, 'Elvis has to hear this'.

Like 'The Wind beneath My Wings', the singer is admitting his selfishness and wishing things had been different. It is a brilliant song, but it is sometimes thought that Brenda Lee recorded it first. Normally a songwriter will give an artist a song and they have to release it within a year, say – and if they don't the songwriter can peddle it elsewhere. In this instance, the system seems to have broken down as Brenda Lee recorded her version for US Decca just a few days after Elvis. She was quicker to get it on the market. It was released in July 1972 and reached No.45 on the US country chart, which was lucky for Elvis as it deserved to go higher. Later on, Johnny Christopher played the song to Willie Nelson and Merle Haggard for their *Pancho and Lefty* album. Merle didn't go for it, but Willie did.

Paul Williams, who wrote for the Carpenters, penned 'Where Do I Go From Here', about someone wanting to get back to the joys of his childhood. The British writer, Clive Westlake, came up with a country ballad, 'It's a Matter of Time': we don't know what happened but he knows that time will heal.

The obvious single from the session was 'Burning Love' which was released as a US single in August 1972. It went to No.2, his biggest hit since 'Suspicious Minds'. It reached No.7 in the UK. It was followed by 'Separate Ways', which was backed by 'Always on My Mind', a great double-sider but a waste of a good song. It did however sell in the country market. 'Separate Ways' made No.20 in the US, while 'Always on My Mind' was No.9 in the UK.

RCA could have issued a great CD from the 'Burning Love' sessions together with recent live cuts, but no, they released *Burning Love and Hits from the Movies*, which had the key track with naff film songs at a budget price on their budget label, Camden. Financially, it was a clever move – a recent hit on a cheapo-cheapo album – and it sold over a million. It was a misleading product though; not many purchasers would have been happy and it drew attention to what Elvis wanted to forget.

Still, the packaging of the full-priced RCA product left much to be desired – the titles were often interchangeable and the covers featured one stage photograph after another. RCA should have looked at what its Japanese counterpart was doing, as their Elvis product was invariably classier.

'Burning Love' became a stage favourite but still Elvis was reluctant to sing it and he sometimes used a lyric sheet as if to say, 'I can't be bothered to learn this song.'

Elvis toured in April, using his private jet. He had to leave the stage in Richmond, Virginia as the fans became hysterical. Two days later he decided to press ahead at Fairgrounds Coliseum in Indianapolis despite thunderstorms. In Albuquerque, Elvis met a girl who was dying of cancer and dedicated 'You Gave Me a Mountain' to her. The shows were filmed for the documentary film, *Elvis on Tour*.

In May, Elvis took a holiday in Las Vegas and went to see his friend Glen Campbell. The audience acted so excitedly on seeing him unexpectedly that he had to leave so that Glen could continue. Glen suggested to Elvis that he should revive 'It's Only Make Believe' and Elvis said, 'No, you should do it, Glen' and it became one of Glen's biggest hits.

In June 1972, Elvis came to New York at last, making his first New York appearance since 1956. Most unusually, he held a press conference before the shows, although not much was said. He told them he owed his success to vitamin E. Colonel Parker told them they would have to pay for their tickets – no comps for Elvis shows.

Elvis was booked into Madison Square Garden for four concerts over three days; in total 80,000 fans saw him perform. He gave a press conference, the last one of his life. It wasn't revealing; he was far more candid on stage.

As the audience arrived for the first show, David Stanley, now training as a bodyguard, saw George Harrison and invited him to meet Elvis. Elvis said, 'Hope you enjoy the show'. 'You don't have to hope. I know I'll enjoy the show,' replied George.

Elvis told George that he and Paul were the most talented Beatles, no mention of John.

David Stanley: 'Elvis had a problem with John Lennon. He didn't like the negative messages within his music. If Elvis was going to contribute a message through his music, it would only be a gospel one. If you asked Elvis about his politics, he wouldn't discuss it. There's a lot of difference between 'Hound Dog' and 'Lucy in the Sky with Diamonds', but as I used to say to Elvis, it's still good music.'

David has other reasons to remember New York City: 'I was on tour with Elvis in New York City and Elvis introduced me to a couple of girls and said, 'I give you the boy, bring me back the man.' I was only sixteen. The man came back. Growing up with Elvis meant growing up real fast. By the time I was 21, I had lived a lifetime. Elvis shared the perks of his life with me and what a way to get broken in – God bless Elvis.'

RCA rush-released *Elvis as Recorded at Madison Square Garden* with 20 songs. The haste was to beat the bootleggers. The complete show was featured, although it was only 45 minutes long, with some songs barely lasting a minute. It was badly mastered as the tapes were speeded up – why? It was the first time that purchasers could officially buy Elvis' versions of 'Never Been to Spain', 'The Impossible Dream' and 'For the Good Times'. Elvis was singing as powerfully as an opera singer and his performance was enhanced by Kathy Westmoreland's high notes and J.D. Sumner's low ones.

Jerry Scheff is playing remarkable runs on his electric bass, almost as though he is upstaging Elvis on 'You've Lost That Lovin' Feelin'' and 'Polk Salad Annie' and the latter features Elvis' most frenzied ending ever. Elvis teases the audience with 'Hound Dog', saying, 'This is a song I sang on *The Ed Sullivan Show* in 1912. (Screaming) You don't know what I'm going to do yet.' He started it with a really funky, Tony Joe White-styled version of 'Hound Dog' and I wish he hadn't switched to the all-out rave up as it is really good. For the first time, the world heard that great final line, 'Elvis has left the building. Thank you and goodnight.'

In July, Elvis was playing around in Memphis – a few weeks of late-night movies, motorcycles, karate lessons and midnight madness, often at the Memphian club.

At one of Elvis' late night film screenings in Memphis, the country singer T.G. Sheppard had brought along a Miss Tennessee and a Miss Rhode Island. Elvis was immediately attracted to Miss Tennessee, Linda Thompson. She saw him again the next night and told Elvis that she didn't want to be a one night stand. They became a team and she even did karate with him. Elvis encouraged The Good Sheppard's career (that's T.G. Sheppard) and bought him his first tour bus.

Elvis brought in other girls including Sheila Ryan, who had been on the cover of *Playboy*. Then Ann Pennington, who became a Playboy centrefold and married Shaun Cassidy. *Playboy* was the one magazine that Elvis couldn't do without and he seems to have regarded each issue as a dating manual.

In 1973, her brother Sam, a former policeman, was appointed head of security for Elvis' team and by all accounts, was very effective. He arranged a target range behind Graceland and he gave Elvis shooting practice. Sometimes he would take Elvis to the police range and they could use machine guns: Elvis loved that. Sam was given a house in the grounds of Graceland as well as two Cadillacs and a Lincoln.

On 27 July 1972, Elvis and Priscilla were formally separated. Priscilla had custody of Lisa Marie but Elvis had visitation rights. She was awarded $100,000 plus $1,000 a month and another $500 for child support.

The new studio album was *Elvis Now*, but despite the title, some songs had been recorded three years earlier. It included the full version of 'I Was Born about 10,000 Years Ago' but despite superb songs such as 'Help Me Make It through the Night' and 'Fools Rush In', it didn't gel as an album. It was outsold by *Madison Square Garden* and the budget *Burning Love*, but there was simply too much Elvis on the market.

In August 1972, Elvis returned to the Las Vegas Hilton, opening on 4 August in a foul mood. He brightened up when Linda Thompson joined him the following day and he brightened up even more when she left, as he started a relationship with the actress Cybill Shepherd.

His moods were evident to the audience and there was erratic behaviour throughout the month. It was partly explained by drugs and he was also over-eating and piling on the pounds. But the main reason was Priscilla. On 18 August he filed for divorce because of 'irreconcilable differences', which was not contested by Priscilla. She did however join him for the final week in Vegas.

Joe Esposito's most demeaning task was to stand in the wings with a spare pair of trousers in case our hero should really let it r-i-i-i-p. Usually he had nothing to do, but during the late show on August 21, Elvis' seam split. He changed pants behind the curtain but kept on singing. After one show, a fan clambered on stage for a Band-Aid that Elvis had flicked off his finger.

In November, the film *Elvis on Tour* was released. The film continued *Elvis: That's the Way It Is*, but the choice of songs (29 this time round) was not as strong and the split-screen technique is now off-putting when seen on a small TV screen. Martin Scorsese was the supervising editor and he created montages from previous films, notably the kissing montage. Elvis wasn't keen at first as he wanted 100% New Elvis, but Jerry Schilling, now working with the filmmakers, talked him round and he liked them. The director Pierre Adidge, who had made Joe Cocker's *Mad Dogs and Englishmen*, died from a spine disorder in 1974 when he was only 35.

Elvis' outfits were becoming more lavish and the film included an interview with Vernon Presley, gospel music with the Stamps, a collage from his many movies (amusingly compiled by Martin Scorsese), a look at Graceland and, for the first time on the big screen, the early Elvis on *The Ed Sullivan Show* singing 'Don't Be Cruel' and 'Ready Teddy'.

Elvis did a short tour in November starting in Lubbock and including El Paso. Vernon Presley was in a good mood in El Paso and he treated the Stanley boys to a couple of hours in a whorehouse. The tour ended on November 18 at the Honolulu International Centre. The following day there was a press conference to announce his next project, a live telecast, *Aloha from Hawaii*, which would be screened via satellite throughout the world.

Lisa Marie came to Graceland for Christmas. She got on fine with Linda Thompson, who received a mink coat. The year ended in typical Elvis fashion with a fireworks war in the grounds of Graceland.

CHAPTER 14

My Baby Left Me

'Elvis would joke and say he was like Clark Kent – he could pop into a phone booth and out would come the guy with the freshly-dyed black hair and the suit with the cape. There he was – Elvis Presley.'

Ronnie Tutt, drummer with TCB band

I. Burger King

There is a humorous but pitiful moment in Alan Bleasdale's play about Elvis, *Are You Lonesome Tonight*, where Elvis is with the Memphis Mafia and calls the kitchen for food. It is a gigantic order and when he has finished, he looks around the room and says, 'You guys want anything?' How true to life was it? How much did Elvis eat and what did he eat? Was he the Burger King?

After Elvis was born in Tupelo, Mississippi, his mother Gladys was haemorrhaging and she was taken to hospital. Elvis went with her and she breast fed him as she recovered.

The young Elvis grew up poor in Tupelo and he was Polk Salad Elvis. His Aunt Lillian had a 'truck patch' for vegetables and he would be served cornbread, fried okra, beans and milk. There wasn't much meat but there was fried squirrel with dumplings, sometimes possum, sometimes rabbit and very occasionally a deer. The squirrels would be skinned, seasoned and fried in butter, so it's best not to eat out if you go to Tupelo. There might be fish but Elvis never liked the smell or the taste of fish.

Elvis ate meat when he could but by his teens, he had developed a passion for junk food. When he went to the cinema, he liked Reese's Peanut Butter Cups (chocolates with a peanut butter filling), Jujubes and Pepsi, and the concept of snacking at the cinema never left him. Similarly, he watched TV with a bowl of cookies on his lap. You can still eat at the Gridiron Restaurant (today Big Bill's BBQ) in Memphis and just like Elvis, enjoy their burgers and thick chocolate shakes with syrup. By a quirk of fate, its address is 4101 Elvis Presley Boulevard.

Elvis developed his favourite snack which was a peanut butter and banana sandwich that was fried on both sides. A friend recalled how Elvis came to see him in 1955 and while he was waiting, Elvis fried himself bacon and eggs.

When Elvis moved into Graceland, Gladys would be preparing his favourite meals. One of his concerns about joining the army was that this would change his habits. However, there is a photo of Elvis with his first army meal – sausages and fried eggs – a sign that he would be okay. Despite his appetite, Elvis was not overweight before he was conscripted and he came out of the army muscular and lean, just right for film work.

Some celebrities can be overweight and it makes no difference. Indeed, judging by the name, it was a marketing ploy for Fats Domino. The big difference is that Elvis was being marketed as a poster boy and so it had to be love me slender. Elvis did add a few pounds during the 60s but he usually worked it off before a film role, maybe by a crash diet, maybe by diet pills. He was overweight in *Paradise, Hawaiian Style* (1965) but it was nothing serious.

In 1963, Elvis appointed a cook for Graceland, Mary Jenkins, and she remained there until he died, and indeed until sometime afterwards. Elvis was to buy her a car and a home and he looked after her and her husband. Her memoir, *Elvis – The Way I Knew Him* (Riverpark, 1984) is derided as an example of how hangers-on have written books, but I disagree. She was crucial to his life (and possibly his death!) and if Elvis could come back, he would probably pick up her book first. Then again, he might go for *The Life and Cuisine of Elvis Presley* by David Adler (Crown 1993).

Mary Jenkins was in the BBC-TV documentary, *The Burger and the King*, under the *Arena* banner in 1995. She came across as a delightful, considerate lady who supplied everything that Falstaff, sorry Elvis, wanted. It was love at first slice. There was no thought that she might be killing him softly with her food.

Having a cook to hand did not stop Elvis eating out and sometimes he and his gang would to go Colette's Italian restaurant in Memphis for a late-night sitting. Elvis would eat three large pizzas in one sitting, each of which would be topped with meat and sauce. Elvis liked to joke that he liked the Colonel's chicken – Colonel Sanders, of course.

Once Elvis had begun to play Vegas, he was looking fit and healthy but things started to slide. Maybe it was work pressure, maybe it was the break-up, maybe it was just heavy eating. He was looking good until 1973 and when things started to go wrong, they happened fast. The jumpsuits only highlighted his condition. He had lost his self-esteem as he didn't want to control himself. As Mary Jenkins said, 'Eating was the only thing that gave him any pleasure.'

There is an element of comfort eating too. When Elvis was in Washington and about to meet Nixon, he filled in the time by consuming a box of 12 honey doughnuts. If he was on a plane, he might eat a pot of yoghurt, either blueberry or peach, and before anyone knew it, he had eaten the whole tray. He ate Krispy Kreme jelly donuts a box at a time: shortly after his death, they opened a branch near Graceland, so there's bad timing for you.

Elvis would invariably sleep through the day and wake up about 4pm. His breakfast was a pint of orange juice, a pot of black coffee, and a six-egg omelette with a couple of pounds of burnt bacon. Indeed, Elvis' favourite compliment was 'That's burnt, man'. A couple of hours later he might be hungry and ask for cheeseburgers and ketchup but no mayonnaise as he considered it bad for his throat.

If he was doing a show, he might have a hearty dinner after he was through, and then have another one. When the shows were over, he might go to bed with a tray of food, which would be removed if he fell asleep. If he woke up in the night in either Graceland or Vegas, there was a well-stocked fridge in the bedroom. He never drank tap water and there were always chilled bottles of Mountain Valley Springwater around. On an average day, Elvis might consume 25,000 calories.

Donna Presley Early is doing her best for him when she says, 'Elvis is from the South and we have some great southern dishes like fried chicken and soups. Of course he ate hamburgers, we all do, but it wasn't to excess. A lot of books and articles exaggerate his food addiction. They keep reproducing the pictures at his last concert but if you look at him, he isn't grossly overweight. It is more like he is bloated with an infection in his body.'

Elvis' fans were sensitive about his weight and disliked jokes about Fat Elvis. Glen Campbell found this out to his cost. 'I knew Elvis well and he once invited me on stage and asked me to do an impression of him. I said that I'd need to put a few pounds first and the whole showroom went quiet. You didn't make Elvis jokes like that, certainly not in front of Elvis.'

Early in 1976, Elvis holidayed in Glendale, in Denver, Colorado and he really went for Fool's Gold Loaf, made by Buck and Linda Scott in their diner. It was a concoction involving peanut butter, jelly and burnt bacon, served in a French stick. A month later Elvis was recording in Graceland and felt peckish. What would satisfy him? He had the answer – Fool's Gold Loaf – and everybody should try it. He said that they should fly to Denver and being Elvis, everybody thought it was a good idea.

Over a thousand miles separates Memphis and Denver but Elvis went there in the middle of the night to get a sandwich. On the plane, Elvis kept awake by eating cookies and drinking Pepsi. Whilst they were flying, Buck and Linda were fulfilling the order, which involved 22 pounds of bacon and 16 jars of peanut butter. Each sandwich contained thousands of calories, so he had a remarkable constitution even if he only ate one of them himself. Three hours later they landed in Memphis and the giant sandwiches were loaded onto the plane. They had cost $40 apiece plus the cost of travel.

In 1975, Elvis met the nurse Marion Cocke in the Baptist Memorial Hospital and he asked her to make a banana pudding. She did that, thinking it would last a few days, but he ate it all at once. Her work was in vain as Elvis was still getting his regular food. Elvis asked Mary to bring in food, hidden amongst his clothing.

In May 1977, he woke up in Baltimore at 4pm and immediately wanted a hot fudge sundae for his breakfast. It was so good that he asked for another. And another. And two more after that. That evening, after eating five hot fudge sundaes, he sang the most anguished version of 'Hurt' he had ever performed. It's way beyond somebody singing a sad song – it's pain at its most exposed. Is it any surprise that he died a few months later?

On 16 August 1977, Mary was away and Pauline Nicholson was cooking for Elvis. He weighed 18 stone – not a massive amount, but it was affecting his health. He was becoming bedridden but that was almost a normal state for Elvis, healthy or ill. Elvis liked to lie in bed, eat and watch TV at the same time. He had designed some special spectacles with the lenses at a 45-degree angle, so that the TV set, Elvis' feet and his head were in a straight line. Elvis could have pitched them on *Dragons' Den*.

Pauline didn't expect to have much to do as Elvis was on a crash diet before his tour. Suddenly he had the urge to eat. Pauline knew he wanted to slim so didn't bring him as much as usual – just four scoops of ice cream and six cookies. Elvis liked a variety of flavours in his ice cream and he would mix them together. This was his last supper.

We will be dealing with Elvis' death shortly, but we can immediately discount one of the theories, that is, that Elvis committed suicide. If he had wanted to die, would he have spent his last week on a diet?

II. Got a Lot o' Livin' to Do, 1973–1975

By 1972, rock was a worldwide phenomenon, and there had been major events like

Monterey, Woodstock and the Isle of Wight festivals. Colonel Parker wanted Elvis at the top of the pack and for once he had a great idea, which became *Aloha from Hawaii*. His initial thought was for a worldwide, closed circuit appearance similar to prize fights but then he switched to a worldwide telecast. Elvis loved Hawaii, and the Honolulu International Centre, which could seat 6,000, would be a suitably exotic and magical location. The deal was agreed in September 1972 and the concert would take place in January 1973. There was talk of an audience of 1,000,000,000, something even larger than the moon landing.

The concert tied in with the Colonel's private agenda. Elvis would be doing a worldwide tour without leaving America. It would be the first show of its kind and a trendsetter. Also, Colonel Parker didn't want to travel as his wife, Marie, was in the early stages of dementia.

To ease negotiations, the Colonel agreed that some proceeds would go to a local charity, the Kui Lee Cancer Fund. It was named after a singer, songwriter and knife dancer who had died in 1966. The fund was to receive $75,000 from the concert.

Elvis was up for *Aloha from Hawaii* but he was not in the best of moods. Irrespective of his own behaviour, he had been cuckolded through Priscilla's affair with Mike Stone and his ego had been bruised.

The director Marty Pasetta told Elvis as tactfully as possibly that he would need to lose some weight, but Elvis knew that and went on a diet. He stopped taking drugs and he got himself down to twelve and a half stone (175 pounds).

Elvis' arrival by helicopter was filmed on 9 January 1973 and a camera crew followed him around Hawaii; some of the footage was shown during the broadcast. There was a dress rehearsal with a full house, which was the fallback. If anything went wrong on the night, they could switch to the recorded performance. Furthermore, four songs were recorded without an audience, three of them with an ethnic flavour: 'Early Morning Rain', 'Blue Hawaii', 'Hawaiian Wedding Song' and 'Ku-u-i-po', and these songs were slotted into the US broadcast, which would give the team time to adjust anything that was going wrong.

The show was beamed around the world via the Intersat IV communications satellite. London was a centre that helped to transmit the broadcast around the world. Oddly, it was not screened in the UK as both BBC and ITV thought the asking price of £25,000 was steep. As a result, the concert does not have the legendary status in the UK that it has elsewhere. Apart from that, the concert was a huge success and showed that Elvis knew how to excite both a live audience and a global audience at the same time. The way the audience screamed at his leg movements in 'Fever' or at his karate chops in 'Suspicious Minds' was undoubtedly duplicated in millions of homes.

The concert became a best-selling double-album. It has since been issued in a legacy edition incorporating the dress rehearsal. There is not much difference between the shows but Elvis added 'Johnny B. Goode', 'I Can't Stop Lovin' You', and a medley of 'Long Tall Sally' and 'Whole Lotta Shakin' Goin' On'.

Despite its celebrity, this is not one of Elvis' greatest performances, probably because he was on his best behaviour. There is little of the looseness of Vegas. He doesn't speak much because there was a huge non-English speaking audience. Just before 'Love Me' he was about to go into a rap, but he admonished himself and started singing. In 'Suspicious Minds', he adds the line, 'I hope this suit don't tear up baby'. He calls Hank

Williams' 'I'm So Lonesome I Could Cry' 'the saddest song I ever heard'.

Possibly Elvis had been told to keep clear of gospel, as this would be transmitted to non-Christian countries. Nevertheless, he performed the ultra-patriotic 'American Trilogy' exceptionally well. It was followed by 'A Big Hunk o' Love', but Elvis loved lunatic running orders. James Taylor's 'Steamroller Blues' was full of innuendo and how was 'I'm a napalm bomb guaranteed to blow your mind' received in Japan? Tasteless or what?

Elvis opened with 'See See Rider' and went into 'Burning Love'. If Elvis disliked this song as much as is reported, would he perform it as his second song? Surely he would have started with songs that had his complete confidence. The set list was different from that of Madison Square Garden, with only seven titles being repeated.

Among the new songs were Marty Robbins' 'You Gave Me a Mountain', Jim Reeves' 'Welcome to My World', and George Harrison's 'Something'. Some thought that he included 'My Way' as a tribute to Sinatra. In view of the tensions between them (chiefly over Juliet Prowse), I doubt that. Possibly Elvis wanted to demonstrate that he could sing it better than Sinatra. He identified with the lyric, although he spent his life doing it Colonel Parker's way.

After the concert, Elvis went to bed – for a whole day! This surely suggested that Elvis was back on the pills. And he was. He returned to those huge meals.

The 1972 Grammy ceremony took place in Nashville on 3 March 1973. Elvis was up for Best Inspirational Performance with *He Touched Me* and he had to compete with Merle Haggard (*Land of Many Churches*) and an instrumental single, the Royal Scots Dragoon Guards' 'Amazing Grace'. So-called 'Jesus Music' had become popular, especially in California, and Elvis' album had that sound. Elvis had his second Grammy.

On 26 January 1973, Elvis was booked for a month at the Las Vegas Hilton and Linda Thompson went as his girlfriend. He missed four shows because of throat problems.

On 18 February, four guys rushed the stage and Elvis said, 'I'll either shake your hands or whip your asses.' They chose the latter and Elvis and his bodyguards set about them with Elvis knocking one assailant into the audience. He received a round of applause for this. Spurred on by this, the next day Elvis asked Red and Sonny to find a hit man who would take out Mike Stone. It's possible that Elvis said that but did he really mean it?

Meanwhile Colonel Parker had been negotiating with RCA and for $5.4m, RCA would retain the rights to all songs that Elvis had recorded up to March 1973. That sounded a lot but Parker had woefully sold Presley short. Even more so, when you consider that the latest management deal gave Parker 50% of his earnings. As part of the package, Presley was committed to two new albums and four new singles a year; that's 28 tracks.

On 7 April, Elvis and his retinue travelled to San Francisco for a karate championship. He wanted to participate but Colonel Parker said he would be breaking a contract in Lake Tahoe, Nevada if he did. This forbade him from appearing within a 300-mile radius within 30 days of the concerts. Elvis watched, annoyed, from the stands.

Starting on the 22 April, Elvis toured for a month, including 25 shows at the Stateline (formerly the Sahara Tahoe Hotel). For most of the time, Elvis was overweight, groggy and unable to focus. After a six-week layoff, Elvis started touring again, playing the Nassau Coliseum, New York, and dates in Nashville, Oklahoma City and Atlanta. His performance in St Louis on 28 June was one of his finest.

When Elvis had met Muhammad Ali, Ali had been taken with his jumpsuits. Elvis had a special robe made for him to wear when he fought Ken Norton in March 1973. It was decorated with rhinestones and had 'People's Choice' on the back. Ali loved it but he lost the fight and never wore it again.

On Saturday evening 21 July 1973, Elvis started a week's recording at Stax Studios in Memphis, only it didn't work out that way. This looked immensely promising. Elvis was recording at a highly successful studio, famous for soul music. He would be recording with his own band and some American Sound musicians (Reggie Young, Bobby Wood and Bobby Emmons). The sessions would be produced by Felton Jarvis, although the official billing was Executive Producer: Elvis Presley, Associate Producer: Felton Jarvis. The intention was to put down 30 songs but Freddy Bienstock hadn't come up with many impressive new songs and Elvis was rejecting far more than he was taking. Elvis used some of them as frisbees.

The eight tracks recorded on the first three days are good but were lacking something, namely Elvis. He didn't have his heart in them and the results were not especially distinctive.

The best performance was his revival of Adam Wade's 1961 hit, 'Take Good Care of Her', which found Elvis in a submissive mood: he couldn't get his girl back but he wished the new man well. It was so unElvis that nobody would have recommended this song to him: ergo, he must have decided to do it himself.

Following 'Polk Salad Annie', Elvis was appreciating Tony Joe White's songs, which were embedded in a Southern lifestyle. 'For Ol' Times Sake' was a song of regret and love lost, not dissimilar to 'For the Good Times', and with an excellent lyric. 'I've Got a Thing About You, Baby' was a funky rhythm with goodtime words, and the result was very enjoyable.

Rosco Gordon had been at Sun but he recorded his best-known song, 'Just a Little Bit', for Vee-Jay in 1960. Elvis' musicians gave this an insidious rhythm but Elvis seemed detached. That applied even more to the sultry revival of a Drifters' B-side, 'If You Don't Come Back' where much of the lyric was sung by the backing vocalists. That was the first Leiber and Stoller song he had recorded in years and he cut a new one, 'Three Corn Patches', a bluesy song about a poor girl with a bulldog. There's a slight pause after Elvis sang, 'She's got big...' and before he adds 'brown eyes': we know what he wants us to think. 'Find out What's Happening' had been a country hit for Bobby Bare in 1968, but here it sounded like something from his film days, despite Bobby Emmons on organ. 'It's Different Now' was rehearsed but not completed and sounded like Bobby Goldsboro singing the verses to 'Honey'.

By far the oddest track was a new song by Mark James, 'Raised on Rock', but surely he didn't write this for Elvis. The song was about growing up in the 50s and loving the music on the radio including 'Hound Dog'. It made no sense at all for Elvis to record this song without modifying the lyric.

Some musicians including James Burton thought that Elvis would be finished after three nights and had booked themselves for other work. Felton Jarvis had to find other musicians quickly and fortunately Donald 'Duck' Dunn and Al Jackson from the Stax studio band were available.

When Elvis turned up that night, he learnt that his personal microphone had been stolen. He was furious and left the building. Felton Jarvis put down some tracks that night and the next, in the hope that Elvis would return, but he didn't. He was to put his voice on 'Girl of Mine' and 'Sweet Angeline' but 'Good, Bad but Beautiful', 'Colour My Rainbow' and 'The Wonders You Perform' were never completed.

Elvis remained touchy all summer. He had a month at the Las Vegas Hilton, performing 59 shows but arguing with everyone. He had a wrestling match in his hotel suite with a young woman and broke her ankle. She pressed charges but they were dropped when Elvis apologised and paid her hospital bills. Elvis hurt his wrist while breaking karate boards. On 2 September, he added a late show at 3am and was overcome with laughter.

There was another incident when Elvis was at the piano playing 'Killing Me Softly with His Song' over and over to Tom Jones, who was at Caesars Palace. When Elvis got up, his road manager Chris Ellis took the piano stool away and Elvis felt insulted. The next day Elvis' bodyguards told Tom that Chris would have to apologise but he refused. When Tom heard of this, he called up Elvis to resolve any misunderstanding.

J.D. Sumner's stepson, Donnie, had sung with the Stamps and had formed his own group, Voice. Elvis told him that Tom was looking for a vocal group and he would arrange an audition. When they came to Vegas, Elvis wanted to hear them first. With their very high and very low notes, Elvis was smitten, deciding to keep them for himself. Elvis had heard Shaun Nielsen (originally Sherrill Nielsen) before and was pleased to have him on board. Elvis gave them a contract, written on toilet paper and worth $100,000 a year. Elvis said, 'I'm gonna be your manager.'

Meanwhile, the RCA contract stipulated that Elvis must start recording again. RCA offered to record him in his living room in Palm Springs in September. There were four musicians: Burton and Hodge, Tommy Hensley (bass) and Donnie Sumner (piano). Donnie brought along Tim Baty and Shaun Nielsen from Voice.

Elvis recorded a ballad about love lost, 'I Miss You', written by Donnie, and 'Are You Sincere', a hit for Andy Williams in 1958, which gets a smoky vocal and a narration from Elvis. Felton asked Elvis to put a vocal on 'Sweet Angeline'. And that was it. It was a lot of effort for seven minutes of music.

'Sweet Angeline' was another British song from the AMMO team – Chris Arnold, Geoff Morrow and David Martin. Chris Arnold: 'Sweet Angeline' started as a melody without any title at all. I had always sung in chapels and church choirs and I have written anthems for choirs to sing. I liked this melody because it had a churchy feel, a kind of solemnity and quiet dignity and simplicity too, like many hymns. We thought we would see if we could get something out of this melody as it would lend itself to his voice. David said, 'How about a girl's name? How about 'Sweet Angeline'?' Elvis was steeped in the gospel tradition and he had recorded some very moving gospel songs. We thought he would make a good job of it and he did.'

On 30 September, Colonel Parker negotiated a contract for future appearances at the Hilton. Elvis was finding a month at a time hard-going and so it would now be for fortnightly engagements.

A week later, Elvis and Priscilla were in court for the divorce settlement. Priscilla was awarded $725,000 plus $4,000 a month and the same again for child support. They left the court together hand in hand.

Elvis was worried about his health. The pills weren't working. He was incontinent and impotent. When he had difficulty breathing, he was admitted to the Baptist Memorial Hospital under the name of Aaron Sivle (well, I ask you) and diagnosed with pneumonia, pleurisy, hepatitis and an enlarged colon. He was addicted to painkillers. His natural cycles were messed up and he was detoxing, but he was insistent on one thing: 'No psychiatrists,' as that wasn't manly.

His erratic behaviour included occasional gunshots at Graceland. In what seems like a prequel to the Oscar Pistorius trial, Elvis narrowly missed Linda Thompson when he put a bullet through the bathroom door. Why did anyone stay with him?

Elvis could be the fiercest of TV critics. When Robert Goulet messed up 'The Star Spangled Banner' before a televised game, Elvis shouted, 'Learn the anthem, you son of a bitch.' He was followed by a commercial for a haemorrhoid ointment, causing Elvis to add, 'Rub that on your ass, you son of a bitch.' He threw his cheeseburgers and milk at the screen and shot it with his Derringer. He told one of his guys to get rid of the TV but he kept it and it was sold at auction in 1994.

A lackey known as Hamburger James had to destroy Elvis' rubbish, especially from hotels, making sure there no drugs left behind or traces of incontinence, in which case he would have to burn the sheets. Elvis thought he had taken some of his possessions including some compromising photos of Priscilla with a girl and he was about catch a plane to sell them to a tabloid. Elvis and his men raced to the airport, where Elvis flashed his narcotics badge and dragged him from his seat. Elvis said, 'James, you have the right to remain silent, you have the right to an attorney,' but he couldn't remember how the rest of it went, so he said, '…and you have the right to all the rest of that shit. Get the fuck into the car!' He let him go so long as he kept his mouth shut.

Another time the singer and TV host, Jimmy Dean, had been made to wait to see Elvis. When he did see him, he said, 'You shouldn't have kept me waiting'. Elvis pulled out his Derringer and said, 'I oughta blow your head off for talking to me like that!'

On the other hand, when one of his backing singers, Joe Moscheo, had his apartment ransacked and his children's bicycles taken, Elvis told him to make a list and 'I will take care of it'.

Elvis was obliged to give RCA 28 new studio tracks in 1973 and so far they had only had 11. He returned to the Stax studio on Monday 10 December 1973 for a week of sessions with a small band – James Burton (lead), Johnny Christopher (rhythm), Ronnie Tutt (drums), David Briggs (piano/organ), Norbert Putnam (bass) and Pete Hallin (keyboards), plus Voice and the Stamps.

Elvis had agreed to the sessions but he didn't want to miss a baseball match which was being televised on the first day. His utterly ridiculous solution was to buy widescreen TVs for the studio. Then he told the staff to take the empty packaging and fill it with hamburgers. There were far too many for the musicians (and Elvis!) and the leftovers were given to the needy. Welcome once again to Elvis World.

Indeed on the fourth day they only cut one song – Jerry Reed's country hit from 1970, 'Talk about the Good Times'. Nothing wrong with the recording – it's rather like a revival meeting – and Elvis was in a good mood, so what went wrong? Someone had forgotten to order the food, so he went home and didn't return.

Elvis sang a new Dennis Linde song, 'I Got a Feelin' in My Body', a gospel song with wah-wah guitar. The track has a good soul groove, but there is too much going on for Elvis to assert his personality.

He recorded 'If That Isn't Love', written by a leading gospel writer, Dottie Rambo from the Rambos. She is best known for 'Holy Spirit, Thou Are Welcome'. Elvis' version of 'If That Isn't Love' is full of passion and he did consider making an album of her songs.

Larry Gatlin was a country songwriter who was making his presence felt with the Gatlin Brothers band. He should have pinned his own hopes on 'Help Me', but the song was recorded by Kris Kristofferson and then Elvis Presley. Larry Gatlin: 'I think some of the Stamps have told Elvis about my songs and I did meet him in Vegas. He was very nice to me and we sat in his suite and he talked about philosophy and religion. I wrote 'Help Me' when I was questioning what I was here for, and it has been recorded by more of my fellow artists than any other. It has done me a lot of good and I thank God for that.' I asked Larry to name his favourite Elvis records. 'Well, I would pick 'Jailhouse Rock', 'Heartbreak Hotel and 'In the Ghetto' off the top of my head but really the two songs he recorded of mine are my favourites – 'Help Me' and 'Bitter They Are, Harder They Fall'.'

There are many strong performances in these sessions and it's good that Elvis was endorsing the mellow blues of 'Good Time Charlie's Got the Blues'. The original version by the songwriter Danny O'Keefe had been recorded at American Sound in 1972: it was a great song but O'Keefe had an irritatingly nasal voice. The song has never been a hit though it has often been recorded, notably by Willie Nelson.

Elvis was interested in contemporary country and he recorded Waylon Jennings' current hit, 'You Asked Me To'. Despite the label credit to Jennings, it wasn't his song, but one by another Nashville outlaw, Billy Joe Shaver. 'Elvis did it as an album cut and my name wasn't on it. They just had Waylon's down there. It was my song really, but I gave Waylon the opportunity to have a piece of it and I kinda fed him the lyrics I wanted. I did that because I love Waylon. I love his version and I love the way Elvis did it too.'

Elvis alighted on a new country song from Troy Seals, 'There's a Honky Tonk Angel'. Conway Twitty had recorded this song but it wouldn't be released until January 1974, when it became a No.1 US country hit. Elvis could have had that hit if he had rushed it out. In the UK, Cliff Richard released it as a single and then, in an unprecedented move, asked EMI to withdraw it as he realised that the song was about a prostitute and it offended his beliefs.

The country songwriter and entertainer, Billy Edd Wheeler, had written 'Jackson' (Johnny Cash and June Carter) and 'Rev. Mr. Black' (Kingston Trio) and he had had a US hit with a tribute to an outside lavatory, 'Ode to the Little Brown Shack out Back' (1964). He had written a desolate ballad of lost love, 'It's Midnight', which appealed to Elvis as he sang it occasionally on stage. In 1979, Billy wrote his biggest hit, 'Coward of the County' for Kenny Rogers.

Billy recalls, 'My co-writer Jerry Chesnut was close friends with Lamar Fike, one of Elvis' gofers, and it was he who took my demos of that and 'Never Again' to Elvis. I remember Jerry calling and asking if I wanted to play a round of golf with him and Lamar. I said, 'No thanks, Jerry. I've seen Lamar hit the ball and it seldom goes farther than eighty yards, sometimes barely getting out of his considerable shadow.' He said, 'Well, you know he's taking our songs to Elvis.' I replied, 'In that case, I don't want to play unless our pal Lamar is playing.' We all went to the golf course. On one hole, I asked Lamar what he shot so I could write his score down. He said, '13.' 'Wait a minute, Lamar,' I said. 'I counted at least 15 strokes. Remember, you whiffed the ball twice.' 'Well, God Almighty!' he exclaimed, 'I didn't know we were playing to PRO rules'.'

But he got the songs to Elvis. 'When Elvis first heard them, he said gruffly, 'Are these about me and Priscilla?' Lamar replied, 'Elvis, not every song I bring you is about you and Priscilla.' On Elvis' initial take of 'It's Midnight', he stopped after the first verse and said to Lamar, 'I can't sing this thing like the demo.' Lamar said, 'Well, cut it the way you feel it.' He then did it exactly like my demo! I've got a live concert recording of 'It's Midnight', but Elvis is pretty high, criticising the décor.'

Elvis didn't need Lamar to pick out Elvis-and-Priscilla songs. He could find them for himself. One of the current hit singles was 'Loving Arms', written by Tom Jans and first recorded by Dobie Gray, and sometimes known by its first line, 'If you could see me now'. It's a wonderfully sensitive pop / country song, very much in Kris Kristofferson's style, and indeed was recorded by Kristofferson and his then wife, Rita Coolidge, in 1974.

Elvis was intent on doing another song on Dobie Gray's album, 'We Had It All', but he changed his mind. He said, 'Everybody will think I am singing about Priscilla.' That song was recorded by Rita Coolidge, so clearly they had similar record collections. If Presley thought that fans might think that, what would they make of 'If You Talk in Your Sleep', another Red West song.

The song, 'She Wears My Ring' was based on 'La Golondrina (The Swallow)' by the Mexican composer Narciso Serradell Sevilla. It had been given an English lyric by the Nashville team, Boudleaux and Felice Bryant. Although it has been recorded by Roy Orbison on his 1962 LP, *Crying*, its potential had not been spotted and it had not been released as a single

In 1968, Gordon Mills, the manager of Tom Jones and Engelbert Humperdinck, thought he might hit the jackpot with Solomon King, who recorded a macho, big-voiced arrangement of 'She Wears My Ring'. His name was really Allen Levy, but he was reluctant to admit it as the stage name suited his ego. It made the UK Top 10 and then was a US country hit for Ray Price. Solomon King had little chart success after 'She Wears My Ring' but he became a favourite on the chicken-in-a-basket cabaret circuit in the north of England. He would close his act with 'God Save the Queen', which you might think was tantamount to disaster, but the audiences loved it especially when he belted out the final note. Elvis would have loved him.

The Irish actor Richard Harris was no great singer but he knew how to sell a song, never better than on 'MacArthur Park' in 1968. He lived in Kensington in London in a house with turrets that resembled a castle, but when he was getting divorced he didn't have much left but a fridge, a bed and a throne in the sitting room. He knew the songwriting/production team, Bill Martin and Phil Coulter, and they adapted a Claude François song, 'Parce que je t'aime, mon enfant', turning it into 'My Boy'.

Bill Martin recalls, 'The demo was just Phil playing and me singing. We gave it to Richard Harris who thought it was phenomenal. Richard was getting divorced and this song was about someone considering divorce. We wrote some other songs around it like 'Proposal'. Richard could identify with them and he loved what we were doing. He had a good timbre to his voice and he had just bought the touring rights to *Camelot*. In one sense, he regarded this album as another exercise on his way to becoming a singer. We took 'My Boy' and Richard Harris to the Radio Luxembourg Grand Prix Music contest in 1971 and we won. 'My Boy' wasn't a UK hit but it did well in America and that is probably how Elvis Presley heard it.'

Elvis started singing 'My Boy' in concert in August 1973. Bill Martin: 'Phil said to me, 'I've heard that Elvis is singing 'My Boy'.' I asked my secretary to take a letter and I started, 'Dear Elvis'. She said, 'Elvis who?' I said, 'Elvis Presley.' She said, 'You can't write to Elvis Presley.' I wrote him several letters, hoping he was going to record it. Elvis did record it in December 1973 and it topped the Adult Contemporary Chart in the US. I've met the recording engineer who told me that Elvis listened to the playback over 30 times. His father Vernon said, 'Hot dog, Elvis, I'm getting tired and hungry, we've got to go home.' I'm sure that Elvis loved that song because it conveyed what he felt about Priscilla leaving him.'

In 1965, the Italian-American singer Al Martino heard a German instrumental by Bert Kaempfert which had been retitled 'Moon over Naples' for the American market. Martino commissioned an English lyric and this became 'Spanish Eyes', a US hit at the time and a UK one, on reissue, in 1973. Presley loved Martino's voice and lovingly recorded the song.

When Chuck Berry was in prison in Springfield, Missouri in the early 60s, he asked a guard for a map of America. The guards assumed he was planning an escape but he was simply writing a song about travelling through the country. The song 'The Promised Land' is about someone from Norfolk, Virginia on his way to Los Angeles with all sorts of diversions *en route* including racial tensions, although that is not spelt out. It's a brilliant song and Berry's superb recording was almost topped by a Cajun treatment from Johnnie Allen in 1970. It would have been good to have heard Elvis with a Cajun feel but his version was very good. He took it much quicker than Chuck Berry, almost at a breathless pace, to give the feeling of being on the move.

In September 1973, Rory Bourke wrote 'The Most Beautiful Girl' for Charlie Rich. He had written 'Patch It Up' for Elvis in 1970 but 'Your Love's Been a Long Time Coming' sounds like a song that was written for Charlie Rich, perhaps emphasised by the prominent piano. It's a good song but the chorus isn't distinctive.

The remaining songs from the sessions were published by Presley but they are reasonable enough – 'Mr. Songman' (Donnie Sumner) and 'Thinking About You' (Tim Baty), both members of Voice, and 'Love Song of the Year' (Chris Christian), which can be seen as an Elvis and Priscilla song.

In 1998, RCA or BMG, or whatever they were calling themselves that week, released an 18-track CD, *Rhythm and Country*, which featured alternate takes from the 1973 sessions. Elvis started singing a snatch of Matt Monro's 'Softly as I Leave You' before going into 'Loving Arms' and he prefaced a slinky 'If You Don't come Back' by la-la-laing 'Come Back to Sorrento' with the Sweet Inspirations. There was also a snatch of 'Muleskinner Blues' and a reference to the time, 'I go crazy at four in the morning.'

Surprisingly, 'If You Talk in Your Sleep' (US No.17, UK No.40) was chosen as the first single from the album, as there were better candidates. That was followed by 'Promised Land' and then 'My Boy'.

The sessions should have made Elvis Presley happier but they didn't – he spent the Christmas season depressed, with long hours alone in his bedroom.

After Elvis' death, Dr. Nichopoulos testified that he had admitted Presley to hospital in 1973 to cure his addiction to Demerol, claiming he often gave Presley placebos instead of the drug. This may be, but Presley would get drugs from other doctors so it was impossible to keep control of what he had.

The doctor advised Elvis against wearing jumpsuits. He thought they were too heavy (and getting heavier), that they were unhygienic and that they impeded his breathing.

Elvis had to get reasonably fit and out of his slump for two weeks at the Las Vegas Hilton. He was starting on January 25, but it was pushed back a day as Sinatra was closing at Caesars Palace and it would be poor publicity to have both events on the same night.

In March 1974, the first of the albums from the Stax sessions was released. Considering several of the songs were sad reminiscences on past loves, the title *Good Times* was rather odd.

Elvis was touring for much of March and British fan Rex Martin was on a mission. He saw 20 shows in 11 different venues, which meant covering 4,500 miles in two weeks. He was still filming and he found it easier to bask in anonymity among 20,000 people in an arena. When Elvis did two shows at the Houston Astrodome, he attracted 88,000 paying customers.

A lively homecoming took place on 20 March 1974, the final night of the tour, at the Mid-South Coliseum in Memphis. This was well away from the Vegas performances and had a carnival atmosphere. Elvis had tremendous fun with 'Steamroller Blues' and although J.D.'s cavernous voice spoils Kris Kristofferson's 'Why Me Lord' in my opinion, Elvis and the audience were enjoying it immensely.

The applause was so ecstatic for 'How Great Thou Art': it couldn't have been any greater for 'Hound Dog'. It was nominated for a Grammy and it was to win Best Inspirational Performance (non-classical), beating Sister Janet Mead with her interpretation of 'The Lord's Prayer', complete with wah-wah guitar.

Elvis was back on tour in May, doing dates in the western states and then a fortnight at the Sahara Tahoe Hotel. Elvis had been offered $1m to tour Australia but had turned it down.

On 20 May 1974, partygoer Edward Ashley was drunk and showing off to some girls. He wanted to introduce them to his 'buddy Elvis', and when he couldn't get into Elvis' suite, he kept turning the power on and off. When David Stanley tried to stop him, Edward turned on him and so Sonny West hit him hard and he fell to the floor. Elvis thought he had come to kidnap Lisa Marie and was ready for action. He had a .45 in one hand and a Thompson submachine gun in the other, with Lisa Marie hiding behind him.

Edward Ashley was handcuffed and they put on a bed. Ironically, he got what he wanted, an audience with Elvis. Elvis asked him what he was doing and instead of replying, he kicked out and hit Sonny. Red West smashed his jaw. Elvis held him forward so that he wouldn't choke on his blood. Edward sued for damages and it cost Elvis a considerable amount to settle. This may be the first time that Elvis thought he might be better off without Red and Sonny.

But that's not all. A waiter called Mario who served Elvis at the hotel told him that his wife was dying of cancer. Elvis went to his house and put his hands on her. The hotel thought Mario was taking advantage of his position and sacked him. Presley lambasted the hotel from the stage, calling them uncaring. The Colonel was furious: this could jeopardise future contracts. Equally mad, Elvis fired the Colonel. The next day Colonel Parker presented Elvis with a bill. The figures were fictitious but they showed that Presley owed him $2m and he would press for payment. Elvis made up with him – reluctantly.

In June, Elvis was touring again and 70 female fans rushed the stage to reach him at the Veterans Memorial Auditorium in Des Moines, Iowa. It was good-natured and Elvis didn't feel threatened. He was laughing and talking with them as they were removed.

On 10 July, there was a cheer for Elvis when he watched the Memphis Grizzlies play basketball. Then he took a holiday in Hawaii.

In August Elvis decided that he wanted a new look and new material for Las Vegas. Among the songs he rehearsed were Olivia Newton-John's 'If You Love Me (Let Me Know)', 'Down in the Alley', 'It's Midnight', 'The Twelfth of Never' and 'Softly As I Leave You'. He found that the audience preferred his old hits and the show went back to what it was.

Elvis was still doing karate. He had got his first black belt in 1960 and on 29 August 1974, on stage in karate garb, he received the eighth degree and was designated a master of the art. A sick one. Presley's bowels were so irregular that he would sleep with a towel around him like a nappy. Two of his Vegas shows were missed through illness.

Yet I have the shows from August 24 and 29 and he sounded fine. 'All Shook Up' and 'Hound Dog' were astonishingly fast and he messed around with J.D. on 'I Got a Woman'. He made fun of 'Fever' and 'Why Me Lord', but he was doing them well. He talked about how he and Red had vandalised a 'big fat angel' that was part of the décor. He said that Charlie handed him his Stay Free pads, and then he said he was only joking and he didn't need them.

Touring in Maryland on 27 September, Elvis came on stage saying 'I just woke up'. He was annoyed that the *Washington Post* had mentioned his paunch. He told the audience that it was his bulletproof vest in case somebody shot him in the belly button.

The closing show in Vegas on 2 September was one of the best, with Elvis on stage for almost two hours. His new girlfriend, Sheila Ryan, was in the audience. She had been the *Playboy* cover girl in September 1973 and Elvis dedicated Don McLean's 'And I Love You So' to her. Priscilla was also in the audience and he said, 'We get along fine, no trouble, but Mike Stone ain't got no balls. Mike is a stud, my ass.' In 1976 Sheila married the actor James Caan, although they divorced a year later.

The next night Elvis was still in Vegas. He went to Tom Jones' show and gave a karate demonstration while Tom sang.

Later in September Elvis went on a spending spree, buying six Continentals and five Cadillacs. He told the showroom, 'Just give Daddy the bill.' Elvis was touring again in late September but he developed a high fever and only spent 30 minutes on stage in Detroit, but he did make a quick recovery. After a return visit to Nevada, he was away for nearly a month on a road trip with his retinue.

Elvis wasn't having much UK chart success in 1974, but the Christmas No.1 was Mud with 'Lonely This Christmas', written and produced by Nicky Chinn and Mike Chapman. Nicky Chinn said, 'It was Mud parodying Elvis Presley, and some people did think it was Elvis at first. Les did a great Elvis on that. We didn't write it that way, it was just how he saw the song.'

Les Gray agreed, 'I was doing an Elvis on that but it was really a send-up of all those smoochy songs. It worked because it can also be taken seriously. I remember playing it at the Liverpool Empire and some of the fans were crying and others were laughing.'

A newspaper report said that Elvis earned $7.5m during the year. If he had, he had spent it as well. One of the world's richest men, Adnan Khashoggi, offered Elvis $10m to play by the Great Pyramid of Giza, which was a great idea – the newest Wonder of the World next to the oldest. Colonel Parker said no. Frank Sinatra was to say yes.

The world's media reported that Elvis was 40, as if there were some special excellence in being able to live that long. In a way there was, as rock music had been destructive. The Righteous Brothers recorded 'Rock'n'Roll Heaven' and there were lots up there – Buddy Holly, Eddie Cochran, Sam Cooke, Gene Vincent, Bobby Darin, Brian Jones, Jimi Hendrix, Otis Redding and Janis Joplin. Although Elvis might pause for breath between songs, at least he was breathing.

Elvis was sent thousands of birthday cards. He received a large box which was said to contain two dogs. Elvis said that there were enough dogs at Graceland and it was to be returned to sender. There was some knocking on the crate and it was two girls. They never saw Elvis, but top marks for trying.

It wasn't just Elvis who was receiving gifts – he was giving as usual. In January, he bought 11 Cadillacs for his friends. Elvis bid for a Boeing 707 which belonged to a disgraced investment banker and friend of Richard Nixon, Robert Vesco, who had left the country but not taken his plane. It had been repossessed. Elvis put down a deposit but he learnt that Vesco's team would claim the plane if it left America. The deal went sour, another indication that Presley was thinking of travelling abroad.

On January 29, Elvis was admitted to the Baptist Memorial Hospital for a check-up, which could be a euphemism for detox.

A week later, Vernon, who had split with Dee, had a heart attack and was taken to the same hospital, where they were put in adjacent beds. Vernon told Elvis that the heart attack was his fault and 'You worried your mama right into her grave'.

In early March, Elvis did three nights of sessions with his road band at the core. Ten songs were recorded and they formed his new album, *Today*. By and large, the songs were well chosen, but there was nothing especially inventive about the music or the arrangements.

One of the biggest singles of the Christmas season had been 'I Can Help', by the singer and songwriter Billy Swan, a superb piece of retro rock'n'roll. Billy had spent some time in Memphis and roomed with Travis Smith, Elvis' uncle, who was on the gate at Graceland. He wrote 'Lover Please' for Clyde McPhatter and he played in Kris Kristofferson's band.

Billy says, 'I wrote 'I Can Help' when my wife was pregnant with our daughter which explains the line, 'If your child needs a daddy, I can help'. I wrote three verses and Chip Young added a guitar solo. The false ending just happened in the studio as did the applause at the end. Elvis recorded 'I Can Help' and he told me he had put a 50s ending on it. I knew what he meant, as 'I Got a Woman' has got one of those stripper endings.'

That ending aside, Elvis stuck close to Billy's original, the main difference being that this was Elvis. Billy Swan: 'Bob Beckham who published the song showed me one of Elvis' belts and asked me if I would ever wear anything like that. I said, 'No, but I'd sure like his socks.' A couple of weeks later Felton Jarvis handed me the very socks that Elvis wore on the session when he recorded 'I Can Help'. They smelt like cinnamon and I still have them. They are longer than the average sock and they are Burlingtons. I should have asked for a jump suit or a sports coat.' Billy had the socks framed, but more to the point, Elvis had recorded a superb version of a fine retro rock'n'roll song.

Another contemporary hit that Elvis covered was 'Fairytale', written by Anita and Bonnie Pointer for the Pointer Sisters. Elvis started singing the song in concert saying it was the story of his life. Elvis' capacity for self-indulgence and self-pity knew no limits. It's a decent song performed country style but the title should have been better placed: you wouldn't pick it up from one hearing.

Marilyn Monroe made her screen début in the 1950 film, *The Asphalt Jungle*. One of its scenes inspired the Nashville songwriter Curly Putnam to write 'Green Green Grass of Home'. It is a tale of a prisoner who dreams of going back home, but when he awakes, he realises he is to be electrocuted. An archetypal country song, it refers to a hometown girl named Mary, a preacher, prison, death and a funeral.

Country singer Johnny Darrell recorded the song in 1964 and then it was a Top 5 country hit for Porter Wagoner. This prompted Jerry Lee Lewis to record it for his 1965 album, *Country Songs for City Folks*. When Tom Jones wanted to record it, the pianist Les Reed wrote a pop arrangement. It became a UK No.1 over Christmas 1966 and went into the US Top 20. When Elvis was driving home for Christmas, he couldn't get the song out of his head. He had someone call the radio station to request repeat plays as he was driving to Memphis. If you're Elvis, you can do that. It wasn't until March 1975 that he recorded Tom's signature song. It's a very good version with an excellent narration but what was the point?

Perry Como had returned to the charts with the Don McLean song, 'And I Love You So', in 1973. Elvis loved this ballad and, as he had being doing it on stage, it made sense to record it. Elvis turned to an old R&B hit for 'Shake a Hand', a success for Faye Adams in 1953 and then LaVern Baker in 1960. It was given a slow, funky, gospel-slanted arrangement.

Charlie Rich had as many dark shadows as Elvis and he too was drawn to songs of remorse, in his case down to alcoholism. Troy Seals wrote 'Pieces of My Life' which Charlie put on his album, *The Silver Fox* (1973). Ray Connolly: 'Some good records came out of the break-up as he was singing sad songs because he felt miserable. 'Always on My Mind' is a very good song and I especially like 'Pieces of My Life', which is great. That is a song of regret, about someone who has thrown the best part of his life away – and he knows it.'

Considering that one of Elvis' best records was 'Trouble' from *King Creole*, it's odd that the songwriter Jerry Chesnut should submit 'T-R-O-U-B-L-E'. Unlike 'D-I-V-O-R-C-E', there is no reason why the words in this song are spelt out, except possibly to emulate Tammy Wynette. It's a good number about a jobbing pianist, quite similar to what Jerry Reed was writing for himself and for Elvis.

Jerry Chesnut also wrote a ballad 'Woman without Love', which had been recorded by Bob Luman and Johnny Darrell. It was about a woman who cried when she thought her man was asleep and the title line sounds dubious today: 'A man without love is half a man, but a woman without love is nothing at all.'

It's hard to see what Elvis got from 'Bringin' It Back', but it was another Priscilla song. Don Reid of the Statler Brothers wrote their 1974 county hit, 'Susan When She

Tried'. It's a song of regret with a hoedown feel, but why did Reid pick the name 'Peggy Harper', the girl who married Paul Simon?

All these songs were included on Elvis' next album, the 10-track *Today*. In addition, he jammed on 'Tiger Man' and cut Cal Smith's 'Country Bumpkin', although the tape has been lost.

On 18 March, he was back at the Las Vegas Hilton for a fortnight, his first appearances for six months. Elvis borrowed a lady's napkin to wipe his nose and at her request gave it back to her. When a girl screamed 'I love you, Elvis', he replied, 'I love you too.' Some guy trying to be funny shouted, 'I hate you, Elvis', to which he responded, 'Fuck you'.

On 1 April, Elvis brought his chow chow Getlo on stage. The dog developed a kidney problem and was then flown by private jet to a recommended vet in Boston but he died in August after an operation.

Lisa Marie was spoilt but we have evidence that Elvis spanked her at least twice. Once when she covered a velvet couch with crayons and once for playing too close to the pool. Many of his associates thought that she was a mini Elvis, awkward, outspoken and wanting to do everything at once. She became acclimatised to his upside down world. Elvis had a pet store open in the middle of the night so that he could buy her a puppy.

Once a fan at the gate of Graceland gave Lisa Marie her camera and $20 for a photo of her dad. Elvis said no and threw the camera in the bushes. Next day the fan wanted it back. 'Tough luck,' said Lisa Marie.

Elvis toured for much of April to June. In May 1974 the young girl met Michael Jackson in Lake Tahoe.

On 11 June, Elvis bought his own jet, a Convair 880 and had it remodelled. He named it the Lisa Marie and now Elvis could travel to concerts and just be in and out without seeing many new faces. He used the jet for his summer tour and by October it would look like a flying palace.

On 20 July in Norfolk, Virginia, Elvis made racial and sexual remarks to the Sweet Inspirations, which were jokes that went wrong. He said of Kathy Westmoreland, 'She will take affection from anybody, any time any place. In fact, she gets it from the whole band.'

The following day he visited a dentist in Greensboro, North Carolina which was usually his excuse to get more drugs. That night he apologised to the Sweet Inspirations on stage, even though the audience wouldn't have known what had happened the day before. Then, to make it worse, he said of Kathy Westmoreland, 'If she doesn't like it, she should get the hell off the stage!'

The next day, the Elvis package had moved to North Carolina. Songwriter Billy Edd Wheeler: 'In 1975 Elvis came to Asheville to play a concert at the Civic Auditorium, but the tickets sold so fast they booked him for two more days. Elvis stopped one show to bring J.D. Sumner downstage. He made a short but touching speech about how long they'd been doing shows together and presented him with a large diamond ring. *The Asheville Citizen-Times* reported the diamond as being worth $35,000. After Elvis' death, J.D. would display his 'Elvis Presley hand' – every ring on it came from Elvis. Also in Asheville, Elvis tossed a guitar into the audience, so they did a big story on the guy who caught it.'

Elvis Presley: Caught in a Trap

Billy continued, 'Lamar Fike invited me to hang out in Elvis' dressing room. We could step from the room and walk up under the stage on either side – a great vantage point to observe women of all ages handing things to Elvis as he gave out scarves...dolls they'd made, flowers, candy, all sorts of items. When Elvis introduced 'It's Midnight', he said, 'Here's a song written by a local boy, a good friend of mine, uh – (He reached into his pocket, pulled out a piece of paper and read from it) – Billy Edd Wheeler.' I said to Lamar, 'What's that all about? He knows my name.' Lamar said that he could not remember names and he'd even do that if it was Liza Minnelli.'

That night Elvis put a bullet through a TV screen, thereby nicking Dr. Nick. On the final show of the tour, also in Asheville on 24 July, Elvis gave away a guitar and two diamond rings. Let the good times roll.

Back in Memphis on July 27, Elvis bought 14 Cadillacs for his friends plus one for a bank-teller, Minnie Person, whom he'd met on the car lot. She was buying a car for her birthday but only but had a limited budget – not any more.

On 16 August, Elvis was flying to Las Vegas but he had problems breathing and the plane was forced to land in Dallas. Elvis was okay in a couple of hours and the journey continued. He only did five shows in Vegas before the shows were cancelled as he was an embarrassment to himself and to the hotel. The press was told that Elvis was suffering from 'extreme fatigue'. On 20 August he had come on stage with water pistols; there was much giggling and laughter and he fired them indiscriminately: the band didn't know whether to continue or not. Throughout the gigs, Elvis was unwell and sweating profusely and from time to time Elvis would ask the Sweet Inspirations to take over.

It's hard to tell how ill he was, as he liked diagnosing himself and then telling his doctors what he wanted. Sometimes they would refuse his requests but not often, as Dr. Nick was given a $750,000 house.

Prescriptions would be issued in everybody's name and the drugs delivered to Elvis. Sonny West was furious when he found his child's name on one of Elvis' prescriptions. Ricky Stanley was arrested for forging a prescription for Demerol, a narcotic for pain relief. Almost certainly he was acting on Elvis' instructions. Elvis would take 30 pills to help him sleep and he would wake up to amphetamines and liquid cocaine.

Dr. Nick thought it was necessary for Elvis to have around the clock medical care to check he wasn't going to OD. Two nurses took shifts to look after him: one was Marion Cocke, the other Kathy Seaman. Elvis would say, 'If Cocke's here, Seaman can't be far behind.' Elvis was turning into Bernard Manning.

Then again Elvis could be active. In October, he bought some three-wheeled motorcycles and he and Linda would ride around Memphis. In a sudden keep fit campaign, he invested in a sauna and racquetball court at Graceland.

In December, he was making up his lost bookings at the Las Vegas Hilton. He was on good form and there were no serious incidents. He was singing 'America the Beautiful' and putting 'Crying in the Chapel' in a medley with 'Rip It Up'. For some months he had been performing 'Softly as I Leave You' as an unusual duet. Shaun Nielsen would sing while Elvis narrated the words, except for the last line where Elvis took over. Its lyricist was Hal Shaper: 'People have their own vision of what songs mean to them. Elvis had heard Jerry Vale in Vegas singing 'Softly as I Leave You' and Jerry told him it was about a man scribbling down a note on his death bed. Elvis believed it to be true and the song became a great favourite of his. He would preface the song by telling the audience this story. I didn't want to tell him this wasn't true as he might have stopped doing my song.'

Elvis was working on New Year's Eve for the first time since 1957. He was at the Silverdome in Pontiac, Michigan, performing to 62,000. The organisers took nearly $1m in ticket money, which was Elvis' highest grossing concert with his highest attendance. It only occurred because the Rolling Stones had cancelled and Elvis was using some pick up musicians as most of his band were unavailable. Elvis split his trousers and he kept on singing when the band started to play 'Auld Lang Syne'.

An audience member ran across the football field with a gun and David Stanley bought him down. The gunman was arrested but let out after a week in a Detroit jail. Elvis called him, 'Hey motherfucker, do you know who this is? I'm your worst nightmare and I'm gonna blow your brains out.' Elvis wanted to fly to Detroit to deal with him but fortunately there was a snowstorm and the plane was grounded. By the next day, Elvis had forgotten all about it.

CHAPTER 15

I Can't Seem to Stand on my Own Two Feet

*'Everytime I look at you I don't understand
Why you let the things you do get so out of hand.'*
Superstar, Tim Rice and Andrew Lloyd Webber

The story of Elvis Presley's life ends here. It's rather like the Beatles' argumentative 'Let It Be' sessions. The official parties would rather that it hadn't been like that. Apple has never reissued the *Let It Be* film and similarly Graceland glosses over the final two years of Elvis' life. But the decline is an important part of the overall story.

If you tour Graceland, they say Elvis died of heart failure. There are no further details or alternative hypotheses.

Elvis was no Howard Hughes; he was making appearances and putting down tracks but there were multiple problems. Things were bad at the start of 1976 and it was evident that it was going to get worse. This chapter, like the others, is in two parts. In the first, we ask 'What if…', what might have happened if Elvis had gone into rehab and got fully committed to his career again. There are some indicators that suggest what could have happened. In the second part, we find out what really happened.

I. What If…

Elvis Presley died on 16 August 1977 and we all wish he hadn't. What if his heart attack had been a wake-up call? What if he had decided at long last to sort himself out? Which might he have done?

Songs were being submitted to Elvis and his advisors all the time and Elvis was hearing songs on the radio that he liked. We can make a reasonably accurate assessment of what would have been on Elvis' next LP.

In January 2004, I saw Elvis Presley's TCB band at the Olympia in Liverpool. The set, though very good, was predictable – with one exception. The bass player, Jerry Scheff, announced that they were going to play a song he had written for Elvis, 'Fire down Below'. It's true, as in October 1976 the backing track had been recorded ready for Elvis' voice. When the TCB Band played it live, it sounded excellent, a forceful rocker like 'Burning Love'. Not only would it have been a good track for Elvis' next album, but it also sounded like a good title.

In January 1977, Elvis Presley went to Nashville for some sessions but flew home instead of going to the studio. It wasn't because he disliked the songs but because he had fallen out with his girlfriend. Backing tracks were recorded but he never added his vocals. They were 'That's What You Do To Me' (written by Bob Morrison and Johnny MacRae and a US Top 10 country hit for Charley McClain in 1978), 'Energy' (by Bob

Morrison and Tommy Roe), 'Rainy Night in Georgia' (Tony Joe White's song which was a US hit for Brook Benton in 1970), 'By Day By Day' (by Dennis Linde), 'Let Me On' (by Layng Martine Jr and recorded by Jerry Lee Lewis on *Killer Country* in 1980) and 'Yes I Do' (Alan Rush).

Dennis Linde, who wrote 'Burning Love', told *Elvis – The Man and his Music*, 'The song 'By Day by Day' had gospel elements to it and I thought he could have done a terrific version. Felton played my demo to Elvis and he liked it.'

Alan Rush was a musician in Jubal with Dennis Linde, which recorded for Elektra. If Felton Jarvis felt that an Elvis session needed a bit of tweaking before release – an extra harmony or some more guitar – he would ask Jubal to resolve it. Another of Alan Rush's songs, 'Wild and Woolly Ways', was recorded by Jerry Lee Lewis in 1978 and would have suited Elvis.

Although a backing track wasn't recorded, there was a good chance that Elvis would record 'Mustang Wine', a song by a maverick songwriter who had moved to Nashville, Steve Earle. In the 1980s this was one of Earle's stage favourites and it was recorded by Carl Perkins.

David Bellamy of the Bellamy Brothers told me, 'Felton Jarvis, who was producing Elvis, got hold of our version of 'Miss Misunderstood' and they cut the backing track for Elvis to add his voice. He was going to put it on his next album and I'm mad at Elvis for leaving before he cut it. After his death, Felton Jarvis brought Carl Perkins in for the vocal but it was in the wrong key for him.' Carl did record the song with a different accompaniment.

We know too that Bruce Springsteen had written a song for Elvis, 'Fire', which would have tied in neatly with 'Fire down Below' and the feeling of 'Burning Love'. It could have been one of his biggest hits, as Springsteen passed it to the Pointer Sisters who took it to No.2 in the US in 1978. David Bowie thought that 'Golden Years' would suit Elvis: he's right but Bowie's image was way out of Elvis' comfort zone. Dolly Parton's 'I Will Always Love You' was still only a country hit and although Elvis recognised its potential to cross over, Dolly wouldn't make a deal with Hill and Range.

When the country singer / songwriter Bob Cheevers lived in Memphis, he collected an annual charity cheque for $50,000 from Elvis Presley in Graceland. In 1963, he got the urge to use the toilet and Elvis told him where it was. 'I took a dump in Elvis' toilet,' says Bob. Years later, Elvis died before he could record one of Bob's songs, 'Big City Gambler', 'and he died on the toilet, maybe the same one.' It's a funky composition in line with the songs Elvis was recording by Jerry Reed.

John Stewart, who wrote 'Daydream Believer', said, 'A friend of mine, John Wilkinson, was playing rhythm guitar for Elvis and he told me that Elvis used to sing 'July You're A Woman' in the dressing room before he went on stage. He never recorded it – it would have been the high point of my life to have Elvis doing one of my songs – but the fact that he loved the song and sang it is enough for me.'

Perhaps because Elvis liked 'July You're A Woman', John Stewart had been asked to submit some new songs to Elvis. He recalls, 'I got a call from RCA Victor, 'Elvis wants you to write a song for him.' He'd broken up with Priscilla and he was singing songs about breaking up with Priscilla. I guess it was so devastating for him that he wanted to sing what he felt, like we all do, I think. I wanted to write one like 'Burning Love', you know, something with that 'Mystery Train' feel. I wrote 'Runaway Fool of Love', sent it in and never heard a word. He never recorded it, but with all these sightings, I haven't given up hope.'

Several writers who had previously written for Elvis had material for him. Elvis liked a new song by George Klein and Mark James' 'Loving You's a Natural Thing' and he was planning a disco single with Mark James' 'Disco Rider'.

Elvis had never completed Mac Davis' 'Poor Man's Gold' at American Sound and Mac had recorded it himself in 1974. It's a sentimental song about the joy of having a new baby and it was worth completing.

Over the years, Paul Evans had written good material for Elvis including 'I Gotta Know', 'Blue River' and 'The Next Step Is Love' and he submitted some new songs shortly before Elvis died. 'I had high hopes for 'Quiet Desperation',' he says, 'and the song is based on the quotation from Thoreau, 'The mass of men lead lives of quiet desperation.' It was going to be shown to Elvis and he never got a chance to cut it.' 'Quiet Desperation' has the same intensity as 'In the Ghetto' and Paul's demo has the changes in dynamics that Elvis loved so much. Paul also submitted a gentle love ballad with gospel overtones, 'Tender Moments', which again would have suited him. Both of Paul's demos are included on his 2003 CD, *Happy Go Lucky Me*.

Elvis was prone to singing brief snatches of songs he liked and on stage in 1975, he broke into another Paul Evans song, 'Roses Are Red (My Love)', a US No.1 for Bobby Vinton in 1962. On several occasions he sang snippets of Roy Orbison's 'It's Over', 'Running Scared' and 'Crying'. Elvis mentioned Jimmy Jones' 1960 single, 'Ready for Love, in rehearsals and he was partial to a 1958 hit, 'The End' by Earl Grant. It was written by Jimmy Krondes and after his death, his son John sang lead vocals in a tribute to Elvis featuring some original musicians, the Hit Making Team.

The British team of Chris Arnold, David Martin and Geoff Morrow had a new song for him. Geoff Morrow: 'We wrote 'Where Would I Be' for Elvis and he was about to record it before he died. Some years ago I saw Gordon Hendricks, the boy who won *Stars in Their Eyes* as Elvis Presley, and he was very good and so I said, 'Let's record this with you'. He did it and it was a lot of fun.'

In the mid-Seventies, Russ Ballard, who had written 'God Gave Rock and Roll to You', met Elvis' music publisher, Freddie Bienstock. 'Freddie heard 'She's so in Love' and said that song would suit Elvis, but he must have some of the publishing. He gave me a contract and it said that in the event of an Elvis Presley recording, Whitehaven Music had to have 50% of the publishing. I suppose it is good management to get as much as you can from the writer, but I would have given the whole song to him for an Elvis cut.' Elvis never got round to 'She's so in Love' but Lulu did cut the song.

There are several favourites that Elvis might have got round to recording at last including 'Uncle Pen' (Bill Monroe), 'Satan's Jewelled Crown' (Louvin Brothers) and 'Since I Don't Have You' (Skyliners). He identified with Kris Kristofferson's songs and he surely would have recorded more of them – 'If You Don't Like Hank Williams (you can kiss my ass)' surely appealed to him, not to mention the killer version of 'Sunday Morning Comin' Down'.

Cliff Richard had a huge UK hit in 1963 with the ballad, 'The Next Time' and the US songwriter Buddy Kaye was pressing Elvis to record it as he felt his version could sell millions.

Two big middle-of-the-road hits appealed to Elvis: Morris Albert's 'Feelings' and the Captain and Tennille's 'Love Will Keep Us Together', which was written by Neil Sedaka and Howard Greenfield. He liked a 1975 country track by the Amazing Rhythm Aces about a dingy affair, 'Third Rate Romance'. Remember too that the TV producer Steve Binder had said to Elvis, 'Would you have recorded 'MacArthur Park' if Jimmy Webb had brought it to you?' and Elvis had replied, 'Definitely.'

For some years, it has been rumoured that Roy Wood had submitted songs to Elvis, but he told me, 'I was with the same publishing company as Elvis and I know he had heard quite a few of my songs and really liked them. I was asked if I wanted to write something for him and I said I could only write songs in his old style. I couldn't do the 'Son of America' stuff'. I wanted to meet him to talk about it but he fell ill and nothing happened.' Which Roy Wood songs did Elvis like? Strikes me that he could have done a fine job of 'Flowers in the Rain'.

Music writer Ray Connolly: 'There are so many missed opportunities. Elvis had the best voice of his generation and he deserved the best songs. Why didn't they ask Paul Simon or Carole King to write for him?' We know that Elvis had little time for John Lennon but why didn't he ask Paul or George for new songs as well as recording 'Yesterday' and 'Something'.

The Irish Elvis, known as The King, made the albums, *Gravelands* and *Return to Splendour*, which featured Presley-styled arrangements of things he didn't record. He never would have recorded 'Sympathy for the Devil' or 'Pretty Vacant' but Queen's hit, 'Crazy Little Thing Called Love', does seem a possibility, although it dates from 1979. The mid-70s hit from The King's repertoire that would be most likely to appeal to the real thing is surely Lynyrd Skynyrd's 'Sweet Home Alabama'. Elvis could have recorded a cracking version of that.

Elvis recorded many songs by Jerry Leiber and Mike Stoller, but they stopped writing for him after an argument with Colonel Parker. Elvis liked their 1977 hit for Elkie Brooks' 'Pearl's a Singer' so let's pretend that he overruled Colonel Parker on this. That song could easily be transferred to a honky tonk and it already has one of those burlesque endings that Elvis loved.

Would Kelly Marie have had a UK No.1 in 1980 with 'Feels Like I'm in Love' if Elvis had stayed alive? Ray Dorset from Mungo Jerry says, 'I wrote it with Elvis Presley in mind and even recorded it Elvis-style on my demo. My producer Barry Murray was about to send it to Elvis when we got a phone call saying that Elvis had died. After that, I put it to bed for a while.'

All of the above is plausible if Elvis returned to work, but the seismic change would have been if he had broken his ties to Colonel Parker or just given the honorary colonel an honorary role. Maybe the TV producer Steve Binder would have been a good choice for a rebooted Elvis. Also, Elvis had invited the TV producer Jack Good to visit him at Graceland but we don't know what he had in mind. Good was a very creative person who masterminded Tina Turner's solo career in the early 1980s.

Surely Colonel Parker's hold on Presley would have ended. Why didn't some other manager like Allen Klein make a bid for Elvis? Admittedly, Klein is a terrible example, but he would have spotted the financial flaws. Maybe Elvis was too loyal to have insisted on an audit. In 1976, both Jerry Weintraub and Tom Hewlett at Concerts West had been thinking of sidestepping Parker in some way, possibly by telling Presley directly that he deserved a much better deal.

Priscilla was to show herself to be an excellent manager after his death – Parker wanted to sell Graceland and she wanted to open it to tourists – and maybe she should have attempted to get Elvis away from the toxic Parker in the mid-70s. She would have seen his return to film-making but exercised more control over their quality. She has said, 'Elvis saw his potential as an actor. He felt he had the dramatic sensibility to pull off challenging parts.'

At the time of his death, Elvis had been talking about having a chain of karate schools and he wanted to make a karate or Kung Fu film like Bruce Lee. If Elvis had made an action film, it would have had the additional benefit of getting him fit again. Elvis did help George Waite by funding a documentary about karate *The New Gladiators,* but it was not released until 2002. It has music by David Crosby and Graham Nash.

Elvis' film career was disappointing. There had been some excellent performances – *Jailhouse Rock, King Creole* – and with the right director, maybe he could have given Oscar-winning performances. Colonel Parker turned down *The Defiant Ones,* directed by Stanley Kramer, which was made in 1958 with Tony Curtis as the prisoner chained to Sidney Poitier.

Once a potential Oscar-winner was passed to Colonel Parker: he was told that this would win Elvis an Oscar but they could only pay $500,000 for his services. The Colonel said, 'No, the fee is still the same – $1m a film, but if my boy wins an Oscar, I'll give you $500,000 back.'

With this attitude, Colonel Parker rejected anything worthy. Elvis would have loved to have been in *West Side Story* but Parker thought not. Elvis would have had no problem with the ballads ('Maria', 'Somewhere') and can't you imagine him enjoying 'Gee, Officer Krupke, krupke you!' and the action sequences. Was *G.I. Blues* really the better choice?

According to Lee Server's biography of Robert Mitchum, intriguingly named after an Elvis song, *Baby I Don't Care,* Mitchum turned up at Elvis' hotel suite with a script in his hand. He wanted Elvis to play his younger brother in *Thunder Road* as he had a theory that anyone who could sing could also act. Mitchum told him of his wild escapades and then said, 'Here's the fucking script. Let's get together and do it.' Elvis said that he would have to discuss it with Parker. 'Fuck that,' said Mitchum, 'I'm talking to you. Let's do it.' 'No,' said Elvis, 'I have to see the Colonel.' The Colonel quoted an astronomical fee for Presley and that was that.

Maybe Parker was right about *Li'l Abner*, as I'm sure Elvis wouldn't have wanted to play in a light-hearted film about hillbillies, based on a comic strip and made in 1959 with Peter Palmer, Stella Stevens and Stubby Kaye.

With rather more class, Elvis could have been right for *The Fugitive Kind* (1960), which had a screenplay by Tennessee Williams, and the role went to Marlon Brando after Parker turned it down. He also rejected *Cat on a Hot Tin Roof* and *Sweet Bird of Youth,* again both Tennessee Williams, and both made with Paul Newman.

Colonel Parker was against a biopic of Hank Williams because Elvis couldn't have the publishing on his Acuff-Rose songs. The film *Your Cheatin' Heart* was eventually made in 1964 with George Hamilton and dubbed vocals from Hank Jr. It was directed by Gene Nelson who directed a couple of Elvis films, but most of all, Hank's widow, Audrey, nixed the idea, fearing that Elvis would steal Hank's glory. Playing Hank Williams is a poisoned chalice; ask Tom Hiddleston.

Parker turned down a film of *The Threepenny Opera* in 1960 and he blacklisted Leiber and Stoller after they had pitched Elvis a musical based on Nelson Algren's novel, *A Walk on the Wild Side*. The film was made in 1962 without songs and starring Laurence Harvey and Jane Fonda.

When he was storyboarding *Midnight Cowboy*, the director John Schlesinger got a memo from the producer: 'If we could clean this up and add a few songs, it could be a great vehicle for Elvis Presley.' Elvis was indeed offered Jon Voight's role but Parker thought such a sleazy film wasn't right for Elvis. Both Jon Voight and Dustin Hoffman were nominated for Oscars.

In the 1960s Colonel Parker had told Norman Taurog that Elvis couldn't play a killer, and by way of contrast, it wasn't a good idea for Elvis to make a guest appearance on his favourite show, *Rowan and Martin's Laugh-In*.

In 1971, Clint Eastwood not only had a hit film with *Dirty Harry* but also a major franchise. The role had been turned down by both Colonel Parker (for Presley) and Frank Sinatra. Elvis loved action movies and he saw the James Bond film, *The Spy Who Loved Me* two days before his death – Elvis as James Bond would have been fanciful, but maybe not to Elvis.

In February 1975, Barbra Streisand and her partner Jon Peters visited Elvis in Las Vegas and asked him to co-star in a remake of *A Star is Born*. Presley would be the falling star and Streisand the rising one, but he was okay with that and he told both Gordon Stoker and Jerry Schilling that he was going to do it. Colonel Parker was less happy, especially as Elvis wouldn't have sole top billing, and he kept raising Presley's fee. Streisand made it with Kris Kristofferson and the film was a major box office hit, grossing $40m in North America alone. How Elvis must have hated seeing the billboards.

Music writer Ray Connolly: 'Maybe the Colonel turned down *A Star is Born* because he thought Elvis wasn't up to it. By then Elvis was on amphetamines, but I think he could have pulled it off. Look at how he slimmed down and came off the drugs for *Aloha from Hawaii*. The billing wouldn't have been a problem. Streisand would have given up her star billing as being alongside Elvis Presley would have made her bigger as well. Maybe Elvis didn't like the fact that he would have to die in the film, but he could have done it well in my opinion.'

It is possible that Elvis never wanted to immerse himself in a role. He would never have had the discipline for a Broadway run and we have noted before that he liked to learn his lines and blurt them out before he forgot them. Therefore if he returned to films, it is more likely that he would gone for light-hearted efforts like *Any Which Way You Can* which had Clint Eastwood co-starring with an orangutan. Elvis did once say, 'All I do is sing to horses, chimps and dogs,' and this would be another example, but somewhat superior. Considering the repetitive nature of so much of his work, *Groundhog Day* was right for Elvis.

Even though Elvis might have never have done Shakespeare, surely he was living it. Is there not a comparison with Hamlet at Elsinore and Elvis at Graceland? Maybe there could have been a restructuring of the staff at Graceland to ensure that the staff were actually contributing to Elvis' success, rather than hampering it.

At the time of his death, Elvis was set to embark on even more touring dates. He wasn't learning new songs but he was preparing to wear his jumpsuit with laser lights. He was in a rut just as when he was making films. He loved Las Vegas as a city and so he enjoyed that lifestyle, but with a new manager, his career could have been much better structured and he could have gone abroad. We know he wanted to tour the UK, Australia and Japan and so a two-year world tour would have done wonders for his career.

While he was in the UK, Elvis might have recorded with local producers, Dave Edmunds and Stuart Colman, both of whom had found new ways of updating rock'n'roll. Similarly, in the States, he could have worked with John Fogerty or Bruce Springsteen.

There was an unexpected development in the 1980s when José Carreras, Placido Domingo and Luciano Pavarotti made million-selling albums and singles. The Three Tenors often recorded with rock stars and Elvis would been enjoyed the challenge. He had found his voice through trial and error but he would have learnt more about holding notes and breath control.

Although Elvis never set out to record duets with other stars, he did perform some in his films, and the ones with Ann-Margret are particularly effective. Parker turned down every request thinking it too much hassle, especially as Elvis would have to share the royalties.

Following Monterey and Woodstock, rock festivals came into their own and even if Elvis were reluctant to take part, it would have been hard to turn down *Live Aid*, especially for such a worthy cause.

Leopards don't change their spots and, by and large, Elvis' characteristics would be unlikely to change much. He was vain and the vast developments in plastic surgery would have intrigued him. In 1973 he did have a little surgery on a potential double chin and to remove fatty tissue around his eyes. There would have been more. If he had remained with Priscilla, maybe they would have discussed it together. Today she looks amazing for someone in her seventies, so how has she managed it?

I love the thought that while Elvis was having his plastic surgery, some guy was in the next bed having surgery to make him look like Elvis. 'Hey,' said Elvis, 'You wanna look like me? You can take my place.' I'd better stop now, as this is how conspiracy theories start.

II. Got a Lot o' Livin' to Do, 1976–1977

After a few days in Memphis, Elvis, Linda Thompson and the retinue flew to Denver, Colorado for a holiday in the snow. Elvis had rented three lavish condos as well as snowmobiles, which, disobeying safety instructions, were used for exhilarating midnight rides down the slopes. Elvis spent his birthday house hunting in Vail, Colorado, looking like a terrorist in his ski mask and jumpsuit. For once, there was no impulse buying and to add to his medical problems, he developed a rash.

The cheque book was out on 14 January as Elvis bought cars for a disc-jockey and some local police officers. They gave him one of their uniforms and he was to wear it at a funeral for one of their number. On 17 January, the police warned Elvis to leave Colorado as he might get arrested for drug possession. He and Linda flew to LA where she auditioned for some TV shows.

RCA had kept so many of Elvis' session tapes that they had at last decided to do something with them. In January 1974 they had released the first in a series of decently packaged LPs called *A Legendary Performer*, which included alternate takes and outtakes that hadn't been heard before. The set was both popular and well-reviewed and led to a growing interest in what Elvis had left behind, leading eventually to the groundbreaking Follow That Dream series.

The real problem was what to do with Elvis now. He didn't mind making records but he couldn't be arsed to go to Nashville or Hollywood. Bringing the mountain to Muhammad, RCA took its mobile studio to Graceland. Elvis would record with his musicians in his Jungle Room, provided the waterfall feature was turned off first.

Over the course of a week, Elvis recorded 12 songs for Felton Jarvis and a further four in October. Elvis appeared at the first session dressed as a Denver policeman. When Colonel Parker arrived to see how the sessions were progressing, Elvis was launching into a porno version of Timi Yuro's hit, 'Hurt'.

Elvis would have known 'Hurt' from Roy Hamilton's recording in 1954 and Timi Yuro's hit single in 1961. Elvis sang the song calmly with a narration and a Conway Twitty croak and then he pulled out all the stops for the final line, rather like his powerful endings for 'Unchained Melody' and 'Softly as I Leave You'. It was a huge roar and you can sense his troubles, his real troubles. Johnny Cash's career ended with an equally intense interpretation of a different song called 'Hurt'.

Another big-voiced emotional ballad was 'Solitaire', written by Neil Sedaka and Phil Cody and a US hit for the Carpenters in 1975. It was the Andy Williams version that made the UK Top 10, but 'Solitaire' was baffling for UK listeners as 'Solitaire' is better known as Patience and indeed, Solitaire is a UK game involving marbles.

Neil Sedaka: 'Solitaire sounds better than Patience as it is a very lonely game where one person plays by himself. I was inspired by Roberta Flack's voice which I loved and I can hear some Chopin in that melody too. I remember Andy Williams asking us to change the lyric. He didn't like 'A little hope goes up in smoke.' It was too spacey for him, but that is something I like about the song. Phil Cody was able to write more poetic lyrics than Howard Greenfield and he could come up with images like that.'

And then Elvis recorded a fine version. 'I'd like to have written for Elvis in the 60s but I always felt that he had very specific writers like Doc and Mort and I wouldn't get in the door. Leba and I did see him at the Las Vegas Hilton. He invited us backstage and he gave Leba a scarf that she has to this day and he and I sat at the piano and sang a gospel song. It was very flattering to hear Elvis do 'Solitaire', but Karen Carpenter sang it beautifully too.' So which version did Neil like best? 'No doubt about that – mine!'

Elvis sang another song from Larry Gatlin, 'Bitter They Are, Harder They Fall', which can be taken as an Elvis and Priscilla song. The song had been a small country hit for Gatlin himself in 1974. Larry Gatlin: 'Elvis wasn't taking care of himself and that would cost him his life, but his voice was still sounding good, and I like what he did with the song.'

Elvis delved back into old country favourites for 'Blue Eyes Crying in the Rain', a hit for Roy Acuff in 1947 and recently revived by Willie Nelson. It is unfortunate that Elvis hadn't gone for a stripped-down arrangement like Willie. There was too much going on and it detracted from the composition. The same is true of Elvis' treatment of George Jones' country hit, 'She Thinks I Still Care'. In 1980, Felton Jarvis took Elvis' voice from an alternative take and added a new backing. It is marginally better but Elvis pitched it wrong. This is a song for man down on his luck and it needed to be more plaintive.

Elvis Presley: Caught in a Trap

What was the point of Elvis singing 'He'll Have to Go' with all the passion of a sleepwalker? Listen to how warmly Jim Reeves sings the song and there's no comparison. Everybody makes bad records but Elvis shouldn't be making bad records.

The bearded balladeer, Roger Whittaker, a British singer born in Kenya, had his only major US hit with 'The Last Farewell' in 1975. It had the feel of an old-time ballad with its talk of war and with 'thee' instead of 'you', although that may have been to get the rhyme right. The arrangement started like a British war film but it's a good interpretation from Elvis, who had been recommended the song by a girlfriend, Barbara Bonner.

'The Last Farewell' was written following a BBC radio series in which Roger had asked listeners for lyrics. 'I figured that it's easy enough to write lyrics and I was proved right. I received half a million lyrics in 13 weeks. We had lyrics from bus drivers, taxi drivers, housewives, everyone. Nearly every song was a love song. I had a small team to sort through them but I did read a hell of a lot of them myself. There wasn't much of a prize on the show but if a record sells a million, then you could have £60,000 in the bank.' So well done, Ron Webster, for co-writing a million seller.

A genuine song of conflict, 'Danny Boy', was written in 1913 by Fred Weatherly with music taken from 'The Londonderry Air'. Conway Twitty had rocked it up for a US hit single in 1959 but Elvis sang it straight.

In 1962 Lonnie Donegan and his guitarist Jimmy Currie took a folk song, 'Wanderin'', which Josh White and Burl Ives had recorded, and they rewrote the lyric and expanded the melody, turning it into 'I'll Never Fall In Love Again.' Lonnie said, 'I took a folk song that wasn't a very long one, and I rewrote the lyrics and added a chorus. That was a deliberate attempt on my part to sound like Ray Charles, but I failed miserably. I didn't sound like Ray Charles and the record meant nothing to the great British public. Later on, Tom Jones was round at my house, thumbing through my records, and he said, 'I don't remember this one, boyo.' He played it and borrowed it and recorded it himself.'

Tom Jones' version of 'I'll Never Fall in Love Again' made No.2 in 1967. It also made the US Top 10, where Sammy Kaye's treatment of the folk song had been a hit in 1950. Lonnie Donegan: 'Tom Jones has told me that 'I'll Never Fall in Love Again' is his favourite song of all-time. Tom was in Las Vegas and Elvis saw his show many times. They hobnobbed and Elvis liked it too and recorded it.' Did Colonel Parker make you give up some of your royalties? 'No, but now you mention it, it's quite surprising, isn't it?'

Yet another British song was 'It's Easy for You' by Tim Rice and Andrew Lloyd Webber, although it didn't come from a musical. Tim Rice remembers, 'Elvis was a hero to both of us and we always hoped that Elvis would sing one of our songs. He was doing covers towards the end of his life – in fact, he did covers for most of his life – and we thought it would be terrific if he would cover something of ours. We sent him the *Joseph* LP, but we never got any response. We knew Freddy Bienstock, who said, 'If you have a couple of original songs for Elvis and if Elvis' company has the publishing, there's a good chance that Elvis will record them.' I thought, 'Great! Publishing is a small deal and Elvis can have my house and my car if he records something of mine.' Andrew and I wrote a couple of songs and one of them was 'It's Easy for You'. We sent it to Freddy in the middle of 1974 and we kept hearing, 'Yes, he's going to record it, he's going to record it', but nothing happened until 1976, one of his last sessions at Graceland.'

But Elvis' regular writers were not at their best. Mark James' 'Moody Blue' sounded like a Tony Christie song from the UK club circuit. Track down Take 3 on *The Jungle Room Sessions* (2000) as Elvis stumbled on his words and went into Mexican. He could have sung this song better as he kept walking around by the piano and then the drums and the engineer had trouble balancing what he was doing.

Dennis Linde's 'For the Heart' was disappointing: it had a funky rhythm but the whole thing was all over the shop. The song had previously been recorded by Teresa Brewer, also produced by Felton Jarvis. Jerry Chesnut was below par on 'Never Again', which he wrote with Billy Edd Wheeler, and why give it an 'American Trilogy' ending? Chesnut's 'Love Coming Down', previously recorded by Razzy Bailey, had possibilities as a country hit but was let down by another 'kitchen sink' arrangement.

The only R&B song was 'Pledging My Love', a success for another Memphis singer, Johnny Ace, in 1954. Ace never enjoyed his success as he chose to play Russian Roulette on Christmas Eve that year and never saw Christmas Day. It was a decent version by Elvis, but you can't beat the cheaply-made but oh so touching original. Paul Simon recorded a tribute song, 'The Late Great Johnny Ace'.

The country songwriter, Layng Martine Jr, felt he had written a good song for Elvis Presley, 'Way Down', and he asked his publisher, Ray Stevens, to help him with a demo. They recorded it as close to Elvis's style as possible with Stevens slowing down the tape to emulate J.D. Sumner. Layng sent it to Felton Jarvis and heard nothing. Having faith in it, he submitted it again, only to be told, 'You know, Elvis has already recorded this.' Layng went to the mixing session and Felton Jarvis told him, 'We're selling excitement here.' It had similarities to 'Burning Love' in that combined a contemporary sound with a 50s feel.

Elvis had decided on a different touring format for 1976 – he would have two weeks on and three weeks off, but he was feeling bad. He started though with just a week in the southern states. On 20 March, a young woman bit Elvis' lip as she went to kiss him and the following day he split another jumpsuit on stage. So much as there can be an average day on the road, this is what it was like for Elvis:

4 pm – Elvis wakes up. Breakfast of two cheese omelettes, a pound of burnt bacon, a melon and black coffee.

8 pm – Getting dressed for the show, while the Stamps are doing their opening set.

8.30pm – Off to the show with his bodyguards and local police, perhaps 15 people.

9 pm – Elvis bursts into 'See See Rider' to open his show. There is an oxygen cylinder backstage just in case…(One night in Tahoe, he brought it on stage, 'You always wondered how I keep my strength up at this altitude. Here it is.')

9.50pm – Bodyguards all around Elvis as he ends with 'Can't Help Falling in Love'. The fans surge forward, and the lower the stage, the more the trouble.

10pm – Elvis is hustled into a limousine and taken to the airport. Dr. Nichopoulos is on hand to bring him down.

10.15pm – Elvis, wearing pyjamas and a bath robe, starts eating – lots.

Midnight in the next city – Elvis puts a jumpsuit over his pyjamas. He's taken to the hotel. Colonel Parker and his team are already there, ready to move to the next city in the morning. More food.

12.30am – Another meeting with Dr. Nichopoulos and then cheeseburgers and ribs.

Elvis' girlfriend, whoever she is, is in the bedroom. Elvis reads the Bible and books on the occult.

5am – After some more pills, Elvis falls asleep.

4pm – Elvis wakes up. Another day, another show.

From time to time, something dragged Elvis out of his lethargy. On 26 March it was witnessing a car accident in Memphis. Elvis got out of his car, pulled out a police badge and offered help.

On 12 April 1976, the building started on Elvis Presley Centre Courts Inc. This was a racquetball project – a form of squash – designed to make Elvis super-rich and Joe Esposito and Dr. Nichopoulos exceedingly wealthy…if it took off. Elvis was getting 25% of the stock for $1.3m and the plan was to build 50 courts in the US. Colonel Parker was furious when he heard of this – Elvis Presley had never endorsed anything and his name was worth far more than this.

In June, ten of the songs from the Jungle Room were issued under the name, *From Elvis Presley Boulevard, Memphis, Tennessee*. The album only sold to dedicated fans but the singles of 'Hurt' (28) and 'Moody Blue' (31, and not on the album) did okay. Although 'Moody Blue' wasn't really country, it became a US country No.1, his last country chart-topper being that other famous country song, 'Jailhouse Rock' in 1957.

On 27 June, Elton John and Bernie Taupin met a drugged and dazed Elvis Presley at the Capitol Centre, Largo, Maryland. It led to Elton and Bernie writing 'Idol' for the October release, *Blue Moves*. As it is a jazz song, listeners might not have picked up that it was about Elvis. After meeting Elvis, Elton said, 'He's not long for this world' and although the song isn't that harsh (or that accurate), it is not a flattering picture. Ironically, Elton didn't learn from Elvis' excesses although he was to combat it with more success.

On 4 July 1976, Elvis appeared before 12,000 people at Oral Roberts University, Tulsa, Oklahoma. He wore his patriotic, bicentennial jumpsuit with the Liberty Bell in studs. It was his heaviest suit at 30 pounds and he hated wearing it.

On 13 July, while Elvis was on holiday in Palm Springs, Vernon, acting on Elvis' instructions, sacked Red West, Sonny West and Dave Hebler. One of the contributory factors must have been the compensation that Elvis had to pay to people they had mishandled.

Elvis was becoming very tired on stage and he looked bloated and ill. On 28 August he gave an incoherent, stumbling, mumbling show at the Hofheinz Pavilion in Houston and was only on stage for 22 minutes.

On 7 September, an exhausted Elvis joined Priscilla and Lisa Marie in Palm Springs. The rest did him some good as the October concerts, especially Minneapolis on 17 October, were much better, but it was a brief respite.

At the end of the month, Elvis bought a Lincoln Continental for J.D. but Linda Thompson told him that she had had enough. His drug use was too much for her to handle. Perhaps the final straw was when Elvis wanted her in the next bed when he was in hospital. Although that ended her relationship with Elvis, she had a new one with his keyboard player, David Briggs.

Not to worry, Elvis met his next partner – Ginger Alden. At first he was going to date her older sister who was Miss USA, but then chose Ginger. Her father, an army officer, was in the draft office when Elvis was enlisted. Within a month he had bought her a Lincoln Continental and a Cadillac. Other girlfriends included a Los Angeles model, Mindy Miller, who was alarmed by his condition and Alicia Kerwin, who was on his final flight to Las Vegas. There was a Memphis schoolgirl, Rise Smith, who soon realised she was out of her depth.

Paul and Linda McCartney, on holiday in Nashville, met someone who knew the late Bill Black's family. His double-bass was standing in a barn and Linda bought it for Paul's birthday. It had some hay in it and a packet for a guitar string. Scotty may have changed a string on stage and dropped the packet in there.

Elvis' people had found out that Red, Sonny and Dave were writing a book about Elvis, and Steve Dunleavy was to put it together. They were offered $50,000 to stop, so Elvis knew he had much to hide. They turned it down: 'Everybody is going to hate me,' said Elvis, 'I'll kill them.' John O'Grady told Elvis that the best way to counter any attack would be to enter rehab immediately. Elvis replied, 'Go to hell!'

Elvis must have wondered how much worse it could get when an equally drugged Jerry Lee Lewis showed up at Graceland with a gun, threatening to shoot him. Fortunately, Elvis wasn't home, although I wonder what would have happened if he had been: two zonked-out patients of Dr. Nick having a go at each other. Jerry Lee's biographer, Chas White (Dr. Rock) says, 'Elvis loved Jerry Lee's piano playing and always liked him. This thing about them being arch-enemies was partly concocted by the media and partly by Jerry Lee himself in his impish ways. When Elvis died, a camera crew went into Jerry's dressing room and he said, 'I'm glad. Now I'll be able to show them who is the King'. He wasn't thinking – he didn't realise that 50 million viewers would hear him say that. Jerry Lee was on about three times as many drugs as Elvis.'

Early in December, Elvis was back in Las Vegas with his weight slightly reduced. On 5 December he sat on a chair to perform as he had sprained his ankle in the bathroom. Not sure I believe this but I've been told that he was doing 'Hurt' so forcefully that the glasses were vibrating on the front tables.

He brought Lisa Marie on stage and gave her a golf cart for Christmas. Elvis gave a few concerts between Christmas and the New Year. He was in excellent form for the New Year's Eve concert in Pittsburgh, and maybe he was the only person ever to lose weight over Christmas.

The New Year started badly as Ginger didn't want to accompany Elvis to some late-night sessions at Buzz Cason's Creative Workshop in Nashville. Elvis went to Nashville but returned the next day without having stepped in the studio. Felton Jarvis, a cool character with immense patience, offered to bring the equipment to Graceland again but Elvis said he was too ill. He was taking pills at a phenomenal rate.

Elvis started touring again in February 1977, his first concert being at the Sportatorium in Hollywood, Florida, close to Fort Lauderdale. Elvis giggled as he sang 'Release Me', another bad sign. On the other hand, he gave a very good show in Charlotte, North Carolina.

On 30 March he changed the first line of 'Can't Help Falling In Love' to 'Wise men know when it's time to go'. The next four dates were cancelled and he spent a week in Memphis Baptist Hospital.

Donna Presley Early: 'My mother said to him, 'Baby, you need to take some time off and get well', and Elvis, thinking of everyone but himself, said, 'Aunt Nash, if I take off six months or a year, that is not a problem for me, but it is for the people who work with me as their livelihoods depend on me. If I don't work, then they don't work and they can't feed their families and I can't do that to them'.'

In May in Landover, Maryland, he said he had to leave the stage for 'nature's call'. He returned to finish his performance.

Elvis was performing until his death but his concerts had become erratic and shambolic. Word was spreading as, for the first time in his life, they were not all sell-outs. Elvis collapsed on stage in Louisville and Dr. Nichopoulos had to bring him round. Elvis now struggled through songs he had sung with ease. You'll have seen him out of breath, looking as though he will never finish 'My Way'. Sinatra at 53 had been too young to sing, 'And now the end is near, And so I face the final curtain', but for Elvis at 42, it was perfect.

According to Paul Anka, Presley changed the nature of 'My Way'. 'That song had resonance for him but not in the way I intended. Given his pathetic state at the end, it was the opposite sense of what the words meant for Sinatra. There was nothing defiant or heroic about Elvis at that point.'

Elvis was worried about the bodyguards' book which would be published soon. It was already being serialised very unflatteringly, *The Sun* running UK exclusives, and Elvis knew it would be hard to reject their claims.

Elvis was pleased that his father and Dee Stanley had had a quickie divorce in the Dominican Republic, but Vernon's health was deteriorating with one cardiac complaint after another. Both Elvis and Vernon had fallen out with the Colonel as they had finally twigged that Elvis was covering his gambling debts in Vegas. The only thing that gave Elvis any satisfaction was riding his motorbike.

'Way Down' was released as a single in June 1977 and the songwriter Layng Martine commented, 'To see my name on a record with Elvis seemed completely impossible.' It was included on Elvis' new album, *Moody Blue,* the title track being a single which had only sold moderately well. There were ten tracks: the six remaining ones from the Jungle Room and four live cuts – 'Let Me Be There' taken from his live album in Memphis and three from the Civic Centre in Saginaw, Michigan: a very passionate 'Unchained Melody' with Elvis at the piano, another Olivia pop / country song, 'If You Love Me (Let Me Know)' and a goodtime version of the Diamonds' 'Little Darlin''. The album was pressed on blue plastic but soon there would be another sure-fire tactic to encourage sales.

Tim Rice: 'The song that Andrew and I wrote, 'It's Easy for You' was the final track on *Moody Blue* and I only had the album a couple of days before his death. I had two days of listening to this wonderful voice making a reasonable fist of our nice but lightweight song. I was so pleased that Elvis had actually spent five minutes learning our song and recording it. Elvis moved to that great jukebox in the sky, and so I had the last track on the last side of his last album while he was still alive. About the same time, I had the last track on the last side of the last album of Bing Crosby which was a song I wrote with Marvin Hamlisch called ironically 'The Only Way To Go', and I thought, 'Oh my goodness, there's a curse here.'

CBS broadcast a TV special, *Elvis in Concert*, which featured two of his latter-day concerts: 19 June at Omaha, Nebraska and 21 June at Rapid City, South Dakota. It was a 50-minute programme with documentary material from Vernon Presley and the fans and just 30 minutes of music. The producers did their best, but Elvis looked unwell and his breathing was bad. Elvis did one of his daft narrations in 'Are You Lonesome Tonight' in Rapid City, but Elvis always struggled with the song. A live version from 1969 where he cracks up was released in 1982 and made the UK Top 30: the public have argued over this – was this evidence that Elvis was strung out or was it just Elvis having fun? In this instance, the latter.

The songs in the documentary were familiar but it wasn't often that he returned to 'Hawaiian Wedding Song'. He was no longer learning new material for the stage but he had a new opening for 'It's Now or Never' in which Shaun Nielsen sang 'O Sole Mio'.

On 24 June, Elvis and his bodyguards were on his way from a stadium in Madison, Wisconsin. They saw someone being beaten up so out stepped Elvis with his police badge and Derringer. He told the lads to take him out instead but Elvis was the peacemaker. Soon everyone was friendly and posing for pictures. Elvis gave them a little lecture about God's good graces and said goodbye.

The next night he apologised for being late at Riverfront Stadium in Cincinnati, Ohio as he had been to the dentist: we've heard that one before. He included 'My Way' but read the lyrics.

The following day was his final concert appearance at the Market Square Arena in Indianapolis, Indiana. He wore his Aztec jumpsuit and included a brilliantly sung version of 'Bridge over Troubled Water'. In a surprisingly apt moment, Vernon Presley appeared on stage with him. Since 1969, Elvis had given 1,120 stage performances, with over 800 of them in Nevada.

Elvis' next concert was in Portland, Maine on August 17 and, as he had no other commitments, he had seven weeks' holiday. At times he was in good spirits, hiring the Libertyland Amusement Park for nine-year-old Lisa Marie and her friends, but there were black moments.

Elvis threw some notes away on 5 December 1976, but they were saved. He was fed up with Vegas and he wrote, 'I feel so alone sometimes, the night is quiet for me. I would love to be able to sleep.' He added, 'I don't know who I can talk to anymore. Or turn to. I only have myself and the Lord. Help me, Lord, to know the right thing.' Wayne Newton has written a song, 'The Letter', around this.

Elvis weighed 18 stone, which isn't excessive for a six foot male, and he was planning rapid weight loss; he wanted to be down to 15 stone for the next dates. He did some exercise, playing racquetball and riding his motorbike. The book, *Elvis – What Happened?*, was published on 1 August 1977. The book was embarrassing enough but the fans might avoid it. However, they couldn't miss the sleazy serialisations in the newspapers. Elvis had a whole other life that relatively few people knew about: millions of people still thought he didn't even smoke or drink. According to the book, Elvis liked to visit a funeral parlour and sit with the corpses.

Donna Presley Early: 'It hurt him terribly to think that three men he had shared his life with and become brothers with had been so disloyal. Elvis was an extremely loyal person and he did call them and say, 'I can't tell you it didn't hurt me because it did, but if you ever need me, I'm here.' Isn't that a wonderful thing to do? I don't know what they were thinking of but it was not something that they should have done. No one is perfect and Elvis certainly wasn't, but neither were they.'

Elvis felt betrayed by the book, which made him out to be worse than the 60s counterculture he had been condemning. David Stanley; 'I was in Mobile, Alabama with him. He was sitting on a bed and saying, 'My life is over'. He felt that he had been exposed and that this life was over. But if he had said, 'Okay' and dealt with his demons in public, the world would have embraced him all the more and he would have remained alive.'

Around the time of his death, Johnny Cash was recording a TV special with Carl Perkins, Roy Orbison and Jerry Lee Lewis. If Elvis could visit President Nixon on a whim, why didn't he just go along to the TV studios and have a great time? Wouldn't that have been the best answer to his critics?

On August 15, Elvis had been out on his Harley. He visited his dentist for genuine dental work at 10.30pm. There was no need to visit the dentist for drugs as Dr. Nichopoulos had completed a prescription for over 600 pills. The singer received 20cc and 50 pills of Dilaudid (a powerful painkiller usually given as a last resort to cancer sufferers), 100 Percodans, 150 Quaaludes, 178 Dexedrine pills, 12 Amytal pills and 100 Biphetamine pills. The pills also indicated his depression. Rick Stanley had been to collect the prescription and when he returned, Presley asked him to pray for salvation with him.

Elvis was back at Graceland in the early hours of the morning. First he wanted peach ice cream and chocolate chip cookies and then he had what he called his 'first attack' about 4am, which was an envelope containing many different pills, prepared by his nurse. Before he went to bed, he kissed Lisa Marie goodnight for the last time.

Around 4.30am, he played racquetball with Billy and Jo Smith; presumably poor Billy and his wife had been sleeping soundly. He was wearing his blue sweater with DEA (Drug Enforcement Agency) on the front. The game continued on and off until 6am and then he played 'Blue Eyes Crying in the Rain'. It would be the last song he would sing: 'Someday when we meet up yonder, We'll walk hand in hand again.' He told the cook that he was not hungry and wanted to rest.

Elvis took some medication to sleep but Ginger sat with him in his bedroom until 9am. He rang Nurse Cocke and asked her to rub his back before he had to leave at 5pm. He told Ginger he was going to the bathroom and he took a book, *A Scientific Search for the Face of Jesus* by Frank Adams, given to him by Larry Geller. There was a barber's chair in the bathroom for when he had his hair dyed and Ginger told him not to fall asleep. Elvis last words were 'Okay, I won't.'

Ginger went to sleep herself and awoke five hours later at 1.30pm. Elvis wasn't next to her. She knocked on the bathroom door and as there was no answer, she looked inside. Elvis was curled up on the floor. She called for Joe Esposito who confirmed that he was not breathing. He called for an ambulance and Elvis was taken to the Baptist Memorial Hospital where he was pronounced dead at 3.30pm. Ginger told Lisa Marie, who immediately wanted to call Linda Thompson, whom she liked very much, and tell her.

Within minutes, the Memphis radio station WMPS broke the story. The hospital, perhaps with prompting from Dr. Nichopoulos, completed a death certificate saying that he had died of heart disease. The coroner told the TV reporters that Elvis Presley had died from cardiac arrhythmia, an irregular heartbeat, but the investigations hadn't been completed.

It was thought to be a heart attack brought on by colonic problems. In short, Elvis Presley was desperate to open his bowels and strained too hard. Had constipation killed the King? An autopsy showed that his bowels were blocked by a clay-like substance which acted as a barrier against his regular food intake.

Donna Presley Early: 'We all knew that Elvis had infirmities in his body and he wasn't well, but Elvis was someone who was larger than life and you could never see anything like that coming. His passing took all of us by surprise and it left a huge hole in our families and in our hearts, but when you love someone and you continue your love for them, they are with you always.'

Dr. Nichopoulos was keen to point out that there was no drug abuse. Almost certainly, he wanted to avoid a full autopsy.

Meanwhile, sensing trouble, Elvis' room was cleared of drugs.

On 17 August 1977, Elvis was meant to be at Portland, Maine. Then he was to play New York, Connecticut, Kentucky, Virginia, North Carolina and on 27/28 August, Memphis. Instead, he would lie in state at Graceland. The gates were opened at 3pm and several thousand mourners saw Elvis, dressed in a white suit made by Lansky's, light blue shirt and silver tie, his body in a white casket. Many thousands didn't get to see him and scuffles broke out. Over 100 fans fainted with the heat.

Elvis' death and its aftermath was to occupy the front pages of national newspapers for over a week. There were 3,000 floral tributes at Graceland.

Bruce Springsteen, who had tickets to see him at Madison Square Garden, said, 'It was like somebody took a piece out of me. There have been pretenders. There have been contenders. But there is only one King.'

President Carter said, 'Elvis' death deprives our country of a part of itself. He was unique and irreplaceable. His music and his personality permanently changed the face of American popular culture.'

James Brown: 'Elvis gave black people a voice.'

Bob Dylan: 'If it wasn't for Elvis and Hank Williams, I couldn't be doing what I do today.'

The Times did not agree. Its uncredited leader proclaimed, 'While Presley himself was an indifferent singer and musician, performing for the most part mediocre songs, a poor actor and it seems, a totally uninteresting person, the phenomenon which he became was of considerable social significance.' It prompted Tim Rice to respond, 'This is simply not true and I would be interested to know which popular singers you consider to be superior to Presley. Or are you unwilling to admit that any popular singers have any merit whatsoever?'

R.G. Short wrote, 'Your leading articles implied that Elvis Presley's huge popularity was somehow in spite of, rather than because of, his music. This sneer is untrue and unfair. People did not buy Elvis Presley's records in order to annoy their parents. They bought them because they derived enormous pleasure from them.'

The funeral, organised at lightning speed, was at Graceland at 2pm the following day. The roads were packed with people and many climbed trees to get a better view. There would also be a candlelit vigil the next night. The hotels were already busy because of a Shriners' Convention, so they became filled to capacity.

The authorities in Memphis didn't like the idea of Presley being buried at Graceland but Vernon saw the Mayor and it was agreed that the bodies could be kept at Forest Hill until Graceland was ready.

The mourners included Burt Reynolds, John Wayne, Ann-Margret and President

Elvis Presley: Caught in a Trap

Kennedy's daughter, Caroline. The service was conducted by the evangelist Rex Humbard. The organist played 'Danny Boy', Kathy Westmoreland sang 'My Heavenly Father Watches over Me', Jake Hess of the Statesmen sang 'Known Only to Him', James Blackwood 'How Great Thou Art', J.D. Sumner and the Stamps 'His Hand in Mine', and Jackie Kahane said, 'Ladies and gentlemen, Elvis has left the building for the last time.' His body was taken three miles to the Forest Hill cemetery.

Donna Presley Early: 'When we headed back to where Elvis was going to be interred, the roads were five or six deep with thousands and thousands of fans. Elvis made a difference to people's lives, he touched people in their hearts and when you can touch people in their hearts, then they raise their children and their grandchildren on you.'

Elvis was placed close to his mother in a mausoleum. But not for long. There were attempts to steal his body, though what the body-snatchers would have done with it is unknown. It was taken back to the cemetery and then Elvis and Gladys were brought to Graceland.

Colonel Parker had been at the funeral, dressed in an Hawaiian shirt, an embarrassment to everyone. Maybe he was having a hard time himself – his wife had dementia and his stepson Bobby had died from multiple sclerosis – but surely all his experience should have stopped him from making ridiculous statements – 'This changes nothing. It's like when he was away in the army. I'll go right on managing him.' Parker was acknowledging that Elvis was worth more dead than alive.

He then flew to New York to see RCA and ensure that they would meet the demands for Elvis products. Several performers have told me that their own records were put on hold as everybody was working on Elvis.

Death had revitalised Elvis' career and yet the US chart placings don't really confirm this story. The US single of 'Way Down' was on the charts for three months and although it didn't climb higher than No.18, it was a No.1 country hit. The album of *Moody Blue* went to No.3, and if the back catalogue was shifting as well, it was not in sufficient quantities to reach the charts.

In the UK, the sales were more noticeable and 'Way Down' was No.1 for five weeks. 'Way Down' became Elvis's 17th number one, putting him on a par with the Beatles. Until 2002, that is.

In the UK, the RCA records were normally pressed at a factory in Washington, County Durham. Because of flagging demand, they had issued 90 redundancy notices. These were withdrawn but the unions objected, saying that the workers must have a 12-month guarantee of work. It was soon resolved as the workers wanted to work and 16 of Presley's 36 albums moved into the Top 200 album sellers.

In the UK, RCA reissued all his No.1 singles at 70p each and a box of all 16 for £12. Seven made the Top 50 on September 3 with 'It's Now or Never' faring best at No.39. On the LP front, *Moody Blue* went to No.3 and a collection of country sides, *Welcome to My World*, which hadn't made the listings early in 1977, was a Top 10 album. It included just one new track, a live version of 'I Can't Stop Loving You'. The most successful of the vintage products was *G I Blues*, reaching No.14. In October, Charly put early performances together with some reminiscences for *The Sun Years*: it made No.31. In 1982, Magnum Force issued an album of broadcast tributes to Elvis, compiled by Tony Prince of Radio Luxemburg.

RCA had licensed tracks for a TV-advertised compilation, *40 Greatest Hits*, on

Arcade and it had topped the album charts in 1975. Arcade's licence to press any more had expired but they continued to do so, enabling the product to return to the top of the album charts. Eventually RCA took over the compilation and marketed it themselves for Christmas 1978. An identical product issued by K-Tel in France was exported to the UK and sold here. There was a successful mail order collection of a 7-LP boxed-set through Reader's Digest.

In Germany, 'Way Down' was No.5 and a reissue of 'Love Me Tender', No.40. In France, 'Way Down' was in the Top 10. It wasn't Elvis' best record by any means and the title was unfortunate but then you can't pick your moment.

Rolling Stone had its writers and designers working for four days straight to produce a special issue devoted to Elvis. The London office solicited opinions from the new British punk scene.

In a wonderfully defiant moment, *Melody Maker* had twin lead stories – one about Elvis Presley, one about the Sex Pistols. A young British singer and songwriter Declan MacManus had made his first album, *My Aim Is True*. He called himself Elvis Costello which now seemed a bad joke. Stiff Records worked this round to Elvis' advantage and it became a seminal New Wave album.

Elvis Costello: 'Declan was a difficult name for people to grasp as it is not very common in England, and MacManus made it even more difficult. If I rang someone to say I was coming down to play, they could never grasp my name, so I needed something easier on the ear. I picked Costello from the family rather than something out of thin air. My first manager chose the Elvis part which was a double dare – you look people straight in the face and say, 'I am called Elvis'. It was outrageous but it was not as much a liability as being called Sid Vicious. I took the name in 1976 and I was putting out records at the back end of 1976 while I was still in a day job. As soon as the first album came out, I had to take the plunge and go professional. A week later I was on the cover of *Melody Maker* and it was like five years' rehearsal for overnight success.' (My friend Steve Davies always refers to Costello as 'the proper Elvis'. Also, there is a French rock'n'roll singer with several albums to his credit known as Jesse Garon, the name of Elvis' twin.)

Elvis Presley died at the very moment that punk was taking off. Johnny Rotten called his death 'fuckin' good riddance to bad rubbish'. Danny Baker at the London punk club, the Vortex, was infuriated by the contempt for Elvis. He told the audience that Elvis was the first punk and got hit by a bottle.

Danny Baker was right. The Clash sang 'No Elvis, no Beatles, no Rolling Stones' but they were wrong and they knew it. Their lead singer, Joe Strummer, like Elvis Costello and Billy Idol was creating his own version of Elvis. The plain-spoken lyrics and bog-standard chords of rockabilly were the inspiration for punk, which was the new rockabilly. Strip away the bedraggled clothes, the unkempt appearances, the safety pins and tattoos, and there was rockabilly. The Vegas Presley was not for them but the 1950s Presley certainly was. Presley's sneer was pure punk.

The outpouring of public grief for a celebrity had never been seen on this level before and there were several comments in the British press that this was tacky and distasteful, that it was somehow typical of Americans, shedding tears for somebody that they hadn't even met. However, it wasn't a one-off and it set a new standard for superstar deaths. We have seen similar displays for John Lennon (1980), Michael Jackson (2009),

Whitney Houston (2012) and David Bowie (2016).

In the next chapter, I will look at some of the sightings of Elvis. Before Elvis, there had been many sightings of Hitler and there have also been many sightings of Lord Lucan and Shergar but so far as I know there have been none for Princess Diana. It seems odd that nobody has claimed to have seen (or to have been healed by) Diana: could it be that the press has curbed such stories as the watchdogs would take a dim view. My own theory is that, although greatly loved, Elvis had become a figure of fun by the time of his death and the sightings continue from that. Diana was a folk hero at the time of her death in 1997 and her death was so unexpected that it was taken far more seriously.

Curiously though the flash cars and the ostentatious bling of the Vegas period became an inspiration for rappers.

Even though there was a studio version, a live take of 'My Way' was the first single to be released after Elvis' death and it went to No.9 in the UK; by reaching No.22 it became the highest-placed version of the song on the US chart. Sid Vicious chose to spit out the words for a single, made with jazz musicians in France, and his version was a UK Top 10 hit in 1978, helped by a video in which he gunned down all in sight before collapsing himself. This version was used at the end of Martin Scorsese's *Goodfellas*. Another wrecked celebrity, Shane McGowan of the Pogues, returned the song to the Top 30 in 1996.

As well as records, the fans were buying posters, souvenir magazines, books, badges and belt buckles – anything with 'Elvis' on it. His last will and testament, dating from March 1977, was selling at £2 a copy, a genuine copy, though not an official product. Priscilla and Ginger were not beneficiaries, although Ginger was a witness to it. He left everything to Lisa Marie, his grandmother Minnie Mae and his father Vernon. If they died, the assets would revert to Lisa Marie at the age of 25. No charities were mentioned.

In 1978 Elvis was nominated for a Grammy for 'Softly as I Leave You'. The category was Best Country Vocal Performance, and which country did the judges have in mind? Willie Nelson with 'Georgia on My Mind' was the popular winner, so much so that one of the losers, Johnny Paycheck, shouted out, 'Way to go, Willie!'

As soon as Elvis had died, Vernon told Dr. Nichopoulos to maintain his payments on a $250,000 loan and said he would no longer be his own doctor. But there was good news for Dr. Nick. At the autopsy, Dr. Jerry Francisco, the Shelby County medical examiner, said that Presley was killed by cardiac arrhythmia and arterial sclerosis. The death was not drug-related, although there were traces of potentially dangerous drugs in his body. Elvis' circulation was unusual for a 42-year-old man. His liver was in bad shape, three times the normal size, his heart was enlarged, twice the normal size, and his colon was twisted.

In 1980, Dr. Nichopoulos was acquitted on grounds of unethical conduct and malpractice but he was convicted of dispensing controlled substances 'not in good faith' to relieve suffering. Nine other patients were listed including Jerry Lee Lewis.

James Thompson and Charles Cole published *The Death of Elvis; What Really Happened* in 1991, which revealed the staggering amount of drugs that Dr. Nichopoulos had prescribed. As a result, the evidence was re-examined and in 1995, Dr. Nick lost his licence. He worked for four years as Jerry Lee Lewis' road manager followed by

Spencer Leigh

six years of pushing papers at FedEx. He then sold his Elvis memorabilia and wrote *The King and Dr. Nichopoulos* in a desperate attempt to clear his name, but offering no explanation for his own behaviour. According to Dr. Nick, Elvis collapsed on the floor and suffocated in the shag-pile. If Elvis had had linoleum in his bathroom, he would still be alive.

CHAPTER 16
I Was Coming Back Anyway

'Bush is comparing me to Elvis. I don't think Bush liked Elvis very much and that's just another thing that's wrong with him.'
President Clinton

I. Goin' Up, Goin' Down

(A) The Imitation Game

Elvis Presley was so distinctive in his jumpsuits that Elvis impersonators were lining up long before his death. Indeed, you could argue that Elvis Presley had become the first Elvis impersonator.

In the mid-70s, Todd Slaughter, who ran the UK fan club, asked Freddie Starr to play the annual convention and but warned him to be careful. The audience would turn on him if that they thought it was a send-up. He did it brilliantly and blew them away.

Tom Jones' road manager, Tony Cartwright, took Freddie to Vegas but he was apprehensive about introducing him to Elvis as Elvis might be offended. When Freddie did meet Elvis, he did an impression and Elvis laughed and said, 'You're good, man.' Elvis gave him a letter of endorsement and so he was close to being the official Elvis Presley impersonator.

His main rival was American TV comedian Andy Kaufman, who often performed as Elvis for comic effect. When he appeared on the 1979 edition of *The Johnny Cash Christmas Show*, he played the Vegas Presley, singing 'That's When Your Heartaches Begin'.

Before his death, Elvis had become such an iconic figure that he had spawned hundreds of impersonators. Colonel Parker hadn't seen this coming and he hadn't liked it, ordering them to stop and threatening to sue. Then he saw how they could help him when Elvis died.

Not wanting to lose out on bookings at the Las Vegas Hilton, Colonel Parker put together *A Tribute to Elvis* with Alan Meyer performing his songs. Images of Elvis were shown as Meyer performed with dancers, singers and musicians. It sold out for 16 weeks with three shows a day. Meyer's single, 'The Lonely King of Rock'n'Roll', didn't make much headway but he was shifting 800 albums a week at his shows. Parker thought this would continue forever and indeed, there are Presley shows in Vegas to this day with similar shows around the world.

Parker didn't benefit from them: one, he lost control of marketing Elvis Presley and two, a totally unofficial market developed of Elvis tribute acts. There is now the Professional Elvis Impersonators Association, but that is the tip of the iceberg as tributes can occur at any time and in any place. I was amongst the bars and restaurants in London Docklands one morning and I saw a team of cleaners at work – dressed in jumpsuits with jet black wigs and stick-on sideburns. Only last week I saw the test cricketer Freddie Flintoff dressed as Elvis and singing his songs in the TV comedy quiz, *A League of Their Own*.

I am sure that there are fine Elvis impersonators in every city and probably every town in the UK. I have been particularly impressed by Chris Clayton in Liverpool but I have no yardstick for comparing him with the rest of the UK. However, he has one of the few tributes that does justice to both the Sun Elvis and the Vegas Elvis. I know too that he performs from a great love of the music and the man himself.

Then again, Billy, an Elvis impersonator from Merseyside, died when a concrete staircase fell on him. He had been singing Elvis songs since the 60s and everybody knew him as Billy Elvis. He was buried in his Elvis outfit and over 100 people went to the funeral dressed as Elvis.

During 2016, Judge Rinder on ITV was hearing a dispute between Patrick Duggan, the owner of the Epstein Hotel in Liverpool, and an Elvis impersonator, Johnny Rocco, who had played the Cavern in the early 60s. Johnny was booked for £300 to entertain at a charity event. He arrived without a band and without backing tapes and sang 'American Trilogy' a cappella. Everybody was sniggering. Patrick refused to pay him, and Judge Rinder agreed.

Although nearly everyone would agree that the 1950s records represent the most creative period of Elvis' life, 80% of the impersonators choose the latter-day Elvis. Why? Because you have to be young and good looking to stand a chance as the young Elvis but you can be any shape you want as the older Elvis. I don't see that as a bad thing – dressing as the older Elvis has provided much fun and entertainment. After all, one of the US TV commercials for Viagra features a rewritten Elvis hit, 'Viva Viagra'.

Donna Presley Early: 'Elvis impersonators are involved in nearly all the Elvis events that I go to and as they want to keep the music alive, that's fine by me. If it is done with integrity and love and honour and wanting to give back to Elvis what he has done for them, that's great.'

Some impersonators take it more seriously than others, but this is not confined to Elvis. I have not personally met anyone who has had his features changed because of Elvis but I have met someone who changed his nose to look like Paul McCartney. A lot of people, both men and women, have had an Elvis tattoo, so that they can wake up to Elvis every morning.

Neither race nor gender is an issue. The scriptwriter Mark Kelly says, 'I went for a meal in a Chinese restaurant in south London and the attraction was Chinese Elvis. On arrival, we were told that he had been double-booked but he should turn up later. His replacement was another Chinese Elvis. He was quite good as a Vegas period Elvis but then the 'real' Chinese Elvis, also a Vegas Elvis, turned up and we had them alternating, though not performing together.'

(B) Elvis Lives

Elvis Presley was pronounced dead at 3.30pm on 16 August 1977 at the Baptist Memorial Hospital in Memphis, Tennessee. Or was he? Over the years, I have assembled

Elvis Presley: Caught in a Trap

newspaper cuttings and press releases on hundreds of musicians and my Elvis files are subdivided by category. It is with some embarrassment that I have one marked *Elvis Lives*. Ever since 1978, I have kept stories about people who thought that Elvis was still alive.

Mostly this is seen as fun and harmless, but there are serious implications. Rock historian and academic Greil Marcus: 'There is a deeply coded impulse in Western culture to refuse to believe that heroes who die prematurely and with their legacies unsettled have actually died. It goes back at least as far as King Arthur and possibly further than that. Billy the Kid died in the 1880s when he was shot by Pat Garrett and in the 1920s you couldn't visit New Mexico without tripping over someone who was claiming to be Billy the Kid. The same thing happened with the aviator Amelia Earhart in the 1930s. The public doesn't want to let them go.' (Don't want to argue with the mighty Marcus but King Arthur was probably fictional.)

The rumours about Elvis' continued existence have subsided by now but around 1993, the odds with the bookmakers, William Hill, on Elvis being alive were 500 to 1. Ciara Parkes of Hammersmith, west London placed a £250 bet with the bookies and was hoping for a £125,000 pay-out. She didn't have a ghost of a chance, but maybe she had been in touch with Liz Prince of Atlanta, Georgia, who claimed a three-year fling with Elvis from 1978 to 1981 and said she received a call from him every Christmas.

The answer to any question in a book title is invariably no, so I was sceptical when the journalist Gail Brewer-Giorgio wrote a book called *Is Elvis Alive?* She reported that when an Elvis lookalike died at Graceland, Elvis saw this as an opportunity to disappear. His gravestone says 'Elvis Aaron Presley' and yet he was born 'Elvis Aron Presley'. Apparently, the King thought it would be bad luck to have his real name on a gravestone.

And that's not all. The first Elvis sighting after his death was by mother-of-five Louise Welling and further sightings followed in Tennessee, Oklahoma, Michigan, Hawaii and New York. In 1989, *The People* reported that they had located Elvis on a farm in Georgia and had the photographs to prove it. Oh yeah?

Elvis sightings have disappeared by now, as Elvis would have to be over 80, but they were rife in the years following his death. Some were serious, some were fun, such as Elvis eating burgers in McDonalds or running a fish'n'chip shop in Yorkshire. It prompted the hit single by Kirsty MacColl, 'There's a Guy Works Down the Chipshop Swears He's Elvis' (1981).

The Southern record producer, Major Bill Smith, discovered Bruce Channel and Paul and Paula, and knew Elvis well. So much so that Elvis called him in 1980 and told him that his 'death' was all part of an insurance fraud.

In 1989, the DJ Tony Blackburn stated that his TV had been taken over by aliens singing Elvis Presley songs. Elvis was using them to thank him for playing his music.

This is Jimmy Webb telling me about his 1993 song, 'Elvis and Me': 'It's a diary entry but it is also a fan story – the fan who still believes he's alive, the fan who thinks he's in that empty chair, the fan who'll buy anything. In the last verse, I say, 'And I know that's wrong, but I just can't set him free', so on another level of perception, it's about the American mysticism of Elvis and the fact that every year, on the anniversary of his death, more and more people show up at Graceland, holding candles in a very eerie vigil, almost expecting a resurrection. Many thousands don't accept the fact that he ever died, so it's a new pop theology and who knows where that leads? How will this guy be perceived 100 years from now? I see people on talk shows saying they've seen him and they are playing taped conversations. Okay, they're fakes but it makes you think twice. The concept of Elvis being alive is more important than whether he really is or not. If so many people want him alive, then he'll be alive. I'd love to be around in a couple of hundred years' time to see how this has mutated. It's an amazing phenomenon and Elvis may be the leader of a new religion.'

If this happens, you can imagine the Elvis commandments: 'Love me tender' and 'Don't be cruel', and you can see the potential for this in Carl Perkins' assessment, 'We've lost the most popular man that ever walked on this planet since Jesus Christ himself was here.'

I'm not sure that Elvis/Jesus comparisons hold any substance but they have amused stoned writers like Hunter S. Thompson and Kinky Friedman (*Elvis, Jesus And Coca-Cola*, 1993). There is a very entertaining painting, *The Last Supper*, with Elvis as Christ by Guy Peellaert, where the 12 disciples are fellow rock'n'roll stars and all sharing burgers and Coke. I'm not sure that the Elvis and Jesus comparisons hold much weight. Elvis was too fond of food for starters and would never have fasted in the wilderness.

If Jimmy Webb's instincts are correct, maybe Elvis will turn out to be the new L. Ron Hubbard, and it is not without irony that Priscilla converted to Scientology in the early 1980s. It was thought that the religion was hoping to capture the considerable funds that Elvis was generating. That hasn't happened, largely because Lisa Marie has broken with Scientology. In her 2012 song, 'So Long', she was putting the religion behind her: 'Religion so corrupt and ruining lives.'

(C) Family Matters
Because Lisa Marie was only a child when her father died, the Memphis courts had to scrutinise any financial dealings on her behalf and this proved to be Colonel Parker's downfall. As soon as Elvis died, Colonel Parker had Vernon Presley sign an authorisation so that he could continue to manage Elvis, but the Memphis courts set this aside – the court was representing Lisa Marie's interests and so all agreements between Elvis and Colonel Parker ended on Presley's death.

The judiciary realised the deals were far more beneficial to Colonel Parker than the Presley family. The court was highly critical of Parker's high percentage and concluded that Presley had been exploited for years. Parker's contract would not be renewed and, although divorced from Elvis, Priscilla would administer the estate until Lisa Marie was 25.

Vernon's health had not been good for many years – at one stage, he and Elvis had been in adjacent hospital beds – and he died of a heart attack on 26 June 1979 at the age of 63. He was buried in Graceland between Gladys and Elvis: some say he shouldn't be between them but he was the head of the family.

David Stanley: 'The only thing that Elvis and Vernon had in common was an incredible sense of humour. If you couldn't cut a joke, you couldn't be around them. Other than that, there were no similarities. Who was Elvis like? Elvis. Who does Elvis remind you of? Elvis. Does Elvis remind you of anyone else? Only Elvis. He was charismatic and he would dominate a room. I could tell instinctively when Elvis was in Graceland and when he wasn't. His presence was inexplicable. His magnetism was beyond comprehension.'

Rocking in the background and taking her snuff was Elvis' grandmother, Minnie Mae. She, Vernon and Elvis' daughter were the only beneficiaries of Elvis' will. Elvis did not leave anything to Colonel Parker, but what can you give a man who already has your soul? Minnie Mae outlived Gladys, Vernon and Elvis, dying in 1980 at the age of 86.

This being America, there have naturally been others wanting a share of the booty. Elvis Aaron Presley Jr, for example, claimed to be the love child of Elvis Presley and Dolores Hart.

Priscilla received a goldmine in the mid-80s when a court ruled that the Presley estate owned his image. This overthrew the standard principle that the dead had no rights.

Colonel Parker was out of the picture. He didn't take on another client, although he did offer Rick Nelson some advice. For all his faults, he had been an important figure in Elvis' life and in the commercial world at large. Surely the aggressive marketing that we often see today owes something to Parker's behaviour.

His wife, Marie, who'd had Alzheimer's for some years and didn't recognise him, died in 1986. To everyone's surprise, Parker then married his secretary Loanne Miller, who was 26 years younger than he was. Parker was in a wheelchair, mostly living in Vegas and still gambling: it seems likely that the casinos gave him special counters so that the bets didn't count. He made occasional public appearances, such as launching the commemorative postage stamp for Elvis' birthday in 1993 and showing he was still stuck on Elvis. At his 85th birthday party, he said, 'I'm still working for you, Elvis,' but this was a vain boast. He died on 21 January 1997 at the age of 87 and, in view of his gambling, it is surprising that he left as much as $900,000.

Just like Elvis, 'How Great Thou Art' was sung at the Colonel's funeral. The hotelier Henri Lewin said, 'You and Elvis are together again. I know you both looked forward to this moment.' I somehow doubt that.

Shortly after his death, the Memphis Mafia was disbanded. Many of them have appeared at Elvis conventions and given talks about the King. Red West became a Hollywood actor, appearing in supporting roles in many films and TV series. Sonny West has done this too, working as a stuntman for some years. Jerry Schilling became the road manager for Billy Joel and Joe Esposito worked for the Bee Gees and Michael Jackson.

Joe's ex-wife Joanie married into the Kardashian family and there are several Presley links here, as the patriarch Robert Kardashian dated Priscilla Presley and then married Kris Jenner, whose husband Bruce had been married to Linda Thompson.

If Elvis had returned in the 1980s, he would have been surprised to see Priscilla running his estate and furthermore, making such a good job of it. From the start, she rewrote history, acting as though they had been eternal lovers and never divorced. In reality, Elvis had tried to woo her back, but she wasn't having any of it. He was acting so irrationally that it would have been walking into hell. She must have been worried whenever Lisa Marie was with him at Graceland: not that she feared for her safety but that the little girl would notice things that she shouldn't.

Priscilla Presley was astute and didn't see Colonel Parker as a Dutch uncle. She knew how show business operated and she realised that Elvis' actual financial assets were nothing compared to the potential of a dead Elvis. As a property, Graceland might fetch a couple of million dollars but if it became a tourist attraction, the rewards could be endless. What is more, she had had the city of Memphis completely on her side.

Fortunately for this venture, Elvis had never thrown much away. He even kept his old shirts. There were eight warehouses packed with his possessions and so a lot of care could be taken in getting Graceland right.

Priscilla wrote a memoir, *Elvis and Me*, in 1985, but it glossed over the most intriguing aspects of their relationship and read like a PR exercise. In 1975, Priscilla broke up with Mike Stone, who became a card dealer in Las Vegas. Priscilla then had a period where she was almost as carefree as Elvis. She lived with a former marine, Mike Edwards and left him for flings with Julio Iglesias, and Richard Gere. She was with the photographer Terry O'Neill for some time and then the film producer and entrepreneur, Marco Garibaldi, with whom she has a son, Navarone.

Priscilla could hardly have welcomed, *Priscilla, Elvis and Me*, written by her former boyfriend, Mike Edwards. Edwards, who had done a photoshoot for *Playgirl*, was with Priscilla for some years. He became an alcoholic, partly because he was replacing Presley in Priscilla's affection, but he provided a level-headed account of life in Presleyworld. According to the book, Mike and Priscilla agreed to an abortion which they both regretted. There were some uncomfortable comments regarding his feelings towards Lisa Marie, who was 13 at the time.

Elvis was unhappy when Hal Wallis had suggested Priscilla could make some films as the camera would love her, but that has proved to be the case. She had success in the TV series *Dallas* as Jenna Wade and in the film franchise, *The Naked Gun* (1988, 1991, 1994), with Leslie Nielsen. She has created the top-selling perfumes, 'Moment' and 'Experiences'.

In recent years, Priscilla has appeared in the UK in pantomime in Wimbledon, Milton Keynes and Manchester, twice as the evil witch in *Snow White and the Seven Dwarfs* in which she sang 'Trouble' and once as the genie of the lamp in *Aladdin*. She had no financial need to do this, although it was good PR for Graceland and something she enjoyed. There is no American equivalent to pantomime but it was surely the inspiration for Elvis' film, *Harem Holiday*. If Elvis had thought about it, he could have turned it into a stage show.

On a more serious note, Priscilla has been campaigning of late to have horse soring outlawed. When Priscilla was with Elvis, she had a pair of Tennessee Walking Horses, but when she found that their talent was acquired through doctoring their feet, she was horrified. It looked as though President Obama would abolish the practice, but President Trump cancelled the bill and it remains to be seen what will happen next.

When Lisa Marie was 20, she married the Chicago musician and Scientologist, Danny Keough. They purchased Buddy Kaye's home in Tarzana, California and their daughter Riley was born in the room where Buddy Kaye had written songs for Elvis. They had a second son, Ben, but divorced in 1994, remaining good friends to this day.

When Lisa Marie was 26, she married the singer Michael Jackson in the Dominican Republic. She said, 'I am very much in love with Michael and I dedicate my life to being his wife,' Well, 19 months of it anyway. They were just very good friends, two people caught up in an extraordinary bubble of extreme fame.

Her third marriage was to the Hollywood leading man and Elvis fanatic, Nicolas

Cage, and her fourth marriage to Michael Lockwood. She and Michael had twins, Harper and Finley, in 2008 and twins ran on both sides of her family. The marriage ended in 2016 with Lisa Marie claiming that he had used her credit cards extensively without her knowledge and she also made some serious allegations about his behaviour. She is said to be broke, owing taxes in both the US and the UK, and she is now living with her daughter Riley. A counter-claim is that she had hidden several million dollars so that it does not form part of the settlement. This is proving very difficult to unravel and only the lawyers are going to benefit.

Lisa Marie has had a sporadic career as a singer and songwriter, both touring and recording, releasing the albums, *To Whom It May Concern* (2003), which sold over a million copies, *Now What* (2005) and *Storm and Grace* (2012). She had had hit singles with 'Lights Out' (2003) and 'Dirty Laundry' (2005). She's certainly no embarrassment to Elvis, and, what's more, she curls her lip like him when she sings. In the court deposition, she claimed that she had made little money from her records. A special exhibition, *Elvis – Through his Daughter's Eyes*, is part of the Graceland experience.

Graceland and its grounds are now a major tourist attraction. Upstairs is out of bounds and so fans can't see Elvis' bedroom or where he died. One upstairs room contains Gladys' clothes, clean and neatly pressed, as though she is going to return. Elvis' cars, including a pink Cadillac, have been lovingly restored and are displayed in a showroom. The humorous travel writer Ian Clayton admits, 'I was very nearly thrown out of Graceland for joking with my mate Kevin Reynolds about how fat Elvis was. The tour guide felt very insulted and said, 'Elvis was never more than 240 pounds'. Kevin said, 'Well, that's fucking fat enough in my book'.'

Somewhat cynically and displaying superiority, Clive James delivered this assessment in *Fame in the 20th Century* (BBC Books, 1993): 'Graceland, where the architectural traditions of Walt Disney, Hugh Hefner and Liberace all came together in one transcendentally tasteless apotheosis, was incorporated as a cash-generating shrine.' It appears even truer today where the number of properties on the estate has increased and you can 'Visit Elvis Presley's Graceland and stay at our new resort.' With amusement park rides, See See Rider has turned into See-Saw Rider.

Graceland has now passed into the hands of really big business. Robert Sillerman's company CKX bought an 85% shareholding in Graceland and this in turn went to Apollo Management, as they purchased CKX for $512m. in 2011. There has been a tie-up with The Beatles Story, with an exhibition in Liverpool, *Elvis and Us* (2011) and there are likely to be further developments.

There has yet to be a permanent Elvis museum in the UK and there may never be. Todd Slaughter opened one in Blackpool but it closed in 1991, having only been open for a year. It cost him his savings and his health. He had a heart transplant in 1994 and recorded a charity single, 'Take Another Little Piece of My Heart'. An Elvis museum on a high street in Islington, London had few original items – a pair of shoes and toothpaste and soap from his plane.

That sounds like nothing, but I admit that I walked across Waterloo Bridge solely to see Elvis Presley's wart on display in Joni Mabe's *Travelling Panoramic Encyclopaedia*, a shrine to everything Elvis. Not only did it contain Elvis' wart (obtained from a hospital) but also a toenail. Mabe had been to Graceland and found it in the shag pile in the Jungle Room. Who else but Elvis, she argued, would be allowed to cut his toenails there? A valid point, but hardly conclusive proof.

Returning to Memphis, the Sun Studio closed in 1959 but it reopened in 1987 and is a combination of a working studio and a tourist attraction. The strands combine when tourists with a bit of cash opt to make a record with the studio's professional musicians and there are hundreds of examples on *YouTube*. Among the records which have celebrated Sun are Chip Taylor's 'I Want the Real Thing' and John Fogerty's two songs, 'Big Train (From Memphis) and 'I Saw It on TV'. Sun's location hasn't changed but the address has, as Union Avenue has become Sam Phillips Avenue. Memphis has a Heartbreak Hotel (hopefully with better room service than the song), a museum for the writer Alex Haley, and the National Civil Rights Museum at the former Lorraine Motel where Martin Luther King was assassinated in 1968.

One of the biggest teenage idols of the new century, Justin Timberlake, was born in Memphis in 1981. There is no Justin Timberlake museum as yet and it remains to be seen whether he has that staying power.

For many years there was discussion as to what to do with Elvis Presley's Circle G Ranch. It is currently being restored and developed. The plans are ambitious and include stage shows, equestrian events and equine therapy.

Elvis Presley's name and reputation is used to attract tourists to Las Vegas. The city hosts over 100,000 marriages a year and you can get married in the *Star Trek* chapel or be given away by an Elvis Presley impersonator. It is easy to see how Elvis songs can replace hymns – 'Love Me Tender', 'Can't Help Fallin' in Love' and 'The Wonder of You'. The British country singer Hank Wangford recalls, 'Las Vegas is a completely potty place, totally mad. My son was married by 'Elvis' in the Viva Las Vegas wedding chapel. If you want your marriage to last, don't get married by 'Elvis' in Las Vegas.'

My friend and Elvis fanatic, Mick O'Toole, never has much money and he has asked me, should he die first, to take his ashes to Graceland. 'Yes,' I said, 'if you leave me the fare.' You may not be permitted to leave ashes at Graceland in which case it would be a furtive operation: perhaps I could get away with the contents of a small envelope tipped on a flower bed.

Mick has never been to Graceland, so it strikes me that the best solution would be, when he has the money, to go and see Graceland for himself. He should wait until he feels he is about to die. Then he joins an official tour to Graceland. Halfway through, he says, 'Sorry, I must go to the toilet.' He rushes up the stairs, down the corridor and straight into Elvis' bathroom. Out of his pocket, he takes out the book about the face of Jesus. He sits down, reads the book and keels over – the ultimate fan's trip.

(D) Stage and Screen

There are so many aspects to Elvis Presley's career that there are numerous ways that it can be treated dramatically. By and large, productions that attempt to tell his full story from birth to death are doomed to failure because it is so rich in characterisation, behaviour and events that it can only ever be a whistle-stop tour.

The first tribute show, opening at the Astoria in the West End of London, in November 1977, was Jack Good's highly successful *Elvis* with three actor/singers playing Elvis: Tim Whitnall brilliant as the young Elvis, Shakin' Stevens making a name for himself as the late 50s/early 60s Elvis, and the unpredictable P.J. Proby being, well,

P.J. Proby as the latter-day Elvis. It was highly entertaining but offered no insights into the King or his lifestyle. It won Best Musical of the Year in the *Evening Standard* Drama Awards. The seat prices ranged from £1.50 to £5.50, which gives you an idea of how long ago this was.

Tim Whitnall was an unknown but perfect as the young Elvis. 'I'd never been to London and I'd never been on a stage before. I simply got on a train and got through the audition. I was in the sixth form on the Friday and singing 'Hound Dog' on the Monday. It seems precocious to say I would get the role but I did have a feeling that I would. It all happened so fast that I didn't have to think.'

Alvin Stardust: 'Elvis had been dead for about half an hour, and some clown phoned me up and said, 'We're looking for someone to play in this thing called *Elvis*.' I said, 'I'm going to put this phone down and if you ever ring me again, I'll get a chair and wrap it around your neck. It is the most disgusting thing I've ever heard of. The guy's only been dead a few minutes and here you are, cashing in.' He said, 'No, it's a tribute.' I said, 'I don't believe in tributes. Someone's making money and it's going into your back pocket.' I put the phone down and left it at that but eventually I went to the Astoria to see it. Tim Whitnall who played the early Elvis was terrific but the fact that he was dressed in a clown's outfit annoyed me. I didn't like the taste of it, but when Shakin' Stevens came on, it was almost like watching Elvis.'

Director Jack Good: 'Of course it was tasteless, but we're talking about rock'n'roll and vulgarity is the essence of rock'n'roll. I didn't mind and I'm sure Elvis wouldn't have objected either. He was probably looking down and saying, 'Thank you, Jack, you've made me slim again, and Proby's singing very well for me'. Proby was wonderful when he was singing, though he shafted me in the end.'

Tim grew up fast as he had to contend with Proby's tantrums: 'There was a boxing day matinee and I felt like I just wanted to go home. Jim had locked himself in his dressing room and he refused to go on. We didn't have an understudy. They put me in a white jumpsuit singing 'In the Ghetto' and the later stuff and looking ridiculous with my light brown hair. The show had to go on and Shaky and I did the whole show between us.'

The production turned Shakin' Stevens into a star. He had played the Welsh club circuit doing rockabilly numbers and perfecting his performance as Elvis in *Loving You*. Now he had hit singles as he revived fairly unlikely old 50s hits – 'The Green Door' and 'This Ole House' among them. Even his tough, no nonsense manager, Freya Miller, was referred to as 'Colonel Parker'.

The semi-official bio-pic, *Elvis – The Movie* (1979) didn't work, although it was directed by John Carpenter and produced by Dick Clark, both of whom should have known better. It was a tacky production where characters introduce themselves by answering the telephone. Unfortunately the ham is so thick, you could sell it at the supermarket. The film was written by Tony Lawrence, who wrote *Paradise, Hawaiian Style*, and it showed. When Elvis moved into Graceland, the first thing he did was hang up his gold records.

The music was okay, as Kurt Russell mimes to Ronnie McDowell's vocal tracks, and the film ended with the Vegas Presley of 1969. Shelley Winters played Gladys Presley while Kurt Russell's dad, Bing, was Vernon. Both Sam Phillips and Priscilla Presley were consultants and the Jordanaires, Charlie Hodge and Kathy Westmoreland took part.

Kurt married the actress who played Priscilla, Season Hubley, although they were to divorce. A fuller version of the film, lasting 150 minutes, was shown on US TV and is on *YouTube*.

This is Elvis (1981) charts Elvis' life through TV and film clips, newsreels and home movies: 50 songs in 100 minutes and even more on the extended 144 minute video release. We have 'Hound Dog' on *The Steve Allen Show*, the best movie sequences ('Teddy Bear', 'Jailhouse Rock'), the homecoming show with Sinatra and the 1968 comeback special. Outtakes from *Elvis: That's the Way It Is* and *Elvis on Tour* are included and you see in close-up how sweaty and bloated he became. The extended version includes Dolores Hart's and Priscilla Presley's home movies. The film is narrated by Elvis from beyond the grave, actually Ral Donner, and it's a ridiculous conceit. Even tackier are the other Elvis Presleys who pop up during the film – Elvis at ten (Paul Boensh III), at age 18 (David Scott), at age 42 (Johnny Harra, in an unenviable role) and, marginally worse, Elvis in hospital played by Dana Markey.

In 1984, there was a UK tour for *Nightmare Rock* starring Peter Straker and Diane Langton in which Sherlock Holmes and Dr. Watson suspect that an Elvis duo are involved in body-snatching. They were hoping to compete with *The Rocky Horror Show* but it didn't last.

In 1985 Alan Bleasdale's play, *Are You Lonesome Tonight?*, directed by Robin Lefèvre, opened at the Liverpool Playhouse. The play started with a funeral and reverted to the moody, middle-aged Elvis reliving his last day on earth and thinking back to his youth (played and sung excellently by Simon Bowman). Martin Shaw from *The Professionals* was brilliant as Presley and didn't do badly on the songs either, but this was a play more than a musical. He was visited by ghosts (Jesse, Gladys) and elsewhere his sacked bodyguards were telling a journalist what Elvis was really like.

It is unwise to reply to criticism and when the *Liverpool Echo* reporter Peter Grant said he hated the play but liked and respected Bleasdale, the playwright responded with 'Mr. Grant claims to like and respect me. The feeling is not mutual.' There were several complaints regarding the bad language, which made it unsuitable as family entertainment. Despite all this, it moved to the West End, was highly acclaimed and won the *Evening Standard* Drama Award for Best Musical. Another critic, Joe Riley, called the play a twentieth-century *King Lear*.

I hope the play hasn't disappeared as there was much good Bleasdale humour channelled through Presley: 'Last night I wanted to make love to a girl with the light on, but she said, 'Oh no' and closed the car door.' It is a deliberately sad and depressing play – the answer to the question, 'Are you lonesome tonight?', being an empathic yes.

In 2003 Simon Bowman returned as the latter-day Elvis in *This is Elvis: Viva Las Vegas*, a UK touring show written by Philip Norman and endorsed by the Presley estate.

The musical *of Jailhouse Rock* was a UK success in 2004, although it was not allowed to use the songs from the film including 'Jailhouse Rock' itself and so it seemed incomplete. Mario Kombou was very good as Elvis and Donna Presley Early came to the UK to promote it,: '*Jailhouse Rock* is about the birth of rock'n'roll and it follows the film very closely as it talks about a young man from the wrong side of the tracks. He gets into a fight and accidentally kills someone and goes to prison. While he is in prison, he finds out who he is and he finds the music and he becomes a superstar. It also tells you about relationships and true friendship and true love, and it is not like you are sitting in the audience watching a musical. It draws you in. You are part of it. The music is fantastic and it will have you dancing in the aisles. We have had a complete age range watching it and everybody is enthralled. Elvis' audience is getting younger and younger and touching people from all walks of life.' The production was good but there is still the opportunity for recreating the movie *Jailhouse Rock* with the original songs on stage.

There have been Elvis characters in numerous films including *Wild at Heart* (1990), *The Adventures of Ford Fairlane* (1990), *Honeymoon in Vegas* (1992), *Kalifornia* (1993) and *My Fellow Americans* (1996). There is Elvis kitsch in many of the scenes in *True Romance* (1993) but it is mostly ignored by the characters. There has been a two-part US TV series, *Elvis* (2005) with Jonathan Rhys Meyers as Elvis and Randy Quaid as Colonel Parker.

Set in a Memphis hotel, the ghost of Elvis loomed large in the film *Mystery Train* (1989) with plenty of weird going-ons but wouldn't you feel weird if you knew the night porter was Screamin' Jay Hawkins? Joe Strummer, Rufus Thomas and Tom Waits made for an eclectic cast.

In 2016 there was *Elvis & Nixon* with Michael Shannon as Elvis and Kevin Spacey as Nixon. It didn't know whether it wanted to stick to the facts or depart from them and it might have been better if it had been played completely as a satire. Kevin Spacey was characteristically fine as Nixon but Michael Shannon didn't look like Elvis and the actor playing Jerry Schilling was better looking that he was. There was little rapport between Elvis and Nixon, and maybe a fictional *Elvis & Clinton* would have been more fun: while Clinton was president, his code name was Elvis so that agents could say, 'Elvis has left the building' while guarding him.

In 2004, Kim Basinger and John Corbett starred in *Elvis Has Left the Building*. The plot revolved around somebody killing off Elvis impersonators. All the impersonators looked ridiculous and included a begging Elvis. At the end, the impersonators climbed onto a hotel roof to get a message from Elvis in the sky. The roof collapsed and the credits read, 'No Elvis impersonators have been hurt during the making of this movie.'

II. Got a Lot o' Livin' to Do, 1977 to the Present

I drafted this chapter in November 2016. The Top 10 best-selling albums included Elvis Presley, Cliff Richard, Michael Ball, Michael Bublé (two entries) and Leonard Cohen: this is 2016? Elvis has just been at No.1, singing with the Royal Philharmonic Orchestra in the Abbey Road Studios in London. The real live Elvis of 1977 would have been mystified, as he never visited London nor sang with the RPO: in many ways, Dead Elvis is having a more exciting life that his real life counterpart and must be far easier to handle.

By definition, Dead Elvis is something that the Live Elvis would know nothing about. While she was performing, Linda Ronstadt was told that Elvis Presley had died, and she went immediately into 'Love Me Tender' by way of tribute. She recorded the song on her next album and a radio disc-jockey cleverly combined the two recordings – Presley (1956), Ronstadt (1978) – to create one of the first electronic duets.

Don't be taken in, as some of these new records may not feature Elvis. In 1978 the relaunched Sun Records, under the ownership of Shelby Singleton, released a single 'Don't Cry for Christmas' by '?'. In my view, the ? of ? & the Mysterians should have complained, but would-be purchasers were led to believe it was Elvis. Then Sun put out an album called *Duets* in which ? sang along with Jerry Lee Lewis. It emerged that ? was Jimmy Ellis, who otherwise worked as the masked Elvis impersonator, Orion – masked because he looked nothing like him. He wasn't bad but a recent TV documentary showed what a sad case he was.

In 2002 Lisa Marie sang 'Don't Cry, Daddy' at a tribute concert for the 25th anniversary of his death. She then sang 'In the Ghetto' with him and the duet, with both of them in black and white, is very effective, right down to her tears at the end. The song was used to make a comment on gun control, something Elvis would hardly endorse. In 2012, she took her father's Sun recording of 'I Love You Because' and added a harmony.

Elvis has often been associated with Christmas albums but I wondered about the announcement for *Christmas Duets* in 2008. Just who had been singing with Elvis? Well, his duet partners were all female country singers – Sara Evans, Amy Grant, LeAnn Rimes, Carrie Underwood, Gretchen Wilson (a blusey, eight-minute 'Merry Christmas Baby'), Wynonna and Little Big Town. You might assume that if Elvis had wanted to sing with Anne Murray or Olivia Newton-John, he would have done so while he was alive. The most interesting track was 'Blue Christmas' with Martina McBride and it was taken from the TV special and the photo-shopping was remarkable as it looked as though she was performing alongside Elvis and his four musicians. He even glanced her way.

The same trick was used for the video of Celine Dion and a small choir singing 'If I Can Dream' with Elvis for *American Idol*. In 2013, Susan Boyle from *Britain's Got Talent* got together with the dead Elvis for 'O Come All Ye Faithful' for a Christmas album on which she sang with a live Johnny Mathis.

In 2011 Barbra Streisand had Elvis as one of her fellow artists for *Partners* in which they performed a three-and-a-half minute version of 'Love Me Tender'. The original recording is nowhere near that long but Barbra has added an introductory verse.

In 2015, Elvis' vocals were given a completely new backing as he was accompanied by the Royal Philharmonic Orchestra for *If I Can Dream*. The press release said that it would win Elvis new fans but more likely, it appealed to old fans who wanted to hear something in a different way. The album, which included a duet of 'Fever' with Michael Bublé, topped the UK album charts. It was followed by the similarly successful, *The Wonder of You*, for Christmas 2016. Although the process was artificial, the sound was better than most would have expected.

In 2016, Cliff Richard was put alongside a 60-year-old recording so that he could record a duet of 'Blue Suede Shoes'. It was very cleverly done but you are trying to spot the joins. It would have been effective to have gone with a ballad: Cliff is 75, Elvis is 21, so it is like Elvis singing with his grandpa.

It is not only duets as from time to time Elvis' old recordings have been given new backings. The first example was the album, *Guitar Man*, in 1981 when Felton Jarvis took his late-60s tracks and gave them contemporary arrangements. It was pointless and the new version of 'Guitar Man' with fresh guitar parts from Jerry Reed sounded a mess, although it sold well.

Since then, many of Elvis' recordings have been doctored in one way or another and often alternative takes are regularly issued. It is often impossible for a casual fan to know whether or not they are buying the original hit recordings.

In 1985 Elvis was brought into line with the *Hooked On...* hit series and six of

Elvis' hit singles were sampled into one single. With the same theme, Jive Bunny and the Mastermixers ran several hits together to create a No.1 single, 'Swing That Mood'. The record company, neatly called Music Factory, hadn't been allowed to use the original RCA recordings so they remade them with Elvis impersonator Peter Wilcox.

In 1995 a live version of Elvis singing 'The Twelfth of Never' at a rehearsal in 1974 was issued as a single. The sticker said it was a 'Recently discovered sensation' but I would hardly go as far: just a nice, one-off workout, which deserved to make the Top 30.

In 2001 an alternate take of 'A Little Less Conversation' was used on the soundtrack of the George Clooney film, *Ocean's 11*. Alerted by the film, Nike wanted it for their TV ads to coincide with the World Cup. The 34-year-old Dutch DJ Tom Holkenborg (Junkie XL) was asked to remix it, adding a modern dance groove and whatever sounds were thought necessary. The Elvis estate thought it was inappropriate for Elvis to be sharing the bill with someone called Junkie XL (or, perhaps, far too appropriate) and the name was shortened to JXL. The reaction to the advert, which featured Eric Cantona, and then the single, was overwhelmingly positive and it was predicted that it would go straight into the charts at No.1. It was Elvis' 18th No.1 and it took him ahead of the Beatles.

In 2005 and to celebrate the 70th anniversary of Elvis Presley's birth, RCA/BMG reissued each of Elvis Presley's 18 UK No.1s in chronological order and on a weekly basis. Two were issued in the first week, 'All Shook Up' (1957) and 'Jailhouse Rock' (1958). Because 'All Shook Up' came with a cardboard storage case to hold all the other singles, it was deemed ineligible for the charts. For the record but not for the charts, 'All Shook Up' sold 17,000 copies that week which would have placed it at No.2, just behind 'Jailhouse Rock' with 21,000. A neat touch was to issue the singles with the original US covers, which had not been seen in the UK before. The singles were also issued on 10-inch vinyl, playing at 45rpm, with sleeves replicating the RCA paper bags of the period with the original serial numbers.

Most critics welcomed these releases but there was an extraordinary outburst from Tim Luckhurst, a columnist for *The Times*, who was dismayed by this attention on Elvis. Resembling that ridiculous leader when Elvis died, Luckhurst wrote, 'Like his fans, Presley was of very limited intellect and he cannot be held responsible for his image. The cleverest thing he did was to die.' He added, 'American giants such as Bob Dylan and Frank Zappa merit our affection. If he had started singing after John Lennon, Presley would not even merit a place on *I'm A Celebrity...Get Me Out Of Here!*' We can only speculate on John Lennon's comments to such risible remarks, but in all probability, he would have written an open letter to *The Times* saying that he wouldn't have found his voice without Elvis. Indeed, Elvis' rasping vocal on 'Jailhouse Rock' could have inspired John's performance on 'Twist and Shout'.

In 1958 'Jailhouse Rock' was the first record to enter the chart at No.1 and in 2005 it became the first record to enter the chart for the second time at No.1. This time, however, its stay at the top was limited as it was replaced by the reissue of Elvis's third UK No.1, 'One Night'. That became the UK's 1000th No.1. Elvis was the first person since John Lennon to replace himself at No.1.

Who could dispute the merit of Elvis having the 1,000th UK No.1? It rekindled interest in the charts and there was speculation as to whether Elvis could continue hitting the top with his former No.1s ('Wooden Heart' anyone?) or if normality would return. 'It's Now or Never' reached No.1 but all the reissues made the Top 5. Ironically. fans were paying full whack for these reissued singles, while Elvis films and CD compilations were given away free with the weekend newspapers.

In January 2006, a fiftieth anniversary reissue of 'Heartbreak Hotel' almost topped the Australian US singles chart. The anniversary was marred by the demolition of the Nashville studio to make a parking lot, but its reverberations will last as long as there is music.

In 2007 there was another series of UK reissues, this time with a box of 18 greatest singles, outside of the UK No.1s. Again the first single, 'Heartbreak Hotel' was ineligible for the charts but each of the subsequent ones made the Top 20 which suggested that the same 5,000 people were buying them each week.

In the midst of this, 'My Baby Left Me', issued by the Memphis Recording Service, made the Top 20. This was a company run by Joseph Pirzada which specialised in good quality packaging of out of copyright recordings, which at the time was anything over 50 years old. The law changed in 2013 but anything issued prior to 1963 is out of copyright in the UK and you don't need permission or need to pay the record company royalties if you issue an album of Elvis' early hits.

The published sales for 2017 calendars in the UK made surprising reading as the contemporary stars were being outsold by Cliff Richard (No.1) and Elvis Presley (No.5). This was almost wholly down to grannypower with Cliff, but I suspect that Elvis had many younger fans.

As well as all these sales, Elvis, or rather Dead Elvis, was on the road in 1998, playing huge arenas around the world, so Elvis was coming to the UK at last. Elvis' first European tour in 1999 featured a light show, original band members, a 16 piece orchestra and Elvis on film with just his vocal track. So Priscilla and Lisa Marie had Elvis back on the road and he wasn't even there. How sad that Colonel Parker, who had died the year before, wasn't able to witness this, which he would have considered the ultimate scam.

But it worked extremely well. With breath-taking technology, Elvis was there in person but on film, and the musicians, his old band and singers, were performing live. They would follow his every move and take their bows when he introduced them. At the end of the show, the audience would be standing, applauding and screaming for someone who wasn't there.

Peter Asher from Peter and Gordon said, 'There was a phase when the band was on the road and Elvis didn't hang out with them at all. He was living his own weird life, and Ron Tutt said that when he went out on the Dead Elvis tour, it was exactly the same (laughs). They showed a film of Elvis introducing the band and the filmed Elvis would say, 'That's Ronnie Tutt', and point at him. Ronnie said it was indistinguishable from playing a real Elvis gig.'

This has been followed in 2016/7 with tours based around the symphonic albums, *If I Can Dream* and *The Wonder of You*, hosted by Priscilla Presley.

Carl Perkins: 'People ask me from time to time, 'Carl, when is this Elvis thing going to die?', and I say, 'Why do you think it ever will? It will not.' Elvis gave the world what it needed at the time, he was handsome, swift-moving, and he wasn't vulgar on stage. You look back at him now and it is all motion and art. He was releasing that feeling right down through his body. He moved his legs like nobody ever did – he didn't realise exactly what he was doing and he couldn't help doing it. Moving is part of the music and if you don't move, something is wrong.'

Acknowledgements

I've been this way since 1956 and so in a way this book has taken me 60 years to write. It has been so entertaining and engrossing to write a book about Elvis and connect the dots on what I knew about him.

My thanks to Andy Peden Smith at McNidder and Grace for his faith in this project and to Linda MacFadyen for arranging the publicity, assisted by Esmee Hoek. Thanks also to Paula Beaton for her diligent editing, Bryan Kirkpatrick of Obsidian Design for setting and designing the book, and to David Charters, Neil Lancaster and Mick O'Toole for commenting on my text and to my wife Anne for several suggestions.

Over the years I have interviewed hundreds of musicians, usually for my BBC Radio Merseyside programme, *On the Beat*. It has been very thought-provoking to go through my files and fish out the Elvis quotes. What I have found is that the stories generally hold up but when they are placed in a time-frame, they often have details wrong: for example, they get the wrong year for meeting Elvis. By and large, I have corrected these details for consistency but no opinions have been changed. The interviewees are:

Chris Arnold, Chet Atkins, Russ Ballard, Bobby Bare, Tony Barrow, Freddie Bell, David Bellamy (Bellamy Brothers), Sid Bernstein, Alf Bicknell, Alan Bleasdale, Pat Boone, Joe Brown, James Burton, Ramsey Campbell, Martin Carthy, Tony Cartwright, Bob Cheevers, Lou Christie, Tommy Collins, Ray Connolly, Elvis Costello, Brendan Croker, Sonny Curtis, Hunter Davies, Maria Davies, Lonnie Donegan, Ray Dorset, Terry Dene, Dion Donna Presley Early, Duane Eddy, Paul Evans, Charlie Feathers, Guy Fletcher, D.J. Fontana, Clinton Ford, Larry Gatlin, Jack Good, Charlie Gracie, Michael Gray, Brian Gregg, Arlo Guthrie, Terry Hamblin, Glen D Hardin, Wee Willie Harris, Ronnie Hawkins, Ben Hewitt, W. S. Holland, Wanda Jackson, Mark Kelly, Barney Kessel, B.B. King, Buddy Knox, Sleepy LaBeef, John Leyton, Gordon Lightfoot, Charlie Louvin, Marshall Lytle (Bill Haley's Comets), Paul McCartney, Roger McGuinn, Tony Macaulay, Greil Marcus, Bill Martin, David Martin, Brian Matthew, Neal Matthews (Jordanaires), Johnny Meeks, Rex Martin, Scotty Moore, Geoff Morrow, Jerry Naylor, Anthony Newley, Ann O'Brien (Vernons Girls), Mick O'Toole, Michael Ochs, Larry Page, Tom Paxton, Trevor Peacock, Carl Perkins, John Phillips, Ken Pitt, P J Proby, Sheila Prytherch (Vernons Girls) Suzi Quatro, Don Randi, Charlie Rich, Cliff Richard, Tim Rice, Wally Ridley, Red Robinson, Johnny Rogan, Tommy Sands, Ray Sawyer (Dr. Hook), Neil Sedaka, Peggy Seeger, Billy Joe Shaver, Mort Shuman, Hank Snow, David Stanley, Hal Shaper, Alvin Stardust, Tommy Steele, Geoff Stephens, John Stewart (Kingston Trio), Big Jim Sullivan, Billy Swan, Rufus Thomas, Johnny Tillotson, Mitchell Torok, Frankie

Vaughan, Bobby Vee, Bobby Vinton, Billy Walker, Ray Walker (Jordanaires), Hank Wangford, Jimmy Webb, Billy Edd Wheeler, Chas 'Dr. Rock' White, Tony Joe White, Slim Whitman, Tim Whitnall, Roger Whittaker, Wally Whyton, Marty Wilde, Roy Wood and Leslie Woodhead.

Bibliography

Books

Elvis: A Biography, Jerry Hopkins (Simon & Schuster, 1971)
Rolling Stone writer, Jerry Hopkins interviewed many of those around Elvis and even though he holds back on criticism, he reveals a highly unusual lifestyle. It is a pity that we had to wait 15 years for a decent biography, but there was no market for fully-researched rock biographies until the late 1960s. Hopkins later wrote *Elvis: The Final Years* and the two books have now been combined.

Elvis, Albert Goldman (Allen Lane, 1981)
The most infamous rock biography of all. The book was Lamar Fike's idea and he shares the copyright with Goldman and a packager, Kevin Eggers. Did Fike know that Goldman would write such a hatchet job? The research was superb but Goldman manipulated it for his own ends, misquoting and misrepresenting his subjects. Goldman was a New York intellectual who had no time for white rock music (as it was stolen from black musicians) or for working people in the South or for those who didn't match his intellect. Elvis lost out on all counts but there are good things in there and it is one hell of a read. The book didn't sell because the fans didn't want it.

Elvis UK, 1956–1986, John Townson, Gordon Minto and Gordon Richardson (Blandford, 1987)
It's one thing to compile a list of all Elvis' UK releases – it's quite another to keep it interesting, so top marks all round. A fascinating study worthy of Sherlock Holmes for its skill in finding spelling mistakes, alternative titles and label errors: what a pity we haven't got Elvis' comments on some of these releases. It is difficult to find your way around the book but that is RCA's fault, not the authors'.

Last Train to Memphis – The Rise of Elvis Presley, Peter Guralnick (Little Brown, 1994)
A superbly researched and beautifully written account of Elvis' early years up to the funeral of his mother. This is for the serious reader, as at the end of 550 pages you are still only in 1958. No one before or since has written about Elvis in such detail. Ground-breaking.

Careless Love – The Unmaking of Elvis Presley, Peter Guralnick (Little Brown, 1999)
Continuing the story of *Last Train to Memphis*, Guralnick takes the story of Elvis up to his death. It's 750 pages this time, and you could spend just as long reading about what happened after his death. It's not afraid to be critical but it is also fair and balanced.

With one exception. No one in the UK took Screaming Lord Sutch seriously: he had little money and the thought that he could have got hold of £1m and presented Elvis in the UK is ridiculous – it was one of his vain boasts.

Heartbreak Hotel: A Tribute to the King in Verse, Jeremy Reed (Orion, 2002)
240 pages of poems about Elvis, all written by one British writer. If you want to read about Elvis' psychedelic recordings, his anti-ageing tips and how he asked Jesus for an angel badge, this is for you.

The Colonel, Alanna Nash (Aurum, 2003)
A fascinating look at the relationship between Elvis and the Colonel from the Colonel's side. The years before and after Elvis are particularly illuminating.

Elvis and Gladys, Elaine Dundy (University Press of Mississippi, 2004)
A scholarly book that is as much about Elvis' ancestry as his relationship with his mother. Great research and very well written but too much is made of the bond between Elvis and his mother: was it really that unusual?

Elvis by the Presleys (Century, 2005)
An intimate look at Elvis' personal life by Priscilla, her parents and sister, Lisa Marie and Elvis' cousin Patsy, who lived at Graceland. More critical than I would have expected. Although many illustrations are revealing and informative, what is the point of a double-page spread of Elvis' touring tipple (Mountain Valley spring water) or Lisa Marie's crayons?

Elvis: My Best Man, George Klein with Chuck Crisafulli (Virgin, 2010)
You don't expect books by Elvis insiders to be particularly good – well, I don't anyway – but George Klein tells his story well and with insight. But was he always on hand to offer advice and friendship as he suggests? George doesn't claim to have invented the wheel, but he gets close.

Elvis Memories, Michael Freedland (Robson, 2013)
A highly-experienced journalist, Michael Freedland visits Tupelo, Memphis, Nashville, Las Vegas and Hollywood to make a series for the BBC; this book fleshes out his thoughts and interviews. All good stuff, but why on earth did he say he wasn't going to talk about films and records?

Elvis Has Left the Building, Dylan Jones (Duckworth Overlook, 2014)
'Punk had set out to destroy Elvis, but never got the chance, as Elvis destroyed himself before anyone else could.' I'd disagree with that, as punk's links to early rockabilly are self-evident – but this is a fine account of what happened in August 1977, with reports from around the world.

Elvis Presley; A Southern Life, Joel Williamson (Oxford University Press, 2015)
Joel Williamson is a university professor who has written on race issues and published the highly acclaimed biography, *William Faulkner and Southern History*. In his introduction he write 'Elvis is the creature of that little postage stamp of earth in north-eastern Mississippi that also gave birth to William Faulkner and Tennessee Williams. Why did America's greatest writer in the twentieth century, America's greatest playwright in the twentieth century and American's greatest entertainer in the twentieth century emerge from the same place?' It's a very good question, which the author makes no real attempt to answer as he gets side-tracked by Elvis Presley's sex life.

Elvis – A Personal Memoir, Chris Hutchins (Neville Ness, 2015)
Chris Hutchins arranged the meeting between Elvis and the Beatles and he often saw Elvis and the Colonel in Las Vegas. The Colonel is much more human in this book than in most others.

Being Elvis: A Lonely Life, Ray Connolly (Weidenfeld & Nicolson, 2016)
Ray Connolly wanted to write this as a first person autobiography, but US copyright laws prevented this. However, he does try to get inside Elvis' head.

Magazines

The monthly *Now Dig This* and quarterly *Elvis The Man and his Music*, both owned by the same company, have consistently published excellent features and news items on rock'n'roll itself and Elvis-related stories, although there is a bit too much moaning and bleating for me. *Elvis The Man and his Music,* which has been published since 1998, is very good at pointing out mistakes in official releases and books on Elvis. They have put me right on so many pitfalls and they have published interviews with people who haven't publicly spoken before. Well done, Trevor.

APPENDIX 1

To Think I Did All That – An Elvis Presley Discography

A complete discography of Elvis Presley would be longer than the text of the book itself as so many tracks have been issued time and again. Multiple takes of the same song have often been released. This discography has been largely compiled around chart placings, so that all Elvis' US and UK chart successes are included. Nothing of significance has been omitted.

Right from the start, there were substantial differences between US and UK releases, primarily because the UK outlet (HMV) didn't like being told what to do: you get the same situation in reverse with US Capitol Records and the Beatles.

Unless otherwise stated, chart placings are according to the US *Billboard* Hot 100 charts and the standard pop charts shown in the *British Hit Singles* books, published by Guinness and then Virgin. The UK chart is purely based on sales, while the US positions are a mixtures of sales, jukebox plays and radio airplay. In recent years, computer downloads and on-line hits have entered the fray, which can throw up anachronisms, to put it mildly.

Don't get me started on all the inconsistencies in listing the two sides of a single together or separately, and the rulings for this have gone back and forth over the years. Then there was the scandal over payola (cash for radioplay) in the late 1950s: this affected chart placings and there could have been a more direct impact with cash paid to the compilers for higher placings.

The albums charts in both the US and the UK are inconsistent, but they're all we've got. The key problem has been in major companies wanting to show their full-price product in the best light. In the UK, the budget and mid-priced albums were originally on the charts but then dropped, but the US has never listed them.

In the early 70s, the UK albums chart included TV-advertised albums on K-Tel and Arcade, but the regular companies complained and so several full-priced albums were dropped from the charts even though they were outselling product from the major labels: someone should have told Decca and EMI to take a running jump, that if a TV album sold more than the others, then it went in the charts. Then Decca and EMI started advertising their own products on TV and wanted them in the charts, so the TV albums returned.

In the 1950s nobody knew what to do with four-track extended-play releases and they appeared on both the singles and albums charts in the US. Then they were dropped completely. In the UK they were placed with the singles at first; later there was a separate EP chart where there was not too much competition for Elvis, so the EP chart became an EP chart.

In addition, this discography shows Elvis Presley's placings on the US Country and US R&B charts as well as unlikely singles doing well in Australia, France, Germany, Norway and Ireland. Again, the definition of what was a country or an R&B record could change from time to time.

Many Elvis fans collect Japanese releases for their beautiful packaging and attention to detail. Invariably though there are annoying typos like 'Heartbread Hotel' and 'Lou're the Devil in Disguise'.

I would comment on four double-CDs I have of Elvis outtakes, *There's Always Me* on the Bilko label. It's my fault I know for buying bootlegs but these CDs are gradually falling apart and 6 of the 8 CDs are now unplayable. We were told that CDs would last forever, but clearly these were of the cheapo-cheapo variety. Guess I shouldn't have trusted a record label named after a comic character.

SUN SINGLES (1954–1955)

The five great singles issued only in America at the time and then predominantly in the South.

That's All Right, Mama / Blue Moon of Kentucky (Sun 209, 1954)

Good Rockin' Tonight / I Don't Care If the Sun Don't Shine (Sun 210, 1954)

Milkcow Blues Boogie / You're a Heartbreaker (Sun 215, 1955) The rarest of Elvis' Sun singles: a mint 45rpm is worth about £3,000 and the 78rpm £1,000.

Baby Let's Play House / I'm Left, You're Right, She's Gone (Sun 217, 1955) (US Country No.5, both sides listed)

I Forgot to Remember to Forget / Mystery Train (Sun 223, 1955) (US Country No.1 for 5 weeks. B-side listed separately, No.11)

Once Elvis joined RCA, Mystery Train was reissued on RCA 6357 and the others followed on RCA 6380-3, respectively.

RCA SINGLES AND EXTENDED PLAY RELEASES (1956– 1959)

Heartbreak Hotel / I Was the One (US RCA 6420, UK HMV POP 182, 1956) (US No.1 for 8 weeks: US Country No.1 for 17 weeks: US R&B No.3: UK No.2; B-side US No.19; US Country No.8) (UK reissue No.10, 1971) (UK reissue with All Shook Up, No.41, 1977) (UK reissue No.45, 1996 included alternative takes of both titles) (Australia No.2, 2006). The UK reissue in 2007 sold enough to be a Top 20 hit but was disqualified as it came with a promotional box. This single is the most complicated entry in this discography as Elvis is always returning to that hotel, so don't let this put you off.

I Want You, I Need You, I Love You / My Baby Left Me (US RCA 6540, UK POP 235, 1956) (US No.1 for 1 week: US Country No.1 for 2 weeks: US R&B No.3, both sides listed: UK No.14; B-side, US No.31)

Tutti Frutti / I Was the One (Australia No.18; B-side No.40) Elvis' first chart entry in Australia. At first, Elvis, Little Richard and Pat Boone were all listed at No.31 with Tutti Frutti.

Hound Dog / Don't Be Cruel (US RCA 6604, UK HMV POP 249, 1956) (US, No.1

for 11 weeks, both sides listed; US Country No.1 for 10 weeks, both sides listed; US R&B No.1 for 6 weeks, both sides listed: UK No.2, *New Musical Express* only listed Hound Dog, but *Melody Maker* had it as a two-sided hit.) (UK reissue: both sides, No.10, 1971) (UK reissue: both sides No.24, 1978) (UK reissue: B-side, No.42, 1992) (UK reissue: both sides No.14, 2007)

In 1956, RCA in the US then released six Elvis singles with little publicity and with few sales, presumably because no one knew about them. Twelve of the tracks formed the first album, *Elvis Presley*, which sold millions. The singles were:

Blue Suede Shoes / Tutti Frutti (US RCA 6636, UK HMV POP 213, 1956) (US No.20, UK No.9) The reason Blue Suede Shoes became a hit is in the text. (UK reissue: No.11, 2007)

I Got a Woman / I'm Countin' on You (US RCA 6637, 1956)

I'm Gonna Sit Right Down and Cry / I'll Never Let You Go (US RCA 6638, 1956)

Tryin' to Get to You / I Love You Because (US RCA 6639, 1956)

Blue Moon / Just Because (US RCA 6640, UK HMV POP 272, 1956) (US No.55, UK No.9) UK B-side was I Don't Care If the Sun Don't Shine and this made No.23 in its own right.

Money Honey / One-sided Love Affair (US RCA 6641, 1956) (US No.76)

Lawdy Miss Clawdy / Shake, Rattle and Roll (US RCA 6642, 1956)

TV Guide Presents Elvis (US RCA G8MW 8705, 1956) Elvis (and Colonel Parker!) were interviewed by Paul Wilder in Lakeland, Florida in August 1956 for a three-part feature in a weekly listings magazine. RCA pressed promotional copies of the interview for radio stations; the local DJs could ask Elvis Paul's questions and he would answer them from the disc.

Love Me Tender / Anyway You Want Me (US RCA 6643, UK HMV POP 253, 1956) (US No.1 for 5 weeks: US Country No.3 both sides listed: US R&B No.3 (what?), UK No.11, Australia No.6 (El's first Top 10 hit in Oz); B-side, US No.20: US R&B, No.12) (UK reissue: No.56, 1987, listed with If I Can Dream)

Love Me Tender EP with Love Me Tender, Let Me, Poor Boy, We're Gonna Move (US RCA EPA 4006, UK HMV 7EG 8199, 1956) (Poor Boy listed on US singles chart, No.24: Love Me listed on US Country No.10: and US R&B No.7: *Love Me Tender* EP on US albums chart at No.22)

The Truth about Me, one-sided flexi-disc (UK Lynchberg, 1956) Elvis talking about his career. *Weekend* contained a coupon you could complete to get the record for free.

Old Shep, one-sided promotional disc (RCA CR 15, 1956) (US No.47) Proof positive that the US charts were dodgy – it was impossible to buy this record and yet it is in the Top 50.

Elvis, Volume 1 EP with Rip It Up, Love Me, When My Blue Moon Turns to Gold Again, Paralyzed (US RCA EPA 992, 1956) (Love Me, When My Blue Moon Turns to Gold Again and Paralyzed all listed on US singles chart, highest placings No.2, No.19 and No.59 respectively.)

Mystery Train / Love Me (UK HMV POP 295, 1957) (UK No.25)

Tutti Frutti (German single, 1957; No.10 in Germany)

Rip It Up / Baby Let's Play House (UK HMV POP 305, 1957) (UK No.27)

Too Much / Playin' for Keeps (US RCA 6800, UK HMV POP 330, 1957) (US No.1 for 3 weeks: US Country No.3: US R&B No.3: UK No.6; B-side, US No.21, US Country No.8)

All Shook Up / That's When Your Heartaches Begin (US RCA 6870, HMV POP 359, 1957) (US No.1 for 9 weeks: US country No.1 for 1 week: US R&B No.1 for 4 weeks: UK No.1 for 7 weeks; B-side, US No.58) (UK reissue of A-side with Heartbreak Hotel, No.41, 1977) UK reissue in 2005 sold enough to be a Top 10 hit, probably a No.1, but was disqualified as it came with a promotional cardboard box.

Teddy Bear / Loving You (US RCA 7000, UK RCA 1013, 1957) (US No.1 for 7 weeks: US Country No.1 for 1 week: US R&B No.1 for 1 week, both sides listed: UK No.3; B-side, US No.20, US Country No.15, UK No.24) (UK reissue: No.14, 2007)

Peace in the Valley EP with Peace in the Valley, It Is No Secret, I Believe, Take My Hand Precious Lord (US RCA EPA 4054, UK RCA RCX 101, 1957). (Peace in the Valley listed on US singles chart, No.25 and *Peace in the Valley* EP on US albums chart at No.3. Go figure.) (UK EP chart, No.12, 1961)

Loving You, Volume 1 EP (US RCA EPA1 1515, 1957)

Loving You, Volume 2 EP (US RCA EPA2 1515, 1957) (Shown on US albums chart at No.18) (On US Country and US R&B, Mean Woman Blues shown at No.11)

Just for You EP (US RCA EPA 4041, 1957) Shown on US albums chart at No.16)

Paralyzed / When My Blue Moon Turns to Gold Again (UK HMV POP 378, 1957) (UK No.8)

(Let's Have a) Party / Got a Lot o' Livin' to Do (UK RCA 1020, 1957) (UK No.2, B-side No.17) (UK reissue: No.14, 2007)

Lawdy Miss Clawdy / Tryin' to Get to You (UK HMV POP 408, 1957) (UK No.15, B-side UK No.16)

Santa Bring My Baby Back to Me / Santa Claus Is Back in Town (UK RCA 1025, 1957) (UK No.7)

Jailhouse Rock / Treat Me Nice (US RCA 7035, UK RCA 1028, 1957) (US No.1 for 7 weeks: US Country No.1 for 1 week: US R&B No.1 for 5 weeks: UK No.1 for 3 weeks; B-side, US No.18: US Country No.11: US R&B No.7) (UK reissue No.42, 1971) (UK reissue No.44, 1977) (UK 25th anniversary reissue No.27, 1983) (UK reissue No.1 for 1 week, 2005)

I'm Left, You're Right, She's Gone / How Do You Think I Feel (UK HMV POP 428, 1958) (UK No.21)

Jailhouse Rock EP with Jailhouse Rock, Young and Beautiful, I Want to Be Free, Don't Leave Me Now, Baby I Don't Care (UK RCA RCX 106, 1958) (UK No.18) Baby I Don't Care listed on US R&B at No.14

Don't / I Beg of You (US RCA 7150, UK RCA 1043, 1957) (US No.1 for 5 weeks: US Country No.2: US R&B No.4: UK No.2; B-side, US No.8: US Country No.4: US R&B No.5) (UK reissue No.14, 2007)

Wear My Ring Around Your Neck / Dontcha Think It's Time (US RCA 7240, UK RCA 1058, 1958) (US No.2; US Country No.3, both sides listed; US R&B No.2 for 3 weeks: UK No.3; B-side, US No.15, US R&B No.10) (UK reissue No.16, 2007)

Hard Headed Woman / Don't Ask Me Why (US RCA 7280, UK RCA 1070, 1958) (US No.1 for 2 weeks: US Country No.2, both sides listed: US R&B No.2: UK No.2: Australia No.2; B-side, US No.25: US R&B No.9) (UK reissue No.15, 2007)

King Creole / Dixieland Rock (UK RCA 1081, 1958) (UK No.2) (UK reissue: No.15, 2007)

One Night / I Got Stung (US RCA 7410, UK RCA 1100, 1958) (US No.4; US Country No.24; US R&B No.10: UK No.1 for 3 weeks: both sides listed on UK chart; B-side in US, No.8) (UK reissue No.1 for 1 week, 2005) The US country market suddenly loses interest in Elvis: was the single too raunchy?

A Merry Christmas EP (UK RCA RCX 121) (UK EP chart, No.16, 1961) A rarity – an EP in a gatefold sleeve.

Elvis Sails EP (US RCA EPA 4325, UK RCA RCX 131, 1958) Press interviews with Elvis as he takes off for Germany.

A Fool Such As I / I Need Your Love Tonight (US RCA 7506, UK RCA 1113, 1959) (US No.2: US R&B No.16: UK No.1 for 5 weeks: Australia No.1 for 6 weeks, Elvis' first No.1 in Australia: Germany No.15: both sides listed on UK chart; B-side in US, No.4) (UK reissue No.2, 2005) Odd that this US No.2 cover of a Hank Snow favourite didn't make the US Country Top 100. More jiggery-pokery, I suspect.

A Big Hunk o' Love / My Wish Came True (US RCA 7600, UK RCA 1136, 1959) (US No.1 for 2 weeks: US R&B No.10: UK No.4: Germany No.23) (B-side in US, No.12, US R&B No.15) (UK reissue No.12, 2007)

Strictly Elvis EP (UK RCA RCX 175, 1959) with Old Shep, Any Place Is Paradise, Paralyzed and Is It So Strange (UK No.26 on singles chart, No.1 for 5 weeks on EP chart)

A Touch of Gold EP (UK RCA RCX 1045, 1959) (UK EP chart No.9)

RCA SINGLES AND EXTENDED PLAY RELEASES (1960–1968)

A Touch of Gold, Volume 2 EP (UK RCA RCX 1048, 1960) (UK EP chart No.8)

Stuck on You / Fame and Fortune (US RCA 7740, 1960) (US No.1 for 4 weeks; US Country No.27; US R&B No.6; UK No.3: Australia No.1 for one week: B-side, US No.17) (UK reissue of A-side: No.58, 1988)

It's Now or Never / A Mess of Blues (US RCA 7777, 1960) (US No.1 for 5 weeks: US R&B No.7: UK No.1 for 8 weeks; B-side, US No.32). The B-side of the UK single was Make Me Know It. (UK reissue No.39, 1977) (UK reissue No.1 for 1 week, 2005)

A Mess of Blues / Girl of My Best Friend (UK RCA 1194, 1960) (UK No.2) (UK reissue with Girl of My Best Friend as A-side, No.9, 1976.) If you can find a UK 78rpm copy of this record, it is worth £400 today: Elvis' most valuable 78rpm – oh, did I say it had to be in mint condition?

Are You Lonesome Tonight / I Gotta Know (US RCA 7810, 1960) (US No.1 for 6 weeks; US Country No.22; US R&B No.3: UK No.1 for 4 weeks; Australia No.1 for 6 weeks, both sides listed; B-side, US No.20) (UK reissue No.46, 1977) (UK reissue No.2, 2003) Elvis' last appearance on the US Country chart until 1970.

Such a Night with Such a Night, It Feels So Right, Like a Baby, Make Me Know It (UK RCA RCX 190) (UK EP chart, No.2)

Wooden Heart / Tonight Is So Right for Love (UK RCA 1226, 1961) (UK No.1 for 6 weeks: Australia No.1 for 4 weeks: Germany No.2) (UK reissue: No.49, 1977) (UK reissue No.2, 2005)

Surrender / Lonely Man (US RCA 7850, 1961) (US No.1 for 2 weeks, UK No.1 for 4 weeks; B-side, US No.32) (UK reissue No.2, 2005)

Elvis by Request EP (US RCA LPC 128, 1961) with Flaming Star, Are You Lonesome Tonight, It's Now or Never, Summer Kisses Winter Tears. Flaming Star listed on US singles chart at No.14. This EP plays at 33rpm, an innovation that didn't catch on.

I Feel So Bad / Wild in the Country (US RCA 7880, UK RCA 1244, 1961) (US No.5: US R&B No.15: UK No.4; B-side, US No.26, In UK both sides listed together with Wild in the Country uppermost.)

His Latest Flame / Little Sister (US RCA 7908, UK RCA 1258, 1961) (US No.4, UK No.1 for 4 weeks; B-side, US No.5, In UK, both sides listed together) (UK reissue No.3, 2005)

Can't Help Falling in Love / Rock-a-Hula Baby (Twist Special) (US RCA 7968, UK RCA 1270, 1961) (US No.2, UK No.1 for 4 weeks, Australia No.1 for 5 weeks: B-side, No.23, UK. Both sides listed together with Rock-a-Hula Baby uppermost: were we mad?) (UK reissue No.3, 2005; reissue deletes the words, 'Twist special'.)

Good Luck Charm / Anything that's Part of You (US RCA 7992, UK RCA 1280, 1962) (US No.1 for 2 weeks, UK No.1 for 5 weeks, Australia No.1 for 6 weeks; B-side, US No.1) (UK reissue: No.2, 2005)

No More / Sentimental Me (German single, both sides listed, No.12, 1962)

Follow That Dream EP (US RCA EPA 4368, US RCA RCX 211, 1962) with Follow That Dream, Angel, What a Wonderful Life and I'm Not the Marrying Kind. Title track was listed on the US singles chart at No.15 and in the UK, the EP was listed at No.34. (UK EP chart No.1 for 20 weeks)

She's Not You / Just Tell Her Jim Said Hello (US RCA 8041, UK RCA 1303, 1962) (US No.5: US R&B No.13: UK No.1 for 3 weeks; B-side, US No.55) (UK reissue: No.3, 2005)

Kid Galahad six-track EP (US RCA EPA 4371, UK RCA RCX 7106, 1962) with King of the Whole Wide World, This is Living, Riding the Rainbow, Home is Where the Heart Is, I Got Lucky and A Whistling Tune. King of the Whole Wide World was listed on the US singles chart at No.30. (UK EP chart No.1 for 17 weeks)

King of the Whole Wide World / Home Is Where the Heart Is (Germany No.26, Norway No.1 for 3 weeks, one week joint No.1 with Little Eva's The Locomotion)

Return to Sender / Where Do You Come from (US RCA 8100, UK RCA 1320, 1962) (US No.2: US R&B No.5: UK No.1 for 3 weeks; B-side, US No.99) (UK reissue No.42

1977) (UK reissue No.5, 2005)

One Broken Heart for Sale / They Remind Me of You (US RCA 8134, UK RCA 1337, 1963) (US No.11: US R&B No.21: UK No.12; B-side, US No.53)

(You're the) Devil in Disguise / Please Don't Drag That String Around (US RCA 8188, UK RCA 1355, 1963) (US No.3: US R&B No.9: UK No.1 for 1 week) (UK reissue No.2, 2005)

Bossa Nova Baby / Witchcraft (US RCA 8243: US R&B No.20: UK RCA 1374, 1963) (US No.8, UK No.13; B-side, US No.32) (UK A-side reissue: No.47, 1987) Elvis' final appearance on the US R&B chart.

Mexico / You Can't Say No In Acapulco (Norway No.7, 1963)

Kissin' Cousins / It Hurts Me (US RCA 8307, UK RCA 1404, 1964) (US No.12, UK No.10; B-side, No.29)

Kiss Me Quick / Suspicion (US RCA 447 0639, UK RCA 1375, 1964) (US No.34, UK No.14) (UK reissue of B-side, No.9, 1976)

Mexico / You Can't Say No In Acapulco (1964: Germany No.23, Norway No.7)

Viva Las Vegas / What'd I Say (US RCA 8360, US RCA 1390, 1964) (US No.29; UK No.17; B-side US No.21, higher than A-side) (UK reissue No.15, 2007)

Viva Las Vegas (US) / *Love In Las Vegas* (UK) EP (US RCA 4382, UK RCA 7141, 1964) with If You Think I Don't Need You, I Need Somebody to Lean On , C'mon Everybody and Today Tomorrow and Forever.(UK EP chart, No.3)

Such a Night / Never Ending (US RCA 8400, UK RCA 1411, 1964) (US No.16, UK No.13)

Elvis for You, Volume 1 EP (US RCA 7142, 1964) (UK EP chart, No.11)

Elvis for You, Volume 2 EP (US RCA 7143, 1964) (UK EP chart, No.18)

Ask Me / Ain't That Lovin' You Baby (US RCA 8440, UK RCA 1422, 1964) (US No.12; B-side, US No.16; UK with B-side promoted as A-side, No.15)

One Track Heart / Roustabout (French single, 1964, No.24 in France)

Blue Christmas / White Christmas (UK RCA 1430, 1964) (UK No.11)

Do the Clam / You'll Be Gone (US RCA 8500, UK RCA 1443, 1965) (US No.21, UK No.19, Australia No.4.)

Crying in the Chapel / I Believe in the Man in the Sky (US RCA 447 0643, UK RCA 1455, 1965) (US No.3, US No.1 for 2 weeks, Australia No.1 for 6 weeks) (UK reissue No.43, 1977) (UK reissue No.2, 2005)

(Such an) Easy Question / It Feels So Right (US RCA 8585, 1965) (US No.11)

I'm Yours / Long Lonely Highway (US RCA 8657, 1965) (US No.11)

Puppet on a String / Wooden Heart (US RCA 447 0650, 1965) (US No.14)

Tell Me Why / Blue River (US RCA 8740, UK RCA 1489, 1965) (US No.33, UK No.15; B-side, US No.95). UK B-side, 'Puppet on a String'.

Tickle Me EP (US RCA EPA 4383, UK RCA RCX 7173, 1965) with I Feel that I've Known You Forever, Night Rider, Slowly but Surely, Dirty Dirty Feeling and Put the

Spencer Leigh

Blame on Me (UK EP chart No.3)

Tickle Me, Volume 2 EP (UK RCX 7174, 1965) with It Feels So Right, (Such an) Easy Question, Long Lonely Highway and I'm Yours. There was no *Tickle Me, Volume 2* in the US. (UK EP chart, No.8)

Blue River / Do Not Disturb (UK RCA 1504, 1966) (UK No.22)

Frankie and Johnny / Please Don't Stop Loving Me (US RCA 8780, UK RCA 1509, 1966) (US No 25, UK No.21; B-side US No.45)

Love Letters / Come What May (US RCA 8870, UK RCA 1526, 1966) (US No.19, UK No.6)

All that I Am / Spinout / (US RCA 8941, UK RCA 1545, 1966) (US No.41, UK No.18; B-side No.40)

If Every Day Was Like Christmas / How Would You Like to Be (US RCA 8950, UK RCA 1557, 1966) (UK No.9)

Indescribably Blue / Fools Fall in Love (US RCA 9056, UK RCA 1565, 1967) (US No.33, UK No.21)

You Gotta Stop / Love Machine (UK RCA 1593, 1967) (UK No.38; both sides listed)

Easy Come, Easy Go EP (UK RCA RCX 7187) (UK EP chart, No.1 for 3 weeks)

Long Legged Girl (with the short dress on) / That's Someone You Never Forget (US RCA 9115, UK RCA 1616, 1967) (US No.63, UK No.49; B-side, US No.92)

There's Always Me / Judy (US RCA 9287, 1967) (US No.56; B-side No.78; both sides listed, Australia No.5)

Big Boss Man / You Don't Know Me (US RCA 9341, 1967) (US No.38, B-side, No.44: France, No.25)

Guitar Man / High Heel Sneakers (US RCA 9425, UK RCA 1663, 1968) (US No.43, UK No.19)

U S Male / Stay Away (US RCA 9465, UK RCA 1688, 1968) (US No.28, UK No.15; B-side US No.67)

Your Time Hasn't Come Yet Baby / Let Yourself Go (US RCA 9547, UK RCA 1714, 1968) (US No.72, UK No.22; B-side US No.71)

You'll Never Walk Alone / We Call on Him (US RCA 9600, UK RCA 1747, 1968) (US No.90, UK No.44) Sylvester Stallone came to Everton, so why couldn't Elvis have come to the Kop?

A Little Less Conversation / Almost in Love (US RCA 9610, 1968) (US No.69; B-side, US No.95)

If I Can Dream / Edge of Reality (US RCA 9670, UK RCA 1795, 1968) (US No.12, UK No.11, Australia No.2; UK B-side, Memories) (UK reissue of A-side: No.56, 1987, listed with Love Me Tender) (UK reissue No.17, 2007)

RCA SINGLES (1969–August 1977)

Memories / Charro (US RCA 9731, 1969) (US No.35)

In the Ghetto / Any Day Now (US RCA 9741, UK RCA 1831, 1969) (US No.3, UK

No.2, Australia No.1) (UK reissue: No.13, 2007)

Clean Up Your Own Back Yard / The Fair Is Moving On (US RCA 9747, UK RCA 1869, 1969) (US No.35, UK No.21)

Suspicious Minds / You'll Think of Me (US RCA 9764, UK RCA 1900, 1969) (US No.1 for 1 week, UK No.2) (UK reissue No.15, 2001) (UK reissue No.11, 2007)

Don't Cry Daddy / Rubberneckin' (US RCA 9768, UK RCA 1916, 1969) (US No.6; US Country No.13; UK No.8; B-side US No.69)

Kentucky Rain / My Little Friend (US RCA 9791, UK RCA 1949, 1970) (US No.16; US Country No.31; UK No.21)

The Wonder of You / Mama Liked the Roses (US RCA 9835, 1970) (US No .9; US Country No.37; UK No.1 for 6 weeks; B-side, US No.65) The first time Elvis had a hit with a live track; he never recorded a studio version. (UK reissue No.48, 1977) (UK reissue No.4, 2005)

I've Lost You / The Next Step Is Love (US RCA 9873, UK RCA 1999, 1970) (US No.32, UK No.9; B-side, US No.33)

You Don't Have to Say You Love Me / Patch It Up (US RCA 9916, UK RCA 2046, 1970) (US No.11, UK No.9; B-side US No.90) (UK reissue: No.16, 2007)

See See Rider (French single) (France No.28)

I Really Don't Want to Know / There Goes My Everything (US RCA 9960, UK RCA 2060, 1971) (US No.21, US Country No.23; B-side, US No.57, US Country No.9, UK No.6; B-side was promoted as A-side in UK.)

Rags to Riches / Where Did They Go, Lord (US RCA 9980, UK RCA 2084, 1971) (US No.45, UK No.9; B-side, US No.33; Ireland No.12)

Heartbreak Hotel / Hound Dog / Don't Be Cruel (UK RCA Maximillion 2014, 1971) (UK No.10, first two tracks listed) The first Presley reissue to make the UK charts.

Life / Only Believe (US RCA 9985, 1971) (US No.53; US Country No.34; B-side, US No.95)

I'm Leavin' / Heart of Rome (US RCA 9998, UK RCA 2125, 1971) (US No.36)

It's Only Love / The Sound of Your Cry (US RCA 1017, 1971) (US No.51) (Not released as a UK single until 1980 – see below)

I Just Can't Help Believin' / How the Web Was Woven (UK RCA 2158, 1971) (UK No.6). One of Elvis' classic tracks and yet not issued as a single in the US.

Until It's Time for You to Go / We Can Make the Morning (US RCA 0619, UK RCA 2188, 1972) (US No.40, UK No.5)

An American Trilogy / The First Time Ever I Saw Your Face (US RCA 0672, UK RCA 2229, 1972) (US No.66, UK No.8) (UK reissue: No.12, 2007)

Burning Love / It's a Matter of Time (US RCA 0769, UK RCA 2267, 1972) (US No.2, UK No.7; B-side, US Country No.36) (UK reissue: No.13, 2007)

Separate Ways / Always on My Mind (US RCA 0815, UK RCA 2304, 1972) (US No.20; US Country No.16, both sides shown; B-side, UK No.9) (UK B-side reissue to promote album of same name: No.13, 1997) (UK reissue No.17, 2007)

Polk Salad Anne / See See Rider (UK RCA 2359, 1973) (UK No.23)

Steamroller Blues / Fool (US RCA 0910, UK RCA 2393, 1973) (Highly confusing chart placings – in the US No.17 with B-side at No.79. Both sides listed on US Country chart making No.31. In the UK, Fool No.15 and No.8 in Ireland.)

Raised on Rock / For Ol' Times Sake (US RCA 0088, UK RCA 2435, 1973) (US No.41, UK No.36; B-side, US No.95)

I've Got a Thing About You, Baby / Take Good Care of Her (US & UK both RCA 0196, 1974) (US No.39; US Country No.4 both sides shown; UK No.33; B-side, US No.63)

If You Talk in Your Sleep / Help Me (US & UK both RCA 0280, 1974) (US No.17: US Country No.6, both sides shown: UK No.40)

My Boy / Thinking About You (US RCA 10191, UK RCA 2458, 1974) (US No.20, US Country No.14, UK No.5; UK B-side, Loving Arms)

Promised Land / It's Midnight (US & UK both RCA 10074, 1974) (US No.14: US Country No.9, both sides shown: UK No.9) Released in the UK on 8 January 1975 with an advertising slogan, 'Happy birthday, my boy'. Perhaps they should have held 'My Boy' back for this event.

T-R-O-U-B-L-E / Mr. Songman (US RCA 10278, UK RCA 2562, 1975) (US No.35, US Country No.11, UK No.31)

Green Green Grass of Home / Thinking About You (UK RCA 2635, 1975) (UK No.29)

Bringing It Back / Pieces of My Life (US RCA 10401, 1975) (US No.65; B-side US Country No.33)

Hurt / For the Heart (US RCA 10601, UK RCA 2674, 1976) (US No.28, US Country No.6, UK No.37; B-side US No.95)

Girl of My Best Friend / A Mess of Blues (UK reissue, RCA 2729, 1976) (UK No.9)

Suspicion / (It's a) Long Lonely Highway (UK reissue RCA2768, 1976) (UK No.9)

Moody Blue / She Thinks I Still Care (US RCA 10857, UK RCA 0857, 1977) (US No.31: US Country No.1 for 1 week, both sides listed: UK No.6; B-side, No.95)

Way Down / Pledging My Love (US RCA 10998, UK RCA 0998, 1977) (US No.18: US Country No.1 for 1 week, both sides listed: UK No.1 for 5 weeks) (UK reissue: No.2, 2005)

ELVIS PRESLEY SINGLES (August 1977 to the Present)

Following the UK success of two reissues, 'Girl of My Best Friend' and 'Suspicion', RCA released 16 singles in May 1977, all of which could be bought individually – but record shops did have free cardboard boxes marked *Presley Gold*, which would fit them all. Following Elvis' death, eight of these singles made the charts, although the highest was 'It's Now or Never' at No.39. My guess would be that they sold better than this and the dealers filled in the chart returns wrongly. There was a similar set in the US called *Elvis Presley – Collectors' Series*; reissues rarely appeared in the *Billboard* charts: they could have sold and the compilers considered them ineligible.

Elvis Presley: Caught in a Trap

From now on, RCA in the UK did not follow the US and showed more initiative with its releases and its promotions, leading to several chart successes.

My Way / America the Beautiful (US RCA PB 11165, UK RCA 1165, 1977) (US No.22, US Country No.2, UK No.9)

Unchained Melody / Softly As I Leave You (US RCA 11212, 1978) (US Country No.6, both sides listed)

Are You Sincere / Solitaire (US RCA PB 11533, 1979) (US Country No.10, both sides listed)

There's a Honky Tonk Angel (who will take me back in) / I've Got a Feelin' in My Body (US RCA PB 11679) (US Country No.6, both sides listed)

It Won't Seem Like Christmas (without you) / Merry Christmas Baby (UK RCA 9464, 1979) (UK No.13)

It's Only Love / Beyond the Reef (UK RCA No.4, 1980) (UK No.3: both sides listed on chart)

Santa Claus Is Back in Town / I Believe (UK RCA No.16, 1980) (UK No.41)

Guitar Man / Faded Love (US RCA 12158, UK RCA No.43, 1981) (US No.28: US Country No.1 for 1 week: UK No.43) This is a revamped version with a new Jerry Reed guitar solo: no point, the original was fine.

Loving Arms / You Asked Me To (US RCA 12202, RCA No.48, 1981) (US Country No.8, both sides listed: UK No.47)

Are You Lonesome Tonight (The Laughing Version) / From a Jack to a King (UK RCA 196, 1982) (UK No.25) Elvis on stage in 1969. It was David Hamilton's *Record of the Week* on BBC Radio 2 and it went to No.1 in Belgium. Not issued as a single in US: RCA might have thought it would not help his legacy. (UK reissue of A-side: No.68, 1991)

The Elvis Medley / Always on My Mind (US RCA PB 13351) (US Country No.31)

The Sound of Your Cry / I'll Never Know (US RCA 232, 1982) (UK No.59)

Baby I Don't Care / True Love (UK RCA 332, 1983) (UK No.61)

I Can Help / The Lady Loves Me (UK RCA 369, 1983) (UK No.30) B-side was duet with Ann-Margret and came with a picture sleeve of them getting married (for the film, but it nearly was for real).

The Last Farewell / It's Easy for You (UK RCA 459, 1984) (UK No.48)

The Elvis Medley / Blue Suede Shoes (UK RCA 476, 1985) (UK No.51) The Elvis Medley was first issued in the US in 1982 and had been prompted by the success of Hooked on Classics and similar releases. This was a late entrant into that market in the UK and released to coincide with the fiftieth anniversary of his birth. No real merit, but may have helped to push his catalogue. Oddly, and this is a mercy, the Elvis songs weren't given a disco beat.

Always on My Mind (Alternate take) / Tomorrow Night (UK RCA PB 49943, 1985) (UK No.59)

Ain't That Lovin' You Baby (alternative fast version) / Bossa Nova Baby (UK RCA

ARON 1) (UK No.47, 1987, both sides listed) Superb picture sleeve.

Love Me Tender / If I Can Dream (UK RCA ARON 2, 1987) (UK No.56) The 12" edition included an extended mix of Bossa Nova Baby.

The Twelfth of Never / Walk a Mile in My Shoes / Burning Love (UK RCA 32012 7, 1995) (UK No.21)

America the Beautiful / Amazing Grace / If I Can Dream (song and video) (US & UK RCA 904022, 2001) (UK No.69) (Release was following 9/11 with proceeds to American Red Cross Liberty Disaster Relief Fund)

A Little Less Conversation (Elvis vs JXL) (Remix, extended remix and original version) (US & UK RCA 74321 943572, 2002) (US No.50, UK No.1 for 4 weeks. Single was No.1 in 26 countries.) (UK reissue: No.3, 2005)

Rubberneckin' (Paul Oakenfold remix) (Remix, extended remix and original version) (US & UK RCA 82876 543412, 2003) (US No.94, UK No.5)

That's All Right, Mama (original and alternative take) / Blue Moon of Kentucky (UK RCA 82876 619212, 2004) (UK No.3) Elvis' first US single makes the UK Top 10 – great to have it in the listings at last.

In 2005, RCA issued all 18 of Elvis' UK No.1s on a weekly basis with a special cardboard box available with the first reissue being 'All Shook Up'. Chart positions shown by original singles.

In 2007 RCA issued another 18 of Elvis' big UK chart hits on a weekly basis, again with a special cardboard box available with the first release, 'Heartbreak Hotel'. Chart positions shown by original singles.

ELVIS PRESLEY ALBUMS

Elvis Presley (US RCA LPM 1254, 1956) (US No.1 for 10 weeks)
Blue Suede Shoes / I'm Counting on You / I Got a Woman / One-Sided Love Affair / I Love You Because / Just Because / Tutti Frutti / Tryin' to Get to You / I'm Gonna Sit Right Down and Cry / I'll Never Let You Go (Little Darlin') / Blue Moon / Money Honey

Rock'n'Roll (UK HMV CLP 1093, 1956) (UK No.1 for 1 week) (Reissue: No.34, 1972)

Listed separately, as the contents differed from the US album with just seven tracks the same: Blue Suede Shoes / I Got a Woman / I'm Counting on You / I'm Left, You're Right, She's Gone / That's All Right, Mama / Money Honey / Mystery Train / I'm Gonna Sit Right Down and Cry Over You / Tryin' to Get to You / One-Sided Love Affair / Lawdy Miss Clawdy / Shake Rattle and Roll

Elvis (US) / *Rock'n'Roll* NO.2 (UK) (US RCA LPM 1382, 1956) (US No.1 for 5 weeks, UK No.3) (Reissue: No.3, 1962)
Rip It Up / Love Me / When My Blue Moon Turns to Gold Again / Long Tall Sally / First in Line / Paralyzed / So Glad You're Mine / Old Shep / Ready Teddy / Anyplace Is Paradise / How's the World Treating You / How Do You Think I Feel

Loving You (US RCA LPM 1515 {12-inch}, UK RCA RC 24001 {10-inch}, 1957) (US

No.1 for 10 weeks, UK No.1 for 3 weeks) (UK reissue No.24, 1967)

On both albums: Mean Woman Blues / Teddy Bear / Loving You / Got a Lot O' Livin' to Do / Lonesome Cowboy / Hot Dog / Party / Blueberry Hill / True Love /

On US album: Don't Leave Me Now / Have I Told You Lately That I Love You / I Need You So

The Best Of Elvis (UK HMV DLP 1159 {10-inch}, 1957) (UK, No.3)

Recycling starts here.

Elvis' Christmas Album (US RCA LOC 1035, UK RCA RD 27052, 1957) (US No.1 for 4 weeks, UK No.2) (Reissue US No.33, 1960) (Reissue UK No.7, 1971)

Santa Claus Is Back in Town / White Christmas / Here Comes Santa Claus / I'll Be Home for Christmas / Blue Christmas / Santa Bring My Baby Back to Me / O Little Town of Bethlehem / Silent Night / Peace in the Valley / I Believe / Take My Hand, Precious Lord / It Is No Secret

Elvis' Golden Records (US RCA LPM 1707, UK RCA RB 16069, 1958) (US No.3, UK No.2) (UK reissue No.21, 1970)

RCA might have not have been too confident about the sales of a *Greatest Hits* album as they included 14 tracks and added a LP-sized photo album of colour portraits. The UK issue replaced four of his recent hits with four Sun titles, which weren't golden records at all. RCA in the UK released it under its more expensive Red Seal brand which made the retail price £2. Still, it was the best-looking album package up until *Sgt Pepper* in 1967.

King Creole (USA RCA LPM 1884, UK RCA RD 27088, 1958) (US No.2, UK No.1 for 7 weeks)

King Creole / As Long as I Have You / Hard Headed Woman / Trouble / Dixieland Rock / Don't Ask Me Why / Lover Doll / Crawfish / Young Dreams / Steadfast, Loyal and True / New Orleans

This was the only one of Elvis' 50s albums to be issued with the same content and the same cover in both the US and the UK.

For LP Fans Only (US), *Elvis* (UK) (US RCA LPM 1990, UK RCA RD 27120, 1959) (US No.19)

On both albums: That's All Right. Mama / Lawdy, Miss Clawdy / Mystery Train / Playing for Keeps / Poor Boy / My Baby Left Me / I Was the One / Shake, Rattle and Roll / I'm Left, You're Right, She's Gone / You're a Heartbreaker

On UK album: Money Honey / I'm Counting on You / Tryin' to Get To You / Blue Suede Shoes

This was the first album not to give the artist's name on the front cover. Most music fans think it is the Rolling Stones who have this honour for their first album but this was five years earlier. There is a colour cover of Elvis the civilian on the front in a red shirt and Elvis the soldier on the back – take your pick. The album is often referred to as *Red Shirt*.

A Date With Elvis (US RCA LPM 2011, RCA RD 27128, 1959) (US No.32, UK No.4)

Another compilation but the UK and US contents had only six titles in common. On the back sleeve, there was a calendar for 1960 with the date of discharge, 24 March, circled. He was to be discharged on 5 March.

50,000,000 Elvis Fans Can't Be Wrong – Elvis' Golden Records, Volume 2 (US RCA LPM 2075, 1959) (US No.31)

Elvis in gold lamé – one of the most parodied album covers of all-time.

Elvis' Golden Records, Volume 2 (UK RCA RD 27159, 1960) (UK No.4) (Reissue No.27, 1977)

Same idea as the previous US album, but the UK issue featured seven singles, both A and B sides, the first time that any album by any artist had been compiled this way. It featured an alternative, slower take of Dontcha Think It's Time: this might have been a mistake but it gave a taste of what was to come.

Elvis Is Back! (US RCA LPM 2231, UK RCA RD 27171, 1960) (US No.2, UK No.1 for 1 week)

Make Me Know It / Fever / The Girl of My Best Friend / I Will Be Home Again / Dirty, Dirty Feeling / Thrill of Your Love / Soldier Boy / Such a Night / It Feels So Right / The Girl Next Door Went A' Walkin' / Like a Baby / Reconsider Baby

G I Blues (US RCA LPM 2256, UK RCA RD 27192, 1960) (US No.1 for 10 weeks, UK No.1 for 22 weeks) (Reissue UK No.14, 1977)

What's She Really Like / Frankfort Special / Wooden Heart / G I Blues / Pocketful of Rainbows / Shoppin' Around / Big Boots / Didja Ever / Blue Suede Shoes (remake) / Doin' the Best I Can / Tonight's All Right for Love (For copyright reasons, replaced by Tonight Is So Right for Love in the UK)

His Hand in Mine (US RCA LPM 2328, UK RCA RD 27211, 1960) (US No.13, UK No.3)

His Hand in Mine / I'm Gonna Walk Dem Golden Stairs / In My Father's House / Milky White Way / Known Only to Him / I Believe in the Man in the Sky / Joshua Fit the Battle / He Knows Just What I Need / Swing Down Sweet Chariot / Mansion over the Hilltop / If We Never Meet Again / Working on the Building

Something for Everybody (US RCA LPM 2370, UK RCA RD 27224, 1961) (US No.1 for 3 weeks, UK No.2)

There's Always Me / Give Me the Right / It's a Sin / Sentimental Me / Starting Today / Gently / I'm Coming Home / In Your Arms / Put the Blame on Me / Judy / I Want You with Me / I Slipped, I Stumbled, I Fell

Blue Hawaii (US RCA LPM 2426, UK RCA RD 27238, 1961) (US No.1 for 20 weeks, UK No.1 for 18 weeks) (Reissue UK No.49, 1977)

Blue Hawaii / Almost Always True / Aloha Oe / No More / Can't Help Falling in Love / Rock-A-Hula Baby / Moonlight Swim / Ku-U-I-Po / Ito Eats / Slicin' Sand / Hawaiian Sunset / Beach Boy Blues / Island of Love / Hawaiian Wedding Song

Pot Luck (US RCA LPM 2523, UK RD 27265, 1962) (US No.4, UK No.1 for 6 weeks)

Kiss Me Quick / Just for Old Time Sake / Gonna Get Back Home Somehow / (Such An) Easy Question / Steppin' out of Line / I'm Yours / Something Blue / Suspicion / I Feel That I've Known You Forever / Night Rider / Fountain of Love / That's Someone

You Never Forget

Girls! Girls! Girls! (US RCA LPM 2621, UK RD 7534, 1962) (US No.3, UK No.2)

Girls! Girls! Girls! / I Don't Wanna Be Tied / Where Do You Come From / I Don't Want To / We'll Be Together / A Boy Like Me, A Girl Like You / Earth Boy / Return to Sender / Because of Love / Thanks to the Rolling Sea / Song of the Shrimp / The Walls Have Ears / We're Coming In Loaded

It Happened at the World's Fair (US RCA LPM 2697, UK RCA RD 7565, 1963) (US No.4, UK No.4)

Beyond the Bend / Relax / Take Me to the Fair / They Remind Me Too Much of You / One Broken Heart for Sale / I'm Falling in Love Tonight / Cotton Candy Land / A World of Our Own / How Would You Like to Be / Happy Ending

Fun in Acapulco (US RCA LPM 2756, UK RCA RD 7609, 1963) (US No.3, UK No.9)

Fun in Acapulco / Vino, Dinero Y Amor / Mexico / El Toro / Marguerita / The Bullfighter Was a Lady / No Room to Rhumba in a Sports Car / I Think I'm Gonna Like It Here / Bossa Nova Baby / You Can't Say No in Acapulco / Guadalajara / Love Me Tonight / Slowly but Surely

Elvis' Golden Records, Volume 3 (US RCA LPM 2765, UK RCA RD 7630, 1963) (US No.3, UK No.6) (UK Reissue No.26, 1977)

Kissin' CousinsS (US RCA LPM 2894, US RCA RD 7645, 1964) (US No.6, UK No.5)

Kissin' Cousins No.2 / Smokey Mountain Boy / There's Gold In the Mountains / One Boy, Two Little Girls / Catchin' On Fast / Tender Feeling / Anyone (Could Fall in Love with You) / Barefoot Ballad / Once Is Enough / Kissin' Cousins / Echoes of Love / (It's A) Long Lonely Highway

Roustabout (US RCA LPM 2999, UK RCA RD 7678, 1964) (US No.1 for 1 week, UK No.12)

Roustabout / Little Egypt / Poison Ivy League / Hard Knocks / It's a Wonderful World / Big Love, Big Heartache / One Track Heart / It's Carnival Time / Carny Town / There's a Brand New Day on the Horizon / Wheels On My Heels

Girl Happy (US RCA LPM 3338, UK RCA RD 7714, 1965) (US No.8, UK No.8)

Girl Happy / Spring Fever / Fort Lauderdale Chamber of Commerce / Startin' Tonight / Wolf Call / Do Not Disturb / Cross My Heart and Hope to Die / The Meanest Girl in Town / Do the Clam / Puppet on a String / I've Got to Find My Baby / You'll Be Gone

Flaming Star and Summer Kisses (UK RCA RD 7723, 1965) (UK No.11)

UK fans had been complaining that they had not been able to buy two songs from *Flaming Star*, the title track and Summer Kisses, Winter Tears. Albert Hand's *Elvis Monthly* had been campaigning for their release and they got their wish in a curious way: this LP included the two tracks but also the eight tracks of the *Loving You* LP and It's Now or Never and Are You Lonesome Tonight. Hard to see whom the LP was aimed at but it did sell.

Elvis For Everyone (US RCA LPM 3450, UK RCA RD 7752, 1965) (US No.10, UK No.8) (Reissue: No.48, 1971)

Your Cheatin' Heart / Summer Kisses, Winter Tears / Finders Keepers, Losers Weepers

/ In My Way / Tomorrow Night / Memphis Tennessee / For the Millionth and the Last Time / Forget Me Never / Sound Advice / Santa Lucia / I Met Her Today / When It Rains, It Really Pours

Harum Scarum (US), *Harem Holiday* (UK) (US RCA LPM 3468, UK RCA RD 7767, 1965) (US No.8, UK No.11)

Harem Holiday / My Desert Serenade / Go East, Young Man / Mirage / Kismet / Shake That Tambourine / Hey Little Girl / Golden Coins / So Close, Yet So Far (from Paradise) / Animal Instinct / Wisdom of the Ages

Frankie and Johnny (US RCA LPM 3553, UK RCA RD 7793, 1966) (US No.20, UK No.11)

Frankie and Johnny / Come Along / Petunia, the Gardener's Daughter / Chesay / What Every Woman Lives For / Look Out, Broadway / Beginner's Luck / Down By the Riverside / When the Saints Go Marching In / Shout It Out / Hard Luck / Please Don't Stop Loving Me / Everybody Come Aboard

Paradise, Hawaiian Style (US RCA LPM 3643, UK RCA RD 7810, 1966) (US No.15, UK No.7) (Reissue: UK No.53, 1980)

Paradise, Hawaiian Style / Queenie Wahine's Papaya / Scratch My Back / Drums of the Islands / Datin' / A Dog's Life / House of Sand / Stop Where You Are / This Is My Heaven / Sand Castles

Spinout (US), CALIFORNIA HOLIDAY (UK) (US RCA LPM 3702, UK RCA RD 7820, 1966) (US No.18, UK No.17)

Stop, Look and Listen / Adam and Evil / All That I Am / Never Say Yes / Am I Ready / Beach Shack / Spinout / Smorgasbord / I'll Be Back / Tomorrow Is a Long Time / Down In the Alley / I'll Remember You

How Great Thou Art (US RCA LPM 3758, UK RCA RD 7867, 1967) (US No.18, UK No.11)

How Great Thou Art / In the Garden / Somebody Bigger Than You and I / Farther Along / Stand By Me / Without Him / So High / Where Could I Go But to the Lord / By and By / If The Lord Wasn't Walking By My Side / Run On / Where No One Stands Alone / Crying In the Chapel / We Call On Him / You'll Never Walk Alone

Double Trouble (US RCA LPM 3787, UK RCA RD 7892, 1967) (UK No.34)

Double Trouble / Baby, If You'll Give Me All of Your Love / Could I Fall In Love / Long Legged Girl (With the Short Dress On) / City by Night / Old MacDonald / I Love Only One Girl / There Is So Much World to See / It Won't Be Long / Never Ending / Blue River / What Now, What Next, Where To

Clambake (US RCA LPM 3893, UK RCA RD 7917, 1967) (US No.40, UK No.39)

Guitar Man / Clambake / Who Needs Money / A House That Has Everything / Confidence / Hey, Hey, Hey / You Don't Know Me / The Girl I Never Loved / How Can You Lose What You Never Had / Big Boss Man / Singing Tree / Just Call Me Lonesome / Hi-Heel Sneakers

Elvis' Golden Records, Volume 4 (US RCA LPM 3921, UK RCA RD 7924, 1968) (US No.33)

Speedway (US RCA LPM 3989, UK RCA RD 7957, 1968)

Speedway / There Ain't Nothing Like a Song / Your Time Hasn't Come Yet, Baby / Who Are You (Who Am I) / He's Your Uncle Not Your Dad / Let Yourself Go / Your Groovy Self (Nancy Sinatra) / Five Sleepy Heads / Western Union / Mine / Goin' Home / Suppose

Elvis – TV Special (US RCA LPM 4088, UK RCA RD 8011, 1968) (US No.8, UK No.2) (Reissue UK No.50, 1978)

Medley: Trouble – Guitar Man / *Medley*: Lawdy, Miss Clawdy – Baby, What You Want Me to Do / *Medley*: Heartbreak Hotel – Hound Dog – All Shook Up – Can't Help Falling In Love – Jailhouse Rock – Love Me Tender / *Medley*: Where Could I Go But to the Lord / Up Above My Head / Saved / *Medley:* Blue Christmas – One Night / Memories / *Medley:* Nothingville / Big Boss Man / Guitar Man / Little Egypt / Trouble /Guitar Man / If I Can Dream

Singer Presents Elvis Singing Flaming Star and Others (US Singer Sewing Machine Company PRS 279, then reissued in 1969 as Elvis Sings Flaming Star RCA Camden CAS 2304, UK RCA Camden INTS 1012, 1968) (UK No.2)

Flaming Star / Wonderful World / Night Life / All I Needed Was the Rain / Too Much Monkey Business / The Yellow Rose of Texas & The Eyes of Texas / She's a Machine / Do the Vega / Tiger Man

Elvis Presley's first budget album, originally only available in the US through Singer stockists. As with many budget albums, the contents were a mish-mash, but there was a great new performance, Too Much Monkey Business, and all yours for £1. Camden was the home of RCA's pressing plant in New Jersey. Many of these albums were pressed on Dynaflex, which didn't look as durable as the standard vinyl and indeed, wasn't used for very long.

From Elvis in Memphis (US RCA LSP 4155, UK RCA RD 8029, 1969) (US No.13, UK No.1 for 1 week)

Wearin' That Loved On Look / Only the Strong Survive / I'll Hold You In My Heart (Till I Can Hold You In My Arms) / Long Black Limousine / It Keeps Right On A-Hurtin' / I'm Movin' On / Power of My Love / Gentle On My Mind / After Loving You /True Love Travels On a Gravel Road / Any Day Now / In the Ghetto / Suspicious Minds / Don't Cry Daddy / Kentucky Rain / Mama Liked the Roses

From Memphis to Vegas – From Vegas to Memphis (US RCA LSP 6020, UK RCA SF 8080/1, double album, 1969) (US No.12, UK No.3)

Disc 1 (from International Hotel, Las Vegas): Blue Suede Shoes / Johnny B. Goode / All Shook Up / Are You Lonesome Tonight / Hound Dog / I Can't Stop Loving You / My Babe / *Medley:* Mystery Train – Tiger Man / Words / In the Ghetto / Suspicious Minds / Can't Help Falling in Love

Disc 2 (Back in Memphis): Inherit the Wind / This Is the Story / Stranger In My Own Home Town / A Little Bit of Green / And the Grass Won't Pay No Mind / Do You Know Who I Am / From a Jack to a King / The Fair's Moving On / You'll Think of Me / Without Love

Let's Be Friends (US RCA Camden CAS 2408, UK RCA Camden INTS 1103, 1970)

Stay Away, Joe / If I'm a Fool (For Loving You) / Let's Be Friends / Let's Forget About the Stars / Mama / I'll Be There / Almost / Change of Habit / Have a Happy

A Portrait in Music (Germany RCA SF 558, 1970) (UK No.36)

Import copies of this German compilation made the UK charts.

On Stage – February 1970 (US RCA LSP 4362, UK RCA SF 8128, 1970) (US No.13, UK No.2)

See See Rider / Release Me / Sweet Caroline / Runaway / The Wonder of You / Polk Salad Annie / Yesterday / Proud Mary / Walk a Mile in My Shoes / Let It Be Me

Almost in Love (US RCA Camden CAS 2440, UK RCA Camden INTS 1206, 1970) (UK No.38)

Almost In Love / Long Legged Girl (With the Short Dress On) / Edge of Reality / My Little Friend / A Little Less Conversation / Rubberneckin' / Clean Up Your Own Backyard / U.S. Male / Charro! / Stay Away, Joe

RCA was flooding the US market with budget releases, which were also issued in the UK. It's hard to see the sense of this as you would have thought the concentration should be on the excellent new material from the regenerated Elvis.

Worldwide 50 Gold Award Hits (US RCA LPM 6401, UK RCA LPM 6401, 4LP box set, 1970) (UK No.49)

Fifty familiar hits and the *Elvis Sails* EP in a box set.

Elvis: That's The Way It Is (US RCA LSP 4445, UK RCA SF 8162, 1970) (US No.21, UK No.12)

I Just Can't Help Believin' / Twenty Days and Twenty Nights / How the Web Was Woven / Patch It Up / Mary In the Morning / You Don't Have to Say You Love Me / You've Lost That Loving Feeling / I've Lost You / Just Pretend / Stranger in the Crowd / The Next Step Is Love / Bridge over Troubled Water

I'm 10,000 Years Old – Elvis Country (US RCA LSP 4460, UK RCA SF 8172, 1971) (US No.12, UK No.4)

Snowbird / Tomorrow Never Comes / Little Cabin On the Hill / Whole Lotta Shakin' Goin' On / Funny How Time Slips Away / I Really Don't Want to Know / There Goes My Everything / It's Your Baby, You Rock It / The Fool / Faded Love / I Washed My Hands In Muddy Water / Make the World Go Away. (Snatches of I Was Born About 10,000 Years Ago played between tracks.)

You'll Never Walk Alone (US RCA CAL 2472, RCA Camden CDM 1088, 1971) (UK No.20)

Inspirational compilation

Love Letters (US RCA LSP 4530, UK RCA SF 8202, 1971) (US No 33, UK No.7)

Love Letters / When I'm Over You / If I Were You / Got My Mojo Working / Heart of Rome / Only Believe / This Is Our Dance / Cindy, Cindy / I'll Never Know / It Ain't No Big Thing (But It's Growing)

C'mon Everybody (US RCA CAL 2518, UK RCA Camden INTS 1286, 1971) (UK No.5)

C'mon Everybody / Angel / Easy Come, Easy Go / A Whistling Tune / Follow That Dream / King of the Whole Wide World / I'll Take Love / I'm Not the Marrying Kind / This Is Living /Today, Tomorrow and Forever

Elvis — The Other Sides, Worldwide Gold Award Hits, Volume 2 (US RCA LPM 6402, 4LP box set, 1971)

Theoretically, Elvis' B-sides, but not as well structured as it should have been for an expensive collection, even if you got an authenticated swatch of Elvis' clothing. Although not issued independently in the UK, 15,000 sets were imported.

I Got Lucky (US RCA Camden CAL 2533, UK RCA Camden INT 1322, 1971) (UK No.26)

I Got Lucky / What a Wonderful Life / I Need Somebody to Lean On / Yoga Is as Yoga Does / Riding the Rainbow / Fools Fall In Love / The Love Machine / Home Is Where the Heart Is / You Gotta Stop / If You Think I Don't Need You

The Wonderful World of Christmas (US RCA LSP 4579, UK RCA SF 8221, 1971)

O Come All Ye Faithful / The First Noel / On a Snowy Christmas Night / Winter Wonderland / The Wonderful World of Christmas / It Won't Seem Like Christmas (Without You) / I'll Be Home On Christmas Day / If I Get Home On Christmas Day / Holly Leaves and Christmas Trees / Merry Christmas Baby / Silver Bells / If Every Day Was Like Christmas

I like seeing Presley listed as the composer of O Come All Ye Faithful and The First Noel. Who would have thought it? And who picks these pathetic album titles – wouldn't *As the Snow Flies* have been a great title for a Christmas album?

Elvis Now (US RCA LSP 4671, UK RCA SF 8266, 1972) (UK No.12)

Help Me Make It Through the Night / Miracle of the Rosary / Hey Jude / Put Your Hand In the Hand / Until It's Time for You to Go / We Can Make the Morning / Early Mornin' Rain / Sylvia / Fools Rush In / I Was Born About Ten Thousand Years Ago

He Touched Me (US RCA LSP 4690, RCA SF 8275, 1972) (UK No.38)

He Touched Me / I've Got Confidence / Amazing Grace / Seeing Is Believing /. He Is My Everything / Bosom of Abraham / An Evening Prayer / Lead Me, Guide Me / There Is No God But God / A Thing Called Love / I, John / Reach Out to Jesus

Elvis Sings Hits From His Movies, Volume 1 (US RCA CAS 2567, UK RCA Camden CDS 1110, 1972)

A car-boot sale of an album – no hits in sight unless you count 'Guitar Man' but that wasn't from a movie.

Elvis as Recorded at Madison Square Garden (US RCA LSP 4776, UK RCA SF 8296, 1972) (US No.11, UK No.3)

That's All Right, Mama / Proud Mary / Never Been to Spain / You Don't Have to Say You Love Me / You've Lost That Lovin' Feelin' / Polk Salad Annie / Love Me / All Shook Up /Heartbreak Hotel / *Medley*: Teddy Bear – Don't Be Cruel / Love Me Tender / The Impossible Dream / Hound Dog/ Suspicious Minds / For the Good Times / American Trilogy /Funny How Time Slips Away / I Can't Stop Loving You / Can't Help Falling In Love

Spencer Leigh

Burning Love and Hits From His Movies, Volume 2 (US RCA CAS 2595, UK RCA Camden INTS 1414, 1972) (US No.22) Back in 1972, it was very unusual to have a recent hit on a budget album.

Separate Ways (US RCA CAS 2611, UK RCA Camden CDS 1118, 1973)

Aloha From Hawaii Via Satellite (US RCA VSPX 6089, UK RCA DPS 2040, 2LP, 1973) (US No.1 for 1 week, UK No.11) Collectors want the quadrophonic version: good luck in finding one.

Disc 1: C.C. Rider / Burning Love / Something / You Gave Me a Mountain / Steamroller Blues / My Way / Love Me / Johnny B. Goode / It's Over / Blue Suede Shoes / I'm So Lonesome I Could Cry / I Can't Stop Loving You / Hound Dog

Disc 2: What Now My Love / Fever / Welcome to My World / Suspicious Minds / I'll Remember You / Long Tall Sally / Whole Lotta Shakin' Goin' On / An American Trilogy / A Big Hunk o' Love / Can't Help Falling In Love / Blue Hawaii / Ku-U-I-Po / No More / Hawaiian Wedding Song / Early Morning Rain

Elvis (US RCA APL1 0283, UK RCA SF 8378, 1973) (UK No.16)

Fool / Where Do I Go from Here / Love Me, Love The Life I Lead / It's Still Here / It's Impossible / For Lovin' Me / Padre / I'll Take You Home Again Kathleen / I Will Be True / Don't Think Twice, It's All Right

Raised On Rock (Worldwide RCA APL1 0388, 1973)

Raised On Rock / Are You Sincere / Find Out What's Happening / I Miss You / Girl of Mine / For Ol' Times Sake / If You Don't Come Back / Just a Little Bit / Sweet Angeline / Three Corn Patches

Elvis – A Legendary Performer, Volume 1 (Worldwide RCA CPL1 0341, 1974 (UK No.20)

This was a new RCA series for its major artists. Some key tracks would be included but it was mostly unreleased or rare material with an illustrated explanatory booklet. These days, with the internet, nothing can be called rare.

Good Times (Worldwide RCA CPL1 0475, 1974) (UK No.42)

Take Good Care of Her / Loving Arms / I Got a Feelin' in My Body / If That Isn't Love / She Wears My Ring / I've Got a Thing About You Baby / My Boy / Spanish Eyes / Talk About the Good Times / Good Time Charlie's Got the Blues

Elvis Recorded Live on Stage in Memphis (Worldwide RCA APL1 0606, 1974) (US No.33, UK No.44)

C.C. Rider / I Got a Woman / Love Me / Tryin' to Get to You/ Medley: Long Tall Sally – Whole Lotta Shakin' Goin' On – Mama Don't Dance – Flip, Flop and Fly – Jailhouse Rock – Hound Dog / Why Me Lord / How Great Thou Art / Medley: Blueberry Hill – I Can't Stop Loving You / Help Me / An American Trilogy /Let Me Be There / My Baby Left Me /Lawdy Miss Clawdy / Can't Help Falling In Love

Having Fun with Elvis (US Boxcar CPM 10818 and reissued as RCA APMI 0818, 1974)

Stage conversation only

40 Greatest (UK Arcade ADEP 12, 2LP, 1974) (UK No.1 for 1 week)

Mammoth, TV-advertised double-album, licensed by RCA and indeed, pressed by them as well.

Hits Of The 70'S (UK RCA LPL1 7527, 1974) (Reissue: No.30, 1977)

As it were, the third LP for the Arcade package as there was no duplication of titles.

Promised Land (Worldwide RCA APL1 10873, 1974) (UK No.21)

Promised Land / There's a Honky Tonk Angel / Help Me / Mr. Songman / Love Song of the Year / It's Midnight /Your Love's Been a Long Time Coming / If You Talk in Your Sleep / Thinking About You / You Asked Me To

Today (US RCA APL1 1039, UK RCA RS 1011, 1975) (UK No.48)

T-R-O-U-B-L-E / And I Love You So / Susan When She Tried / Woman Without Love / Shake a Hand / Pieces of My Life / Fairytale / I Can Help / Bringin' It Back / Green, Green Grass of Home

The Elvis Presley Sun Collection (UK RCA Starcall HY 1001, 1975) (UK No.16)

The editor of the *NME*, Roy Carr, persuaded RCA in the UK to put his Sun masters onto one LP. Tremendous cover – Shakin' Stevens built a whole career around this pose – and possibly the greatest album of all-time. But it's not got Harbour Lights.

Pictures Of Elvis (UK RCA Starcall HYY 1023) (Reissue No.52, 1977)

Elvis – A Legendary Performer, Volume 2 (Worldwide RCA CPL1 1349, 1976)

The discovery of a new Sun performance, Harbour Lights, was the highlight of this collection of largely outtakes and unissued material.

By now you are probably getting lost in view of all the new product and the remarketing of old tracks that was taking place in the 70s. This discography only shows a part of it, as there were many other budget albums and several reissues of complete albums. Camden was going berserk by taking their existing releases and repackaging them as double or triple album collections. Budget albums were excluded from the album charts so we don't really know how they sold, but it was probably a licence to print money.

However, Elvis, like the Beatles, the Rolling Stones and soon Queen, were very rarely licensed for multi-artist compilations. As a consequence, Elvis was invariably omitted from such albums as *The Best Rock'n'Roll Album in the World…Ever!* which couldn't live up to their titles without Elvis. Everything changed when 50 year old tracks went out of copyright.

Elvis Presley's Greatest Hits (Reader's Digest RDS 9001/7, 7LP, 1975)

Six albums of hits and another of film songs – 107 songs in all and the mail order sales hit 250,000 in seven years.

From Elvis Presley Boulevard, Memphis, Tennessee (US RCA APL1 1506, UK RCA RS 1060, 1976) (UK No.29)

Hurt / Never Again / Blue Eyes Crying In the Rain / Danny Boy / The Last Farewell / For the Heart / Bitter They Are, Harder They Fall / Solitaire / Love Coming Down / I'll Never Fall In Love Again

The original cover stated 'Recorded live' but this had to be removed as these were studio recordings.

The Sun Years (Charly SUN 1, 1977) (UK No.31)
Not the Sun tracks but interviews and memories of Elvis.

Elvis In Demand (UK RCA PL 42003, 1977) (UK No.12)
The smorgasbord of Elvis Presley is getting ridiculous as now the Elvis fans choose what they would like on an album. Ultimately, you will be able to go into a shop, tell the clerk what you want and the album will be produced. Interesting though that they should include the Dylan song, 'Tomorrow Is a Long Time'. It sold 40,000 in the first week of release, so it's not for me to mock it.

The Elvis Tapes (UK Redwood RED 1, 1977)
Elvis' press conference in Vancouver in 1957 with DJ Red Robinson.

Welcome To My World (US RCA APL1 2274, UK RCA PL 12274, 1977) (UK No.7)
Country performances, mostly from the early 70's.

Moody Blue (US RCA AFL1 2428, UK RCA PL 12428, 1977) (US No.3, UK No.3)
Unchained Melody / If You Love Me (Let Me Know) / Little Darlin' / He'll Have to Go / Let Me Be There / Way Down / Pledging My Love / Moody Blue / She Thinks I Still Care / It's Easy for You

Elvis In Concert (US RCA APL2 2587, UK RCA PL 02587, 2LP, 1977) (US No.5, UK No.13)
In the wake of his death, RCA had reissued five of his film albums (which surely should have been put on hold) and then in November, released this double-album based on his 1977 tour and CBS TV special.

He Walks Beside Me (US RCA AFL1 2772. UK RCA PL 12772, 1978) (UK No.37)

Elvis Sings for Children and Grownups Too (US RCA AFL1 2772)

Elvis – The 56 Sessions, Volume 1 (UK RCA PL 42101) (UK No.47)

Elvis' 40 Greatest (UK RCA PL 42691, 2LP, 1978) (UK No.40)
RCA reissue of Arcade best-seller as Arcade had now lost its licence.

Elvis – A Legendary Performer, Volume 3 (US RCA CPL1 3078, UK RCA PL 13082, 1978) (UK No.43)
Highlights are 'Danny', which had been dropped from *King Creole* and seven minutes of Paul Wilder's 1956 interview with Elvis for *TV Guide*. A 16-page LP sized booklet of memorabilia too and some copies pressed as picture discs. The picture discs were imported for sale in the UK as a limited edition, but as they quickly showed up in discount bins; something went wrong or RCA was not telling the truth.

Our Memories Of Elvis (US RCA AQL1 3279, RCA PL 13279, 1979) (UK No.72)
The cover photograph shows Vernon Presley and Colonel Parker outside Graceland. The idea was to take original tracks of Elvis with the rhythm section and without overdubs. The intention was to offer pure Elvis, but they were mostly ballads ('My Boy', 'Solitaire') which worked better with a full accompaniment.

Our Memories Of Elvis, Volume 2 (US RCA AQL1 3448, UK RCA PL 13448, 1979)

Well, someone liked the first volume. This album included Elvis' jam session around 'Don't Think Twice, It's All Right'.

Love Songs (UK K-Tel NE 1062, 1979) (UK No.4)

Another TV advertised package, Elvis' first for K-Tel.

Elvis Sings Leiber And Stoller (UK RCA International INTS 5031) (UK No.32)

Fantastic songs, fantastic performances, all in mono and good sleeve notes too.

Elvis Aron Presley (Worldwide RCA CPL8 3699, 8LP, 1980) (US No.27, UK No.21)

Eight albums of Elvis for around £35, although I bought mine in a sale at Our Price for £10, one year after release. Just 15,000 copies had been imported from the US. The full concert at Pearl Harbour in 1961 is included. Very funny outtakes to 'A Dog's Life'. Three sides featured Elvis in concert in June 1975, but complete Elvis concerts are often dull as he keeps chatting about girls he's going to kiss and the scarves he's going to dole out – who cares?

We are told that this project was conceived and produced by Joan Deary: considering that the early Presley releases were very scant with the credits, it is impressive that Joan Deary has her name on the package 26 times. She was good on what had previously been released and what hadn't but she wasn't so hot on what was good and what was not: deary deary, in fact.

Elvis Presley (UK, Imp IMP 113, 1980)

The Wonderful World Of Elvis Presley (UK, Imp IMP 204, 2LP, 1980)

Marks & Spencer offer Elvis albums for Christmas but they were poorly marketed and most people didn't notice they were available. Those that did probably thought that they were poor Camden-style compilations. There weren't many sales so the albums are now, paradoxically, highly collectable.

Inspirations (UK K-Tel NE 1101, 1980) (UK No.4)

Guitar Man (US RCA AAL1 3917, UK RCA RCALP 5010, 1981) (UK No.33)

The original idea was to take recordings of Elvis and add new backings and duet vocalists, such as Elvis and Jerry Reed singing Guitar Man. Colonel Parker nixed that but new backings were added with Jerry playing Guitar Man. All seems a bit pointless.

This Is Elvis (US RCA CLP2 4031, UK RCA RCALP 5029, 1981) (UK No.47)

Double-album tied in with the documentary film, *This Is Elvis,* mostly of familiar material.

The Ultimate Performance (K-Tel NE 1141, 981) (UK No.45)

TV-advertised compilation from live albums.

The Million Dollar Quartet (UK Charly SUN 1006, 1981)

Taking a chance, Charly Records at last issues a legitimate version of the Million Dollar Quartet. Many other versions appear over the years, some with additional material. Best is on RCA PL 90465 in 1993.

Elvis' greatest shit!! (RCA Victim SUX 005, 1982)

A bootleg selection of Elvis' worst tracks and outtakes, mostly from his films, and presented in the worst possible taste. On the label it says, 'The King of Rock'n'Roll?

You gotta be kidding!'

20 Greatest Hits, Volume 2 (UK RCA INTS 5116, 1982) (Reissue: UK No.98, 1985)

The Sound Of Your Cry (US RCA RCALP 3060, 1982) (UK No.31)

The Ep Collection (UK RCAEP 1, 1982) (UK No.97)

11 UK EP releases in a special wallet. Regarded as an album for chart purposes.

Romantic Elvis (RCA RCALP 1000, 1982) / *Rockin' Elvis* (RCA RCALP 1001, 1982) (UK No.62)

What would RCA think of next? This was a twofer and so they came onto the charts as one item.

Memories Of Christmas (US RCA CPL1 4395, 1982)

It Won't Seem Like Christmas Without You (UK RCA INTS 5235, 1982) (UK No.80)

Jailhouse Rock / Love In Las Vegas (UK RCA RCALPP 9020) (UK No.40, 1983) An Elvis picture disc makes the album charts.

I Was The One (UK RCALP 3105, 1983) (UK No.83) A follow-up to the Guitar Man LP. This time Elvis' early successes are given new backings, but how can you improve on those wonderful guitars on Little Sister?

Elvis – A Legendary Performer, Volume 4 (US RCA CPL1 4848, UK RCA PL 84848, 1983) (UK No.91) Unissued performances from 1954 to 1972 including a laughing Wooden Heart and a funky Reconsider Baby.

I Can Help (UK RCA PLP 89287, 1984) (UK No.71) Seventies hits on a picture disc.

Elvis' Golden Records, Volume 5 (US RCA AFL1 4941, 1984) Not released in the UK, but copies imported from Germany.

The First Live Recordings (UK RCA PG 89387, 1984) (UK No.69)

A Golden Celebration (RCA CPM6 5172, 6LP, 1985) Issued for the 50th anniversary of Elvis' birth and far superior to the *Elvis Aron Presley* box set, including full versions of his early TV appearances. Elvis on top form nearly all the time.

Reconsider Baby (US RCA AFL1 5418, UK RCA OK 85418, 1985) (UK No.92) Blues tracks from over the years and a shame that Elvis never made a blues album.

Rock'n'roll – The Early Years (UK RCA NL 90085, 1985) The first time Elvis appears on a rock'n'roll compilation, but then it is on RCA.

Ballads (UK Telstar STAR 2264) (UK No.23) More TV-advertised Elvis.

Essential Elvis (UK RCA PL 89979, 1986) Taking over from the *Legendary Performer* series with a lot more outtakes.

The Complete Sun Sessions (UK RCA PL 86414, 2LP, 1987) Not quite complete but getting there.

Presley – The All-Time Greatest Hits (UK RCA PL 90100, 2LP, 1987) (UK No.4) Heavily-promoted package for his tenth anniversary of death.

The Memphis Record (UK RCA 86221, 2LP, 1987) Distinctive mock newspaper cover and those Memphis sessions of 1969 hold up well together.

The Alternate Aloha (UK RCA PL 86985, 1988) This was the previous day's performance, recorded as a back-up.

Stereo '57 (ESSENTIAL ELVIS, VOLUME 2 (UK RCA PL 90250, 1989) (UK No.60) Some early stereo recordings were made in what was known as 'binaural'. It was thought that they had been destroyed but some were still around.

The Fifties Interviews (UK Magnum Force MFLP 074, 1989) Round about here, everything was issued on CD and vinyl was being phased out; the catalogue numbers were becoming barcodes and one compilation followed another.

Hits Like Never Before (Essential Elvis, Volume 3) (UK RCA PL 90486, 1990) (UK No.71) 'When I Got Stung' breaks down, Elvis goes into 'When Irish Eyes Are Smiling', and 'Steadfast, Loyal and True' has a piano accompaniment but nothing startling.

Great Performances (UK RCA PL 82227, 1990) (UK No.62) A hits collection, but the opening track is 'My Happiness', first time on vinyl.

For The Asking (The Lost Album) (US RCA/BMG 07863 610242, UK RCA PL 82227, 1990) The non-film tracks that Elvis recorded in 1963 were used on bonus tracks and the B-sides. Why didn't they constitute an album at the time? Good idea to do it now.

Collectors Gold (UK RCA 3LP or 3CD box set, 1991) (UK No.57) Three CDs marked *Hollywood*, *Nashville* and *Live in Las Vegas*. On the *Hollywood* CD, when Elvis is amusingly chided for taking too many takes, he points out that he once got up to 60 takes and the record never came out. This is all good fun but the ribbing could have gone the other way. The original 'Flaming Star', that is 'Black Star', is included. In the fadeout for 'Roustabout', Elvis sings, 'I'm a raving maniac.' The live six minute workout of 'What'd I Say' is not as inviting as it sounds as it is too fast and mostly instrumental: there is a classic Vegas moment where Elvis starts 'Loving You' and then decides to sing 'Reconsider Baby'.

From The Heart – His Greatest Love Songs (UK No.4, 1992)

The King Of Rock'n'roll – The Complete 50s Masters (5CD, 1992)

From Nashville To Memphis – The Essential 60s Masters (5CD, 1993)

The Essential Collection (UK No.6, 1994)

Amazing Grace (2CD, 1994) 55 sacred performances including a jam session with the Stamps

Walk A Mile In My Shoes – The Essential 70s Masters (5CD, 1995)

Elvis 56 (UK No.42, 1996) Neat packaging with hardback cover and vintage session shots.

Always On My Mind – Ultimate Love Songs (UK No.3, 1997)

Blue Suede Shoes (UK No.39, 1998)

A Touch Of Platinum (1954–1966) (2CD, 1998)

A Touch Of Platinum, Volume 2 (1967–1977) (2CD, 1998) Mostly rarities and alternative takes.

Artist Of The Century (30 CDs in a box and a standard 3CD collection, 1999) Duplication at a premium – there is some logic in having different performances of

Heartbreak Hotel but not five versions of the same original studio cut, no matter how wonderful it is.

The 50 Greatest Hits (UK No.8, 2CD, 2000)

The Live Greatest Hits (UK No.50, 2001)

Live In Las Vegas (4CD box-set) The first CD is a full concert from Las Vegas in August 1969. The CD concludes with a six-minute rap from Elvis about his career full of classic one-liners, but it's weird – nobody else spoke like this.

The 50 Greatest Love Songs (UK No.21, 2CD, 2001)

30 Number 1 Hits (US No.1, UK No.1, 2002) This was issued in a 2CD special edition, with the second CD consisting of outtakes. His first stab at Heartbreak Hotel has none of the excitement of the issued 45, but no one had turned on the echo chamber. The package contains six pages of fans talking about Elvis, with 80 lines to a page on the CD booklet, had RCA gone mad?

Today, Tomorrow And Forever (4CD box set, 2002)…and to commemorate the 25th anniversary of his death, four CDs of alternative takes, effectively four CDs of tracks that Elvis had rejected.

Second To None (US No.3, UK No.4, 2003)

Christmas Peace (UK No.41, 2003)

Concert Anthology, 1954 – 1956 (Red Line, 2CD, 2004) Appearances from *Louisiana Hayride* and a second CD of live performances with overdubbed, additional musicians including Slim Jim Phantom from the Stray Cats. There have been many releases of the *Hayride* material, the first album being in 1983.

Elvis By The Presleys (US No.15, UK No.13, 2 CD, 2005) Promotional link with TV film and book.

The Complete Elvis Presley Masters (30CD, 2010) 711 masters and 103 bits and pieces.

In addition, RCA created a Follow That Dream series for collectors. These took the original album and added outtakes, usually to make a 2CD package, so a purchaser might buy 30 minutes of the original album and 90 minutes of outtakes. There have been 150 releases, all beautifully packaged

Elvis At The Movies (Marks & Spencer, 2005) M&S trying again, but did anyone buy it?

If I Can Dream – Elvis Presley And The Royal Philharmonic Orchestra (US No.21, UK No.1, 2015) Elvis back on top and recording in Abbey Road with the RPO. A classy product and the public bought it.

Way Down In The Jungle Room (UK 16, 2CD, 2016) All the Jungle Room tracks with outtakes.

The RCA Albums Collection (60CD, 2016) A 60 CD box and retailing at around £170, which works out at under £3 an album but bear in mind that it includes the film dross. The press release says that Elvis has sold 135m albums in the US alone, and RCA should know. As well as 57 album reissues, often with bonus tracks, there are 3CDs of what they call rarities, but we know better. Personally, I am never too happy with these mammoth projects – whenever I buy an album or a CD, I like to play it right away so that I can check there are no faults: obviously, it is impossible with a package like this

The Wonder Of You – Elvis Presley And The Royal Philharmonic Orchestra (US No.47, UK No.1, 2016) There is a special boxed vinyl/CD edition with additional tracks including a duet of Just Pretend with the Soviet-born, German star Helene Fischer.

APPENDIX 2
ELVIS FOR EVERYONE

Answer Versions
'Old Shep (The Dog's Side)' – Bobby George (1953)
'You're a Dirty Hound Dog' – Mickey Katz (1956)
'Hound Dawg' – Homer and Jethro (1956)
'Oh, How I Miss You Tonight' – Jeanne Black (US No.63, 1961), Jim Reeves (1960) It was written as the original answer version to 'Are You Lonesome Tonight' in the 1920s but Jeanne Black clearly intended it as a response to Elvis)
'Yes I'm Lonesome Tonight' – Thelma Carpenter (US No.55, 1961), Dodie Stevens (US No.60, 1961), Linda Lee, JoAnne Perry)
'Hey Memphis (Little Sister)' – LaVern Baker (1961)
'Don't Want to be Another Good Luck Charm' – Jo (1962)
'Just Tell Her Jane Said Hello' – Gerri Granger (1962)
'Don't Want Your Letters (Return to Sender)' – Gerri Granger (1962)

Sampling Elvis
'The Flying Saucer' – Buchanan and Goodman (US No.3, 1956) The first record to sample Elvis. Asked what he would do if he saw a flying saucer, he replies, 'Just take a walk down lonely street'. Presley appears on their follow-ups, 'Buchanan and Goodman on Trial', 'Santa and the Satellites' and 'The Flying Saucer No.2': in that last one, Elvis saves the world. How does he feel about it? 'I'm a little mixed up but I'm feeling fine.'
'Dear Elvis' – Audrey (US No.87, 1956) Another cut-in record
'Outer Space Looters' – Mad Martians (1957) Elvis is taking on the aliens who stole his teddy bear.
'Swing the Mood' – Jive Bunny and the Mastermixers (US No.11, UK No.1 for 5 weeks, 1989) Elvis back on top with snatches of 'Hound Dog', 'All Shook Up' and 'Jailhouse Rock'.
'Elvis on the Radio, Steel Guitar in My Soul' – KLF (1990) Eerie soundscape with samples from In the Ghetto. Strangely haunting.
'In The Ghetto' – Three 6 Mafia (2008) Samples Elvis' 'In the Ghetto' with their own song.

Songs About Elvis While Elvis Was Alive

'Heartbreak Hotel' – Stan Freberg (US No.79, 1956)

'I Want Elvis for Christmas' – Holly Twins (1956) A heartbreak Noël with Eddie Cochran as Elvis and written by Bobby Darin.

'I Wanna Spend Xmas with Elvis' – Little Lambsie Penn (1956) The same Bobby Darin song with a different arrangement.

'Elvis Presley for President' – Lou Monte (1956) …and why not? There's been worse.

'My Boy Elvis' – Janis Martin (1956) There is a complete compilation album *The Female Elvis*, on Bear Family, released in 1987.

'The Elvis Blues' – Otto Bash (1956) Otto's girl sees Elvis and doesn't want Otto anymore. As well as several novelty songs, Cy Coben wrote 'Nobody's Child'. The single was on RCA and so this must have shown to Elvis and the Colonel before release.

'Elvis and Me' – The Kids (1957)

'Hey Mr. Presley' – Pete De Bree and the Wanderers (1957) Telling Elvis' story via his song titles and sounding like him too.

'New Angel Tonight' – Red River Dave (Dave McEnery) (1958) A tribute to Gladys.

'(I Wanna Be) Elvis Presley's Sergeant' – Bobolinks (1958)

'All American Boy' – Bill Parsons (actually, Bobby Bare)(US No.2, 1959, UK No.22, 1959) A year later Bare released 'I'm Hangin' Up My Rifle'. UK versions from Marty Wilde and Rory Storm and the Hurricanes.

'Gonna Get Even with Elvis Presley's Sergeant' – Janie Davids (1958)

'Don't Knock Elvis' – Felton Jarvis (1959) A gushing testimonial from his future producer.

'My Baby's Crazy 'Bout Elvis' – Billy Boyle, Mike Sarne (both 1962)

'Tupelo Mississippi Flash' – Jerry Reed (1967), Tom Jones (1970). T.J. Thorpe of the Rubettes says, 'It's a great comic song and I'm dumb-stuck at the rhythm that Jerry Reed kicks up on a nylon string guitar.'

'Elvis' – Steve Barlby (1970)

'Went to See the Gypsy' – Bob Dylan (1970) Is it about Presley? Did their meeting go like that? No one really knows. There has been talk of a lost Dylan / Presley session for years, akin to the one Dylan did with Johnny Cash. I haven't given up hope.

'The E.P. Express' – Carl Perkins (1975)

Songs About Elvis Once Elvis Was Gone

'The Day the Beat Stopped' – Ral Donner (1977)

'I Remember Elvis Presley' – Danny Mirror (UK No.4, 1977) …but do we remember Danny Mirror? Eddie Ouwens (Danny Mirror) was behind 'Ding A Dong' by Teach-In.

'The King is Gone' – Ronnie McDowell (US No.13, 1977) On the Scorpion label, no less.

'The Lonely King of Rock'n'Roll' – Alan Meyer (1977)

'The Gate' – George Owens (1977) The gate (not the gatekeeper) at Graceland on his former boss.

'He Ate Too Many Jelly Donuts' – Rick Dee & his Cast of Idiots (1977) Too early to be releasing a record like this.

'Loving You' – Donna Fargo and The Jordanaires (1977) The standard Elvis song with a narration about Elvis, comparing him to J.F.K. and delivered at breakneck speed.

'I Dreamed Elvis Sang My Song' – Don Todd (1977) Talk of opportunism: Don Todd wants his songs recorded, so how about putting them onto a single and imagining that Elvis was singing them?

'Welcome Home Elvis' – Billy Joe Burnette (1977). To the melody of 'Peace in the Valley', Billy Joe as Jessie Garon welcomes his twin to Heaven. Billy Joe is the son of Dorsey Burnette and was in Fleetwood Mac for many a year but he slipped up here.

'Hound Dog Man's Gone Home' – Arthur Alexander (1977)

'Candy Bars for Elvis' – Barry Tiffin (1977)

'Elvis and Marilyn' – Leon Russell (1978)

'You Were the Music' – Kathy Westmoreland (1978)

'The Whole World Misses You' – Carl Perkins (1978) Produced by Felton Jarvis.

'To Elvis with Love' – Brenda Joyce (1979) Elvis is now with the only king 'who is greater than you are'.

'King Rocker' – Generation X (UK No 11, 1979) A song about Elvis' influence on the Beatles. Elvis could mime a lot better than Billy Idol.

'Hound Dog Man' – Lenny LeBlanc (US No.58, 1977), Roy Orbison (1979), Glen Campbell (1980).

'King's Call' – Phil Lynott (with Mark Knopfler on guitar) (UK No.35, 1980: remix, UK No.68, 1987) Getting drunk when Elvis died.

'There's a Guy Works Down the Chipshop Swears He's Elvis' – Kirsty MacColl (UK No.14, 1981)

'Jesus Mentioned' – Warren Zevon (1982) 'Can't you just imagine digging up the King, begging him to sing?' Not really.

'The King's Last Concert' – Red Sovine (1982) A trucker on speed imagines he is seeing Elvis perform, but Elvis has died and so has he.

'I Know Why You Cried The Day Elvis Died' – Boxcar Willie (1982) Boxcar felt the same way when Hank Williams died.

'Elvis Presley Boulevard' – Billy Joel (1982) The merchandise has got him: 'They were selling plastic souvenirs of Elvis on the cross.'

'Riding with the King' – John Hiatt (1983)

'You're Messin' with the King of Rock'n'Roll' – Ian Hunter (1983, but not released until 2017) Hunter's response to Albert Goldman.

'Elvis Presley and America' – U2 (1984)

Elvis Presley: Caught in a Trap

'Johnny Bye-Bye' – Bruce Springsteen (1985) Rewritten Chuck Berry.

'Graceland' – Paul Simon (1986) About visiting Elvis' home but more about Simon's hang-ups.

'The Birth of Rock'n'Roll' – Carl Perkins (1986) You'll have gathered by now that Carl was preoccupied with writing about Elvis.

'A Country Boy Who Rolled the Rock Away' – David Allan Coe (US Country No.44, 1986) Tribute to Hank Williams, Buddy Holly and Elvis.

'Big Train from Memphis' – John Fogerty (1987)

'American Roulette' – Robbie Robertson (1987) Tribute to James Dean, Elvis Presley and Marilyn Monroe.

'Why Can't They Leave Him Alone' – Mark Haley (1987)

'Elvis Has Left the Building' – Frank Zappa (1988)

'Personal Jesus' – Depeche Mode (US No.28, UK No.13, 1989) Written after reading Priscilla Presley's memoir. Covered by Johnny Cash (2002) and Marilyn Manson (2004).

'Eternal Flame' – Bangles (US No.1, UK No.1, 1989) Cover by Atomic Kitten (UK No.1, 2005) Written about the eternal flame at Elvis Presley's graveside.

'The King is Gone' – George Jones (1989) Graceland meets Bedrock: 'Yabba-dabba-do, the king is gone and so are you.' Most poignant line, 'Elvis said, 'Find them young'.'

'I Saw Elvis in a U.F.O.' – Steven Bays (1989)

'Elvis' Rolls Royce' – Leonard Cohen with Was Not Was (1990)

'Elvis is Dead' – Living Colour (1990) A song about Elvis sightings with a guest appearance from Little Richard: 'To all you pimps making money off of his name, How do you sleep, don't you feel ashamed?'

'Black Velvet' – Alannah Myles (US No.1, UK No.2, 1990) Myles' boyfriend saw fans going to a candlelight vigil in Memphis and wrote the song. Original version was by Robin Lee (US Country No.12, 1990)

'Fight the Power' – Public Enemy (1990) 'Elvis was a hero to most, but he never meant shit to me.'

'Mission Drive' – The Wonder Stuff (1991) 'I've never loved Elvis and I've never sung the blues.'

'Calling Elvis' – Dire Straits (UK No.21, 1991)

'Godfather of Rock'n'Roll' – Carl Perkins (1991) Still at it.

'Walking in Memphis' – Marc Cohn (US No.13, UK No.22, 1991) 'There's a pretty little thing, Waiting for the King, Right down in the Jungle Room.'

'The Letter' – Wayne Newton (1992) Written about the note Elvis wrote in his suite in Vegas a few months before he died – see text.

'Elvis on Velvet' – Stray Cats (1992) 'Thy kingdom come, thy will be done, thy records will be re-released.'

'Irish Elvis Presley' – Brendan Shine (1992)

'Elvis and Me' – Jimmy Webb (1993)

'Elvis Impersonator' – Manic Street Preachers (1996) Mocking the Blackpool impersonators: 'American trilogy in Lancashire pottery'.

'I'm Turnin' Into Elvis' – Bruce Springsteen (live in Memphis, 1996)

'From Galway to Graceland' – Richard Thompson (1996) Sensitive song about an obsessive fan.

'Elvis Has Left the Building' – Old Dogs (1998) Lead vocalist, Jerry Reed, on a Shel Silverstein song.

'Porcelain Monkey' – Warren Zevon (2000) Warren Zevon on a visit to Graceland is attracted to Elvis' bric-a-brac.

'Flying Elvis' – Leilani (UK No.73, 2000) 'I hope you don't think I'm being selfish, I don't marry a flying Elvis.' Flying Elvis are skydivers who appear in *Honeymoon in Vegas* (1992). A flying Elvis was killed in a skydiving accident in 2011.

'Lights Out' – Lisa Marie Presley (UK No.16, 2003) Lisa Marie notes the space for her in the family plot.

'Real Good Looking Boy' – The Who (2004) Roger Daltrey wants to grow up like Elvis. Melody includes a snatch of 'Can't Help Falling In Love'.

'Advertising Space' – Robbie Williams (UK No.8, 2005) Robbie Williams has called this his 'Candle in the Wind'. He wrote it after watching Christian Slater in *True Romance* speak to the spirit of Elvis. Brilliant video with Robbie in an Elvis quiff shot in Blackpool – in the final sequence, he goes through some Graceland gates and performs at a bingo hall.

'Elvis at the Wheel' – Al Stewart (2005) Elvis meets Stalin in the Arizona desert.

'King of the Mountain' – Kate Bush (UK No.4, 2005) Linking Elvis' death to Rosebud in *Citizen Kane*.

'Did You Know Elvis' – Jimmy Velvet and David Allen Coe (2007)

'Singing with Angels' – Suzi Quatro with James Burton and the Jordanaires (2011) (Suzi Quatro; 'The Jordanaires told me that they were often asked to sing on tribute records, but Ray Walker said that it was the best Elvis tribute he'd heard. You can make tributes too sentimental but I think I got it about right.')

'Elvis and the Disagreeable Backing Singers' – Neil Innes (2013)

'I Can See Elvis' – The Waterboys (2014)… about to murder the Colonel.

'Elvis Presley Blues' – Tom Jones (2015)

Tribute Albums

Pat Boone Sings…Guess Who (1964)

The Guitar that Changed the World – Scotty Moore (1964)

Blues for Elvis – King Does the King's Things – Albert King (1970)

Rockabilly Jive – Jerry Foster with Scotty and D.J. (1970)

Vince Eager Pays Tribute to Elvis (1971)

My Farewell to Elvis – Merle Haggard (1977)

Elvis' Favourite Gospel Songs (Sung at His Funeral) – J.D. Sumner and the Stamps (1977)

Tony Crane Sings Elvis Presley (1978) A live recording by the lead singer of the Merseybeats

I've Been Away for a While Now – Ral Donner (1980) Includes speech from Donner and eulogy from Ray Walker of the Jordanaires.

Sounds like Elvis – Ral Donner (1986)

Class of '55 – Carl Perkins, Jerry Lee Lewis, Roy Orbison and Johnny Cash (1986) The Class of '55 pay tribute to Sun Records, Elvis and of course themselves on this oddball album. Paul Kennerley writes about Elvis in 'We Remember the King', but he could be writing about Jesus.

The King and Eye – The Residents (1989) Experimental rock with a storyline linking the various covers.

The Last Temptation of Elvis (NME 2CD set for Nordoff-Robbins, 1990) Bruce Springsteen, Paul McCartney, Robert Plant, Dion and many more sing Elvis.

Our Tribute to Elvis – Terry Dene and the Runaways (1992)

It's Now or Never (All-star, country-based tribute produced by Don Was, 1994)

Blue Suede Sneakers (1995) Suzy Bogguss, Rodney Crowell, Ronnie Milsap and Brian Setzer perform Elvis songs for kids.

All The King's Men – Scotty Moore, D.J. Fontana and friends (1997)

Elvis – Still Alive Volume 1 (1997) and *Volume 2* (2000). Mostly UK contemporary rock'n'roll acts singing Elvis, including DiMaggio Brothers and Darrel Higham. The country singalong of 'I Love You Because' by Rick Hollow is engaging and inventive.

Honeymoon in Vegas (1999) Billy Joel, Willie Nelson and others perform Elvis songs for a Hollywood soundtrack.

Like Elvis Used to Do Billy Swan (recorded at Sun, 1999)

Peter and Ted singen Elvis – Peter Kraus and Ted Herold (2000). Two German hit-makers at the forefront for recording local versions of Elvis' hits. The album features 20 Elvis hits in German.

In the Ghetto – The Songs of Elvis (Castle, 2CD, 2002) All the Elvis covers to hand in the Pye catalogue, several of them very dodgy.

The Gregorian Chants of Elvis Presley – Brotherhood of St Gregory (2003) Should monks be singing about good luck charms?

The Elvis Connection – Elvis Connection (2005) Ronnie McDowell, The Jordanaires, Scotty Moore, D.J. Fontana and Millie Kirkham. The package includes a bonus CD of the backing tracks, so you too can be Elvis.

My Happiness – Amanda Lear (2014)

All About Elvis (3CD, 2015) Nearly 100 examples of tribute records, covers and singers who want to be Elvis, all pre-1963.

Spencer Leigh

Acknowledging Elvis – Songs

'Lewis Boogie' – Jerry Lee Lewis (1958) 'Cruise on down to ol' Memphis town, That's where that Presley boy sang, 'You ain't nothin' but a hound'.'

'The Old Payola Roll Blues' – Stan Freberg (US No.99, 1960) Clyde Ankle acts humble in front of the press: 'Oooh, I'll never replace Elvis. He's the King all right.'

'You're the Top' – Edd Byrnes (1960) 'You're the top, You're a Presley sideburn.'

'It Won't Happen With Me' – Jerry Lee Lewis (1961) 'If you loved Elvis Presley, it wouldn't last very very long, You'd get sick and tired of seeing him wiggling past your door.'

'1977' – The Clash (1977) The punk credo: 'No Elvis, Beatles or the Rolling Stones'.

'A Rock'n'Roll Fantasy' – Kinks (US No.30, 1978)

'I Will Rock and Roll With You' – Johnny Cash (1978)

'My My, Hey Hey (Out of the Blue)' and 'Hey Hey, My My (Into the Black)' – Neil Young (1979)

'Elvis Should Play Ska' – Graduate (1980) Graduate became Tears For Fears.

'Child of the Fifties' – Statler Brothers (1982)

'Tupelo' – Nick Cave (1985)…and your point is?

'Bloc Bloc Bloc' –OMD (1985)

'Christmas in Dixie' – Alabama (1985) Praise for Graceland's lights.

'Free Fallin'' – Tom Petty & the Heartbreakers (1989)

'Fight the Power' – Public Enemy (UK No.29, 1989) 'How can you say Elvis is the King when Little Richard and all those other guys put it down before him?'

'(Don't Step in) My Blue Suede Shoes' – Clive Gregson and Christine Collister (1989)

'57 Channels' – Bruce Springsteen (UK No.32, 1992) Bruce has a gun and 'in the blessed name of Elvis, I just let it blast.'

'Man on the Moon' – R.E.M. (US No.30, UK No.18, 1992) A tribute to comedian Andy Kaufman that asks, 'Hey Andy, are you goofing on Elvis?'

'You and Your Heroes' – Da Lench Mob (US, 1992) Black rappers' view of American history: 'Take it from Da Lench Mob, Elvis is dead as a door knob, Never been caught for all the songs he stole, And you put James Brown on parole?'

'Ain't Hurtin' Nobody' – John Prine (1995) 'You can fool some of the people part of the time, But 50,000,000 million Elvis Presley fans can't be all wrong.'

'Baby's Got a Thing about Pat Boone' – Rhythmaires (2001)

'Singing Elvis' – The Men They Couldn't Hang (2003)

'Elvis Ain't Dead' – Scouting for Girls (UK No.8, 2007)

'I Made a Mistake' – Willie Nelson (2017) 'I feel a little like Elvis when he was alone.'

Elvis Presley: Caught in a Trap

Acknowledging Elvis – Cultural References

The leader of the Troggs, Reg Ball, became Reg Presley in 1965.

Aladdin Sane – David Bowie (1973). The cover shows Bowie with the TCB logo. He considered arranging some Presley songs for Iggy Pop but it never happened.

Keith Moon wore a gold lamé suit in *Stardust* (1974). It was purchased by Sid Vicious.

Gunfight at Carnegie Hall – *Phil Ochs (1970, released 1975)* Rebel folk-singer in gold lamé. Discussed in text.

Evel Knievel's costumes were inspired by Elvis.

Declan Patrick MacManus became Elvis Costello in 1976.

London's Calling – The Clash (1979) No direct Elvis references but look at the lettering and style of the cover – it was their first album and it copied Elvis' first album.

A Date with Elvis – The Cramps (1986) No Elvis songs at all and the album is dedicated to Ricky Nelson. In the psychobilly band's rewriting of history, the young Elvis was a drug dealer who hung around the Sun Studios selling speed to musicians.

'Shoplifters of the World Unite' – The Smiths (UK No.12, 1987) Elvis cover pic on sleeve.

Bono wore a gold lamé suit on U2's *Zooropa* tour in 1993.

Dead Elvis – Death in Vegas (UK LP chart, No.52, 1997)

100,000,000 Bon Jovi Fans Can't Be Wrong – Jon Bon Jovi (4CD and DVD box set, 2004)…but they might be. Jon Bon Jovi in a gold lamé suit for the cover.

Reintarnation – k.d. lang (2006) Compilation again using the 1956 album cover.

50,000 Fall Fans Can't Be Wrong – The Fall (2008) Double-album of minor successes with Mark E. Smith parodying the Elvis cover.

Lilo and Stitch (2012). Animated film with Kauai Lilo, an Elvis fan and Stitch, an alien.

At the UK general election in 2014, David Bishop stood for the Bus-Pass Elvis Presley Party in Kettering, which was said to be part of the Church of the Militant Elvis. Whatever, the candidate received more votes than the Liberal Democrats.

I Can't Believe It's Not Elvis

The Eagles – 'Tryin' to Get to You' (1954) Things working in reverse here as Elvis followed this demo by a Washington DC group, except for the sax break.

Johnny Burnette – 'Oh Baby Babe' (1956) Copies Elvis himself; Scotty, Bill and D.J; and the song too.

Gene Vincent – 'Be-bop-a-Lula' (1956) Nowadays we would say that Gene Vincent himself sounds totally unique but he was trying to sound like Heartbreak Hotel.

Eddie Cochran – 'Twenty Flight Rock' (1956) It was presented in *The Girl Can't Help It* as a parody, but it was the real thing.

John Hampton – 'Honey Hush' (1957) Vocal so incoherent that it sounds like a Stan Freberg parody. Great fun.

Charlie Gracie – 'Fabulous' (1957) (US No.16, UK No.8, 1957)

Conway Twitty – 'It's Only Make Believe' (US No.1, UK No.1, 1958), 'Make Me Know You're Mine' (originally submitted to Elvis but he didn't record it), 'Lonely Blue Boy' (originally 'Danny' for Elvis) (US No.6, 1960)

Sonny Lowery – 'Goodbye Baby Goodbye' (1958)

Johnny Rivers – 'Baby Come Back' (1958) Outrageous! Johnny Rivers takes the Christmas content out of 'Santa Bring My Baby Back To Me' and copies Elvis note for note. The listed songwriter, Johnny Ramistella, is Johnny himself: he was only 16 and it's a brilliant copy, if that isn't an oxymoron.

Johnny Powers – 'Be Mine, All Mine' (1959) Sun Records too.

Vince Taylor – 'Brand New Cadillac' (1959) An American based in Hounslow and promoted by Jack Good as the local Elvis. He found success in France and David Bowie sang his praises.

Bruce Channel – 'Run Romance Run' (1959) Bruce soon had a style of his own.

Chubby Checker – 'The Class' (US No.38, 1959) Chubby impersonates Elvis singing 'Mary Had a Little Lamb'.

Johnny Restivo – 'The Shape I'm In' (US No.80, 1959) Paul Simon on guitar.

Ben Hewitt – 'I Ain't Givin' Up Nothin'' (1959) Hewitt did the demo of 'Dontcha Think It's Time for Elvis'.

Wanda Jackson – 'Let's Have a Party' (US No.37, 1960, UK No.32, 1960) Okay, she's a girl, but her version is as exciting and as raucous as Elvis'. Other Elvis girls are Janis Martin and Alis Lesley.

Jett Powers (P.J. Proby) – 'Loud Perfume' (1960) Great title!

Danny Rivers – 'Hawk' (1960) A UK Top Rank single ripping off 'Fever' but spooky and fun.

Ral Donner – 'The Girl of My Best Friend' (US No.19, 1961), 'You Don't Know What You've Got' (UK No.25, US No.4, 1961), 'Please Don't Go' (US No.39, 1961) and many more. The best of Elvis impersonator and his best copycat performance is 'Rip It Up' (1979).

Davy Kaye – 'In My Way' (1965) If Joe Meek had produced Elvis. Spoken intro to celebrate ten years of Elvis.

David Bowie – 'Friday on My Mind' (1973) The Easybeats' hit as if done by Elvis.

Viv Stanshall in the Bonzo Dog Band – 'Canyons of Your Mind' (1968). Viv loved impersonating Elvis and he revived 'Suspicion' (1970).

Les Gray in Mud – 'Lonely This Christmas' (UK No.1, 1974)

Freddie Starr – 'White Christmas' (UK No.41, 1975) Starr's Elvis is excellent and his Hitler is good too. His best straight Elvis is 'I Love How You Love Me' (1989) but Elvis wouldn't have had such a tacky production.

Robert Plant in Led Zeppelin – 'Candy Store Rock' (1976)

Robert Gordon with Link Wray – 'I Want To Be Free' (1978)

Elvis Presley (Michael Conley) – 'Tell Me Pretty Baby' (1978) This was promoted as an early track recorded by Elvis in Phoenix in 1954. When it went to court, Conley admitted that he had made the record at the suggestion of his manager.

Orion – 'Ebony Eyes' (1978), 'Crazy Little Thing Called Love' (1981) In 1978 when the world was swamped with Elvis imitators, Orion tried to distance himself with 'I'm Not Trying to Be Like Elvis', but no none believed him. In the final verse, he wonders if Elvis is now trying to sound like him. Orion is fun when he sings others' hits as Elvis might have done them. He was shot by two no-marks who thought he was a cop. He was later murdered in his pawnshop. Queen's original was inspired by Elvis anyway.

Waylon Jennings – 'Nobody Knows I'm Elvis' (1994) Waylon with the perfect disguise.

Elvis McPresley – 'My Christmas Days / Scottish Trilogy' (1996) "Technical advisor to Elvis Presley – Colonel Tom McParker"

The King – *Gravelands* (1999) and *Return to Splendour* (2000). Can you imagine Elvis singing 'Whiskey in the Jar', 'Voodoo Chile', 'No Woman, No Cry' or 'Twentieth Century Boy'? Belfast-born postman Jim Brown is The King singing hits from other dead rockers on two albums. I'm tempted to write 'Return to Sender', but he's good.

Notable Cover Versions

'All Shook Up' – Ry Cooder, Humble Pie, Billy Joel (UK No.27, 1992), Paul McCartney, Cliff Richard, Suzi Quatro

'Always On My Mind' – Willie Nelson, Brenda Lee

'Anything that's Part of You' – Billy J Kramer, Charlie Landsborough

'Are You Lonesome Tonight' – Bryan Ferry, Brian Hyland, Eden Kane, Barry Manilow, Mavericks, Anne Murray, Helen Shapiro, Frank Sinatra, Tiny Tim

'Baby I Don't Care' – Buddy Holly (UK No.12, 1961), Don McLean, Joni Mitchell, Queen

'Baby Let's Play House' – Buddy Holly, Sleepy LaBeef, Don McLean, Joni Mitchell, John Prine, Queen, Cliff Richard, Rory Storm and the Hurricanes

'Blue Moon' – Cowboy Junkies (combined with an original song as 'Blue Moon Revisited', 1988), Bob Dylan

'Blue Moon of Kentucky' – Ronnie Hawkins, Tom Petty

'Blue Suede Shoes' – Johnny Hallyday, Carl Perkins

'Burning Love' – Arthur Alexander (original), Melissa Etheridge. Travis Tritt

'Can't Help Falling In Love' – Andrea Bocelli, Bono, Perry Como, Bob Dylan, Hall and Oates, Stylistics (UK No.4, 1976), Corey Heart (US No.24, 1987), Lick the Tins (lively folk version, UK No.42, 1986), UB 40 (US No.1 for 7 weeks, UK No.1 for 2 weeks, 1993), Andy Williams (UK No.3, 1970), Russell Watson (UK No.69, 2006)

'Crawfish' – Marianne Faithfull

'Danny' – Conway Twitty (song recorded as 'Lonely Blue Boy') (US No.6, 1960), Cliff Richard, Marty Wilde

'Devil in Disguise' – Trisha Yearwood

'Didja Ever' – Michael Barrymore

'Don't Be Cruel' – Bill Black's Combo (US No.11, 1960), Cheap Trick, Neil Diamond,

Spencer Leigh

José Feliciano, Bryan Ferry, Jerry Lee Lewis, Barbara Lynn (US No.93, 1963), Billy Swan (UK No.42, 1975)

'Down in the Alley' – Ronnie Hawkins, Jeff Healey

'Follow that Dream' – Blow Monkeys, Bruce Springsteen

'A Fool Such As I' – Petula Clark (as 'Prends Mon Coeur'), Bob Dylan, Davy Kaye (Richie Blackmore lead guitar, great solo), Hank Snow

'Girl Next Door (Went A'Walkin')' – Thomas Wayne

'The Girl of My Best Friend' – Bryan Ferry

'Girls, Girls, Girls' – Joe Brown, Coasters (original), Fourmost

'Got a Lot o' Livin' to Do' – Pogues (fast Irish cajun)

'Guitar Man' – Jesus and Mary Chain, Jerry Reed (original)

'Hard Headed Woman' – Wanda Jackson, Suzi Quatro

'Have I Told You Lately That I Love You' – Eddie Cochran

'Heartbreak Hotel' – Dread Zeppelin, Stan Freberg (US No.79, 1956), Frijid Pink (US No.72, 1970), Homer and Jethro (as Hart Brake Motel, 1956), George Jones (as Thumper Jones), Roger Miller (US No.84, 1966)

'Hound Dog' – Bryan Adams, Jeff Beck, Chubby Checker (with twist lyrics), Everly Brothers, Jimi Hendrix, Homer and Jethro (as 'Houn' Dawg'), Beverley Knight (with Jools Holland), John Lennon, Robert Palmer, Little Richard, Sex Presleys, Status Quo, James Taylor, Big Mama Thornton (original), Robin Trower, Dickie Valentine (faster than Elvis plus 'Hound Dog' as performed by Mr. Magoo and Edward G. Robinson)

'I Don't Care If the Sun Don't Shine' – John Leyton

'I Forgot To Remember To Forget' – Johnny Cash

'I Got Stung' – Paul McCartney

'In the Ghetto' – Lena Martell, Candi Staton

'It's Now or Never' – Paul McCartney, Wet Wet Wet

'Jailhouse Rock' – Dion, Frankie Lymon, Mötley Crüe, Queen, Patti Smith, Alvin Stardust, ZZ Top

'Lawdy Miss Clawdy' – Lloyd Price (original), Travis Tritt, Steve Young

'Let's Have a Party' – Wanda Jackson (US No.37, UK No.32, 1960), Robert Plant (an arrangement full of surprises), Rivieras (US No.99, 1964)

'Little Sister' – LaVern Baker (as 'Hey Memphis'), Ry Cooder, Marty Wilde, Dwight Yoakam

'Love Me' – Nicolas Cage (film, *Wild at Heart*), Mavericks (slow burning Raul Malo vocal), Wild Angels

'Love Me Tender' – Kenny Ball & his Jazzmen, Tony Bennett ('A lot of folk don't know this song was written by Elvis Presley' says Tony Bennett: well, they don't know it because it isn't true.), Richard Chamberlain (US No.21, UK No.15, 1962), Shawn Colvin (who calls the song 'a lullaby'), Amy Grant, Holly Johnson, Linda Ronstadt, Percy Sledge (US No.40, 1967), Link Wray

'Mean Woman Blues' – Dion, Jerry Lee Lewis, Roy Orbison (US No.5, UK No.3, 1963)

'A Mess of Blues' – Tom Jones

'Milkcow Blues Boogie' – Eddie Cochran, Flamin' Groovies, Steve Marriott's All Stars, Ricky Nelson, Jody Reynolds

'Mystery Train' – Jeff Beck & Chrissie Hynde

'No Room to Rhumba in a Sports Car' – Viv Stanshall ('I mucked around with it and wrote new verses but the song is absolute trash. I wonder what persuaded him to do that.')

'Old Shep' – Clinton Ford (UK No.27, 1959), Mike Reid (*Eastenders* actor doing it Cockney-style), Freddie Starr ('When I was a boy and old Shep was a frog')

'One Night' – Billy Joe Burnette, Joe Cocker (as 'One Night of Sin')

'Paralyzed' – Terry Dene, Emile Ford

'Return To Sender' – Dave Kelly

'Shoppin' Around' – Danny Boy et ses Pénitents (as 'Je ne veux plus être un dragueur')

'Song of the Shrimp' – Townes Van Zandt

'Steadfast, Loyal and True' – Aaron Neville

'Stuck on You' – Suzy Bogguss

'Surrender' – Lesley Garrett

'Suspicion' – Bonzo Dog Band (with narration), Steve Forbert, Terry Stafford (US No.3, UK No.31, 1964), Dwight Yoakam. 'It's a paranoid version of 'Save the Last Dance for Me',' says Steve Forbert.

'Suspicious Minds' – Candi Staton (wonderfully sultry), Dee Dee Warwick (US No.80, 1971)

'That's All Right, Mama' – Johnny Cash and Bob Dylan (with Carl Perkins on guitar, unissued at time, 1969), Bob Dylan, Paul McCartney

'Trouble' – Emile Ford

'T-R-O-U-B-L-E' – Travis Tritt

'Tryin' To Get To You' – Animals, Ricky Nelson, Roy Orbison (as part of the Teen Kings)

'Viva Las Vegas' – Dead Kennedys, Dale Watson, Bruce Springsteen, ZZ Top (UK No.10, 1992)

'Wear My Ring Around Your Neck' – Ricky Van Shelton

'Wooden Heart' – Kenny Ball & his Jazzmen, Gus Backus, Chordettes, Joe Dowell (US No.1, 1961), Nanci Griffith, John Holt, Bobby Vinton (US No.58, 1975)

'Young and Beautiful' – Aaron Neville (beautiful five-minute jazz version)

…and that's it. Spencer has left the building.

INDEX

Aberbach, Jean and Julian 50, 59, 62, 75
Ace, Goodman 62
Ace, Johnny 276
Acuff, Roy 30, 54, 67, 274
Adams, Nick 131
Addams Family 62, 118
Adele 35
'After Loving You' 176, 210
Agnew, Spiro 234
'Ain't That a Shame' 8, 49
'Ain't That Loving You, Baby' 121
Alden, Ginger 120, 278, 281, 285
Ali, Muhammad 117, 254
'All American Boy' 124
Allen, Steve 69–70, 136, 223
'All I Needed Was the Rain' 192
Allison, Mose 15–6
'All Shook Up' 94, 98–101, 201, 260, 299
'All That I Am' 185
'Almost' 203
'Almost Always True' 161
Aloha from Hawaii (TV special) 206–7, 248, 252–3
'Also Sprach Zarathustra' (*2001* theme) 242
'Always on My Mind' 245–6
'Amazing Grace' 239
'America the Beautiful' 265
'American Trilogy, An' 1–2, 244, 253, 289
Ames, Brothers, 159
'And I Love You So' 261, 263
Andress, Ursula 161, 167
'And the Grass Won't Pay No Mind' 208
'Angel' 163
'Angelica' 214
Animals, The 10
Anka, Paul 6, 279
Ann-Margret 56, 144, 162, 170–2, 188, 194, 196, 198,
218, 224, 273, 282
'Any Day Now' 215, 217
'Anyone Could Fall in Love with You' 172
'Any Place Is Paradise' 74
'Anything that's Part of You' 163, 167
'Any Way You Want Me' 70–1, 76
Arden, Don 56, 136
'Are You Lonesome Tonight' 99, 127, 143, 147, 158, 188, 200, 280, 317, 333
Are You Lonesome Tonight (play) 147, 248, 295
'Are You Sincere' 255
Armstrong, Louis 24, 100
Arnold, Chris 211, 216, 240, 255
Arnold, Eddy 21, 45, 54–5, 58–60, 74, 159, 189, 192, 210, 215, 232
Asher, Jane 188
Asher, Peter 300
Ashley, Edward 260
'Ask Me' 169
'As Long As I Have You' 118
Asner, Ed 165
Atkins, Chet 21, 32, 49, 59–60, 74, 76, 121, 141, 148, 158.
'Auld Lang Syne' 266
Austin, Gene 54
Avalon, Frankie 139, 162
Axton, Mae Boren 46, 60–1
Axton, Hoyt 244

'Baby I Don't Care' 103
'Baby, Let's Play House' 45–7, 50
'Baby What You Want Me to Do' 174, 200–1, 219
Bacharach, Burt 159, 214
Baker, Danny 284
Baker, LaVern 5, 40, 160, 170, 263
Ballard, Russ 269
Band, The 9, 19
Bare, Bobby 124, 254

'Barefoot Boy' 172
Barrow, Tony 181–2
Batchelor, Ruth 140, 165
Baum, Bernie – see Giant, Bill
Baxter, Art 92
'Beach Boy Blues' 161
Beach Boys, The 33
'Beale St Blues' 24
'Bear Cat' 27
Beard, Chris 200
Beatles 11, 28, 32–3, 45, 48, 55, 64, 66, 75–6, 91, 106, 120, 136, 144, 151, 172, 174–6, 178, 181–3, 191, 196, 204, 210, 236, 267
Beaulieu, Ann and Joseph Ann 126–7, 129, 151, 190
Beaulieu, Priscilla – see Presley, Priscilla
'Be Bop A Lula' 32, 89–90
'Because of Love' 166–7
Becker, Ken 146
Bee Gees, The 154
Belafonte, Harry 106, 198
Belew, Bill 205–7
Bell, Freddie 66–7
Bellamy, David 268
Bennett, Roy C – see Tepper, Sid
Bennett, Tony 127, 233
Benton, Brook 182
Berle, Milton 66, 68
Berlin, Irving 109
Bernard, Bert and George 126
Bernero, Johnny 47
Bernstein, Sid 229
Berry, Chuck 24, 31, 78, 85, 100, 136, 138, 169, 197, 259
Bicknell, Alf 181–2
Bienstock, Freddy 129, 145, 159, 198, 207–8, 211–2, 214, 231–2, 239–40, 254, 269, 275
'Big Boots' 145
'Big Boss Man' 191, 201
'Big Hunk o' Love, A' 121, 126, 187, 245, 253

Binder, Steve 199, 203, 205, 216, 270
'Bitter They Are, Harder They Fall' 257, 274
Black, Bill 37, 43, 45, 50, 60–1, 66, 68, 71, 101, 107, 278
Blackboard Jungle (film) 49
Blackburn, Tony 289
Blackman, Joan 162, 165
'Black Star' 148
Blackwell, Otis 70, 74, 98, 141, 166–7, 169,178
Blackwood Brothers 59, 150
Blake, Peter 191
Bleasdale, Alan 93, 147, 249, 296
Blossoms, The 203
'Blueberry Hill' 99
'Blue Christmas' 107, 200, 298
'Blue Eyes Crying in the Rain' 274, 281
Blue Hawaii (film) 159, 161–3, 177, 190, 194, 215
'Blue Hawaii' (song) 53, 161
'Blue Moon' 40
'Blue Moon of Kentucky' 38–9, 41–2, 49–50
'Blue on Blue' 159
'Blue River' 169
'Blue Suede Shoes' 60, 63–7, 75, 146, 200–1, 298
Bogart, Humphrey 71, 152
Bolger, Ray 67
Bonner, Barbara 275
Boone, Pat 8, 40, 49–50, 71, 73–4, 85, 88, 96, 100, 102–3, 109–10, 138, 154, 171, 176, 183, 193–4
'Bosom of Abraham' 240
'Bossa Nova Baby' 169
Bova, Joyce 243
Bowie, David 134, 148, 196, 268, 342
Box Tops, The 25, 208, 213
Boyle, Susan 298
Bradley, Arlene 132
Bragg, Johnny 27–8, 149
Brand, Neville 72
Brando, Marlon 9, 55, 71, 114, 148, 205
Brel, Jacques 211
'Bridge over Troubled Water' 230, 234, 280
Briggs, David 277
'Bringin' It Back' 263
'Britches' 148
Bronson, Charles 165
Brooks, Dudley 99, 104
Broonzy, Big Bill 6, 23
Brown, Earl 201
Brown, James 282
Brown, Joe 48
Brown, Roy 40
Bryant, Boudleaux and Felice 74, 258
Bublé, Michael 298
Buchanan and Goodman 69
Buffett, Jimmy 10–1
'Bullfighter was a Lady, The' 168
Bürgin, Margrit 123, 132
Burnette, Dorsey and Johnny 25, 45, 71, 105, 138, 153, 208
'Burning Love' 221, 244–6
Burton, James 105, 138, 155, 217–20, 230–1, 241, 244, 254, 256, 338
Bush, Kate 34–5
Butler, Jerry 6, 214, 244
Butterworth, Donna 185
Bye Bye Birdie (play and film) 143, 194
Byers, Joy 169
Byrds, The 33, 204

Cage, Nicolas 292
Cahn, Sammy 222
Campbell, Glen 174, 223, 246, 251
Campbell, Ramsey 72, 162
'Cane and a High Starched Collar, A' 148
'Can't Help Falling in Love' 161–3, 165, 201, 219, 278
Carey, Michele 197–8
Carroll, Ronnie 93
Carson, Wayne 245
Carter, President Jimmy 153, 282
Carter Family (including Anita and June) 3, 20, 28, 47, 131, 257
Carthy, Martin 88
Cartwright, Tony 206, 216–7, 219–20, 229, 233, 287

Cash, Johnny 3, 18, 21, 29, 45, 47–51, 59, 64, 79–85, 149, 163, 169, 194, 217, 281
Rosanne Cash 24
'Casual Love Affair' 28, 25
'Chains of Fools' 207
Change of Habit (film) 199, 211, 216, 221
Charles, Ray 5, 31, 35, 45, 170, 187, 189, 208, 210, 213
Charro! (film) 202, 216
'Charro!' (song) 203
Checker, Chubby 165
Cheevers, Bob 258
Chesnut, Jerry 257, 263
Chinn, Nicky 261
Christie, Lou 140
Christopher, Johnny 245–6
Clambake (film) 147, 154, 189–90
'Clambake' (song) 189
Clapton, Eric 7, 27
Clark, Dick 124, 138
Clark, Petula 188, 191, 198
Clayton, Chris 288
'Clean Up Your Own Backyard' 202
Clement, Jack 82–5
Clinton, President Bill 287, 295
Coasters, The 100, 107, 114, 165, 178
Cochran, Eddie 43, 106, 140
'C'mon Everybody' 170
Cocke, Marion 251, 265
Cole, Nat 'King' 39, 62, 188
Collins, Tommy 46
'Colour My Rainbow' 255
Como, Perry 65, 87, 94, 228, 237, 263
'Confidence' 189
Connolly, Ray 11, 14, 17, 88, 152, 190, 263, 270, 272, 306
Cooder, Ry 160–1
Cooke, Sam 6, 147, 184
Coolidge, Rita 258
Costello, Elvis 13–4, 284
Cotton, Billy 87
'Could I Fall in Love' 189
Coulter, Phil 258
Cramer, Floyd 60, 121, 141,

157
'Crawfish' 119, 125
Croker, Brendan 45
Crombie, Tony 92
Crosby, Bing 99, 107, 161, 193, 279
Crudup, Arthur 'Big Boy' 4–5, 37–8, 44, 59, 63, 75
'Crying in the Chapel' 132, 150, 181, 187, 265
Curtis, Sonny 49
Curtis, Tony 77
Cymbal, Johnny 231

Daniels, Charlie 169
'Danny' 118
'Danny Boy' 175, 275, 283
Darby, Ken 73
'Dark Moon' 176
Darin, Bobby 107, 138–9, 194, 213
'Datin'' 186
Davies, Hunter 183
Davies, Gladys and Maria 220, 226, 234–5
Davies, Oscar 55
Davis, Jimmie 54
Davis, Mac 199, 202, 209–10, 212, 269
Day, Annette 188
Dean, James 55, 58, 114, 117
Dean, Jimmy 98, 256
Dean, Quentin 198
Dekker, Desmond 90
Del Rio, Dolores 148
DeMetrius, Claude 62, 107
Dene, Terry 88, 92, 115–6, 125, 195
Denny, Jim 41, 104
'Devil in Disguise' 169, 211
Diamond, Neil 208, 223
Diddley, Bo 6, 10, 63, 160
'Didja' Ever' 145
Dion 140
'Dirty, Dirty Feeling' 143
Diskin, Tom 45, 55, 199, 212
'Dixie Fried' 81
'Dixieland Rock' 118
Dixon, Willie 10
'Dog's Life, A' 185
'Doin' the Beat I Can' 146

'Dominick' 113
Domino, Fats 8, 36, 49, 99, 219
'Doncha Think It's Time' 119–20
Donegan, Lonnie 18, 275
Donner, Ral 143, 164, 296
Donovan, Jason 79
'Don't' 107, 119
'Don't Ask Me Why' 118
'Don't Be Cruel' 70–1, 76–7, 105–6, 201, 248
'Don't Cry Daddy' 210, 298
'Don't Forbid Me' 85
'Don't Leave Me Now' 99, 104, 108
'Don't Think Twice, It's All Right' 241
'Do the Clam' 173–4, 180
'Do the Vega' 170
Dorset, Ray 270
Dorsey, Jimmy and Tommy 63–4
Dorsey, Rev Thomas A 98
Double Trouble (film) 153, 188–9
Douglas, Donna 184
Dowell, Joe 164
'Down by the Riverside' 183
'Down in the Alley' 187, 260
'Do You Know Who I Am' 214
Drifters, The 62, 109, 114, 130, 133, 213, 241, 254
Duggan, Patrick 288
Dundy, Elaine 12
Dunleavy, Steve 153, 278
Dunn, Donald 'Duck' 214
Durden, Tommy 60–1
'Drums of the Islands' 185
Dylan, Bob 21, 33, 58, 79, 187, 196, 214, 229, 237, 241, 282, 335

Earle, Steve 268
Early, Donna Presley 17, 182, 186, 188, 250–1, 279–80, 282, 289, 296–7
'Early Morning Rain' 238, 241
'Earth Angel' 126
'Earth Boy' 166
Eastwood, Clint 148, 192,

291, 272
Easy Come, Easy Go (film) 187–8
'Echoes of Love' 170
Eddy, Duane 86, 140
'Edge of Reality' 197
Edwards, David 'Honeyboy' 6
Edwards, Mike 292
Edwards, Sherman 145
Egan, Richard 72–3
Eisenhower, President Dwight D 159
Ellis, Jimmy 298
Elvis (second US LP) 75
Elvis (1979 bio-pic) 295–6
Elvis' Christmas Album 101, 103, 106, 109–10, 175, 238
'Elvis has left the building' 78, 219, 247, 283, 297, 305, 337–8 (This saying has a complete social history of its own.)
Elvis on Tour (film) 244, 248
Elvis Presley (first US LP) 64, 67
Elvis – That's the Way It Is (film) 230, 234
Elvis – What Happened (book) 153, 279–80
Emerson, Billy the Kid 44–5
Emmons, Bobby 209, 254
Epstein, Brian 55–7, 181–2
Escott, Colin 81
Esposito, Joe 153–4, 190, 198, 248, 276, 281, 291
Evans, Mal 181–2
Evans, Marilyn 80, 83, 132
Evans, Paul 62, 139, 148, 158, 165, 169, 231, 269
'Evening Prayer, An' 240
Everly Brothers 10, 32, 74, 86, 115, 132, 142, 184, 227

Fabian 139–40, 148–9, 194
Fabares, Shelley 179, 185, 189
'Fabulous' 105–6
'Faded Love' 232
'Fair's Moving On, The' 212
'Fairytale' 263

Faith, Adam 195–6
'Fame and Fortune' 142
Farrell, Glenda 172
'Farther Along' 186
Faulkner, William 9
Feathers, Charlie x, 38, 45–7, 50–1
Federal Bureau of Investigation (FBI) 67–8, 128, 236–7
Ferris, Bob 60
'Fever' 143, 168, 226, 252, 298
Fields, W C 53
Fike, Lamar 14, 21, 122, 124, 126, 128–9, 154, 168, 211, 232, 257–8, 265
'Finders Keepers, Losers Weepers' 170
'Find out What's Happening' 254
Finkel, Bob 199–200, 202
'Fire' 268
'Fire Down Below' 267
'First in Line' 74
'First Time Ever I Saw Your Face, The' 238
'Five Sleepy Heads' 191
Flaming Star (film) 148–9
'Flaming Star' (song) 148, 321
Flamingos, The 89, 99, 175
Fletcher, Guy 197, 211, 231
Flett, Doug 197, 211, 231
Flintoff, Freddie 288
'Flip, Flop and Fly' 46, 63
'Flying Saucer, The' 69, 333
Fogerty, John 294
Foley, Red 17, 21, 71, 96, 98, 121
Follow that Dream (film) 163, 177
'Follow that Dream' (song) 163
'Folsom Prison Blues' 64
Fonda, Jane 236
Fontana, D J 42–4, 48, 60, 67, 70, 107, 141, 199
'Fool' (Last, Sigman) 245
'Fool, The' (Hazlewood) 174, 191, 232
'Fool, Fool, Fool' 45
'Fools Rush In' 241
'Fool Such As I, A' 121, 189

Ford, Clinton 93
Ford, Tennessee Ernie 20
'For Lovin' Me' 238, 241
'For Ol' Times Sake' 254
Fortas, Alan 155, 199
'For the Good Times' 245, 247
'For the Heart' 276
'Fort Lauderdale Chamber of Commerce' 180
'Fountain of Love' 165
Four Amigos, The 168
Francis, Connie 29
'Frankfort Special' (spelling mistake on album) 144
Frankie and Johnny (film) 180, 183–4
'Frankie and Johnny' (song) 183–4
Franklin, Aretha 207, 218
Frazier, Dallas 182, 212, 233, 240
Freberg, Stan 62
Freed, Alan 40, 57
'From a Jack to a King' 175, 210
Fuller, Dolores 167
Fun in Acapulco (film) 168
'Funny How Time Slips Away' 219, 232
Fury, Billy 95–6, 119, 165, 170, 179, 211

Garland, Hank 107, 121, 141
Garrett, Lesley 156
Gatlin, Larry 257, 274
Geller, Larry 155, 178, 182–3, 220, 281
'Gentle on My Mind' 213–4
Gentry, Bobbie 8, 34
Gere, Richard 292
'Get Along Home, Cindy' 233
'Get Back 160, 210, 244
Giancana, Sam 224
Giant, Bill with Bernie Baum and Florence Kaye 119, 164, 169, 210, 233
'Giddy-Up A Ding-Dong' 67
G I Blues (film) 127, 143–6, 187, 223–4, 271
Girl Can't Help It, The (film) x

Girl Happy (film) 179–80
'Girl Next Door Went a'Walkin'' 143
'Girl of Mine' 255
'Girl of My Best Friend, The' 143, 146
Girls! Girls! Girls! (film) 165–8
'Girls! Girls! Girls!' (song) 165
Gleaves Cliff 153
Gold, Wally 146, 163
Goldman, Albert 8, 12, 61, 154, 172, 304
'Gonna Get Back Home Somehow' 164–5
Good, Jack 92, 95–6, 119, 138, 190, 270, 294–5
'Good Luck Charm' 163, 168
'Good Rockin' Tonight' 40–1
'Goodtime Charlie's Got the Blues' 257
Goodwin, Laurel 166
Gordon, Rosco 26, 254
Gordy, Emory 246
'Got a Lot o' Livin' to Do' 99, 105
'Got My Mojo Workin'' 6, 233
Goulet, Robert 125, 256
Grammys 187–8, 215, 237, 253, 260, 283
'Graceland' (song) 11
Gracie, Charlie 96, 105–6
Graceland Too (museum) 15
Graham, Bill 102–3, 131
Grand Ole Opry (radio show) 20–1, 38, 41, 104
Grant, Currie 126–7
Grant, Earl 269
Grant, Peter 229
Grant, President Ulysses S 3
Gray, Les 262
Gray, Michael 120
Great Escape, The (film) 166, 179
Greene, Shecky 66
'Green Green Grass of Home' 263
Gregg, Brian 92
Griffith, Andy 46
Grob, Dick 155

Elvis Presley: Caught in a Trap

349

Groom, Bob 12
Guerico, Joe 242
Guitar, Bonnie 175
'Guitar Man' 192, 199, 201, 298
Gunter, Arthur 45
Guthrie, Arlo 214
Guthrie, Woody, 33, 214

Haggard, Merle 217, 229, 246, 253
Haley, Bill and his Comets 36, 49–50, 55, 57, 62, 68–9, 90, 123, 161
Hall, Rich 85
Hamblin, Terry 100
Hamburger, James 256
Hamilton, Roy 193, 214, 274
Hammond, John 5, 33
Handy, W C 2, 23–4
'Harbour Lights' 37
'Hard Headed Woman' 118–9
Hardin, Glen D 88–9, 227–8, 237, 242
Harem Holiday – UK title for *Harum Scarum*
Harman, Buddy 121, 141–2, 169, 186
Harmony, Dorothy 132
Harris, Richard 184, 258
Harris, Wee Willie 88
Harris, Wynonie 40, 130
Harrison, George 88–9, 104, 118, 246–7, 253
Hart, Dolores 105, 118, 132, 180, 291, 296
Harum Scarum (film) 184, 292
'Have I Told You Lately that I Love You' 99
'Hawaiian Sunset' 161
'Hawaiian Wedding Song' 161–2, 225, 279
Hawkins, Ronnie 18, 140, 187
Hawkins, Screamin' Jay 297
Hazlewood, Lee 3, 192, 232
'Heartbreak Hotel' 32, 51, 60–7, 69, 88–9, 200–1, 242, 300
'Heart of Rome' 232

Hebler, Dave 153, 155, 276, 278
'He Is My Everything' 240
'He Knows Just What I Need' 149
'He'll Have to Go' 275
Hellions, The (film) 165
'Help Me' 257
'Help Me Make It through the Night' 241, 248
'Here Comes Santa Claus' 107
Hess, Jake 186, 215
Heston, Charlton 224
He Touched Me (gospel album) 240–1, 253
Hewitt, Ben 100, 119–20, 136–7
'He's Your Uncle, Not Your Dad' 191
'Hey Jude' 210, 241
'Hi-heel Sneakers' 192
Hill, David 98, 104
Hill, Marianna 186
Hill and Range – see Aberbach
Hilton, Ronnie 228
His Hand in Mine (gospel album) 149–50, 186
'His Hand in Mine' (hymn) 150, 283
'His Latest Flame' 159–60, 164, 186
Ho, Don 155
Hodge, Charlie 123, 125, 143, 154–5, 174–5, 199, 218, 232, 295
Holland, W S 45, 64–5
Holly, Buddy 10, 32, 49
'Holly Leaves and Christmas Trees' 238
'Home Is Where the Heart Is' 165
Hope, Bob 62
Hopkins, Jerry 12, 122, 242–3, 304
'Hot Dog' 99
'Hound Dog' 26–7, 29, 67–71, 76–7, 201, 242, 244, 254, 260
House, Son 5–6, 16
Houston, Cissy 218
'How Can You Lose What You Never Had' 190

'How Do You Think I Feel' 74
Howe, Bones 199
How Great Thou Art (gospel album) 186–7, 190
'How Great Thou Art' (hymn) 103, 260, 283, 291
Howlin' Wolf 10, 11, 26
'How's the World Treating You' 74
'How the Web Was Woven' 231
'How Would You Like to Be' 167
Hubbard L Ron 290
Humperdinck, Engelbert 206, 217, 227, 232, 240
Humphries, Patrick 161
Hunter, Ivory, Joe 99, 107, 175, 241
'Hurt' 274, 277
Husky, Ferlin 107
Hutchins, Chris 182, 306
Hyland, Brian 138

'I Almost Lost My Mind' 66
'I Beg of You' 99, 119
'I Believe' 98
'I Believe in the Man in the Sky' 150
'I Can Help' 262
'I Can't Stop Loving You' 210, 219, 234, 244, 283
'I Don't Care If the Sun Don't Shine' 29, 41, 180
'I Feel So Bad' 157
'I Feel that I've Known You Forever' 164
'I Forgot to Remember to Forget' 47, 60
'I Got a Feeling in My Body' 256–7
'I Got a Woman' 45, 60, 63, 260, 262
'I Got Stung' 121
'I Gotta Know' 143, 148
'I Have Only One Girl' 189
'I, John' 240
'I Just Can't Help Believin'' 230–1
'I Love You Because' 37, 298
'I Miss You' 255
'I Need Your Love Tonight'

121, 126
'I Need Somebody to Lean On' 169
'I Need Your Love Tonight' 121, 126
'I Need You So' 99
'I Really Don't Want to Know' 232
'I Slipped, I Stumbled, I Fell' 157–8, 161
'I Understand' 122, 173
'I Want to Be Free' 104, 154
'I Want You, I Need You, I Love You' 66, 68–9
'I Was Born About 10,000 Years Ago' 231–2, 241, 248
'I Washed My Hands in Muddy Water' 232
'I Was the One' 62, 64
'I Want You with Me' 159
'I Will Be Home Again' 123, 143, 154
'I Will Be True' 241

'If Every Day Was Like Christmas' 154, 188
'If I Can Dream' 200–1, 203
'If I'm a Fool' 213
'If I Can Get Home on Christmas Day' 239
'If That Isn't Love' 257
Ifield, Frank 156
'If I Were You' 233
'If You Don't Come Back' 212, 254
'If You Love Me (Let Me Know)' 260, 279
'If You Talk in Your Sleep' 154, 258–9
Iglesias, Julio 292
'I'll Be Back' 185
'I'll Be Home' 89
'I'll Be Home for Christmas' 107
'I'll Be Home on Christmas Day' 242
'I'll Be There' 212–3
'I'll Hold You In My Heart (Till I Can Hold You in my Arms)' 210
'I'll Never Fall in Love Again' 275
'I'll Never Let You Go' 40

'I'll Remember You' 185
'I'll Take Love' 187
'I'll Touch a Star' 167
'I'm Comin' Home' 158
'I'm Counting on You' 62
'I'm Falling in Love Tonight' 167
'I'm Gonna Sit Right Down and Cry Over You' 63
'I'm Leavin'' 241
'I'm Left, You're Right, She's Gone' 44, 46, 47
'I'm Movin' On' 213
'I'm Not the Marryin' Kind' 163
Imperials Quartet 186, 188, 218, 228, 240, 244
'Impossible Dream, The' 243, 247
'I'm So Lonesome I Could Cry' 253
'I'm Yours' 159, 165
'Indescribably Blue' 175, 187
'Inherit the Wind' 211
Ink Spots, The 29, 99, 173, 182
'In My Father's House' 150
'In My Way' 157
'In the Ghetto' 126, 209–10, 216, 229, 234, 298
'Is It So Strange' 84, 99, 126
'It Ain't No Big Thing' 233
'It Feels So Right' 141
It Happened at the World's Fair (film) 167
'It Hurts Me' 169, 200–1
'It Is No Secret' 98
'It Keeps Right on a-Hurtin'' 213
'It's a Matter of Time' 246
'It's a Sin' 159
'It's a Wonderful World' 178
'It's Carnival Time' 178
'It's Easy for You' 275, 279
'It's Impossible' 243
'It's Midnight' 154, 257–8, 265
'It's Nice to Go Travelling' 142
'It's Now or Never' 143, 146–7, 165, 189, 300
'It's Only Love' 242

'It's Only Make Believe' 6, 32, 246
'It's Over' 243
'It's Still Here' 241
'It's Your Baby, You Rock It' 232
'It Won't Seem like Christmas' 239
'(It Wouldn't Be the Same) Without You' 35
'I've Got a Thing about You, Baby' 234
'I've Got Confidence' 240
'I've Lost You' 231

Jackson, Al 254
Jackson, Michael 264, 285, 291–2
Jackson, Wanda 19–20, 46, 131
'Jailbait' 133
Jailhouse Rock (film) 78, 103, 106–8, 201, 296–7
'Jailhouse Rock' (song) 107–8, 149, 299
James, Clive 177, 293
James, Harry 30
James, Mark 212, 242, 245, 254, 269, 276
Jarrett, Michael 239, 241
Jarvis, Felton 175, 186, 207–09, 213, 228, 239, 254–5, 263, 268, 274, 276, 278, 298
Jefferson, Blind Lemon 5, 83
Jeffries, Herb 132
Jenkins, Mary 156, 250
Jennings, Waylon 22, 257
Jive Bunny 299
John, Elton 34, 277
'Johnny B Goode' 219, 252
Johnson, Lonnie 40
Johnson, Robert 5–7
Jones, Carolyn 118
Jones, Casey 4
Jones, George 43
Jones, Jimmy 269
Jones, Tom 12, 34, 67, 96, 152, 196–7, 214–6, 227, 233, 255, 258, 261, 263, 275, 287 (Many references for Tom but maybe they're only just beginning now

he is linked with Priscilla Presley)
Joplin, Janis 5
Jordanaires, The 59, 64, 68, 70–1, 77, 96–8, 103, 105, 107, 121, 145–6, 149–50, 165, 167, 169, 189, 218, 295, 338
'Joshua Fit the Battle' 149
Juanico, June 131
'Judy' 159
'Just a Little Bit' 254
'Just Because' 40
'Just Call Me Lonesome' 192
'Just for Old Times' Sake' 165
'Just Pretend' 231
'Just Tell Her Jim Said Hello' 163
'Just Walkin' in the Rain' 28

Kaempfert, Bert 145
Kahane, Jackie 243, 283
Katzman, Sam 172, 183
Kaufman, Andy 287
Kaye, Buddy 170, 269, 292
Kaye, Florence – see Giant, Bill
Keisker, Marion 29, 35–6, 129
Kennedy, Caroline 283
Kennedy, President John F ix, 172
Kennedy, Robert 2, 199
'Kentucky Rain' 154, 211, 214
Kenwright, Bill 126
Kerkorian, Kirk 215
Kelly, Mark 288
Kesler, Stan 47, 74, 96, 213
Kessel, Barney 69, 152, 167
Keystone Kops, The 166
Khashoggi, Adrian 262
Kidd, Johnny 32–3
Kid Galahad (film) 165
'Killing Me Softly with His Song' 255
King, B B 4, 6–7, 23, 26, 39
King, Martin Luther 208
King, Solomon 258
King Creole (film) 110, 117–20

'King Creole' (song) 118
Kingston Trio, The 1, 143
Kinks, The 33
Kinn, Maurice 109
Kinsey, Alfred 130–1
Kirkham, Millie 107
Kissin' Cousins (film) 171–2, 176–7
'Kissin' Cousins' (song) 176
'Kiss Me Quick' 159, 164, 175
Klein, George 135, 153, 209, 269, 305
'Known Only to Him' 150, 283
Knox, Buddy 115
Kristofferson, Kris 2, 22, 197, 241, 245, 257–8
Krolik, Alvin 170
Krushchev, Nikita 113–6
'Ku-U-I-Po' 252

LaBeef, Sleepy 42–3, 48
Lacker, Marty 154, 191, 208–9
'Lady Loves Me, The' 170
Lanchester, Elsa 187
Landau, Dr Laurenz 128
Lange, Hope 157
Lansbury, Angela 162
Lansky Brothers 25, 282
Lanza, Mario 31, 146, 156
Last, James 245
'Last Farewell, The', 275
Laughton, Charles 75–6, 187
'Lawdy Miss Clawdy' 63, 200, 216
Lawrence, Tony 295
'Lead Me, Guide Me' 240
Ledbetter, Huddie (Leadbelly) 130
Lee, Brenda 127, 154, 245
Lee, Kui 186, 252
LeGault, Lance 172, 190, 199
Leiber, Jerry and Mike Stoller 27, 74, 104, 108, 118, 143, 163, 165, 169, 270, 272
Leigh, Suzanna 184–5
Lennon, John 25, 55, 120, 210, 229, 247, 285, 299
'Let It Be Me' 227

'Let Me' 73
'Let Me Be There' 279
'Let's Be Friends' 216
'Let's Forget about the Stars' 202
'Let Us Pray' 216
'Let Yourself Go' 201
Lewis, Jerry Lee 79–85, 133–6, 138, 156, 263, 278, 285–6
Leyton, John 179
Liberace 14–5, 67, 102, 293
'Life' 232
Lightfoot, Gordon 208
'Like a Baby' 143
Lincoln, President Abraham 1, 3
Linde, Dennis 244–5, 256, 268, 276
'Little Bit of Green, A' 211
'Little Cabin on the Hill' 232
'Little Darlin'' 279
'Little Egypt' 179, 201
'Little Less Conversation, A' 197, 299
Little Milton 41
Little Richard 26, 63, 73–4, 89–90
'Little Sister' 159–60, 244
Live a Little, Love a Little (film) 197
Locke, Dixie 78, 131
Logan, Horace 43, 78
Lolita (novel, film) 133, 161
'Lonely Man' 156
'Lonely This Christmas' 261–2
'Lonesome Cowboy' 6, 99–100
Long, Shorty 63, 70
'Long Black Limousine' 209
'Long Legged Girl (With the Short Dress on)' 188–9
'Long Lonely Highway' 165, 169. 180
'Long Tall Sally' 33, 66, 73–4, 90
Lord Boothy 95
Lord Soper 92
'Lord's Prayer, The' 242
Loren, Sophia 118
Louisiana Hayride (radio show) 39, 42, 48, 64

Louvin Brothers 63
'Love Comin' Down' 276
'Love Letters' 167, 188, 232
Love Machine, The' 187
'Love Me' 77, 200
'Love Me, Love the Life I Lead' 241
Love Me Tender (film) 72–3, 83, 88, 94, 196
'Love Me Tender' (song) 73, 76, 77, 142, 151, 201
'Love Me Tonight' 169
'Lover Doll' 118
'Love Song of the Year' 259
'Loving Arms' 258
Loving You (film) 6, 72, 94, 98–9, 104, 194
'Loving You' (song) 99, 105, 331
Luckhurst, Tim 299
Luman, Bob 105, 138, 263
Lund Jana 105
Lynch, David 21
McBride, Martina 298
McCartney, Paul 44, 89, 119, 192, 278
MacColl, Kirsty 289
McCoy, Charlie 187/8, 192, 230, 238
McDowell, Ronnie 295
McFarland, John Leslie 141, 188
McGuinn, Roger 139, 181
McGuire, Phyllis 224
MacLaine, Shirley 184
McPhatter, Clyde 115, 130, 214, 262
McPresley, Elvis x, 342
Mabe, Joni 290
Macaulay. Tony 239–40
'Make Me Know It' 141
'Make the World Go Away' 232
Malarkey, Michael 80
'Mama Liked the Roses' 210
Mann, Carl 158
Mann, Herbie 217
Mansfield, Jayne x
Mansfield, Rex 121, 125, 129
'Mansion over the Hilltop' 150

Marcus, Greil 289
'Marguerita' 168
Martin, Bill 258–9
Martin, David 211, 216, 255
Martin, Dean 29, 41, 66, 72, 143, 175, 200
Martin, Freddy 66–7
Martin, Rex 226, 260
Martindale, Wink 69
Martine Jr, Layng 276, 279
'Mary in the Morning' 231
Martino, Al 31, 91, 259
'Matchbox' 83
Matson, Vera 73
Matthau, Walter 118
Matthew, Brian 93–4
Matthews, Neal 146, 189
'Maybellene' 31, 46
Mayfield, Curtis 213
'Mean Woman Blues' 99
Meeks, Johnny 178
'Memories' 199–200
'Memory Revival' 212
Memphis Mafia – see Chapter 9, Part 1 and entries for individual members
Memphis Minnie 23
Memphis Slim 23
'Memphis, Tennessee' 24, 169
Mercer, Johnny 110, 241
'Merry Christmas, Baby' 239, 298
'Mess of Blues, A' 8, 141–2, 146, 311
Meyer, Alan 287
Milete, Shirl 214, 232
'Milkcow Blues Boogie' 6, 43–4
'Milky White Way' 179
Miller, Ned 175, 210
Millins, Mike 212
Million Dollar Quartet, The (Play) 79–85
Mills, Gordon 258
Milsap, Ronnie 214
'Miracle of the Rosary' 241
'Miss Misunderstood' 268
Mitchell, Guy 176
Mitchum, Robert 270
Mobley, Mary Ann 183

Moman, Chips 207–13, 221, 230
'Mona Lisa' 175
'Money Honey' 62
Monroe, Bill, 38, 41, 84, 232
Monroe, Marilyn 77, 131, 263
'Moody Blue' 276–7
'Moonlight Swim' 162–3
Moore, Mary Tyler 216
Moore, Scotty 36–7, 40, 44–5, 47, 49, 60–1, 71, 96–7, 100, 107, 118, 141, 143, 160, 167, 199–200
Moreno, Rita 132
Morrison, Jim 205
Morrow, Geoff 211, 216, 240, 269
'Movie Magg' 81
'Mr Songman' 259
Mud 261
Mullaney, Jack 180
Muppet Show, The 8
Murphy, Senator George 235–6
'My Babe' 219
'My Baby Left Me' 63, 66, 300
'My Baby's Gone' 44
'My Boy' 258–59
'My Happiness' 29, 31, 59
'My Heart Cries for You' 176
'My Little Friend' 214
'Mystery Train' 28, 47–8, 234
'My Way' 220, 242, 253, 279–80, 284
'My Wish Came True' 107

Naked Gun, The (film) 292
Nashville (film) 22
Naylor, Jerry 45
Neal, Bob 39–40, 48
Nelson, Gerald 187
Nelson, Gene 177
Nelson, Ricky 43, 98, 105, 109, 138, 144, 171, 179, 194, 217, 219, 241, 291
Nelson, Willie 22, 246, 257, 274, 285
'Nearer My God to Thee' 244

Spencer Leigh

'Never Again' 276
'Never Been to Spain' 243
'Never Ending' 170
'Never Say Yes' 185
Newbury, Mickey 1–2, 244
New Gladiators, The (film) 271
'New Orleans' 117
Newley, Anthony 125, 195, 219–20
Newman, Lionel 73
Newton, Wayne 280
'Next Step Is Love, The' 231
Nicholson, Pauline 251
Nichopolous, Dr George 153–4, 156, 188, 239, 260, 265, 276, 278–9, 281, 285–6
'Night Rider' 164
Nixon, Hershel 101
Nixon, President Richard 206, 236–7, 250, 296
Nielsen, Leslie 292
Nielsen, Shaun (Sherrill) 255, 265, 279
Noone, Peter (Herman) 180
'No Room to Rhumba in a Sports Car' 168
'Nothingville' 199

Oates, Warren 185
O'Brian, Hugh 77
Ochs, Phil 229–30
'O Come All Ye Faithful' 298
O'Curran, Charles 161
'Ode to Billie Joe' 8, 34, 192
Odetta 1–2
Odets, Clifford 157
O'Grady, John 220, 224, 235, 278
'Old MacDonald' 188–9
'Old Shep' 17, 25, 74–5, 93–4
'O Little Town of Bethlehem' 107, 110
'On a Snowy Christmas Night' 239
'One Boy, Two Little Girls' 172
'One Broken Heart for Sale' 167

'One Hundred Years From Now' 233
'One Night' 99, 123, 200–1, 299
'One Sided Love Affair' 63
'Only Believe' 232
'Only the Lonely' 210
'Only the Strong Survive' 6, 214
Orbison, Roy 195, 210, 258, 269
Orion 298, 343
'O Sole Mio' 146
Otis, Clyde 71, 119
O'Toole, Mick 294
Owens, Buck 22

Pachucki, Al 208
'Padre' 241
Page, Larry 92
Page, Patti 161
Paget, Debra 72, 127, 172
Paradise, Hawaiian Style (film) 165, 180–1, 184–5, 295
'Paralyzed' 74
Parker, Junior (Herman Parker) 28, 47
Parker, Ed 155
Parker, Marie (Marie Mott, Col Parker's first wife) 53, 56, 147, 199, 252, 283, 291
Parker, Loanne (Loanne Mott, Parker's second wife) 291
Parker, Patricia 233
Parker, Colonel Tom
  Background 52–4
  Carnival life 54
  Managing Eddy Arnold 21, 54
  Agency with Hank Snow 41, 45–6, 55, 62
  Honorary title 54, 129, 158
  Advising Tommy Sands 55
  Gambling 66, 216, 220, 279
  Comparison with Brian Epstein 56–7, 174, 181–2
  Working as 'Technical Advisor' 104, 144
  Suspicions of Gladys Presley 101, 122
  Films involving Parker's lifestyle 104, 177
  Dislike of Memphis Mafia 152–3
  Death 291
Parker, Colonel Tom and Elvis Presley
  First seeing Elvis 54–6
  Isolating Elvis 58, 123, 149
  Management contracts 48, 121, 181
  Merchandise xi, 50, 77, 94, 142, 184, 244
  From Sun to RCA 50, 55
  Breaking contracts 55
  Relationship with Elvis 56, 83 (on holiday together!), 184, 189, 225, 237, 263 (Elvis fires him but it didn't last!), 270–1
  Management style 56–7, 62, 68, 74
  Deals for films 71, 72
  Booking Elvis 63, 93, 114, 127, 142, 144, 159, 162
  Publishing arrangements 2, 61, 65, 69, 71, 73, 84, 109, 126, 158, 174, 180, 212, 275 (see also Aberbachs and Bienstock, Freddy)
  Putting Presley in army 76–7, 96, 102, 110, 125
  Turning Presley into all-round entertainer 97, 109
  Press conferences 106, 120, 246
  Going behind Parker's back 107, 163, 229, 276
  Parker on Elvis' girlfriends 132, 171, 188, 224
  Talk of touring outside USA 166, 181, 218, 229, 243, 262
  Others using the Presley name 172, 191, 253
  Parker and imitators 109, 287
  Setting up TV special 198
  Contracts for Vegas 215, 226, 235

Contracts for touring US 228–29
Setting up *Aloha From Hawaii* 251–2
Selling back catalogue to RCA 253
Film roles rejected 271–2
Parker at recording session 274
Post-Elvis 282, 290–1, 328
Parnes, Larry 165
Parrish, Julie 184
Parsons, Bill 124
Parton, Dolly 22, 268
'Party' 100
Paseta, Marty 252
'Patch It Up' 231, 259
Patton, Charley 3–4, 8
Paxton, Tom 63
Payne, Jack 87
'Peace in the Valley' 96, 98, 101
Peacock, Trevor 93
Pearl, Minnie 54
Peck, Gregory 193
Peellaert, Guy 290
Pennington, Ann 247
Perkins, Carl 45, 47, 49–51, 59–60, 64–6, 74, 79–85, 105, 268, 290, 300–1
Peter, Paul and Mary 3, 238, 240
'Petunia, The Gardener's Daughter' 183
Phillips, Dewey 38, 44, 69
Phillips, John 21, 182
Phillips, Sam 7, 11, 26–9, 31, 35–51, 55, 62, 64, 70, 79–85, 150, 158, 200, 294–5
Pickett, Wilson 210
'Pieces of My Life' 263
Pierce, Webb 21, 44, 46, 56, 74
Pitney, Gene 214, 231, 244
Pitt, Ken 136
Pittman, Barbara 74, 132
Plant, Robert 160
Platters, The 67, 182
'Playing for Keeps' 74, 96
'Please Don't Drag That String Around' 168
'Pledging My Love' 276

'Pocketful of Rainbows' 146
Poindexter, Doug 35, 38
'Polk Salad Annie' 228, 247, 249, 254
Pomus, Doc and Mort Shuman 48, 139–42, 145–6, 150–1, 154, 156–7, 159–60, 163, 169–70, 175, 177, 210, 221
'Poor Boy' 73, 76
'Power of My Love' 211, 214
Prell, Milton 263
Presley, Dee (Dee Stanley: Vernon's second wife) 125, 147, 150–1, 155, 279
Presley, Elvis
  Birth 14/5
  Childhood and education 12–3, 25
  Church and gospel music 16–7, 41, 60, 83, 97–8, 174–5, 228, 244, 247. See entries for *His Hand in Mine*, *How Great Thou Art* and *He Touched Me*.
  First guitar 17, first public appearance 17, RCA session 60, national TV appearance 63, Vegas show 66–7, first film 71–2, first *Ed Sullivan Show* 75, first screen kiss 105, first show at International, Las Vegas 215
  Clothes and appearance: shopping on Beale 25, hair 77–8, 83, 104, 120, gold lamé suit 76, actress sacked for being too tall 149, jump suits 204–7, 277
  Employment: cinema usher 25, delivery man 25, 29
Promotion: singing radio ad 42, *TV Guide Presents Elvis* 309, 328, *The Truth About Me* 309
  Meeting Buddy Holly 49, Pat Boone 49, 109, Bill Haley 123, football with Ricky Nelson 171
  The greatest recording session by anyone

anywhere at any time! 70–1
On black music 73–4, 100, 282
Stage controversy 96, 107, reactions to criticism 76, 95, UK reaction 87–91, 94, 108, Sinatra's hatred 102 but note U-turn 142
'World's most eligible bachelor' 78
Recording: multiple takes 99, 103, home recordings 126, 173–5, messing around with lyrics 222–5, 233
Anger mismanagement 101, 256, 260, 264, 266, wants contract on Mike Stone 253, making arrests 256, 280
Graceland purchased 101–2, 110
Vehicles: car ownership 103, 235, 262, motorbikes 177, 180, Lear Jet 188
Army drafted 75–6, 102, serving 113–4, 117–129
Generosity 120, 153 (plastic surgery!), 180, 188, 225, 235, 262, 264–5, 277
Girlfriends 131–3, sexual stamina 126, 144, 'Little Elvis' 157, paternity suit 233, use of *Playboy* as dating manual 166, 247, 261, blackmailed 128
Memphis Mafia 152–6, forms football team 171
Gluttony xi, 154, 156, 249–51, diet pills 191, 252
Nicknames 155, 157, 217, 256, 277
Drugs 156, 168, 225, 264–5, 281, 286
Vocal range vii, 156
Honorary awards: Colonel Elvis 156, Sheriff Elvis 178, Top Young American 237
Charity work 159, 252
Favourite films 166, 179

Circle G Ranch 155, 188, 217, 294
Guns and rifles: 17, 56, 72, 153, 188, 235, 243, 247, 256, 260, 266
Karate 126, 142, 149, 155, 198, 205, 220, 223–4, 247, 253, 255, 261, 271
Health: 223, 239, 256, 260–2, 277–8
Album never made 267–70, films never made 270–2
Death ix, 281–2, funeral 282–3
Links to punk music 283
Tribute acts 287–8, Elvis Lives! 288–90, Dead Elvis 297–301
Presley, Gladys and Vernon (Elvis' parents)
  Family background, marriage and birth of twins 12–3
  Vernon in jail 15–6
  Move to Memphis 17
  Witnessing contracts 43, 48, 55
  Relationship with Parker 57, 78
  Singing together 98
  Moving into Graceland 101
  In *Loving You* 104–5
  Death of Gladys 122
Presley, Priscilla, (Priscilla Beaulieu)
  Recommends 'American Trilogy' 8
  Birth 125
  Meeting Elvis in Germany xi, 126–9, 137, 159
  Pining for Elvis 143, 150
  Graceland, 168, 170–2, 181
  Engaged to Elvis 187
  Marries Elvis 146, 190, 192
  Birth of daughter 197
  Sexual tension 198
  With Mike Stone 199, 243–4, 292
  Elvis and Priscilla songs 212–4, 245, 258, 263–4, 268, 274
  Elvis commenting on stage 224, 233, 242, 261
  Separated and divorced 247–8, 255
  "Compromising photographs" 256
  Still seeing Elvis 277
  Managing estate 270, 290–1
  Scientology 290
  Boyfriends 291–2
  Film and stage appearances 292, 295–6, 300
  Memoir 304, 337
Presley, Vernon (Elvis' father)
  Enjoyment of sex 124, 248
  Marriage to Dee Stanley 125, 150–1
  Relationship with Beaulieus 127, 168
  Relationship with Memphis Mafia 152–5, 277
  Watching the bills 201, 235
  On screen 248
  In studio 210, 259
  In hospital with Elvis 262
  On stage with Elvis 280
  Death of Elvis 283
  Will 285
  Death 290–1
  Portrayed in film 294
Presley, Jessie Garon (twin brother), 14, 66
Presley, Lisa Marie (daughter)
  Birth 197
  Childhood 244–5
  Custody 247–8
  Potential kidnap 260
  Gifts from Elvis 263, 278, 280
  Plane named after her 264
  On stage with Elvis 278
  Death of Elvis 281
  Beneficiary 285–90
  Scientology 290
  Four marriages 292–3
  Records 293, 297
  Memoir 304
Presley, Minnie Mae (grandmother) 13, 25, 122, 153, 285, 291
Presley, Reg 177
Presley, Vester (uncle) 14, 181
Price, Lloyd 63
Price, Vincent 202
Priemal, Heli 127
Princess Diana ix, 285
Prisonaires, The 27–8, 41, 149
Proby, P J 8, 137–8, 171, 198, 294–5
'Promised Land' 136, 259
Prowse, Juliet 144, 146, 162, 227, 253
'Puppet on a String' 180
'Put the Blame on Me' 159
'Put Your Hand in the Hand' 241
Putnam, Curly 263
Prince, Tony 284
Putnam, Norbert 239, 256

Quatro, Suzi 76, 118, 338
'Queenie Wahine's Papaya' 185

Rabbitt, Eddy 211, 231
Race, Steve 87
'Race with the Devil' 90
'Rags to Riches' 233
Rainey, Ma 5
Rainmaker, The (film) 72
'Raised on Rock' 254
Randle, Bill 50
Randolph, Boots 142, 157, 167, 232
Randi, Don 201
Ray, Johnnie 28, 40–1, 61–2, 88, 99, 109, 130
'Reach Out to Jesus' 241
'Ready Teddy' 74, 76, 248
Rebel without a Cause (film) 58, 72
'Reconsider Baby' 84, 143, 159, 331
Reed, Jerry 167, 192,–3, 197, 256, 298
Reed, Jimmy 200

Reeves, Glen 61
Reeves, Jim 21, 59, 126, 158, 175, 253, 275
'Release Me' 227
'Relax' 167
'Return to Sender' 166–7
Rey, Alvino 161
Rice, Tim 275–6, 279, 282
Rich, Charlie 158, 183, 259, 263
Richard, Cliff 92, 95, 118, 164, 179, 195, 197, 257, 269, 298, 300
Ridley, Wally 87, 91–2
Riley, Billy Lee 207
'Rip It Up' 74, 90, 265
Rivers, Johnny 169
Robbins, Harold 117
Robbins, Marty 46, 168, 233, 243, 253
Robertson, Don 62, 146, 158–9, 163, 165, 167–69
Robey, Don 27
Robinson, Red 68–9, 106
'Rock-a-hula Baby' 161, 165
'Rock Around the Clock' 36, 49, 62
'Rocket 88' 36
Rodgers, Jimmie 13, 20
Roe, Tommy 186, 268
Rogers, Kenny 1, 103, 257
Rolling Stones, The 6–7, 24, 136, 266
Ronstadt, Linda 297
'Roses Are Red' 159, 270
Rossington, Norman 188
Roustabout (film) 155, 177, 331
Royal Philharmonic Orchestra 297–8, 300, 333
'Rubberneckin'' 211, 218
'Runaway' 219, 227
'Runnin' Scared' 232
Russell, Kurt 14, 167, 295–67
Ryan, Sheila 247, 261
Rydell, Bobby 144, 194

Sands, Tommy 48–9, 55, 140, 194, 196
'Santa Bring My Baby Back (To Me)' 107
'Santa Claus Is Back in Town' 107, 200

'Santa Lucia' 170
Saperstein, Hank 77, 94
'Satisfied' 40
'Saved' 201
Savile, Jimmy 165
Sawyer, Ray 46–7
Scheff, Jerry 218, 220, 225, 242, 247, 267,
Schroeder, Aaron 71, 75, 104, 107, 141, 146, 163
Schilling, Jerry 155, 182, 235–6, 291
Scorsese, Martin 248
Scott, Lizabeth 104
'Scratch My Back' 185
Seal s, Troy 257, 263
Seaman, Kathy 265
Sedaka, Neil 137–8, 270, 274
'Seeing Is Believing' 241
'See See Rider' 5, 227, 276
'Sentimental Me' 159
'Separate Ways' 154, 245–6
Sex Pistols, The 284
'Shake a Hand' 263
'Shake, Rattle and Roll' 45, 47, 63, 65
Shaper, Hal 265–6
Shaver, Billy Joe 257
Shaw, Martin 147, 296
Shea, George Beverly 103, 150, 187, 240
Sheeley, Sharon 138
Shepherd, Cybill 248
Sheppard, T G 247
'She's a Machine' 187
'She's Not You' 162
'She Thinks I Still Care' 274
'She Wears My Ring' 258
Sholes, Steve 50, 70, 87, 96, 106, 141, 158, 164, 169
'Shoppin' Around' 146
Shore, Dinah 41
Shuman, Mort – See Pomus, Doc
Siegel, Don 148–9
'Signs of the Zodiac' 203
'Silent Night' 107, 110
'Silver Bells' 240
Silvers, Phil 67, 75, 111, 120
Simon, Paul 11, 32, 183, 196
Sinatra, Frank 14–5, 29–30,

Elvis Presley: Caught in a Trap

58, 75–6, 79, 102, 108, 112–4, 142, 144, 146, 152, 193, 215, 222, 234, 262
Sinatra, Nancy 3, 129, 142, 191, 198, 215, 221
'Singing Tree' 192
Slaughter, Todd 287, 293
'Slicin' Sand' 161
'Slowly but Surely' 170
Smith, Bessie 5, 227
Smith, Billy and Jo 153, 182, 281
Smith, Gene 153
Smith, O C 209
'Smokey Mountain Boy' 171
'Smorgasbord' 185
Snow, Hank 22, 41, 44, 46, 55, 59, 62–3, 71, 213
Snow, Jimmy Rodgers 44
'Snowbird' 232, 241
'So Close, Yet So Far' 183
'Softly As I Leave You' 260, 265–6, 285
'So Glad You're Mine' 63, 75
'So High' 186
'Soldier Boy' 124, 141, 174
'Solitaire' 274
'Somebody Bigger than You and I' 186
'Something' 210, 253
'Something Blue' 169
'Sometimes I Feel Like a Motherless Child' 201
'Song of the Shrimp' 166
'Sound Advice' 163
'Sound of Your Cry, The' 233
South, Joe 227
'Spanish Eyes' 259
Spector, Phil 160, 198
Speedway (film) 192, 197
Speer Family (Brock and Ben) 59, 62
Spinout (film) 153, 185
Springfield, Dusty 24, 208, 231
Springsteen, Bruce 34, 69–70, 268, 282
Stafford, Terry 164, 168
Stamps Quartet 244, 255, 257, 276
'Stand by Me' 186

Stanley, Billy 155
Stanley, David 147, 155, 181, 210, 218, 237, 243, 246–7, 260, 266, 281, 290–1
Stanley, Dee – See Presley, Dee
Stanley, Rick 155, 265, 281
Stanshall, Viv 168, 342
Staple Singers 8
Stapleton, Cyril 87
Star Is Born, A (film) 272
Starr, Freddie 287, 342
Starr, Randy 189
'Stay Away' 192
Stay Away, Joe (film) 192, 197
'Stay Away, Joe' (song) 192
'Steadfast, Loyal and True' 118
'Steamroller Blues' 253
Steele, Barbara 148–9
Steele, Tommy 92–3, 126, 192
Stefaniak, Elisabeth 124–5
Stephens, Geoff 232
'Steppin' Out of Line' 161, 165
Stevens, Shakin' 294
Stevens, Stella 166
Stewart, Billy 207
Stewart, John 27, 68, 108, 268–9
Stoker, Gordon 59–61, 70–1, 76, 98, 218, 226
Stone, Mike 198, 233, 243–4, 253, 261
Storm, Tempest 132
Storm, Warren 83
Strange, Billy 199, 202
'Stranger in My Own Home Town' 213–4
Stardust, Alvin 119, 295
Standwych, Barbara 179
Stoller, Mike – See Leiber, Jerry
'Stranger in the Crowd' 231
Stray Cats, The 43
Streisand, Barbra 31, 196, 218, 270, 298
'Stuck on You' 98, 141
Stylistics, The 163
'(Such an) Easy Question' 165

'Such a Night' 130, 142
Sullivan, Big Jim 95
Sullivan, Ed 55, 63, 75–6, 94–6, 144, 177, 248
'Summer Kisses, Winter Tears' 148
Sumner, Donnie 256, 259
Sumner, J D 244, 247, 255, 264, 283
'Suppose' 175, 191
'Surrender' 146, 150, 156
'Susan When She Tried' 264
'Suspicion' 167
'Suspicious Minds' 211–2, 221, 252
Swan, Billy 262–3
'Sweet Angeline' 255
'Sweet Caroline' 208, 227
Sweet Inspirations xi, 155, 218, 228, 259, 264–5
'Swing Down Sweet Chariot' 149, 159, 203
'Sylvia' 232, 241

'Take Good Care of Her' 254
'Take My Hand, Precious Lord' 98
'Talk About the Good Times' 256
Tatham, Dick 87
Taurog, Norman 143, 145, 165, 180, 188, 271
Taylor, Chip 294
'Teddy Bear' 96, 105, 120, 212
'Tell Me Why' 99
'Tennessee Waltz' 21, 174
'Tennessee Saturday Night' 75
Tharpe, Sister Rosetta 87
'That's All Right, Mama' 4–5, 31, 37–9, 42, 45–6, 200, 208
'That's Someone You Never Forget' 159, 165
'That's When Your Heartaches Begin' 29, 98–100, 148, 287
'There Ain't Nothing Like a Song' 191
'There Goes My Everything' 232
'There's a Brand New Day

on the Horizon' 179
'There's Always Me' 158
'There's a Honky Tonk Angel' 257

Tepper, Sid and Roy C Bennett 100, 104, 117, 145–6, 161, 165, 170, 179–80, 184, 191
Tyler, Judy 108
'This Land is Your Land' 214
Thompson, Dave 155
Thompson, Linda 155, 175, 247–8, 253, 256, 273, 277, 281, 291
Thompson, Sam 155, 247
'They Remind Me Too Much of You' 167
'Thing Called Love, A' 240
This Is Elvis (1981 film) 143, 296
'This Is Our Dance' 232
'This Is the Story' 211–2, 240
'This Time' 210
Thomas, B J 207, 212, 230, 241
Thomas, Rufus 26–7, 39, 41, 200, 208, 296
Thornton, Big Mama 26–7, 67
'Three Corn Patches' 254
'Thrill of Your Love, The' 143
Tickle Me (film) 81
'Tiger Man' 201, 220, 264
Tillotson, Johnny 203
Timberlake, Justin 294
'Today, Tomorrow and Forever' 170
'Tomorrow Is a Long Time' 187
'Tomorrow Never Comes' 232
'Tomorrow Night' 40, 181
'Tonight is So Right for Love' 145
'Tonight's All Right For Love' 145
'Too Much' 75, 96
'Too Much Monkey Business' 197
Torok, Mitchell 44

'Treat Me Nice' 103
Tracy, Kim 125
'Trouble' 118, 201, 292
'T-R-O-U-B-L-E' 263
Trouble with Girls, The (film) 203–4, 222
'True Love' 99
'True Loves Travels on a Gravel Road' 213
'Tryin' To Get To You' 32, 45, 47, 200
Tschechowa, Olga and Vera 127–8, 132
Tubb, Ernest 37, 42, 84
'Tupelo Mississippi Flash' 15, 191, 335
Turner, Ike 26, 36
Tutt, Ronnie 218, 225, 242, 249, 300
'Tutti Frutti' 63, 73–4, 89–90
'Tweedle Dee' 43
'Twelfth of Never, The' 299
'Twenty Days and Twenty Nights' 231
Twitty, Conway 6, 22, 32, 98, 118, 196, 257, 275

'Unchained Melody' 274, 279
Underwood, Charles 83
'Until It's Time for You to Go' 241
'Up Above My Head' 201
'U S Male' 167, 197
USS Arizona 159, 181

Vale, Jerry 266
Valentino, Rudolph ix, 183
Vallee, Rudy 194, 197
Vaughan, Frankie 93, 96
Vaughan, Malcolm 92
Vee, Bobby 74, 138, 140–1, 160
'Venice Blue' 174
Vernons Girls 94
Vincent, Gene 32, 46, 62, 65, 78, 89–90, 205
Vinton, Bobby 108, 139, 158–9
Viva Las Vegas (film) 170–1, 177, 194, 204, 294, 296
'Viva Las Vegas' (song) 169, 171, 215

Viva Las Vengeance (novel) 180
Voice 255, 259

Wagoner, Porter 205
Wakely, Jimmy 35, 40
'Walk a Mile in My Shoes' 227
Walker, Billy 35, 39, 43
Walker, Ray 144–5, 150, 189, 218
Walker, Scott 211
Walker, T-Bone 58
Walk on the Wild Side (film) 163
Walley, Deborah 185
Wallis, Hal 71–2, 127, 166, 177, 180, 184–5, 292
'Walls Have Ears, The' 166
Wangford, Hank 294
Ward, Billy and his Dominoes 130
Warhol, Andy 149
Waters, Muddy 6
'Way Down' 276, 279, 283–4
Wayne, Sid 145, 170, 233
Wayne, Thomas 143, 187
'Wearin' That Loved On Look' 212
'Wear My Ring Around Your Neck' 119
Webb, Jimmy 9, 289–90
Webber, Andrew Lloyd 275
'We Call On Him' 192
'We Can Make the Morning' 241
'We Had It All' 258
Weintraub, Jerry 22, 228, 270
Weisman, Ben 74, 141, 145, 168–70, 233
Welch, Raquel 178
'Welcome to My World' 253
Weld, Tuesday 157, 195
Welk, Lawrence 177
Wells, Kitty 186
'Went to See the Gypsy' 79, 335
'We're Comin' in Loaded' 166
'We're Gonna Move' 73
West, Mae 177

West, Red 25, 122, 124, 153–4, 159, 165, 171, 174–5, 188, 190, 208, 239, 241, 245, 258, 260, 276, 278, 291
West, Sonny 153–4, 236–7, 243, 260, 265, 276, 278, 291
'Western Union' 167, 170, 191
Westlake, Clive 231, 246
Westmoreland, Kathy 247, 264, 283, 295
West Side Story (film) 193, 271
'What a Wonderful Life' 163
'What'd I Say' 135, 170, 191, 331
'What Every Woman Lives For' 184
'What Now, What Next, Where To' 169
'What's She Really Like' 146
Wheeler, Billy Edd 257–8, 264–5, 275
'When I'm Over You' 232
'When It Rains, It Really Pours' 49, 99, 181
'When My Blue Moon Turns to Gold Again' 74, 200
'When the Saints Go Marching in' 173, 183
'Where Could I Go But to the Lord' 201
'Where Did They Do, Lord' 233
'Where Do I Go from Here' 246
'Whistling Tune, A' 165
White, Bukka 16
White, Chas 'Dr Rock' 90, 278
White, Jack 29
White, Tony Joe 118, 228, 244, 247, 254, 268
'White Christmas' 107, 109
Whitman, Slim 39–40, 167
Whitnall Tim, 294–5
Whittaker, Roger 275
'Who Am I' 214
'Who Needs Money' 189
'Whole Lotta Shakin' Goin'

on' 80, 133, 232, 252
'Why Me, Lord' 260
Whyton, Wally 95
Wilde, Marty 48, 116, 118, 144, 166
Wild in the Country (film) 156, 182
'Wild in the Country' (song) 151, 157
Wilson, Eileen 183
Williams, Andy 2, 162, 198, 219, 239, 255, 274
Williams, Big Joe 10
Williams, Hank 21, 27–8, 30–1, 36, 41–2, 60, 164, 253, 271–2
Williams, John 268
Williams, Tennessee 9, 157, 271
Willis, Chuck 5, 157, 227
'Willow Weep for Me' 126
Winehouse, Amy 35
Winfrey, Oprah 13
'Winter Wonderland' 240
Wise, Fred 104, 141, 145, 159, 168
'Witchcraft' (Bartholomew, King) 169
'Witchcraft' (Coleman, Leigh) 142
'Without Love' 214, 237
'Without You' 28, 37
'Wolf Call' 181
'Woman without Love' 263
'Wonderful World' 197
'Wonder of You, The' 93, 228, 294, 298, 300
'Wondrous Place' 119, 169
'Wonderful World of Christmas, The' 239
Wood, Anita 104, 120, 124–5, 132, 143, 167–8, 173
Wood, Bobby 209, 213
Wood, Natalie 58, 132
Wood, Roy 270
'Wooden Heart' 145, 151
Woodhead, Leslie 113–4
'Words' 219
Wright, Frank Lloyd 152
Wynette, Tammy 11

'Yellow Rose of Texas, The' 170
'Yesterday' 210
'Yoga Is as Yoga Does' 187
'You Asked Me To' 257
'You Can't Say No in Acapulco' 168
'You Don't Have to Say You Love Me' 231
'You Don't Know Me' 189, 192
'You Gave Me a Mountain' 243, 246, 253
'You Gotta Stop' 187
'You'll Be Gone' 155
'You'll Never Walk Alone' 192, 215
'You'll Think of Me' 210–1, 221
Young, Faron 84, 126
Young, Reggie 209
'Young and Beautiful' 103, 108
'Young Dreams' 118
'Your Cheating Heart' 28
'Your Groovy Self' 192
'You're a Heartbreaker' 44
'You're My World' 182
'You're the Boss' 170
'Your Time Hasn't Come Yet, Baby' 191
'You've Lost that Lovin' Feelin'' 230

Elvis Presley: Caught in a Trap

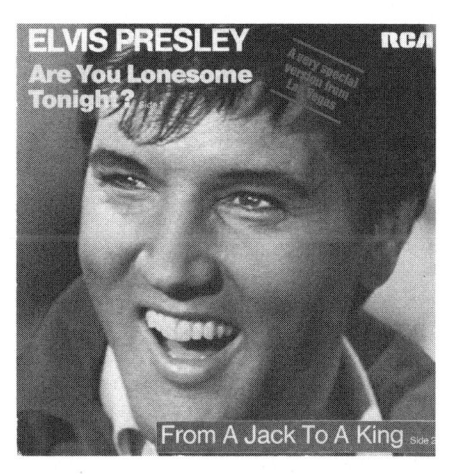

FRANK SINATRA
An Extraordinary Life

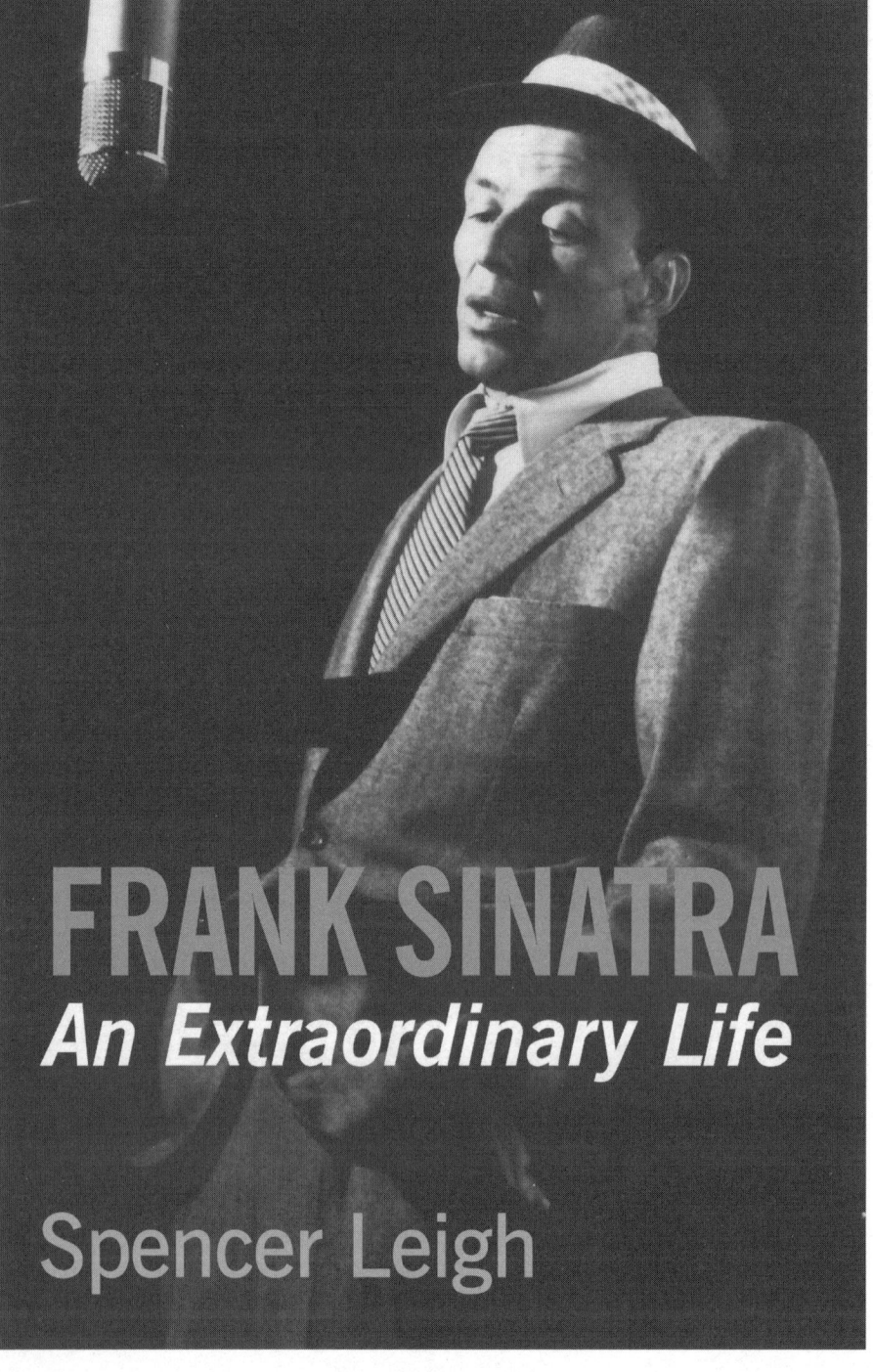

Spencer Leigh

ISBN 9780857160867

SIMON & GARFUNKEL
Together Alone

Spencer Leigh

ISBN 9780857161505

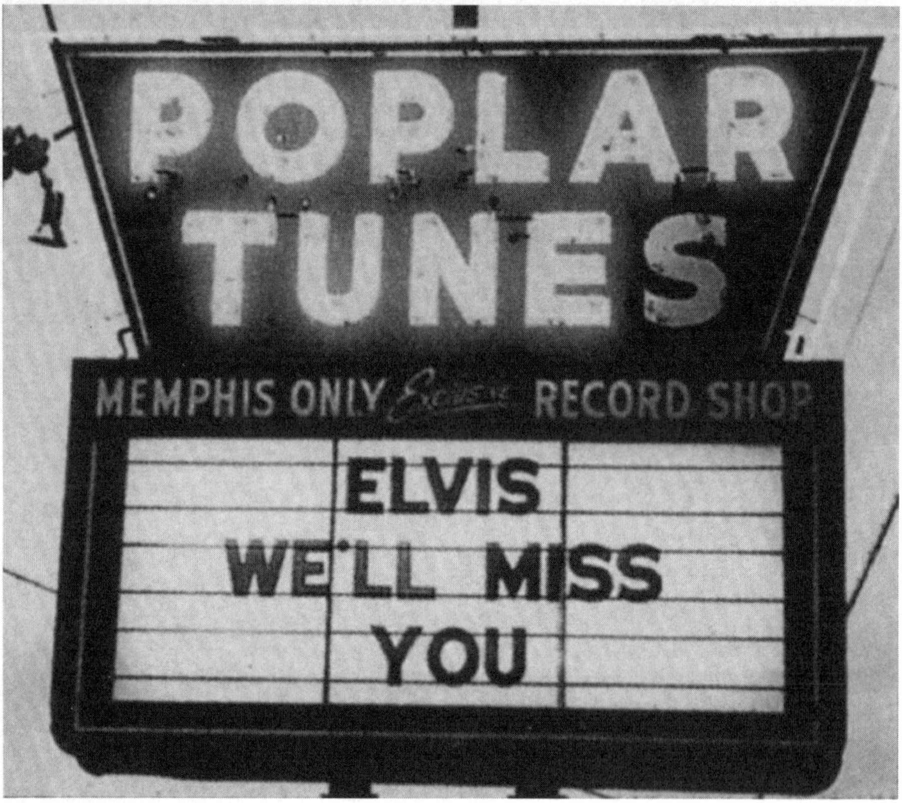
POPLAR
TUNES
MEMPHIS ONLY RECORD SHOP
ELVIS
WE'LL MISS
YOU